D1192948

FROM WITHOUT THE FLAMINIAN GATE

FROM WITHOUT THE FLAMINIAN GATE

150 Years of Roman Catholicism in England and Wales

1850–2000

Edited by

V. ALAN McCLELLAND and MICHAEL HODGETTS

DARTON · LONGMAN + TODD

First published in 1999 by
Darton, Longman and Todd Ltd
1 Spencer Court
140–142 Wandsworth High Street
London SW18 4JJ

ISBN 0–232–52177–8

A catalogue record for this book is available from the British Library.

Designed by Sandie Boccacci
Phototypeset in 9/12½pt Stone Serif by Intype London Ltd
Printed and bound in Great Britain by
The Cromwell Press, Trowbridge, Wiltshire

In memory of Nicholas Wiseman whose pastoral letter of 7 October 1850, issued '*Without the Flaminian Gate of Rome*', marked the beginning of one hundred and fifty years of the spiritual, social and material advancement of a community.

CONTENTS

LIST OF ILLUSTRATIONS

between pages 206–207

INTRODUCTION

Forty-one years elapsed from the issue of Nicholas Wiseman's pastoral letter announcing the erection of an English and Welsh hierarchy of bishops on 7 October 1850 and the demise of his immediate successor in the archiepiscopal see of Westminster on 14 January 1892. The national reaction to Manning's death, appropriately symbolised by the placing of Queen Victoria's wreath on his grave in Kensal Green Cemetery, was a far cry from the frenzied animosity unleashed against Catholics by the Liberal Prime Minister, Lord John Russell, in 1850 in his efforts to stoke the fires of religious intolerance against the Puseyite faction in the Anglican Church. *The Times* thought Wiseman should flee the wrath of the country and the Cardinal recorded he was the recipient of worrying threats, one of which intimated he would be shot the moment he ascended the pulpit of his pro-cathedral. Guy Fawkes night in 1850 witnessed the rekindling of the atmosphere of the Gordon Riots of 1780 in fury at what was declared to be the 'insolent and invidious aggression by the Pope upon our Protestantism'.

On the day Cardinal Manning succumbed to a fatal attack of pneumonia, the *Daily Chronicle*, while paying tribute to the Sisyphean character of Wiseman's task in London and to the leadership he provided, declared Manning's fame rested upon other enduring foundations. It was 'the common property of the English people, as his virtues and excellences were emphatically of the English type'. Consequently, the whole English-speaking race, 'Catholic and Protestant, religious and indifferent', lamented his passing. Manning's life and public commitment had affected the national conscience. It was said that while those who visited him in death may not have understood his theology, their hearts had been deeply touched by his essential humanity.

London had never witnessed such an impressive funeral for an ecclesiastic as it experienced in January 1892 and the death of any future cardinal archbishop was not to see its repetition. On the first day of Manning's lying in state, it was estimated that fifty thousand people paid their respects. At his funeral, which took six hours to complete, sixty carriages preceded the hearse from Brompton Oratory, where the Requiem Mass was celebrated, to Kensal Green and one hundred and eighty-four carriages followed in sombre cavalcade. Long streams of representatives of the Irish National League, the Phoenix Temperance Society, the Good Templars, the Watermen and Lightermen, the Operative Bakers, the

Dockers' Union, the London Trades Council, the Gas Workers, the Railway Workers, the Coal Porters, the Covent Garden Porters and many others, followed on foot. The crowds lining the four-mile processional route, on a bitterly cold and dank day, were estimated at five hundred thousand in number. Yet the overwhelming characteristic of the dense crowds awaiting the arrival of the cortège at Kensal Green was its level of visible material poverty.

Writing in the *Catholic Times* shortly after Manning's death, Canon William Barry surveyed this *bouleversement* in fortune. For him, the achievement of Manning's twenty-seven-year episcopate lay in its advocacy of 'an organic and organising Catholicism' that both nationally and internationally was intended to make 'an end of dynastic quarrels between Church and State'. For Charles Gatty, on the other hand, Manning's achievement had been that he had succeeded in presenting the Catholic Church in a new aspect to the Protestant British public by his essential Englishness and by the way he led his 'timid phalanx' into the thick of the fight against statism and secularism. Gatty maintained Manning 'held out the right hand of fellowship from the fortress of his own firm faith to all souls of any denomination who obeyed the light of conscience and strove to do the will of God' – no mean an objective today for a Church approaching the beginning of the third millennium!

Reflecting on his return from a tour in Ireland in the late summer of 1858, Wiseman had been sufficiently percipient to see the role that would inevitably be played by the Irish diaspora in the presentation of the human face of Catholicism to an hitherto largely indifferent and sceptical English nation. Frequently, Wiseman has been regarded as a man in a hurry, primarily concerned with rapid progress towards a 'conversion' of England. This simplistic view does him less than justice, making little allowance for his realisation of the enormity of the task confronting the new bishops in 1850 in the forging of a coherent and cohesive community. Time would be needed for such momentum to grow for, as he put it, 'social progress does not move by a sudden rush; it goes forward gradually'. The momentum was to be sustained by the investment of the Church's limited resources into the provision of elementary education for the poor, by the development of a rich array of charitable institutions inspired by religious communities of women and men and by lay confraternities, by the nurturing of a suitably educated middle and professional class of laymen in both old and new colleges located around the country and by a carefully formed and trained pastoral clergy. Brilliant acquisitions to the Church as the converts of the nineteenth century were, with the towering influence of Newman at their head, the social message of care and compassion was at least as important a drive as that of intellectual debate in the construction of a community that would appeal to men's hearts and lead to national acceptance and spiritual regeneration. It is with examining the validity or otherwise of this view that the present volume of essays is essentially concerned.

To celebrate the centenary in 1950 of the Apostolic Letter *Universalis Ecclesiae* which established the modern English hierarchy, the Catholic bishops of England and Wales commissioned one of their colleagues, George Andrew Beck, then coadjutor to Bishop Arthur Doubleday of Brentwood, to prepare a volume of essays to celebrate a century of achievement. The outcome was a remarkable book in the comprehensiveness of its range and the quality of its contributions. It has retained its standing to this day as an essential reference book of its period. Little, indeed, would be gained from attempting to replicate Beck. Nevertheless, as Bishop Daniel Mullins of Menevia pointed out to the Catholic Record Society, almost half a century has now elapsed since 1950 and it is opportune to bring the story up to date. The Catholic Church has undergone important reorientations in its structure, mission and presentation in recent years, not least as a result of the Second Vatican Council (1962–65), which have had far-reaching consequences. The aftermath of the Council has seen the emergence of 'maximising' and 'minimising' camps in relation to changes proposed or propagated in the Council's name. Consequent debate has threatened to fracture the increasingly fragile concept of community that had been consistently nurtured in the years from Wiseman to Heenan. For this reason, this volume of essays embraces the last one hundred and fifty years, rather than concentrating exclusively upon the changes of the last fifty. Within such a time-context, the impact of recent developments, as the Church comes to grips with the pressures of modern living while trying to preserve what is of lasting value in its inheritance, its approach and its teaching, can be more readily appreciated.

Three essays in the volume are concerned with historical analyses of the period, the first considering the formative years of the community after the restoration of the hierarchy and the second reflecting upon the years from the advent of Vaughan to Westminster in 1892 to the death of Arthur Hinsley in 1943, years of 'equipoise' as Dr Sheridan Gilley has called them. The third component of the trilogy, the final contribution to the volume, is of a somewhat different genre in that it not only contemplates development since 1943, but analyses some of the challenges confronting the Church in England and Wales as it reaches the year 2000. The history of the Catholic Church in Wales is the subject of discrete treatment. The formation of the diocesan priesthood, the nature of sacerdotal studies, the development, expansion and contraction of religious life for women and men are subjects for special attention in the book, as are the roles of lay people, their family life and marital concerns, the education of their children, their contribution to political, social and cultural life and their interaction with the society of which they form a distinctive and clearly recognisable part. While *From Without the Flaminian Gate* is not designed as a comprehensive study of all aspects of Catholic life and advancement since 1850, contributions have been situated within the wider spectrum of community growth and awareness.

The volume does not end on a note of nostalgia for what has been, still less does it rest in a paean of contentment or self-satisfaction. Rather it poses a set of questions which will present themselves with considerable urgency in the new millennium. Will their solution still be addressed from that concept of 'other-worldliness' that Bishop Beck detected as the dominant 'if not immediately evident' characteristic of Catholics? For him 'only in function of this eternal outlook can the "this-worldly" activity of Catholicism be rightly appreciated and understood' (*The English Catholics*, p. 604).

The editors wish to record their thanks to the Council of the Catholic Record Society for entrusting to them the production of the volume and to Morag Reeve of Darton, Longman and Todd for her understanding, patience and encouragement. A special word of thanks is offered to Fr Ian Dickie of the Westminster Diocesan Archives and to Bishop Daniel Mullins for supplying particular illustrations for the text.

The editors are especially grateful to Abbot Charles Fitzgerald-Lombard and Dom Daniel Rees of Downside Abbey for their assistance in supplying material for the cover design.

CONTRIBUTORS

Dom Aidan Bellenger is a monk of the Benedictine Abbey of Downside in Somerset. He was educated at Finchley Grammar School and Jesus College, Cambridge, where he received his PhD in 1978 for his work on 'French Exiled Clergy in Great Britain during the French Revolution'. Theological studies at Downside Abbey and the Angelicum University, Rome, led, in 1988, to ordination. He has published several books, contributed to many others, and written numerous articles principally on Anglo-French relations, the history of monastic and religious orders, and the English Catholic community. A former headmaster of Downside School, he lectures in history at several universities. He is a Fellow of the Society of Antiquaries, the Royal Historical Society and the Royal Society of Arts.

Peter Doyle read history at Cambridge. He obtained his doctorate in ecclesiastical history from London University and has lectured in social and religious history at De Montfort University, Bedford, where he became head of the Department of Arts and Humanities. Author of *Westminster Cathedral: 1895–1995*, he has recently been involved in a major revision of *Butler's Lives of the Saints*.

Sheridan Gilley is Reader in Theology at Durham University. His recent publications include *Newman and his Age* and *A History of Religion in Britain* (edited with W. J. Sheils). The third volume of essays on the Irish in Modern Britain, which he has edited with Roger Swift, will be published as *The Irish in Britain: The Local Dimension* in 1999. He is writing a biography of Wilfrid Ward.

Michael Hodgetts is volumes editor of the Catholic Record Society and a former editor of *Recusant History*. He has been chairman of the Church Music Association, head of religious education in a comprehensive school, and a member of the Translations Sub-committee of the International Commission on English in the Liturgy (ICEL). He was created a Knight of St Gregory by Pope John Paul II in 1990.

Edward Hulmes some time Spalding Professorial Fellow in Comparative Theology at Durham University, is a former Director of the Farmington Institute at Oxford and is a member of the Centre of Theological Inquiry at Princeton. He has published on aspects of the study of Islam, on inter-faith encounter and on Catholic education.

V. Alan McClelland has worked in three universities, occupying chairs in two of them. He has written and edited several books and contributed to others, mainly in the fields of nineteenth-century ecclesiastical and educational history and in denominational education. He was the first Anatole von Hügel Fellow at St Edmund's College, Cambridge and edits *Recusant History* for the Catholic Record Society of which he is the current chairman. Professor McClelland is a foundation fellow of the Maryvale Institute where he also functions as Dean of Graduate Research.

Daniel J. Mullins is Bishop of Menevia and previously was Auxiliary Bishop of Cardiff where he was Vicar General. A graduate of the University of Wales, having obtained first class honours in Welsh, he has served as the bishop responsible for higher education to the Bishops' Conference of England and Wales and also as chairman of the national committee for catechetics. A Fellow of University College, Cardiff and of St David's University College, Lampeter, Bishop Mullins is president of the Catholic Record Society.

Susan O'Brien is Deputy Vice-Chancellor of Staffordshire University and has taught history in colleges and universities for twenty years. She has been Pro-Rector of Liverpool Hope University College and Dean of Humanities at Anglia Polytechnic University in Cambridge. She has been chairperson of the directors of the Margaret Beaufort Institute of Theology, Cambridge, since 1995.

Joseph Pearce is a full-time writer living in Norfolk, author of *Wisdom and Innocence: A Life of G. K. Chesterton*; *Tolkien: Man and Myth*; *Literary Converts* and *Solzhenitsyn: Prophet and Loss*. His first novel, *The Three Ys Men*, was published in 1998. He has lectured on nineteenth-century themes and, in particular, on the Catholic Literary Revival.

James Pereiro, a priest of the Opus Dei Prelature, is the author of *Cardinal Manning: An Intellectual Biography* and holds degrees in history, sociology and education. He has written on historical and theological themes in journals and collective volumes. The theology of the laity, in its historical development and practical expression, is one of his main fields of research. Dr Pereiro is currently chaplain at Grandpont House, Oxford.

Jeffrey Paul von Arx is a Jesuit and Dean of Fordham College in Fordham University, New York City. Formerly he was Department Head of History at

Georgetown University in Washington, DC. Fr von Arx, who also has interests in Irish and Australian history, has published in late nineteenth-century British intellectual history and in the history of the Catholic Church in Britain.

Michael Walsh is librarian of Heythrop College, University of London, and has written extensively on religious matters past and present including several books. Among the latter are *The Popes: An Illustrated History* and *Roots of Christianity.*

Maurice Whitehead is a senior lecturer in Education in the University of Hull, a member of the Council of the Catholic Record Society and editor of the *European Journal of Teacher Education.* Formerly on the staff of Wimbledon College, he has published on the historical and contemporary development of English Catholic education and is the author of *The Academies of Reverend Bartholomew Booth in Georgian England and Revolutionary America.*

Michael Williams is a priest of the Birmingham archdiocese and former head of studies in theology at Trinity and All Saints' Colleges in Leeds. For thirteen years he taught the history of theology at the English College, Lisbon, where he was Vice-President. Mgr Williams has written histories of the Venerable English College, Rome and St Alban's College, Valladolid. He is currently preparing a history of Oscott College.

Edward Yarnold is a Jesuit and University Research Lecturer in Theology at Campion Hall, Oxford University. He was a member of the Anglican–Roman Catholic International Commission for more than twenty years. He has written and edited several books on liturgical, theological and ecumenical subjects, most recently *Anglican Orders* in collaboration with Bishop Christopher Hill. He has been Visiting Professor at the University of Notre Dame and at a number of other American universities.

ONE

THE FORMATIVE YEARS, 1850–92

V. ALAN MCCLELLAND

Robert Seton, the first Transatlantean to study at the Roman Accademia of Noble Ecclesiastics, an exclusive staff college for the public service of the Church, has left on record his view that community life there 'was like that of Saint Augustine and his friends after his conversion',[1] an existence characterised by comradely talk, laughter, courteous mutual deference, common study and camaraderie. In 1861, it was a cosmopolitan residence of some six nationalities, numbering among them four future cardinals, a patriarch, two archbishops, two bishops, a delegate apostolic and two canons of St Peter's. The table was delicate, with aromatic wines served from a special vineyard near Ancona and a plentiful supply of fish, to say nothing of gourmet eels from the Commachio near the mouth of the Po. It is quite an intellectual challenge to speculate upon what the staid, widowed and abstemious former archdeacon of the Anglican diocese of Chichester, Henry Edward Manning, made of this privileged abode of his post-ordination studies for the Roman Catholic priesthood when he entered the Accademia a decade before Seton in the summer of 1851. At forty-three years of age, Manning was older than most of his new companions and the year of his arrival was the momentous one in which Lord John Russell's anti-popery legislation embedded in the Ecclesiastical Titles Act unleashed the enmity of Protestant Englishmen against the new bishops of the restored Catholic hierarchy of 1850. Catholics, however, were inured to the manifestations of persecution and, although the restoration of the hierarchy had not met with universal acclaim among them, the outbreak of Protestant intolerance acted as a bonding force in the process of dampening down internecine strife and in enabling the community to defend Wiseman and his episcopal confrères in establishing a new ecclesiastical polity.[2]

A CATHOLIC REVIVAL

Nicholas Wiseman was a genuine European with an international reputation for scholarship and his perspective of the agitation of 1851 was influenced by convictions he shared with Catholic apologists in Munich and Paris that commitment to Christianity and to Catholicism was needed for the salvation of the modern world.[3] The new apologetic was skilfully delineated in his Donatist article in the *Dublin Review* of 1839, a presentation which, in particular, opened a vista for John Henry Newman that was destined to convey him progressively to his Armageddon six years later. Wiseman (as with W. G. Ward subsequently) was convinced that an English Catholic 'has a very far closer corporate connection with a French or Italian Catholic, than with an English Protestant',[4] a belief arising, as Wiseman put it, from a realisation that 'if the Church is to be heard because Christ teaches in it, the Church is *infallible*, – even as Christ is . . .'[5] The logic in this theology was direct and simple, yet it had profound implications for nineteenth-century ecclesiology. For Wiseman, it meant 'there is no middle point between private judgement and the infallible authority of a living Church which, being universal, can command particular Churches as well as individuals'.[6] The statement embodied an ecclesiology that Wiseman, and Manning who followed him, were to propagate with unswerving devotion in the forty-two years they guided the development of the Roman Catholic Church in England and Wales. The message gained in significance as the Church of England became increasingly fixated upon navel-contemplating disputes on doctrinal issues, disestablishment and ritualism.[7]

Manning was distanced from coping with the immediate aftermath of 1851. Apart from summer breaks in England necessitated by his delicate health (he suffered from a chest weakness that occasionally manifested itself in the expectoration of blood and led him to suspect the onset of the consumption that carried off his young wife of twenty-five in 1837), the Roman Academia was to be a second home for him until 1854, the year in which Rome was vibrant with prelates and pilgrims for the declaration by Pope Pius IX of the dogma of the Immaculate Conception of the Blessed Virgin Mary. Manning's years in Rome were stirring years, the declaration of 1854 only marking the zenith of that nineteenth-century Catholic revival in Europe of which the English Tractarian Movement and its consequences were but a minor exemplification.[8]

Coming as it did so recently after the Pope's return to Rome from exile in Gaetà, the declaration of an *ex cathedra* utterance, in the face of political unrest in Europe and despite renewed onslaughts of liberal anti-clericalism, gave occasion for a new display of the efficacy of Catholic unity, testifying to the universality of the Church.[9] The dogma was proclaimed without benefit of General Council, but after consultation with bishops and theologians. Not only did it affirm the truth of original sin but, in a challenge to the homocentric philosophy of contemporary liberalism, posited the need for man's continuing redemption. As significantly, perhaps, it constituted a clear manifestation of the functioning of the Petrine legacy within the Church and, hence, of the role of papal infallibility in her teaching and evangelising imperatives.[10] It was the definition of the Immaculate Conception in 1854 that, according to Manning, 'powerfully awakened in the minds of both clergy and laity the thought of infallibility'.[11] Newman's theory of the development of Christian doctrine (which aroused the ire of another convert to Rome, the poet Aubrey de Vere, who considered it to be 'as full of fallacies as the sea is full of fish'[12]) enabled him to greet the definition of 1854 as an exemplification of the setting of faith and tradition within a true theological dynamic.[13] It was a theory, of course, that was to serve equally well in 1870 in relation to the Vatican Council's formal definition of papal infallibility.

It has recently been argued that the Catholic revival of the mid-nineteenth century was strongly influenced by the figure and charism of Pio Nono himself 'whose change of heart from his early liberalism had done nothing to diminish his warmth of personality and irresistible charm'.[14] Around his ageing and corpulent figure developed a personality cult, perhaps 'unique in the history of the Holy See'.[15] Bishop Francis Amherst ascribed part of the papal charm to Pius's accessibility to visitors, to his regular walks among the people of Rome and to the ability he cultivated to direct attention to individuals 'as though the one before him were the only object of his care'.[16] Anne Pollen describes how Pius used to engage in conversation the nine children of Manning's former Anglican curate, Charles La Primaudaye, who had converted in 1850. The Pope would tease the youngest child as '*la figlia del sole*' on account of her blond hair.[17] It was in essence the Pope's vulnerability, his good humour, his uncomplicated but sincere spirituality and his openness to people[18] that helped to confirm de Vere's view that on joining the Church of Rome, he was exchanging a lawless freedom for a glorious liberty and avoiding 'the cramping narrowness of a formal or sectarian interpretation of Christianity'.[19]

In de Vere's writings the sense of a momentous period of confidence in the Catholic Church and of commitment to her authoritative role as teacher and spiritual guide is discernible. In his receptivity, he cannot but have been influenced by Manning as the two journeyed to Rome in 1851 following de Vere's submission to the Catholic Church at Avignon on 15 November. The debt is pointed out in his likening of Manning in a letter to Lady de Vere to 'a saint of old' who had stepped out of a painting by Raphael or Perugino. What he admired was Manning's 'union of grace, decisiveness and sanctity', a trinity of descriptors he also found applicable to Pio Nono. De Vere's analysis of Manning predated by half a century the similar judgement of the logical positivist, Frederic Harrison. But it was praise, indeed, coming from de Vere, who could be unduly caustic in his description of people, once categorising English society women as both hard and 'without *chiaroscuro*' and, again, remarking about a fat child on one occasion that 'it is good to have something to grow out of'.

There is very little doubt the Roman experience was a tremendously formative one upon many of those exposed to it.[20] It has been observed that, in the 1850s, more English than ever before went to Italy 'with Murray's guidebook in their hands, to gaze on the forum, to view the statues in the Vatican galleries and to experience the pomp of St Peter's'.[21] The highlight of such visits was to see and, if possible, to meet with the Pope himself, a memorable aspiration for increasing numbers of middle-class English people as well as for the wealthy and titled.

Wiseman certainly never lost his love of the Eternal City. It remained a constant stimulus to the furthering of his conviction that his essential role in England after 1850 was the intellectual one of purging eighteenth-century scepticism by bringing to bear upon it the culture, authority and influence of a continental scholarship, tempered and humanised by the experience of Catholicism. Some, however, thought about Wiseman as did Walter McDonald, a distinguished alumnus of Maynooth who would be named to a chair of theology there in 1881. Son of a tenant farmer in Co. Kilkenny, McDonald was but eleven years of age when Wiseman died in 1865 but he remembered vividly the magnificence of his obsequies by which a repentant London made some reparation for the hysteria with which his appointment had been received fifteen years earlier. 'Think of Wiseman,' McDonald mused in his autobiography,

> with the genius for literature that produced *Fabiola* in scraps, at spare half hours, and with the scholarship and eye for world problems that gave us lectures of so many kinds; think of the man whose article in *The Dublin Review* shook Newman's soul and at length converted him; think of him taken from his desk to work out the details of the re-establishment of the hierarchy of England, and at the administration of a diocese like Westminster, poverty-stricken, in the metropolis of the wealthiest and most anti-Catholic people in the world! . . . What a legacy he would have left us had he been allowed to remain at his books![22]

Wiseman would have eschewed such well-meaning sentiments: he knew his task in London, above all, was one demanding intellectual strengths of a high order.

Not least among Wiseman's concerns was the necessity of confronting that element of native Cisalpinism, prevalent among the old recusant families, which owed its resilience to the struggles of the gentry with the Vicars Apostolic over an acceptable form of an oath of allegiance to the Crown. By the time of Catholic Emancipation in 1829, Cisalpinism (a peculiarly English variant of French Gallicanism or eighteenth-century German Febronianism) had become marked by antipathy to the growing influence of the middle-class followers of O'Connell and by a resentment at the prominence being given to Irish ecclesiastical affairs in English planning and policy.[23] The sense that Catholics were members of an international body with strong links to the faith and interests of fellow Catholics elsewhere was singularly absent from Cisalpine thought patterns. As Wilfrid Ward put it, Cisalpinism merely 'witnessed to the remnant of national Catholicism'.[24] While acknowledging the supremacy of the papacy in theological terms, it was concerned to preserve its independent life in matters of ecclesiastical organisation and control.

In his study of the English Catholic community, John Bossy has argued the latter increased considerably during the eighteenth and early nineteenth centuries.[25] It was poised to continue its advance before the advent of the major famine years in Ireland that were to lead to what Squire de Lisle epitomised as that 'wretched and untameable race' constituting a catalytic revitalising force within the community. A figure of eighty thousand Catholics in England and Wales has been postulated for the second half of the eighteenth century, some twenty thousand more than the Parliamentary 'Papist Returns' of 1767 indicated.[26] By 1851, that number had increased to form almost 3½ per cent of the total population of England and Wales, the increase being largely drawn from the immigrant Irish in the post-1845 famine years. Although it must not be assumed that all Irish male immigrants were unskilled labourers, such a phenomenal growth in numbers presented grave problems for ecclesiastical policy in England and Wales. Certainly, the Irish presented a challenge and opportunity for Catholic philanthropy in the building of churches, schools, clubs and charitable institutions and they provided the indigenous Catholic population with a higher social profile in their understanding of the needs of the poor and underprivileged than had been the case hitherto. Indeed, from 1850 until the death of Cardinal Manning in 1892, it was the great achievement of the Roman Catholic Church in England and Wales that it became manifestly as conscious of problems engendered by social deprivation outside its own confessional identity as it did of those within.

VIGOUR IN UNITY

It was inevitable that in the pursuit of a policy for coping with its own social ills, the Catholic community needed a specific direction, a co-ordination of policy, effort, decision-making and resourcing that presented both a challenge and an ecclesiastical imperative for the newly established hierarchy. It would, however, be too simplistic to imagine that a conscious realisation of the need for strength in unity somehow suddenly presented itself with the appointment of Wiseman to Westminster in 1850. Vicars Apostolic, the form of ecclesiastical government prior to the restoration of the hierarchy, produced powerful episcopal figures such as John Milner in the Midland District (1803–26) and William

Poynter in the London District (1812–27) who struggled, with varying degrees of success, to secure proper episcopal direction of effort. Catholic lay magnates were frequently resentful of such effort making inroads into their own traditional power base and exposing them to the public notice of particularly suspicious or prejudiced Protestant neighbours. Historians have portrayed Catholics as forming an entity apart from the nation in 1850. For David Newsome, the Catholic families 'in their indigenous strongholds, proudly and aloofly aristocratic' rested uneasily 'among the rank and file (mainly immigrant Irish), the lowest of the labouring class with many destitute'. Hence, the argument evolves, 'until the influx of the Anglican converts in the 1840s and 50s, English Catholicism was a social anomaly' because 'it had no middle'.[27] This is a neat perception, in the genre of John Henry Newman's romantic portrayal of Georgian Catholicism as a period of stagnation and decay[28] which was propagated in his 'Second Spring' sermon preached before the Synod of Oscott in 1852. Such broad-brush categorisation leaves many questions unanswered and is as unrealistic as that which characterises the early years of the restored hierarchy as mainly preoccupied with the introduction of ultramontane structures and attitudes. While it is undoubtedly true that the great achievement of Wiseman from 1850 to 1865 and of Manning from 1865 to 1892 lay in the rapid advance they made in blending three potentially divisive constituents of English Catholicism and, in so doing, preparing the way for the emergence of a robust Catholic middle class, it is important to recognise that the central preoccupation of the first twenty years of the restored hierarchy was an essentially pastoral revolution that left the faithful more cohesive in worship and, in the words of Olaf Blum, 'more actively devout' than at any time during the previous hundred years.[29] The pastoral revitalisation was the spiritual and liturgical catalyst that greatly facilitated the essential bonding processes.

The text selected by Manning for the panegyric he was to preach at the spectacular funeral of Wiseman in February 1865 was 'Let Nehemias be a long time remembered, who raised up for us our walls that were cast down, and set up the gates and the bars, who rebuilt our houses'. In this way, Manning emphasised his appreciation of Wiseman's pioneering attempt to create a synthesis of Roman Catholic life in England. Slowly, social groupings had become less exclusive, partly affected by rapid industrialisation and the need for a new sense of professionalism in public life, partly as a consequence of intermarriage between new converts from the Anglican Church and 'old Catholics', and partly, subsequent to the definition of 1854, by closer ties of Catholic life with Rome, a city in which, in the view of the Bishop of Northampton 'the churches stand wide open to receive and welcome all' and 'the rich, the poor, the simple and the learned, are of one mind in the presence of Pius IX'.[30]

Manning in 1865 looked upon education as the panacea by which converts, indigenous Catholics and immigrant Irish could become united in sympathy more effectively than in any other area of social work. By its agency the course of mutual tolerance and co-operation could be advanced. If the aid of educated converts could be enlisted in a crusade against the forces of nineteenth-century materialism, especially in the task of defining anew the attitude of religion to science and industry, other groups would be stimulated by the example. Similarly, if indigenous Catholics and converts could be encouraged to undertake the task of educating the Irish and the poor generally, then new religious attitudes to faith would be defined and new horizons of ecclesiastical unity approached.

Such a course of action could best be pursued by the conception of ultramontanism as a principle of cohesion. Two years before the death of Wiseman, Manning outlined in the *Dublin Review* what he saw as the needs of the Catholic Church in England and the effort required to meet them. Essentially, there was a twofold task, one of spiritual regeneration and one 'to ripen and to elevate the social and political life of men by the Church's influences of morality and of law'.[31] He posited the act of the restoration of the hierarchy as of pivotal significance in the process, for without it 'Catholicism would have languished, its efforts would have wanted unity and permanence', in addition to its productiveness being but partially developed.[32]

Manning argued that the advent of the hierarchy had

> ingrafted the Catholic Church in England upon the episcopate of the world, and the influx of the universal church came into it once more with the full tide of life and vigour. The result was dioceses, cathedrals, chapters, missionary parishes. Then councils, provincial and diocesan, then the provisions and traditions of the common law, adjusted by the Holy See to the condition of [the] country. Then an intimate union of action and counsel with Rome, such as before had not been attainable.[33]

Consequently, he argued, every bishop in the hierarchy became a conduit of the spirit and mind of the Holy See to his diocese 'with a fulness and minuteness not possible in the vast vicariates of other days'.[34] Manning's day was to be the day of the bishops.[35]

In specific terms, Manning's blueprint for the future was heavily concerned with education. For the priesthood, proper diocesan seminaries were needed, for the poor and middle classes an adequate system of schooling had to be constructed, for the better educated 'a higher literary and scientific education' was required, 'analogous, in fact to that furnished by the Protestant universities'.[36] There were other identified needs: more experience in public life for the laity (twenty-four Catholics represented British constituencies in Parliament, albeit some of them for only a short time, between 1829 and 1885[37]), a society for foreign missionary endeavour, the growth of a Catholic literature. Manning was firmly convinced that 'in twenty years Rationalism will inundate England' as a consequence of which 'unbelief will be more widely spread'.[38] He was not alone in his apocalyptic vision. Friedrich von Hügel, in his relationship with Newman, contemplated 'how one so good, and who had made so many sacrifices to God, could be so depressing'. He attributed the disposition to Newman's difficulty 'in surmounting his deeply predestinarian, Puritan training'.[39] Evangelical influences left a permanent propensity in both Manning and Newman to declare opposition to a world marked by processes of expediency and materialism and by an increasing unbelief. Von Hügel remarks how Newman, in his Oratory church at Edgbaston, 'used to preach so fiercely to his young men against "their second-rate imitations of polished ungodliness" '.[40] For both Manning and Newman, the Church's educative and missionary enterprise arose out of a divine mandate based upon truth and faith.

Emmet Larkin has shown how increased centralisation of the Church's structures, direction and organisation in the pontificate of Pius IX was accompanied, paradoxically, 'by an increasing ascendancy of the more relaxed and less rigorist moral theology of St Alphonsus de Liguori, with a greater emphasis on the Incarnation than the Atonement, and as a God of love rather than of fear',[41] a direction in personal devotion best exemplified in England by the teaching of Faber, the endeavours of Coffin and the preaching of newly established religious orders and congregations. Increased Marian devotion after 1854 helped greatly to soften the harshness of earlier apologetic. In Ireland, Cardinal Paul Cullen's ultramontanism, while influential in the process of effecting radical reform of the Irish Church and in removing the corruption, superstition and episcopal ineptitude which confronted him in many areas of church life, was accompanied by a revitalisation of religious devotion that was to prove as permanent as it was spectacular.[42]

Larkin has contended that Cullen, by the effect of his ultramontanism, was able to assure Irish Catholics psychologically 'that they would never be absorbed by the greater English culture because the historical identity of that English culture was itself profoundly rooted in its Protestantism and could not, therefore, without becoming something other than it was, accommodate an ultramontane and Tridentine Irish Catholicism'.[43] The argument can similarly be related to Manning. Fundamentally, von Arx has argued,

> if the Church were to fulfil its mission of acting effectively for Christian goals in a pluralistic political world no longer based on Christian values, the Church must act at the direction of a single authority. That unity of belief and action was a defining characteristic of the Church was self-evident to Manning and had been . . . decisive as a motive for his conversion.[44]

If the Church in England had a spiritual and temporal message to convey to the nation, it could only do it effectively by speaking with one voice and in unity within itself. The temporal message was clear as Manning delineated it in his *England and Christendom*, published in 1867. The Church

> is eminently in England, as the Church of God must always be in all lands, the Church of the poor. It is not the Church of the Crown, certainly. It is not the Church of the aristocracy. It is not the Church of the landlords, in Ireland or in England . . . it is the Church of the poor.[45]

In Manning's view, the First Vatican Council, at which he played a significant part, defined the nature of the Petrine primacy, not for a temporal end but 'to guard the Divine deposit of Christianity, and to vindicate the Divine certainty of faith'.[46] Indeed, he saw the Council as freeing the Church from the danger of political domination, as releasing her from the shackles imposed by the *ancien régime*. The Church's success in England, as he intimated in his far-sighted speech at the Council itself on 23 May 1870, would no longer be judged by a head count of converts but by how far the teaching of the Church had penetrated the thought-processes of the English nation and by the change in political and social attitude Catholic truth could generate. This view was a remarkable sea-change from Wiseman's stance of thirty years before, when he declared 'few more pernicious sacrifices have been made to the false divinities worshipped by the age, than that of denying the spirit of proselytism to be inherent in Catholicity'.[47] While disowning an intermeddling and intrusive spirit, Wiseman had seen the essence of proselytism as 'a steady, unceasing desire to bring others to the possession of the same truth as we hold, a prudent yet zealous endeavour to recommend that truth by word and action'.[48] By contrast, Manning possessed no grand plan for the conversion of England. By strengthening and educating the Catholic community, by speaking with one voice on matters of faith and morality, by involving the Church in processes of social welfare, by standing firm for Christian mores, a change in mental attitudes might ensue. Bishop Amherst put the issue in a nutshell on the eve of the Council:

> The struggle in a few years will be between Catholicity and infidelity, as it is on the Continent – at least in France, Spain and Italy; and though infidelity will carry off a very great number, the sense of the necessity of religion will prevail over a vast crowd of people whose only refuge will be the Church.[49]

Cisalpine attitudes were outdated after the Council. They were anathema because they were seen to fragment the visible unity of the Church, because they prognosticated hesitancy in direction, because they put at risk long-term missionary endeavour and ecclesiastical *stabilitas*. Manning's vision of the Church after 1870 was similar to that of Canon William Barry when he wrote that the papacy 'is now the head of a worldwide voluntary association which wields no sword but its faith, and which owes nothing to secular governments'.[50] Manning's support, too, for the episcopacy when in conflict with hitherto largely free-lancing independent religious orders and congregations needs to be seen within such a context. The securing of the Bull *Romanos Pontifices* from Leo XIII in 1881 regulated the relationship between bishops in their dioceses and religious orders or congregations operating therein. Leo's support of the diocesan bishops demonstrated 'a recognition of the changing complexities of socio-religious organization in Europe', as Oliver Rafferty has stated it, although it was many of the Orders that had kept the ultramontane spirit alive 'in the face of Gallican-type hierarchies in several countries'.[51]

In 1873, Manning plainly outlined the nature of his variety of ultramontanism. It consisted of three elements: recognition of the separation of spiritual and civil powers; a claim for the Church (resting upon the guidance of the Holy Spirit) that she had the sole right to define doctrines of faith and morals; an acceptance that the Church had the duty to fix the limits of her own jurisdiction within her own proper sphere.[52] These principles, he affirmed, 'are of the substance of Christianity' and

> no man can deny any one of them without denying the office and even the existence of the Christian Church or without affirming the preposterous and monstrous doctrine that the revelation of Divine truth is to be judged and disposed of by royal mandates, legislative enactments, and civil tribunals, which is the lowest and basest form of Erastianism.[53]

The same point was emphasised in a paper Manning gave to the Academia of the Catholic Religion, an association formed by Wiseman to engage the laity in debate of topical issues of the day. In 1873, Manning declared 'the natural antagonist of Caesarism is the Christian Church, with all its liberties of doctrine and discipline of faith and jurisdiction, and the vindication of these liberties of the Church in their highest and most sacred form is ultramontanism . . .'[54] David Newsome has put it succinctly: 'The monster which threatened to devour people's liberty was not the Pope, but the so-called "German Liberalism" which the *Kulturkampf* had unmasked.'[55]

Some historians have seen Manning's paper on 'Caesarism and Ultramontanism' as the most controversial public pronouncement he ever made.[56] This is because of the positive contribution he considered the Church was poised to make in the development of the new democratic processes of the last quarter of the nineteenth century. His vision was to form a blueprint for the future, a contribution that was to be envisaged as collaborative with other Christians in the design to infuse the secular State with Christian attitudes towards government and morality. This was a realistic approach because Manning considered the Church of England to be already disestablished to all intents and purposes.[57] Implied in the approach was a new irenicism, a desire to collaborate with other Christian denominations when common interests were threatened by the overweaning power of an essentially secular State.[58] After 1871 the power of the papacy rested upon its moral influence alone. The same could be said of the prestige and authority of the Archbishop of Westminster. Wilfrid Ward pointed out that because of Manning's 'internal belief in and devotion to the Church, and his readiness to champion its claims, even where they were unpalatable to his fellow-countrymen', he 'ultimately won the respect of the bulk of Englishmen and greatly diminished the national prejudice against his co-religionists'.[59]

CATHOLICITY AND INFIDELITY

The challenge, Manning discerned, would present itself in education, in the area of labour rights and with regard to social deprivation, in the field of marriage law and on issues of public and private morality. His ultramontanism led him to evolve a theological stance that made it imperative for the English Catholic Church to assume the mantle of spokesperson for and protector of the British working man. To achieve that with any prospect of pastoral success, the Church had to speak with an international and authoritative voice: 'Catholics cannot meet without being forced into the time-spirit,' he warned his listeners in 1865;

> the Middle Ages are passed. There is no zone of calms for us. We are in the modern world, in the trade winds of the nineteenth century, and we must brace ourselves to lay hold of the world as it grapples with us, and to meet it intellect to intellect, culture to culture, science to science.[60]

In proportion as the Church, through her members, 'regains the intelligence of the English people, the hearts of men will turn to it *sicut torrens in austro*'.[61] The instincts of the English people he believed to be largely Christian and, based upon this conviction, he preached 'the Church is nowhere so vigorous than when it is in closest sympathy with the people'.[62] He looked to Ireland, Poland, America and Australia for exemplars.

To the horror of many of the recusant families, Manning seemed to wish to identify Catholics in England with 'the poor of Ireland and the poor of England mingling together in poverty, labour, mutual kindness and marriages which unite both races in the unity of Faith'.[63] The Catholic Church was no longer 'an exotic in England', like 'an air-plant suspended over the soil, without root in the earth'.[64] It was now 'deep in the clay, like the tap root of our old forest tree, which pierces downwards, and spreads on every side with an expanding and multiplying grasp'.[65] He saw English Catholics of the mid-nineteenth century as 'interwoven with the whole population' and forming 'a solid and sensible bulk in our cities and towns, and one more firmly rooted where these are largest, as in London, Liverpool, Manchester and Glasgow'.[66]

The landed recusant families were not enamoured at this social and ecclesiastical reorientation and, least of all, with the identification of the English Catholic

Church with the poor. Furthermore, they resented the usurping role they considered converts and middle-ranking Catholics were beginning to play at the centre of the Church in England. Barbara Charlton of Hesleyside was to remark in her acerbic diary, 'The depression of the old Catholic type seems to have come on very rapidly, occasioned, it may be presumed, by an influx of converts and colonists.'[67] The latter category encapsulated the Irish, characterised as 'all dirty, and helpless, sackless and unworthy objects'. She never knew 'to what degree of perfection Irish filth could be raised until I visited the Hibernian colony in Bristol'. She considered 'duplicity went hand-in-hand with dirt'.[68] Concern for the masses, however, was a main characteristic feature of ultramontane religious thought, evidenced not only in the public stance of a Manning or a Cullen but also in the policy of Cardinal Pie in Poitiers and Cardinal Von Geissel in Cologne. Its incisiveness arose not merely from a reinvigorated interpretation of the Christian message but also from the necessity confronting many national churches in the wake of rapid industrialisation and its social manifestations. Ultramontane support for a wide range of charitable associations and the mushrooming of nineteenth-century congregations of priests, brothers and nuns did much to humanise and assuage the worst examples of deprivation and acted as a bonding and unifying force within the Catholic body.

Manning's call, therefore, for Catholics to brace themselves to face the modern age presaged a message of hope for the future of the Catholic community. Its importance has recently been emphasised by Mary Heimann in her study of Catholic devotion which underpinned community growth and change. She has shown that

> the spiritual life of the nineteenth-century Catholic was increasingly bound up with his social rôle within the wider Catholic community, not only through his church, school, hospital, and at times of socially recognized importance such as his birth, marriage and death but also in his leisure hours, his insurance policies and in the direction of his spiritual growth.[69]

Furthermore, she emphasises that the Catholic revivalist devotions of the century, 'far from exacerbating differences between Irish and English, old Catholics and converts, ultramontanes and liberals, effectively provided a common language to articulate that specifically religious dimension of life which was shared by Catholics as Catholics'.[70]

When Manning took possession of his titular church in Rome in March 1875 (that of Sts Andrew and Gregory on the Coelian Hill), he viewed the political turmoil that was ravaging Europe. Pius IX had endured the loss of the Papal States and had been insultingly treated by the Risorgimento, France had experienced the Commune and the associated murder of Georges Darboy, the Archbishop of Paris. Spain had suffered civil war from 1868 to 1874 and the Spanish Church was under siege. Germany was rejoicing in the ascendancy of Protestant Prussia over her Catholic neighbours. On that bitterly cold day in Rome which nearly brought on the death of one English observer, Dom David Hunter Blair OSB,[71] Manning spent some time in understanding and sympathising with those whose hearts were failing on account of the days being evil and the strengthening international tide towards unbelief.[72] Using his customary messianic style, he urged his hearers to 'stand firm in the Faith', to be strong and of perfect heart, for 'Come what may, there is yet a future more glorious and fruitful than the past. We have no cause for despondency, but ought to be hopeful and courageous.'[73] It was a curious brand of optimism when all seemed likely to be at risk but events were to show that his conviction in the regenerative effect of the First Vatican Council was not misplaced. A reflowering of Catholicism, perhaps a more devout, but certainly a more socially aware Catholicism, emerged as the idea of the confessional State receded. The old man was to live to receive with great joy the encyclical *Rerum Novarum* in 1891, a pronouncement on social questions that went far to realise his vision of the Church becoming the champion of the working man.

Ultramontanism and Tractarianism were variants of the same fundamental yearning for the reaffirmation of apostolic authority.[74] Both were concerned with the nature of that authority and with the issue of the freedom of the Church from political interference or control in the areas of faith and morals. Both were insistent that the Church should have freedom to organise her life and polity in relation to the teaching of Christ without fear of State oppression or intervention. There is thus essential truth in Bishop Geoffrey Rowell's view that

> as the Catholic Church in Europe in the aftermath of the French Revolution saw the growth of the ultramontane movement, which stressed the authority of the papacy over against national churches which could be controlled by secularizing and unsympathetic governments, so the Oxford Movement can be seen in part as a parallel English movement.[75]

Both movements led to a more intimate relationship between theology, ethics and personal sanctification, the fruits of what Manning, with directness, called 'practical Christianity'. This led in turn to a greater understanding of the doctrine of the Mystical Body of Christ and to the missionary legacy inherent in that belief. The significance of good works in the salvific process had been an essential core in evangelicalism, the progenitor of much that was distinctive in Tractarianism.

A major stimulus to the growth of the active apostolate among the people had been Wiseman's early encouragement of 'the Italian mission', introduced into the country from Italy, the religious congregations of Paul of the Cross and Antonio Rosmini in particular. Bishop Louis Charles Casartelli of Salford saw this 'mission' as a centrifugal force, with its evangelising endeavour among the poor of cities and towns and especially in the heart of rural parishes neglected by the Established Church. It helped to dispel the insularity and religious exclusivity of indigenous English Catholics while introducing an almost evangelical approach to repentance and conversion. Casartelli, referring to 'the Italian mission', doubted 'even such a vital force as that of the Oxford Movement would have been able to produce the far-reaching effects which are attributed to it'.[76]

The Oxford Movement, however, was more than an insatiable yearning for the romantic in stone and liturgy that would enhance the dignity of Christianity and awaken dormant spirituality, more than a desire for the return of primitive practice in the interests of revitalising sacramental and doctrinal life, more than a need for spiritual certitude or the authentication of ecclesiastical credentials. It was, rather, a renaissance in the understanding of the foundation and role of authority within the Church from which all authenticity stemmed, the need to convince oneself that the Anglican Church was more than 'a serviceable breakwater against errors more fundamental than its own'.[77] Both the evangelical and Catholic revivals weakened the credentials of the Church of England as a Church and State establishment.[78]

Animated as so many of the Oxford converts to Roman Catholicism were by the treasure they had so recently discovered, and enamoured by the strong links the restored Catholic hierarchy was forming with the See of Peter,[79] they were personally enraptured by Rome itself, which 'shed upon them all that soothing equanimity that was her own special gift'.[80] Of course, not all the converts had been to Rome or had met with Pius IX. At least five hundred Oxford men and two hundred Cambridge men followed Newman into the Church of his adoption in the immediate aftermath of 1845. Few had enjoyed personal experience of the diurnal round of the Catholic Church in England, let alone on the Continent. Hardly any had contacts with local Catholic clergy whether English or Irish. To these men, Rome was little more than a high-minded reality and their obedience to her was based essentially upon theological conviction. While there was danger in this situation of the reality not living up to expectation, it is remarkable how the devotion to the Pope inspired the lives of so many converts. Thomas William Allies devoted the years from 1861 to 1895 to the completion of his volumes on *The Formation of Christendom*. 'After the work of saving my soul,' he wrote in his journal, 'it is my work in life to defend the See of Peter.'[81] Manning, from his own pastoral experience as Anglican and Roman Catholic, was sympathetic to the desires of the converts and conscious of their obligations, obfuscations and uncertainties. He knew better than most the inner turmoil by which they were beset and the bleak economic future forced upon many married convert clergymen.

Spurning imperfection as they saw it, the convert clergymen sought perfection in their new home. Some of them, such as Richard Waldo Sibthorpe,[82] were disappointed and returned to their former allegiance, a few for a time, others permanently. Those who remained Catholics searched for a new role to fulfil and an appropriate livelihood for their families to enjoy. In this quest the idea of teaching assumed a prominence for educated convert married clergy for whom there could be no openings in the Catholic celibate priesthood. Many such men had been prominent figures as Anglicans and 'understood dimensions of English life from which the old (English) Catholics had been removed'.[83] In particular, 'they had a working knowledge of the fine line between politics and philanthropy in areas of social importance' and in this 'they were set apart from "old Catholics" '.[84] The absence of a similar intellectual ability and experience among many of the indigenous Catholics provided a ripe breeding ground for misunderstanding and for the germination of differences and tensions. The philanthropic work for the poor which marked the social conscience of many converts won a popular base for ultramontanism. Having a clear perception of the need ahead of them, many converts wished to arouse indigenous Catholics to begin a process of reform and saw their own role as that directed to a raising of the level and tone of the whole Catholic community.

Allies, who was converted to Catholicism in 1850, typified the dilemma of some married converts. 'I feel like the man', he wrote, 'who rode his horse over a bridge of boats one night and when he saw what he had done next day, died of fright.' Overnight he had become a layman 'without *status*, with great desires and aspirations, which were often damped by poverty and its attendant ills'. He had come 'out of Anglican pastures into the back street of things Catholic'. Added to which there was 'the coldness of friends who now knew him no more'.[85] Nevertheless, Allies was to fare better than some others. Through the good offices of Wiseman he was appointed Secretary of the Poor School Committee (the Catholic substitute for the National Society and the British and Foreign Schools Society), a post he held from 1853 to 1890.

Another convert, J. M. Capes, had a high-minded mission in his sights: 'I soon made up my mind', he wrote, 'it was my function to devote myself to promoting that general culture of the English Catholic body in which, as I soon found, they were grievously deficient.'[86] He was able to persuade himself that there were many Catholics who hailed the introduction of the new converts, 'not merely on theological grounds, but because they expected from them an infusion of that love of science and literature whose absence they themselves had been long deploring'.[87] The indigenous priests, he considered, were poorly trained, their studies being confined 'to the acquisition of such authors of dogmatic and moral theology as will enable them just to pass muster at ordination and to act as confessors'.[88] He attributed the lack of theological culture to a history of over-dependence upon the old landed families for support and sustenance. The families had not been interested in having a learned clergy, but only 'massing priests' who could serve as domestic chaplains and, perhaps, help in the surrounding area.

Capes and others took up the issue in the pages of the *Rambler*, a journal of the liberal left, loyal to the papacy, but determined to reform the educational inefficiencies of the old generation of indigenous Catholics. The need was palpable. W. G. Ward considered that when 'a Protestant meets a Catholic in controversy, it is like a civilized man meeting a barbarian'.[89] Even Newman nostalgically feared he had set his face towards the wilderness.

In 1849, Ward pointed out in the columns of the *Rambler* that

> there is no recognised system whatever among us which so much as professes to train the noble or the wealthy for their high and responsible positions: there is no recognised system whatever which so much as professes to train up persons who may be really fitted to teach the secular branches of education in our colleges.[90]

And yet, the journal was to argue 'the problems of human life, its happiness for this life, and the life to come, is to be solved by the acquisition of knowledge and by the labours of the schoolmaster'.[91]

At the root of the problem was alleged to be the mixed system of clerical and lay education in the chief Catholic educational establishments. Priests and religious occupied the majority of the teaching posts and they thus presented a solid front against the employment of married clerical converts. The *Rambler* complained, 'We have found the middle of the nineteenth-century arrive without the establishment of a single purely ecclesiastical or purely secular, seminary in Great Britain.'[92] The Church was already stretching her resources in trying to meet the requirements of the Poor School Committee. If the middle classes were to be properly educated it could only be done by separating the education of priests from that of lay boys in those colleges which were heirs to the exiled continental traditions.

Attacks on the low intellectual level of indigenous English Catholics were based upon exaggerations. Oscott College had been among the pioneers in seeking affiliation with London University in 1839 and in entering students for the London Matriculation examinations: it gained its first BA graduate in 1848.[93] By 1842, Ushaw, Stonyhurst, Prior Park, Downside and St Edmund's College at Ware had all been affiliated to London University and a major realignment of the studies in the affiliated colleges had begun to take shape as the relationship developed. The *Rambler*, however, felt this process was insufficient. Capes warned: 'Vain will be every apparent improvement if we ignore the momentous difference between the life of the priest and the layman and are content to perpetuate a system which more or less brings them up in one indiscriminate crowd.'[94] Meantime, the frustration of many converts continued, leading Edmund S. Ffoulkes to remark: 'We have, everyone of us, had the cold shoulder given to us when we asked for work, or else encouraged to seek employment in any calling, no matter how secular.'[95] Allies bemoaned 'living the life of a clerk, occupied mainly with petty routines' when his natural desire was 'to study and write'.[96]

Some of the converts undoubtedly were unduly demanding and expected change to be effected too rapidly. Others managed to make satisfying careers for themselves – Thomas Arnold, Thomas William Marshall and Scott Nasmyth Stokes became inspectors of schools; Frederick Barff (a former Anglican curate in Hull) became a chemist of some distinction; Robert Ornsby, John Hungerford Pollen and Thomas Scratton were employed as university teachers and/or artists; W. G. Ward, Henry Bacchus, Capes and Simpson followed careers as writers or journalists or teachers; Edward Badeley and Edward Bellasis made their futures in law. Nevertheless, the educational reform the converts were urging represented a mark of common sense. By the date of Manning's death in 1892, nine dioceses had established their own seminaries for the education of priests and thus effectively broke the traditions of the education of lay and clerical students together, although the practice did linger on.

It was the hierarchy's achievement that by the death of Manning, the Catholic community had become less inward looking, better educated, more socially aware and more loyally Roman than it was at any earlier period in the century. This was achieved, in human terms, by the insight and inspiration of the bishops and their single-minded approach to what Manning considered to be the chief aberration of the nineteenth century – 'the intellectual perversion', as he called it, 'of those who have rejected all revelation and all belief in God, and all moral conception of the nature of man'. He declared it was 'to rectify and to restore the intellect of [the] day'[97] that he and his co-religionists were called to labour. As the century closed, the terms ultramontane, Cisalpine and Tractarian began to assume merely an historic resonance. The sanctification of the intellect was to be 'the proper work of [all] those who have the light of faith and of men who desire the welfare of their fellows'.[98] It can be maintained it was in the pursuit of this irenic aim that the Roman Catholic Church began to grow faster in Great Britain than did the general population, increasing from a figure of some 1,680,000 Catholics in the closing years of Manning's episcopate to one of nearly five millions in 1969.[99]

NOTES

1. Archbishop Seton, *Memories of Many Years 1839–1922* (John Long, London, 1923), p. 141.
2. J. D. Holmes, *More Roman than Rome* (Burns & Oates, London, 1978), pp. 55f.
3. W. Ward, *Ten Personal Studies* (Longmans, Green & Co, London, 1908), p. 201.
4. W. G. Ward, *The Authority of Doctrinal Decisions* (Burns, Lambert & Oates, London, 1866), p. 102.
5. N. Wiseman, *The High Church Claims* (Catholic Institute, London, 1836), Tract 16, no. 2, p. 34.
6. Wiseman, *Claims*, p. 36.
7. G. I. T. Machin, *Politics and the Churches in Great Britain 1869 to 1921* (Clarendon Press,

Oxford, 1987), p. 7. See also J. Pereiro, *Cardinal Manning: An Intellectual Biography* (Clarendon Press, Oxford, 1998), *passim*.

8. W. M. Brady, *Annals of the Catholic Hierarchy in England and Scotland*, AD 1585–1876, etc. (John Mozley Stark, London, 1883), p. 383.
9. A. Mills, *The Life of Pope Pius IX*, 2 vols (D. Lane, London, 1877), vol. I, p. 162.
10. D. Newsome, *The Convert Cardinals* (John Murray, London, 1993), p. 271.
11. H. E. Manning, *The True Story of the Vatican Council* (Henry S. King & Co, London, 1877), p. 43. It was the example established in 1854 that Pius XII followed on 1 November 1950, in defining the doctrine of the Assumption of the Blessed Virgin Mary.
12. W. Ward, *Aubrey de Vere* (Longmans, Green & Co, London, 1904), p. 145.
13. E. R. Norman, *The English Catholic Church in the Nineteenth Century* (Clarendon Press, Oxford, 1984), pp. 326–7.
14. Newsome, *Convert Cardinals*, pp. 268–9.
15. Ibid.
16. Dame Mary Frances Roskell, *Memoirs of Francis Kerril Amherst, DD, Lord Bishop of Northampton*, ed. H. F. J. Vaughan (Art & Book Company, London, 1903), pp. 226–7. Amherst was Bishop of Northampton from 1858 to his resignation in 1879. He was writing in 1859.
17. Anne Pollen, *John Hungerford Pollen, 1820–1902* (John Murray, London, 1912), pp. 249–50.
18. Notice the regular contact the students of the Oblates of St Charles in Rome had with Pius IX between 1862 and 1872, in V. A. McClelland, '"*O Felix Roma!*": Henry Manning, Cutts Robinson and Sacerdotal Formation 1862–1872', *Recusant History*, vol. 21, no. 2 (1992), pp. 180–217.
19. W. Ward, *Aubrey de Vere*, p. 213. See also P. J. Cronin, *Aubrey de Vere* (Askeaton Civic Trust, 1997), p. 58. Letter quoted of de Vere to Mrs Sarah Coleridge, 15 November 1851.
20. A good account of this is provided in Madeleine Beard, *Faith and Fortune* (Gracewing, Leominster, 1997), Part 1, pp. 3–60.
21. C. T. McIntire, *England Against the Papacy, 1858–1861* (Cambridge University Press, 1983), pp. 34–5.
22. W. McDonald, *Reminiscences of a Maynooth Professor* (Jonathan Cape, London, 1926), p. 394.
23. Norman, *English Catholic Church*, pp. 51–2.
24. W. Ward, *Ten Personal Studies*, p. 157.
25. J. Bossy, *The English Catholic Community 1570–1850* (Darton, Longman & Todd, London, 1975), *passim*.
26. Norman, *English Catholic Church*, pp. 205–6.
27. D. Newsome, *The Victorian World Picture* (John Murray, London, 1997), p. 66.
28. S. Gilley, *Newman and His Age* (Darton, Longman & Todd, London, 1990), pp. 272–3.
29. See C. O. Blum, 'St George Mivart' (Notre Dame, doctoral dissertation, 1996), p. 20, for a more general treatment of this theme.
30. Roskell, *Amherst*, pp. 226–7.
31. H. E. Manning, 'The Work and Wants of the Catholic Church in England', *The Dublin Review* (July 1863), reprinted in his *Miscellanies*, vol. I (Burns & Oates, London, 1877), p. 29.
32. Manning, 'Work and Wants', p. 37.
33. Manning, 'Work and Wants', p. 43.
34. Ibid.
35. Peter Doyle, 'Episcopal Authority and Clerical Democracy: Diocesan Synods in Liverpool in the 1850s', *Recusant History*, vol. 23, no. 3 (1997), p. 431.
36. Manning, 'Work and Wants', p. 43.
37. See J. A. Stack, 'Catholic Members of Parliament Who Represented British Constituencies, 1829–1885: A Prosopographical Analysis', *Recusant History*, vol. 24, no. 3 (1999), pp. 335–63.
38. Manning, 'Work and Wants', p. 70.

39. F. von Hügel, *Essays and Addresses on the Philosophy of Religion*, Second Series (J. M. Dent, London and Toronto, 1926), p. 242.
40. Von Hügel, *Essays*, p. 265.
41. E. Larkin, 'Cardinal Paul Cullen' in J. P. von Arx (ed.), *Varieties of Ultramontanism* (Catholic University of America Press, Washington, DC, 1998), p. 64.
42. Larkin, 'Cullen', pp. 68, 79.
43. Larkin, 'Cullen', p. 84.
44. Jeffrey Paul von Arx, 'Cardinal Henry Edward Manning' in *Varieties of Ultramontanism*, p. 100.
45. H. E. Manning, *England and Christendom* (Longmans, Green & Co, London, 1867), pp. xxxix, xliii.
46. H. E. Manning, *The Vatican Decrees in their Bearing on Civil Allegiance* (Longmans, Green & Co, London, 1875), p. 9.
47. N. Wiseman, *The High Church Claims* (Catholic Institute of Great Britain, London, 1839), Tract 17, no. 3, p. 62.
48. Ibid.
49. Roskell, *Amherst*, p. 277. Amherst was writing in 1868 in anticipation of the First Vatican Council.
50. William Barry, *The Coming Age and the Catholic Church: A Forecast* (Cassell, London, 1929), p. 35.
51. Oliver P. Rafferty SJ, 'The Jesuit College, Manchester, 1875', *Recusant History*, vol. 20, no. 2 (1990), p. 302.
52. H. E. Manning, *Ultramontanism and Christianity*, printed in his *Miscellanies*, vol. II (Burns & Oates, London, 1877), p. 197.
53. Ibid.
54. H. E. Manning, *'Caesarism and Ultramontanism'*, paper read before the Academia of the Catholic Religion, 23 December 1873, printed in *Miscellanies*, vol. II, p. 162.
55. Newsome, *Convert Cardinals*, p. 341.
56. See Jeffrey Paul von Arx SJ, 'Archbishop Manning and the *Kulturkampf*', *Recusant History*, vol. 21, no. 2 (1992), p. 255.
57. Von Arx, 'Manning and the *Kulturkampf*', p. 256.
58. Von Arx, 'Manning and the *Kulturkampf*', p. 264. John T. Smith, *Methodism and Education 1849–1902* (OUP, Oxford, 1998), pp. 168–74, shows how closely Manning worked with the Wesleyan, James Rigg, on the Cross Commission, 1886–88. Manning believed in the universality of the work of the Holy Spirit in the world – see James Pereiro, *Cardinal Manning: An Intellectual Biography* (OUP, Oxford, 1998), pp. 337f.
59. W. Ward, *Ten Personal Studies*, p. 262.
60. H. E. Manning, 'On the Subjects Proper to the Academia' in H. E. Manning (ed.), *Essays on Religion and Literature by Various Writers* (Longman, Roberts & Green, London, 1865), p. 51.
61. Manning, 'Subjects', p. 66.
62. H. E. Manning, 'The Centenary of St Peter and the General Council', Pastoral Letter, 1867.
63. Manning, *England and Christendom*, p. xcviii.
64. Ibid.
65. Ibid.
66. Ibid.
67. L. E. O. Charlton (ed.), *The Recollections of a Northumbrian Lady 1865–1866* (Jonathan Cape, London, 1949), p. 90.
68. Charlton (ed.), *Recollections*, p. 228.
69. Mary Heimann, *Catholic Devotion in Victorian England* (Clarendon Press, Oxford, 1995), p. 136.

70. Heimann, *Catholic Devotion*, p. 137.
71. D. Hunter-Blair, *A Medley of Memories* (Edward Arnold, London, 1920), p. 71.
72. Manning's address on taking possession of his titular church in Rome, 31 March 1875, is quoted in Brady, *Annals*, p. 390.
73. Ibid.
74. See P. Vaiss (ed.), *From Oxford to the People* (Gracewing, Leominster, 1988), p. viii.
75. G. Rowell, *The Vision Glorious* (Oxford University Press, 1983), p. 4.
76. L. C. Gasartelli, *Sketches in History* (R. & T. Washbourne, London, 1906), p. 240.
77. See W. G. Ward, *The Oxford Movement* (London, n.d.), esp. p. 84.
78. Machin, *Politics*, p. 7.
79. D. McElrath, *The Syllabus of Pius IX: Some Reactions in England* (Bibliothèque de l'Université, Bureau de la Revue, Louvain, 1964), p. 6.
80. M. Andrieux, *Daily Life in Papal Rome* (George Allen & Unwin, London, 1968), p. 182. What was true of the eighteenth century in this regard was equally true of the nineteenth.
81. Mary H. Allies, *Thomas William Allies* (Burns & Oates, London, 1907), p. 141. See also my chapter, 'The Most Turbulent Priest of the Oxford Diocese: Thomas William Allies and the Quest for Authority, 1837–1850' in V. Alan McClelland (ed.), *By Whose Authority? Newman, Manning and the 'Magisterium'* (Downside, Bath, 1996), pp. 273–90.
82. The new study of the religious development of Sibthorpe upon which Michael Trott is currently engaged is eagerly awaited. Currently the standard work remains J. Fowler's *Life* published in 1880 and an interesting but misleading essay in C. Sykes, *Two Studies in Virtue* (Collins, London, 1953). A short essay has been published by M. Clifton in *A Victorian Convert Quintet* (Saint Austin Press, London, 1998). Sibthorpe does not gain a mention in Beard's *Faith and Fortune*.
83. Mary G. Holland, *The British Catholic Press and the Educational Controversy 1847–1865* (Garland, New York and London, 1987), p. 50.
84. Ibid.
85. M. H. Allies, *Allies*, pp. 66, 67.
86. J. M. Capes, *To Rome and Back* (London, 1873), p. 272.
87. Ibid.
88. Capes, *Rome and Back*, p. 267. Also his *Reason for Returning to the Church of England* (London, 1871), p. 65.
89. Bernard Ward, *The Sequel to Catholic Emancipation*, 2 vols (Longmans, Green & Co, London, 1915), vol. 2, p. 236.
90. *The Rambler* (February 1849), p. 449.
91. *The Rambler* (October 1851), pp. 332–3.
92. *The Rambler* (December 1848), p. 238.
93. See my *English Roman Catholics and Higher Education 1830–1903* (Clarendon Press, Oxford, 1973), pp. 56f., where the subject is treated in detail.
94. *The Rambler* (December 1848), p. 241.
95. *The Union Review*, vol. I, no. 4 (1864), pp. 677f.
96. M. H. Allies, *Allies*, pp. 69, 70.
97. Manning, *Miscellanies*, vol. II, pp. 309–10.
98. Ibid.
99. Machin, *Politics*, pp. 12–13.

TWO

THE YEARS OF EQUIPOISE, 1892–1943

SHERIDAN GILLEY

The period between 1892 and 1943 was one of equipoise in the Roman Catholic Church in England, an era of steady expansion largely untroubled by internal dissent. The rival religious revivals of the nineteenth century, Anglican, Nonconformist and Catholic, had fought themselves to a standstill against a backdrop of increasing unbelief. The Roman Catholic Church had grown most from small beginnings, yet was the least obviously English of all the main churches. Most Roman Catholics in England were either of Irish birth or descent, were poor or very poor, and had interests quite different from those of their English Catholic co-religionists. Yet, with occasional friction, the Irish seemed content with an overwhelmingly English hierarchy and a mostly English priesthood; indeed in Lancashire, even English priests, 'by dint of living among the Irish', wrote an inspector of schools who knew them well, 'nearly always have a noticeable brogue'.[1] Except for the brief flurry between 1900 and 1910 over Modernism, a subject which has received an attention disproportionate to its importance to the great majority of humble and not especially literate Catholics, the period was unmarked by the great controversies of mid-Victorian Catholicism.

This internal peace of the Church was that of Catholics everywhere. Its faith was settled. The infallibility and universal jurisdiction of the papacy were defined at Rome in 1870, and the latter was made the more effective by the codification of canon law begun by Pius X in 1904, and completed by his successor Benedict XV in 1917. The collapse of the great European Empires in 1918 left the papacy free to appoint to bishoprics almost everywhere, without interference from the state, for the first time in the Church's history. From 1878, the Encyclicals of Pope Leo XIII declared the Thomism of Aquinas the basis of the Church's official theology and philosophy, while Leo's social encyclicals, especially *Rerum Novarum* in 1891, defined a Catholic third way between the extremes of liberal laissez-faire capitalist individualism and collectivist secular socialism. Leo's Social Catholicism became a concrete reality across much of Catholic Europe, through the creation of Catholic political parties, trades unions, peasant co-operatives and popular systems of education in areas where Catholic practice remained strong and even strengthened, in northern France, Spain and Portugal, the southern Netherlands and Flanders, western and southern Germany and Austria, and in a great Slav belt from Lithuania and Poland through Slovakia and Croatia.[2] The experience of the English Church, however, was like that of other English-speaking democracies, in which the Church did not encourage the creation of separate Catholic political parties and trades unions. 'Social and political divisions within the Catholic community, the long-standing British antipathy to confessional political parties, and a lack of funds and ambition have all conspired to make political Catholicism almost invisible in the twentieth century.' Yet there was a Social Catholicism and a Catholic politics, and a 'Catholic critique' of British society, especially on the political left,[3] even if this had to contend with a strain of Catholic conservatism which did much to counteract it.[4]

In its experience of comparative political stability, English Catholicism was also markedly different from the rest of the European Church. It was largely unaffected by the two world wars, and only in a degree by the Catholic revolution in Ireland, which began in 1916 and ended in the next decade in civil war. British Catholics underwent nothing to compare with anticlerical persecution and disestablishment in France in 1905 and the puppet Vichy regime in 1940; in Italy, first anticlerical attack and then the rise of Fascism; in Germany, the fall of the Second Reich, the Weimar Republic and the rise of Nazism; the Second Republic, civil war and Franco in Spain; in central and eastern Europe, the collapse of the Catholic Habsburg empire, and later the Nazi and Bolshevik tyrannies. The product of these vicissitudes was the right-wing character of a good deal of European Catholicism, which was an embarrassment to many British Catholics. But the Leonine doctrine that the Church could coexist with any form of political regime which fell short of active persecution of the Church left Catholics in England free, as in the predominantly Protestant British Empire and the United States, to profit from the rise of democracy, with its concomitant freedom for Catholicism. The result was the divergence of Anglo-American Catholicism from the Catholicism of much of Europe, so that where Europe developed a 'closed Catholicism' of the right, Anglo-American Catholicism developed an 'open Catholicism' of the left.[5]

The English Church was, however, quite as much as its sister churches elsewhere, also heir to a global process of clericalisation. Thus by 1890, in all religious matters, the Catholic clergy were undisputed masters of the laity, and the bishops of the clergy, thereby reversing the relationships in which the post-Reformation Catholic Church in England had its origin. More particularly, the

Bull *Romanos Pontifices* in 1881 had established episcopal control of the religious orders, abolishing the freedoms of the biggest orders, the Benedictines and Jesuits, to attend to their own corporate interests first. There was, however, a more important contrast between late Victorian Catholicism and Catholicism by 1943. The nineteenth-century Catholic revival began in parallel to the Protestant revival, indeed in some ways as a consequence of it. The preaching of Christ's passion as a remedy for personal sin was common to the Baptist Charles Spurgeon's Metropolitan Tabernacle and the Brompton Oratory. But the twentieth-century expansion of the Catholic Church occurred against the backdrop of decline in the other churches, and in spite of the loss to secularism if not to unbelief of large numbers of the children of the Irish immigration. 'It is hardly too much to say', writes Peter Clarke, 'that during the twentieth century, Great Britain lost its historic identity as a Protestant nation.'[6] The consequence was that the Catholic Church in England in 1850, a body quite inconsiderable beside the massed ranks of the Establishment and Nonconformity, was probably in terms of practising adherents the largest church in England by 1950, almost as a rival Establishment, with a prominence and profile made the more conspicuous by the decline in the forces of popular anti-Catholicism. The era between the world wars especially was something of a golden age in the history of Catholicism in England.

This change occurred over fifty years, in less than a single lifetime, one dominated by the three Cardinal Archbishops of Westminster, Vaughan, Bourne and Hinsley. Each was in his own way characteristic of his period, and each embodied its distinctive character in the changing fortunes of the Roman Catholic Church in England.

VAUGHAN

Herbert Cardinal Vaughan was a survivor from the heroic era of the mid-Victorian Roman Catholic revival, having served as a young man as Vice-President of St Edmund's, Ware and as a member of Henry Edward Manning's Oblates of St Charles. This community was modelled on the Oblates of St Ambrose founded by St Charles Borromeo, and served as the right hand to Cardinal Wiseman, being more Roman than Rome down to its shoe buckles and stockings. Vaughan and the Oblates were party to the eradication by Wiseman and Manning of any hint of lay control of the English Catholic Church and of the lingering spirit of Anglo-Gallicanism. Vaughan sided with Manning in opposing the plan for Newman's Oratory in Oxford and, as editor-owner of the *Tablet*, strongly commended the definition of papal infallibility at the First Vatican Council. An ascetic who wore a spiked bracelet, his greatest work as a priest was the creation of a new missionary congregation, St Joseph's Society centred at Mill Hill, whose first enterprise was the evangelisation of American negroes. This largeness of spirit extended into his labours to the overwhelmingly Irish diocese of Salford. He was Manning's ally in the Crusade of Rescue to save Catholic children from non-Catholic institutions. He was, moreover, an expert administrator and something of a showman, and no one was a more expert beggar or knew better the value of money for religious purposes. His foundations in Salford included St Bede's Commercial College; to protect its neighbourhood, he acquired the adjoining Manchester Aquarium, and tried for a time to manage it as a public attraction, despatching a trusted Monsignor to the docks to buy an alligator and cockatoos. Vaughan's favourite devotion was to the Sacred Heart, which he did everything to encourage. In succeeding to Westminster, he represented the spirit of continuity with the work of his predecessor in the creation of a self-confident and proselytising Catholic Church.

There were, however, discontinuities between his regime and that of his greater predecessor. He came from an old border family, the Vaughans of Courtfield.[7] As a dazzlingly handsome young man, compared by his younger contemporary Wilfrid Ward to Sir Galahad, his main interests were in country sports, saying his rosary as he knelt with his gun behind a hedge, and he would have been the local squire had he not become a priest. His mother was a convert evangelical who prayed that all her children would enter the religious life; ten of them responded to her call, two of them becoming archbishops and another the Abbot of Fort Augustus. Her influence survived in Vaughan's *amitiés religieuses* with Lady Herbert of Lea,[8] the mother of the thirteenth and fourteenth Earls of Pembroke, and with Alice Ingham, the Rochdale foundress of the Franciscan Missionary Sisters of St Joseph. Manning thought he lacked humour, and sent him Sheridan's plays *The Critic* and *The School for Scandal*. 'You would be holier and happier if you would enter into such things with patience and learn to laugh. You are grim and truculent.'[9] Where Manning was born into the purple of commerce, Vaughan's background was that of an instinctive rural squirearchical Toryism, and he had no sympathy for Manning's great enthusiasms for social justice, Ireland and temperance, which he attributed to 'senile decay'.[10] Their disagreement over temperance had lasting consequences, for Manning struck him from the list of his executors, and Vaughan was unable to persuade the others to stop the journalist Edmund Sheridan Purcell from making a gross misuse of Manning's papers in his notorious biography of the Cardinal.[11] The publication was happier in its consequences, for it made it possible for the brothers Wilfrid and Bernard Ward, the younger sons of W. G. 'Ideal Ward', to write their excellent ecclesiastical biographies and histories of the nineteenth-century Catholic Church in England, on the principle that the Church's best defence was the sympathetic but critical presentation of the truth.[12]

In background, then, Vaughan was representative of the aristocratic and gentry interest in British Catholicism, some of it arising from traditionally recusant

Catholic families, some of it the consequence of conversion to Rome in the nineteenth century. Some seventy-six Catholic aristocrats, male and female, converted to Rome between 1850 and 1900.[13] In 1895, there were forty-three British Catholic peers with seats in the Lords and fifty-three Catholic baronets,[14] as well as scores of landed Catholic county families, some of them the more distinguished for being untitled. At the head of the aristocracy was the devout fifteenth Duke of Norfolk, who built great Catholic churches at Arundel and Norwich and was Postmaster General in Salisbury's Conservative cabinet between 1895 and 1900. The most distinguished of the converts were the lay Marquess of Ripon, himself the son of a Prime Minister, a former Liberal Minister and Grand Master of the English Freemasons, and in his greatest office, the only Catholic Viceroy to India;[15] and the Marquess of Bute, a considerable scholar and archaeologist and the richest man in Britain, the owner of the Cardiff docks. Bute was the model for Disraeli's Lothair, and a lavish supporter of Catholic church building as well as of great Gothic palaces for himself. It is claimed that he could read twenty-one languages and he gave the Church a splendid if neglected treasure in his complete translation of the Roman Breviary. He also subsidised the singing of the whole Latin office in a tin cathedral in Oban. Bute's remark, 'Isn't it perfectly monstrous that St Magnus hasn't got an octave?'[16] obscures his real scholarly seriousness, but it suggests something of the conservative, romantic, aristocratic and antiquarian frame of mind which found Catholicism so attractive.[17] The *reductio ad absurdum* of this outlook was W. G. Ward's eldest son Edmund Granville, a priest manqué, who inherited the great family estates on the Isle of Wight and was accustomed to tour religious houses, promising large legacies in return for the right to act as master of ceremonies; he is said to have once dosed the Benedictines of Fort Augustus with a favourite purgative and then taken the community for a drive. His marriage was annulled and he left twice the value of his estates to the Church, creating a situation which drove his heir Wilfrid to an early grave.

In such a world, as W. H. Auden put it, Baptists 'were persons who came to the back door, not the front', but conversion to Catholicism 'was rather like having an illegitimate baby, an unfortunate event but something which can happen in the best families'.[18] The value of such high society conversions was sometimes disputed. One irritated reader of the *Tablet* remarked,

> When we hear of a Catholic movement among the English dissenters, or when some dozen shopkeepers in London or Liverpool seek to be received at the nearest Catholic chapel, I shall begin to believe in the conversion of England. Until then, the less we pride ourselves in conversions, the better.[19]

The comment points to the comparative weakness of Catholicism in the great bulwark of English religion, the middle class: Catholicism was disproportionately strong precisely where English Christianity was comparatively weak, at the opposite ends of the social scale, among the aristocracy and the poor.

Yet the Church seemed to want to appear as a kind of alternative Establishment, and Vaughan differed from Manning in making a priority the construction of Westminster Cathedral, the masterpiece of John Francis Bentley.[20] It was built of ten million bricks in the Byzantine style to discourage comparisons with the High Gothic Westminster Abbey. Byzantine had the further advantage over Gothic that its decoration was not intrinsically part of its structure, so it could be left to a later generation to sheathe the bare walls with mosaic and marble. This left the cathedral without the debt which was the bane of so many churches and an obstacle to their consecration. Remembering the medieval Benedictines of Westminster, Vaughan invited monks from Downside to Ealing in west London, with the aim that the community should also sing the daily office in the cathedral, but when they insisted on undertaking pastoral activity, invading the sphere of the secular clergy, Vaughan turned for help to the Abbey of Solesmes. The proposal for French monks was anathema to the new English Benedictine Abbot-President, the medievalist Francis Gasquet, and in the end the services were left to the Cathedral Chapter.[21] Vaughan inspected the unfinished shell of his great enterprise, accompanied by child 'Crusaders' from the Crusade of Rescue, who began 'upsetting loads of mortar, overturning piles of bricks, and mixing sand with putty, to their hearts' content . . . He was content to feel that for those children their first recollection of his cathedral would be associated forever with a happy memory.'[22] Vaughan died on the Feast of the Sacred Heart. His obsequies were the first ceremonial in the unfinished church, which stands at the heart of the capital as a symbol of the energies and aspirations of late Victorian Catholicism.

THE CATHOLIC COMMUNITY

By the 1890s, this achievement was a most impressive one in areas which had received large numbers of Irish immigrants from the 1840s, largely concentrated in London and in Lancashire, the only county with two dioceses, Liverpool and Salford, and in some of the industrial towns of North-Eastern England. The immigrants of mid-century were usually the poorest of the poor, poorer even than many of those who managed to migrate to America or Australasia, and were often ill schooled in the disciplines of Tridentine Catholicism. This radically improved from the 1850s if not before, but Britain remained 'a curious middle place',[23] being neither mother Ireland nor entirely remote from her, like the Irish in the British Empire overseas or the United States. Despite some few exceptions to the rule, the Irish were too dispersed through the host population to be strictly described as living in 'ghettos'. Their concentration, however, in particular places made the Church's pastoral task of teaching them possible. So, too, did the slackening of the incoming immigrant tide. The actual numbers of Irish-born declined from six hundred thousand in 1861 to about a third of a million in 1921, though the figures conceal the arrival of new immigrants and the emigration of old ones to the New World. The Catholic population, as distinct from the Irish one, is more difficult to estimate: the Church's figure in 1916 of 1,885,655 has an illusory precision, and Roman Catholic statistics are described by the experts as 'the most difficult types of church membership data to handle',[24] being based upon the impressions of parish priests rather than on any rigorous mode of actual counting.

The four biggest concentrations of Irish Catholics were in Liverpool, London, Manchester and Glasgow, and while two-thirds of immigrants were outside these centres, 'the vast majority remained townsmen'.[25] They continued to be affected by 'the familiar signs of deprivation (poor housing, menial employment, and criminality)',[26] and their existence as a community was essentially one provided by the expanding institutions of their Church, architecturally prominent in the buildings of chapel and school. Thus the single parish of Holy Trinity, Dockhead, in Bermondsey in 1840 had grown by 1900 into a body of five churches served by five priests, though 'more money was spent on schools – teachers and buildings – than on priests and churches',[27] and in the schools, Catholicism was properly taught, through preparation for first communion and confession, regular prayers, services, processions and catechesis.

The schools were established at great cost to the Church. The Education Act of 1870 created popularly elected School Boards to fund non-denominational Board Schools, while the voluntary religious schools had to subsist on Privy Council grants. Under this pressure, many Anglican voluntary schools were surrendered to the School Boards, while the Catholic Church, insisting on the right of parents to educate their children in their own faith, continued to open new schools, which were largely financed by house-to-house street collections. The Church wanted the introduction of rate aid for Voluntary Schools, a measure also supported by many Anglican churchmen, and embodied in the Conservative government's Education Act of 1902, which pleased Catholics and most Anglicans, as 'it entailed the abolition of all school boards in England and Wales and the bestowal of rate aid on all voluntary schools',[28] considerably reducing the pressure on Catholics to find the salaries for their teaching staff.

The educational issue posed a dilemma for Irish Catholics, as it aligned them with the Tory Party rather than with the Liberals who were their allies in the matter of civil rights, Home Rule and land reform in Ireland. In the East End, Irish Catholics and Jews were united in defence of the Act of 1902.[29] Yet there was an ambiguity at the heart of the Catholic school, whose double aims were 'incorporation and denationalisation', in providing a twofold system of confirming young Catholics in their faith, while integrating them into English society. There was virtually no attempt in the schools to conserve or create an Irish national culture, except in the sense of making much of St Patrick's Day, on which even Vaughan could claim to be 'in heart . . . an Irishman'.[30] The survival of Catholicism was undoubtedly reinforced by Irish national feeling, while a minority from the 1880s were attracted to the revivals of Gaelic sport and the Gaelic tongue, and the principal organs of Irish nationalism in England provided some of the social cement to Catholic institutions. But even at their height in 1890, the biggest of the nationalist political associations under the control of the Irish Parliamentary Party, the Irish National League, had only forty-one thousand members, a small minority of the practising Catholic body, while the professional political organisers in any era were vastly outnumbered by priests and religious.[31]

Thus there was only one constituency in England in which the Irish were sufficiently numerous to return their own MP, the Scotland Division of Liverpool, held from 1885 by T. P. O'Connor, known as 'Tay Pay'.[32] Irish Catholics were generally too few or too poor to do more than help to confirm the election of a sitting member of their choice, generally a Liberal. Where they were most numerous, as in Lancashire, they were likely to raise up a larger Tory Protestant host against them. The Irish Catholic journalist Charles Diamond had strong Nationalist interests, and in 1884 he founded the *Irish Tribune* in Newcastle, and went on to establish what were ultimately a chain of about forty local Catholic publications loosely based around the London *Catholic Herald* and the *Glasgow Observer*; but the community he served was essentially a church-based one, which was partly the creation of Irish loyalties but was destined to survive them.[33]

The Church, however, dominated by English priests and bishops, had to tread warily where nationalism was concerned. Bishop Thomas Whiteside in Liverpool was soundly beaten when the Irish refused to support his candidate in a School Board election in 1892, and was more careful afterwards, though he removed two priests at Barrow in 1902 for their over-involvement in Nationalist politics.[34]

Yet the Church was still defined by its Irish faithful where tensions between Protestant and Catholic remained strong. Where Bermondsey could hold its first street procession in 1907, without public disquiet, indeed with some friendly public interest, the activities of the Bermondsey-born Protestant preacher George Wise in Liverpool kept that most sectarian of English cities in a state of civil war. The confrontation of Orange and Green in Liverpool was partly sustained by Welsh and Irish Protestants – indeed the latter, who had probably constituted a sixth of Liverpool's population in 1841, may well be the origin of the city's sectarian tradition. There was little of this tradition in other northern enclaves like Manchester and Newcastle, where at least after 1868, 'anti-Catholicism was never again a major issue in local politics'.[35] Indeed only in Liverpool was there the savage polarisation of rival religious neighbourhoods as in Belfast. The biggest explosion occurred in 1909, in the aftermath of a Catholic street procession and an attack by police on crowds of Protestant protesters,[36] though Catholics claimed that the main provocation came from Wiseites rather than from the mass of Protestants. The depth of sectarian animosities in Liverpool and, to a lesser degree, in other parts of Lancashire, resembled those in Northern Ireland more than in most of mainland Britain, but it is sometimes difficult to distinguish anti-Irish prejudice from a more doctrinal anti-Catholicism in the lingering tradition of English hostility to Rome.

Yet if the overtly Nationalist community was smaller than the churchgoing one, the latter also had its problems in converting belief into practice, minimally defined as attendance at Sunday Mass and annual confession and communion. Despite the increase in the number of churches and priests in Bermondsey by 1900, Mass-going figures were not much above those in mid-century. The Church's greatest problem was the lapsation from the faith of its poorest members, which was said to have made Vaughan weep. Certain neighbourhoods were almost uniformly bad, and one London priest briskly described a section of his flock to the social investigator Charles Booth as 'incarnate mushrooms'.[37] Men lapsed rather than women, and adolescent boys rather than men, the Church's best chance of recovering them lying in marriage to a practising Catholic. By the 1890s, with the fall of the number of immigrants, many of the parishes in the great urban conurbations had settled into a steady pattern of practice and non-practice with a gradation of commitment,

> ranging from a lack of involvement which rendered a person ecclesiastically 'invisible', to use of the Church for baptism, to attendance at Mass, to Easter Communion, to membership of a Confraternity. At least part of the purpose of missions was to inspire people to move to the last two stages.[38]

Figures from the diocese of Salford suggest that there were considerable fluctuations from one of these categories to another: a religious census in Manchester in 1900 indicated that 43 per cent went to communion at Easter, a percentage varying from 24 per cent at St Edmund's, Miles Platting, to 82 per cent at St Alban's, Ancoats, with most parishes hovering between a half and a third, and the highest attendances in middle-class parishes.[39] In Manchester, 'a sensible guess would be: the devout accounted for 5 per cent of Catholics, those who frequently attended to their devotions amounted to 35 per cent, those who infrequently did so, 40 per cent, whilst those who rarely if ever attended Mass came to 20 per cent.'[40] A mission might secure a higher attendance over a short period, but any sensational growth was quickly lost, the Church's achievement lying more in the creation of a steady core of fully practising Catholics with a wider penumbra of semi-practising and believing ones. Thus whereas in the 1850s, the orders which conducted missions, the Passionists, Redemptorists and Rosminians, were engaged in missionary activity to largely unchurched bodies of immigrant Catholics, by the 1890s, they were increasingly given over to the labour of reviving or confirming the faith of Catholics in well-established parishes. Much of the original excitement and spontaneity of the early years of these orders were lost. Their task now was 'not to convert non-Catholics but to bring non-conforming Catholics into line',[41] to reclaim the detached or semi-detached members of existing congregations and to strengthen and confirm the structures and institutions of Catholic parochial life.[42]

This life was also sustained by some spectacular growth in the religious orders. 'By 1900, there were 33 male and 49 female religious communities in the Archdiocese of Westminster, 22 and 42 respectively in Birmingham, 17 and 14 in Clifton, and 17 and 35 in Hexham.'[43] Partly as a result of the expulsion of the religious orders from France in the early 1880s and the first years of the twentieth century, there was a great increase in the numbers of convent schools for girls, a large number of whom were not Catholic, but who came during their childhood and adolescence under a single-minded Catholic influence. Active nuns did a vast amount of work in the Church's social welfare institutions. The older orders of English Catholicism also grew, none more so than the Jesuits, from 507 members in 1885 to 807 in 1925.[44] The other large old order of the recusant Church, the Benedictines, underwent a fundamental change in its constitution in 1899, when it was turned from a centralised missionary order into the more normal type of monastic institution with independent and autonomous abbeys. Nonetheless, like other orders, Benedictines and Jesuits continued the recusant tradition of serving large numbers of parishes. Increasingly, both Benedictines and Jesuits were to turn their private schools into the Catholic equivalents of Eton and Harrow as well as recruiting grounds for themselves.

ANGLICAN ORDERS

It was one thing to copy Anglicans, quite another to unite with them. Vaughan was the dedicated opponent of the attempts to promote Anglican–Roman Catholic ecumenism by Charles Lindley Wood, second Viscount Halifax, President of the Anglo-Catholic English Church Union, and the Abbé Fernand Portal.[45] Their enterprise was repugnant to the mass of Anglican Protestants as to most English Roman Catholics, the Protestant viewpoint being precisely that of Roman Catholics, that Anglican ministers were not Catholic priests. Pope Leo appointed a papal Commission to consider the matter in 1896. In its final form it comprised the French historian, Louis Duchesne; a Jesuit, Emilio de Augustinis; a future papal Secretary of State, Pietro Gasparri, the main reviser of the Church's canon law; and an English secular priest, T. B. Scannell, all of whom were in some degree favourable to Anglican orders or thought them doubtful. The English members nominated by Vaughan were Canon James Moyes, the Benedictine historian Francis Gasquet, and a Franciscan, David Fleming, who, with the Spanish Capuchin, Calasanzio de Llaveneras, and the Commission's chairman and secretary, Marcello Cardinal Mazzella and Rafael Merry del Val, were all opposed. The Commission remained divided, but was followed by Leo XIII's letter *Apostolicae Curae* of 13 September 1896 dismissing Anglican orders as 'absolutely null and utterly void', on the grounds that the Edwardine and Elizabethan ordinals lacked the 'form' and 'intention' of ordaining a sacrificing priesthood. The Anglican Archbishops of Canterbury and York replied in *Saepius Officio* that in the Preface to its Ordinal, the Church of England had expressed its intention to retain the orders of bishop, priest and deacon as of Apostolic origin, but that the Roman definition of priesthood in terms of offering the Eucharistic sacrifice was neither Scriptural nor patristic nor in accordance with Eastern Orthodoxy.[46] Perhaps the greater significance of the controversy was for the Church of England, in inducing an anxiety about the validity of Anglican orders, which made relations with the other Protestant churches difficult, and led to the participation in the consecration of Anglican bishops of 'Old Catholic' bishops ultimately deriving their orders from the eighteenth-century Dutch Catholic schism of Utrecht, whose orders were valid even in Roman terms. Vaughan feared that any admission of the validity of Anglican orders would discourage Anglican conversions to Rome; indeed he and his theologians thought that *Apostolicae Curae* would encourage them. The Converts' Aid Society, founded in 1896, sought to aid former Anglican clergy and Sisters with practical assistance towards their new Catholic life.

Some Anglican clergymen doubted the validity of their own orders, and obtained reordination from a source which Rome recognised. Thus the Vicar of All Saints', Lambeth, Frederick George Lee, the Rector and Vicar of East and West Torrington, Lincolnshire, Thomas Wimberley Mossman, and possibly an Anglo-Catholic layman, J. T. Seccombe, a Norfolk doctor and magistrate, were consecrated bishops in Italy by an unknown prelate or prelates in 1877. Lee and Mossman imparted their orders to other worried clerics; both were received into the Catholic Church (Mossman by Manning) on their deathbeds.

One product of their frame of mind was Arnold Harris Mathew, born Matthews, an Anglican who had become a Roman Catholic priest and then a Unitarian, returned to the Anglican ministry, assumed an Italian name and title, married, claimed the Irish earldom of Llandaff, and was reconciled to Rome as a layman. Mathew, however, then came under the influence of the Modernist ex-Jesuit George Tyrrell, with whom he collaborated on an edition of H. C. Lea's anti-Catholic *History of Sacerdotal Celibacy*; and of Richard O'Halloran, a choleric Irish secular priest in Ealing who refused Vaughan's order to retire in favour of the Benedictines and maintained a schismatic congregation of loyal parishioners. O'Halloran persuaded Mathew that large numbers of dissident Roman Catholics desired a purely Catholic Church, and four Old Catholic bishops ordained

Mathew a bishop in Utrecht in 1908. This placed him in a line of episcopal descent deriving through Bishop Bossuet from Pope Urban VIII's nephew, Antonio Cardinal Barberini.[47] Mathew's own flock was negligible, but he passed his orders on to others, including Anglicans, with a resulting proliferation of tiny ecclesiastical bodies with panoplied bishops possessing valid orders, the largest being the Liberal Catholic Church which was part of the theosophical movement.[48] This kind of fantasy possessed the gifted Frederick William Rolfe, the self-styled 'Baron Corvo', who was accepted and then rejected for training for the priesthood in the Scots College in Rome, and who imagined himself as pope in his novel *Hadrian VII*.[49] Rolfe's aesthetic fascination with the externals of Catholicism was common among the decadents of the 1890s, and sometimes led to serious conversions, though Aubrey Beardsley and Oscar Wilde were only received into the Church on their deathbeds.

PROTO-MODERNISM

The most learned Catholic of his day, Baron Friedrich von Hügel, the son of an an Austrian and a Scotswoman, thought that Cardinal Manning had died leaving Catholics 'without ideas for real, detailed guidance'.[50] The Modernist controversy was foreshadowed during Vaughan's episcopate in his reluctant condemnation of the convert St George Jackson Mivart, whose essay in the *Nineteenth Century* in December 1892, entitled 'Happiness in Hell', was put on the Index. Vaughan excommunicated him after further articles in 1900. Mivart, who had been received into the Church in 1844, and been Professor of Biology at Manning's Catholic University College in Kensington, was a brilliant anatomist whose works included a monograph, *The Common Frog* (1874) and a paper in the *Transactions* of the Zoological Society 'On the Axial Skeleton of the Ostrich', and perhaps most famously, *The Cat* (1881), 'which for fullness and accuracy of detail and lucidity of exposition is worthy to rank with Huxley's "Crayfish" '.[51] Mivart was also a meticulous dissector and critic of Darwin's evolutionary theory, but his own ideas led him into perilous theological areas in which he was less well qualified.[52] Vaughan refused him a Catholic burial in 1900, but when approached by the dead scientist's friends, who claimed that the balance of the scientist's mind had been disturbed, left the issue to be resolved by his successor.

Mivart was not alone in his heterodoxy, but at first he seemed to have few fellow-Catholic critics of the same eminence. The worries of the bishops about unorthodox opinion in the Church resulted in a joint pastoral letter from the hierarchy, 'The Church and Liberal Catholicism', published in 1900, which condemned such Catholicism as an infection invading the Catholic body from the popular principle outside it. The pastoral taught that the true Church consisted of the *Ecclesia docens*, the teaching Church, identified in the apostolic office of pope and bishops; and the *Ecclesia discens*, the Church taught, consisting of the whole body of the faithful, indeed even of the bishops in their private capacities. The errors of the Liberal Catholic included a false understanding of doctrinal development, by which old dogmas could be superseded or updated in the light of new knowledge, and a semi-rationalism induced by indiscriminate reading.[53] Wilfrid Ward, himself something of a liberal, but fundamentally orthodox, wrote that the Encyclical was justified against an 'extreme left' of minor journalists in the Church,[54] and he later thought that the letter had pushed the Jesuit George Tyrrell into it.[55] Von Hügel in turn was critical of his friend Ward's criticism.[56] The papal condemnation of Modernism was to make these distinctions much clearer. Yet at a time when a leading Methodist could say, 'I hold that, when the Methodist Conference has spoken, no man has a right to have a conscience against it',[57] Rome's views were less distinctively Roman than they might later seem to be.

Vaughan's episcopate has been interpreted as the high point of ultramontane triumphalism,[58] but he was responsible for one liberal measure, the lifting in 1895 of the ban on Catholic attendance at Oxford and Cambridge, which was important to the educated Catholic élite.[59] The *Tablet* remained Vaughan's mouthpiece, with a tradition of weekly meetings between the archbishop and the editor, who from 1884 was Vaughan's nominee J. G. Snead-Cox. Snead-Cox held the post for a record thirty-six years, and became Vaughan's biographer. The paper was anti-Irish, conservative and ultramontane, but also intelligent and intellectually respectable, and the editor was retained by Vaughan's successor Bourne.

THE SUCCESSION TO VAUGHAN

Vaughan wanted as his successor Rafael (María José Pedro Francisco Borja Domingo Gerardo de la Santísma Trinidad) Merry del Val, who was born in England, of mixed Spanish and British descent, the son of the Secretary of the Spanish Legation, later ambassador at Vienna. His maternal great-grandfather, Don Pedro Juan de Zulueta, first Count de Torre Díaz, was a liberal exile from Spain. His son, Merry del Val's grandfather, the second Count, conformed to the Church of England, but with his Scottish-Dutch evangelical wife, was carried by the Oxford Movement back to the Church of his Catholic baptism.[60] The family was completely Anglophone, and Merry del Val was educated at Ushaw College in England as well as in Belgium and Rome at the Accademia dei Nobili Ecclesiastici, but his complex of international aristocratic connections, also to be seen in the Church's two greatest lay scholars, Lord Acton and the Baron von Hügel, suggests something of the international character of Catholicism in its élites, in contradiction to Archbishop Edward White Benson's famous denigratory remark that the Roman Church was no more than 'the new Italian mission' in England.[61]

Such internationalism, however, sometimes cut the other way, even for Catholics: Merry del Val could be termed a 'Cockney Spaniard',[62] while Vaughan, in paying tribute to the young von Hügel's high qualities, wrote to Lady Herbert of Lea, the Baron's future mother-in-law, 'That he is not an Englishman is probably a defect which neither regeneration nor salvation will ever be able to cure or atone for . . .'[63]

A good deal hung on Rome's choice of a new archbishop for Westminster. There was no obvious successor to Vaughan, as there had been to Manning. The Westminster Chapter of secular canons sent to Rome a list of three (or a *terna*) consisting of Merry del Val and two Benedictines, Francis Gasquet and Bishop John Cuthbert Hedley of Newport and Menevia, also a considerable scholar. The Duke of Norfolk opposed the appointment of a 'foreigner' like Merry del Val, who went on to become Secretary of State to Pope Pius X and the hammer of the Catholic Modernists. The Irish Patrick Cardinal Moran, Archbishop of Sydney, happened to be in Rome at the time of the nomination to Westminster, and disliked the Benedictines, one of them Vaughan's brother, who had preceded him in his Australian see; he now opposed the appointment of Gasquet or Hedley. The English bishops had added to the list the Bishop of Southwark, Francis Bourne, the son of an English civil servant and an Irish mother. Bourne became the fourth Archbishop of Westminster and the longest reigning, with an archiepiscopate of almost thirty-two years.

BOURNE

Bourne was a reserved and undemonstrative man, a devout administrator rather than a prophet, indeed a 'dry old stick'[64] on one view of him, an impression reinforced by his singularly unctuous and over-defensive biography, by the editor of the *Tablet*, Ernest Oldmeadow.[65] Bourne had passed through the two major English religious establishments of St Edmund's Ware and Ushaw, both children of Douai, and had been finally formed at St Sulpice. Bourne was the first Rector of the new Southwark seminary of Wonersh, but his deepest loyalty was to St Edmund's, where in 1904 he reopened the diocesan seminary, and also extended the school, hoping to make it the Catholic Winchester.

Early in his archiepiscopate Catholic England came of age, when Pope Pius X in his Constitution *Sapienti Consilio* of 29 June 1908 declared England no longer a missionary territory by removing it from the immediate jurisdiction of the Sacred Congregation of *Propaganda*, with the United States, Canada, Holland and the Duchy of Luxembourg. In the same year, King Edward VII, accompanied by Queen Alexandra, became the first ruling British monarch since James II to attend Mass 'in his State capacity', when they were present at the requiem for the assassinated Portuguese King Carlos I in St James', Spanish Place.[66] Protestant criticism of this made the King vulnerable to pressure later in the year, when there was a magnificent Eucharistic Congress in London, with Vincenzo Cardinal Vannutelli as Papal Legate.[67] The arch-Protestant John Alfred Kensit's 'Kensit Crusade' and other extremist Protestant societies protested at the Catholic plan for a procession of the Blessed Sacrament around Westminster. According to the letter of the third Catholic Emancipation Act, of 1829, Roman Catholic ritual and the wearing of canonical vestments in public by the clergy were still illegal outside churches and private houses, although the Catholic Sir Edward Henry, the Commissioner of the Metropolitan Police, had given permission for the procession without, according to his own account, having been told that it would involve the carrying of the Host. Instead of simply declaring the procession illegal, an oddity in a country in which such processions were becoming increasingly common, the Prime Minister, Asquith, who was under pressure from Edward VII and from the Home Secretary, Herbert Gladstone, tried to persuade Bourne to call off the affair, using as an intermediary the reluctant Lord Privy Seal, the Catholic Marquess of Ripon. In a compromise, Bourne retained the procession through the streets with the dignitaries in choir dress rather than vestments, and the religious orders with their habits over their arms and without the Blessed Sacrament. Bourne also made public the government's actions, winning in both Catholic and conservative newspapers like *The Times* and the *Standard* a minor diplomatic triumph at its expense.[68] In the aftermath, Ripon took the occasion to retire from politics and the government lost a by-election at Newcastle upon Tyne, allegedly through its loss of the Catholic vote. Catholic street processions were authorised in the Relief Act of 1926.

Bourne presided over a major diocesan reorganisation, in 1911, when Rome raised the sees of Liverpool and Birmingham to archbishoprics with provinces. The first Archbishop of Liverpool, Thomas Whiteside, was an astute ecclesiastical politician described by the Liberal minister Augustine Birrell as 'the mildest man who ever slit a throat'[69] but although Liverpool was the most Catholic of great English cities and Lancashire the most Catholic of English counties, with 15 per cent of its population Catholic, against a national proportion of 5 per cent, the English national leadership remained attached to Westminster. In 1911, Bourne was made a cardinal. In a further expansion of the hierarchy, Brentwood and Lancaster became dioceses in 1917 and 1924. Bourne's chief ambition, however, was to unite Westminster and Southwark in a single diocese for London, reversing the division of the capital so resented by Cardinal Wiseman at the restoration of the hierarchy in 1850. Bourne threatened the Southwark Chapter with excommunication when they tried to appoint a Vicar Capitular during the vacancy after his departure, and secured the election as his successor of his protégé, Peter Amigo, a young Gibraltarian, who was to hold the see for forty-five years.

In 1907, however, Bourne quarrelled with Amigo over the rectorship of Wonersh, and over his disastrous legacy to Amigo of diocesan debt, partly caused by the financial incompetence of Canon Edward St John, who also ran the diocesan rescue work for children, and by two lay advisors, one a confidence trickster, the other a speculator with diocesan money on the Stock Exchange. Bourne was still a diocesan trustee. He took St John's side in the row with Amigo, and when Amigo took his troubles to Rome in 1910, tried to get him transferred to the diocese of Plymouth while urging the union of Westminster and Southwark. The Southwark Chapter withdrew its speech of congratulation to Bourne as Cardinal, and a public meeting and a diocesan petition signed by all but six of the diocesan clergy protested against any redivision. Rome ruled in Amigo's favour in the dispute about finance in 1912, but Bourne pressed his plan, and was so sure of success that Archbishop Ilsley of Birmingham, on opening his advance copy of the *Catholic Directory* for 1913, found a map in which London was shown as a single diocese. Amigo insisted on the removal of the map, and Bourne had little support from the other English bishops. A Roman document of 1917 seemed to promise the rearrangement, but Bourne had to apologise for its mistranslation. Bourne tried again with new schemes for redrawing the dioceses in 1921 and 1925, and the matter was only finally shelved with the succession of Hinsley to Westminster: Hinsley had been Amigo's agent in Rome, and told him that 'they had far more important matters to attend to'.[70]

MODERNISM

Bourne was hardly more intellectual than Vaughan, but he was slow to condemn intellect in others. One of his first acts was to permit Mivart's reburial in St Mary's Cemetery, Kensal Green, and the new archbishop did little to hunt out 'Modernists' in his diocese after the condemnation of the Modernist heresy by Pius X in 1907 in the Bull *Pascendi* and the decree of the Holy Office, *Lamentabili*, followed by the universal imposition of the anti-Modernist oath in 1910 upon the clergy. There is so little balance in either the older or the recent writings on this subject that the historian finds himself treading on eggshells and likely to offend either the traditionalist critics of Modernism or its galaxy of recent supporters. Thus the definition of Modernism varies from a short-lived movement, between 1890 and 1910, in which truth defeated the hydra of heresy, to an 'intellectual crisis' in English Catholicism,[71] or 'the painful and often tragic beginning of a significant success, of a rich and fruitful renaissance of Catholic life, thought and spirituality, which came near to fruition in the nineteen-sixties',[72] only to be then outmoded by more contemporary concerns. Another difficulty is partly that Modernism was not so much a 'movement' as Friedrich von Hügel's postbag, his correspondence with theologians, philosophers and biblical scholars. Thus the 'Modernists' included the perfectly orthodox French lay theologian, Maurice Blondel, whose 'method of immanence' was a 'preparation for the Gospel', rather than a denial of divine transcendence; Wilfrid Ward, who merely wanted the Church to emerge from a state of intellectual siege; and the brilliant New Testament scholar, Alfred Firmin Loisy, who viewed Christ as a limited first-century Jew who, by great good fortune, had inadvertently founded the Catholic Church.

No orthodox Church could tolerate Loisy's views, but they were swallowed hook, line and sinker by the most original British Catholic theologian of his day, the Anglo-Irish convert and Jesuit, George Tyrrell, whose writings in other ways constitute a profound apologetic defence of Catholicism. Tyrrell wrote a good deal of his more radical work anonymously, and he died excommunicate while still insisting, as the chalice and host on his gravestone declared, that he had remained a Catholic priest. Bourne allowed his biographer and apologist Maude Petre a requiem in the archdiocese of Westminster, but Amigo refused her burial in Southwark.[73] Von Hügel was protected by his lay state, and his *magnum opus*, *The Mystical Element of Religion* (1908), was uncontroversial, being based upon the life of the fifteenth-century St Catherine of Genoa. He disapproved of the immanentist strand in Modernism anyway, combining, in a manner deliciously satirised by Tyrrell, Loisy's radical views of the New Testament with a deep devotional and prayer life of a very traditionally Catholic kind.

The immediate consequences of the papal condemnation of Modernism are not easily summarised. *Pascendi* urged the establishment of diocesan Vigilance committees, but even in Southwark, whose committee was especially vigilant, the full result was the departure of two clergy to the Church of England and the censure of two or three others.[74] On the one hand, some of the best scholars of the Church – the liturgist Edmund Bishop,[75] Herbert Thurston[76] and Cuthbert Butler[77] – were profoundly disheartened, and deliberately avoided or discouraged research in the difficult area of Christian origins. Others, like the mystical writer Evelyn Underhill, who was in devotion a Roman Catholic in all but name, were deterred from formally becoming Catholic. A few Catholic priests left the Church, the most able, after Tyrrell, being Alfred Fawkes, who reverted to the Anglican ministry.[78]

On the other hand, some of the most brilliant of the converts were primarily attracted to Rome by its resolute resistance to Modernism, in contrast to the Church of England. As Ronald Knox, who was received into the Church in 1917, recalled,

> I came into the Church, it seems to me, in a white heat of orthodoxy,

> Manning's disciple rather than Newman's; and when I took the anti-Modernist oath, it was something of a disappointment that the Vicar-General was not there to witness the fervour I put into it – he had gone out to order tea.[79]

The brilliant minds of the Church, like the Jesuit Martin D'Arcy, were for the most part members of religious orders and devoted to the defence and exploration of orthodoxy. D'Arcy's finest work, *The Mind and Heart of Love* (1945), was an intellectually scintillating mix of psychology, metaphysics and mystical theology, arguing that truth is known in love.[80] Generally speaking, however, the parochial clergy were unreflectively and instinctively orthodox, absorbed in practice rather than interested in theory. This was part of the Church's institutional strength, and there remains a question whether any church can, in the Modernist manner, query its own fundamentals and survive.

It is striking that the few British Modernists had so little interest in social and political radicalism, unlike their Italian brethren;[81] indeed there was no stouter political conservative than von Hügel. This may well have blunted their appeal to British radicals, whose interest in religion was as a great popular force, and for whom radicalism had to be more than a matter of scholarship or theology. The Church's later convert, Gilbert Keith Chesterton, published in 1908 his fundamental defence of the mainstream Christian tradition in *Orthodoxy*, and always trusted the instincts of common people over the learning of the scholars. 'It may be (I do not know and I do not care)', he wrote of Modernism, 'that Catholic Christianity is just now passing through one of its numberless periods of undue repression and silence. But I do know this, that when the great flowers break forth again, the new epics and the new arts, they will break out on the ancient and living tree.'[82]

Though the anti-Modernist oath was to be applied in all clerical appointments until the 1960s, the anti-Modernist campaign itself ceased with the death of Pope Pius X in 1914. His successor Benedict XV dismissed Merry del Val as Secretary of State; indeed one of the earliest documents the new Pope is said to have opened was a denunciation of himself as a Modernist addressed to his predecessor.[83] The anti-Modernist mood had been fatal to ecumenism, which then sank beneath other preoccupations and the First World War. The Vatican and Cardinal Gasparri, however, gave encouragement to the meetings at Malines in Belgium between 1921 and 1925 of Catholic and Anglican theologians, under the presidency of Cardinal Mercier. The participants included both the veterans Halifax and Portal, as well as such distinguished Anglican scholars as G. K. A. Bell and Charles Gore. Though Merry del Val was strongly opposed to the meetings, and Halifax regarded Bourne as an enemy of the exchanges, in fact Bourne cautiously favoured them, in spite of his increasing annoyance at the failure of the participants to keep him fully informed. Indeed Bourne instructed the *Tablet* in 1923 to give 'the most sympathetic and cordial treatment' to Cardinal Mercier's pastoral on reunion, at a time when the journal was publishing articles hostile to the Malines conversations by three conservative Jesuits, Francis Woodlock, Joseph Keating and Leslie Walker.[84] The meetings found a surprising agreement on an honorary primacy for the pope, the sacrificial character of the Eucharist and the divine origins of episcopacy, but the lack of English Catholic participation and English Catholic suspicion would probably have doomed the talks to failure, even if Mercier had not died in 1926. The new Primate of Belgium, van Roey, presided over a further meeting in 1926, and Bourne proposed the continuation of the conversations to the Anglican Archbishop Randall Davidson as late as 1928. Bourne, however, had only one supporter in the English hierarchy on the issue, the scholarly Louis Charles Casartelli, Bishop of Salford, and the general view among the bishops was that there should be no compromise with error. Again, as in the 1890s over Anglican orders, English Catholics argued against Malines that it discouraged Anglicans from submitting to Rome, and that the way forward lay not through corporate reunion with the Church of England, but by individual conversions.

CONVERSION AND COMMUNITY

It was an essential part of the character of the Church that it made converts from other communions, even if some old-fashioned Catholics, like Ronald Knox's fictional Dr Catacomb, 'never thought of a convert but as a bird which had flown into the room by accident, to the embarrassment of its occupants'.[85] Conversion to Rome was not merely a change in individual conviction: it had important social consequences. Most converts were humble folk converted by being drawn into a Catholic milieu, most normally by marriage to a Catholic, so that most conversions were a consequence of the Irish immigration. The implications of intermarriage, however, were complicated by the *Ne Temere* decree of 1907, which declared illicit those marriages by Catholics that had not been contracted in the presence of a priest. Both Irish Catholic communal pressures and the Church discouraged mixed marriages between Catholics and non-Catholics, even with a priest, and even when the non-Catholic agreed to bring up any children of the union as Catholics. Unmixed marriages were still the majority in 1939: 68.5 per cent of Catholic marriages were unmixed and took place before a priest. On the other hand, mixed marriages had become more common than in 1900, and their consequences could be heavy for both partners.[86] James Callaghan's father left the Church when the priest forbade him to marry a non-Catholic, and his offspring were reared as Baptists. Yet the Church sometimes benefited from circumstances in which the stronger faith of the Catholic partner brought about conversion to Catholicism,[87] and some

Protestants were also hostile to mixed marriage: the Anglican Bishops of Burnley and Blackburn both warned against it, while 'in Salford, even slum Protestants suffered a loss of status if they married an Irish Catholic'.[88] In this the marriage by a Protestant to a Catholic could signal the Protestant's loss of community, like conversion itself, which must have tempted some Protestants to go the whole hog and convert on marrying. On the other hand, the Catholic marrying a Protestant might, like Callaghan senior, cease to be a Catholic by conforming to his spouse's religion.

The actual numbers of converts are listed in the *Catholic Directory* from 1911, when they were probably underestimated at 3,609. In the following year they were 6,511, and they rose to a peak of 9,367 in 1915 before falling to 8,501 in the following year. They rose again steadily to a new peak of 12,621 in 1920, and then fell to 11,621 in 1921, hovering between the eleven and twelve thousands until 1936, when there was a fall to 10,617. This figure remained steady until 1940, but fell into four figures until the end of the war. The figures correspond to periods of rises and falls in Protestant church membership, suggesting the oddly ecumenical conclusions that the Catholic Church gained large numbers of converts when the other churches were doing comparatively well, and that it suffered when they did; and, contrary to commonsense assumptions, that religion does not flourish in time of war.[89] Over time, the number of converts was significant – some 746,000 between 1900 and 1960[90] – so that a large part of the Catholic population was Catholic by deliberate choice and not by birth. Of course, this came nowhere near the Church's stated aim, and especially that of the Guild of Our Lady of Ransom, founded in 1887 by Fr Philip Fletcher, himself a convert, the conversion of England as a whole.[91]

Striking conversions were good publicity, and any well-known individual received into the Church could expect to be welcomed by the Catholic press. There was an extensive literature recording these trophies. Successive editions of W. Gordon Gorman's *Converts to Rome*[92] received their final if still not very accurate edition in 1910, the year of the Diamond Jubilee of the hierarchy.[93] The work is a treasury of forgotten worthies, many of them with a literary bent, and the huge uncharted seas of Victorian and Edwardian fiction give up their dead in these pages. Here, for example, lies John Ayscough, the literary alias of Monsignor Francis Bickerstaffe-Drew, a count, according to the *British Museum Catalogue of Printed Books*, the author of at least twenty-three novels, the convert son and grandson of Anglican clergymen and an army chaplain. In this respect, the size of the English Catholic sub-culture can be greatly underestimated, a point implicit in the listing of some three thousand tales and novels by English-speaking Catholics in the catalogue revised in its sixth edition by Fr Stephen Brown SJ in 1940,[94] a great number of them by converts or the children of converts. Here the dominant influence was that of John Henry Newman, the perfect demonstration that a Catholic could be a great thinker, scholar and literary man. It is also notable that some of the very best scholars received into the Church, like the liturgist Edmund Bishop and the historian Christopher Dawson, have a literary elegance traceable to Newman.[95] Like Wilfrid Ward, Dawson was a distinguished editor of the *Dublin Review*, and maintained its high intellectual standard and content.[96] The literary influence crosses the theological one, and Gorman also bears witness to the Catholicising work of the High Church movement in the Church of England.

These two influences, the literary and the Catholic, combined in two of the best-known converts of the early part of the century, Robert Hugh Benson and Ronald Knox. Benson was the youngest son of Edward White Benson, Archbishop of Canterbury; Knox was the youngest son of E. A. Knox, the evangelical Bishop of Manchester. Both had formidably literary siblings. Benson was brother to A. C. Benson, Master of Magdalene College, Cambridge, and author of 'Land of Hope and Glory'; E. F. Benson achieved fame with his 'Lucia' and 'Mapp' novels, and collectively the output of the three brothers and two sisters runs to hundreds of volumes. They also wrote endlessly of themselves. Knox's three brothers included the editor of *Punch*, a famous ancient linguist and cryptologist, and a leading Anglo-Catholic scholar-priest. Benson's outpouring of novels and other works came to an abrupt end with his premature death in 1914. He left his little manor of Hare Street as a country residence for the Archbishops of Westminster. His best work is a collection of Catholic supernatural tales, *The Light Invisible*, and his futurist fantasy *The Lord of the World*, in which the Second Coming sees the Church reduced to the pope and eleven disciples. His writings have a curious period flavour which is part of their fascination.[97] Knox's two great works, his translation of the Bible and his monograph, *Enthusiasm*, lie beyond this period, but his countless books include sermons, apologetic and even six detective novels, written to fund his chaplaincy at Oxford.[98]

The whole significance of conversion subtly changed in the 1920s, when there were strong new intellectual currents, Fascist and Communist. 'With Europe possibly on its last legs from its recent attempt to kill itself, Dada, Cubism, and the rest must have seemed like graffiti on a cathedral wall. It was an excellent time for Rome to stand still.'[99] This gave Roman Catholicism the polemical advantage of knowing its own mind with a degree of intellectual sophistication at a time when other churches seemed increasingly a prey either to fundamentalism or doubt, so that submission to Rome might be called an intellectual and social fashion, as indeed some saw it,[100] if this phrase were not quite so unfair to the spiritual and moral earnestness of the lifelong commitments which were the consequence. The master convert-makers were the Jesuits, whose fashionable Mayfair church, Farm Street, had a roll listing its three thousand converts instructed between 1910 and 1935, led by the ninth Duke of Marlborough. The Jesuit house next door, for the Society's writers, was described by Evelyn Waugh as 'superbly ill-furnished. Anglicans can never achieve this ruthless absence of "good-taste".'[101] The greatest converter among the Jesuits and Waugh's own instructor was the brilliant Martin D'Arcy, who lived at Campion Hall from 1927, and reinforced Knox's influence on the undergraduates. Another famous Farm Street convert-maker was the prolific writer Fr C. C. Martindale, remembered in the memoir of the convert actor Robert Speaight 'as leaning out of his window, sighing for the soul of a stoker to save, and only discovering a duchess',[102] though he converted stokers as well.

The convert-priests also gave a literary air to the convert mind, and the Church's greatest convert of this century, Gilbert Keith Chesterton, the very model of a Johnsonian literary man, had worked out a Catholic philosophy for himself, not unassisted by his Anglo-Catholic wife, long before he became a Roman Catholic in 1922. Chesterton formed a physically impressive literary triptych with Hilaire Belloc,[103] whose mother was the ex-Unitarian Birmingham writer Bessie Rayner Parkes, and the convert novelist Maurice Baring.[104] Chesterton himself created the most famous priest in English fiction, based in character, if not appearance, on the Irish Monsignor John O'Connor; but a part of Chesterton's enormous literary work, with that of Belloc, a former Liberal MP disillusioned by the corruptions of Liberalism, was devoted to the Distributist movement, which favoured small businesses and peasant proprietorship over monopoly capitalism and state socialism. A succession of periodicals, *The Eye Witness* (1911–12), *The New Witness* (1912–23) and *G.K.'s Weekly* (1925–36), were as much social as political in content, and influenced such communal ventures as the convert sculptor Eric Gill's community at Ditchling,[105] whose chaplain, the uncompromising advocate of social reform, the Irish Dominican Fr Vincent McNabb,[106] was more famous for his speaker's stand in Hyde Park.[107] The Ditchling experiment attracted a wealth of talent, including the Welsh poet and painter David Jones, the typographer René Hague,[108] and Hilary Pepler of the St Dominic's Press. McNabb was one of the stars of the Catholic Evidence Guild, founded in 1926 by Wilfrid Ward's daughter Maisie and her husband Frank Sheed to take Catholicism to the market place. Their publishing house, Sheed and Ward, was one significant influence on the Catholic revival. One of the profoundest minds of the movement, whom our generation may recover, was the convert-historian Christopher Dawson, whose vision of Catholicism was as the fulfilment and completion of all human culture and history which is implicit in the very meaning of 'Catholic'.

The influence of inter-war Catholicism was, therefore, more cultural than political, sometimes through contact between Roman and Anglo-Catholics, as in the circle around C. S. Lewis and J. R. R. Tolkien at Oxford. Oxford was the centre of the Dominican revival, through the house created in 1922 by the great Dominican Provincial Fr Bede Jarrett, whose intellectual offspring gave a new lustre to Dominican thought. The Cambridge house of the order was founded by two tertiaries, the convert Professor Edward Bullough and his wife Enrichetta.

The Dominican publication *Blackfriars* rivalled the *Month*.[109] Otherwise, the two most celebrated of inter-war converts were the novelists Evelyn Waugh and Graham Greene, though their conversions, according to one jaundiced commentator, 'only served to increase their woe'.[110] In 1933, Waugh came under the lash of the editor of the *Tablet*, Ernest Oldmeadow, for the obscene, immoral and sacrilegious character of his novel *Black Mischief*. Oldmeadow was a former Nonconformist minister, 'a genial, humorous man of the world with wide interests, a *bon vivant*, too, who could be very witty on congenial subjects',[111] but perhaps in this matter, as in his stern rebuke to Ronald Knox in 1926 for a comic news broadcast on a wildly imaginary riot in London,[112] he was still the Nonconformist minister. The *Tablet* was Bourne's property. Its views, though Oldmeadow's, were thought to reflect the Cardinal's, and it even published in support of Oldmeadow's stand a letter from the birth-control advocate, Marie Stopes. The young Tom Burns instigated on Waugh's behalf a letter of protest against Oldmeadow, signed by the Jesuits D'Arcy, C. C. Martindale and R. H. J. Steuart, the Dominican Bede Jarrett and Eric Gill, the very cream of intellectual Catholicism.[113] Waugh had printed, but did not publish, an attack on Oldmeadow in the form of a letter to Bourne in defence of his book: 'Your Eminence's patronage', Waugh wrote, 'alone renders this base man considerable.'[114] On Bourne's death, Burns bought the *Tablet*, with Douglas Woodruff and A. H. Pollen. Under the editorship of Woodruff, the paper remained anti-Irish and perhaps a shade too sympathetic to Franco and Mussolini, but with its redesign by the great letterer, Stanley Morison, it also signified the intellectual and literary brilliance of inter-war Catholicism. It reflected the oddity that, in a Protestant nation, so much of the responsibility of defending orthodox Christian doctrine now rested upon Roman Catholics.[115]

POLITICS

Despite the radical intellectual fringe, perhaps most pronounced among McNabb and the Dominicans, most converts were conservatives with a small c. The natural alliance for the majority of Catholics from 1906 was with the Liberal Party which favoured social welfare legislation and Home Rule for Ireland. But the Nonconformist and radical supporters of the Liberal administration which was elected with a large majority in 1906 strongly opposed rate aid to voluntary education, partly out of the antagonism of chapel to church, partly out of an anti-Catholic hostility to 'Rome on the rates', and there was a campaign of resistance to the payment of rates by leading Dissenters, especially in Wales. The compromise bill in 1906 was unsatisfying to radical Dissenters as well as to most Anglicans and Catholics, though the Irish leader John Redmond, in consultation with Bourne, sought to improve it by amendments, against the adamant opposition of the Duke of Norfolk. Further bills in 1907 and 1908 also ran into decisive opposition in the Lords, so that the benefits of the 1902 Education Act remained in force until 1944.[116] It is notable, however, that the attempt by Bishop Casartelli of Salford to intervene in politics through the Catholic Federation which he set up in 1906 collapsed in the Manchester North West by-election in 1908.[117] Catholics in England never took to forming Catholic political parties.

The other two main political changes for Catholicism came with the rise of the Labour Party and the First World War. The first meant a gradual drift of the Catholic vote to Labour from the Liberals with that of the mass of the working class. Labour began with a general enthusiasm for secular education which became less emphatic as it approached power. Secularist education, however, was one aspect of secular socialism which was clearly condemned by the Church, but the issue was muddied by the larger one as to whether Labour was socialist in any sense, as well as in the sense condemned by the Church. Significantly, the most thorough discussion of the issue was not in England but in western Scotland, where John Wheatley founded a Catholic Socialist Society in 1906, while the warmest support for the election of Labour candidates came from the Archbishop of Glasgow, John Maguire, at the 1908 Eucharistic Congress, even though the Glaswegian Church was secretly entirely opposed to Wheatley's socialism.[118]

In England, a compromise seems to have been found without verbal fireworks. Bourne's Lenten Pastoral in 1918 recognised in working-class unrest 'the true lineament of the Christian spirit', while in 1924 he wrote 'that our Labour Party's programme contains nothing which threatens religion. No doubt there are extremists among them, but the Party as such has nothing in common with the Socialists of the Continent.'[119] The matter surfaced most dramatically in 1926, when at High Mass in Westminster Cathedral, Bourne condemned the General Strike of that year as 'a sin against the obedience which we owe to God, . . . and against the charity and brotherly love which are due to our brethren'.[120] Here was the paradox of the head of a working-class church condemning the strike, while mediation was sought by Randall Davidson, the primate of a middle-class one. More characteristic of Bourne was his statement, a month after the appearance of Pope Pius XI's social encyclical *Quadragesimo Anno* in 1931: 'I think it will be generally admitted that very few members of the Labour Party would base their desire for social reform on the principles which His Holiness has so rightly and so strongly condemned.'[121] He had, therefore, already made it clear that the Labour Party's principles did not amount to the continental-style secularist socialism under the ban of the Church. In this, the most conservative prelates were pragmatists, and followed their flocks rather than leading them.

The Church was, like the great majority of English institutions, thoroughly patriotic during the First World War, and could draw on public outrage over the German sack of Catholic Belgium, which was a central plank of British propaganda: a favourite atrocity story was the raped Belgian nun, and many Belgian refugees found a refuge in Britain. Again, the hundreds of thousands of Catholics in the British and dominion armies, including a disproportionate number of Catholics from Ireland, conveyed a strong impression of the Catholic contribution to the war. By contrast, the determined and principled peace-making efforts by Pope Benedict XV were an embarrassment, as were the activities of a small number of Catholics in the Guild for the Pope's Peace, founded by E. I. Watkin and Wilfrid Meynell. A much greater embarrassment was the Easter Rising in Ireland in 1916, a revolution which came as a bolt from the blue, made a prominent use of the symbols of the Catholic faith, and enjoyed a leadership of 'traitors' who died like Christian heroes.

Bourne was thought to lack sympathy for Ireland. It was his rival, Peter Amigo, who welcomed the Irish Nationalist Archbishop of Melbourne, Daniel Mannix, to London in 1920, and gave the absolution at the funeral of the Lord Mayor of Cork, Terence MacSwiney, who after the burning of his city by the Black and Tans, had died on hunger strike in Brixton gaol. Ten thousand people marched with MacSwiney's coffin from Southwark Cathedral to Euston Station. Amigo's forthright denunciation of the atrocities of the Black and Tans in Ireland brought an outraged reaction from the conservative and patriotic Catholic Union. Bourne somewhat balanced matters by holding in Westminster Cathedral a solemn requiem for the three Catholics among the British officers shot in their beds in Dublin on Bloody Sunday. The Catholic press and clergy were divided on the issue of whether MacSwiney's death was murder or suicide, and the patriotic Cardinal Gasquet tried ineffectively to get him condemned as a suicide by Rome.[122]

The subsequent disappearance of nearly all the Irish Catholic MPs at Westminster left Catholics with very few representatives in the House of Commons, the chief being T. P. O'Connor, who held his seat until his death in 1929, the last survivor of a bygone age. On Bishop Beck's view in 1950,

> the height of Catholic influence was reached about the period when the Liberal Government of 1906 took office. The Irish influence in the House of Commons was then at its strongest . . . Nothing in Catholic public life has replaced it . . . Politically, since the withdrawal of the Irish Members, the Catholic influence has, on the whole, been negligible . . .[123]

On the other hand, there was no great issue between the wars on which the Church felt a special need to mobilise Catholics, given that British administrations were either Conservative or minority ones or coalitions, with the effect if not the intention of maintaining the status quo.

With declining immigration, the Irish-born were also a declining proportion of the Church's congregations. Thus by 1900, only a third of the Catholics in Manchester were Irish-born, a figure which had fallen to a sixth in 1931, by which date only two-fifths of the hundred and thirty thousand Catholics in the city were of immediate Irish descent. The reluctance of the English clergy to appeal to Irish patriotism contributed to the progressive redefinition of a Catholicism which ignored Ireland in its school curricula, which was wed less and less to Irish nationalism, and was progressively less Irish.[124]

There were not many English Catholic Labour MPs, certainly none to rival John Wheatley, the Irish-born MP from the East End of Glasgow who in 1924 became the first Labour Minister for Housing. Best known were Joseph Tinker, a former miner, and the 'dockers' MP' James Sexton.[125] It is not clear if the anti-Catholic vote actually exceeded the Catholic, and representation in Parliament depended upon alliances between Catholics and other portions of the working class at a lower level. In the Manchester Whit Walks, Catholic Labour councillors walked behind the parish clergy, while in Stepney in East London, the Labour Party was run by a condominium of Irish Catholics and Jews under the leadership of a Jewish politician, 'Morry' Davis, an alliance 'strengthened in the period 1916–22 by the shared hostility of both Jews and Irish in east London to the use made of the Defence of the Realm Act to deport Jews and (in the wake of the Easter 1916 Irish uprising) to imprison Irishmen without trial'.[126] In the Deerness valley in County Durham, Catholic miners replaced Methodists in the control of the mining unions in the 1930s.[127] This was significant of the supplanting of one working-class church by another. In such matters, as in others, the Church 'was an organic, accepted feature of working-class life'.[128]

The social prestige of seigneurial Catholicism survived the war intact, and the few Catholic Tory MPs had this kind of background, like the Duke of Norfolk's brother Lord Edmund Talbot, the Conservative chief whip, Francis Blundell of Crosby Hall and Sir Gerald Strickland of Sizergh Castle.[129] It is difficult to form a statistical picture: some families died out; others survived.[130] Many of the converts were also of conservative temper, and Gorman in his listing of converts was anxious to refute the ancient slur that Catholicism was a religion of disloyalty:

> In yielding allegiance to the Old Faith the convert becomes no less loyal to his native country. His Gracious Majesty King George V has not in the thousands enumerated in these pages lost a single subject; rather has he gained, for loyalty like all the virtues only grows stronger in the fuller life.[131]

The importance of Catholics of higher rank should not be exaggerated: with some three hundred thousand adherents, the diocese of Salford boasted only one gentry family, the de Traffords, and the main strength of the Church remained much further down the social scale. The statistical prominence of Lancashire also continued: 'By 1939 the industrial North-West, consisting of Lancashire and parts of Cheshire, contained some 820,000 Catholics, twice as many as the industrial North-East or Greater London and eight times as many as the industrial Midlands.' The number of priests and churches in the North-West about doubled between 1921 and 1965. Liverpool seemed to some more Irish than English, Preston, with its magnificent churches, was a veritable citadel of the faith, while St Mary's, Chorley, with a hundred thousand annual communions from its 1,500 communicants, had a claim to be one of the most practising Catholic parishes in the world.[132]

The Catholic population was by then, however, also spreading through the cities of the new consumerist south. John Carmel Heenan's first curacy in Barking in the 1920s was a ministry to a social mix which became more complicated with a degree of Catholic *embourgeoisement*, as some at least moved up the social scale in the general improvement of living conditions. 'Most of the congregation were poor,' Heenan recalled.

> The men worked on buildings, on roads and in various factories around Barking Creek. Of the Irish most had come to Barking when Ford's factory was transferred from Cork to Dagenham. Many of our girls were employed making tin boxes or in the asbestos factory – some, indeed, contracted the fearful disease asbestosis.

Beside these were the commuters of New Barking, with their own excellent school and chapel,

> typical of the white-collared working class usually referred to as lower middle class. The Catholics in this part of the town were nearly all exemplary. They first showed me . . . that people who take pride in their homes, make sacrifices for their children's education and pay their debts are usually also the most dutiful Catholics.

On the other hand, Heenan was shocked by the lapsed, who

> were all my friends and came to me for every kind of help. They would do anything I asked – except perform their spiritual duties . . . The Mass-missers were almost always feckless in everything they did or, rather, failed to do. Those whose homes were dirty, whose children were neglected, were rarely practising Catholics. The lapsed were usually also in arrears with rent and hire purchase payments. They were pathetic, friendly people. They were for me a source of disillusionment. These people were the 'God's poor' I had dreamed about.[133]

Their wages might be higher than those of some practising Catholics; but they were not the poor in spirit. Heenan wrote of their 'tragic apostasy', and thought them simply faithless. He discontinued the practice of visiting the homes of the lapsed for the contribution which had at one time been paid towards the

Catholic school (failure to pay was still deemed unlucky). One may discount something here for Heenan's own lower middle-class background, for he did not value the residual Catholicism which the non-practising might be thought to hold. His picture, however, is significant. The bustling parish of Barking, with its hospital, substantial working-class membership, its confraternities and Society of St Vincent de Paul to aid the poor, some of them deeply undeserving, and its steady and increasing flow of vocations into the religious life, was in many ways a continuation of its Victorian predecessor; but it also indicated the growth of a new suburban commuter-land Catholicism, in which the most active parishioners were increasingly middle class.

The spread into commuter land was served by an increasing number of secular priests: in 1910, 3,835; in 1920, 4,528; in 1930, 4,484; in 1940, 5,642. The number of clergy doubled between 1880 and 1920. The annual number of ordinations almost doubled between the wars, from 119 in 1913 to 215 in 1939, this being rather below the peak of 260 in 1936. The priesthood grew by 29.8 per cent between 1931 and 1941. To some extent this increase drew on clergy from Ireland: between the 1890s and the 1920s in the diocese of Salford, the proportion of the Irish clergy rose from 38 per cent to 46 per cent, at a time when there was a sharp decline in the Irish-born proportion of the Catholic population.[134] This in turn reflected the flourishing condition of Catholicism in Ireland.

> By the end of the nineteenth century Irish-trained priests were arriving in increasing numbers: All Hallows College, Dublin, was specifically dedicated to the training of priests for England and overseas, while the seminaries at Thurles, Carlow, Kilkenny and Wexford, although primarily serving local needs, maintained a strong sideline in training priests who were available to be incardinated elsewhere. Some of these men, together with most of those who came from Maynooth, were merely on loan and would return to Ireland when a vacancy occurred in their home diocese.[135]

Few were promoted: there were very few Irish-born bishops in the English hierarchy. The most venerable was probably Richard Lacy, for fifty years (1879–1929) the first Bishop of Middlesbrough; but though born at Navan in County Westmeath, his priestly training was a conventional British one, first at Ushaw and then in Rome.[136] Even rarer was an Irish Nationalist prelate in an English see like William Cotter, Bishop of Portsmouth (1910–40), who stage-managed Daniel Mannix's controversial visit to Britain in 1920, and sang the requiem in Southwark for Terence MacSwiney.[137]

This expanded clerical body was the basis of a highly clerical Catholicism, and of a culture of the presbytery, of the shared reading, humour, knowledge of the world and fund of anecdotes and stories of a professional caste. A liking for boxing, racing and golf was not unknown, though the clergy were still forbidden to go to the theatre. The accompanying picture was one of uniformity: the existence of a single liturgy, the stress on the ministry of the Sacrament rather than the Word and the long period of clerical training made the priest almost classless in ministering to quite different social classes. In many respects, the rich of Mayfair and the poor of Salford were receiving much the same sort of ministry, a ministry centred on the Mass and loyal to the Pope and Rome.

The religious and moral content of Catholicism was in some ways nothing special, in other ways quite distinctive. The Church's teaching on questions of sexual morality was for the most part that of the other churches, except in the obvious matter of contraception, and even here it was closer to public opinion than was later to become the case. Only in 1930 did the Lambeth Conference of the Church of England gave a very qualified acceptance to the case for birth control, while declaring that the 'primary and obvious method is complete abstinence from intercourse (so far as may be necessary) in a life of discipline and self-control'. Even this was over the objections of some of the Church's most distinguished members; its greatest theologian, Charles Gore, 'was quite overcome with grief' by the decision,[138] and was a tireless propagandist for the League of National Life, an anti-contraceptive body containing Anglicans, Dissenters and Jews as well as Roman Catholics. A great many people no doubt had no strong opinion on the matter, but an astute priest like Heenan in Barking, with a phalanx of well-esteemed doctors in his train, could draw on the opposition to contraception of 'most of the professing Christians in the town', and bring enough of the community together to prevent the establishment of a Marie Stopes clinic from public funds.[139] Only about a tenth of the male population made use of the condom, which was more generally accepted after 1940, and it seems that the substantial fall in the size of non-Catholic families in the first half of this century was without benefit of contraceptive devices. No medical schools gave instruction in the subject until after 1945.[140] So much has opinion on this subject changed that the modern biographer of the Anglo-Catholic Dorothy L. Sayers is bewildered by her subject's strong if muddled dislike of contraception.[141]

Divorce also remained as difficult as ever, and in one matter morality became tighter, in that a notorious divorce in 1926 caused an Act of Parliament which banned, except for the judge's summing up, the sort of sensational publication of the details of divorce cases which had so delighted the Victorians.[142] A great number of Anglicans and Nonconformists still accepted the duty of Sunday worship, and indeed were stricter Sabbatarians than Catholics. Many Protestants thought the Church of Rome louche in this and in her approval of gambling, and positively scandalous in her annulment laws, which were looser than the then discipline of the Church of England. The ninth Duke of Marlborough and his wife Consuelo née Vanderbilt were granted a civil divorce in 1921, after she had successfully sued for the restoration of her conjugal rights; but the subsequent Catholic dissolution of their marriage – which, as *Burke's Peerage* said, in a phrase which may have been suggested by the Duke, was 'declared null and void by the Sovereign Pontiff 19 Aug. 1926'[143] – was a cause of considerable scandal to Protestants.

These high matters were quite beyond the experience of the ordinary parish priest, whose main preoccupations would probably include the indebtedness of his church, a regular round of house visiting to keep in contact with his parishioners and in some cases to ensure they came to church; and in poorer parishes, breaking up fights on Saturday nights in public houses. The rector sometimes visited the richer houses, the curate the poorer ones. In poor areas, the clergy were in constant demand for the last rites from sick parishioners who regarded the presence of the priest gratis as worth more than that of a doctor. As a school inspector recalled the disruption of his cosy evenings spent with the mission priests, with the local Catholic doctor and one or two more favoured laymen:

> . . . the heavy work undoubtedly comes at night. The door bell seems to get no rest; sometimes it is a drunken woman, who comes to take the pledge, just as a wealthier drunkard might ask for a bottle of seltzer; sometimes a request for worldly advice or assistance; sometimes, and many times, an urgent demand for a speedy visit to Biddy, who is 'dyin' entirely,' but turns out to be dismally drunk. The whole force of the mission is sometimes called out, and then, even when the inspector was playing his annual rubber, it was with much difficulty that a quorum could be kept.
>
> In the small hours of the morning the flock break out afresh. Patsey is brought home helpless at 2 A.M., Michael has his head cut open at 3; Molly upsets the lamp, and sets the baby on fire at 4. In each and every case his reverence is brought down to give the last rites to the afflicted person, and in each and every case he finds that he might as well have gone on with his sleep.[144]

This observer saw this as 'drudgery with the halo of martyrdom';[145] he also noted that Catholic clerics were 'singularly free from that professional, unreal manner affected by some [Anglican] clergymen, and by nearly all Dissenting ministers'.[146] The priest would say his daily Mass as well as two Sunday Masses, and conduct baptisms, weddings and funerals. In middle-class areas especially, in the seminaries and in churches belonging to the orders, there were choirs, and the High Mass on Sundays and great festivals and Vespers and Benediction would be sung to music of a high order, now hardly obtainable outside Westminster Cathedral and the Oratories. Indeed the English Catholic tourist, pilgrim or seminarian abroad would wonder why these things were so much more slovenly in Catholic climes, even in Rome. The English laity were particularly well served by a long tradition of bi-lingual Missals, by which the Latin of the liturgy could be understood by a glance at the adjoining column of English translation. The Society of St Gregory encouraged lay participation in the liturgy, and in 1930, a cheap little volume of *Plainsong for Schools*, containing a wealth of simple Gregorian chants, was published with a Foreword from the Archbishop of Liverpool. It quickly sold a hundred thousand copies, and was supplemented in 1934 by a further volume containing the music for more Masses, hymns, sequences and motets, including no fewer than six settings for the Benediction hymn *O Salutaris* and four for the *Tantum ergo*. This was quite apart from a wealth of vernacular hymnody in the Duke of Norfolk's compilation, with Charles Gatty, *Arundel Hymns* (1902), and *The Westminster Hymnal*, authorised by the hierarchy in 1912, edited by the convert musician Sir Richard Terry and containing hymns both ancient and modern.

There were other forms of participation in worship from the genuflections and crossings of the Mass to vernacular rosaries and devotions before particular shrines and statues. Catholic churches were generally conceded to have a distinctive atmosphere, compounded of a concern for sacramentals as well as sacraments, of the lingering fragrance of incense and melted beeswax, of the multiple side altars and chapels with their candles guttering against coloured plaster, alabaster and marble, and of the intense quiet of a distant Low Mass magically broken by bells at the elevation of the host and chalice. At one extreme there was a Carthusian simplicity; at the other, an overpowering richness. Part of the Church was anxious to show the Englishness of its own particular spiritual tradition.[147] This was implicit in the beatification of one hundred and thirty-six English martyrs in 1929 (in addition to the fifty-four beatified in 1886), and the canonisation of St Thomas More and of St John Fisher in 1935: their original feast day was 9 July. There were also commemorations of local *beati*, saints and martyrs in the calendars of particular dioceses, and of St George as the patron saint of England. Their supernatural aid was near, and miracles were always possible, though More and Fisher were canonised 'equipollently' on the basis of their cult, without miracles. At the very edge of the Catholic spiritual continuum was the cult of the mystic Teresa Helena Higginson (1844–1905), whose bilocations, assault by the Devil and mystic marriage were like those of some continental *beatas*. Her distinctive devotion, to the Sacred Head of Our Lord, was eventually condemned in Rome, and in 1937–38 there was vigorous controversy between defenders of her cult and its critics, but however outrée she appeared to critical minds like Fr Herbert Thurston's, she belonged to a Catholic ethos which seemed as if it would last forever.[148]

HINSLEY

Bourne died in the very first hour of 1935, and was buried in the Galilee Chapel in his beloved St Edmund's. His successor Arthur Hinsley was born in a joiner's cottage near Selby in Yorkshire, taught at Ushaw, founded the St Bede's Grammar School in Bradford, was an advisor to the irascible Peter Amigo of Southwark, and was steeped in the Roman spirit: as a petition to make him a bishop in Gasquet's papers put it, 'La chiesa cattolica in Inghilterra ha bisogno dello spirito di Romanità.'[149] He had been away from England for years as the reforming Rector of the English College in Rome, where he was known as 'the Boss', acquired the students' summer residence at Palazzola and saved a large part of the College from demolition to make way for a street market, through a campaign waged at a distance through the columns of *The Times*. Much less of a disciplinarian than his successor, Godfrey, his rectorate was the high point of the College's influence on the Church in England, producing a galaxy of bishops: 'Griffin, Heenan, Masterson, Grimshaw, Dwyer, Rudderham, Restieaux, Ellis, Tickle, Halsall, Pearson were all students under Hinsley.'[150] For a time it seemed that there were three qualifications for a bishopric in England: to be a baptised Catholic, male, and an alumnus of the English College. 'The first two conditions, we were told, were sometimes dispensed with,' recalled Anthony Kenny, 'but the third never.'[151]

Hinsley went on to become Apostolic Delegate to British Africa, and was afterwards plucked from semi-retirement in Rome to lead the Roman Catholic Church in England. This was in preference to the Irish-born Archbishop Richard Downey of Liverpool, a see more closely associated in the public mind with the Irish immigration. The elderly stop-gap candidate turned out to be a pastoral genius. He began by a round of friendly visits to the presbyteries of his diocese, even intruding into the kitchens to interview the housekeeper and maids and to thank them for their work, and concluding with a general blessing. He also dropped into churches during the diocesan mission services to deliver a heartfelt Roman *ferverino* on the love of God from the altar steps.[152] Hinsley was raised to the sacred purple in 1937. He had a difficult course to steer in a Europe poised between Fascism and Communism, and earned the displeasure of Rome by describing the Pope as 'a helpless old man' in the course of a superb denunciation of the Italian invasion of Abyssinia. Like many parish priests, he severely discouraged the Irish Catholic inclination to join Oswald Mosley's blackshirts.

Indeed Hinsley's strong sense that Roman Catholicism was being compromised by the Vatican's relations with Italian Fascism complicated the most notable innovation of his early years, the appointment of the first Apostolic Delegate to Great Britain, a move greatly desired in 1935 by Bishop Amigo, still smarting from his long conflict with Bourne, to provide a check on the power of the

Cardinal Archbishop, with its tendency to take Rome's authority to itself. Pius XI had already erected five Apostolic Delegacies, including Hinsley's to British Africa, and the British Minister in Rome, D'Arcy Godolphin Osborne, urged the creation of a British curial cardinal to represent the interests of Catholics in the Empire.[153] The Vatican first tried the waters with the appointment of William Godfrey as Apostolic Visitor to the seminaries of England, Scotland and Malta in 1938, and then created a permanent Apostolic Delegation from November. The office was strictly speaking an ecclesiastical and not a diplomatic one like a nunciature, but the negotiations for it took place between Rome and the Foreign Office without any reference to Hinsley (or the English hierarchy), who in a letter to Cardinal Pacelli as Secretary of State, at first opposed the move as 'in the highest degree provocative of religious bigotry and political bitterness'; 'an Apostolic Delegate, . . . even though he might be an Englishman, would be looked upon as an agent of Mussolini in the interests of the Rome-Berlin axis.'[154] In the end, the letter was not sent, and Godfrey and Hinsley 'developed . . . a good working relationship based on mutual respect',[155] while the Foreign Office continued to make use of Hinsley, who was to show his mettle as a national leader at a time of war.

Hinsley was driven to resign from his Vice-Presidency of the League of Nations Union by its left-wing politics and persistent pacifism, and opposed the anti-war propaganda of the semi-pacifists of *Pax*, Donald Attwater, Eric Gill and Edward Watkin. More controversially, against the reservations of some ordinary Catholics and of the Dominican *Blackfriars*, Hinsley wholeheartedly defended the Nationalist cause in Spain and kept a signed photograph of Franco on his desk. Spain, however, was a special case. Hinsley was embarrassed in 1940 by the Pétainist sympathies of Michael de la Bedoyere's *Catholic Herald*, and defended the Allied cause to neutral Catholic states, while striving to see that Russian entry into the war did not mean lasting injury to Poland or advance the cause of Communism. He became a national figure through his patriotic radio broadcasts, within Great Britain and to Catholic countries abroad, which gave him a stature personally higher than that of the Archbishop of Canterbury. His most striking imaginative ecumenical venture, however, was the wartime crusade of the 'Sword of the Spirit', a religious and patriotic movement initiated by Catholics for European spiritual renewal, with a predominantly lay committee and with Hinsley as President, involving other churches, including the Archbishops of Canterbury and York and Bishop Bell of Chichester, as well as refugee European Catholics. In 1941, a new Constitution clearly placed the movement under the authority of the Catholic bishops, reducing the non-Catholic members to second-class status, so a separate non-Catholic body was created with which the 'Sword' shared a joint committee. Hinsley, who was reprimanded by Rome for publicly saying the Lord's Prayer with the Anglican Bishop Bell of Chichester, cautiously 'gave instructions that, at joint meetings, if prayers were led by a non-Catholic, Catholics present might join in with the Our Father, but should remain silent during any other prayer'.[156] Archbishop Downey banned the movement in his diocese, some of the bishops were not prepared to pray with non-Catholics, and the 'Sword' had little influence in northern England.

Hinsley's broadcasts and his modest ecumenical measures, however, secured him the sympathy of a great many non-Catholics, as was to appear when he died in 1943. His requiem and funeral was a national and international occasion, more so than any archbishop's since Manning's obsequies in 1892, and was attended by two of the foremost Anglican bishops, of Chichester and Gloucester, by the Greek Archbishop Germanos, by General de Gaulle representing France and General Sikorsky representing Poland. He had enjoyed the double benefit of the allegiance of a Church completely united in itself, and secure in its teaching, now reaching out with some diffidence from that untroubled centre, to the Christians of other communions. It was a position which his more recent successors might envy.

In so far as spiritual results are quantifiable, the Catholic Church in England was a success, a success which lasted into the 1960s. In the words of A. J. P. Taylor, 'The Roman Catholics held up best.'[157] 'After 1910 Catholic and Protestant experience became even more diverse: for in 1910 the membership of the major Protestant churches was more than twice as great as the estimated Catholic population, while, by 1970, the estimated Catholic population was rather greater than the membership of the major Protestant churches.'[158] As Dr Fielding writes, 'It is the success of the Church, not its failure, that seems most striking.'[159] It was from 1918 that the history of the Catholic and Protestant churches clearly diverges, as the former continued to expand while the latter underwent a marked decline. There was a continuing growth in the number of Catholic parishes, schools and religious orders. Thus in Bermondsey by the 1930s, Catholic church attendance for the first time outstripped the Anglican, even though the 'very devout' amounted to only 20–30 per cent of the local nominally Catholic population.[160] The inter-war period was especially notable for the great public processions which brought Catholicism on to the streets. In the Friday Whit Walk in Manchester, some twenty thousand adults and children, marshalled in parishes and led by Catholic priests, magistrates and politicians, squeezed into Albert Square in front of the great Gothic town hall to receive the Bishop's benediction and to sing the battle hymn of a militant Catholicity, the Victorian convert Frederick Faber's 'Faith of our Fathers'. There was a similar grandeur to the Corpus Christi procession through the streets of Middlesbrough. Great crowds assembled for the Masses and rallies to mark the centenary of Catholic Emancipation in 1929. The larger parishes also regularly manifested their particular kind of triumphalism, which 'compacted their own solidarity while still proclaiming separation from the world outside':

> Week by week they continued throughout the liturgical year, the indoor and outdoor processions, rhythmically swaying their way by aisle and nave, through terraced street and suburban avenue, safely girt about by the episcopal *cordon sanitaire* of Catholic Action and the confident certainty of doctrinal belief. The serried ranks of the faithful in the sashes and regalia of their individual parish organisations thundered forth the four-square Victorian hymnody,
>
> Faith of our Fathers, Holy Faith,
> In spite of dungeon, fire and sword . . .
>
> which soared above the tossing banners of the myriad parochial guilds, the shy blue veils of the Children of Mary and the weeping black mantillas of the Wayside Sodality . . . All life was there: colour, sound, ritual, liturgy, devotion, worship, community, not excluding ostentation, management and authoritarianism for those so minded.[161]

There are two sorts of contemporary judgement on this community. On the one hand it is denigrated by some post-Vatican II Catholics as the 'ghetto Catholicism' of a 'fortress Church'.[162] On the other hand it is significant that this world, which was at its height in the 1940s and lasted until the 1960s, is recalled by many Catholics with the nostalgia with which socialist historians recall the solidly working-class communities between the wars. The very prevalence of the word 'community' in modern Catholic rhetoric – among some of the clergy, it seems to have all but supplanted 'church' – suggests what has been lost. A final judgement ought to be suspended until it finds an historian comparable to Mary Heimann in her work on Victorian Catholic devotion.[163]

The particular Roman Catholic achievement was to have built up a church, principally from a social class which was largely absent from the churches of other denominations, and to have become a large part of the Christian face of England, with a considerable share of its learning and culture, wit and wisdom. It was a position that would only be eroded in more recent years.

NOTES

1. E. M. Sneyd-Kinnersley, H.M.I., *Some Passages in the Life of One of H.M. Inspectors of Schools* (Macmillan & Co Ltd, London, 1913), p. 184.
2. Tom Buchanan and Martin Conway (eds), *Political Catholicism in Europe 1918–1965* (Clarendon Press, Oxford, 1996).
3. Tom Buchanan, 'Great Britain' in Buchanan and Conway (eds), *Political Catholicism*, p. 248.
4. See Bernard Aspinwall, '*Rerum Novarum* and the Church in the Transatlantic World' in *Rerum Novarum: Écriture, Contenu et Réception d'une Encyclique* (École Française de Rome, 1997), pp. 465–95. Also published in another useful collection, as '*Rerum Novarum* in the Transatlantic World' in Paul Furlong and David Curtis (eds), *The Church Faces the Modern World: Rerum Novarum and its Impact* (Earlsgate Press, Hull, 1994), pp. 205–40.

5. John H. Whyte, *Catholics in Western Democracies: A Study in Political Behaviour* (Gill and Macmillan, Dublin, 1981), pp. 74–5.
6. Peter Clarke, *Hope and Glory: Britain 1900–1990* (Penguin Books, London, 1996), p. 161.
7. A Mill Hill Father, *Remembered in Blessing: The Courtfield Story* (Sands & Co, London, 1955).
8. Shane Leslie (ed.), *Letters of Herbert Cardinal Vaughan to Lady Herbert of Lea, 1867 to 1903* (Burns & Oates, London, 1942).
9. J. G. Snead-Cox, *The Life of Cardinal Vaughan*, 2 vols (Herbert and Daniel, London, 1910), vol. I, p. 458.
10. Snead-Cox, *Vaughan*, vol. I, p. 477.
11. Edmund Sheridan Purcell, *The Life of Cardinal Manning*, 2 vols (Macmillan, London, 1895); Sheridan Gilley, 'New Light on an Old Scandal: Purcell's Life of Cardinal Manning' in Aidan Bellenger (ed.), *The Opening of the Scrolls* (Downside Abbey, Bath, 1987), pp. 166–98.
12. On Wilfrid especially, see Maisie Ward, *The Wilfrid Wards and the Transition*, I: *The Nineteenth Century* and II: *Insurrection versus Resurrection* (Sheed & Ward, London, 1934 and 1937); Mary Jo Weaver, 'A Bibliography of the Published Works of Wilfrid Ward', *The Heythrop Journal*, vol. XX, no. 4 (October 1979), pp. 399–420.
13. 'Appendix G', Vicary Gibbs (ed.), George Edward Cokayne, *The Complete Peerage of England Scotland Ireland Great Britain and the United Kingdom* (St Catherine Press, London, 1913), vol. III, pp. 639–41.
14. *The Catholic Directory 1895*, pp. 72–82.
15. J. P. Rossi, 'Lord Ripon's Resumption of Political Activity, 1878–1880', *Recusant History*, vol. XI (1971), pp. 61–74; Dermot Quinn, *Patronage and Piety: The Politics of English Roman Catholicism, 1850–1900* (Stanford University Press, 1993), pp. 87–121, 139–60.
16. J. Mordaunt Crook, *William Burges and the High Victorian Dream* (John Murray, London, 1981), p. 257.
17. See Madeleine Beard, *Faith and Fortune* (Gracewing, Leominster, 1997).
18. W. H. Auden, 'Introduction' in Anne Fremantle, *The Protestant Mystics* (Mentor Books, New York, Toronto and London, 1965), p. 37.
19. Quinn, *Patronage and Piety*, p. 101.
20. Winifride de L'Hôpital, *Westminster Cathedral and its Architect*, 2 vols (Hutchinson, London, 1919).
21. Réne Kollar, *Westminster Cathedral: From Dream to Reality* (Edinburgh, 1987); Peter Doyle, *Westminster Cathedral, 1895–1995* (Geoffrey Chapman, London, 1995).
22. Robert O'Neil MHM, *Cardinal Herbert Vaughan: Archbishop of Westminster, Bishop of Salford, Founder of the Mill Hill Missionaries* (Burns & Oates, London, 1995), p. 371.
23. David Fitzpatrick, 'A Curious Middle Place: The Irish in Britain, 1871–1921' in Roger Swift and Sheridan Gilley (eds), *The Irish in Britain 1815–1939* (Pinter Publishers, London, 1989), pp. 10–59.
24. Robert Currie and Alan Gilbert, 'Religion' in A. H. Halsey (ed.), *Trends in British Society since 1900: A Guide to the Changing Social Structure of Britain* (Macmillan, London, 1972), p. 407.
25. Currie and Gilbert, 'Religion', p. 14.
26. Currie and Gilbert, 'Religion', p. 29.
27. Alan B. Bartlett, 'The Churches in Bermondsey 1880–1939' (University of Birmingham PhD, 1988), p. 311.
28. G. I. T. Machin, *Politics and the Churches in Great Britain, 1869 to 1921* (Clarendon Press, Oxford, 1987), p. 263.
29. Geoffrey Alderman, *London Jewry and London Politics 1889–1986* (Routledge, London, 1989), pp. 48–9.
30. Steven Fielding, *Class and Ethnicity: Irish Catholics in England, 1880–1939* (Open University Press, Buckingham and Philadelphia, 1993), p. 42.

31. Swift and Gilley (eds), *The Irish in Britain*, p. 7; Fitzpatrick, 'A Curious Middle Place', pp. 33–44; Alan O'Day, 'The political organization of the Irish in Britain, 1867–90' in Swift and Gilley (eds), *The Irish in Britain*, pp. 183–211.
32. L. W. Brady, *T. P. O'Connor and the Liverpool Irish* (Royal Historical Society and Humanities Press, London and New Jersey, 1983).
33. Owen Dudley Edwards and Patricia J. Storey, 'The Irish Press in Victorian Britain' in Roger Swift and Sheridan Gilley (eds), *The Irish in the Victorian City* (Croom Helm, London, 1985), pp. 174–6.
34. Caroline L. Scott, 'A Comparative Re-examination of Anglo–Irish Relations in Nineteenth-Century Manchester, Liverpool and Newcastle-upon-Tyne' (University of Durham PhD thesis, 1998), p. 215.
35. Scott, 'Anglo–Irish Relations', p. 114.
36. Frank Neal, *Sectarian Violence: The Liverpool Experience, 1819–1914: An Aspect of Anglo–Irish History* (Manchester University Press, 1988), pp. 230–4.
37. Hugh McLeod, *Class and Religion in the Late Victorian City* (Croom Helm, London, 1974), p. 76.
38. Bartlett, 'Churches in Bermondsey', p. 103.
39. Fielding, *Class and Ethnicity*, p. 49.
40. Fielding, *Class and Ethnicity*, p. 55.
41. Fielding, *Class and Ethnicity*, p. 50.
42. John Sharp, *Reapers of the Harvest: The Redemptorists in Great Britain and Ireland 1843–1898* (Veritas Publications, Dublin, 1989).
43. Derek Holmes, *More Roman than Rome: English Catholicism in the Nineteenth Century* (Burns & Oates and Patmos Press, London and Shepherdstown, 1978), pp. 250–1.
44. Francis Edwards, *The Jesuits in England: From 1580 to the Present Day* (Burns & Oates, London, 1985), p. 242.
45. Régis Ladous, *Monsieur Portal et les Siens* (Les Éditions du Cerf, Paris, 1985).
46. R. William Franklin (ed.), *Anglican Orders: Essays on the Centenary of Apostolicae Curae, 1896–1996* (Mowbray, London, 1996); Christopher Hill and Edward Yarnold (eds), *Anglican Orders: The Documents in the Debate* (Canterbury Press, Norwich, 1997).
47. Peter F. Anson, *Bishops at Large* (Faber and Faber, London, 1954), pp. 156–215.
48. Peter Washington, *Madame Blavatsky's Baboon: Theosophy and the Emergence of the Western Guru* (Secker & Warburg, London, 1993).
49. A. J. A. Symons, *The Quest for Corvo* (Penguin, London, 1934); Miriam J. Benkovitz, *Frederick Rolfe: Baron Corvo: A Biography* (Hamish Hamilton, London, 1977).
50. M. Ward, *The Wilfrid Wards and the Transition*, vol. I, p. 205.
51. 'Mivart, St George Jackson', *Dictionary of National Biography.*
52. Jacob W. Gruber, *A Conscience in Conflict: The Life of St George Jackson Mivart* (Columbia University Press, New York, 1960).
53. Mary Jo Weaver (ed.), *Letters from a 'Modernist': The Letters of George Tyrrell to Wilfrid Ward 1893–1908* (The Patmos Press and Sheed & Ward, Shepherdstown and London, 1981), pp. 131–57.
54. Wilfrid Ward, 'Liberalism and Intransigence', *The Nineteenth Century*, vol. 47 (June 1900), pp. 960–73; M. Ward, *The Wilfrid Wards and the Transition*, I, p. 327.
55. See on Tyrrell, David G. Schultenover SJ, *George Tyrrell: In Search of Catholicism* (The Patmos Press, Shepherdstown, 1981); Nicholas Sagovsky, *'On God's Side': A Life of George Tyrrell* (Clarendon Press, Oxford, 1990).
56. Lawrence F. Barmann, *Baron Friedrich von Hügel and the Modernist Crisis in England* (Cambridge University Press, 1972), pp. 149–53.
57. George Osborn, Professor at Richmond College. Cited Alan Turberfield, 'A Critical Appraisal

of the Rev. Dr John Scott Lidgett, 1854–1953, Theologian, Educationalist and Ecclesiastical Statesman between 1890 and 1920' (University of Oxford DPhil thesis, 1998), pp. 27–8.

58. Holmes, *More Roman than Rome*, pp. 199–248.
59. V. Alan McClelland, *English Roman Catholics and Higher Education 1830–1903* (Clarendon Press, Oxford, 1973), pp. 369–428.
60. F. A. Forbes, *Rafael, Cardinal Merry del Val: A Character Sketch* (Longmans, London, 1932); Pio Cenci, *Il Cardinale Raffaele Merry del Val* (Rome, 1933); Marie Cecilia Buehrle, *Rafael Cardinal Merry del Val* (Sands and Co, London, 1957).
61. A. C. Benson, *The Life of Edward White Benson, sometime Archbishop of Canterbury*, 2 vols (Macmillan, London, 1899), vol. II, p. 372.
62. Shane Leslie, *Cardinal Gasquet* (Burns & Oates, London, 1953), p. 81.
63. Barmann, *Modernist Crisis*, p. 2.
64. Adrian Hastings, *A History of English Christianity 1920–1990* (SCM Press and Trinity Press International, London and Philadelphia, 1991), p. 144.
65. Ernest Oldmeadow, *Francis Cardinal Bourne*, 2 vols (Burns & Oates, London, 1944).
66. Oldmeadow, *Bourne*, vol. I, pp. 349–52.
67. *Report of the Nineteenth Eucharistic Congress, held at Westminster from 9th to 14th September 1908* (Sands and Company, London, 1909).
68. G. I. T. Machin, 'The Liberal Government and the Eucharistic Procession of 1908', *The Journal of Ecclesiastical History*, vol. XXXIV (1983), pp. 559–83.
69. J. A. Hilton, *Catholic Lancashire: From Reformation to Renewal 1559–1991* (Phillimore & Co, Chichester, 1994), p. 107.
70. Michael Clifton, *Amigo – Friend of the Poor; Bishop of Southwark 1904–1949* (Fowler Wright, Leominster, 1987), p. 50.
71. William J. Schoenl, *The Intellectual Crisis in English Catholicism: Liberal Catholics, Modernists, and the Vatican in the Late Nineteenth and Early Twentieth Centuries* (Garland Publishing, Inc., New York and London, 1982).
72. Nicholas Lash, 'Modernism, Aggiornamento and the Night Battle' in Adrian Hastings (ed.), *Bishops and Writers: Aspects of the Evolution of Modern English Catholicism* (Anthony Clarke, Wheathampstead, 1977), p. 52.
73. Clyde F. Crews, *English Catholic Modernism: Maude Petre's Way of Faith* (Notre Dame, Indiana, 1984); Alec Vidler, 'An Abortive Renaissance: Catholic Modernists in Sussex', *Renaissance and Renewal in Christian History, Studies in Church History*, vol. XIV (Basil Blackwell, Oxford, 1977), pp. 377–92.
74. Clifton, *Amigo*, pp. 33–6.
75. Nigel Abercrombie, *The Life and Work of Edmund Bishop* (Longmans, London, 1959).
76. See on Thurston, Joseph Crehan SJ, *Father Thurston: A Memoir with a Bibliography of his Writings* (Sheed & Ward, London, 1952).
77. David Knowles OSB, 'Edward Cuthbert Butler: 1858–1934' in *The Historian and Character and other Essays* (Cambridge University Press, 1963), pp. 264–362.
78. On Underhill, see Ann Loades, *Evelyn Underhill* (Fount, London, 1997), pp. 3–4; on Fawkes, see Alec R. Vidler, *A Variety of Catholic Modernists* (Cambridge University Press, 1970), pp. 155–60.
79. Ronald Knox, 'After 33 Years', Preface to *A Spiritual Aeneid* (Burns Oates, London, 1958), p. xx.
80. H. J. A. Sire, *Father Martin D'Arcy: Philosopher of Christian Love* (Gracewing, Leominster, 1997).
81. Michele Ranchetti, *The Catholic Modernists: A Study of the Religious Reform Movement 1864–1907*, tr. Isabel Quigly (Oxford University Press, London, 1969), p. 95.
82. Maisie Ward, *Gilbert Keith Chesterton* (Sheed & Ward, London, 1944), p. 171.

83. Eamon Duffy, *Saints and Sinners: A History of the Popes* (Yale University Press, New Haven, CT, 1997), p. 251.
84. Michael Walsh, *The Tablet 1840–1990: A Commemorative History* (The Tablet Publishing Co, London, 1990), p. 35.
85. Ronald Knox, *Barchester Pilgrimage* (London, 1936), p. 82.
86. Buchanan, 'Great Britain', p. 252.
87. Fielding, *Class and Ethnicity*, p. 59.
88. Fielding, *Class and Ethnicity*, p. 71.
89. Robert Currie, Alan Gilbert, Lee Horsley, *Churches and Churchgoers: Patterns of Church Growth in the British Isles since 1700* (Clarendon Press, Oxford, 1977), p. 190.
90. Buchanan, 'Great Britain', p. 250.
91. Fr Philip Fletcher, ed. George E. Anstruther and William Spence, *Recollections of a Ransomer* (Sands & Co, London, 1928).
92. W. Gordon Gorman, *Converts to Rome: A Biographical List of the More Notable Converts to the Catholic Church in the United Kingdom during the last Sixty Years* (London, 1910).
93. Gorman mysteriously refers to it as the Golden Jubilee (*Converts*, p. ix).
94. Stephen J. Brown SJ, *Novels and Tales by Catholic Writers* (Central Catholic Library, Dublin, 1940).
95. It should perhaps be noted that Bishop's early love of Newman later turned to dislike.
96. Stratford Caldecott and John Morrill (eds), *Eternity in Time: Christopher Dawson and the Catholic Idea of History* (T. & T. Clark, Edinburgh, 1997).
97. A. C. Benson, *Hugh: Memoirs of a Brother* (Smith, Elder & Co, London, 1915); C. C. Martindale SJ, *The Life of Monsignor Robert Hugh Benson*, 2 vols (Longmans, London, 1917).
98. Evelyn Waugh, *The Life of the Right Reverend Ronald Knox* (Chapman & Hall, London, 1959); Thomas Corbishley SJ, *Ronald Knox the Priest* (Sheed & Ward, London and New York, 1964).
99. Wilfrid Sheed, *Frank and Maisie* (Chatto & Windus, London, 1986), p. 65.
100. Robert Graves and Alan Hodge, *The Long Week-end: A Social History of Great Britain 1918–1939* (Faber & Faber, London, 1950), pp. 127–8.
101. Sire, *D'Arcy*, p. 59.
102. Robert Speaight, *The Property Basket: Recollections of a Divided Life* (Collins & Harvill, London, 1970), p. 126. See Philip Caraman, *C. C. Martindale: A Biography* (Longmans, London, 1967).
103. Robert Speaight, *The Life of Hilaire Belloc* (Hollis & Carter, London, 1957); A. N. Wilson, *Hilaire Belloc* (Hamish Hamilton, London, 1984).
104. Laura Lovat, *Maurice Baring: A Postscript with Some Letters and Verse* (Hollis & Carter, London, 1947).
105. Gill's halo as the greatest of modern Catholic sculptors has been dented by the revelations of his sexual antinomianism. Compare Robert Speaight, *The Life of Eric Gill* (Methuen & Co, London, 1966), and Fiona MacCarthy, *Eric Gill* (Faber & Faber, London, 1989). After his death, an archbishop ordered that Gill's statue of a monkey be removed from his carving of St Thomas More in Westminster Cathedral.
106. Ferdinand Valentine OP, *Father Vincent McNabb, O.P. The Portrait of a Great Dominican* (London, Burns & Oates, 1955).
107. E. A. Siderman, *A Saint in Hyde Park: Memories of Father Vincent McNabb, O.P.* (The Catholic Book Club, London, 1950).
108. Barbara Wall, *René Hague: A Personal Memoir* (The Aylesford Press: The Wirral, 1989).
109 Aidan Nichols, *Dominican Gallery: Portrait of a Culture* (Gracewing, Leominster, 1997).
110. A. J. P. Taylor, *English History 1914–1945* (Clarendon Press, Oxford, 1965), p. 180.
111. Walsh, *Tablet*, p. 33.
112. Ronald Knox, 'A Forgotten Interlude' in *Essays in Satire* (Sheed & Ward, London, 1928), pp.

279–87: also Waugh, *Knox*, pp. 190–1: '. . . Sir Theophilus Gooch, who was on his way to this station, has been intercepted . . . and is being roasted alive.'

113. Martin Stannard, *Evelyn Waugh: The Early Years 1903–1939* (J. M. Dent & Sons, London, 1986), pp. 321, 336–8, 348, 350, 375–6, 405, 417; Selina Hastings, *Evelyn Waugh: A Biography* (Sinclair-Stevenson, London, 1994), pp. 282–4.
114. Mark Amory (ed.), *The Letters of Evelyn Waugh* (Weidenfeld and Nicolson, London, 1981), p. 78.
115. And their Anglo-Catholic brethren. See Maurice Cowling, *Religion and Public Doctrine in Modern England*, 2 vols (Cambridge University Press, 1980 and 1985).
116. John Cashman, 'The 1906 Education Bill: Catholic Peers and Irish Nationalists', *Recusant History*, vol. 18, no. 7 (October 1987), pp. 422–39; V. Alan McClelland, 'Bourne, Norfolk and the Irish Parliamentarians: Roman Catholics and the Education Bill of 1906', *Recusant History*, vol. 23, no. 2 (October 1996), pp. 228–56.
117. Hilton, *Catholic Lancashire*, p. 102.
118. Sheridan Gilley, 'Catholics and Socialists in Glasgow, 1900–30', in Swift and Gilley (eds), *The Irish in Britain*, pp. 212–38.
119. Buchanan, 'Great Britain', pp. 259, 264.
120. Stuart Mews, 'The Churches' in Margaret Morris (ed.), *The General Strike* (Penguin, London, 1976), p. 330.
121. Sidney Z. Ehler and John B. Morrall (eds), *Church and State Through the Centuries: A Collection of Historic Documents with Commentaries* (London, Burns & Oates, 1954), p. 411.
122. Stuart Mews, 'The Hunger-strike of the Lord Mayor of Cork, 1920: Irish, English and Vatican Attitudes' in W. J. Sheils and Diana Wood (eds), *The Churches, Ireland and the Irish, Studies in Church History*, vol. 25 (Basil Blackwell, Oxford, 1989), pp. 385–400.
123. George Andrew Beck, 'To-day and To-morrow' in *The English Catholics 1850–1950* (London, Burns & Oates, 1950), p. 603.
124. Mary Hickman, *Religion, Class and Identity: The State, the Catholic Church and the Education of the Irish in Britain* (Avebury, Aldershot, 1995).
125. Hastings, *English Christianity*, pp. 142–3.
126. Alderman, *London Jewry*, pp. 84–6.
127. Robert Moore, *Pit-men, Preachers and Politics: The Effects of Methodism in a Durham Mining Community* (Cambridge University Press, 1974), p. 214.
128. Fielding, *Class and Ethnicity*, p. 55.
129. Hastings, *English Christianity*, pp. 141–2.
130. See for Lancashire, Hilton, *Catholic Lancashire*, pp. 116–17.
131. Gorman, *Converts*, p. x.
132. Hilton, *Catholic Lancashire*, pp. 109, 119.
133. John C. Heenan, *Not the Whole Truth* (Hodder & Stoughton, London, 1972), pp. 72–3.
134. Fielding, *Class and Ethnicity*, p. 43.
135. Charles Fitzgerald-Lombard, *English and Welsh Priests 1801–1914: A Working List* (Downside Abbey, Somerset, 1993), p. xiv.
136. Robert Carson, *The First Hundred Years: A History of the Diocese of Middlesbrough 1878–1978* (The Middlesbrough Diocesan Trustees, 1978), pp. 73–9.
137. Mews, 'Hunger-strike', pp. 389–90, 394.
138. G. L. Prestige, *The Life of Charles Gore: A Great Englishman* (William Heinemann Ltd, London and Toronto, 1935).
139. Heenan, *Not the Whole Truth*, pp. 82–8.
140. Taylor, *English History*, pp. 165–7.
141. Barbara Reynolds, *Dorothy L. Sayers: Her Life and Soul* (Hodder & Stoughton, London, 1993), p. 112.

142. Taylor, *English History*, p. 170.
143. *Burke's Peerage, Baronetage and Knightage* (96th edition: Shaw Publishing Co, London, 1938), p. 1691.
144. Sneyd-Kinnersley, *Some Passages*, p. 186.
145. Sneyd-Kinnersley, *Some Passages*, p. 185.
146. Sneyd-Kinnersley, *Some Passages*, p. 191.
147. See, for example, Maisie Ward (ed.), *The English Way: Studies in English Sanctity from St Bede to Newman* (Sheed & Ward, London, 1934).
148. Cecil Kerr, *Teresa Helena Higginson, Servant of God, 'The Spouse of the Crucified', 1844–1905* (Sands & Co, London, 1927); John Davies, 'Traditional Religion, Popular Piety, or Base Superstition? The Cause for the Beatification of Teresa Higginson', *Recusant History*, vol. 24, no. 1 (May 1998), pp. 123–44.
149. Michael E. Williams, *The Venerable English College, Rome: A History* (Associated Catholic Publications, London, 1979), p. 161.
150. Ibid.
151. Anthony Kenny, *A Path from Rome: An Autobiography* (Oxford University Press, 1986), p. 53.
152. John C. Heenan, *Cardinal Hinsley: A Memoir* (Burns, Oates & Washbourne, London, 1944), pp. 81–3.
153. On Osborne see Owen Chadwick, *Britain and the Vatican during the Second World War* (Cambridge University Press, 1986).
154. Thomas Moloney, *Westminster, Whitehall and the Vatican: The Role of Cardinal Hinsley, 1935–43* (Burns & Oates, London, 1985), pp. 96–7.
155. Moloney, *Westminster*, p. 101.
156. Michael Walsh, *From Sword to Ploughshare: Sword of the Spirit to the Catholic Institute for International Relations 1940–1980* (Catholic Institute for International Relations, London, 1980).
157. Taylor, *English History*, p. 169.
158. Currie, Gilbert and Horsley, *Churches and Churchgoers*, p. 29.
159. Fielding, *Class and Ethnicity*, p. 78.
160. Bartlett, 'Churches in Bermondsey', p. 346.
161. Moloney, *Westminster*, p. 242. The first line of the hymn ends 'living still', not 'Holy Faith', which is the chorus. The quotation as given correctly reproduces the usual confusion in performance.
162. E.g. 'It would seem that the days of substantial thought-control over all aspects of social life, powerful especially in the defensive ghettoes of the fortress Church, are now well and truly over.' Michael P. Hornsby-Smith, *Roman Catholic Beliefs in England: Customary Catholicism and Transformations of Religious Authority* (Cambridge University Press, 1991), pp. 226–7.
163. Mary Heimann, *Catholic Devotion in Victorian England* (Clarendon Press, Oxford, 1995).

THREE

SEMINARIES AND PRIESTLY FORMATION

MICHAEL E. WILLIAMS

A comprehensive study of the English seminaries has still to be written.[1] But the story of their development and a consideration of some of the problems encountered in the past can perhaps help towards an understanding of inherited attitudes that still have an influence in the post-Vatican II Church.

THE FIRST ENGLISH SEMINARIES

The sacred ministry that involves the public duties of saying Mass, hearing confessions and preaching calls for a special sort of preparation. In the course of centuries various practices have been in operation, ranging from cathedral and monastic schools to a period of apprenticeship served under an experienced priest in a parish. In Europe it was the expansion of learning at the Renaissance that, on the eve of the Reformation, drew attention to the ignorance of many of the clergy. Both Catholic and Protestant reformers were anxious to remedy this state of affairs. However, it was not until the Council of Trent that the Catholic Church ordered that all bishops should set up colleges that would be 'perpetual seed-plots (seminaries) of ministers of God'. This took place at the twenty-third session of the Council in 1563. Five years later in 1568 William Allen opened his college at Douai. But Douai College was more a response to the religious situation in England than it was to the conciliar decree. Like the fathers at Trent, Allen was concerned about the preparation of candidates for the priesthood in the post-Reformation world. But whereas Trent envisaged an embattled but basically stable church, Allen was faced in England with a complete breakdown of the Church's authority and organisation that called for more than just a reform in clerical education. The Tridentine disciplinary decrees set out to strengthen the role of the bishop in the diocese, but none of those who exercised the office of bishop in England were in communion with Rome and the whole ecclesiastical system was under the control of the Crown.

Allen became the unofficial spokesman of all those who still professed loyalty to Rome and his concerns at Douai were wider than clerical education. The pastoral services he had to provide for the English Catholic exiles included a general university education now denied them in England. He was able to respond to some of the measures suggested by the Tridentine reformation decrees, but not being in episcopal orders himself and there being no English ordinaries to whom he could refer, one of the essential elements in the conciliar scheme of seminaries was absent. Any college that might be established would have no clear authority to whom its rector would be responsible either spiritually or financially. In Trent's vision it was the diocesan bishop either personally or, more usually, through consultation with his priests and diocesan officials, who set up the seminary, decided whom to admit, determined the teaching staff and the course of studies according to the requirements of the diocese. In England, however, there was no such ecclesiastical structure. But there were still men willing to work as priests there and very soon the religious orders, Benedictines, Franciscans and especially the recently founded Jesuits, sent their own missioners. Following the example of Douai, other colleges were established on the Continent of Europe which provided education for the exiles and maintained a supply of priests to work in England. Generous patrons and donors, including the Holy See and the Catholic monarchs, gave financial support. Bishops in foreign parts welcomed and assisted the English seminarian exiles and the Jesuits administered the English seminaries in Rome, Valladolid and Seville. But the linchpin of the Tridentine reform, the diocesan bishop, was absent from the English scene. A network of contacts among the laity enabled the missionary priests to circulate when they arrived back in their home country. For a time there was an 'archpriest' in charge, but the reluctance of Rome to appoint a bishop-in-ordinary meant that the English Catholics, while holding firmly to the notion of episcopacy, were in fact living in a non-episcopal local church. This lack of direction affected in a special way those clergy who did not belong to any of the religious orders. Under James II the country was divided into four districts and Vicars Apostolic were appointed, but these were not diocesan bishops and they were dependent on Rome and the Congregation of *Propaganda Fide*.[2] Moreover, although the Vicars Apostolic had men in training at all the seminaries abroad, it was only at Douai and Lisbon that the college rectors were secular priests. In Rome and in Spain the Jesuits were in charge of the administration and at times this led to complications, as they were not always aware of the requirements of the Vicars Apostolic.

In the course of time, because of a less rigorous application of the penal laws and the way in which English public opinion reacted to the attacks on religion in the wake of the French Revolution, Catholic seminaries and schools began to be established in England towards the end of the eighteenth century. At the end of the Napoleonic period when the work of restoration was in hand, three of the colleges abroad, in Rome, Valladolid and Lisbon, resumed their full activity. Douai, the jewel in the crown, was not reopened, but its tradition continued on English soil, at Ushaw in the north and Ware in the south. In the Midlands it was joined by Oscott, whose origins were native English. By reason of their location these three English seminaries fell neatly under the responsibility of the Vicars Apostolic of the Northern, London and Midland Districts.[3] But in 1840 the number of districts was doubled and this meant that there were now eight Vicars Apostolic who shared between them the resources of the three seminaries at home and the three abroad. During the years of its existence Douai had developed a certain tradition of independence from episcopal control, and this was to manifest itself in a sense of the autonomy of the President of the seminary in the administration of its affairs.[4]

THE RESTORATION OF THE HIERARCHY AND SOME SURVIVING DOUAI TRADITIONS

In 1850 the restoration of the hierarchy and the re-emergence of dioceses meant that for the first time since the Council of Trent England had episcopal rule. But the change in the administrative division of the country from eight vicariates to thirteen dioceses further complicated matters. All the seminaries at home and abroad were now administered by secular priests, but the three overseas colleges were situated outside the English bishops' territory and the fact that the colleges at home were located in the dioceses of Westminster, Birmingham and Hexham suggested that these bishops had a particular if not sole responsibility.

In 1852 the First Provincial Synod of the restored hierarchy did not tackle the matter of any sharing in episcopal control or finance of the seminaries, but it did call attention to one of the stipulations of Trent that had never been strictly adhered to by the English colleges at home or abroad. Trent had envisaged that the seminaries would cater for boys from an early age (twelve years) and would be for the exclusive use of candidates for the priesthood. As far as England was concerned, the college at Douai had to meet the many needs of the English Church. Not only was it obliged to provide for the formation of prospective priests, it had also to attend to the education of the laity. Because of the penal laws, admission to the ancient universities of Oxford and Cambridge was not possible for those who were loyal to the papacy. So the seminary at Douai had a double role, the education of clerics and the education of the laity. There was no serious practical difficulty about this since the latter could be conveniently catered for in the early part of the course where the humanities were studied as a necessary preliminary to the ecclesiastical studies of philosophy and theology.

This system proved successful and the practice was continued not only in Douai's direct successors at Ushaw and Ware but also at Sedgley Park School and Oscott, where lay and church students were educated together. One of the effects of this arrangement was to bind together future clergy and laity as common schoolfellows. But when the hierarchy was restored, there was a feeling among some of the bishops that this tradition should be broken and the strict Tridentine seminary should be introduced into England. At the insistence of Thomas Grant, the Bishop of Southwark, in 1852 the First Provincial Council of Westminster stated: 'We hold it would exceedingly avail to the increase of religion if seminaries could be established in which the clergy could be educated apart from others.' Although this resolution was passed, its implementation was difficult to achieve and, as we shall see, the 'mixed' Douai tradition has had its supporters up to the present day.[5] At the time, however, there was a measure of support for the Roman and Tridentine view to be found in the seminaries themselves. A convert who entered the College of St Edmund, Ware, to study for the priesthood at the age of twenty-four, wrote that he and his fellow seminarists 'were all mixed up with future lords, earls and other lay students, who at the end of each vacation used to return from London with London news and London pleasures . . . I got more harm than good from such conversations.' At Ushaw the President, Charles Newsham, complained of the 'very great want of a spirit of piety, faith and religion in the clergy'.[6] Every effort was made at Ushaw to ensure that lay boys were in the minority and in 1840 Bishop Walsh of the Midland District considered sending the lay students away from Oscott. They were in the majority and it was 'difficult to prevent a worldly spirit' in the house.

CARDINAL WISEMAN AND EPISCOPAL JURISDICTION OVER THE SEMINARIES

Apart from the distinct nature of clerical education and its relationship to Catholic education in general, there is another theme that runs through the history of the English seminaries since 1850. If clerical education is to be considered as primarily the responsibility of each bishop and his diocese, as Trent suggests, then it will be difficult to set up a uniform national policy. Because of the diversity between the dioceses in needs and requirements, and also the disparity in financial and human resources, it would not be possible for every diocese to have its own seminary. Trent was well aware of this, and in its decree allowed for the coexistence of the provincial seminary, which brought about co-operation between richer and poorer dioceses. But such co-operation between bishops can sometimes be as difficult as co-operation between the diocesan and regular clergy. Each of the bishops in the newly restored hierarchy was very conscious of his newly acquired power and jurisdiction and the opportunities this gave for the growth of the Church in England in the diocese entrusted to his care.[7] One of the results of this was not only a tension between the competence of the bishops and the rectors of the seminaries, but also among the bishops themselves and their rights over their own diocesan subjects.

In the North of England, the Bishops of Liverpool, Beverley, Salford and Hexham each wanted an equal share in the government of Ushaw College. The President, Newsham, saw that such a division of interests created an obstacle to the smooth and efficient administration of college affairs. Wiseman, a former seminary rector, defended Newsham and declared that Ushaw was a corporate body and the President and superiors were not servants of the bishops, since the college was not a seminary in the Tridentine sense.[8] An example of independent episcopal action can be seen in Bishop Goss of Liverpool's decision in 1857 to make the lay school of St Edward's into a junior diocesan seminary for the district of Lancashire. Ushaw saw this as a challenge to its own position as the place for priestly training in the North. It reacted against Liverpool by deciding to build a junior seminary of its own and many of the clergy rallied to support the plan.[9]

After several years of discussion and wrangling, some measure of agreement was reached when *Propaganda Fide* in 1863 decided that the spiritual jurisdiction and care of the students was to be placed in the hands of the ordinary in whose diocese the colleges were located. This favoured the Bishops of Westminster, Birmingham and Hexham. However, 'temporal matters' which were taken to include such things as studies, discipline and day-to-day government and administration, were to be entrusted to boards or panels of bishops. Ushaw was to be cared for by the northern bishops plus Shrewsbury; Ware was to be the concern of Westminster and Southwark. As to Oscott, the President, James Spencer Northcote, seemed to be much more interested in the college's general educational role and only twelve of his 123 boys were destined for the ecclesiastical state.[10] However different the circumstances in the North, Midlands and London, the three places that trained senior seminarians in England were more like regional seminaries than diocesan ones under the sole control of the local bishop and his chapter. Although the principle or ideal was that each diocese should have its own seminary, the particular situation in England and the lack of adequate resources meant that some form of regionalism was the only solution.

Wiseman had spent more than half his life in a seminary. He was a boy at Ushaw from 1810 to 1818, in Rome at the English College as a student, professor and rector from 1818 to 1840 and Rector of Oscott from 1840 to 1847. As Archbishop of Westminster he became directly responsible for St Edmund's, Ware. Two features stand out in his relationship with St Edmund's. First of all there was the appointment of W. G. Ward, a convert and a layman, as professor of dogmatic theology, which was not well received by the bishop-coadjutor, Errington, and other members of the clergy. Even more controversial was the presence on the teaching staff of members of the Oblates of St Charles. Wiseman always entertained broad views of the Church's role in society and he appreciated the work of the religious orders. The Oblates dated from a group of priests in Charles Borromeo's Milan of 1578 who drew their strength from their life in common. They put themselves at the disposal of the bishop in a way that the older traditional orders did not. When in 1855 Herbert Vaughan, who had been designated at the age of twenty-three to be the Vice-President at St Edmund's, together with three other members of the staff joined the Oblates, there was an immediate reaction. The presence of this group, although pleasing to a man like Henry Edward Manning, did not meet with universal approval in the diocese. The chapter took exception to this situation on the grounds that the Council of Trent had stipulated that the control of the diocesan seminary was to be exercised by the bishop and diocesan officials appointed by him. The Oblates were not ordained *ad titulum missionis* but *ad titulum patrimonii.* They were not strictly diocesans and hence it was argued they ought not to have any part in running the seminary. Here perhaps we have an echo of past prejudices of the English secular clergy against the religious orders. Wiseman defended the Oblates on the grounds that the English seminaries were not strictly Tridentine seminaries. The matter was referred to Rome who eventually referred it back to the provincial synod.

TWO NEW OVERSEAS SEMINARIES

It was in the midst of these discussions that Sir John Sutton, a recent convert to Catholicism, proposed to Bishop Grant of Southwark and Cardinal Wiseman the foundation and endowment in Belgium of a new English college. There was already a well-established English community in Bruges and this included several influential Catholics. The English Canonesses of St Augustine, who had been established there in 1624, had to leave for England in the upheaval of 1794, but they returned to Bruges in 1802 and since that date their school had flourished. They benefited from the Catholic revival consequent upon the liberation from Dutch Protestant rule and the restoration of the diocese of Bruges in 1835.[11] Sutton's projected English College would be for the teaching of theology to future priests and so, in this sense, a seminary. However, it would not be exclusively clerical in intent, since it would also undertake the teaching of English literature to Belgian nationals. Wiseman was hesitant about adding to the overseas colleges. The old English colleges abroad had arisen out of the strict educational needs of the Catholic community in England. This offer of a new college seemed to have been prompted by the personal piety of an individual

English convert and by a desire to support a newly established Catholic country. But in the end Wiseman agreed to it, and the college began on a small scale with mixed Belgian and English superiors and with seven seminarians taken from six English dioceses. The college remained in existence from 1858 to 1873. By the end of its brief life every diocese in England and Wales had sent at least one student there, and it was also supported by two of the Scottish Districts. Vocations were sought from those born in the Low Countries and in Germany, and the registers tell us that there were about 120 ordained priests who had done at least part of their training at Bruges. The college did not long survive after the founder's death. There were legal disputes about the ownership of the seminary building and some of the assets, and a decision was made to close.

Although Wiseman relinquished his rectorship of the *Venerabile* when he returned to England in 1840, he still had a keen interest in English seminary affairs in Rome. This was to lead to another more durable foundation in the nineteenth century. It was Mgr Talbot, Wiseman's representative in Rome, who first seems to have appreciated the special need to accommodate those Anglican clergmen who had converted to Rome and wished to be priests in the Roman Catholic Church. Wiseman took up the suggestion of having a shortened course of study adapted for older men and without the system of discipline suited to a community of young and less mature seminarians. It was fitting that this seminary should be in Rome so that the 'Roman spirit' would be imbibed. Rooms were acquired near St Peter's and the *Collegio Ecclesiastico* came into being.[12] The college began with just six students, but it has continued and grown despite several interruptions and name changes. At present it is well known in the Catholic world as the Pontifical Beda College. In many ways it was the most innovative of all the English seminary developments in the nineteenth century. Its story also shows a willingness on the part of Rome to modify some of the strict requirements of training in order to accommodate Anglican converts. The revised course was tailored to the needs and capacities of older and more experienced men and lasted for four years, not the customary six, with lectures in English, not Latin. Because of financial difficulties, for twenty years (1855–75) the College was lodged in a wing of the *Venerabile*. Although there were advantages in some association between younger and older men called to the same vocation, difficulties arose from having two distinct communities under the same roof.

It was during this period that the Oblates of St Charles come into the picture again. In 1861 Wiseman and Manning had withdrawn them from the staff in the college at Ware. But in 1868, largely due to Manning's influence (he was now Archbishop of Westminster in succession to Wiseman), there was a change of rector at the *Venerabile* and an Oblate, Henry O'Callaghan, was appointed to this post. He had previously been a member of the staff at St Edmund's and was well connected with people in Rome.[13] It was during O'Callaghan's regime that numbers at the Beda began to decline. One of the reasons for this was O'Callaghan's tightening up of the rules at the *Venerabile* and the ending of the practice that allowed students in their final year to transfer to the less restrictive *Collegio Pio*. The political situation in Italy that was to culminate in the loss of the Papal States and the taking of Rome in 1870 dissuaded many from residing in Rome. There was a period when there were no students at the Beda and the college existed in name only. It was only after the Bull *Apostolicae Curae*, declaring Anglican Orders null and void, that there was a new influx of students and eventually in 1917 the Beda was able to resume a separate existence in another part of Rome. The Beda like the *Venerabile* kept its corporate continuity during World War II by residence in England. It has not been troubled by staffing difficulties as have some of the other seminaries abroad, since its situation in Rome has meant that there was never any serious shortage of approved and willing qualified priests and teachers ready to give their time to the education of future priests. It has also managed to persuade bishops from English-speaking countries outside England and Wales to send men there for their studies.

CARDINAL MANNING AND THE PRIESTHOOD

To understand many of the ideas about the priesthood that lay behind the disputes about the seminaries in the second half of the nineteenth century one cannot do better than consult Manning's *The Eternal Priesthood*.[14] This book sought to put into practice in the England and Wales of the nineteenth century the ideals of the Council of Trent. For three hundred years the Catholic scene at home had missed out on a truly native implementation of the Tridentine decrees. It had had to be content with establishments abroad that were only intended originally as provisional measures until the time when dioceses were restored. *The Eternal Priesthood* not only sets out a traditional Catholic theology of the priesthood but at the same time it relates the work of the priest to a particular local context.

Manning was of the opinion that the English diocesan clergy had a too low estimate of their calling and so he stressed that the priestly vocation is a special sharing in the priesthood of Our Lord and this sets the priest apart from others. It is as if his dedication to prayer and service of others places him in a distinct class of society. This becomes apparent in chapter eighteen which concerns the priest's house. We read that the presbytery is not like other houses in the district. Not only is it distinguished by its simpler style of furniture and the presence of sacred pictures on its walls but it is marked by its well-ordered regularity and punctuality. The clergy house has servants but of advanced age. No women take their meals with the priests. There is no suggestion of a flexible timetable, still less of an open house. Visitors are expected to abide by the timetable of the priests. To a late twentieth-century reader this speaks of a bygone age when society was stable and had its fixed boundaries and limits. But although there is the separation of priest from people, the priest is not a solitary figure. He shares a common table and common recreation with the other priests resident in the presbytery. They are expected to take their recreation together and not go outside the house.

The picture painted by Manning places the priest among the professional classes. The conditions described would also be applicable to the life of many Anglican clergymen in so far as the house was a family home. The difference was that the Anglican was usually a married priest with his wife and family, whereas the Catholic was one of a group of celibate clergy living in community. This can help us understand Manning's attraction to the Oblates of St Charles. If Trent were to be followed strictly, these ideals and this style of living would begin at the age of twelve in the junior seminary. Manning was well aware of the break that would come when it was time to leave the seminary for the parish. He appreciated the effect of the loss of the familiar surroundings and enclosed life of the seminary. But this was no argument for changing the system. Rather was it an invitation to build invisible walls and not seek the society offered by the world. Although the presence of other priests under the same roof would not be in the category of friendship and familiarity as the world knows it, nevertheless this companionship was necessary. He said,

> Priests dwelling alone are in an abnormal, unecclesiastical, unsacerdotal state which often has grave dangers, and is not free from many disadvantages. The liberty of living alone is not wholesome; and the loss of the daily discipline of self-abnegation in living with others is a privation of much good.[15]

These attitudes were not peculiar to Manning and they must be borne in mind if we are to understand the debates about the seminaries that took place throughout the nineteenth and early twentieth centuries. The seminary was a time of preparation for this ideal life of the priest. Moreover the stability and regularity of life in the presbytery, with its implications of apartness, was often a factor that encouraged vocations. It was a time when the clergy were no longer being recruited exclusively from the gentry or merchant classes. Many of the new proletariat, especially the immigrants from Ireland, were coming forward and they often saw in Manning's ideal of the priest an incentive to rise to a higher standard of living, materially as well as spiritually.

So much for the ideal. It was to find expression in a series of events which took place fairly rapidly and followed a recognised pattern. Acting on his principles, in 1869 Manning disturbed the existing situation by opening a new establishment at St Thomas's Hammersmith which was to replace St Edmund's Ware as the diocesan seminary for Westminster. True, it was not a seminary in the full Tridentine sense, since there were no young boys. But the students of philosophy and theology were transferred from St Edmund's to Hammersmith, and Ware became a school for lay boys. This arrangement had its repercussions outside the diocese since the Southwark diocesan students at Ware were now left on their own, and it was to be another twenty years before their diocese was able to establish its own seminary at Henfield (1889), and only in 1891 was the new seminary at Wonersh completed.[16] In 1873, four years after the opening of Hammersmith, Ullathorne, the Bishop of Birmingham, followed Manning's precedent. Oscott's predominantly lay and public-school style of administration rendered it far from ideal for priestly formation and the bishop established a seminary at Olton on the other side of the town to which he sent some of the philosophers and theologians from Oscott. As was the case with Ware, other dioceses who had students at Oscott were affected by these changes.

In 1875 Bishop Vaughan of Salford was commissioned by the hierarchy to make a visitation of the overseas seminaries. He published his report in 1876.[17] Among the resolutions was one to make Lisbon into a junior seminary solely, and Valladolid a senior seminary alone. This attempt to simplify, so that all those studying humanities would be grouped in one place and all those doing philosophy and theology in another, did not take into account the traditional way of life of the two colleges concerned, whereby the existence of a lower house and a senior house was part of the structure that encouraged a development and mutuality between the aspirants to the priesthood from boyhood to manhood. This had been the tradition at Douai, a tradition still maintained at Ushaw. Neither did these proposals of Vaughan take into account the different circumstances of the Church in Spain and Portugal. Moreover, any changes in the overseas seminaries would have to be acceptable to all the English and Welsh bishops, since these institutions recruited from the whole country and were responsible to the whole hierarchy and not to one particular bishop. They were by their constitutions linked with Rome and *Propaganda Fide* and often had 'Protectors' who placed them in the context of the Church in the territory where they resided. This could not be neglected even though their main purpose was to prepare men for the English mission.

Following on the changes occasioned by the establishment of seminaries at Hammersmith and Olton there were other developments. The Bishop of Beverley opened a seminary in Leeds which was at first intended for students completing their course at Ushaw.[18] Bishop Cornthwaite of Beverley contended that the new seminary at Leeds would not affect Ushaw or break his promise to support that college. The Bishop of Liverpool, O'Reilly, had already shown his desire for control over vocations by turning St Edward's into a junior diocesan seminary. Now in 1877 he launched an appeal to build a senior seminary and the foundation stone was laid at Upholland in 1879. Other dioceses followed suit. Small seminaries were opened at Salford in part of the cathedral house (1883), at Nottingham in Derby Road near the cathedral (1883), for Northampton at Shefford in Bedfordshire (1884), and at Clifton.

The closure of Olton in 1889 is not to be regarded as a setback or reversal to this policy since it was associated with the end of lay education at Oscott, which now for the first time became an exclusively clerical establishment. So, by the end of the 1880s, not counting schools like those at Sedgley Park and Ware, which still accepted prospective clerical candidates along with lay boys, there were nine seminaries in England in addition to the four overseas establishments. Of the fifteen dioceses in England and Wales, nine had their own seminaries, the remaining six dioceses sending their students to an extra-diocesan seminary.

This adoption of the Tridentine regulations in such a short space of time was prompted by Manning's own enthusiasm for a renewed clerical training. The number of clergy in the whole country was rising and in the 1880s new dioceses were created at Middlesbrough and Portsmouth. Although diocesan seminaries could fulfil a valuable function in providing either part of the course of studies or a short post-ordination training, it was too much to expect each diocese to provide a full course of training from the age of twelve as Trent had suggested. Despite the lack of financial resources and manpower, little attention seems to have been paid to the idea of a seminary common to several dioceses, a possibility for which Trent had allowed.

Difficulties in staffing the seminaries were no new thing. In the eighteenth century the expulsion of the Jesuits from Spain meant that the English secular clergy had to take over the administration of the college in Valladolid in 1767. When the Society of Jesus was suppressed by the Pope in 1773 the management of the College in Rome was entrusted to the Italian secular clergy. In the nineteenth century anticlerical legislation brought about the closure of many Catholic theological faculties on the Continent, and the English colleges had to follow the long-standing practice of Lisbon, all the teaching being now undertaken by the resident English college staff in the college itself. Adding to the number of seminaries at home only aggravated this situation. The diocesan clergy had not a sufficient pool of qualified priests to run the existing seminaries, let alone the new ones that were mushrooming in the latter part of the century. What is more, the English universities were unable to provide a qualification in the sacred sciences acceptable to the Roman authorities and so there seemed to be no alternative to a period of study abroad in a foreign Catholic university.

CARDINAL VAUGHAN AND THE CENTRAL SEMINARY

When Herbert Vaughan was transferred to Westminster on the death of Manning in 1892, the policy concerning the seminaries had to be reviewed. As has been pointed out,[19] Vaughan and Manning were in close agreement about the preparation of priests in the seminary, but Vaughan was more aware of the English Catholic Church's lack of resources to implement the ideal of each diocese having its own seminary. A high quality of teaching and adequate library resources called for a regional or provincial seminary to which several dioceses contributed both professors and students. Something on these lines was already in existence in Ushaw. So it was that Vaughan closed the Hammersmith seminary in 1893 and the students were sent, not back to St Edmund's Ware, but to Oscott. Oscott was to become a central seminary. Some of the newer diocesan seminaries that had been opened had not proved viable, and so to Oscott students were now directed from the dioceses of Birmingham, Westminster, Clifton, Newport, Plymouth, Northampton, Portsmouth and Southwark. The last-named diocese sent its students to Oscott as a temporary measure until its own diocesan seminary was ready at Wonersh. Ullathorne had already removed the last remaining lay students from Oscott and it, not Olton, was now the seminary for the diocese of Birmingham. The plan was that Birmingham would supply the buildings and the library and other dioceses would endow chairs of theology, canon law and Scripture and pay an agreed pension for the maintenance of their students. There was to be no compulsion on the bishops to send their students to Oscott – it was left to their own discretion – but the arguments from the point of view of finance and provision of staff were strongly in favour of the new scheme.

The Holy See agreed to the plan[20] and in July 1897 Oscott became *de jure* as well as *de facto* a central or common seminary for the dioceses of Westminster, Birmingham, Clifton, Portsmouth, Northampton, Newport and the Vicariate of Wales. The Bishop of Birmingham, Ilsley, had acted as Rector of Oscott for some years. To mark the transition from diocesan to central seminary, he resigned the office of Rector and Mgr Parkinson was appointed to this post. The college now contained seventy-four students, of whom twenty-nine belonged to Westminster and twenty-six to Birmingham. All the existing teaching staff remained and this meant that, for the time being at least, the opportunity to widen the resources was not taken, and the new central seminary depended too much and rather unfairly on the Birmingham clergy. But the staff that had been assembled under Parkinson could hold its own with any in the country. During these years of change in the Midlands and the South, Ushaw continued to supply priests for the Northern dioceses, although its hegemony was somewhat challenged by the new seminaries at Leeds and Liverpool.

An insight into Vaughan's own personal approach to clergy formation can be gained from a perusal of his *The Young Priest*. This series of conferences was edited and published after his death.[21] As well as theological and doctrinal reflections on the life of the diocesan priest, he calls attention to the need for the priest to exercise self-denial in his life so as to make clear his distinction from members of the laity and his not sharing in the fashions of the day. He lays great stress on the need for direction during the early years of the ministry. He says that the secular clergy have a disadvantage, compared with the religious orders, because they lack the training that a novitiate can provide. They are left too much to themselves for direction and growth in sanctity and often their spiritual development does not match the physical, rational and emotional maturation that takes place in their early priesthood. Vaughan was in favour of an extension of the period of preparation after ordination and in Salford he set up a house of pastoral theology next to the cathedral and under the eye of the bishop. However, he realised that unfortunately this ideal was difficult to put into practice and it often became necessary to 'plunge the young priest into the excessive and exhaustive occupation of a large mission before the chrism is dry'.

Francis Bourne, the Bishop of Southwark, agreed with Vaughan as to the need to improve the academic standards of the clergy, but he wished to retain a place for the diocesan seminary because it was here that the bishop could be in touch with his future priests and, in turn, they could learn the customs and traditions of the diocese.[22] Moreover, he thought that it was not necessary for every priest to be an expert theologian – the clergy was made up largely of general practitioners. He was of the view that the very early Catholic schooling of boys should be in common. But when a boy of whatever age formed a serious wish to be a priest, then it was fitting that he should enter a place where he could associate with others of like mind. He quoted examples of boys not so separated who had continued a 'mixed' education and had developed a critical and discontented attitude which manifested itself when they entered a seminary later. Bourne's idea was that up to about the age of fourteen, boys would be educated together, after which they would be segregated and those wishing to be priests would enter a seminary. There they would remain until ordination. After ordination it would be possible for the more gifted to specialise in sacred studies, and for this they would go to an overseas university such as Louvain or Fribourg where they could enter university life and mix with the laity as well as clergy.

When Bourne succeeded Vaughan at Westminster there were once more changes in seminary policy. One of his first acts as Archbishop of Westminster was to withdraw the Westminster students from Oscott and return them to St Edmund's. This sounded the death knell of the Central Seminary. Although seminarians were once more being educated with the laity at St Edmund's, this was not like the old days. The seniors, philosophers and theologians, were henceforth to be housed in a separate building, Allen Hall, and the juniors were marked off from the lay boys by the house system. There were to be two houses, Talbot and Challoner, for the lay boys and one house, Douglass, for the church students. Douglass House, Bourne maintained, was 'a true junior seminary in accordance with the rules of Trent'. The church students shared the college chapel with the divines and the classroom with the lay boys, but in all else they led a separate existence. This was certainly an ingenious solution for Bourne and the diocese of Westminster, but the effect could not be confined to one diocese. The example shown by the Cardinal and its effect on Oscott meant that there was no longer any national plan as Vaughan had envisaged.

HIGHER EDUCATION FOR THE CLERGY: A UNIVERSITY LINK?

The rescript from *Propaganda Fide* in 1867 forbidding Catholics from attending the universities of Oxford and Cambridge was followed by a letter to the bishops urging them to found a Catholic university. The story of the short-lived Catholic University College of Kensington and the proposed Institute of Higher Studies in London is the story of both lack of academic and financial resources and the Catholic community's failure to come to an agreed policy.[23] But when the rules concerning attendance at the universities were relaxed there arose the question as to whether clerics would be allowed to take degrees. This would not be a matter of personal preference but would imply a decision by a bishop to send a priest to the university for a specific purpose, such as the future provision of qualified teachers in Catholics schools and colleges that were conducted by the secular clergy. At this stage there was no possibility of Catholic priests graduating in theology at a 'Protestant' university – their studies would be in the secular arts or sciences. Although some welcomed this as a way of adding academic respectability to the many existing Catholic educational establishments, there was little enthusiasm from the majority of the bishops. What progress was made was due to the efforts of St Edmund's Ware to open a daughter house in Cambridge. At the beginning it was not easy to recruit priests[24] and there was reluctance to make up the numbers by accepting lay students in the residence, as there was care to segregate the clergy from the laity. For many years the regime of the priest students at Cambridge closely resembled the life of a seminary, and freedom to take part in university activities was seriously restricted. As late as 1938, when Mgr Godfrey made his apostolic visitation of the seminaries in England, St Edmund's House Cambridge came under his scrutiny. But subsequent events have taken St Edmund's out of the control of the hierarchy, and since 1996 it has become a full college of the University of Cambridge.[25]

THE ENGLISH SEMINARIES UP TO THE SECOND VATICAN COUNCIL

It was during the long episcopacy of Bourne at Westminster (1903–35) that the seminaries in England took a form that was to remain basically unchanged up to the Second Vatican Council. Ushaw was supported by the Northern bishops, Oscott was under the Archbishop of Birmingham, St Edmund's Ware under

Westminster, while Wonersh was in the care of the Bishop of Southwark. These four had been supplemented by St Joseph's Seminary Leeds (1878–1939) and, after extensive rebuilding in the twenties, by Upholland for the diocese of Liverpool (1883–1974). Those dioceses that did not have a seminary of their own were accommodated in existing seminaries either in England or abroad. The staffing of the seminaries became the main responsibility of those dioceses where the colleges were located. But although there was a general commitment of the hierarchy to maintain the seminaries and provide students, there was no specific obligation on individual bishops to contribute a regular quota of students or professors to a specific seminary. The professors were always priests and inevitably their theological qualifications and degrees would have been obtained abroad in a Catholic institution on the Continent, most commonly in Rome. There were some teachers in the seminaries who had no officially recognised theological qualification but these were in the minority. The professors' theology and method of teaching reflected the state of studies in the Catholic Europe of the day. But when they returned to England from their foreign training to work in distinctively English conditions, these foreign influences were often muted or at least made to fit in with current English Catholic thought.

The courses in all the colleges resembled each other in so far as they followed a scheme of two years of philosophy followed by four years of theology using a neo-scholastic approach. The textbooks and many of the lectures were in Latin and followed the pattern in vogue on the Continent of Europe. Studies were of a 'professional' nature and were intended to fit the students to pastoral practice by instruction in canon law and competence in administering the sacraments, especially the sacrament of penance. Dogmatic theology and church history were usually presented in an 'apologetic' or 'controversial' manner so as to defend the Church against attack and manifest the falsity of other forms of Christianity, especially Protestantism. As part of the training it was considered necessary to be able to answer charges and give simple explanations and so provide answers for the enquiring or doubting mind. This also applied to philosophy. This rational practicality of the courses was something inherited from the post-Reformation history of Europe and was particularly applicable to England, where Protestantism had triumphed over Catholicism. At its worst, the course of studies followed a textbook or the professor's notes so slavishly that it insulated the students from any original thought of their own. Little attention was paid to the possibility of a student having anything to offer the Church from his own reflections or spiritual experience.

The system of five seminaries at home and three (plus the Beda College) abroad, servicing all the dioceses of England and Wales, was supported by a series of junior seminaries and schools which educated boys from an early age preparatory to their entrance into the seminary proper. In some places this function was performed on the same site as the senior seminary although in separate buildings, as at Ware, Ushaw and Upholland. A similar 'lower house' was to be found abroad at Valladolid until 1915, and Lisbon until 1949. Southwark students went to Mark Cross (1924–70) as a preparation for Wonersh and cassocks were worn from an early age. Just as the junior seminaries at Ware and Ushaw were not strictly Tridentine seminaries since they also catered for lay boys, so for many years Oscott and the Birmingham diocese used the separate establishment of the school at Sedgley Park (1763–1873) and later at Cotton (1873–1987) as a place for nourishing vocations where church students were known as such but received the same general education as other Catholic boys. In addition to these places there were other colleges run by religious orders which catered specifically for young men who had a vocation but were not yet ready to enter a major seminary. Since 1918 the Jesuits at Campion House, Osterley, have assisted the first steps of many to the priesthood, both diocesan and religious.[26] A similar task was undertaken by the Carmelites at Llandeilo and Aberystwyth in Wales.

Shortly after the Second World War new diocesan junior seminaries were established. The colleges at Tollerton (Nottingham) and Thistleton/Underley (Lancaster) were originally intended as schools for prospective priests, but later lay pupils were also recruited. The most original foundation in the post-war years, however, was that of Archbishop Masterson of Birmingham who opened a college at Grove Park in Warwickshire. This house, rented from the Dormer family, was intended to ease the break that occurred when boys entered the senior seminary. Although not perhaps realised at the time, this was an implicit criticism of the senior seminary, whose way of life and arcane learning were so different from what schoolboys or even 'late' vocations had experienced, no matter how devout their life as members of their local parish. Grove Park became an obligatory half-way house for Birmingham candidates for the priesthood. Whether they had been to Cotton or not, they were not exempt from this preparatory period before entering Oscott. Masterson made it something of a showpiece and several other English bishops sent some of their students there whether they were intended for Oscott or some other seminary. It also aroused the interest of bishops overseas.[27] The experiment lasted from 1948 to 1966 and outlived Masterson. The financial and other drawbacks of a rented property were one reason for its failure, but its existence also meant an increase in the seminary course of at least a year added to the six years spent at Oscott. Above all, there was the matter of the timetable. What were these young men to do during their stay in this old country house? Was it a novitiate or simply an opportunity to accustom the students to certain modes of clerical behaviour? In the end it became a way of relieving an already crowded programme at Oscott by providing an introduction to the Scripture course and practice in singing plainsong and performing full Catholic ceremonial and rites they had not witnessed in their home parishes. It came as no surprise when Archbishop Dwyer closed Grove

Park in 1967. Not was there much regret! It was only much later (1998) that the real need and possible structure of a pre-seminary year began to materialise.

WILLIAM GODFREY AND THE SEMINARY SPIRIT

If there was one person who expressed the spirit that lay at the heart of the English seminary in the thirty years preceding the Second Vatican Council it was William Godfrey. Not only was he a professor at Ushaw and Rector of the *Venerabile* in Rome, but he was Apostolic Visitor to the English seminaries in 1937 and the first Apostolic Delegate to Great Britain from 1938 to 1953. He went on to complete his career as Archbishop of Liverpool and finally Cardinal Archbishop of Westminster, dying before the Council completed its work. His importance does not lie in the originality of his ideas but in the way in which he imbibed, propagated and reflected the fears and modest hopes of a certain circle that flourished both in Rome and among English Catholics. Externally, from the 1930s there was an expansion in English Catholicism. There were a number of distinguished converts, many new churches and schools were built, there was no scarcity of vocations and priestly ordinations were relatively high.[28] But behind all this lay an element of narrowness, caution and restraint. When Godfrey first appeared in Rome as Rector of the English College, succeeding Arthur Hinsley, there was a detectable chill in the air that contrasted with the warmth of his predecessor. As a young professor at Ushaw he had written *The Young Apostle*[29] and this very ordinary work is typical of his life and entire career. It is a faithful representation of the current orthodoxy.

The Young Apostle follows in the tradition of Manning and Vaughan, but Godfrey's attempt to transpose their ideas to the twentieth century became less convincing as the years passed and one generation of seminarians followed another. The book is based on a series of conferences to young seminarians. He traces their steps from their first entrance into the junior seminary right through their course of studies and training to their ordination as priest. It is in a way autobiographical, and has something of the air of a Good Student's Diary. It is within the structure of seminary life, the daily routine and yearly progress that he expounds the ideals and spirituality of the diocesan priest. Significantly the book stops at ordination – there is little about life in the parish. At the beginning he cites Lahitton's *La Vocation Sacerdotale* and the controversy it provoked that led to its official approval and endorsement by Pius X.[30] This work states that no one has ever any right to ordination before his being freely accepted by a bishop. Vocation to the priesthood does not as a general rule consist in a certain aspiration on the part of the subject, or an invitation of the Holy Spirit to him to take up this way of life. Nothing further is required beyond the call of the bishop than a right intention together with suitable gifts of nature and grace, uprightness of life and sufficiency of knowledge. The student is thus relieved of the burden of passing judgement on his own suitability. That is a matter for the bishop and superiors to decide. The concerns of the candidate should centre around the purity of his intention, i.e., he should not be concerned for personal comfort or preferment or see the priestly life in terms of an easier way to save his soul. That he has a right intention can be discerned by how faithfully he follows the rules and regulations of the seminary. It is the implications drawn by Godfrey that are to be noted. It would seem to him that the spirituality of the seminary is best understood by attending to the highly structured daily and yearly programme and timetable.

Quite apart from the periodic days of retreat and recollection and regular talks by the spiritual director or invited preachers from outside, there were frequent addresses by the rector or vice-rector that dealt with particular matters of order and discipline. Many of Godfrey's contemporaries as rector were disciplinarians: Emery at Oscott, Dean at Upholland, Henson at Valladolid, Cullen at Lisbon. The day was heavily timetabled and ruled by bells. This was calculated not only to keep the students busy but also to create in them an ability to switch from one occupation to another by never allowing them to concentrate on one item for any length of time. This was considered a good preparation for the varied demands made on the priest in the parish. Rules and regulations were intended to form character. Godfrey said 'The rules strike at the will and they do so because the will needs to be struck *scalpri salubris ictibus et tunsione plurima*'.[31] They 'help to supress the strong instinct towards self-indulgence that makes itself felt in the heart of every human being'. Moreover, he said, we must remember that these rules were drawn up by wise and holy men and they can be said to be the expression of God's own will. It was in this spirit that rectors extolled the merits of arbitrary rules, that is, rules that have no other purpose than to instil obedience to authority and discomfort to self. By the close of the twentieth century this rigid framework has been eroded and with it the spirituality it inspired.

Godfrey's views were shared in most parts of the Catholic world, but they had a particular value in England since they could be related to the penal times. Godfrey's own devotion to the English Martyrs sometimes suggested a connection between the hardships of seminary life and the rack and gallows of the sixteenth century. But it also recalled a time when the priest on the mission was a loner. He had not only to care for those in his charge but for his own salvation too. Often he could not rely on regular association with fellow priests and a spiritual director and so he had to develop a self-made, do-it-yourself spirituality. As a preparation for this, detachment was a characteristic of the way of life of the seminarian. On the one hand he was detached from home and family – visits home were forbidden and holidays kept to a minimum. On the other hand, even within the clerical community he had to keep to himself. There were times when he was alone, and even speaking to or visiting the rooms of his companions was not allowed. Privacy had to be respected and particular friendships were discouraged, not only for the sake of an harmonious community but for the individual's own good. Solitude was a special virtue for the diocesan priest. There were times when he had to keep to his room and this place was not simply a student's room, but had some of the characteristics of the monastic cell.

However, despite this apartness the student in the seminary was also a member of a community that enjoyed a common life of prayer, study, eating and recreation. Although they lived together there was never complete sharing. The college assembled together in church frequently during the day. But morning meditation, Mass, visits to the Blessed Sacrament, public recitation of the rosary and night prayers formed part of the public duties, and the prayer on these occasions was according to fixed and approved formulae. So when the post-conciliar liturgical reforms were introduced, the flexibility and spontaneity that were now permitted in public prayer were something quite alien to the system hitherto in practice.

SINCE THE SECOND VATICAN COUNCIL

The Second World War did not bring about any fundamental changes in seminary life. Those in holy orders, and this included those who had received the tonsure and so were clerics, were exempt from military service. Numbers in the seminary declined, but there was never any fear that there would be closures on this account. Overseas colleges suffered the most, but at the end of the war the colleges in Rome, Valladolid and Lisbon were reopened. It is only since the death of Pius XII (1958) that things have begun to change. There are now no longer any junior seminaries in Britain. Even those started since the war have closed. This is not entirely because of a lack of vocations. The reasons include the general falling out of favour of the boarding school, the inadvisability of separating young children from their parents, and also the difficulty for the Church in providing standards of education that are comparable to those in ordinary schools. Some might think that it is by no means clear that the average Catholic school is able to provide an atmosphere that is conducive to the fostering of a vocation to the priesthood, and one cannot be sure that the present arrangement will remain for ever. But there have also been closures in major seminaries. Both Upholland in Lancashire and the English College in Lisbon have ceased to be. Allen Hall, the seminary at St Edmund's College, Ware, moved into London shortly after the Jesuit house of studies at Heythrop transferred from Oxfordshire to become a college of the University of London.

These changes need to be considered as part of the many developments in the Church's educational scene. The last thirty years of the century have witnessed the rise and fall of the colleges of education. At one time in the seventies there were fifteen Catholic colleges. Now there are only three. Perhaps more important than the reduction in the overall number of seminaries is the change that has come about in those that remain. The ending of the isolation of the seminary is most spectacular in the move of Allen Hall to Chelsea, but the other seminaries have strengthened their links with universities: Ushaw has links with Durham, Oscott with Birmingham and Wonersh with Surrey. But whereas in the fifties there was concern about the academic standards of the clergy,[32] interest has now turned more to the nature of the priesthood and the reasons why a priest might need a different theological education from that offered by the university. Practical pastoral experience has now entered the seminary curriculum and this has resulted in a reduction in the time spent on pure academic study. It has also removed the isolation of the seminary from the life of the parish. Not only do students spend part of their time outside the walls of the seminary, but the seminary is more accessible to the laity and lay men and women can assist in various ways in the formation of future priests. One result of this is that the seminary of today has less of the air of being a self-contained community and the tendency to an exclusive clubbishness among the clergy has been halted. Changes in the ministerial structures of the Church such as the institution of the permanent diaconate (1968) and the abolition of the tonsure, minor orders and subdiaconate (1972) have led to a rethinking about the role of the clergy. The active participation of the laity in the liturgy has brought together priest and people in a new way. The increasing realisation of the importance of the priestly nature of the laity by reason of baptism must, however, not be allowed to diminish the special place of the ministerial priesthood.[33]

The Catholic ordination of former Anglican priests who are married has put the topic of priestly celibacy to the fore once more. Whereas in the 1970s defections from the priesthood and laicisations were the cause for much anxiety, in the nineties scandal has arisen from cases of gross clerical misconduct in the matter of child abuse. These and other factors have had their effect on vocations to the priesthood and have led to much soul-searching as to the formation of priests and the training they receive in the seminary. Compared with the problems of today, those of the nineteenth century seem very trivial indeed. There is no lack of debate and discussion at both the local and international level, although the arguments tend to be repetitious. Rome makes its views known but the local hierarchies have much more freedom about their course of action than was the case with England one hundred years ago when *Propaganda Fide* was still in charge. Today the bishops do not contend so much among themselves, but there is a seeking for the common good. Whatever the future, the preparation and training of candidates for the priesthood will always have a special place in the life of the Church and be the concern of bishops, priests and laity.

NOTES

1. A number of studies of individual seminaries have been published: B. Ward, *History of St Edmund's College, Old Hall* (1893); W. Croft, *Historical Account of Lisbon College* (1902); F. A. Gasquet, *A History of the Venerable English College, Rome* (1920); T. Hooley, *A Seminary in the Making* [Wonersh] (1927); D. Milburn, *A History of Ushaw College* (1964); M. E. Williams, *The Venerable English College, Rome: A History 1579–1979* (1979); M. E. Williams, *St Alban's College, Valladolid: Four Centuries of English Catholic Presence in Spain* (1986); J. Champ (ed.), *Oscott College 1838–1988: A Volume of Commemorative Essays* (1988). The only attempt at an overall picture is G. Culkin, 'The English Seminaries', *The Clergy Review*, vol. 35 (1951), pp. 73–88.
2. B. Hemphill, *The Early Vicars Apostolic of England 1685–1750* (1953).
3. The proposal that Downside should become a seminary was resisted by the Benedictines. For this and Bishop Baines's attempt to open a seminary at Prior Park see E. Norman, *The English Catholic Church in the Nineteenth Century* (1984), pp. 89–96.
4. The way in which this tradition continued in the President of Ushaw is treated by D. Milburn, *A History of Ushaw College*, p. 206.
5. It has been argued that in Liverpool during the episcopate of Goss (1856–1872), where this policy of segregation was adopted, the clergy grew up to have a deep suspicion of the world, a narrow view of theology that precluded a commitment to study after leaving the seminary. P. Doyle, 'The Education and Training of Roman Catholic Priests in Nineteenth-Century England', *Journal of Ecclesiastical History*, vol. 35 (1984), pp. 208–19. It has to be remembered however that the publication of the Syllabus of Errors in 1864 supported the idea of a withdrawal of the Church from secular life.
6. Quoted by Culkin, 'English Seminaries', pp. 76–7.
7. P. Doyle, 'Episcopal Authority and Clerical Democracy: Diocesan Synods in Liverpool in the 1850s', *Recusant History*, vol. 23 (1997), pp. 418–33.
8. Milburn, *History of Ushaw*, pp. 183–4, 202–4. 'Ushaw did not regard itself as a formal diocesan seminary and retained a fiercely guarded independence of the northern bishops' (Norman, *English Catholic Church*, p. 179).
9. Milburn, *History of Ushaw*, pp. 192, 198.
10. For the story of the trial of Northcote, Ullathorne's opening of Olton and the change of Oscott into a school see C. Butler, *The Life and Times of Bishop Ullathorne* (1926), vol. I, pp. 171–4. J. Champ, 'The Crown of the Diocesan Structure' in *Oscott College*, pp. 96–103.
11. For Bruges and English Catholics, see Stephen H. Hancock, 'From Hagiography to History', *Recusant History*, vol. 23 (1997), pp. 358–9. For Bruges seminary, see Stewart Foster, 'The Life and Death of a Victorian Seminary: The English College Bruges', *Recusant History*, vol. 20 (1990), pp. 272–90.
12. The College soon adopted the name *Collegio Pio* as a mark of respect to Pius IX. M. J. McConnon, 'The Pontifical Beda College: A History', *Beda Review*, vol. 12 (1985), pp. 2–10.
13. P. Doyle, 'Pastoral Perfection: Cardinal Manning and the Secular Clergy' in W. J. Shiels and D. Wood (eds), *The Ministry Clerical and Lay*, Studies in Church History 26 (1989), pp. 385–96. V. Alan McClelland, '"*O Felix Roma*!" Henry Manning, Cutts Robinson and Sacerdotal Formation 1862–1872', *Recusant History*, vol. 21 no. 2 (1992), pp. 180–217.
14. *The Eternal Priesthood*, originally published 1883, 23rd edition 1950.
15. As Doyle notes ('Pastoral Perfection', p. 391), chapter 18 reflects many of the decrees of the Provincial Council of 1873.

16. Hooley, *Seminary in the Making*, pp. 15–34.
17. H. Vaughan, *Report of the Conditions of the English Catholic Colleges in Italy, Spain and Portugal* (Salford, 1876).
18. G. T. Bradley, 'Leeds Seminary: an Experiment in Clerical Education' in R. E. Finnigan and G. T. Bradley (eds), *Catholicism in Leeds: A Community of Faith 1794–1994* (1994).
19. For the relationship between Vaughan and Manning, see Norman, *English Catholic Church*, p. 354.
20. J. G. Snead-Cox, *The Life of Cardinal Vaughan* (1910), vol. II, pp. 34–69.
21. H. Vaughan, *The Young Priest: Conferences on the Apostolic Life*, ed. J. S. Vaughan (1904).
22. See letter of Bourne quoted in Snead-Cox, *Vaughan*, Vol. II, pp. 52–5. Bourne had been the first rector of the Southwark seminary.
23. V. A. McClelland, *English Roman Catholics and Higher Education 1830–1903* (1973), pp. 277–97.
24. One of the first graduates from St Edmund's was Thomas Williams (future Archbishop of Birmingham). When he was appointed to Cotton he was the only member of the teaching staff to hold an English university degree.
25. Garrett Sweeney, *St Edmund's House Cambridge: The First Eighty Years: A History* (1980); M. Walsh, *St Edmund's College, Cambridge 1896–1996: A Commemorative History* (1996); V. A. McClelland, 'St Edmund's College, Ware and St Edmund's College, Cambridge: Historical Connections and Early Tribulations', *Recusant History*, vol. 23 (1997), pp. 470–82.
26. See Clement Tigar SJ, *Edmund Lester S.J.: A Memoir* (1937).
27. Oscott College Archives, The Grove Park Diaries.
28. For an overview of this period see A. Hastings, *A History Of English Christianity 1920–1985* (1986), pp. 276–87.
29. *The Young Apostle* (London, 1924).
30. Canon Joseph Lahitton, *La Vocation Sacerdotale* (1912). The official approval of the book is to be found in *Acta Apostolicae Sedis*, 15 July 1912. Shortly before his death in the mid-1980s, Archbishop Dwyer of Birmingham made favourable references to this work in *Some Definite Service*, a guide to vocations to the priesthood edited by M. Sharkey.
31. The quotation is from a hymn in the office of the dedication of a church and the translation reads '[fashioned] by the salutary blows of the chisel and much buffeting from the hammer'.
32. At a conference on Catholic higher education held at St Mary's College, Strawberry Hill in September 1958, one of the subjects that came up for discussion was the relationship between the seminaries and the universities. The then Bishop of Salford, Rt Rev. G. A. Beck, presided and remarked, 'The fundamental question in priestly training, however, will not be solved merely in the intellectual order or in terms of academic standards', *Dublin Review*, no. 491 (Spring 1962), pp. 35–42.
33. 'Instruction on Certain Questions regarding the Collaboration of the Non-ordained Faithful in the Sacred Ministry of the Priest' (13 November 1997).

FOUR

THE IRON FORM: CATHOLICS AND PHILOSOPHY BETWEEN THE COUNCILS

MICHAEL HODGETTS

There seems something of an iron form here, tho' I may be wrong.

(J. H. Newman, 8 February 1847 (*Letters and Diaries* XII, p. 32)

The centennial volume edited by Bishop Beck in 1950 contains a shrewd essay on diocesan structures by Morgan Sweeney and one on Newman by Humphrey Johnson in which he coined the apt and scathing phrase 'tabloid apologetics'.[1] But it contains no direct discussion of theological or liturgical issues, which in essentials had been settled for good by the Code of Canon Law and the encyclicals of Pius XII. Admittedly, some points remained uncertain, such as whether the indulgence for the Litany of Loreto at Benediction could be gained if the musical setting only had one *Ora pro nobis* for every three invocations.[2] Mgr Ronald Knox had just completed a best-selling translation of the Bible which had broken with the hallowed principle that a faithful version is one that cleaves to the structures and diction of the Latin.[3] For twenty years, from his parish in the Black Country, Canon F. H. Drinkwater had been urging a more imaginative teaching of the Catechism – though the text itself was, of course, canonical and unalterable. Some intellectuals were reading Karl Adam and other German and French writers who advocated an approach to theology which was not that of Gibbons, Sheehan and Ripley[4] and had rightly been disapproved of by the Pope that year in *Humani Generis*. Despite the Council of Trent, some cranks were even arguing that English might be used in the liturgy.[5] But none of this should be allowed to confuse the faithful, and (apart from one sentence on the Knox Bible) none of it is mentioned in Beck. Modernism was still perceived as a threat, and Newman, though he might have admirers on the Continent, was still suspect in some quarters in England.[6]

During the last fifty years these omissions have been more than made good; and there is now a familiar and predictable track through the Victorian disputes which *were* touched on by Beck's contributors, notably by Johnson himself, J. J. Dwyer and H. Outram Evennett: Genesis, geology and Darwin; the Temporal Power of Pius IX; the universities and the Oxford Oratory; the *Rambler*, the Syllabus of Errors and Vatican I.[7] But there is still room for a brief consideration of scholastic philosophy as it was understood at this time in England and Wales (both qualifications are important). The distinguished philosophers who have devoted themselves to the study of St Thomas since Vatican II have been concerned with his own writings and those of his contemporaries and sources, not with the scholastic manuals, which were at best second-hand versions and which have now disappeared from library shelves. Gerald McCool's *The Neo-Thomists* (Marquette University Press, 1994) does not mention a single British or Irish neo-scholastic. That may be fair comment, but still leaves an historical gap, since the content of Latin manuals and lectures was understood (or not) by English students in the light of English textbooks, whose authors' interests and presuppositions were not always transparent. Moreover, the tidy dichotomy, in fashion since the 1960s, between Aristotle and St Thomas on the one hand and a 'scriptural' or 'historical' or 'experiential' approach on the other, is at least partly false, since what was taught under the name of Thomism, both here and on the Continent, was much of it Platonist and Cartesian.

It is commonly supposed that in *Aeterni Patris* (1879) Leo XIII laid down a minutely detailed programme of Thomism, and therefore that neo-scholasticism, like other forms of truth, was always and everywhere the same. This is an exaggeration. The Jesuits still read Suarez and the Franciscans St Bonaventure and Scotus. Moreover, *Aeterni Patris*, though exalting St Thomas and complaining that he is more quoted than read, is a survey of the whole Christian philosophical tradition in which no particular Thomist theses are prescribed.[8] Not until 1914 did the Congregation of Seminaries publish a list of twenty-four such theses, in response to seminary lecturers who wanted to do the right thing but were not sure what it was.[9] Even that is far from a complete syllabus. Of the twenty-four, I-XII are on metaphysics, XIII-XVI on psychology, XVII-XXI on perception and XXII-XXIV on knowledge of God. There is nothing on human society, despite St Thomas's constant use of Aristotle's *Politics*; nothing on human action from the *Secunda Pars*, which many consider to be his greatest achievement; nothing even on the natural law (though this and human action would be dealt with in moral theology); and nothing on the most characteristic Thomist doctrine of all: that grace perfects nature and does not destroy it. In *Deus Scientiarum Dominus* (1931) the Congregation went further and laid down a pattern for the training of priests throughout the world; but the philosophical content is a mere list of tracts to be covered *ad methodum et principia S. Thomae Aquinatis*, except that 'in speculative questions . . . the so-called scholastic method' was required,[10] meaning the method of the seminary manuals since the late seventeenth century.[11]

There was therefore room for manoeuvre, which was used on the Continent and in England by Fr Bede Jarrett as Dominican Provincial.[12] But only at the *Venerabile* in Rome was it possible both to study in an English college and to gain a degree in philosophy or theology which was recognised by the Holy See. Consequently, the teaching of these subjects in English seminaries was too much influenced by the arid and legalistic approach of the Gregorian University, whose courses the English College followed.[13] This was no accident: from the 1860s onwards the College came to be seen as a means of ensuring that the education and administration of the English clergy were controlled by men imbued with the 'Roman spirit', and this despite the fact that until 1931 doctorates of philosophy and theology could be gained there merely by completing undergraduate courses of three and four years.[14]

The inadequacies of the Gregorian have been described by former students from Wilfrid Ward, William Barry and George Ambrose Burton in the 1870s and 1880s to Sir Anthony Kenny in the 1950s;[15] they need no rehearsing here. But there was another influence on English scholasticism which has been less remarked on. In 1896 and 1897 the Jesuits and Benedictines opened at Oxford what later became Campion Hall and St Benet's Hall. (The Oxford Blackfriars did not follow until 1922.) In 1902 an optional special subject on 'The Outlines of Scholastic Philosophy' was added to the Greats course, which was then the only one at Oxford to include philosophy at all. This required the study, from original texts, either of St Anselm, Abelard and John of Salisbury or of St Thomas, St Bonaventure and Scotus.[16] One of the Thomistic texts was the *Summa contra Gentiles* I-III, and it was for this course that Fr Joseph Rickaby SJ made his translation of it (1905) under the title *Of God and his Creatures*.[17] But Greats also required the study of Plato and Aristotle (commonly *The Republic* and the *Nicomachean Ethics*) and of the central questions of philosophy in the light of current debates; and here, whatever Manning and Vaughan might have feared, the effect was to reinforce certain elements in neo-scholasticism, rather than to raise doubts about them.

The dominant philosophical fashion in Edwardian Oxford was Idealism, which went hand in hand with a preference (reminiscent of medieval debates) for the high-minded Plato over the earthy Aristotle. Though all of Plato had been included in the Oxford Classical Texts by 1908, much of Aristotle had to wait until the 1950s and the *Eudemian Ethics* until the 1990s. Among educators and leader-writers the moral excellence of Plato was hardly questioned until the publication in 1945 of Sir Karl Popper's *The Open Society and Its Enemies*. Idealism sounded edifying, but, as Elizabeth Anscombe once remarked in another context,

'It is, I think, quite characteristic of very bad degenerations of thought on such questions that they sound edifying.'[18] It encouraged windy generalities, colourful metaphor in place of argument, a contempt for science and a sympathy for authoritarian governments. All of these were thought by some to be in the spirit of scholasticism: even in the 1960s, the fashions for Teilhard de Chardin and for existentialism owed something to their traditional virtues of being pretentious and obscure.

For this thumb-nail sketch I shall quote particularly from three books which appeared between 1926 and 1935. T. J. Walshe's *Principles of Catholic Apologetics* (1926) was written in response to 'a suggestion from a high ecclesiastical quarter',[19] perhaps Cardinal Bourne, and is described on the title-page as 'A Study of Modernism based chiefly on the Lectures of Père Garrigou-Lagrange, O.P.'. Fr Martin D'Arcy's *St Thomas Aquinas* (1930) was the work of a distinguished Jesuit who was tutor in philosophy at the English College in Rome in 1925–6[20] and afterwards Master of Campion Hall; it was also singled out for criticism by G. K. Chesterton in his *St Thomas Aquinas* (1933).[21] R. P. Phillips's *Modern Thomistic Philosophy* (1934–5) was the outcome of his teaching at Wonersh. These books can therefore be taken as authoritative statements of views which were imposed on students as 'what the Church teaches'. For this country they are certainly more representative than Mercier, Gilson or Lonergan.

PSYCHOLOGY AND ANTHROPOLOGY

Whether Catholics went on to doctorates in Rome or left school at fourteen, their introduction to philosophical questions was by way of the *Catechism of Christian Doctrine*, which, though based on Challoner's *Abridgement of Christian Doctrine*, had been much revised, not always for the better, during the nineteenth century.[22] Right from the beginning, it uses the (unexplained) concepts of 'body' and 'soul' in a way which assumed and inculcated a Platonist and Cartesian understanding of human nature.

3. *To whose image and likeness did God make you?* God made me to his own image and likeness.
4. *Is this likeness to God in your body or in your soul?* This likeness to God is chiefly in my soul.
5. *How is your soul like to God?* My soul is like to God because it is a spirit and is immortal.
6. *What do you mean when you say that your soul is immortal?* When I say that my soul is immortal, I mean that my soul can never die.
7. *Of which must you take most care, of your body or of your soul?* I must take

> most care of my soul; for Christ has said, 'What doth it profit a man if he gain the whole world, and suffer the loss of his own soul'.

This way of putting it implies that a human person is a spirit only temporarily imprisoned in a body, and it is significant that the eleventh article of the Creed, on the resurrection of the body, has only two questions (128–9), and that the Four Last Things (Q. 332) do not include it. Here is the root of what Dom Illtyd Trethowan called 'anti-humanist tendencies . . . lurking behind unintelligent forms of asceticism, a certain contempt for thinking and especially for art, [and] various kinds of pessimism, prudery and pietism'.[23] The reminiscences of some former nuns and convent schoolgirls suggest that this was a real danger.

Mgr Ronald Knox observed that 'the age which immediately followed the Counter-Reformation was, on the whole, an age of introverts', whereas St Ignatius had intended his Exercises for thoughtless extroverts.[24] One consequence of this mood, and of attempts to promote silent devotion at Mass, was a subordination of the Thomist distinction between common and particular prayer to the other Thomist distinction between vocal and mental prayer.[25] It is often supposed that recusant Catholics were more introverted than most because they had to 'supply [their] want of publick Assemblies by a greater diligence in private Devotions'.[26] But it is arguable that if anything the gap, or gaps, between body and soul, vocal and mental, liturgy and devotion, may have widened when intimate attic chapels or Georgian Masshouses were replaced by elongated Victorian churches with Puginesque 'skreens' and it became fashionable to think that the Word should only become flesh in a medieval idiom. Subsequently, despite the urgings of Pius X that congregations should sing the Ordinary of the Mass, the practice of all responding at Low Mass, the so-called Dialogue Mass, only came in, haltingly and against some episcopal opposition, during the 1940s and 1950s.[27] How far introversion and scrupulosity could go in the era of *Brideshead* is shown by the fact that in 1947 the editor of the Goodliffe Neale missal thought he should reassure those who used it: 'There is no necessity to pay such close attention to one's book that one would scruple to raise one's eyes to watch the movements of the celebrant at the altar.' And, although he printed the Ordinary chants as an appendix, he urged as the ideal: 'a devout gathering entirely animated with the same faith . . . silent in their befitting manifestation of this faith, making the same inclinations of adoration, their exterior attitude conforming with their interior devotion in union with the whole assembly'.[28] This is more than a reminder that prayer is 'the raising up of the mind and heart to God' (*Catechism*, Q. 141): it is a dissociation of 'exterior' and 'interior' which risks giving as much weight to the emotions of the worshipper as to the action of Christ in his Church and which, since whatever the Church did followed necessarily from first principles, was likely to go with a two-substance psychology.

What in fact seems to have happened was that the Aristotelian and Thomist view was expounded in seminary lectures, while the Platonist and Augustinian one was assumed for purposes of devotion, especially as it made survival after death much easier to explain. This compromise proved awkward when the dogma of the Assumption was defined in 1950. If the disembodied soul already enjoys the beatific vision, what is the point of the Assumption, or of our own resurrection, which, unlike that of Christ, has no apologetic uses? Even a fine theologian like Mgr H. Francis Davis was unconvincing here, with expressions such as 'strife between body and soul' and 'man is a spirit spiritualising some of this world's matter'.[29] In 1959, a controversy in the *Newman Philosophy of Science Bulletin*, arising out of a review by Anthony Kenny of Teilhard's *The Phenomenon of Man*, showed that some eminent Catholic scientists regarded the Cartesian account of body and soul as the only Catholic one.[30] But perhaps that is not surprising, when Ripley could state authoritatively: 'It is certain that, in addition to the pain of loss, the souls in purgatory suffer torment of the senses. It is most probable that this pain is caused by real fire, though there is no dogmatic definition on the subject.'[31] Here there is a clear assertion of the Cartesian view that a disembodied soul can exercise functions proper to an organism: a view which St Thomas denies and which was not required of the Greeks by the Council of Florence nor of the Church at large by that of Trent.[32]

These questions surfaced again in 1970 with the publication of the Order of Funerals translated by the International Commission on English in the Liturgy. The Conciliar directive for the revision had been that it should express 'the Paschal nature of Christian dying',[33] which means the hope that we who have shared in the death of Christ will also share in his resurrection. Given the Platonist and Cartesian associations of the word 'soul' in English, how was *anima* to be rendered? The job would have been easier if the anthropology and imagery of the Latin texts had been consistent, but they were not: they were from a wide variety of periods and sources and, even after revision, anomalies remained. One prayer contains a petition that the *anima* of the deceased will be resuscitated on the last day: clearly *anima* here, like the Greek *psyche* and the Hebrew *nephesh* in some contexts, must be understood as 'life' or 'person', rather than 'soul'. There was the further snag that in English any pronouns used of 'soul' must be neuter, in contexts where 'he' or 'she' will have occurred a line or two before. The translators of 1970 therefore avoided using 'soul' as much as they could: a decision which was much criticised and which seems to have been the reason why the English and Welsh hierarchy commissioned an alternative version of its own. In 1979 the Congregation for the Doctrine of the Faith put out a statement (*Recentiores Episcoporum Synodi*) in which it conceded that the scriptural usage of *anima* was inconsistent but nevertheless maintained that some word was necessary to express what it stood for.[34] The ICEL revision of 1982–5, which *has* been approved by the English and Welsh bishops, uses 'soul' more freely, on a principle which I have described as 'wherever the logic of the prayer demands it and sparingly on other occasions where the problems could be overcome'.[35] But there is no perfect solution.

Meanwhile, the two-substance psychology has brought about a dichotomy between 'pastoral' and 'aesthetic' considerations in art, music and architecture. What conforms to, or is tolerated by, canon law and the rubrics, is good for the soul; if the bodily senses are repelled by what is mawkish, slovenly or downright ugly, they will just have to offer it up. Even Sir Richard Terry, the founder of the choral tradition at Westminster Cathedral, could write in 1932: 'The actual merits of any music written for the Church are of secondary importance to its character. This would appear so obvious that it seems superfluous to mention it.'[36] That is not the mind of the Missal, which has much to say about the quality and authenticity of liturgical materials,[37] nor of St Thomas, who, in discussing the Word of God, says that the characteristics of a word (or of any form of expression) are, or should be, *integrity*, consonance and radiance.[38] Where the prime emphasis is on what Ernest Oldmeadow in 1929 called a 'churchly' style,[39] there will be a damaging dissociation between life and worship. The same goes for the disregard of natural symbols, so that the restoring to its proper time of the Easter Vigil, with its profound imagery of darkness, fire and light, was a step towards psychological as well as rubrical reintegration.[40] But some of its implications were resisted. The rubric at the beginning of the *Exultet* said, *Accenduntur candelae populi de cereo benedicto, et luminaria ecclesiae.*[41] Experts held that the comma separated *de cereo benedicto* from *luminaria ecclesiae*, which therefore meant the electric lights, and that the practice of singing the *Exultet* in a darkened church dominated by the pillar of fire in the sanctuary was incorrect. The 1966 translation for England and Wales rendered baldly, 'The lights of the church are switched on', so making it clear that imagery should not be allowed to become more than a legal fiction.[42]

PERCEPTION AND LANGUAGE

St Thomas criticises 'the Platonists' for holding that 'the soul is in the body like a sailor in a boat'.[43] Anyone who does think on those lines will be tempted to think of perception on the model of a sailor in a submarine, uncertainly constructing the hostile world outside from a series of electronic flashes and bleeps, and concerned that an evil demon may have jammed the radar. The scholastics therefore devoted much energy to the pursuit of a 'criterion of certitude' by which any desired statement could be shown to be true by definition. To an English reader, the discussion is remarkably reminiscent of Locke, Berkeley and Hume and of the logical atomists between the wars.[44] Phillips, for instance, having established that 'I, as an individual thinking subject, exist' and that 'the extra-mental and corporeal world' also exists, proceeds by way of four chapters on universals to the conclusions that 'all existential judgements (e.g. Peter is white) are subject to error, inasmuch as they are not directed towards the formal object of the intellect, viz. nature or essence', and that 'that judgement is to be considered true which cannot be denied without involving a denial of the first principles, and which is therefore, in a sense, contained in them'.[45] It follows from this, though Phillips does not say so, that we can never be certain that anyone has been baptised, married, ordained or elected pope. This inconvenient position is the outcome of four other features of neo-scholasticism: minor logic; the doctrine of abstraction; the doctrine that truth consists in contemplation of universals; and the assumption that there is, or ought to be, only one language. All of these are in St Thomas, and all, with qualifications, can be defended: the question is rather what writers of this generation made of them in the light of Hegel.[46]

Courses in scholastic philosophy always began with minor logic: the theory of terms, statements and syllogisms based on the Aristotelian *Organon* and transmitted to the Middle Ages through Boethius and the twelfth-century debate on universals. But, apart from some notorious problems in the logic itself, not easily grasped by young men coping for the first time with lectures in Latin, the ontology of the *Organon* is inconsistent with that of Aristotle's own *Physics* and *Metaphysics*;[47] and the ideal set out in it, that of a rigorous series of deductions from self-evident principles, is not characteristic of either Aristotle or St Thomas, who prefer to begin with questions, rather than theses. It was in the scholastic manuals, rather than in the medieval *quaestiones*, that the ideal of the *Organon* was realised, and then only at the cost of leaving out whatever would not fit into the system.

The doctrine of abstraction can conveniently be set out in the words of Copleston's *History of Philosophy*, perhaps the most impressive work by an English neo-scholastic:

> Although sensation is an activity of soul and body together, the rational and spiritual soul cannot be affected directly by a material thing or by the phantasm . . . which arises in the imagination and which represents the particular material object perceived by the senses . . . There is need, therefore, of an activity on the part of the soul, since the concept cannot be formed simply passively. This activity is the activity of the active intellect which 'illumines' the phantasm and abstracts from it the universal or 'intelligible species' . . . As he held that the intellect knows directly the essence, the universal, St Thomas drew the logical conclusion that the human mind does not know directly singular material things . . . Nevertheless, even after abstracting the intelligible species, the intellect exercises its activity of knowing only through a 'conversion', a turning of attention to the phan-

> tasms in which it apprehends the universals, and in this way it has a reflexive or indirect knowledge of the particular things represented by the phantasms.[48]

It is noticeable in this account that, as usual among scholastics, the agent is not the person but 'the soul', 'the mind' or 'the intellect', a use which makes a two-substance psychology hard to avoid. More serious, all 'knowledge' is assimilated to acquaintance with universal objects, despite the insistence elsewhere that truth is to be found formally in complete judgements. From this it follows that a language consists primarily of names for such objects, with the corollary that there can be only one correct language: that in which the names and the objects correspond one to one in the same structure. This is a doctrine strikingly similar to that of Russell and the early Wittgenstein,[49] and it is open to the same objections. Further, it appears that each of us applies these names independently to our own abstracted intelligible species, with no allowance for the communal and conventional elements in language. Phillips dismisses briefly and in passing what he calls 'the interesting suggestion [of the Vicomte de Bonald] that man cannot think without words';[50] nowhere does he ask whether it was odd of Descartes to wonder in seventeenth-century French whether there existed any seventeenth-century Frenchmen. Scholastics were committed to the doctrine of a private language, which providentially just happens to be the same for all of us.

Whether this was what St Thomas meant was and is another matter. In 1924, in one of a series of lectures to mark the sescentenary of St Thomas's canonisation, Professor A. E. Taylor questioned the doctrine of abstraction as 'hard to reconcile with the character of our knowledge in pure mathematics', though he insisted that

> a theory of perception . . . which is to meet the requirements of modern science . . . will have to combine, as [St Thomas] at any rate meant to combine, the two complementary positions that our knowledge of the world around our bodies is mediated in fact by highly complicated processes of a very special kind and that as *knowledge* it is *direct, unmediated* apprehension, not of 'ideas' or 'images' but of actual physical reality.[51]

Thirty years later, in 1957, Peter Geach explained and defended St Thomas's account of the *conversio ad phantasmata* (while inveighing against the 'abstractionism of his *soi-disant* followers') by arguing that 'judgements about directly sensible particulars are to be analysed as judgements of general content standing in some special connexion with certain sense-experiences': in other words,

> What we may call the intelligible content of the judgement is the same in all judgements expressible as 'That flash was before this bang', regardless of which flash and bang are in question . . . The special reference to *that* flash

> and *this* bang comes in . . . in a sensory context in which the hearer notices a flash and a bang.[52]

But scholastics were too concerned with the contemplation of discrete universals to be interested in judgements in contexts in which they were actually used. Their examples were drawn from a very small traditional stock, analysis of which was at best perfunctory.

A corollary to the doctrine of abstraction was that there were three degrees of it, which allowed there to be three, and only three, modes of science. In ascending order, these were physics (which dealt with quality), mathematics (which dealt with quantity) and metaphysics (which dealt with essence). Since the modern natural sciences are mathematical, they did not fit into this scheme, and so their practitioners were severely rebuked for what D'Arcy called 'a bastard mode of knowledge . . . [which] is merely preparing for itself a final disappointment'.[53] (Rather in the same spirit, some elderly Greats dons in the 1920s tried to explain to Einstein certain considerations of Idealist logic which would have refuted the theory of relativity.[54]) The twenty-four theses (XVIII) laid down that there were degrees of intellectuality corresponding to degrees of immateriality, but not that there were only three of them, nor that all questions in one subject had to fall within the same degree. This was prudent, as the three degrees are inextricably entangled with Neoplatonism.[55] Nevertheless, they were put to students as self-evident fact, without consideration of their complex and fascinating origins from Pythagoras onwards, and as a straitjacket within which all intellectual endeavour must be confined.

The philosophy of language affected all Catholics through its consequences for biblical and liturgical translation. A great loosening was brought about here by the Knox Bible (1944, 1949)[56] and by the Finberg-O'Connell missal (also 1949).[57] Even in the seventeenth century, however, Catholic translators were more ready than Protestants to mirror current speech,[58] and Knox quotes a splendid Georgian version which for James 2:3 has, 'And he says to the fine suit of clothes, Sit you here; that's for quality'.[59] Knox himself thought that equal blame for our 'miserably low' standard of religious translation from the 1840s on should attach 'to the men who went with Newman and to the men who stayed behind with Pusey'.[60] Among Catholics, however, the scholastic account of meaning undoubtedly encouraged the notion that 'faithful' means 'literal', a notion which is still unquestioned by many critics of ICEL. In my own view, as one of the contributors to the new version, the main defect of the hastily translated Missal of 1973 was rather its inattention to rhythm, the outcome of a habit of treating words as purely intellectual counters and ignoring the breathing, the *spiritus*, by which they exist.[61] But in an age of print this is a common weakness, not least in the critics' proposed amendments. It is not cured by translating word for word.

HISTORY

A necessary consequence of scholastic epistemology, and of the principle that nothing could be certain unless it was deduced from 'the nature of being', was a marked disapproval of history. Even Philip Hughes was driven to say, 'History may confirm the truth of a thesis known to us by surer means; it rarely proves a thesis';[62] the one reference to the Renaissance in Phillips is as follows:

> The triumph of the Nominalism of Ockham was the destruction of medieval scholasticism, for henceforward philosophy is mere juggling with words, which, by hypothesis, can have no relation to reality. At the same time the Humanists of the Renaissance were directing attention to the value of positive studies, such as history, thus giving support to the anti-intellectualist view of the world . . . 'It is a great mistake to conceive this historical revolt [i.e. the revival of the historical spirit at the Renaissance] as an appeal to the reason. On the contrary, it was through and through an anti-intellectualist movement. It was a return to the contemplation of brute fact; it was based on a recoil from the inflexible rationality of medieval thought'.[63]

The quotation is from A. N. Whitehead, the Cambridge metaphysician and collaborator with Bertrand Russell;[64] the sentiment is reminiscent of Bradley's assertion that if the choice must be made between 'a great historical fact' and 'a high abstract principle', then 'the issue I must decide in favour of the principle and the higher truth'.[65]

Many English ecclesiastics were convinced that there often were such choices, and that they must be decided as Bradley would have decided them. There was still the 'perennial endemic fidget about scandal'. There was the controversial need to represent every action of the Elizabethan government, and anyone who conformed to the Elizabethan Settlement, as actuated by deliberate malice. There was Aristotle's dictum that a science is about 'what is universal and cannot be otherwise',[66] which led him to say that poetry is more scientific than history[67] and St Thomas to say that the doings of Abraham, Isaac and Jacob are not matter for a science but only *exempla* or *auctoritates*.[68] There was the fact that history was not an academic subject in England until 1850, and even then was looked on at first as 'an easy school, for rich men'.[69] There was a justified fear that Modernism would dissolve all faith into subjective emotion, and there were the pronouncements of the Biblical Commission, to which all Catholics were obliged to give interior assent.[70]

On the other hand, there were considerations which pointed in another direction. There is a good deal of historical matter in Aristotle, who indeed seems to have given the Greek word *historia* the meaning which it has had ever since.[71] In the seventeenth century, history had developed on the Continent at least partly as 'a refutation of Cartesian philosophy'.[72] By the 1890s it was a serious academic subject in England, even if there was a lingering assumption that it was for those, like Belloc, whose classics were not up to reading Greats.[73] And the pronouncements of the Biblical Commission, once their double and triple negatives are disentangled, are usually of the form that such-and-such a critical conclusion had not been proved, so leaving scope for further investigation.[74]

The approved response to the Modernist crisis is better represented, however, by Walshe's adaptation of Garrigou-Lagrange (1926). Apart from a preface on palaeontological discoveries and two chapters on 'pantheistic' and Bergsonian evolution,[75] the first 200 pages of this book are concerned with the possibility, suitability and credibility of revelation in the abstract and with the classifying of theories about criteria and motives.[76] Only then does Walshe consider the Gospels. He quotes the usual *testimonia* from the Apostolic Fathers and refers, briefly and at second hand, to the archaeological work of Sir William Ramsay in Asia Minor.[77] But he prefers to rely on a general principle that the New Testament writers are 'sincere',[78] and it is easy to see why. A historian goes by something like Newman's principle that certitude is reached by an accumulation of probabilities: except where the evidence is very thin, no single strand in the rope bears all the weight, and one or more strands may break without the whole rope giving way.[79] So a historian can admit that the evidence on a particular point is inconsistent or inconclusive, and still claim to have written a true account of his subject. But a scholastic has to have a universal and necessary principle, which can only be certain if it is true by definition and so immune from empirical correction. There may not be a doubt, but it is always possible to imagine a doubt, against which his conclusion must be secured in advance.[80]

The embarrassments that this may cause are well illustrated in D'Arcy's *The Sense of History: Sacred and Profane* (1959). Much of this is a handy survey of what has been said about history by philosophers and theologians (St Augustine, Bossuet, Vico, Hegel, Toynbee, Henri Marrou, Paul Tillich) and in Chapter 1 there are discussions of such historical questions as the provenance of the Bayeux Tapestry and the site of Emmaus. But about halfway through it becomes clear that D'Arcy is still looking for universal objects to contemplate, and to allow this he is ready to admit 'both genuine universals and fictitious ones in moderation', where the latter term covers expressions like 'the Middle Ages' or 'the Baroque period'.[81] In one sense, this is a reasonable extension of the Thomist account of understanding as the grasping of structures (forms) apart from the matter by which they exist. Without being metaphysicians, people can and do talk about the structure of a fugue, the structure (or structures) of the Church or even the structure of politics at the accession of George III. But D'Arcy's willingness to accept 'fictitious universals' only 'in moderation' shows that he was uneasy about his own solution. Where do you draw the line, and how? Is Bismarck's foreign policy a universal? Or *Domesday Book and Beyond*? As a scholastic, D'Arcy holds that to answer a question is to become acquainted with an abstract object, and yet such objects are not to be multiplied *praeter necessitatem*.

A notable omission from *The Sense of History* is any discussion of whether or in what sense the Scriptures are, or contain, history. For this, two reasons can be suggested. The first is that in the 1950s this was still a touchy subject, so much so that the copious notes to the Knox Old Testament (1949) and to the definitive edition of the whole Bible (1955) give no dates or contexts for the various books (though such points are discussed in his *New Testament Commentary* of 1953–56 and, briefly, in some separate editions of the New Testament). The second, and more likely, is that D'Arcy is less concerned with asking how historians reach the truth than with the metaphysical pattern of history-as-a-whole, as in *The City of God*.[82] It is significant that, with reservations, D'Arcy admires Arnold Toynbee, whose work displays a high degree of abstraction from contingent facts and whose 'answer to the meaning of history would lie in religion, and in particular in the Christian religion'.[83] But this admiration means that he is uncritical of Toynbee's starting point, which he sums up as follows:

> [Toynbee] accepts, with qualifications, the Aristotelian distinction between the techniques of history, science and fiction . . . Where the data are few, all that we can do is to ascertain and record them; where the data are too numerous to tabulate, we have to survey them and formulate some laws; where finally the data are innumerable, we have to use the technique of fictions.[84]

Such a starting point leads straight to a position which since the 1960s has become very common and which can be summed up in a sentence from Xavier Léon-Dufour: 'In modern language, we should say that [the early Christians] had an existentialist, rather than a positivist, attitude to history.'[85] This way of putting it owes something to the old dichotomy between the Jesus of history and the Christ of faith. But behind this it assumes another one, which is implicit in D'Arcy and Toynbee: that between a neutral body of atomic facts – hard, separable granules of truth – and a set of personal and emotional attitudes which a historian may adopt towards them and in the light of which he imposes his 'interpretation' on them. This is to confuse history with annals and to assume that an 'historical fact' comes ready packaged to be picked off the shelves of some intellectual supermarket. It is, rather, whatever is asserted by a true answer to a question with its verb in a past tense; and of such questions there is an infinite variety. Indeed, an original historian is someone who can ask new questions and answer them from evidence which no one else had thought of using for that purpose. You cannot say a priori what evidence may answer what question; and it is misleading to think of a hierarchy with 'brute facts' at the bottom and wider and wider generalisations in strata above them. At any time, the Synoptic Problem might be settled by the discovery of two square inches of papyrus.

In Britain we may be more sceptical about such atomic facts, after the failure of the analytic movement between the wars to find any, despite twenty years of sustained and sophisticated enquiry.[86] On the Continent, however, this episode and its lessons are not as well known as they should be; and it was from there that most English Catholics acquired their philosophy during the 1960s and 1970s. Sometimes the fly does not want to get out of the bottle.

METAPHYSICS

The function of metaphysics in a Christian philosophy is threefold: to consider patterns in the visible world which imply that it is created, and therefore that there is a Creator; to consider what the fact of creation implies about our due response to our Creator; and to explain how, and how far, it makes sense to talk about the Creator in terms drawn from creation, without which we cannot even say 'Our Father'. Chesterton remarked that this in turn implies what is found in St Thomas: 'a strong personal interest in things subordinate and semi-dependent . . . [and in] a hierarchy of higher and lower liberties'.[87] This came to St Thomas from the biological and social writings of Aristotle, with the consequence that, for instance, the argument from design would consider, not only the movements of the planets, as in Plato, but also such phenomena as the ability of turtles to navigate two thousand miles to Ascension Island to breed. It follows that even a metaphysical argument must begin from contingent fact, and therefore that it may have to be reconstructed with advances in science, as Rickaby pointed out with gusto in the notes to *Of God and His Creatures*.

Until the 1860s it was possible to keep these elements in balance. At Oscott in the 1830s, metaphysics was still being taught in conjunction with Virgil's *Georgics* and 'natural philosophy';[88] and at the same time Wiseman was lecturing in Cardinal Weld's apartments at the Palazzo Odescalchi on 'The Connexion between Science and Revealed Religion'.[89] But one effect of the controversies associated with Darwin, Huxley and Mivart was a certain shyness about the doctrine of creation and a rather desiccated understanding of natural law, which depends on the doctrine of creation. This showed in 1968 in the controversy over *Humanae Vitae*, and it still shows today in the reluctance of clergy to preach about creation. Meanwhile, one effect of the 1917 Code of Canon Law (which, like any workable law, had to be univocal) was to foster the idea that analogical predication was a necessary fiddle for talking about God, and one which had to be argued for at great length, rather than a feature of any natural language.

In 1914 Bertrand Russell observed tartly that many philosophers were 'less anxious to understand the world of science and daily life than to convict it of unreality in the interests of a super-sensible "real" world'.[90] His gibe was aimed at the Oxbridge Idealists, but many scholastics would have regarded it as a fair description of their task, and indeed as a compliment. D'Arcy is scathing about the 'partiality and prejudice' of all subjects other than metaphysics, and insists that we should argue solely from 'the general character of reality [and] the principle of contradiction'.[91] Joseph Maréchal's *Le Point de Départ de la Métaphysique* (1923–6), which was still the foundation of the Gregorian course in the late 1950s, is a Kantian transcendental deduction of the whole of scholastic metaphysics from the form of the judgement, on the assumption (also Kantian) that all judgement can be reduced to the subject, copula and predicate of traditional logic.[92] This could be represented as despoiling the Egyptians or meeting a current objection on its own terms;[93] but it is hard to avoid a suspicion that such writers rather enjoyed dismissing the common world, and their manner of proceeding certainly had two undesirable consequences. One of these was a reluctance to admit that the Five Ways begin from ascertainable facts (*constat quaedam . . .*);[94] the other was an offhand and contemptuous treatment of 'adversaries', whose errors, by definition, had no right to a fair hearing. Compared to the 'defence of the ontological value of primary notions and principles of reason',[95] the accurate statement of other views, and of the arguments for them, was a minor consideration.

Scholastics found in the Idealists an element which corresponded to the Platonic tradition in St Thomas. That this could be understood positively was shown at the time by Fr Victor White OP[96] and others. But too often it tended, in the words of Dom Bede Griffiths, 'to draw Christian mysticism away from its sacramental and corporate, in a word its incarnational character, and to make it appear a solitary and ascetic ideal'.[97] The manuals were Platonist in the sense of holding that to exist means to be incapable of changing, and that this is only true of pure Forms or universals. As Gilson wrote of St Augustine,[98] they showed 'a marked tendency to reduce the existence of a thing to its essence and to answer the question, "What is it for a thing to be?" by saying, "It is to be that which it is" '. One consequence was a habit of talking about entities denoted by the definite article and an adjective, such as 'The Real', or by the definite article and a singular noun where a class was meant, such as Vaughan's 'The Professor', who after 1870 would 'no longer be able to devote his days and nights to sapping the foundations of that Church for whose good estate he offers the Adorable Sacrifice the next morning'.[99] Such entities might not actually exist, but they were more real, and statements about them were more true, than any matters of contingent fact.

Such language might be explained, like the Syllabus of Errors, in terms of 'thesis' and 'hypothesis', or as corresponding to a scientific model. But, unlike such a model, it aimed at superseding observations, rather than unifying them; and it created a tension about which Michael Williams has written:

> There is a distinction between life as it is lived and enjoyed in practice and the official line which always states the ideal [as if it were fact]. The Roman is able to live in these two worlds without feeling the tension, but there are a great many who are unable to bear it and break under the strain.[100]

Moreover, although there was some justice in the claim that the analyses of act, potency and so on were merely technical articulations of common sense, the scholastics' own language made it unconvincing. Platonist ontology dictated the use, wherever possible, of abstract nouns rather than finite verbs. English scholastics also acquired from the Idealists a taste for high-flown tropes and metaphors, which, like some current academic jargon, served to impress upon others the profundity and importance of their subject. So D'Arcy explains that

> Being frowns down upon us like a mountain shrouded in mist. It is one, and it is all that is . . . The form is intelligible but, like Samson, it has lost its native strength because of its paramour [matter] and is 'silent at the mill with slaves'. It shines for others and not to itself . . . Pure potency is just what is not nothing: it is indistinctness, the principle of indefiniteness, multiplicity, barbarism waiting to be civilised, a formless void distinct from nothingness only by a capacity to receive form. By form alone does it rise to its destiny and 'inherit the earth'.[101]

And Phillips does his best to frighten students off metaphysics at the outset by warning them: 'We ascend, as it were, into the stratosphere of knowledge and breathe an air so rarefied that it could not support mental life unless we were first trained in abstract thinking in the more congenial climates of natural philosophy.'[102] Such flourishes have little in common with the lucid and businesslike distinctions of St Thomas.

Rarefied or not, metaphysics has political and social implications. Plato held that his Guardians, who could see the Forms, ought therefore to have absolute power and maintain it by methods which included the control of education, nocturnal arrests and the brainwashing of dissidents.[103] Discussing Abelard in 1946, Meyrick Carré wrote: 'In our own day there has been a portentous revival of extreme Realism in European politics.'[104] Many British Catholics openly admired Mussolini. At the end of his *Aquinas*, D'Arcy wrote:

> The vigour of the modern Thomist movement promises well for its future, and the spirit of the age seems to be favourable to it. Whether we turn to the political world or the world of art and literature, we witness the same phenomenon. *L'Action Française* and the political systems in Spain and Italy stand for the intellect as against sentiment. Form and order are to have precedence over, or at any rate direct, the general will.[105]

Similarly, at the end of his *Apologetics*, Walshe held up to Catholics the example of Constantine the Great, that would-be *episcopus ad extra*, and continued: 'The State cannot tolerate *per se* (*i.e.* without a just cause) that which is evil and injurious to God. *Per accidens* the worship of unbelievers and of heretics may be tolerated to avoid greater evil. But the Catholic State cannot by law sanction freedom of worship.'[106]

Such *dicta* might suggest that, if the Battle of Britain had gone the other way, there would, as in France, have been Catholic collaborators with the new order, despite the sturdy patriotism of Cardinal Hinsley. But Walshe's integrist sources reflected the recent history of the Church in France rather than in England, and his two pages on civil authority are a mere distortion of the subtle and complex elements which were later explored by Thomas Gilby OP in *Principality and Polity in St Thomas Aquinas* (1958).[107]

DIVIDING AND COMPOUNDING, 1950–65

It would be inaccurate and unjust to leave the impression that ecclesiastical scholarship was dormant in this country. Apart from those episcopal polymaths John Cuthbert Hedley of Newport (1837–1915) and George Ambrose Burton of Clifton (1852–1931), there were figures like Victor Schobel, who taught at Oscott from 1886 to 1895;[108] Abbot John Chapman of Downside (1865–1933), who was reputed to have read the whole of Migne; and Adrian Fortescue (1874–1923), who was most famous for his *Ceremonies of the Roman Rite Described* (1919) but should be remembered rather for his interest in patristics and the Eastern Church and for his edition, annotated in Latin, of Boethius's *De Consolatione Philosophiae.*[109] The necessary emphasis on Latin, and to a less extent Greek, in junior seminaries gave many clergy a competent knowledge of classical literature and the ability to read the Fathers in the original, even if the manuals made this a work of supererogation. Nevertheless, it is possible to feel that the best work was done where the theses were least restrictive. In 1956 Mgr Knox wrote that 'our Catholic apologetic, nearly all of it, strikes the modern reader as inhuman' and criticised 'the pettifogging appeal to isolated Scriptural phrases, torn from their context'. Instead, he looked forward to 'that great work of apologetics, some day to be written, which shall suggest to the reader that in approaching Christian theology he is approaching something that is alive, not a series of diagrams'.[110] Knox's own conferences at the Oxford chaplaincy[111] represent the best that could be done within the Euclidean framework of the manuals, but it is clear that he found it irksome and, as he said in one of them, 'essentially unreal'.[112]

Ten years later, Knox's distant aspiration was a fact in the documents of Vatican II, which have since been followed by a new *Catechism* based on them. Fundamental to these was a radically different philosophy of language, though here, paradoxically, it was Pius XII who undermined scholasticism by conceding in *Divino Afflante* (1943) that Scripture should be interpreted in the light of its own literary forms. (Already in 1930, F. A. Blanche had shown that St Thomas did not have a mathematically exact terminology of the sort ascribed to him by the manuals, and that to him the decisive consideration was *usus*, ordinary language.[113]) At the time, such literary forms were understood to be merely a Semitic foible of 'people in those remote times';[114] still, there was an obvious corollary, and in *Humani Generis* (1950) the Pope thought it necessary to reiterate the privileged status of scholastic terminology. But in his opening speech to the Council, Pope John XXIII shocked the curia by quoting, not only Cicero on history as the *magistra vitae*, but also St Thomas on the distinction between the substance of the faith and the manner of its expression,[115] so setting the agenda for the whole Council, and especially for the documents on Revelation, Christian Unity and the Eastern Churches.[116] After that, scholastic terminology could still be regarded as the most illuminating but not as uniquely correct.

The notion of 'language games' and its consequences for epistemology, psychology and intention, had become familiar to anyone reading philosophy in a British university after the posthumous publication (1953) of Wittgenstein's *Philosophical Investigations*. For Catholics, it was natural to see it as a general theory of which the literary forms of *Divino Afflante* were a special case. In the same way, Gilbert Ryle's *The Concept of Mind* (1949) had something in common with St Thomas on *anima*; John Austin's Oxford lectures on performative utterances threw a new light on the sacraments; Stephen Toulmin's *The Uses of Argument* (Cambridge, 1958) considered logic from a standpoint similar to that of Newman; and Peter Geach's *Mental Acts* (1957) combined St Thomas with modern logic and the thinking of Wittgenstein, one of whose pupils he had been. Running through all of these was an emphasis on language as a common possession, a series of public conventions, and so on a rejection of the isolated Cartesian self. They might, therefore, have furnished a valuable element in the thinking of the Council from 1962 onwards. They were, however, almost unknown to scholastics, though at Hawkesyard Cornelius Ernst was introducing students to Wittgenstein, and at the *Venerabile* Alan Clark (later Bishop) was introducing them to *The Concept of Mind*,[117] while at the Gregorian Fr Gonzalez di Caminero was an enthusiastic admirer of Ryle.[118] Most ecclesiastical philosophers thought of British philosophy as identical with the logical positivism of Ayer's *Language, Truth and Logic* (1936); and, if they shared Knox's dissatisfaction, they looked rather to the Continent for fresh inspiration.

This can be seen in Dom Illtyd Trethowan's *Essay in Christian Philosophy* (1954), of which he wrote in the preface:

> The conclusions to which these chapters come differ, to a greater or lesser extent, from those which are most commonly met with today in books by

> Christian philosophers; I find St Augustine or Scotus more enlightening on some issues than St Thomas, and MM. Blondel and Le Senne more sympathetic than M. Maritain. Thus I am between two fires. On the one side is the scepticism of the average modern philosopher, on the other what I would venture to describe as the dogmatism of the conventional Thomist philosopher.[119]

Following Georges van Riet's *L'Épistémologie Thomiste* (Louvain, 1946), Trethowan traced and criticised scholastic views from 1850 to 1950, complaining that

> Even those who maintain most firmly the *union* of soul and body and the veridical character of sense-knowledge continue to ask the Platonist questions: How can the material world act upon the mind? How can what is nobler be thus subject to what is baser?[120]

But he then paints himself into a corner by adding:

> The Christian philosopher is always a Platonist in the basic sense that he recognises two levels in our experience . . . We may take our analysis a stage further by proposing that these two levels refer to two classes of objects, traditionally described as 'material' and 'immaterial'.[121]

Once the question is put in those terms, the same problem returns in a different guise: at the end, Trethowan can only commend French writers like Le Senne, Marcel and Lavelle,[122] whose manner has much in common with that of the Idealists.

After the Council, however, when seminaries began to establish contacts with British universities, what had been written off on both sides as 'mere juggling with words' began to be taken seriously by both. A notable landmark here was the conference held at Downside in April 1963, whose proceedings were edited by John Coulson as *Theology and the University*.[123] A generation later, Aquinas is again a contemporary voice in secular philosophy, while theologians and Christian philosophers have absorbed and refined what is valuable in Wittgenstein and his successors. Catholics are now used to working within a wider academic community, a state of affairs which discourages either uncritical admiration or uncritical condemnation, and also means that the Church in this country is not saddled with Catholic universities on the American model, with their problems of funding and of reconciling orthodoxy with academic independence. If D'Arcy, Walshe and Phillips are compared with, say, Brian Davies' *The Thought of St Thomas Aquinas* (Oxford, 1992), there is a striking change in both spirit and content. The 'external world' no longer has to be proved or discounted; valid insights from whatever source are given due credit, as they were by St Thomas himself; above all, there is a willingness to begin with questions rather than theses, and to admit that some of the answers may not be known.

In the 1990s, this academic reconstruction is affecting Catholic schools, in two ways. First, there are now Advanced Level courses in philosophy and in religious studies with a philosophical component, which are being taught in Catholic schools as in others. Second, after the rejection by many teachers in the 1960s and 1970s of almost any intellectual element in religious teaching (itself a consequence of the earlier divorce between devotion and apologetics), there is an increasing appreciation that authentic devotion depends on sound theology. This shows in a steady demand for the postgraduate Catholic Certificate in Religious Studies and for diploma and degree courses, including those run from Maryvale. Both these and the sixth-form courses may include the doctrine of analogy, the foundations of ethics and St Thomas's metaphysical explorations of the Trinity, but they do not commit students to the Cartesian and Idealist doctrines of the manuals. It still seems to be axiomatic that (unlike the medieval carols) hymns for use by children should have no theological content whatever, but perhaps in time it will be accepted that, here also, sentiment is not enough.

It may well be true, as McCool thinks, that neo-scholasticism, as formerly understood, is now a closed chapter.[124] But it may also be true that in another fifty years the authentic revival of St Thomas will be seen to have begun, rather than ended, with Vatican II, and that a distinctive and important contribution to it has been made by philosophers in this country. As Newman wrote, rather surprisingly perhaps, towards the end of the *Apologia*:

> If there is one consideration more than another which should make us English grateful to Pius the Ninth, it is that, by giving us a Church of our own, he has prepared the way for our own habits of mind, our own manner of reasoning, our own tastes, and our own virtues, finding a place and thereby a sanctification, in the Catholic Church.[125]

NOTES

1. G. A. Beck (ed.), *The English Catholics, 1850–1950* (1950), p. 263.
2. *Clergy Review*, 33 (January-June 1950), pp. 183–4.
3. 'Let [the translator] try to render the sense of Scripture plainer to us by whatever means he will, but let him adhere (or rather, let him cleave) to the good old-fashioned diction which was good enough for our forefathers, and is still better for us because for us it is still more old-fashioned': R. A. Knox, *On Englishing the Bible* (Burns Oates, 1949), p. 13.
4. James Gibbons, *The Faith of our Fathers* (Baltimore, 1876); Michael Sheehan, *Apologetics and Catholic Doctrine* (Dublin, 1918); Francis Ripley, *This Is the Faith* (Birchley Hall Press, 1951).
5. S. J. Gosling, 'Vernacular in the Liturgy', *Clergy Review*, 33, pp. 361–75.
6. Johnson in Beck, *English Catholics* pp. 263–4. Cf Martin D'Arcy SJ in Maisie Ward (ed.), *The English Way* (Sheed & Ward, Ark Library edn, 1934), p. 328: 'The ghosts of Bunyan, of Hooker and Laud, of the Cambridge Platonists and Bishop Butler flit across his pages and

speak in his voice; middle-class sentiment makes him truly Victorian, and he speaks with the accent of Oxford.'

7. Beck, *English Catholics*, ch. 8, 10, 16 (pp. 243–64, 291–321, 475–514).
8. *Acta apud Sanctam Sedem*, 12 (1879), pp. 97–115.
9. *Acta Apostolicae Sedis* (hereafter *AAS*), 6 (1914), pp. 383–6.
10. *AAS*, 23 (1931), pp. 253, 263, 271–2.
11. Aidan Nichols OP, *The Shape of Catholic Theology* (T. & T. Clark, 1991), pp. 321–2.
12. Allan White OP in Dominic Aidan Bellenger OSB (ed.), *Opening the Scrolls: Essays in Catholic History in Honour of Godfrey Anstruther* (Downside, 1987), pp. 222–32.
13. M. E. Williams, *The Venerable English College, Rome: A History, 1579–1979* (Associated Catholic Publications, London, 1979), pp. 129–31, 143–4, 147, 158–61, 163.
14. Williams, *Rome*, pp. 118, 120, 123, 160.
15. Williams, *Rome*, pp. 130–1, 141–2; Anthony Kenny, *A Path from Rome* (Sidgwick & Jackson, 1985), pp. 43–51, 74–79, with due credit to Lonergan and Flick.
16. This special subject was last set in 1965.
17. *Of God and His Creatures*, p. vii.
18. E. Anscombe, *Philosophy*, 33 (1958), p. 11.
19. T. J. Walshe, *The Principles of Catholic Apologetics* (Sands, 1926), p. xviii.
20. Williams, *Rome*, p. 158.
21. G. K. Chesterton, *St Thomas Aquinas* (1933) in *Collected Works* (Ignatius Press, San Francisco), vol. II (1986), pp. 514–15 (in ch. 6, 'The Approach to Thomism').
22. J. D. Crichton, 'Challoner's "Catechism" ', *Clergy Review*, 63 (January-June 1978), pp. 140–6; Crichton, 'Challoner and the "Penny Catechism" ', *Recusant History*, vol. 15 (1979–81), pp. 425–32.
23. I. Trethowan OSB, *An Essay in Christian Philosophy* (Longmans, 1954), p. 16.
24. R. A. Knox, *Enthusiasm* (Clarendon Press, Oxford, 1950), p. 246.
25. *Summa Theologiae* (hereafter *ST*) II–II.83.12; 84.2.
26. *A Manual of Prayers and other Christian Devotions* (Henry Hills, 1686), pp. 178–9.
27. J. D. Crichton, H. E. Winstone and J. R. Ainslie (eds), *English Catholic Worship* (Geoffrey Chapman, 1979), pp. 42–3, 52–4, 57, 60–1, 67–8.
28. *The Roman Missal . . . in Latin and English* (Goodliffe Neale/Brepols, no. 2539, 1947), pp. 25–6.
29. H. Francis Davis, *The Assumption* (Our Lady of Walsingham Lecture Group/Legion of Mary, Birmingham, 1950), p. 4.
30. *Newman Philosophy of Science Bulletin*, nos. 37–39, reprinted in Laurence Bright OP (ed.), *Readings in the Philosophy of Science: Papers from the Philosophy of Science Group Quarterly Bulletin, nos. 1–50* (Newman Association Philosophy of Science Group, 1964), pp. 165–212.
31. Ripley, *This Is the Faith*, p. 353. Cf. p. 340: '[Hell] is certainly a place, and it seems from Sacred Scripture that it is within the earth, though there are many theories on this point.'
32. Josef Neuner SJ and Jacques Dupuis SJ, *The Christian Faith in the Doctrinal Documents of the Catholic Church* (Theological Publications in India, Bangalore, 1996), nos. 2308–10 (pp. 944–6); *ST* I.75.6.ad 3; 77.8.
33. *Sacrosanctum Concilium*, para. 81: '*Paschalem mortis christianae indolem*'.
34. *AAS* 71 (1979), p. 939.
35. Hodgetts, 'Revising the Order of Christian Funerals' in Peter C. Finn and James M. Schellmann (eds), *Shaping English Liturgy: Studies in Honor of Archbishop Denis Hurley* (The Pastoral Press, Washington, DC, 1990), pp. 199–218, esp. pp. 208–10.
36. Sir Richard Terry, *Music of the Roman Rite* (Burns Oates, 1932), p. 52.
37. *Roman Missal* (1970), General Instruction, paras. 253, 263–4, 272, 279, 283–5, 288, 290, 292, 305–6, 311–12.

38. *ST* I.39.8.
39. Ernest Oldmeadow, 'The Catholic Church and Music' in *Catholic Emancipation 1829–1929: Essays by Various Writers* (Longmans, 1929), p. 140.
40. Optional from 1951 to 1955, mandatory from 1956 onwards.
41. *Ordo Hebdomadae Sanctae Instauratus* (1956), Easter Vigil, para. 11A.
42. *The New Order of Holy Week* (Burns Oates, 1966), p. 129.
43. *Summa contra Gentiles* (*SG*) II. 57 (= Rickaby, *Of God and His Creatures*, p. 118).
44. J. O. Urmson, *Philosophical Analysis: Its Development between the Two World Wars* (Clarendon Press, Oxford, 1956).
45. R. P. Phillips, *Modern Thomistic Philosophy* (Burns Oates & Washbourne, 1934, 1935), vol. II, pp. 47–64, 121–2, 133.
46. Chesterton's ire was provoked by D'Arcy's remark (in *St Thomas Aquinas* (2nd edition, Clonmore & Reynolds, Dublin, 1953), p. 59) that 'a certain likeness can be detected between the aim and method of St Thomas and those of Hegel'. Cf. n. 21 above.
47. Daniel W. Graham, *Aristotle's Two Systems* (Clarendon Press, Oxford, 1987).
48. F. C. Copleston SJ, *A History of Philosophy*, vol. II (Burns Oates, 1948), pp. 388–91.
49. Cf. A. Kenny, *Downside Review*, 249 (Summer-Autumn 1959), pp. 217–35.
50. Phillips, *Philosophy*, vol. II, pp. 132–3.
51. A. E. Taylor, 'St Thomas as a Philosopher', in Aelred Whitacre OP and others, *St Thomas Aquinas* (Basil Blackwell, Oxford, 1925), pp. 59, 61.
52. P. T. Geach, *Mental Acts* (Routledge & Kegan Paul, 1957), pp. 63–4, 130–1.
53. D'Arcy, *Aquinas*, p. 143.
54. Hugh Lloyd-Jones, *Greek Studies in Modern Oxford* (Clarendon Press, Oxford, 1961), p. 20.
55. Cf. Henry Chadwick, *Boethius: The Consolations of Music, Logic, Theology and Philosophy* (Clarendon Press, Oxford, 1981), pp. 69–111.
56. Cf. Knox, *Englishing the Bible* (n. 3 above).
57. Finberg-O'Connell used Knox for the readings.
58. David Crane, 'English Translations of the *Imitatio Christi* in the Sixteenth and Seventeenth Centuries', *Recusant History*, vol. 13 (1975–6), pp. 79–100. The comment quoted is on pp. 93–4.
59. Knox, *Englishing the Bible*, pp. 18, 42.
60. R. A. Knox, *On English Translation: The Romanes Lecture 1957* (Clarendon Press, Oxford, 1957), p. 12.
61. Hodgetts, 'The English Tradition and Liturgical Reform', *Clergy Review*, vol. 61, no. 11 (November 1977), pp. 434–40; Hodgetts, 'Sense and Sound in Liturgical Translation', *Worship*, vol. 57, no. 6 (November 1983), pp. 496–513.
62. Philip Hughes, *Rome and the Counter-Reformation in England* (Burns Oates, 1942), p. 428.
63. Phillips, *Philosophy*, vol. II, p. 88.
64. A. N. Whitehead, *Science and the Modern World* (Cambridge, 1925), p. 10.
65. Quoted in John Passmore, *A Hundred Years of Philosophy* (Pelican, 1968), p. 61, from F. H. Bradley's *Presuppositions of Critical History* (1874).
66. *Nicomachean Ethics*, VI, 1139–40; X, 1180b23.
67. *Poetics*, 1451a36 ff.
68. *ST* I.1.2.
69. Sir Richard Southern, *The Shape and Substance of Academic History* (Clarendon Press, Oxford, 1961), p. 12.
70. *Acta Sanctae Sedis*, 11 (1907), pp. 723–6.
71. Simon Hornblower, *Thucydides* (Duckworth, 1987), pp. 7–12.
72. R. G. Collingwood, *The Idea of History* (Clarendon Press, Oxford, 1946), p. 63. Collingwood

was both an Idealist metaphysician and a distinguished archaeologist and historian of Roman Britain.

73. Robert Speaight, *The Life of Hilaire Belloc* (Hollis & Carter, 1957), pp. 32, 76–8.
74. But in the atmosphere of the time it was not easy to distinguish between a duty to believe that, say, Isaiah 40 – 66 were by the same author as Isaiah 1 – 39 and a duty to believe that it had not been proved (in 1908) that they were by different authors.
75. Walshe, *Catholic Apologetics*, pp. v–xx, 58–69, 81–102.
76. Walshe, *Catholic Apologetics*, pp. 25–214.
77. Walshe, *Catholic Apologetics*, p. 227.
78. Walshe, *Catholic Apologetics*, pp. 229–33.
79. *Grammar of Assent*, chs 8–9; *Essay on Development*, ch. 3.
80. Wittgenstein, *Philosophical Investigations* (1953), I, para. 84.
81. M. C. D'Arcy SJ, *The Sense of History: Secular and Sacred* (Faber & Faber, 1959), p. 139.
82. D'Arcy, *History*, pp. 204–17.
83. D'Arcy, *History*, p. 114.
84. D'Arcy, *History*, pp. 109–10.
85. Xavier Léon-Dufour, *The Gospels and the Jesus of History*, tr. John McHugh (Fontana, 1970), p. 187.
86. See Urmson, *Philosophical Analysis*, n. 44 above.
87. Chesterton, *Aquinas*, p. 527.
88. Oscott College archives, MS 330 (examinations timetable, Christmas 1833).
89. London, 1836; cf. Wiseman, *Recollections of the Last Four Popes* (Hurst & Blackett, n.d.), pp. 258–60.
90. B. A. W. Russell, *Our Knowledge of the External World* (The Open Court Publishing Company, 1914), p. 45.
91. D'Arcy, *Aquinas*, pp. 48, 59.
92. D'Arcy, *Aquinas*, p. 203n, describes it succinctly as 'Thomism reset in Kantian language'.
93. But Austin Farrer, *Finite and Infinite* (second edn, 1959), p. x, wrote bluntly: 'This [Kantian] centring of metaphysics in the act of thought is vicious.'
94. *ST* I.2.3, in various forms at the beginning of each Way.
95. Walshe, *Catholic Apologetics*, pp. 44ff.
96. Victor White OP, *God the Unknown* (Harvill Press, 1956), pp. 62–71 (first publ. in *The Eastern Churches Quarterly* in 1941); Taylor, 'St Thomas', pp. 46–59.
97. Quoted by White, *God the Unknown*, p. 62.
98. Étienne Gilson, *God and Philosophy* (Yale, 1941; Yale Paperbound, 1959), p. 61.
99. Quoted e.g. by M. Trevor, *Newman: Light in Winter* (Macmillan, 1962), p. 474.
100. Williams, *Rome*, p. 145.
101. D'Arcy, *Aquinas*, pp. 79, 86–7.
102. Phillips, *Philosophy*, vol. II, p. 157.
103. Plato, *Republic* 376–403, 414–15, 457–61; *Laws* 909a.
104. Meyrick H. Carré, *Realists and Nominalists* (Oxford, 1946), p. 38.
105. D'Arcy, *Aquinas*, p. 204.
106. Walshe, *Catholic Apologetics*, p. 376.
107. Published in the USA as *The Political Thought of St Thomas Aquinas*.
108. Mervyn Tower, 'A Missing Link: Oscott's Bavarian Connection, Victor Schobel, 1848–1915' in Judith F. Champ (ed.), *Oscott College 1838–1988: A Volume of Commemorative Essays* (1988), pp. 141–56.
109. *De Consolatione Philosophiae Libri Quinque Quos denuo recognovit . . . Adrianus a Forti Scuto* (Burns Oates & Washbourne, 1925). The introduction, appendices and index, also in Latin, were added after Fortescue's early death by Canon George Smith.

110. R. A. Knox, 'Towards a New Apologetic', *The Month*, New Series 21 (January-June 1959), pp. 160, 165.
111. R. A. Knox, *In Soft Garments* (Burns Oates, 1942); *The Hidden Stream* (Burns Oates, 1952).
112. Knox, *Hidden Stream*, p. 76.
113. F. A. Blanche, 'Sur la langue technique de Saint Thomas d'Aquin', *Revue de Philosophie*, 30 (1930), pp. 7–30.
114. *AAS* 35 (1943), p. 315: *'remota illa Orientis saecula'*.
115. Cicero, *De Oratore* II.9.36; *ST* I.29.3.
116. Cf. *Dei Verbum* 12, 23, 24; *Unitatis Redintegratio* 4, 11, 17; *Orientalium Ecclesiarum* 2, 6.
117. Fergus Kerr OP, *Theology after Wittgenstein* (Blackwell, Oxford, 1986), p. viii; Anthony Kenny, *A Path from Rome*, p. 50.
118. As I discovered during an oral examination in June 1959, though the question began as one on Scotus.
119. Trethowan, *Christian Philosophy*, p. v.
120. Trethowan, *Christian Philosophy*, p. 42.
121. Trethowan, *Christian Philosophy*, p. 41.
122. Trethowan, *Christian Philosophy*, pp. 171–82.
123. Darton, Longman & Todd, 1964. Cf. Charles Davis in *Downside Review*, 265 (October 1963), pp. 307–16, and the review of *Theology and the University* by Maurice Couve de Murville (now Archbishop of Birmingham) in *Downside Review*, 269 (October 1964), pp. 355–9.
124. McCool, *The Neo-Thomists* (Marquette University Press, 1994), p. 161.
125. J. H. Newman, *Apologia* (World's Classics edition, 1964), p. 279.

FIVE

RELIGIOUS LIFE FOR WOMEN

SUSAN O'BRIEN

> The world that spawned religious life, even the religious life of this century, is not the world we're living in . . . It is at best a difficult time for religious communities. The glory days of large congregations, bulging novitiates and growing institutions is long gone for most communities, but clearly remembered nevertheless.[1]

In writing these words at the end of the twentieth century, Joan Chittister, Benedictine nun and at one time President of the United States Leadership Conference of Women Religious, brought together personal experience and historical reflection. Like others writing on the subject of contemporary religious life at this time, she captured a particular moment in the history of that life for women in western Christendom. The number of women entering religious congregations and still active in them had been in decline for more than twenty years.[2] In Britain journalists captured the moment too with headlines such as 'Convents: on a wing and a prayer' and 'Wanted: more nuns' to recount news of sisters withdrawing from convent schools or selling large properties for which they no longer had a use.[3] It was a transitional time when those still actively involved were conscious of themselves as the turning point at the end of a particular historical era, able to describe and analyse what was passing without being able to discern, as yet, what future shape religious life would take within their own culture.[4] While remaining committed to their own individual calling and to the God-given value of the religious life more generally, many were able to recognise that a particular epoch of the history of that life was drawing to a close throughout western society along with the second millennium.[5]

This epoch had its starting point around 1800 with the emergence of the first of literally hundreds of new and re-established women's congregations founded in the aftermath of the French Revolution.[6] An historian of nineteenth-century

French Catholicism, Ralph Gibson, described these hundreds of separate actions as a movement to re-Christianise the Church.[7] Not confined to France, this movement of unenclosed apostolic sisters spread outwards to the rest of the western Catholic Church. So powerful was it that by the end of the century when Catholics spoke of 'nuns' they were usually referring not to enclosed contemplative nuns but to apostolic sisters living under simple vows. Even though sisters with simple vows were not granted the full status of 'religious' by Rome until Pope Leo XIII's *Conditae a Christo* in 1900, the Catholic community and the Vatican had accorded them this status de facto decades before.

The first half of the nineteenth century was distinctive not only for the proliferation of new congregations and the scale of their membership but also for the effective establishment of a new form of government for apostolic women religious. The chief innovation was papal approval for a female Superior General who was to receive her authority directly from Rome. All attempts to establish this kind of government, usually involving heroic effort by individual women, had been rejected by the Church in earlier centuries. Even so, female apostolic congregations had 'evolved irregularly but relentlessly, tolerated and even encouraged for reasons of social and ministerial necessity'.[8] Before 1800 they were organised as diocesan institutes under the jurisdiction of the local bishop, some following their own rule and others following a Third Order Rule of one of the older orders, such as the Franciscans or Dominicans. The new papal congregations were able to develop centralised structures and systems of administration which, through the authority of the Superior General and her councillors, gave women religious much greater control of the direction of their congregation, the use of its resources and the employment of their sisters. For the first time in the history of the religious life, communities of women could belong to and direct unified congregations transcending both diocesan and national boundaries. Now they, like the Jesuits and other men's orders, could more readily innovate new forms of apostolic activity according to their own perceptions of what was needed, and respond to requests from any part of the world. Although sisters continued to be circumscribed by their dependence on priests and bishops and on gender-based structures and attitudes,[9] they also experienced more autonomy than most other contemporary women.

International apostolic congregations grew at a phenomenal rate, but never to the exclusion of older forms of religious life. Contemplative orders, such as the Benedictines and Carmelites, continued to recruit members throughout the nineteenth and twentieth centuries, having their own cycle of expansion and contraction. Large numbers of new diocesan institutes were also formed in many countries. Moreover, the worldwide expansion of the Irish Sisters of Mercy, an apostolic congregation whose houses were governed independently of one another under a single Rule, shows how effectively this more traditional form of government could be applied to modern society given the right kind of leadership and circumstances.[10] But the dominant form of religious life in the modern period was that of the apostolic sister in a congregation governed by a sister Superior General.[11] Its dominance and success was no coincidence. In this structure and culture women had created a form of religious life which enabled them to respond to what they (and the Church at large) saw as the rationalist challenge of the Enlightenment and the French Revolution, and to the welfare and spiritual needs of the new urban and industrial poor. From its origins onwards the history of the modern congregation was closely intertwined with the broader societal changes of which it was a part.

In the first half of the twentieth century women's congregations continued to grow, responding in this period to the new missionary and welfare imperatives they saw in the worldwide imperialism created by a growing nationalist culture and in further industrial development and the growth of the welfare state.[12] They consolidated in structure and style between the 1920s and the 1950s so that by 1960 congregations had all the appearance of strong and enduring organisations. But, as the modern industrial and imperial epoch faded during the later years of the twentieth century, these same congregations ceased to travel along an accustomed trajectory of consolidation and growth and instead underwent dramatic change. By 1960 women were no longer coming forward in such large numbers, a trend which was dramatically heightened after 1965. Numbers also reduced significantly after 1965 as a consequence of a movement out of religious life by professed sisters.[13] At the same time, but not to be seen as simple cause of membership loss, the Catholic Church experienced the Second Vatican Council (1962–65). Complex forces of change were unleashed to work their way through the Church in many different ways. Among them was a near-revolution in many women's congregations who took to heart the theology of the Second Vatican Council and translated it into new styles, new structures and, most seriously, into a new consciousness about the purposes and presence of active religious life in Church and society.

By the 1990s Western society at large had faced and begun to work through challenges to traditional forms of authority, including those of age, class, race and gender. Post-colonial political regimes and societies had replaced colonialism throughout the world and Western societies had begun to respond to the profound changes in economic and social organisation produced by the technological revolution of the micro-chip. The social and mental worlds that had given birth and purpose to the modern religious congregation in the early nineteenth century, and those that had sustained it in the first half of the twentieth, had indeed changed in fundamental ways. During the 1990s, when documents issued by Rome reflected a determination to stem the flow of some post-Vatican II changes, including some of those in religious life, there was little inclination among sisters to attempt to turn back the clock for, as one put it: 'Spending time and energy yearning for the return of a mythical past while the present swirls perilously around us . . . only holds us back . . . from moving forward in holy ways in a post-modern world.'[14]

The history of sisters and nuns in England and Wales since 1850 must be seen within this larger historical and geographical context if it is to be explained and understood. Although much more research is needed (particularly for the period 1914–65), it is perhaps timely to draw on the work that has already been completed and to suggest some lines of thought for further exploration, for this is a subject which merits continued movement out of the margins of history.[15] In 1950 when Bishop Beck's survey of Catholic history since 1850 was published, it included two essays which approached the same task of synthesis: Dom Edward Cruise's 'Development of Religious Orders' and Rev. W. J. Battersby's 'Educational Work of the Religious Orders of Women'.[16] Their endeavour to provide a summary overview was novel and taxing, given the limited nature of the primary sources and historical writing available at the time,[17] but Battersby's study in particular pointed historians directly to the subject of the modern women's religious congregations and to the existence of a considerable secondary literature written by sister and priest historians.[18] Topics explored by these earlier Catholic writers have become of much greater interest to a broad range of scholars since the 1950s because of changes in the nature of history as an academic discipline. The new social history writing of the 1960s, concerned with 'history from below', was augmented rapidly by the intellectual forces associated with the women's movement and the politics of cultural pluralism in the 1970s. Between them these social and intellectual movements have established that history without recognition of gender is at best partial and that the history of communities, including modern communities, must pay proper attention to religious beliefs and practices if it is to be intelligible. Scholars have a new and enlarged set of questions about the interplay of class, ethnicity and gender in religious experience itself and in the life of the organised Church;[19] about the part played by religious belief and practices in the development of individual and community self-definition;[20] about the meaning of visual iconography and the language of prayers and hymns; and about 'the relationship between the churches and social and cultural life at the grass roots'.[21] These larger questions translate readily into an agenda for writing a new type of convent history. How, for example, did the class and ethnic origins of the sisters affect the organisation and culture of the convent?[22] What has been the interplay of gender and authority as between religious superiors, bishops and priests?[23] How did the spiritual life of the convent influence girls and women in the Catholic community? What meanings do convent rituals and architecture hold?[24] It now seems possible to explore the past with greater openness than previously and, as one sister historian writes, not only to celebrate and restore but to acknowledge and then seek to understand the darker aspects of some of the human relations involved, for 'research has also uncovered . . . harsh and cruel regimes in orphanages . . . patterns of dependence and undue deference to authority. For women, religious and otherwise, are not just the innocent victims of history.'[25] These newer perspectives take their place alongside some of the more traditional ones about the impact of institutional and doctrinal changes on the organisation of religious life or the impact of church and state relationships over, for example, questions of funding for education and welfare provision.

Materials for writing this history are relatively plentiful and have become much more accessible since the Second Vatican Council and its promulgation of the 'Decree on the Appropriate Renewal of the Religious Life'. By emphasising that renewal must be grounded in an understanding of history, this Council document made the proper maintenance and ordering of congregational archives an imperative. Implementation of the decree has led many congregations to re-write biographies of their founders and foundresses, to publish key documents of their history and, of central importance to other historians, to appoint archivists who have organised the archives.[26] As a consequence of all this activity interested scholars have extensive archival material available to them and there is no longer any good reason for sisters and nuns to be omitted from histories of the English Catholic Church.[27] If, at the end of the twentieth century, the history of women religious continues to be less well integrated into the social and religious history of England than might be warranted, this is no longer to be explained by reference to Protestant hegemony or to the ghetto mentality of the Catholic community, but by the amount of primary research and writing still waiting to be undertaken.

THE FIRST PHASE: FOUNDATIONS AND INNOVATIONS, 1840–1900

In 1840 the English Catholic community could lay claim to fewer than twenty convents and an even smaller number of convent schools and welfare institutions. By 1880 the *Catholic Directory* listed more than three hundred convents offering extra-parochial opportunities for worship and devotions and administering a well-developed system of Catholic educational and welfare services. Within a single generation religious sisters had established a network of convents and teaching and welfare institutions across the country and had made themselves an integral part of the Church. Theirs was a generation consciously pioneering a way of life unfamiliar, even alien, to English culture. Led by a number of noteworthy and strong individuals, communities of apostolic sisters during this first phase were characterised more by their responsiveness to situations and individuals than by conformity to formulas. Moreover, they were willing to persist in the face of a range of difficulties which included financial hardship, several court cases and media 'scandals' of national prominence, a lengthy anti-convent campaign led from Parliament and periodic conflicts within their own congregations and with their own clergy over issues of authority. Most began in genuine poverty but succeeded in creating significant administrative and physical structures such as schools, orphanages, women's refuges, nursing homes and asylums. Beyond this, they laid down the organisation and finances for the large-scale building and missionary projects undertaken by later generations. Some aspects of their history reflect the ways that Catholic culture was set apart and different from the rest of society, but in other ways the endeavours undertaken by religious sisters were characteristic of Victorian institution-building and Victorian social reform movements. Themes of risk-taking, innovation, leadership and institution-building in a context of poverty characterise this first phase, as does the international mix of congregations and sisters and the importance of French models and customs.

The establishment of the English hierarchy in 1850 greatly accelerated but did not initiate the advent of convents throughout the country. Even before Catholic Emancipation in 1829, there were a small number scattered through the countryside. Apart from the exceptional Bar Convent in York, founded by Mary Ward's Institute of the Blessed Virgin Mary in 1686, and its sister convent in Hammersmith, London (which did not survive into the nineteenth century),[28] the first convents in England after the Reformation were English communities of enclosed nuns whose houses had been founded on the Continent from the late sixteenth century onwards and who had been allowed by the British government to settle in England when they were threatened with persecution at the time of the French Revolution.[29] The English convents of Benedictines, Poor Clares, Dominicans, Carmelites, Teresians and Canonesses settled in England with the aid of the Catholic gentry families whose sisters and daughters had for generations filled their choir-stalls.[30] Although the presence of convents of contemplative nuns and convent schools in places such as Winchester and Chelmsford marked a significant break with post-Reformation history and made a difference to a small section of the community, their migration did little to bring the English Catholic community into line with developments in the active religious life for women innovated on the Continent during the previous century and a half and reinvigorated after the French Revolution.

A movement to adopt the modern type of religious life and adapt it to English circumstances started fitfully in the 1830s, quickened in pace during the 1840s and achieved real momentum during the 1850s. Two complementary forces made this possible: one was the new status of Catholicism and of the clergy which began with emancipation and continued with the establishment of the hierarchy, and the other was the commitment and zeal of Catholic women in France, Belgium, Ireland and England.[31] Clerical leaders, freed from the prohibitions of the penal laws but now facing the impact of industrial urbanisation and the impact of Irish immigration, energetically set about establishing an infrastructure of dioceses, seminaries, parishes, schools and Catholic institutions. Familiar with the scores of religious congregations founded in France and Belgium[32] and with the rapid growth in the number of sisters in Ireland,[33] the clergy and leading members of the Catholic laity accepted without question or debate that apostolic religious sisters would be essential to the process of creating a missionary and fully functioning national Catholic Church. It seemed obvious to them that they should ask for help from the existing congregations.

Bishops, priests and laity who petitioned superiors to send sisters from France and elsewhere usually met with a favourable response. Leaders such as Sophie Barat (Sacred Heart), Euphrasie Pelletier (Good Shepherd) and Catherine McAuley (Mercy) recognised the spiritual and welfare needs of England's predominantly working-class Catholic community and they were further advised by women from England who entered their congregations. Already committed to working on an international scale, they believed England to be fruitful missionary territory on its own account and a practical route into other English-speaking countries. First to respond was Madeleine D'Houet, foundress of the Faithful Companions of Jesus, who sent sisters to Somers Town (London) as early as 1830, followed by the Irish Presentation Nuns sent to Manchester (1836). For London, the Sisters of Mercy came to Bermondsey from Cork (1839), the Good Shepherd nuns to Hammersmith from Angers in France (1841), the Society of the Sacred Heart from Paris to Roehampton after a short stay at Berrymead (1842). Sisters of Providence came to Loughborough from Italy (1843), Sisters of Notre Dame de Namur to Penryn in Cornwall (1845) and Daughters of the Heart of Mary from Paris to London (1846). Starting with the Sisters of the Assumption who went from Paris to Richmond in Yorkshire in 1850, the 1850s and every decade thereafter saw congregations arriving with great regularity.[34]

As a result of concerted efforts from both sides of the channel the Francophone influence on English convent history – and thereby on English Catholicism – was considerable. By 1887 thirty-two of the sixty-two apostolic congregations working in England had come from France, with a further five from Belgium. In addition to the sheer variety and range of their Catholic social action, the French congregations brought to an inexperienced English Catholic culture an expertise in the practice of religious life which could not otherwise have been achieved with such ease and rapidity. Through the training they gave to the founders of new congregations in Ireland and England and through their own direct involvement in England, the customs, disciplines and devotions practised in these congregations were an important component of English Catholicism. From matters organisational, such as the ordering of novitiates and the keeping of records, to matters devotional and spiritual, such as the training of sodality members, the catechising of children and adults, the decoration of altars and the manner of keeping feasts, they established standards and patterns which were all the more powerful in the context of the relatively open and rapidly developing Catholic culture of England.[35] During the 1850s and 1860s, in their schools, sodalities, sewing circles, orphanages and other residential homes, these congregations created a physical environment and an atmosphere which had not been previously available to ordinary Catholics.

To these 'imported' congregations were added the first new congregations to be founded on English soil since the Reformation.[36] In all, twelve surviving new foundations of apostolic sisters were made in England between 1840 and 1880 and three more were added by 1900. A further congregation, the Sisters of Charity of St Paul the Apostle, which had begun its work at Banbury in Oxfordshire in 1847 as a branch of the Chartres mother-house, was given papal approval in 1864 to become an English congregation independent of Chartres and to be governed by an elected sister Superior General.[37] The group of English foundations was almost evenly divided between congregations of Third Order Dominicans and Franciscans on the one hand and congregations of the new type with centralised government. Some remained small while others developed an international dimension and grew quite rapidly. (See the table of Congregations of Sisters founded in England 1845–95 on p. 116.)

Two general characteristics of the English founders and foundations are worth noting for their own sake and for what they reveal about the English Catholic community more generally, the first being the striking number of foundations made by converts to Catholicism. Converts to Catholicism made a major contribution to the formation of Catholic bodies in nineteenth-century England in general and particularly to the founding of women's congregations. The daughters of 'old Catholic' or recusant gentry families had founded the post-Reformation continental English convents and in the nineteenth century many became nuns and sisters in congregations such as the Daughters of Charity of St Vincent de Paul, the Religious of the Sacred Heart and in the enclosed orders, but few entered any of the modern 'native' English foundations and none became the foundress of one. Instead the English foundresses were, generally speaking, women whose individual and family faith histories were complex and had involved a significant level of spiritual and religious change. Seven had been baptised and confirmed as Anglicans, another as an Irish Episcopalian and a further one, Cornelia Connelly, was brought up a Presbyterian, and baptised in the Episcopalian Church of the USA in her early twenties before becoming a Roman Catholic a few years later. Many of them had experienced life in other religious congregations before making a new foundation and three had lived for varying periods as sisters in one of the new Anglican sisterhoods.[38]

A second striking feature of new English foundations was their strong drive to create more opportunities for working-class women to enter the religious life and, moreover, to do so in capacities other than as lay-sisters undertaking domestic service. As Bishop Turner of Salford wrote in support of the fledgling Cross and Passion community:

Year*	Name of congregation	Place	Founder	Religious upbringing
1845	Dominican Third Order Congregation of St Catherine of Siena (Stone)	Coventry	Margaret Hallahan	Roman Catholic
1846	Society of the Holy Child Jesus	Derby	Cornelia Connelly	Presbyterian, then US Episcopalian
1851	Poor Sisters of Nazareth	London Hammersmith	Victoire Lamenier	Roman Catholic
1852	Cross and Passion	Manchester	Elizabeth Prout	Anglican
1855	Dominican Third Order Congregation of St Rose of Lima	Stroud	Mary Teresa Matthews	Anglican
1859	Missionary Franciscan Sisters of the Immaculate Conception	Bayswater London	Elizabeth Lockhart	Anglican
1864	Sisters of Charity of St Paul the Apostle	Banbury	Geneviève Dupuis	Roman Catholic
+1866	Dominican Third Order Our Lady Help of Christians [authorised from Dominicans, Stroud]	Haverstock Hill, London	Rose Corbett	not known
1868	Franciscan Congregation of the Five Wounds	Hackney London	Mary Francis Basil	Anglican
1869	Poor Servants of the Mother of God	Fleet St London	Fanny Taylor	Anglican
1877	Little Company of Mary	Nottingham	Mary Potter	Roman Catholic
1877	Dominican Third Order Congregation of the Holy Rosary	Harrow	Catherine Bathurst	Anglican
1880	Franciscan Missionaries of St Joseph	Rochdale	Alice Ingham	Roman Catholic
1884	Sisters of St Joseph of Peace	Nottingham	Margaret Anna Cusack	Irish Episcopalian
1888	Franciscan Sister Minoresses	Soho	Margaret Murphy	Roman Catholic
1895	Franciscan Missionary Sisters of Littlehampton [from FM of St Joseph]	Hampstead	Margaret Manning	Anglican

+ Never became a separate congregation with its own constitutions, but had several daughter houses before joining with all the other Dominican houses listed as a part of the Dominican Sisters of the English Congregation of St Catherine of Siena, taking the Stone Constitutions (1929).

* Dates given for foundation can vary, sometimes being taken from the date of first vows and sometimes slightly later. Dates given here are taken from internal congregation sources.

> Its object was to afford pious and industrious young females an opportunity of embracing a state of religious perfection to which many of the humbler classes aspire without having the means of obtaining the object of their pious wishes. The purpose for which it was established has realised our expectations.[39]

By 1912 this congregation was asking for a dowry or teaching qualification but in its early phase it enabled millworkers, former domestic servants and needlewomen to enter and, in some cases, to become teachers. One of its postulants was Alice Ingham, former millworker and shopkeeper who entered in 1865 but concluded that her vocation lay elsewhere. In 1871 Alice Ingham began a community in her home town of Rochdale which later became the Franciscan Missionaries of St Joseph. Her earliest companions were from the local industrial working class and by 1900 almost the entire number of postulants, about one hundred and fifty in all, had been drawn from this class, about one-third of them having been millworkers. As Franciscan Missionaries these women of little formal education held responsible positions, went to Borneo as missionaries and became highly respected in their congregations for their hard work, spiritual advice and practical intelligence.[40]

Some of the orientation of the English foundations reflected the social origins of the foundress who, as in the case of Margaret Hallahan, Elizabeth Prout, Alice Ingham and Margaret Murphy, was herself a member of the skilled or unskilled working classes. But it was matched by others, like Fanny Taylor, the daughter of an Anglican rector, who recognised that the economic facts of life conspired to limit the opportunities for women of the poorest classes to live the religious life. One of Fanny Taylor's primary concerns, when making her foundation, had been to find a way for a community of poor women to support itself and still conduct its works of charity and mercy. After thorough research she concluded that 'a laundry [was] the only sure means of support' and took the congregation into the commercial laundry business.[41] So completely did she realise her original intentions that by 1900 almost all of the congregation's 500 postulants had come from poor rural Irish homes and the congregation was able to operate five convents in Ireland, one each in Rome and Paris and eleven in England.[42]

By 1880 the English, Irish and Francophone congregations were not only affording the opportunity for thousands of women to 'embrace a state of religious perfection' but also providing a considerable range of educational and social services to the Catholic community and to others. They had not reached this position without encountering difficulties. Risks had been taken: Superior Generals abroad sent groups of sisters into almost unknown settings, often not able to speak English and, during the 1840s and 1850s, unable to wear their religious habits in public.[43] Individuals often risked much more. Cornelia Connelly, for example, was not only an American citizen who accepted the recommendation of Nicholas Wiseman, then Rector of the English College in Rome, that she should make the first totally new foundation in England, but she was also a wife and mother who trusted her own reputation and the well-being of her children to God, the Church and her canonically separated husband.[44] Although hers was a dramatic overturning of social norms, other conventions were set aside by bishops and superiors during this early phase. Many superiors, for example, were extremely youthful: Mother Mary Clare, Superior of the Cork convent of the Sisters of Mercy, was sent to England in 1839 as their first Superior in England when she was in her mid-twenties, the same age at which Sr Helen Down was put in charge of the first group of youthful sister missionaries from the Franciscan Missionaries of St Joseph to Borneo. Such initiatives did not always have happy results, as the detailed investigation of the Great Convent Scandal involving the Mercy sisters in Hull has shown.[45] But overall, the new congregations succeeded because by taking some risks they were able to attract other women to share in their 'holy adventures'. In the case of the new congregations members might, for example, have to take private vows in experimental communities which had no formal status. In international congregations they had to be willing to go wherever they were required, often beginning with a novitiate in France or Belgium.

Little of this commitment could be taken for granted in early Victorian Britain, even given the large numbers of Irish vocations,[46] for the culture did not provide support for the nuns' way of life. On the contrary, there was widespread publicly voiced hostility to the vows of obedience and celibacy and the removal of women from the family. The anti-convent dimension of the larger mid-Victorian Protestant–Catholic rivalry manifested itself on occasion during the 1840s and 1850s in physical attacks on convents and sisters and, from 1851 to the mid-1870s, in a parliamentary campaign for government inspection of convents in the name of protecting 'helpless women'.[47] Protracted though this campaign was, and significant for what it symbolised, it did not have a major impact on the spread of convents or the attractiveness of the life to aspirants.

Historians have tended to focus on these threats from outside the Catholic community, but in reality they were of less significance to the security of congregations than the challenges from within during this formative period. As Margaret Thompson concluded from her own extensive researches into American congregations, 'The most pervasive pattern I encountered within women's religious orders was that of *conflict*.' She classifies these conflicts as of two main kinds: disputes among sisters and gender-defined confrontations between women and men. 'Incidents of this [latter] sort were more common than those involving only nuns; indeed, they occurred without exception in every one of the approximately 175 communities on which I have done any research.'[48] Tensions between benefactors and sisters, or between a local priest and the convent over its conduct and management, were not infrequent. For the new English foundations conflicts over the control and direction of embryonic communities, some of which occurred between senior members of the congregation and others between the foundress and a priest or bishop, could be serious. Cornelia Connelly faced a challenge to her authority (including the unauthorised expenditure of a large sum of money) from one of her most valued members who was also a personal friend of influential Catholics, including John Henry Newman. The departure of this sister caused considerable further difficulties.[49] In the case of Alice Ingham's struggling community, her hard-taken decision to move from Rochdale to Mill Hill, London, and take on the domestic work for the Mill Hill Fathers, in part to gain formal approval for her community's work, split her community.[50] But the most severe tests for any congregation were those between bishops and superiors over the constitutions and rule. Mary Potter was given valuable support by Bishop Bagshawe of Nottingham but

> he was convinced that the community needed his guidance and made sure that obedience to the diocesan was part of the rule. He went so far as to dismiss Potter as the superior . . . She gained permission to go to Rome and stated, 'Who was it went out with a sling? I feel like that going to Rome. I must rely on God.'[51]

Another foundress who made a personal visit to Rome about constitutions was Geneviève Dupuis, who needed approval for separation from her French motherhouse at Chartres in order to create a fresh foundation in England. Her own wish was for an institute of Pontifical Rite with its vesting of authority in a Superior General elected by General Chapter: the wish of her bishop and supporter, Bishop William Ullathorne, was for an institute overseen by himself as Bishop of Birmingham with other bishops having the role of superior of any house in their dioceses. Although Rome's ruling included 'prohibition to nominate any father superior', the issue was taken up again in 1888 by Ullathorne's successor Bishop Ilsley, and he and Mother Dupuis remained locked in conflict over questions of authority and government until she died in 1903.[52]

While such matters absorbed significant amounts of time and energy and caused suffering,[53] they did not altogether prevent the development of any of the congregations. Nor were initiatives stopped by the undoubted financial hardship so commonly experienced in opening a new house during this period. Foundations were often begun in the kind of poverty described by Mary Potter, foundress of the Little Company of Mary:

> Here at Hyson Green I was wandering alone, then sleeping in an old dilapidated place in the midst of mortar and rubbish of all kinds, with doors that would not fasten. I remember putting a pickaxe against the door to fasten it. In working for God you must not look for personal comfort.[54]

An authoritative study of convent finances is overdue, but there are indications that initial pump-priming funding often came from benefactors among the established Catholic families such as the Norfolks, Petres, Arundells, Dalkeiths, Towneleys and Cliffords,[55] and there were occasional gifts from mother-houses outside England to the English missions and in some cases the dowry of a wealthy member.[56] Regular and reliable income came from government subsidies to Roman Catholic schools for teacher salaries and the income earned by sisters who taught in fee-paying schools or ran laundries, to which was added a stream of small gifts in money and in kind from the less wealthy. The impression gained from all the evidence is of a highly efficient financial operation in which little was expended on the sisters' costs and a high proportion was reinvested in their mission and activities.

The range of activities undertaken by sisters were well established by 1880 but were not static. New ideas for Catholic institutions involving religious sisters, such as the Catholic Children's Rescue and Protection Society established by Bishop Herbert Vaughan of Salford in 1886, were regularly introduced.[57] The main works were: crèches, schools (state elementary and private convent schools), industrial schools and teacher education; retreat work, catechetics and religious instruction; hospital, prison and parish visiting and welfare support in working-class districts; homes for orphans or children unable to be supported by their families, the physically handicapped and the elderly; women's refuges, reformatories and hostels for working-class young women; and, to a lesser extent, dispensaries, home nursing, convalescent homes and hospitals. Some congregations had a specialised field of activity, such as the Good Shepherd nuns in 'rescue' work, the Augustinian Sisters of Bruges who nursed mentally ill women, and the Little Sisters of the Poor with their homes for the indigent elderly, while a number specialised in education. Most, however, had a cluster of activities which crossed welfare work and elementary teaching. Of all these missions education dominated. Sr Mary Linscott, historian of the Sisters of Notre Dame, notes that after the Education Act of 1870 'the great drive led by the Bishop of Salford and the Voluntary Schools Association raised the number of Catholic elementary schools from 350 to 1066 in thirty years', of which the Notre Dame share was a further twenty-three schools.[58] Such was the emphasis placed on the establishment of Catholic elementary education by the hierarchy that even congregations not created for this work found themselves being pressed into it. The Little Company of Mary, for example, although founded to be present with the dying, immediately 'at the insistence of the Bishop, gathered the children together and began a school',[59] and the Poor Servants of the Mother of God soon found themselves teaching in elementary schools. Sisters conducted elementary schools across the country. The same was true of private convent schools. 'Very probably the Church in England had, in proportion to the number of Catholics, more convent schools than the Church in any other part of the world',[60] which met a wider demand from outside the Catholic community for the formation as well as the education of young women.

A number of the 'apostolates' established by sisters paralleled the new professions for women which themselves had emerged from the philanthropic and charitable activities previously undertaken voluntarily and on a smaller scale by the leisured classes. Although it is not yet a part of the historical literature on the subject, a case needs to be made for the significant contribution that Roman Catholic religious congregations made to the training of women for public life, bringing expertise from other countries to England during the middle decades of the nineteenth century and finding in the Catholic Church an extensive sphere of operation. This was certainly Florence Nightingale's view as expressed in her correspondence with the newly converted Henry Manning:

> You do know now what a home the Catholic Church is. And what is she to you compared with what she would be to me? No one can tell, no man can tell, what she is to women, their training, their discipline, their hopes, their home . . . For what training is there compared to that of the Catholic nun? . . . I have seen something of different kinds of nuns, am no longer young and do not speak from enthusiasm but from experience. There is nothing like the training (in these days) which the Sacred Heart or the Order of Saint Vincent gives to women.[61]

There are echoes of the same response in the writings of contemporary Christian feminists such as Bessie Belloc and Anna Jameson.[62] Evidence to support Nightingale's personal conviction can be found across the congregations, but a few examples will have to serve as illustrative of the more general point.

The Sisters of Notre Dame de Namur, whose teacher training college opened at Mount Pleasant in Liverpool in 1856 under the principalship of Frances Lescher (Sr Mary of St Philip), were acknowledged by government inspectors and teacher educators in Britain and elsewhere as leaders in the fields of initial and in-service education for teachers. The congregation had been founded by Julie Billiart for education, especially the education of girls regardless of social class. It had rapidly seen the importance of teacher education and had fifty years' experience of training teachers before the college in Liverpool was opened. Mère Julie's approach, represented in maxims such as, 'You must teach them to think. If they simply memorise and repeat, they will never understand what they are doing', underpinned the classroom methodologies taught at Mount Pleasant and it was well known that the training given at Mount Pleasant was different from that in other colleges, meeting the requirements of the official Codes without being constrained by them.[63] Student results, measured in terms of the government's examinations, 'were unparalleled in the history of Training Colleges'[64] but the sisters offered a far broader curriculum and philosophy than was required for national certification.[65] For more than twenty years Mount

Pleasant was the sole provider of female Catholic teacher education in Britain, training almost all those who went on to headships and many who later held positions of responsibility in other religious congregations.

In the care of the elderly poor the Little Sisters of the Poor created an environment and type of provision which struck many English contemporaries as novel and beneficial.[66] Similarly, the Little Sisters of the Assumption worked with those who could not afford to pay, disregarded religious affiliation and adopted what would later be called 'a holistic approach'. Founded to support working-class families affected by illness or recent childbirth, they were an early form of combined health and social services, offering poor families a mix of qualified home nursing, health visiting and home help services.[67] Some congregations, including the Religious of the Sacred Heart and the Poor Servants of the Mother of God, ran their own printing presses and trained sisters as compositors and printers. Among Benedictine nuns the learning of Latin and the revival of the monastic chant, which began in the late nineteenth century, required technical training and the establishment of new standards.[68] Religious sisters were by no means always professional or well trained for the works they undertook: several congregations, for example, launched themselves into parochial schools with no teacher training and little English. Others ran somewhat old-fashioned seminaries for young ladies, teaching a range of accomplishments in a family atmosphere, and there is much that we do not know about the standards and characteristics of all residential homes in this period. But until the 1890s many religious congregations can properly be described as in the vanguard of training and education for their own members and students and as leaders in the development of professional practices and standards for women.

By the 1890s the active religious life for women in England had already begun to move from a pioneering phase to one of consolidation. Patterns of recruiting sisters, for example, became settled and conventional, drawing strongly on Catholic schools,[69] and systems of support were better established. The Catholic community had come to expect the presence of sisters and the larger society had come to accept, with more or less grace, that convents and sisters were in England to stay.

CONSOLIDATION AT HOME AND MISSION OVERSEAS, 1900–1962

> I have been a nun, or rather, to use the correct term, a religious sister, for forty years. I am aware therefore that for half of my religious life I experienced the triumphalist, outwardly rock-like immobility of the pre-Vatican II Church, and loved it.[70] (Sr Prue Wilson RSCJ, 1984)

> I have been a member of a Roman Catholic religious community of inter-

> national dimension for over forty years. The first twenty-five years were happy active years, lived in the stable framework of a way of life that changed little from day to day and seemed geared to remaining so forever.[71]
> (Sr Ruth Duckworth SC, 1979)

For most committed Catholics coming to adulthood in Britain between 1910 and 1950 Catholicism had a timeless feel about it. Could it ever have been different? In fact, it had been very different in the nineteenth century but by the 1920s Catholics had successfully created their own institutional life, from cradle to grave, for body and soul, and had begun to forget that it had been otherwise. Between 1910 and 1950 lay the two world wars, a depression, and considerable upheaval in the political world ending with a bifurcation into communist and capitalist spheres of influence. All the more reason for the Church to make itself solid and sure, self-contained and at the same time missionary. For the time being the future held small adjustments, but there were no major changes foreseen or wanted by most Catholics. Religious sisters seem to have shared this world-view and their institutional life reflected it.[72] Perhaps it was inevitable, as a number of sociologists studying the religious life have concluded, that after a pioneering period there should follow one of regularisation and greater conformity.[73]

If consolidation was inevitable, sociologically speaking, the tendency was given considerable impetus by the conservative anti-Modernist movement in the Church whose most powerful expression in relation to sisters and nuns was the new Code of Canon Law of 1918. Some aspects of the Code were anticipated in 1900 with the constitution *Conditae a Christo* and in the *Normae* of the following year. This legislation recognised sisters under simple vows as 'real religious' for the first time, thus removing the ambiguity which had existed for more than two centuries. At the same time it created a rigorous and more uniform system for granting official approval to new congregations, and spelt out the rights of bishops and the rights and duties of superiors. Although the ambiguity had caused some difficulties in the nineteenth century it had also created the room for experiments and innovations to take place and much of this capacity was lost once the newly classified congregations came within the orbit of the new Code of Canon Law. The Code's rejection of Modernism can be seen in its implicit rejection of the attitudes and goals of the contemporary women's rights movement and the explicit regulations and control mechanisms:

> Specifically, regulations governing cloister (enclosure) became obligatory, which meant that even on the most active orders a degree of enclosure was imposed . . . This made the apostolic orders less able to respond to the needs of the world . . . canonical hours laid down a detailed prescription of the manner and content of prayer . . . Among the tasks now deemed unsuitable

> for nuns were the care of babies, the nursing of maternity cases and the staffing of co-educational schools.[74]

All of this was regulated through a quinquennial report comprising the answers to 105 questions to be completed by the superior, signed by her councillors and the bishop and submitted to Rome. 'Underlying the precise provisions of the canonical code was a new stress on centralism, rigid hierarchy and distinct channels of obedience . . . One consequence of this was the further elevation of the Mother Superior.'[75] It is likely that the Vatican was acting to ensure that some of the more anarchic moments of the past would not be repeated in the future, and also to be consistent in its regulation of women accorded the status of religious. That it did so at the height of its anxiety about Modernism had a powerful impact. In her study of women religious, Sara Maitland concludes that the legislation 'had a major effect on the way their [sisters'] history has developed', limiting their freedom to act from the inside out and increasing any tendencies towards deference and conformity.[76]

It is within this theological, psychological and legal framework that we must set the experience of Sisters Ruth Duckworth and Prue Wilson and countless other sisters who, with hindsight, acknowledge the truth of Maitland's analysis but who also experienced the 1930s, 1940s, and even 1950s as stable, confident and full of activity for the congregations.[77] These features were most manifest in the steady and sizeable flow of well-catechised Catholic young women into novitiates, the construction or adaptation of impressive buildings and the growth of Catholic institutional provision staffed by sisters. They could also be seen in the absence of internal and external conflict and the slowing down in the number of new foundations made. There were signs of a continuing inspiration for innovation, but less powerfully than previously and less significant than the trend to stability in matters of government, finances and mission. During this period three other trends were significant for the overall direction of the religious life. First, the very strong thrust to missionary activity outside Europe and the English-speaking world, which was important to both active congregations and contemplative orders. Second, the engagement with public authorities as the state itself became increasingly involved in education and welfare provision. Third, there was renewed vigour in the contemplative life, which showed itself most visibly in the foundation of new Carmels through the inspiration of Mother Mary of Jesus, but which was also seen in the completion of the liturgical revival in Benedictine communities under the guidance of Dame Laurentia McLachlan of Stanbrook Abbey. All three trends originated at the end of the nineteenth century but had their fullest and most characteristic expression after 1900 and meant religious lives spent fully engaged in a wide range of works and spiritual activities.

Lives like that of Margaret Thornton, Religious of the Sacred Heart, who entered in 1917, a few months after leaving the Sacred Heart school at Roehampton where she had gained the *Prix d'Excellence*. She began teaching in 1920 at the congregation's school in Hammersmith and while teaching full-time achieved a first-class degree in geography as a London University external student followed by a PhD in sociology. During the 1920s and 1930s Mother Thornton moved between school-teaching and teacher-training, diligently preparing herself from 1933 to 1937 to become a founder member of a new Sacred Heart college planned for Bombay. Instead, she found herself posted to Shanghai in China in 1939 as professor and Dean of Studies at Aurora University, a Jesuit university recognised by the Chinese authorities. Here she worked for fifteen years through war, Japanese occupation and internment by the Japanese army, staying on until expelled by the Chinese Communist government. In the meantime she learned spoken Cantonese and Mandarin. As a Communist victory became inevitable she and Father Aidan McGrath, a Columban missionary priest, laid plans for the Legion of Mary to be the active force for Catholicism in Communist China. Her practical contribution was the creation of a cadre of girls and women who could sustain the faith under suppression. In 1952 Mother Thornton was the last Sacred Heart sister to leave Shanghai, arriving in Hong Kong to a gala reception. On her way home to Britain she wrote:

> I have been having an unforgettable time these months – a few obvious disadvantages of course, but I would not for the world have missed our Chinese Catholic youth standing up to the Communists, calling their bluff when no one else dared resist and putting the whole fight into the open as a religious one. It was just like living in the early Church, everyone in the full supernatural and prepared for anything . . .[78]

After only a short period back in Britain and the United States, Mother Thornton took up a new post lecturing at the University of the Sacred Heart in Tokyo where among her hundreds of students was included Michiko, later Crown Princess of Japan. Her final task in the Far East, begun in 1963 at the age of 65, was to supervise the physical and intellectual construction of the congregation's new college for women in Seoul, South Korea and 'on retirement' to become executive secretary of the Korean Association of Voluntary Agencies. Not all religious lives could be lived so heroically, but Mother Thornton's is none the less emblematic of the period in its institutional security and strength, its purposefully directed activism, missionary effort, engagement with civic authorities and its professional work for girls and women. (Emblematic of religious life in this period too was her own very extensive and firmly committed family, which included three Sacred Heart nieces and two Benedictine nephews.) It is worth exploring each of these features in a little more detail for religious congregations as a whole.

Institutional security and strength is most obviously measured in the size of the congregations, the scale of their operations and the growth of formal buildings.

For many (although not all) of the congregations established in the nineteenth century, the 1920s and 1930s witnessed the peak for both total size of membership and new recruits to the congregation: 1938 was the peak year for the Sisters of Charity of St Paul, for example, with 708 members in the English province,[79] and that for the Faithful Companions of Jesus was a little earlier in 1925,[80] while the peak decade for recruitment to the Sisters of Notre Dame with 242 new entrants was the 1930s[81] and both decades between 1910 and 1930 saw the Sisters of the Cross and Passion admit about 160 to their novitiate, a significantly higher intake than the decades before and after.[82] In its centennial history, the Franciscan Missionaries of St Joseph describe the novitiate as 'bursting at the seams' between 1926 and 1933, when it was moved to somewhere larger.[83]

After 1900 congregations opened houses to fill the remaining spaces in the nation's conventual map: on the south coast and in the South-West during the first decade of the century (where many convents from France took refuge following the 1904 religious laws), and in East Anglia during the 1920s. Physical building and the establishment of new organisations and institutions followed the steady expansion. It was after the First World War that many congregations constructed or adapted imposing buildings to serve as novitiates and provincial houses, in part because of their own needs but at a pace created by the requirements of the new Canon Law. In 1920, Notre Dame, for example, bought and adapted a very large house on the edge of Ashdown Forest in Sussex and continued to develop this magnificent building and estate until moving to a much smaller novitiate in Wigan in 1969. Other new imposing buildings established in the first half of the twentieth century included teacher training colleges,[84] houses of study in London, Oxford and Cambridge for sisters and other Catholic women studying for degrees,[85] convalescent homes and hospitals,[86] and children's homes. The cost of these initiatives could be considerable and was often borne by the congregations themselves, like the construction of St Paul's School for Girls in Edgbaston, Birmingham, to which the Sisters of St Paul contributed £12,000 against £279 from other donors.[87]

In a number of ways, however, even this level of activity at home was eclipsed by the effort and achievements of missionary activity overseas. Missionary work exerted a considerable appeal to religious sisters, active and contemplative, being given an extra impetus by Popes Benedict XV (*Maximum Illud*, 1919) and Pius XI (*Rerum Ecclesia*, 1926). A significant number of new congregations were founded specifically for missionary work[88] while most existing congregations added the missions to their existing works. In some cases they put a considerable strain on their resources to meet the new demands: the Religious of the Sacred Heart, for example, staffed 141 houses worldwide in 1915 from a total of 6,444 religious, but in 1946 only a marginally larger number (6,570) staffed 179 houses.[89] On a smaller scale but with as much impact on their own community, the Ursulines of the Greenwich community sent one sister to Cuba, one to Thailand, another each to Brazil, Naxos, South Africa and Soweto before 1945, and the Carmel at Darlington sent out a group of experienced nuns to make a foundation at Johannesburg in 1931. The Society of the Holy Child opened its first mission in Africa – in Nigeria – in 1930 and, like so many congregations, set in motion a dynamic which is still working its way through the congregation, religious life and the Church at the end of the century. Here is an aspect of the history of women's congregations which remains to be researched and which will make a significant contribution to our understanding of the congregations themselves, to the history of Christian missions and to the history of the localities in which they operated.[90]

Setting aside the effects and impact of missionary activities on indigenous populations, the 'missions' enabled many women from England, like Margaret Thornton, to act with their eyes focused rather more on gospel imperatives than those of Canon Law and to remain at the cutting edge of the Church's work. The missions, moreover, proved to be the psychological space within which the Church at large could move beyond some of its self-imposed gender constraints. This was most strikingly the case in respect of medical work, which can serve as illustrative of the general point. In earlier centuries religious sisters had pioneered nursing and health-care work. Just at the point when women were entering the medical service as trained midwives and doctors, the Catholic Church legislated against religious sisters practising as midwives, made other nursing practice more difficult and ruled out the concept of a sister-doctor. A wedge was successfully driven into this position primarily with the needs of 'mission countries' in mind. The pioneer was Dr Agnes McLaren, a Scottish Catholic doctor, friend and fellow campaigner for women's rights with Sophia Jex-Blake and Josephine Butler, who founded St Catherine's hospital for women and children in Rawalpindi in India and travelled to Rome five times 'trying to obtain permission for religious women to practise medicine expressly so that they could go to India'.[91] After her death her vision was taken up by an Austrian doctor, Anna Dengel, who was practising medicine in Derbyshire and went to work in St Catherine's. She undertook a 'holy experiment' when in 1925 she established the Society of Catholic Medical Missionaries within which medically qualified women took a public mission vow and private religious vows. Dengel (and her clerical supporters) continued to pursue the goal of full congregational status for her Society (which also meant Vatican recognition of sister-doctors). In 1936 the Sacred Congregation of *Propaganda Fide* 'issued an instruction encouraging religious women to study and practise medicine in its full scope',[92] and in 1941 the Society of Catholic Medical Missionaries became a congregation with public vows. Others, such as the Franciscan Missionaries of the Divine Motherhood, entered the medical field and the number of sister-midwives in particular grew significantly. Health care for women and children, as McLaren and Dengel had predicted, became one of the primary contributions of religious sisters to developing countries.

The professionalism of such sisters and their necessary engagement with the public authorities was a significant feature of this period. As the educational and welfare state grew in organisational reach and formality, so the apostolates of religious congregations had to respond to state and public requirements. As sister-historian Dr Mary Linscott put it, 'The period of self-sufficiency was over',[93] or, in the words of Hope Stone, another historian of religious life, 'They began by giving charitable assistance to the poor, then became professionally committed as they met government qualifications.' In education, the 1902 Balfour Act added to the impact of the 1870 Forster Act, leading to the movement for grant-aided publicly inspected Catholic high schools to follow the publicly funded and inspected elementary schools. In addition to gaining qualified teacher status, some sisters began to take university degrees from the first years of the twentieth century and others to qualify formally through professional bodies for welfare and medical work. With new confidence and a firmer place in the larger society, congregations established a range of organisations to improve their co-ordination, public accountability and lobbying strength, such as the Association of Convent Schools (1928) and the Annual Conference of Catholic Colleges. The trend was towards public inspection of all Catholic welfare and charitable enterprises and for the congregations to work with the state in much of its provision for the less well off. For the moment this did not give rise to many questions. Nuns were still fulfilling apostolates which were distinctive, in part because their work was embedded within Catholic organisations, more often than not directed and owned by the congregations, but also because before the 1960s they were also still undertaking professional social and educational works which other Catholic women either did not undertake at all, or only for a short period before marriage and motherhood.

If active sisters retained a strong sense of their distinctiveness in this period against a backcloth of increasing integration with public service standards and norms, neither the general public nor nuns themselves had any questions about the distinctiveness of contemplative orders. It remains to be explored and explained why there was a revitalisation of the contemplative life in the period and to plot its timing more precisely. For the Benedictines at Stanbrook it may have come from the glory of the restored chant and the vigour of life in the choir which made its own compelling case to so many (relatively speaking) young women, including a high proportion of intellectual and well-qualified women. However, a different explanation is needed for the remarkable expansion of the Carmelite Order, thirty-three houses being founded between 1907 and 1940, twenty-five of which were established after the First World War. The human dynamic in this expansion was Mother Mary of the Blessed Trinity (Thompson) who founded the Carmel in Notting Hill (1878) from which all the later foundations came. Some connection between the devastating human and spiritual impact of the Great War and this movement seems likely (as it does for the growth in the contemplative life for men after the Second World War).

By the 1950s, the perspicacious inside the Church and its religious congregations were beginning to sense that the era of growth, stability and certainty of purpose was about to change. Cardinal Suenens's penetrating analysis, *The Nun in the World* (1962), voiced concerns which were in anticipation of the Second Vatican Council but did not spring unheralded. At a time of continued large-scale institutional operation and, for many congregations, healthy recruitment, his sounding of warning notes must have seemed strange – but proved to be prophetic:

> We no longer live in an age where daily lives were solidly framed in tradition, and institutions were there to safeguard values that were never called in question. On all sides tradition is foundering and conformism falling into ruins . . . Our planet has seen more revolutionary development in the last quarter century than in all the preceding nineteen . . . And that, whether we like it or not, is how we stand today.[94]

Amidst all this change, he argued, religious sisters had remained cut off from the world around them and were now lagging behind 'the general evolution of women'.[95]

SINCE VATICAN II

> I lived through the irruption into Vatican II of the unseen inward turmoil of the Church and by it was shaken out of my complacency. Finally, I am still here, observing with misgiving the conservatism which is again taking us over both inside and outside the Church. (Prue Wilson RSCJ, 1984)[96]

> The last fifteen years have seen changes so radical and so far-reaching that [the past] . . . seems to belong to another age . . . (Ruth Duckworth SC, 1979)[97]

The Catholic community in general, the religious sisters themselves, and other interested observers seem to agree that nuns – particularly nuns in English-speaking countries – have changed more since the Second Vatican Council than any other distinct group in the Church.[98] There is much less agreement about the value and appropriateness of the changes. Nevertheless, the readiness of the sisters themselves to engage in public discussion of their life and in public debate on the nature of the Church has been one of the distinctive features of religious life during the last thirty years. Other participants reflecting on the religious life for women have included Vatican officials, secular clergy and male religious, academics and journalists. Between them they have produced Vatican documents, doctoral theses and books on the theology, sociology, anthropology and psychology of contemporary religious life, personal reflections and autobiographical writing, essays published in religious journals, articles in the religious weekly press, and the proceedings of symposia and conferences.[99] In general, the literature has emphasised three related influences for change in religious life during this period: the theology of the Second Vatican Council; the changed nature of gender relations and thinking about gender in society at large; and the radically changed demography of membership of the religious congregations in the developed world.

Membership in the late twentieth century has been diminishing and the congregations ageing. Where many congregations had admitted cohorts of between ten and twenty postulants annually between 1910 and 1960, the number dropped sharply into single figures in the 1960s and then continued to fall for the next two decades until the annual number of postulants might be nil, or only one or two. In 1989 the total number of new women entrants to the active religious life in England and Wales across all congregations (of which there were about 300), was thirty-one and that to the contemplative life across all orders was twenty.[100] For Ireland in the same year, the total figure had dropped to seventy-five.[101] Traditional novitiates became unviable and the role of novice mistress had to be re-thought, leading the Conference of Major Religious Superiors to establish a permanent Vocations Centre in 1979 'to co-ordinate the work of religious vocations promoters in England and Wales'.[102] Over the three decades from the mid-1960s the drop in recruitment has inevitably reduced the size of each congregation. According to a newspaper report at the start of 1996, the total number of nuns and monks in England and Wales had fallen by a third during the previous decade, from some 15,000 to 10,000.[103] This was mirrored, with some differences, in the individual congregations.[104] Perhaps even more significantly, the drop in recruitment has led to a steadily rising age profile, a situation compounded by the departure of a significant number of sisters in their twenties, thirties and forties who left in the ten years after Vatican II.[105] During the 1980s and 1990s the leaders of congregations had to face the implications of their ageing communities: in 1995, for example, of the 338 sisters in the Sisters of Charity of St Paul the Apostle in Britain, only thirty-five were under the age of 50; of the 357 Sisters of Notre Dame more than 240 were over retiring age (many of them still very active).[106] Although precise figures are quite difficult to come by and are not always available in a disaggregated form, the overall direction and pace of the demographic change is indisputable.

Between 1965 and the early 1980s the dramatic demographic changes were working hand in hand with transformations in the thinking of the congregations about their mission and values. This thinking was undertaken in the context of Vatican II theology and ecclesiology, for the Council required and urged on all religious orders and congregations a 'constant return to the sources of all Christian life and to the original spirit of the institutes, and their adaptation to the changed conditions of our time'.[107] The 'return to sources', which often led women religious to the rediscovery of the radical nature of their foundations and early members, was grounded in two profound Council insights which run throughout the major documents. The first was that 'there is no case for the traditional view that religious life is "superior" to other forms of Christian living, to be protected from outside contamination by elaborate structures, regulations and distinctive life-styles'.[108] This the sisters drew from the document *Lumen Gentium* with its proclamation of the universal holiness of 'the People of God' rooted in the baptismal promises of all Christians.[109] The second insight lay in a new attitude towards 'the world': the Church regarding itself as a timeless entity separate from the world, which it saw as an ever-changing adversary, was transformed in the opening sentence of *Gaudium et Spes* into the Church as a community 'truly and intimately linked with mankind and its destiny'. The new thinking, developed further by the Synod of Bishops in 1971 with the document *Justice in the World*, was seen as having radical implications for religious sisters as they worked out its meanings for themselves.

In that spirit the religious congregations responded when, in obedience, they followed the Council's requirement to 'renew' themselves by rewriting their constitutions in the light of their own origins and the needs of the age, and to do so by consulting widely within the congregation and through Special General Chapters. What followed was a period described in all the sisters' accounts of it, formal and informal, as exhilarating and 'heady'. Sisters 'wrestled with concepts such as collegiality, availability, open church, subsidiarity, the option for the poor, through Chapters, Assemblies, meetings, discussions, lectures and questionnaires. Topics hitherto sacrosanct were held to the light and examined.'[110] In rewriting their Rules and Constitutions most congregations, inevitably, re-assessed their apostolate and their way of life. The outcomes were dramatic, often experimental and sometimes painful for individual sisters and the rest of the Catholic community.

After an initial phase of vigour and optimism, what followed in the 1970s was a period of demoralisation and unease as the difficulty of the tasks emerged. Congregations experienced the loss of many members and the public voiced doubts about the changes. The most visible signs to the rest of the community, and most often commented upon, were the experiments in modifying the habit and the gradual dismantling of the 'mystery of convent life'. Symbolic and internal changes (which also included removing the distinctions between 'lay' and 'choir' sisters where this division had existed) were accompanied by the dismantling of many of the institutional structures and services that the sisters had long provided to the community; instead they shifted their emphasis 'to respond to the social conditions in which life was being lived'.[111]

Outside observers saw the withdrawal of sisters from large-scale institutions and, above all, from private convent schooling as the consequence only of the reduction in numbers, but in fact it was derived from a combined effect: demographic change *and* the renewal process. During the 1980s, as the withdrawals took effect, the Catholic community often reacted strongly and critically to the loss of 'their sisters' from Catholic institutions, and particularly from convent schools. 'We did all we could to warn everyone and explain why the school would have to close because of the shortage of sisters,' wrote one sister later. 'Some parents said angrily "Why aren't there Sisters?" I answered "Have you done anything to encourage your daughters to think about religious life? Where do you think Sisters come from?" '[112] According to one newspaper report the number of sisters teaching in convent schools fell from 1,063 in 1974 to 300 in 1987.[113] By the end of the 1980s the traditional convent school was an institution of the past. The withdrawal of the sisters from such archetypal Catholic institutions had both real and symbolic significance and, when it occurred before numbers absolutely dictated it, demonstrated the determination of the sisters to 'renew'. 'It's not that we think education isn't important,' stated one Sacred Heart headmistress. 'In fact sisters in our order are still involved in state schools. We just feel the needs of the poor are greater';[114] and Sr Mary Quaine of the Sisters of Notre Dame represented many sisters during the 1980s in her view: 'we are no longer needed as nurses or teachers and we see our task now in a wider context . . . we must go where lay people cannot because of their family and financial commitments.'[115]

The decision about 'where to go', about where to put the commitment and energy of the congregation and of individual sisters, was no longer a semi-automatic, predictable matter. By the 1980s, and following the phase of exhilaration and then demoralisation, many congregations were developing sophisticated, realistic and more challenging processes for determining their future. As Sara Maitland discerned as early as 1983, 'the sense that the worst is over is clear among many nuns. The price has been paid, now there is work to be done.'[116] Two major trends can be perceived in apostolates adopted from this point onwards. The first was the movement into what can, broadly speaking, be seen as psychologically based activities such as spiritual direction, retreat-giving, counselling, and therapeutic work with individuals. The other was a movement into more challenging activities of a social and even political nature, by engaging once again with the most marginal groups and organisations: refugees and illegal immigrants, travellers, people with AIDS, alcoholics and very disadvantaged families in inner cities. Often these two trends came together in a particular new initiative, such as the Fireside Centre opened by the Sisters of Charity of St Paul the Apostle in central Birmingham for the homeless and needy,[117] the experimental Emmaus Community in Sunderland formed by two Jesuits, a Sister of St Joseph of Peace and a Daughter of Charity for 'non-church-based social ministries' in what is described as an 'unchurched area' of the town,[118] or The Sanctuary opened by the Little Company of Mary in Nottingham for alcoholics and their families, and their work in Cardiff supporting the terminally ill in their homes.[119]

All these changes tended to take the sisters out of large-scale institutions, and by the end of the twentieth century the shift from institution-based apostolates had become very marked. It was accompanied by a physical shift out of large-scale convent buildings into smaller houses, by many more individually negotiated apostolates, and by much greater collaboration between religious sisters and professionals and volunteers from outside their congregation. Thus the Sisters of Notre Dame between 1960 and 1990 bought some thirty smaller houses, and 'by 1990 there were only five houses with communities of more than twenty sisters, these mainly sick and elderly'.[120] Collaboration with others became normal: the Fireside Centre, for example, 'is a collaborative ministry with many volunteers, religious and lay, ecumenical and inter-faith in character',[121] while the Emmaus Community works with lay community associates, and the Little Company of Mary project had, by 1994, some one hundred volunteers working with the small group of sisters. Moreover, fewer sisters were conducting their works of charity and mercy *within* organisations controlled by their congregation and many more were working in, for instance, non-governmental organisations, ginger groups and charities and in chaplaincy services in state institutions. In some cases their role in such organisations was pivotal and pioneering. Sister Bridget Tighe, for example, a Franciscan Missionary of the Divine Motherhood and a trained midwife, spent most of her life as a sister working in primary health care in hospitals run by her congregation, including seventeen years in Jordan. During the late 1980s she took a theology degree at Cambridge University followed by an MSc in Social Administration at the London School of Economics and was expecting to return to health-care work when, in 1994, she was invited to apply for the post of first Principal of the Margaret Beaufort Institute of Theology in Cambridge, 'an innovative Catholic venture educating women in theology, spirituality and leadership in lay ministry in an ecumenical setting'.[122] When she accepted this post, Sr Bridget was employed by a Board whose members represented eleven different women's congregations and the four other Christian colleges of the Cambridge Theological Federation. Her own congregation, in supporting her acceptance of the post, had thus permitted a significant change of apostolate. It has been this kind of engagement, which they see as prophetic and pioneering and thus in keeping with their historic foundation, that many congregations have been seeking for their small number of active sisters. Little is understood at large, as yet, about the contributions being made by religious sisters to a wide range of organisations and the extent to which they are providing something distinctive or even unique as a result of their spiritual formation and commitment. Although this kind of presence is more difficult for the sociologist or historian to keep track of or even discover, what cannot be doubted is the strategic policy decision taken by congregations to work in this way and that the origins of the policy lie in their interpretation of the Second Vatican Council.

Equally, the renewed congregations' commitment to the developing world, which after the collapse of Soviet Communism included Eastern European countries, has been a marked trend. The congregations in England and Wales have not responded to shrinking numbers by withdrawing from such missionary situations but, on the contrary, have tended to concentrate a higher proportion of human and financial resources in them. It seems likely that the twenty-first century will see a renewal of the religious life for women in countries such as Albania, Poland and Romania as a result of the initiatives begun by congregations in the British and Irish provinces at the end of the twentieth century.[123] Meanwhile, in the earlier missionary countries of Africa and Latin America, the Far East and Indian subcontinent, a considerable effort has been made within religious congregations to transfer leadership and authority from western to indigenous sisters and to remove any barriers which limit the role that sisters from developing countries might play in the congregation worldwide. In 1996 the theologian Sr Teresa Okure reflected on this process as it had involved herself, as the first African sister of the Society of the Holy Child Jesus:

> As I see the growth in vocations in the Society today, where the former West African Vicariate has now become a full-fledged African Province, one which has already produced three African provincials and a general councillor, I feel that [God] has fulfilled the hope he gave me at the beginning. This hope was that I could become a means through which others would come to join the Society and in fact the Society has been greatly enriched, rejuvenated and renewed by its African members.[124]

The growth in the number of sisters outside of Europe, North America and Australia, referred to by Teresa Okure, is yet another element making an impact on the international congregations, by changing their membership in ways which lie beyond the scope of this chapter to discuss.

Influenced not only by demographic change and by Conciliar and post-Conciliar theology, religious sisters have also responded to the more generalised social dynamic offered by the women's movement and the radical shift in social perceptions about questions of gender relations. There are a number of reasons for their response, some of which derive from their own history as women's organisations run by and for women, and providing for the education and health care of girls and women. Also important is the influence that the culture of the USA, with its progressive and democratic impulses, has had on women religious in Europe, more particularly on English-speaking religious. Just as congregations and sisters in England in the nineteenth century were profoundly influenced from France, so in the late twentieth century they have been stimulated constantly from North America. Significant numbers of members and leaders of these international congregations are drawn from the United States, so that the North American no-nonsense approach to questions of equality, inclusiveness and power-sharing has undoubtedly had its impact.[125] Moreover, a considerable number of senior sisters from the British province have undertaken sabbatical study in the United States over the past thirty years. Writing about the Cross and Passion sisters in the British Province, Sister Anna Maria Reynolds paid tribute to the 'forward-looking stance of American women religious' which she noted 'had resulted in new ministries, spiritual and social'.[126] These new ministries have included challenging the Church itself about its own structures and behaviour in so far as they have inhibited what sisters see as the gospel imperative to equality and inclusiveness:

> Religious communities of women have given institutional outlet to the movement for the use of universal language in liturgy and church documents, the modelling of women as preachers of the Word and the question of women's ordination . . . The impact of all these activities lies less in the activities they generate than it does in the doubts they raise, both inside and outside of the institution.[127]

The President of the Conference of Religious of England and Wales, for example, sent a letter on behalf of Conference members to the Hierarchy and all religious in 1994 concerning the language in the liturgy and in church documents, such as the recently published Universal Catechism. The Conference requested 'the appropriate office in Rome to set up a commission to study the theological implications involved in the use of inclusive language', noting that 'changes have been taking place in people's perceptions and therefore in the meaning of such words as "men", "brethren" and "sons" '.

> When many women hear these words in the liturgy, or read them in official Church documents, they do feel excluded. To continue to use such language is an injustice, considering women represent half (and often more than half) of the active Christian community, and considering the movement the world over to give women their proper place. Religious women are perhaps more aware than most of the issues and feel hurt that they are not heard.[128]

As the authors and officiators of new forms of liturgy, as the writers of books on women in the Church, and as the active participants in a number of groups promoting justice for women within the Church, individual women religious have innovated and taken risks on behalf of the community as a whole.[129] Although this activity has involved a minority, they have had the tacit support of a larger number of sisters.

By the end of the twentieth century all congregations were pursuing the goals of revitalised charisms with improved levels of theological and professional formation, together with a greater collaboration across congregations and between congregations and others, and overall, a replacement of uniformity per se with a uniformity in diversity. Such was the theme of the submission by the religious of England and Wales to the Synod on Religious Life, held in Rome in 1994.[130] Such was the spirit in which Sr Ruth Duckworth could say:

> And where are we going? We cannot know, nor do we need to know – but we believe that our movement has been in a good direction. We do not think that all is now done that needs to be done. On the contrary we have a strong suspicion that change has come to stay. But we do know that we are more alive, more vitally united, freer to love and serve; and we are content not to see the future, since not to know the future is something to do with what we call faith.[131]

NOTES

1. Joan Chittister OSB, *The Fire in These Ashes: A Spirituality of Contemporary Religious Life* (Kansas City, 1996), pp. vii & 1.
2. 'The number of nuns and monks in England and Wales has fallen by a third in a decade [from 15,000 to 10,000] . . .', *The Times*, 1 January 1996; *Briefing*, vol. 20, no. 13 (15 June 1990). For the United States see the comprehensive study by D. J. Nygren and M. D. Ukeritis, *The Future of Religious Orders in the United States: Transformation and Commitment* (Westport and London, 1993).
3. *The Times*, 1 January and 5 February 1996.
4. See *The Way Supplement* 65 (Summer 1989) dedicated to 'Religious Life in Transition'.
5. The idea of epochs or phases in religious life has come largely from the academic analyses of religious men and women. See, for example, the works of G. A. Arbuckle, H. Ebaugh, T. Flannery, M. Neal, and D. Ó'Murchú. It is echoed in recent histories of women's congregations celebrating 150 years in Britain: Cross and Passion Sisters, Society of the Holy Child Jesus and Sisters of Notre Dame de Namur. Philip Sheldrake, 'Revising Historical Perspectives', *The Way Supplement* 65 (Summer 1989) provides a valuable challenge to the idea that there is a single historical line of development in the religious life.
6. M. Ewens, *The Role of the Nun in Nineteenth Century America* (New York, 1978), p. 255, and C. Langlois, *La Catholicisme au féminin: les congregations françaises à supérieure au xix siècle* (Paris, 1984), p. 67.
7. R. Gibson, *A Social History of French Catholicism, 1789–1914* (London, 1989), p. 105.
8. M. S. Thompson, 'Women, Feminism and the New Religious History' in P. R. Vandermeer and R. P. Swierenga (eds), *Belief and Behaviour: Essays in the New Religious History* (New Brunswick, 1991), pp. 136–63.
9. James Walsh, 'Historical Perspectives and Ideal Demands,' *The Way Supplement* 37 (Spring 1980), pp. 34–6. L. M. Jarrell, 'The Development of Legal Structures for Women Religious Between 1500 and 1900: A Study of Selected Institutes of Religious Life for Women' (PhD thesis, Catholic University of America, 1984).
10. R. B. Savage, *Catherine McAuley: The First Sister of Mercy* (Dublin, 1949), pp. 261–2.
11. Dominant because this was the direction in which many of the diocesan foundations also moved.
12. Mary Linscott SND, 'Women Religious in the Church', *The Way Supplement* 19 (Summer 1973), pp. 54–5.

13. See, for example, G. Hollingsworth, *Ex-Nuns: Women Who Have Left the Convent* (London, 1985).
14. Chittister, *Fire in These Ashes*, p. vii.
15. For recent studies see: Catriona Clear, *Nuns in Nineteenth Century Ireland* (Dublin, 1987); P. J. Gilbert, 'In the Midst of a Protestant People: The Development of the Catholic Community in Bristol in the Nineteenth Century' (PhD thesis, University of Bristol, 1996); J. P. Marmion, 'Cornelia Connelly's Work in Education 1848–1879' (PhD thesis, University of Manchester, 1984); M. G. McClelland, 'The First Mercy Nuns: A Nineteenth Century Case Study', *Recusant History*, vol. 22, no. 2 (October 1994), pp. 199–221; H. Stone, 'Constraints of the Mother Foundresses: Contrasts in Anglican and Roman Catholic Religious Headship in Victorian England' (PhD thesis, University of Leeds, 1993).
16. G. A. Beck (ed), *The English Catholics, 1850–1950* (London, 1950).
17. Both benefited, as do all historians of religious congregations since 1949, from the considerable work of compilation undertaken by Peter Anson, *The Religious Orders and Congregations of Great Britain and Ireland* (1949). See also F. M. Steele, *The Convents of Great Britain and Ireland* (1923).
18. For example, M. C. Chambers, *The Life of Mary Ward*, 2 vols (London, 1882); A Sister of Notre Dame, *Sister Mary of St Philip* (London, 1922); A Member of the Society, *The Life of Cornelia Connelly* (London, 1922); *Life of The Venerable Madeleine Louise Sophie Barat* (Roehampton, 1900); F. C. Devas, *Mother Magdalen Taylor* (London, 1927); Fr Stanislaus, *Life of the Viscountess de Bonnault D'Houet* (London, 1916); Fr Bertrand Wilberforce (ed.), *A Memoir of Mother Francis Raphael* (London, 1923).
19. See H. McLeod, *Religion and Society in England, 1850–1914* (London, 1996) and Vandermeer and Swierenga (eds), *Belief and Behaviour.*
20. See L. Colley, *Britons: Forging the Nation 1707–1837* (London, 1992); L. Davidoff and C. Hall, *Family Fortunes: Men and Women of the English Middle Class, 1780–1850* (London, 1987); S. Gilley, 'Vulgar Piety and the Brompton Oratory, 1850–1860' in R. Swift and Sheridan Gilley (eds), *The Irish in the Victorian City* (London, 1985).
21. J. Wolffe (ed.), *Religion in Victorian Britain*, vol. V, *Culture and Empire* (Manchester, 1997), p. 9.
22. S. O'Brien, 'French Nuns in Nineteenth-Century England', *Past and Present*, no. 154 (February 1997), pp. 142–80.
23. J. McNamara, *Sisters in Arms: Catholic Nuns through Two Millennia* (London, 1996); M. Thompson, 'Women, Feminism'.
24. P. Curran, *Grace before Meals: Food Ritual and Body Discipline in Convent Culture* (Urbana, 1989).
25. A. Murphy SHCJ, '150 years of SHCJ History', *Society of the Holy Child Jesus*, Issue 1, 'Beginnings' (1996), p. 6.
26. The work of the Catholic Archive Society, founded in 1979, has been invaluable. See *Catholic Archives*, the Journal of CAS, published annually since 1981.
27. A considerable amount of research on women religious in the modern period in France, Belgium, United States and Australia has now been published and the Network for the History of Women Religious, which has held four conferences in the United States, has played an important role in encouraging scholarship.
28. H. J. Coleridge (ed.), *St Mary's Convent, Micklegate Bar, York [1686–1887]* (London, 1887); S. O'Brien, 'Women of the English Catholic Community: Nuns and Pupils at the Bar Covent, York, 1680–1790' in J. Loades (ed.), *Monastic Studies* (Bangor, 1990), pp. 267–82; D. Evinson, *'Pope's Corner'* (London, 1980), pp. 3–15.
29. P. Guilday, *The English Catholic Refugees on the Continent, 1558–1795* (London, 1914); and essays in various volumes of *Recusant History.*
30. See Anson, *Religious Orders and Congregations* for a brief history of their locations.

31. D. T. J. (Aidan) Bellenger, 'France and England: The English Female Religious' in F. Tallett and N. Atkins (eds), *Religion, Society and Politics in France since 1798* (London, 1991); S. O'Brien, 'French Nuns' and '*Terra Incognita*: The Nun in Nineteenth Century England', *Past and Present*, no. 121 (November 1988), pp. 110–40.
32. For example the Daughters of Charity of St Vincent de Paul (1633), Religious of the Society of the Sacred Heart (1800), Notre Dame de Namur (1804), the Faithful Companions of Jesus (1820) and the Good Shepherd Nuns (1835).
33. Presentation Nuns (1777), the Irish Sisters of Charity (1815), the Loreto Sisters (1820) and the Sisters of Mercy (1831).
34. They included such well-known congregations as the Little Sisters of the Poor (London, 1851), the Ursulines (London, 1851) and the Daughters of Charity of St Vincent de Paul (Sheffield, 1858).
35. There is some debate about the importance of various influences on English Catholic piety. See M. Heimann, *Catholic Devotion in Victorian England* (Oxford, 1995); J. Crichton, 'Popular Devotion in Victorian England', *Month*, 2nd ser., xxix (1996); D. Holmes, *More Roman than Rome: English Catholicism in the Nineteenth Century* (London, 1978); O'Brien, 'French Nuns', pp. 147, 167–73, and 'Making Catholic Spaces: Women, Décor and Devotion in the English Catholic Church, 1840–1900' in D. Wood (ed.), *The Church and the Arts*, Studies in Church History 28 (Oxford, 1992).
36. It is likely that more initiatives were taken than are to be found in existing listings since not all sources survived, and not all initiatives led to the formation of a separate congregation.
37. G. V. Hudson, *Mother Geneviève Dupuis* (London, 1929); J. J. Scarisbrick, *Selly Park and Beyond: The Story of Geneviève Dupuis and the Congregation of the Sisters of Charity of St Paul the Apostle* (1997).
38. Fanny Taylor spent six months as a postulant in Devonport with the Society of the Most Holy Trinity before volunteering to nurse in the Crimea, where she was received into the Roman Catholic Church. Elizabeth Lockhart and Mary Francis Basil became Roman Catholics only after having entered Anglican sisterhoods: in Lockhart's case as one of the founding members of St Mary's Wantage, and in Basil's after eighteen years as a senior member of the Society of St Margaret, East Grinstead.
39. E. Hamer, *Elizabeth Prout 1820–1864* (London, 1994), p. 136.
40. S. O'Brien, 'Lay-Sisters and Good Mothers: Working-Class Women in English Convents, 1840–1910' in W. Sheils and D. Wood (eds), *Women in the Church*, Studies in Church History (Oxford, 1990), pp. 53–65.
41. MS Annals for 1870, Archives of the Poor Servants of the Mother of God, Roehampton.
42. Cornelia Connelly had wanted to insist that vocations should not be refused on financial grounds, writing to Bishop Grant: 'I wish you would remember my Lord that we only want to *labour* for our support as mendicant orders beg . . . If we sink into making provision for our support, *not* imitating our Blessed Lord, we shall not be blessed.' R. Flaxman, *A Woman Styled Bold: The Life of Cornelia Connelly, 1809–1879* (London, 1991), p. 284.
43. The older prohibitions were re-stated in Lord Derby's Proclamation of 1852 which forbade public display of Catholic symbols.
44. Flaxman, *A Woman Styled Bold, passim*.
45. M. G. McClelland, 'The First Hull Mercy Nuns', pp. 199–221.
46. A model for the vital topic of membership is to be found in S. Hoy, 'The Journey Out: The Recruitment and Emigration of Irish Religious Women to the United States, 1812–1914' in J. Hoff and M. Coulter (eds), 'Irish Women's Voices: Past and Present', *Journal of Women's History*, vol. 6, no. 4/vol. 7, no. 1 (Winter/Spring 1995), pp. 64–98. The proportions of first-generation Irish women in English convents varied with time and between congregations.
47. W. L. Arnstein, *Protestant versus Catholic in Mid-Victorian England: Mr Newdegate and the Nuns*

(London, 1982), p. 67; D. Paz, *Popular Anti-Catholicism in Mid-Victorian Britain* (Stanford, 1992).

48. Thompson, 'Women, Feminism', p. 142.
49. Flaxman, *A Woman Styled Bold*, pp. 208–27.
50. *The Franciscan Missionaries of St Joseph: Centenary 1883–1983* (1983), pp. 11–22.
51. P. Dougherty, *Mother Mary Potter: Foundress of the Little Company of Mary, 1847–1913* (Rome, 1961), p. 134, and Elizabeth West LCM, unpublished papers.
52. Scarisbrick, *Selly Park and Beyond*, pp. 14–29. See Stone, 'Constraints on Mother Foundresses', chapter 2.
53. After years of re-drafting constitutions and seeking approval, from 1874 to 1877 the Society of the Holy Child Jesus was forced to live under a rule written by Bishop Danell without attention to their past experience and with him as superior. Elected by the sisters as superior general in 1877, Cornelia Connelly died in 1879 still not knowing whether the Society would be permitted to follow her spiritual vision and constitutions.
54. M. Motherway, 'Archives of the Little Company of Mary', *Catholic Archives*, no. 14 (1994), p. 14.
55. See, for example, references to benefactors in *Pioneer Sisters of Charity of St Vincent de Paul in Great Britain and Ireland* (1955).
56. For example, the gift of Laura Petre (Sister Mary of St Francis) to the Sisters of Notre Dame de Namur subsidised the building of Mount Pleasant College in Liverpool. The case of Cox v Manners 1871, involving a woman 'who willed part of her estate to the Dominican convent at Carisbrook and part to the Sisters of Charity of St Paul the Apostle', established the legal validity of gifts to a convent. Arnstein, *Protestant versus Catholic*, p. 162.
57. *Franciscan Missionaries of St Joseph: Centenary*, p. 27.
58. M. Linscott SND, *Quiet Revolution: The Educational Experiences of Blessed Julie Billiart and the Sisters of Notre Dame* (Glasgow, 1966), p. 121.
59. Motherway, 'Little Company of Mary', p. 14.
60. A. Hastings, *A History of English Christianity, 1920–1990* (3rd edn, 1991), p. 144.
61. Shane Leslie, 'Forgotten Passages in the Life of Florence Nightingale', quoted in M. Ewens, 'Removing the Veil' in R. Ruether and E. McLaughlin (eds), *Women of Spirit* (New York, 1979), p. 259, and Shane Leslie, *Henry Edward Manning: His Life and Labours* (1921), p. 109.
62. B. R. Belloc, *Historic Nuns* (London, 1898); A. Jameson, *Sisters of Charity and the Commerce of Labour* (1859).
63. Linscott, *Quiet Revolution*, p. 40.
64. Rev. Frederick Fuller, 'The Churches Train Teachers' (PhD thesis, University of Exeter, 1973), p. 390. I am indebted for this quotation to Kim Lowndes who is completing a PhD at Liverpool Hope University College on women and denominational teacher education in Liverpool and Warrington.
65. See A Sister of Notre Dame, *Sister Mary of St Philip (Frances Mary Lescher): 1825–1904* (1922), especially chapters X, XI and XII.
66. Charles Dickens wrote of them: 'A few women, feeble in frame but strong in heart and mind, without publicity, or subscription dinners or charity sermons . . . patiently go round collecting from one house to another these scraps, wherewith, in humility and tenderness, they nourish the poor', F. Trochu, *Jeanne Jugan* (2nd English edn, 1960), p. 161.
67. See M. Lonergan LSA, 'The Archives of the Anglo-Scottish Province of the Little Sisters of the Assumption', *Catholic Archives*, no. 11 (1991), pp. 17–21; E. Whitehead, *A Form of Catholic Action* (1947).
68. Benedictines of Stanbrook, *In a Great Tradition* (1956), pp. 116ff.
69. Registers of novices provide evidence that in the founding years congregations accepted

more older women and more widows (always few in number), and that there were more converts.

70. P. Wilson RSCJ, *My Father Took Me to the Circus* (London, 1984), p. 3.
71. S. Maitland, *A Map of the New Country: Women and Christianity* (London, 1983), p. 81.
72. E.g. 'Little change occurred in the number of Notre Dame convents and lifestyle up to the second world war', *Jubilee, Sisters of Notre Dame de Namur Celebrate*, p. 54.
73. E.g. G. A. Arbuckle, *Out of Chaos: Refounding Religious Congregations* (New York, 1988).
74. Maitland, *Map of the New Country*, pp. 56–7.
75. Ibid.
76. Maitland, *Map of the New Country*, p. 59.
77. For a discussion of the degree to which Catholics had a stable and distinctive subculture before the 1950s see M. Hornsby-Smith, *Roman Catholics in England: Studies in Social Structures since the Second World War* (Cambridge, 1987). Although Hornsby-Smith cautions against the 'myth of a golden age' and argues for the diversity and lack of security in the Church in the nineteenth century, his conclusion that a distinctive subculture had dissolved by the 1980s underscores its existence in the period between 1900 and 1950.
78. Typed MS, 'Sister Margaret Thornton 1898–1977', Sacred Heart Archives, Roehampton.
79. Scarisbrick, *Selly Park and Beyond*, pp. 87–8.
80. MS typescript, 'Statistical Information Prepared for the 1988 Chapter', FCJ Archives, Broadstairs.
81. MS 'Entry and Clothing Register', SND Archives, Woolton, Liverpool.
82. MS Registers, Cross and Passion Archives, Great Billing, Northampton.
83. *Franciscan Missionaries of St Joseph*, p. 43.
84. Four new training colleges were opened between 1900 and 1910.
85. In Cambridge the Institute of the Blessed Virgin Mary and Canonesses of St Augustine; in Oxford the Sisters of Notre Dame, Sacred Heart, Holy Child Jesus.
86. See Scarisbrick, *Selly Park and Beyond*, p. 43 for example.
87. Scarisbrick, *Selly Park and Beyond*, p. 35.
88. E.g. Benedictine Missionary Sisters; Missionary Sisters of Our Lady of Africa; Sisters of Our Lady of the Missions; Society of the Catholic Medical Missionaries; African Missionary Sisters; Franciscan Medical Missionaries.
89. Williams, *Society of the Sacred Heart*, p. 185.
90. The Roman Catholic dimension has yet to be included in the growing literature on women and missions: see S. Gill, *Women and the Church of England from the Eighteenth Century to the Present* (London, 1994), pp. 173–205; S. Gill, 'Heroines of Missionary Adventure: The Portrayal of Victorian Women Missionaries in Popular Fiction and Biography' in A. Hogan and A. Bradstock (eds), *Women of Faith in Victorian Culture* (London, 1998), pp. 172–85; *Women's Studies International Forum*, vol. 21, no. 3 (1998), special issue on 'Women, Imperialism and Identity'; and Lavinia Byrne, *The Hidden Journey: Missionary Heroines in Many Lands* (London, 1993).
91. L. M. Major, 'The Central Archives of the Society of Catholic Medical Missionaries', *Catholic Archives*, 8 (1988), pp. 73–82. See also, Katherine Burton, *According to the Pattern: The Story of Dr Agnes McLaren and the Society of Catholic Medical Missionaries* (1946).
92. Major, 'Catholic Medical Missionaries', p. 74.
93. Linscott, *Quiet Revolution*, p. 122.
94. L. Joseph Suenens, *The Nun in the World Today: New Dimensions in the Modern Apostolate* (London, 1962), pp. 4–5.
95. Suenens, *The Nun*, p. 18.
96. Wilson, *The Circus*, p. 3.
97. Maitland, *Map of the New Country*, p. 81.

98. Maitland, *Map of the New Country*, p. 68; *The Way Supplement* 65 (Summer 1989).
99. In addition to works cited elsewhere, see also: M. Bernstein, *Nuns* (London, 1976); S. Campbell-Jones, *In Habit: An Anthropological Study of Working Nuns* (London, 1979); M. Loudon, *Unveiled* (London, 1992); Union of Superiors General, *Consecrated Life Today: Charisms in the Church for the World* (Papers from International Congress, Rome, 1993: St Paul's Press, 1994); *Proceedings of the Carondelet Conference on the Future of Religious Life* (Minnesota, 1990); M. A. Neal, *Catholic Sisters in Transition: From the 1960s to the 1980s* (Wilmington, 1990). This is a small selection of a large literature.
100. *Briefing*, vol. 20, no. 13 (15 June 1990).
101. 'Vocations in Ireland', *Briefing*, vol. 20, no. 12 (1 June 1990).
102. *Signum*, vol. 7, no. 7 (4 May 1979). The CMRS was itself established as a consequence of conciliar recommendations. It later changed its name to Conference of Religious (COR).
103. *The Times*, 1 January 1996.
104. The total membership of the Little Company of Mary, for example, had halved to about 500 within a generation: *The Times*, 1 January 1996.
105. Estimated for Britain at around 12–18 per cent. Maitland, *Map of The New Country*, p. 78.
106. Scarisbrick, *Selly Park and Beyond*, p. 89; *Jubilee: Sisters of Notre Dame de Namur Celebrate*, p. 61.
107. *Perfectae Caritatis*, n. 2.
108. A. M. Reynolds, *Heralds of Hope* (Strasbourg, 1989), p. 35. I am indebted to Sr Reynolds' summary.
109. *Lumen Gentium*, n. 32.
110. *Jubilee: Sisters of Notre Dame Celebrate*, p. 58.
111. *Jubilee*, pp. 58–9.
112. Scarisbrick, *Selly Park, and Beyond*, p. 64.
113. *Daily Telegraph*, 25 February 1987, p. 11.
114. *Daily Telegraph*, 25 February 1987, Sr Elizabeth Smith RSCJ.
115. Quoted in 'Nuns Retreat from Habits of the Past', *The Observer*, 2 February 1986.
116. Maitland, *Map of the New Country*, p. 79.
117. Scarisbrick, *Selly Park and Beyond*, p. 51.
118. *Signum*, vol. 23, no. 5 (May 1995).
119. *Catholic Archives*, no. 14 (1994), pp. 15–16.
120. *Jubilee: Sisters of Notre Dame Celebrate*, p. 59.
121. Scarisbrick, *Selly Park and Beyond*, p. 51.
122. Taken from the 1998 brochure of the Margaret Beaufort Institute of Theology.
123. For example, the Faithful Companions of Jesus, Sisters of Charity of St Paul the Apostle.
124. *History: Society of the Holy Child Jesus*, Issue I, 'Beginnings' (1996), p. 100.
125. Wilson, *The Circus*, p. 4: 'Of course, the convergence in the 1960s of the insights of the women's movement with those of women religious was an important part of our growing self-awareness, especially in the U.S.A.'
126. Reynolds, *Heralds of Hope*, p. 39.
127. Chittister, *Fire in These Ashes*, p. 13.
128. *Signum*, vol. 22, no. 17 (September 1994), pp. 14–15.
129. For example, via such organisations as Catholic Women's Network, the experimental Websters Women's Resource Centre in London and the central organising committee for the first Women's Synod (to be held at Liverpool Hope University College in July 1999), and in such writings as Sr Lavinia Byrne's *Woman at the Altar* (London, 1994).
130. *Signum*, vol. 22, no. 10 (May 1994). See also A. Flannery, *Towards the 1994 Synod: The Views of Religious* (Dublin, 1993).
131. Maitland, *Map of the New Country*, pp. 81–2.

SIX

RELIGIOUS LIFE FOR MEN

D. AIDAN BELLENGER

In the summer of 1965, at the end of the Second Vatican Council, there was a Vocations Exhibition at Earls Court, a venue in London better known for less religious gatherings. It had something about it of the self-congratulatory feeling of the Hierarchy Centenary Celebrations of 1950. It was seen at the time as 'a vigorous manifestation' of the variety of the forms of 'dedicated' Christian life. It had about it, too, something of the 1960s with a nuns' fashion show revealing the diversity of religious habit and in some cases the distinctive wear 'before and after modernisation'.[1] Self-confidence and an attempt in 'the swinging sixties' to make things seem relevant revealed two contradictory trends which have characterised the religious life of the last thirty years – a mature organisational structure shown in a great multitude of churches and religious houses across the land, and an increasingly ageing population of religious to man them. This chapter tries to put this present condition in context.

The contribution of the male religious to the life of the English Catholic community has been a great one, even if it has been delivered in a diffuse and sometimes haphazard way and is difficult to quantify. It is the nature of the beast. Among the charisms in the Church the various religious societies of men are not part of the hierarchical structure, with which, indeed, they have been often in conflict. In the case of the individual monks and religious, like Ullathorne in the nineteenth century and Hume in the twentieth century, who have played a prominent role in episcopal leadership, they have always brought with them something of a wider and outsider's vision which has made their contributions all the more memorable. Each religious carries with him not only his own personality but the insights of his spiritual formation and community. According to the 1983 Code of Canon Law,

> In the Church there are many institutes of consecrated life, with gifts that differ according to the grace given them; they more closely follow Christ

> praying, or Christ proclaiming the Kingdom of God, or Christ doing good to people, or Christ in dialogue with the people of this world, but always Christ doing the Will of the Father.[2]

The life of those who follow the path of 'consecrated life' is always one of dialogue between *traditio*, the passing on of the insights of the past, and *renovatio*, renewing the life of the institute to make its witness viable in the society within which it finds its mission. Often, perhaps surprisingly, *renovatio* is found through *traditio*. 'The whole patrimony of an institute must', the canonists remind us, 'be faithfully preserved by all. This patrimony is composed of the intentions of the founders, of all that the competent ecclesiastical authority has approved concerning the nature, purpose, spirit and character of the institute, and of its sound traditions.'[3]

In the ebb and flow of the history of the male religious, 'sound traditions' are not always apparent and, for the converts of the 1840s like Newman, it was difficult to find an appropriate home, a satisfactory compromise as it were, between clerical Oxford and the Carthusians. In the 1840s traditional religious orders were still recovering from a century of Enlightenment and revolution which had stigmatised the religious orders in general and the monks in particular as upholders of all that was obscurantist and backward-looking.[4] Newman was to become a great spokesman for the Benedictines, but it was not the English Benedictines of his epoch that he looked to for the reconversion of England. To him the life of the ideal monk was not one of activism, so characteristic of his monastic contemporaries, but solitude and contemplation, one of whom it could be said that 'the very air he breathes is peace'.[5] The Benedictines were not for him, and he famously advised the young and earnest Gerard Manley Hopkins to opt for the Jesuits, a society not adapted enough for the spirit of the age for himself,[6] rather than the Benedictines.[7] For the great and learned Order of Preachers he had little enthusiasm. 'If indeed', he wrote on 6 July 1846, 'we could be Dominicans *teaching* it were well. Meanwhile I am doubting whether the Dominicans have preserved their traditions – whether it is not a great idea extinct.'[8]

Newman's coldness towards the older orders was much influenced by their character in the 1840s. They remained wedded to a recusant past where family connections and missionary networks seemed to matter more than the fundamentals of the institutes' tradition. There was a lingering Gallicanism inbred from centuries of formation in France which reminded the converts too much of their rejected Anglicanism. Ultramontanism was to be the chosen instrument to undo English national apostasy. Even the Society of Jesus seemed past its best. Since the sixteenth century the Jesuits had played a crucial part in the organisation and manpower of the English Mission, forming almost a church within a church.[9] The closure of the Continental houses during the French Revolution and the official papal suppression of the whole Society failed to destroy it.[10] The Benedictines, numerically inferior to the Jesuits, recovered from the revolutionary dislocation and continued in reduced circumstances, rather like distressed gentlefolk determined not to disappear from view but looking for a new role.[11] Even the friars, greatly depleted, continued to exist if not to flourish.[12] During the High Victorian period it was more recent institutes which attracted popular attention and appeared for a while to offer more opportunities for the aspirant. Despite the preference of the Oxford converts for the *Romanità* of the Oratorians, Passionists and Redemptorists, however, the older-established English orders and societies, gradually renewed and transformed and restored to self-confidence, have, in the hundred and fifty years since 1850, probably made the greatest contribution to the Catholic community.

THE MONASTIC TRADITION

The second half of the twentieth century has seen the Benedictines return to the centre of national consciousness with a long-serving Benedictine Archbishop of Westminster and many ecumenical and public celebrations like the fourteenth centenary in 1997 of the arrival of St Augustine at Canterbury. The Benedictines were an integral part of the medieval English Church in a way in which no other order was, with monks staffing the royal chantry at Westminster Abbey and the metropolitan church of Canterbury, as well as many other cathedral priories. Many of its abbots were called to Parliament. There were numerous great abbeys and not a few great monks. All this went with the Reformation, and although the Benedictines as revived in the early seventeenth century saw themselves as successors to the Black Monks of the Middle Ages, their renewed congregation was in many ways quite different. It shared, no doubt, and perhaps with more enthusiasm, the missionary zeal which had brought the Roman monk Augustine and his companions to Kent in 597, but its structure was organised on lines which had more in common with the orders of the Reformation than with those of the High Middle Ages. It lacked the traditional abbatial role of individual monasteries with local autonomy and territorial stability so crucial to the Benedictine ideal, and was administered by a single superior, an elected President General who ruled with a regimen and a four-yearly General Chapter which elected him and the other congregational officials. The monk's formation and profession was made to an individual community, of which there were three by 1850, St Gregory's (Downside), St Lawrence's (Ampleforth) and St Edmund's (Douai, France), but once on the English mission the monks became part of a missionary province, either Canterbury or York. The province of York comprised all the missions of the six northern counties along with Derbyshire, Cheshire, Nottinghamshire and Lincolnshire. The province of Canterbury embraced the rest of England and Wales. The system was to remain intact until the last decade of the nineteenth century.[13]

The missionary spirit of the English Benedictines scaled new heights in the half-century after the restoration of the hierarchy both at home and abroad. In 1838 there were thirty English Benedictine missions in England and Wales. By 1900 there were sixty-two. One particular area of growth was South Wales where a succession of Benedictine bishops, starting with Joseph Brown, first Bishop of Newport and Menevia, continuing with Cuthbert Hedley, and concluding with Romanus Bilsborrow, first Archbishop of Cardiff, gave leadership to the Church. The mission life was not always an easy one and could, as in the case of the Benedictine martyrs of charity, who stood alongside their secular brethren in the typhoid epidemic of the 1840s, lead to early death. The most heroic exercise of Benedictine missionary activity was, however, not in the British Isles but in the establishment of the Australian Catholic Church. As early as 1817 the English Benedictines became involved in the vicariate of Mauritius which was ecclesiastically responsible for most of the southern hemisphere. In 1834 Bede Polding, a Downside monk, was made Vicar Apostolic of New Holland and, in 1842, first Archbishop of Sydney, an office he held until his death in 1877, when he was succeeded by Bede Vaughan, another Downside monk and brother to Cardinal Herbert Vaughan. In Australia a new church was established, with its own institutions, colleges of higher education and religious orders, on a small scale, perhaps, but with an integrity and sense of confidence which put their English co-religionists to shame.

The missionary work of the Benedictines was accompanied by the beginning of other enterprises, especially the development of boarding schools. At one stage, about 1860, the college at Ampleforth numbered about one hundred students, even if fifty was a more common roll. Ampleforth and Douai remained predominantly schools for the training of 'church boys', students intended for the priesthood, and it was said that by 1900, six hundred priests and sixteen bishops had been educated at St Edmunds, Douai, mainly for the secular priesthood. Only Downside educated a significant percentage of lay pupils, and Downside was a very small and domestic 'academy' until the First World War. The school showed what could be achieved by a resident community, and the missionary bishops like Brown and Ullathorne shared with their episcopal colleagues a desire to return to a restored hierarchical discipline in which the religious orders were to play a less proactive and independent role. Indeed, Ullathorne, through his work in Australia, the beleaguered Western District and as first Bishop of Birmingham, may have appeared the very model of a Benedictine missioner, yet at heart he was a monastic romantic whose religious name, Bernard, reflected an attraction towards 'reformed' back-to-basics monasticism and whose characteristically outspoken words to his brethren always called for a more primitive observance of their Rule.[14]

The gradual rebuilding of the English communities in England allowed monastic blueprints to be considered, and the plans prepared by Pugin for the monastic church and buildings at Downside were a vision of possible things temporarily impossible through lack of cash. There were more solid manifestations of a 'reformed' monasticism. The buildings at Belmont in Herefordshire were envisaged as the seat for a Benedictine bishop, a cathedral priory (a scheme for another cathedral priory at Westminster was also briefly canvassed) and as a central missionary college for the Benedictines. Instead Belmont became a beacon for those among the English Benedictines who wanted a full liturgical and community life.[15]

The English Benedictines were able to gain experience and example from the various stricter 'monastic' communities which were established during the nineteenth century. The Cistercians of Mount St Bernard in Leicestershire[16] were successors to the monastery at Lulworth in Dorset, a community in exile from the French Revolution which had an abbot by the time it left England in 1817.[17] The first building at Mount St Bernard was opened in 1837 and this was replaced in 1844 by a purpose-built Pugin monastery. In 1848 the community was raised to abbatial status. A few years later, in 1856, Wilfred Alcock, an Englishman who had become a member of the Subiacan Province of the reformed Cassinese Congregation in Italy, started the community at Ramsgate. Monastic buildings were soon built adjoining the Pugin church, already existing, in which the architect had been buried in 1852. In 1896 the community became an abbey. Although the Cassinese monks were engaged in missionary activity in the Isle of Thanet, serving at one time 2,000 parishioners, and in New Zealand, their community life was far nearer to the 'classic' Benedictine model than that of their English Benedictine confrères.[18] In 1876, at the invitation of Bishop Ullathorne, the monks of the Beuronese Congregation, a German grouping, were invited to Birmingham and established a monastery at Erdington which flourished until anti-German feeling during World War I forced its closure and the transfer of its fine church in the Birmingham suburbs to the Redemptorists. Beuron was attracting English-speaking monks on the Continent and the Belgian abbey of Maredsous, closely associated with Erdington, had as members the future Abbot of Downside, John Chapman, and the martyrologist and antiquarian, Bede Camm. Influential though the Cassinese and Beuronese monks were on the English monastic tradition, it was France which perhaps provided the best examples of the full monastic life.[19]

Bismarck's *Kulturkampf* was reflected in the continuing atmosphere of the French Third Republic and the Anti-Association Laws passed by the fiercely anticlerical Combes were to force the English monks of Douai Abbey back to England in 1903. During the Third Republic a number of French communities established themselves in England, which they saw as a safe refuge for religious houses – ironically, given the centuries of anti-Catholic persecution. In 1882 some monks of La Pierre-qui-Vire in Burgundy moved to the site of the Cistercian medieval abbey of Buckfast in Devon. Some remnants of the old building were incorporated in the new monastery commenced in 1884 and completed in 1938. Much of the work was done by the monks themselves, and this captured the public imagination as much as the rebuilding of a medieval monastery. Elevated to abbatial status in 1902, Buckfast had the character of a great monastery of the Middle Ages in a way that no other foundation had at that time.[20] In its learned abbot, Anscar Vonier, it had a spiritual leader of the first rank.[21] Buckfast was eventually, in 1960, to join the English Benedictine Congregation and to be a pioneer in monastic hospitality and accessibility to visitors. In 1896 the monks of Solesmes made a foundation at Farnborough in Hampshire attached to the mausoleum of Napoleon III. Farnborough, transferred to the Subiaco congregation in 1946, became a great scholarly community under its abbot, Fernand Cabrol, and was much associated with liturgical and patristic research. Solesmes itself was in exile on the Isle of Wight from 1901 and a new abbey, built by the monk-architect Paul Bellot, was opened in 1912. The Solesmes community returned to France in 1922, but in 1937 Quarr became an abbey in its own right with an enviable tradition of chant and erudition as well as of full observance.[22] The most dramatic manifestation of the French monastic contribution was St Hugh's Charterhouse, in Sussex. The last English Carthusian had died in 1825 and the new monastery, on a gigantic scale, was opened in 1873 with its church consecrated in 1883. Manning, fond of the image, said that 'the Carthusians have built, not a convent, but a city', and it was seen by the authorities of the Grand Chartreuse as a potential house of refuge if active persecution of religious broke out, as seemed increasingly possible.[23]

The conflict between Church and State in the last quarter of the nineteenth century which led to the establishment of French monasteries in England coincided with a reclassification of aim and objectives in the Catholic Church itself, given focus in the declaration of papal infallibility at the First Vatican Council of 1870. There was also a rediscovery of Christian roots, and the fourteenth century of St Benedict's birth in 1880 led to much heart-searching and declarations of monastic ideals. In that year the *Downside Review* was begun as a quarterly of monastic thought and the Downside monk, Aidan Gasquet, later a cardinal and Librarian of the Holy Roman Church, began his historical work which, for all its flaws, was to contribute considerably to the scientific understanding of the monastic life.[24] Stirrings within the English Congregation had included, under the inspiration of Abbot Guéranger of Solesmes, the creation of a 'perfect' monastic enclosure (for women) at Stanbrook in Worcestershire,[25] and a new monastic foundation at Fort Augustus in Scotland by the self-exiled Downside monk, Jerome Vaughan, on Beuronese lines.[26] In Rome Jerome Vaughan, among others, had been agitating for a reform which would bring the English Benedictines into line with the developing new *order* of the monastic life. In May 1881 an Apostolic Visitation of the English Benedictines was announced by Rome and the visitor was named as Boniface Krug, the American-born prior of Monte Cassino.[27]

Krug's report, published in July 1882, recognised the unique missionary character of the Congregation, and called for abbeys to be erected and new constitutions to be prepared. A decade of intense debate raged in the Congregation with the monastery of Downside in favour, predominantly, of a more monastic Congregation and Ampleforth and Douai far more attached to the mission. In 1890 the Apostolic letter *Religiosus Ordo* abolished the missionary provinces and put the missionaries under the priors of their houses of origin. In 1899 *Diu Quidem* elevated the three priories of Douai, Ampleforth and Downside to abbatial status. Despite the conflict the Benedictines were strengthened in number and by 1905 there were 280 monks of whom some 150 were working on the mission.[28]

Since 1900 the resident communities of the English Congregation have provided the main focus for the life and work of their monks. The original three abbeys have been joined by Belmont, which became an abbey in 1920, and two foundations from Downside, Ealing and Worth, both now autonomous communities.[29] The daily round of the monasteries, in particular the *Opus Dei*, has returned to the forefront of the English Benedictine life, but as to work, the most important developments were in the world of education. All the abbeys of the Congregation have had a school at some time or another and four still survive in England. Downside School was reordered by Leander Ramsay, headmaster from 1902, on the model of an English public school, especially Wellington College, which seemed to the convert Ramsay to have the right combination of godliness and good learning. Reforms included the founding of a cadet corps, a house system and boy prefects.[30] At Ampleforth the house system was developed still further and under its great heads, Edmund Matthews and the legendary Paul Nevill, developed into the biggest Catholic boys' boarding school, which it remains (1998).[31] At Douai another influential (and long-reigning) headmaster, Ignatius Rice, built up a reputation for an excellent Benedictine education. Recognition from the educational establishment came with the election of the headmasters of the schools to the influential Headmasters' Conference, Downside in 1913, Ampleforth in 1917, Douai in 1920. Worth, originally a preparatory school for Downside, opened its senior school in 1959, very much in the style of its three senior predecessors, while Ealing opened a day school in 1902 which is now the largest of all the Benedictine schools.[32]

Schools required schoolmasters with adequate academic qualifications, and the Benedictines made close contacts with the universities. St Benet's, the Oxford house established by Ampleforth in 1896, eventually became a recognised private hall of the university and presented students for degrees.[33] Benet House, the Downside residence at Cambridge, established in the same year, never attained the status of its Oxford sister. Cambridge was less open to 'sectarian' 'colleges', and all the undergraduates had to matriculate through established houses of the university.[34] Cuthbert Butler and Hugh Connolly, both very distinguished scholars, became the first Catholic priests to proceed to the degree of BA at Cambridge since the Reformation. Both were members of Christ's College, a house which was to matriculate a great number of Downside's most celebrated scholars. One of the best-known monks of the century, David Knowles, who eventually became Regius Professor of Modern History at Cambridge, began his university career at Benet House.[35]

David Knowles had a long and well-documented feud with Downside and the English Benedictine Congregation over the nature of the monastic life. A disciple of Cuthbert Butler, the chief spokesman of the monastic reform party at Downside in the 1880s and 1890s, he believed that the boarding schools and the civilised English balance of the communities were not monastic enough. He became, before his defection from the community, the prophet of what became in the 1930s the 'Usque movement' (from a phrase in *Religiosus Ordo* which declared the English Congregation to be *usquequaque monastica*), a return to monastic origins, Cistercian in its radicalism, which led to appeals to Rome and the transfer of some monks to 'stricter' houses, to Mount St Bernard, to Caldey (where Cistercian monks had arrived in 1929),[36] to Quarr (where one of them, Aelred Sillem, became the first English abbot), to the Charterhouse and elsewhere. The movement itself fizzled out, but it reflects the constant call for reform which is at the heart of monastic life, and the monastic atmosphere of Knowles gradually permeated the Downside consciousness and much of the English Congregation. The intellectual work of the English Benedictines had been concentrated on historical studies with notable medievalists predominant. The polymath Abbot Christopher Butler of Downside was a Scripture scholar and philosopher who became noted for his radio broadcasts[37] and, as Auxiliary Bishop of Westminster to Cardinal Heenan, continued the tradition of Benedictine bishops which culminated in the appointment of Basil Hume as Archbishop of Westminster in 1976.[38]

The learned and educational work of the English Benedictines (with their continuing work on the missions) is one reflection of the monastic ideal. Another is provided by the foundations which come from the work of Aelred Carlyle whose Anglican Benedictines, at Caldey Island from 1906, were received into the Church in 1913. The revival of the religious life in the Church of England led many to make the move from Canterbury to Rome. The community moved to Prinknash Park, near Gloucester, in 1928 and was affiliated to what is now the Subiaco Congregation.[39] Foundations were eventually made at Farnborough (1947) and Pluscarden in Scotland (1948). The monks of these monasteries wear a white habit and live an austerely monastic life with little external apostolate.[40]

Among their number was Bede Griffiths, one of those most closely involved in the dialogue between Christianity and the Eastern religions.[41]

The original character of each Benedictine foundation is reflected in another White Benedictine house, of the Olivetan Congregation, Cockfosters in London, founded in 1936 by Constantine Bosschaerts. It was in the forefront of the liturgical movement, combining community and parish. Its long-serving prior, Edmund Jones, who died in 1985, was active in the ecumenical movement, in communications and in the co-operation of monks and nuns in what was effectively a dual house. He founded the more contemplative double house at Turvey in 1980.[42] At Cockfosters among more recent enterprises has been the establishment of a centre based on the spiritual teaching of John Main, once a monk at Ealing, who sought to revive a practice of prayer dating back to the Desert Fathers.[43] Building anew within an established tradition long remained characteristic of Benedictinism, but the years since Vatican II have shown signs of decline. In 1965 there were 727 Benedictine monks in England; by 1996 there were 479, a reduction of 34 per cent. Nevertheless the scale remains impressive and the number of abbeys remains constant.[44]

THE JESUIT MISSION

The Jesuits have been the most influential of the religious groups over the last century and along with the Benedictines they have shown remarkable staying power. They have benefited, too, from the scale of their manpower. In 1925 the English Jesuit Province had grown to 807 members as compared with the 507 of 1885.[45] In 1925 the total of regular clergy listed in the *Catholic Directory* was 1,433.[46] It must be realised however, that not all Jesuits were priests. Nevertheless, the proportion is striking. In the days of persecution most Jesuit activity in England was dedicated to the mission, providing priests for Catholic centres, often isolated, frequently one-man enterprises. By 1850 the emphasis was shifting. Stonyhurst College in Lancashire was the Society's first headquarters, an educational and cultural centre of great strength, entirely staffed by Jesuits, providing education for Jesuits and lay-pupils alike.[47] It was joined by many other establishments. Jesuit colleges – like Beaumont in Old Windsor (1861) and Mount St Mary's at Spinkhill near Sheffield (1842) – were accompanied by a string of Jesuit grammar schools. In the Province from the 1850s onwards parochial activities were being concentrated in important centres of population, with large resident communities of fathers backed up by well-maintained and staffed schools at both a primary and secondary level, with the Jesuits confining their teaching mainly to the secondary age-group. Many great churches were built, as illustrated by Preston in Lancashire where a string of fine buildings culminated in the Gothic extravaganza of St Walburge's towering over the railway line, its great spire challenging and surpassing so many of the towers of medieval England.[48]

Gothic, too, was the new Farm Street church in London's West End opened in 1849. Gothic emphasised Englishness as against the baroque exuberance of the Oratory and, with all the ambiguities of the word 'Jesuit' in the English anti-Catholic tradition, the presentation of Englishness was always important. Farm Street began to receive its first convert almost at once and the church has remained one of the most public aspects of the Jesuit apostolate. It has always drawn a mixed congregation but its reputation as a 'fashionable' church, reflected in the extraordinary success of Father Bernard Vaughan's much over-subscribed series of sermons on 'The Sins of Society', later published, was part of the contribution made by the Jesuits to the gradual acceptance of Catholics into English society. As early as 6 March 1882 Queen Victoria and Princess Beatrice stopped at the gates of Beaumont College and graciously received a loyal address from the boys underneath a triumphal floral arch especially constructed for the occasion.[49] On 18 October 1990 Queen Elizabeth II visited Stonyhurst College and was presented with a piece of tartan worn by Charles Edward Stuart.[50] It seemed that not even a Jacobite memento could cast doubt on the Jesuits' loyalty.

It would be simplistic, however, to associate the Jesuits, even in their most imperial period during Stonyhurst's period of predominance, with 'the Establishment', or one area of the Church's mission. The work of the English Jesuits has always been difficult to categorise. Overseas missions, first in British Guyana, later in Southern Africa and India, provided an important service for the wider Church and represent the continuing commitment to the Third World and, more recently, to radical 'liberation' theology, which has formed as important a thread in the English Jesuit mentality as has 'social' Catholicism. The Jesuit journals, *The Month* and *The Way*, have made a continuing contribution to the Church's intellectual life. Individual Jesuits have been able to make a great contribution to the apostolate of the pen and, more recently, to broadcasting. Noted writers include Bernard Bassett, spiritual writer and historian, Philip Caraman, historian, Frederick Copleston, historian of philosophy, Martin D'Arcy, philosopher and man of letters, Gerard Manley Hopkins, poet, Cyril Martindale, prolific author and apologist, Joseph Rickaby, philosopher, Walter Sidegraves, astronomer, and Herbert Thurston, controversialist and savant. This is only a selective list but it reveals something of the quality and diversity of the modern English Province.

The intellectual life of the Province has been directed in recent years, with a falling manpower characteristic of all the male religious orders since Vatican II, to specialised minorities and towards tertiary education. Campion Hall, Oxford, founded in 1896, established in new buildings designed by Lutyens in 1935, and Heythrop College, an affiliated college of London University since 1971, are the flagships, but the foundation of the Catholic Workers' College, now Plater College, Oxford, earlier this century, reveals the breadth of interest. Most of the Jesuit schools, including Stonyhurst itself since 1985, are under lay heads but retain a Jesuit personality and often at least some Jesuit presence. The Jesuit way has a strong support from the laity through the practice of the Spiritual Exercises, which go to the heart of the Ignatian approach. The Exercises consist of a course of meditations divided into four 'weeks' which can be lengthened or shortened depending on need and circumstance and they can be used by anyone, lay or clerical. The *Ratio Studiorum*, the definitive version of which appeared in 1599, is the system of Jesuit education which can be used to organise a course of studies without direct Jesuit supervision. The spirituality and resilience of the Society owes much to this dual inheritance.

THE RETURN OF THE FRIARS AND CANONS REGULAR

The figure of St Francis has been one of the most acceptable of religious icons throughout the period covered by this survey, a saint admired by all Christians. The Franciscans, however, have never seemed to benefit from this identity and remain, as compared to the Jesuits and Benedictines, a surprisingly small religious order in England. The English Province of Friars Minor, known as 'Friars of the Strict Observance' or 'Recollects', had an active apostolate in the late seventeenth and eighteenth century and a house of formation at Douai. The closure of their French house seems to have hit them very hard and despite attempts at increasing vocations, by the time of their chapter in 1838, with only nine dispirited and ageing friars remaining, it seemed as if the time for the English Franciscans was up. Attempts to revive the Friars Minor from Belgium were made as early as 1849 but it was really only in 1861, with the foundation of Gorton Monastery in Manchester and the construction of its vast church, that Franciscan fortunes recovered. Their mission was concentrated in the inner cities and included Forest Gate in London's East End, where a secondary school was also established. In 1973 the Franciscans established a house of studies in Canterbury and became associated with the new University of Kent. They also made a big contribution to overseas missions, especially in India, South Africa and Peru.[51]

The Capuchins, unrepresented in England since their days at the Stuart Court in the seventeenth century, were helped by the gift made by a convert peer, Viscount Feilding, of a church and convent at Pantasaph in North Wales. The four original friars, none of them English, were soon attracting native vocations. From Pantasaph the friars went out conducting missions and retreats and, in time, established other houses. By 1873 there were enough English friars for an English Province to be formed. The establishment of Greyfriars, Oxford, revived the learned tradition of the order and provided a base for the literary activities of Father Cuthbert (Hesse), whose books *The Life of St Francis* (1912) and *The History of the Capuchins* (1928) contributed to an increasing awareness of the life and spirituality of St Francis in the Catholic community and beyond.[52] The Conventual Franciscans, under the Maltese Father Bonaventure Scerberras, established a mission at Portishead near Bristol in 1907 and a second house in Rye, Kent, in 1910. With the establishment of houses in Liverpool and Manchester a number of English friars joined the Conventuals, who in 1955 (by which time there were about forty friars living in six houses) erected a separate Province. They took an active part, along with the Minors, in establishing the Franciscan study centre in Canterbury.[53]

The English Dominicans, like the Franciscans, had suffered badly in the early nineteenth century from dislocation and lack of vocations, although they retained important missions at Hinckley and at Leicester. The revival of the Dominican ideal in nineteenth-century France under Jandel and Lacordaire had a faint reflection in England with the opening of study houses at Woodchester in Gloucester and Hawkesyard in Staffordshire (1894) as well as the foundation of inner-city priories, with magnificent 'preaching' churches in Haverstock Hill, London, and in Newcastle, but it was only during the twentieth century that the Dominicans acquired a distinctive and significant character. This owed much to the drive and personality of Bede Jarrett (1881–1934) who was English Provincial from 1916 for some sixteen years. Educated at Stonyhurst and at Oxford, where he took a first in Modern History, he sought to engage the Dominicans in active intellectual work as well as widening their involvement in the overseas missions. At the centre of his activity was the foundation of Blackfriars, Oxford, which was to provide a focus for teaching and contact with the wider academic world.[54] Jarrett's appeal was personal and immediate and during his provincialate and afterwards the English Dominicans produced, or gave a home to, a great number of individuals whose contribution, at first sight, seems highly individualistic, with such extraordinary characters as Vincent NcNabb in the forefront.[55]

A present-day Dominican, Aidan Nichols, has suggested (1997) in his *Dominican Gallery*[56] that discounting the short-lived 'New Left' Catholics of the 1970s, the 1930s were the last period in which an attempt was made to present a Catholic interpretation of English history and culture through the search for a new order of society, and that the Dominicans were at the heart of it. He isolates certain themes, including the aesthetics of Gill, the beginning of Jungian psychology, Distributist economics, the emergence of English Dante scholarship, and the environmentalism of the 'back to the land' movement. He takes seven Dominicans to illustrate his thesis: Victor White, theologian and psychologist, Gerald Vann, spiritual writer, Thomas Gilby, philosopher, Sebastian Bullough, aesthetician and exegete, Gervase Mathew, Byzantinist and English medievalist, Kenelm Foster, student of Dante and Petrarch, and Conrad Pepler, critic of culture and theologian of mysticism. He argued that despite their contrasting personalities they had a common vision based on the power of Catholic Christianity in general and Thomism in particular to illuminate the world. The continuing intellectual vitality of the Dominican way, despite the many defections and difficulties which beset the English Dominicans in the years around Vatican II, is a tribute to that common culture, and towards the end of the century, with Timothy Radcliffe as the first English Master General of the Dominicans, the Preachers remain buoyant. The Dominican contribution has been largely an intellectual one but, as with the Jesuits, there has been an active political involvement especially with the peace movement. For many years the English Dominican School at Laxton (now closed) was the only religious-run Catholic boarding school without a cadet corps. The Dominicans, too, through their pioneer conference centre at Spode House, through their publications like *New Blackfriars*, and through their tertiaries, have had a profound impact on lay spirituality.

The Carmelites have also contributed in this direction although their influence has been less obviously high profile. The English Carmelite friars, a small group at the best of times, had died out in 1849 with the death of Francis Willoughby Brewster, who described himself as having 'no Superior, no inferior, being the last man'.[57] As with the Franciscans, the Carmelites come in several varieties. The Discalced Carmelites arrived in London in 1862 at Wiseman's invitation and established the Carmelite church in Kensington under the leadership of Herman Cohen, a convert Jew who was to die a martyr of charity ministering to French prisoners during the Franco-Prussian War. In Kensington and elsewhere the Carmelites promulgated their spirituality and gave noted retreats.[58] The Carmelites had strong English traditions, holding their first general chapter at Aylesford in Kent in 1247 and electing as their Prior General Simon Stock, an Englishman, to transform their eremitical way of life into that of an order of mendicants, the Whitefriars. Some seven centuries later, in 1948, negotiations began which were to bring back the remains of Aylesford into Carmelite hands, and a group of Calced Carmelites came into residence by the end of 1949. Relics of St Simon Stock were translated from Bordeaux in July 1951 and in the same year, too, the Carmelites of England became a Province independent from Ireland.

Cardinal Heenan, whose motto was '*sub umbra Carmeli*', 'under the shadow of Carmel' (after his second name, Carmel), reopened the outdoor church at Aylesford in 1965. The reconstruction of the shrine and priory at Aylesford owed much to the three Lynch brothers from County Wicklow. Some Irish Carmelites had come to Kent as early as 1926 and it was Elias Lynch, the eldest of the brothers, then resident at Faversham, who masterminded the acquisition of Aylesford. His youngest brother, Kilian, Prior General of the Order, gave the project all the support he could, and the third brother, Malachy, became the house's first prior and chief fund-raiser. Under him it became a popular Marian shrine. 'Father Malachy Lynch was one of the great religious beggars of the present century. He was quite shameless about this, and with justification; for', as Brocard Sewell remembers,

> he used to remind us in the talks that he gave at the weekly Conventual Chapter, the Carmelites are by origin a mendicant order. He really did trust in providence, and practised the virtue of magnificence, to which it belongs, Saint Thomas Aquinas tells us, to spend largely in the pursuit of noble objects; providence, he believed, would, through the intercession of Our Lady and Saint Joseph, provide for all the community's financial needs. To raise funds for the restoration of the priory and the building of the shrine he issued shares in what he called 'Our Lady's Company'; shares which were unredeemable and paid no interest. The idea caught on, and the money came pouring in. When asking for huge bank loans and overdrafts to pay for all the work that was going on, he would astonish bank managers by naming the Blessed Virgin as guarantor.[59]

The ability of the religious orders to receive public confidence and to raise sums of money sufficient to build large churches was shown also in the establishment of the Servites in London. A Florentine order of the thirteenth century in origin, and with a well-developed 'third order' and nuns, the Servites sent two of their brethren, Philip Bosio and Augustine Morini, to London in 1864. They arrived, clad in black satin; an Italian tailor had assured them that was what English gentlemen wore.[60] They spoke little or no English. In the early part of 1867 they were allocated a portion of the then vast Oratory parish to serve as a new parish. This was eventually to be the site of their priory in Fulham Road. The priory church was opened in 1875, and in the years that followed, the Italian founding fathers were being replaced by English recruits and the friars were finding some influential benefactors, including Charles Robertson, who bequeathed them the site of the present Servite house at Begbroke near Oxford. In 1899 the Servites had their first English superior and in 1914 an English Province was established. They continued to maintain a specific spirituality. 'Don't you think', wrote Father Morini to a friend in 1866,

> the spirit of our Order can be defined more or less as the Apostolate of Charity, brought about and maintained by true humility arising from contemplation of the Passion of Our Lord and the Sorrows of Mary? In the last analysis it is the spirit of Sacrifice. Our principal purpose is the propagation of devotion to the Sorrows of Mary.[61]

The Servites were unknown in medieval England but the Augustinian Friars, generally known as the Austin Friars, were numerous. They returned to England the same year as the Servites, 1864, and established a priory at Hoxton in the

East End of London, a very poor and populous district. The friars, like most of their charges, were from Ireland, and included among their number a remarkable pastor, Michael Kelly, who was to be in Hoxton from 1864 until his death in 1914. The number of English houses of the order had reached fourteen by 1994 and this included a second substantial parish priory in London, at Hammersmith, established in 1903, and a private school, Austin Friars, founded in 1950 at Carlisle. In 1953 a medieval house of the order, Clare Priory in Suffolk, came into their hands, and as in the cases of Aylesford and Buckfast, religious life returned to a dissolved foundation. In 1977, the previously Irish-governed English communities were formed into an Anglo-Scottish Province.[62]

The Augustinian Friars, who emerged in a similar way to the Carmelites and Servites as orders of friars in the thirteenth century, owed their way of life to the inspiration of St Augustine of Hippo. Many religious founders were inspired by the Augustinian model. The Augustinians of the Assumption, founded in 1845, in France, and dedicated in a typically French Catholic way to undoing the French Revolution, came to England in 1901 and included among their members George Andrew Beck, the future Archbishop of Liverpool and the editor of the 1950 Hierarchy Centenary volume.[63] Augustine, too, had inspired the Canons Regular to live a life in community. The principal centre of the Augustinian canons was, for most of the period covered by this book, at Bodmin in Cornwall, where, before the Reformation, the order had a house. The canons, under the Italian Felix Menchini, arrived at Bodmin in 1881 and with a succession of superiors, notably Walter Aloysius Smith and Richard Alphonsus McElroy, built a priory, and a church which was to become in many ways the spiritual heart of Catholic Cornwall.[64] The resident community was, at its height, about ten in number with non-resident canons, as many as seven in number, living in outlying parishes, The canons had a school at Datchet near Windsor and, for some time, a house of studies at Hoddesden in Hertfordshire. Their work is now concentrated in London at Hornsey in the north and Eltham in the south. The Canons Regular of the Immaculate Conception, founded in France in 1866, came to England in 1932 and at Harlow, Essex, built one of the most ambitious parish churches of its period.[65]

Another family of canons, the White Canons, or Norbertines, or Premonstratensians, came to England in two groups. One group came from the Abbey at Tongerloo in Belgium and settled at Crowle in Lincolnshire in the 1870s; from it houses were established as far apart as Manchester and Spalding. In 1882 the Provençal house of Frigolet sent some canons to Storrington in Sussex where the Duke of Norfolk provided his patronage. At Storrington, established as a shrine of Our Lady of England, the canonical life flourished in the middle part of the present century and having been transferred to the jurisdiction of Tongerloo in 1953, Storrington became, in 1962, the first independent house of the Premonstratensians to be established in England since the Reformation.[66] The ordered life of a Canon Regular, whose principal obligation is *Laus Dei in Choro*, is the product of a settled church.

THE MISSIONARY CONGREGATIONS

Wiseman in 1850 favoured those orders, or societies, who placed less emphasis on the choir and more on missionary action. His support was crucial in the encouragement and growth of the orders most associated with the Catholic revival of the Victorian period. Their success, however, owed more to the boundless energy and missionary zeal of their founding fathers.

One congregation, the Institute of Charity, generally known as the Rosminians after their founder, Antonio Rosmini, had a profound effect on English Catholicism within a few years of its foundation in Italy in 1828. Luigi Gentili had come to England as early as 1835, with two other fathers, to take on the troubled Prior Park project in Bath, a college and a potentially influential spiritual centre founded by Bishop Augustine Baines, the flamboyant and far-sighted, if somewhat extravagant Vicar Apostolic of the Western District.[67] It was not with this, however, that Gentili was to make his greatest impact but in the Midlands, newly industrialised, where, under the patronage of Ambrose Phillipps de Lisle, he set out with fierce energy to convert England: 'People shout at you that they are free, but they are slaves to a nobility that wallows in opulence. This idea of independence which in fact they have not got, acts like a drug and hides from them their temporal and spiritual ruin.'[68] In a few years Gentili founded the parish of Loughborough, organised the building of Ratcliffe College in Leicester (opened, with buildings by Pugin, in 1847),[69] established the Sisters of Providence and began a great series of missions and retreats. Before his death in 1848 in Dublin of 'famine fever' he had preached fifty-one missions, each of a fortnight, in all the great industrial towns, given fifteen clergy retreats, twenty-one retreats to religious, and sermons without number – eight hundred, it is said, in his last eighteen months. It is claimed that not only did he receive up to three thousand converts into the Church but that his attire, the Roman collar, and the clerical dress of cassock, cincture and biretta, influenced all who came after him. Moreover, he preached the first public mission in 1839 at Spetisbury, near Blandford, Dorset, and the first public retreat at Prior Park in 1836, as well as encouraging processions in honour of the Blessed Sacrament and Our Lady.[70] Such inspirational leadership was difficult to sustain, but new Catholics were attracted to the Institute and among them was William Lockhart who in 1874 bought Ely Chapel in London, now known as St Ethelreda's, Ely Place, the only pre-Reformation church building in London in Catholic hands and one of the few in England.[71] Other work started by the Rosminians included parishes in

Wales, overseas missions and, for a time, reformatory schools – a veritable catalogue of activity.

The Rosminians in the 1830s and 1840s were breathing new life into the English Church and they were soon joined by others equally afire with evangelical zeal. The Passionists, founded in the eighteenth century by St Paul of the Cross, were an order dedicated to the preaching of missions and retreats. Dominic Barberi, ordained in 1818 as a Passionist, had an early devotion to the conversion of England, but it was not until 1841, following a preliminary visit in the previous year, that he finally settled in England. The first Passionist monastery in England was opened at Aston, Staffordshire, on 17 February 1842. Despite an unprepossessing appearance and poor English, his popular appeal and his ability to cope with insults made him a great evangelist. His was no triumphalism without content, but an attempt to bring back people to Christ. He died at Reading, in the Railway Tavern, in 1849 after seven years of retreat-giving and constant activity. He is perhaps best remembered as the priest who reconciled Newman, but he is also the only one, so far, of the nineteenth-century apostles of the 'Second Spring' to have been beatified, on 27 October 1963.[72] George Ignatius Spencer, son of Earl Spencer, one of the Cambridge converts of the 1830s, joined the Passionists, and added social status to great ardour. Those who felt uncomfortable with a foreigner might feel more at home with an English aristocrat.[73] As with the other orders, a London base was soon acquired with a foundation in Highgate in 1858. It was said that Wiseman wanted his new Rome of London to be surrounded by the great churches of the various religious orders, and the dome of St Joseph's on London's northern heights reflects this ambition. The present church was opened in 1889. It has ten purpose-built confessionals, which emphasised the work of its founders.[74]

The Redemptorists, another eighteenth-century foundation, seemed to answer Wiseman's need for a group of clergy who would arouse the slumbering energies of congregations in which 'stronger excitement is required than the voice of ordinary admonition'. The Redemptorists saw their charism as 'Apostles abroad and Carthusians at home'. From humble beginnings in the 1840s the Redemptorists centred themselves at Clapham in South London where, after 1847, they ran a model 'parish' and also, in Thomas Edward Bridgett, provided one of the outstanding Victorian Catholic apologists. It was not the pastoral ministry, nor the 'apostolate of the pen', which occupied most of their attention. Their principal work, a task they shared with the Passionists, was the holding of missions, short, sharp, religious campaigns using the full panoply of Victorian piety to revitalise or awaken a religious spirit in a locality and to establish the identity of the resident Catholics. Victorian Catholicism, for the first time since the Reformation, was generating a vital parish life. 'The work of parochial missions', John Sharp, a recent historian of the Redemptorists, has suggested, 'in helping to establish this Catholic identity was an essential procedure, as well as contribution to the building up of parishes and the cementation of regular parochial life, on which the long-term success of the missions depended.' Missions could be the crucial period in the development of a parish and the work of the Redemptorists in this direction deployed every ecclesiastical, not to say theatrical stratagem. One sermon so moved a man in the congregation at one mission that he shouted out self-accusingly, 'Stop! I'm the man – I've crucified the Lord.' Personal salvation, as with the Evangelical Protestant and the Salvation Army, was linked to the great social issues of the day, especially the problem of alcoholism. In the short term the Redemptorists seem to have been successful. In Washington, County Durham, a usually full lock-up on pay-day was almost empty during a retreat. There were no Catholic drunks that week.[75]

The 'shock-troopers' were to introduce vitality and prayer, and then the secular clergy were to take over and build up the community. But in some poor areas the orders sometimes remained. The Oblates of Mary Immaculate, a French order founded in 1816 with an intention of evangelising the poor, came to England in 1843 and to London in 1865, at the – by then – ailing Wiseman's invitation, to establish missions at Tower Hill and Kilburn. Tower Hill was in the Docklands and in the parish at one time there were 6,000 resident Catholics. It was a fluctuating population and needed much financial support from the outside. Kilburn became, in an expansive period for the Church after World War II, a gigantic parish with a ministry to Irish immigrants and the homeless.[76] Many other 'apostolic' orders were drafted into England's cosmopolitan Catholic community. The Society of the Catholic Apostolate, or Pious Society of Missions, established in 1835 by Vincent Pallotti and generally known as the Pallottines, were invited by Wiseman to look after the Italian community in London.[77] Many of the new orders were French in origin, well suited by their understanding of 'de-Christianisation' to deal with the conversion of England. London was often their starting point. From 1850, thirteen years after their foundation as a society, the Marist Fathers at Spitalfields, a traditional French area, evangelised a district adjacent to Tower Hill with similar problems.[78] In more recent times, since 1968, the Marists have managed the national Shrine of Our Lady at Walsingham in Norfolk.[79] Others, like the Fransalians, the Fathers of St Edmund and the Sons of Mary Immaculate, made English foundations and, in most cases, attracted English recruits. In time the various groups became familiar parts of the English Catholic community. Even the most 'Continental' of congregations could take on an English character.[80]

CLERICAL INSTITUTES, RELIGIOUS BROTHERS AND LAY FRATERNITIES

Newman saw the Oratorian way of life as proposed by St Philip Neri as a halfway house between the secular and the regular priesthood. 'Altogether it seems rather the age for external secularism,' he told John Bernard Dalgairns, one of his closest disciples, 'with a gentle inward bond of asceticism – and this is just Oratorianism.'[81] Newman placed the perfection of the Oratorian in the common life.[82] An English Oratory was established by a papal brief of 24 November 1847 in which Newman was made superior and his abode fixed in Birmingham. The Birmingham Oratory was inaugurated in 1848. In the same year another Oxford convert, Frederick William Faber, and his companions, resident temporarily at Cotton Hall in Staffordshire, were admitted as Oratorians and in 1849 went to London where, in 1850, the London Oratory became autonomous.[83] It was not until 1993 that a third Oratory, in Newman's beloved Oxford, was inaugurated in what had been the Jesuit church of St Aloysius. This was perhaps an appropriate monument to the great Oratorian cardinal, declared venerable but not yet beatified at the century's end.[84]

The London Oratory became a centre first for the rich devotional life for many of the Irish immigrants to London.[85] Father Faber, flamboyant and sentimental, composed many hymns which remained standard for generations including one, 'Faith of our Fathers', whose very words captured the Catholic mentality of an age of triumphant ultramontane Catholicism in a way that perhaps only a recent Catholic convert could. The Oratory was also a centre of 'fashionable' Catholicism and its domed church in Knightsbridge, where the original Oratory had been transferred from the Holborn area, became one of the most frequented and familiar of London's Catholic centres, a place of prayer and rich musical liturgy. The first generation of Oratorians, with Newman at the forefront, were a learned community of writers, but later generations, many still attracted as converts from the Church of England, have concentrated their attention on their community and pastoral responsibilities.[86]

Communities of secular clerics seemed very well adjusted to the spirit of the nineteenth century and the Victorian cardinals were all involved in one way or another with such groups, which have tended to have shorter life-spans than the Oratorians. Thus Wiseman, with Manning as superior, established in his diocese a house of 'free-lance' priests living in community and forming in principle a kind of task-force at the bishop's disposal. They were known, after St Charles Borromeo, the great Catholic Reformation Archbishop of Milan who had a similar group, as the Oblates of St Charles. Their Rule, drawn up by Manning, was approved by Rome and their community was established at Bayswater in 1857. The Oblates continued until Vatican II but with Manning's death they lacked motive force.[87] Even more short-lived, but still significant in the number of missions they established, were the priests of the Institute of St Andrew, yet another convert's creation, in this case George Bampfield. They aimed at evangelising North London and the southern fringes of Hertfordshire.[88]

The English Catholics looked far beyond the borders of their own country. The British Empire and Commonwealth saw to it that, throughout much of the last hundred and fifty years, the English Catholic community made a crucial contribution to the missions in British territory, especially in Africa. The older orders, as we have seen, made their mark, but there was plenty of space for expansion. Cardinal Vaughan, much influenced by the French 'Missions Étrangères' society and its college in the rue du Bac in Paris, in 1866 established a college at Mill Hill in the developing suburbs of North London to educate missionaries.[89] At first the college concentrated its efforts on providing clergy to minister to America's black Catholics but eventually the priests emanating from Mill Hill divided into two groups: the American-based Josephites (not to be confused with the Josephites from the diocese of Ghent who concentrated on educational work[90]) working still among black people, and the St Joseph's Foreign Mission Society, familiarly known as the Mill Hill Missionaries. As the ecclesiastical scramble for Africa paralleled the political one, various other groups arose in England. These included the French White Fathers[91] and the Society for the African Missions,[92] the Holy Ghost Fathers, begun in France but much promoted in America,[93] and, more recently, a number of Italian-based societies including the Consolata Fathers from Turin[94] and the Comboni Fathers from Verona.[95] The continuing vitality of the missionary ideal was shown in the pooling of resources in the establishment of the Missionary Institute in London, at Mill Hill, the centre of Cardinal Vaughan's activities.

In the work of education as a specialised minority the Salesians, founded by John Bosco in 1859, arrived in England, at Battersea, in 1887, and opened schools which complemented their overseas mission work.[96] Most of the congregations referred to so far, including the Salesians, have been clerical institutes, most of them priests or training for the priesthood. Such institutes have stood the test of time well if the raw statistics are reliable. Thus, according to the *Catholic Directory* there were 1,433 'regular clergy' in 1925, 1,971 in 1959, 2,530 in 1975 and 1,888 in 1995. Yet what these figures do not reveal is a continuing difficulty in recruitment, which has been particularly acute in the orders of non-ordained brothers. Their work in the provision of secondary education was substantial. The De la Salle brothers (the Brothers of the Christian Schools), the Xaverians, the Brothers of Mercy, the Marist Brothers and the Irish Christian Brothers, among others, established many schools across the country, most of which survive and flourish under lay management.[97] Religious Brothers like the Alexians and the Brothers of St John of God, both established in England before the end of the nineteenth century, provided and continue to provide selfless medical support.[98] Sometimes, as in the case of many of the brothers, the life-span of an order's vitality is short-lived, but its contribution is nevertheless essential for the development of the local church. Knowing when to let go of a project and hand it on to others is a valuable gift of religious discernment.

The disappearance and the decline of religious orders is nothing new in the history of the Church[99] but the continuing vitality of the ideal is shown in the new forms of the life which have continued to emerge. Many begin as secular movements and gradually take on the characteristics of a religious order. Thus a group of priests led by René Voillaume following the spiritual teachings of Charles de Foucauld (1858–1916) became the 'Little Brothers of Jesus', combining a deeply contemplative life in small communities with working in ordinary workplaces.[100] The fraternity began in 1933 and became a Pontifical Institute in 1968. The Opus Dei movement, begun in 1928 by Josemaría Escrivá de Balaguer in Spain as an organisation of lay people, eventually became an international network of the apostolic life.[101]

The diversity and vitality of the male religious in the English Catholic community is particularly striking given the relative smallness of the Catholic population. Indeed, practically every religious order that aspired to more than a local apostolate succeeded in finding a foothold in England, bringing with them the many spiritual and cultural riches of their various traditions. Some came to avoid persecution. Others arrived to participate in the missionary opportunities provided by a growing Catholic population and a developing empire. Still others came to learn English, a language which has outlived every other form of British imperial hegemony. The great possibilities of the rich mix provided by these religious were somewhat muted by the necessity for all the societies, however eremetical and contemplative their origins, to make a living by doing the same kind of pastoral and educational work in parishes and schools which made them far more uniform than was the case with the religious sisters. Such work also brought them into conflict with the diocesan authorities.

'*ROMANOS PONTIFICES*' AND ITS AFTERMATH

The restoration of the hierarchy in 1850 came to a church deeply divided in its ecclesiastical government. The traditional rivalry between the religious orders, enshrined in the English Catholic sub-culture by jokes about Benedictines, Franciscans and Jesuits, was combined with a struggle between regulars and seculars for control of the hearts and minds of the Catholic population. Missions and Mass centres had often been established with little or no reference to the appropriate ecclesiastical superior, if he could be identified, and the shadowy territorial authority of the Vicars Apostolic played into the hands of the regulars, especially the well-established, well-connected and to some extent well-funded Benedictines and Jesuits. With the restoration of the hierarchy the bishops gradually redressed the balance. A battle was waged between the bishops and the regulars, especially in the 1870s, with the developing city of Manchester as its vortex. A dispute between the then Bishop of Salford, the future Cardinal Vaughan, and the Jesuits over the control of Catholic education in the city mirrored the growing feeling among the increasingly dominant secular clergy – 'Our Lord's own Order', as Manning rather defensively described them – that *they* should be in the front line of influence on the new generation of the Catholic middle classes. Education was too critical a matter, in the mind of Manning, Vaughan and others, to be left to the Jesuits. Indeed, Manning considered the Jesuit system outmoded for the Victorian city. Vaughan championed the cause, and spent long months in Rome pushing his arguments, which he saw as a dispute on 'matters of discipline affecting the working of the Church in Great Britain'. The papal constitution of Leo XIII, *Romanos Pontifices* (8 May 1881), was the reward of his labour.[102]

This document clearly defined the rights of the English bishops in their own dioceses and upheld the episcopal privilege of supervising all their missions (what we would now call parishes) whether their pastors were secular or regular. Parish schools and the colleges of religious orders were subject to episcopal visitation. Missions, even those served by religious, could be decided by the diocesan bishop and a secular parish priest appointed. *Romanos Pontifices* was an important moment of definition. The work of the religious was to be in future less independent than before and more integral to the diocesan model. Religious were to be more concerned with the charismatic formation of the Church than with its administrative structure.[103]

The religious orders, nevertheless, throughout the last hundred and fifty years have played a crucial role in the development of the English Catholic community, especially in its spiritual life. 'The Religious Orders', wrote Bishop George Ambrose Burton of Clifton on 1 June 1903, 'have ever been the Church's finest bulwark. It is they who have given to orthodoxy its stoutest champions and cleverest expounders, to the Holy See its bravest defenders, to the good their brightest models, to the wayward their sternest reprovers.'[104] This is not fashionable language, but it expresses, somewhat flamboyantly, why throughout the last hundred and fifty years the religious orders have both fulfilled many individual vocations and contributed greatly to the vigour of the Church. Each new generation brings its own problems but the continuing influence of such monastic teachers as Thomas Merton far beyond his own Cistercian Order, and such groups as the Protestant monks of Taizé are only two examples of a continually renewing tradition which goes back to the Apostolic roots of Christianity.[105]

NOTES

1. *Tablet*, 3 July 1965, pp. 736–7, 742.
2. *Code of Canon Law* (English Translation) (London, 1983), Canon 577.
3. *Code of Canon Law*, Canon 578.
4. See D. A. Bellenger, '"Superstitious Enemies of the Flesh"? The variety of Benedictine Responses to the Enlightenment' in N. Aston (ed.), *Religious Change in Europe 1659–1914* (Oxford, 1977), pp. 149–60.

5. See A. Clark, 'The Return to the Monasteries' in D. Rees (ed.), *Monks of England: The Benedictines in England from Augustine to the Present Day* (London, 1997), p. 215.
6. R. Addington, *The Idea of the Oratory* (London, 1966), p. 102.
7. R. B. Martin, *Gerard Manley Hopkins: A Very Private Life* (London, 1991), pp. 175–6.
8. Quoted in B. Bailey, D. A. Bellenger and S. Tugwell (eds), *Letters of Bede Jarrett* (Bath, 1989), p. viii.
9. See F. Edwards, *The Jesuits in England* (London, 1985), and B. Bassett, *The English Jesuits* (London, 1967).
10. See, for example, T. E. Muir, *Stonyhurst College 1593–1993* (London, 1992), especially pp. 60–72.
11. See Rees, *Monks of England*, esp. chs 10–12.
12. See, for example, G. Anstruther, *A Hundred Homeless Years: English Dominicans 1558–1658* (London, 1958).
13. See D. Lunn, *The English Benedictines, 1540–1688* (London, 1980) and G. Scott, *Gothic Rage Undone* (Bath, 1992).
14. See D. A. Bellenger, 'Revolution and Emancipation' in Rees, *Monks of England*, pp. 199–213.
15. See Clark, 'Return to the Monasteries', *passim*, on the gradual monastic reform of the English Benedictines.
16. See L. J. Lekai, *The Cistercians: Ideals and Reality* (Kent State, 1977).
17. See D. A. Bellenger, *The French Exiled Clergy in the British Isles after 1789* (Bath, 1986), pp. 83–90.
18. See D. Parry, *Monastic Century: St Augustine's Abbey Ramsgate (1861–1961)* (Tenbury Wells, 1965).
19. See D. Rees, 'The Benedictine Revival of the Nineteenth Century' in D. H. Farmer, *Benedict's Disciples*, 2nd edition (Leominster, 1995), pp. 324–49.
20. See J. Stéphan, *A History of Buckfast Abbey* (Bristol, 1970).
21. Stéphan, *Buckfast*, pp. 318–31. See also E. Graff, *Anscar Vonier* (London, 1957).
22. P. F. Anson, *The Religious Orders and Congregations of Great Britain and Ireland* (Worcester, 1949), pp. 36–8.
23. See, for a popular account, R. B. Lockhart, *Halfway to Heaven* (London, 1985).
24. See M. D. Knowles, 'Cardinal Gasquet as Historian' in M. D. Knowles, *The Historian and Character and other Essays* (Cambridge, 1963), pp. 240–63.
25. See The Benedictines of Stanbrook, *In a Great Tradition* (London, 1956), pp. 55–7.
26. See Clark, 'Return to the Monasteries', pp. 223–4.
27. Clark, 'Return to the Monasteries', pp. 224–8.
28. Clark, 'Return to the Monasteries', p. 232.
29. See B. Whelan, *The History of Belmont Abbey* (London, 1959) and R. Kollar, *Westminster Cathedral* (Edinburgh, 1987).
30. See H. van Zeller, *Downside By and Large* (London, 1954).
31. See J. McCann and C. Cary-Elwes, *Ampleforth and its Origins* (London, 1952).
32. See R. Kollar, *Return of the Benedictines to London: A History of Ealing Abbey* (Tunbridge Wells, 1989).
33. See H. Wansbrough and A. Marett-Crosby (eds), *Benedictines in Oxford* (London, 1997).
34. See P. Jebb, 'Benet House, Cambridge', *E.B.C. Symposium* 15 (1997), pp. 48–51.
35. See C. N. L. Brooke (ed.), *David Knowles Remembered* (Cambridge, 1991).
36. R. Howells, *Total Community: The Monks of Caldey Island* (Tenby, 1975).
37. See D. A. Bellenger in *DNB 1986–1990* (Oxford, 1996), pp. 55–6.
38. See e.g. T. Castle (ed.), *Basil Hume* (London, 1986).
39. See P. F. Anson, *Abbot Extraordinary: A Memoir of Aelred Carlyle* (London, 1958).
40. See A Monk of Prinknash, *Prinknash Abbey* (n.d.), and the journal *Pax* edited from Prinknash.

41. K. Spink, *A Sense of the Sacred* (London, 1988).
42. 'Dom Edmund Jones, OSB, A Celebration of his life and work', *Christ the King, Cockfosters, Parish Magazine, Special Edition* (June 1985).
43. P. Harris (ed.), *John Main by Those who Knew Him* (London, 1991).
44. See Rees, *Monks of England*, p. 248.
45. Edwards, *Jesuits in England*, p. 242.
46. *The Catholic Directory* (1925), p. 609.
47. Muir, *Stonyhurst*.
48. See N. Pevsner, *Buildings of England: North Lancashire* (Harmondsworth), pp. 199–200.
49. Edwards, *Jesuits in England*, p. 204. See also B. Bassett, *Farm Street Church* (London, 1948).
50. Muir, *Stonyhurst*, p. 144.
51. See also H. Docherty, 'The Friars Minor in England, their Historical Continuity', *Clergy Review*, 37 (1952), pp. 332–51, Father Thaddeus, *The Franciscans in England, 1600–1850* (London, 1898), pp. 106–7; J. R. H. Moorman, *The Franciscans in England* (London, 1974), pp. 98–111.
52. See *Capuchin Ordo* (Bristol, 1963), pp. 52–62, for a necrology of Capuchins to that date.
53. Moorman, *Franciscans*, pp. 109–10. The Franciscan tradition continues to inspire new groupings. In 1909 the Society of the Atonement, founded in 1898 by an Episcopalian priest in the United States, became Catholic and is known as the Friars of the Atonement. In 1908 Father Paul Watson (1863–1940), their founder, inaugurated the annual week of prayer for Christian unity. These Friars have a presence in London.
54. See Bailey *et al.*, *Bede Jarrett*, and also A. White, 'Father Bede Jarrett and the Renewal of the English Dominican Province' in D. A. Bellenger, *Opening the Scrolls* (Bath, 1987), pp. 216–34.
55. See F. Valentine, *Father Vincent McNabb* (London, 1955).
56. A. Nichols, *Dominican Gallery: Portrait of a Culture* (Leominster, 1997).
57. L. C. Sheppard, *The English Carmelites* (London, 1943), p. 75.
58. Sheppard, *English Carmelites*, pp. 75–8. See also B. Zimmerman, *Carmel in England* (London, 1899).
59. B. Sewell, *The Habit of a Lifetime* (Padstow, 1992), pp. 115–16. See also E. Fielding, *Courage to Build Anew* (London, 1968).
60. G. M. Corr, *Servites in London* (Newbury, 1952), p. 15.
61. Corr, *Servites*, p. 100.
62. M. B. Hackett, 'The Irish Augustinians in England and Scotland, 1539–1992' in F. X. Martin (ed.), *The Irish Augustinians in Rome, 1656–1994 and Irish Augustinian Missions throughout the World* (Rome, 1994), pp. 57–81.
63. Anson, *Religious Orders*, pp. 18–22.
64. See A. Whitehead, *Ninety Years in Cornwall* (Bodmin, 1971).
65. Anson, *Religious Orders*, pp. 54–5.
66. H. M. Gillett, *Shrine of Our Lady of England at Storrington* (Storrington, 1954). See also *White Canons Centenary Issue* (Storrington, 1971), which contains some details of Norbertine Canons who worked in England.
67. J. S. Roche, *A History of Prior Park College* (London, 1931).
68. C. R. Leetham, *Luigi Gentili* (London, 1965).
69. C. R. Leetham, *Ratcliffe College 1847–1947* (Leicester, 1950).
70. Leetham, *Luigi Gentili*, esp. pp. 372–5.
71. K. Cunningham, *St Ethelreda's, Ely Place* (London, 1992).
72. See A. Wilson, *Blessed Dominic Barberi* (London, 1966).
73. See Father Pius, *Life of Father Ignatius of St Paul* (Dublin, 1866).
74. A. Rottmann, *London Catholic Churches* (London, 1926), p. 218.

75. J. Sharp, *Reapers of the Harvest: The Redemptorists in Great Britain and Ireland 1843–1898* (Dublin, 1989).
76. See *Centenary Brochure of the Oblate Fathers, Tower Hill, 1865–1965.*
77. F. M. Steele, *Monasteries and Religious Houses of Great Britain and Ireland* (London, 1903), p. 165.
78. Anson, *Religious Orders*, pp. 121–2.
79. R. Connolly, *The Slipper Chapel* (Great Wakering, 1975), p. 15.
80. C. Fitzgerald-Lombard, *English and Welsh Priests 1801–1914* (Bath, 1993), lists all known members of religious orders ordained between those years, pp. 154–263. It provides an invaluable guide.
81. Addington, *Oratory*, p. 104.
82. Addington, *Oratory*, p. 126.
83. See M. Napier and A. Laing, *The London Oratory Centenary 1884–1984* (London, 1984).
84. The first Oratorians arrived at Oxford to take up residence in September 1990 and the formal establishment of the Oxford Oratory was announced on 14 May 1993. See J. Bertram, *St Aloysius Parish Oxford* (Oxford, 1993).
85. S. W. Gilley, 'Vulgar Piety and the Brompton Oratory, 1850–1860', *Durham University Journal*, 43 (1981).
86. See Napier and Laing, *London Oratory.*
87. Steele, *Monasteries*, pp. 144–8.
88. Steele, *Monasteries*, p. 135. S. M. Foster, '"*Et in Suburbia Ego*": Father Bampfield and the Institute of St Andrew', *Recusant History*, 23 (1997), pp. 434–49.
89. R. O'Neill, *Cardinal Herbert Vaughan* (London, 1995), pp. 105–207, 303–30.
90. See Anson, *Religious Orders*, p. 119.
91. Anson, *Religious Orders*, pp. 147–8.
92. Anson, *Religious Orders*, p. 19.
93. Anson, *Religious Orders*, pp. 110–11.
94. T. Kennedy (ed.), *Men Religious in the Church* (n.d.), p. 34.
95. Kennedy, *Men Religious*, p. 33.
96. Anson, *Religious Orders*, pp. 139–41; Steele, *Monasteries*, 183–7.
97. See W. J. Battersby, 'Secondary Education for Boys' in G. A. Beck (ed.), *The English Catholics, 1850–1950* (London, 1950).
98. Anson, *Religious Orders*, pp. 17–18, 117–18.
99. See R. Hostie, *Vie et Mort des Ordres Religieux* (Paris, 1972). One modern congregation, the Servants of the Paraclete, founded in 1947 in the USA, is dedicated to looking after priests and religious with serious problems.
100. R. Voillaume, *Au Coeur des Masses; La Vie Religieuse des Petits Frères du Père de Foucauld* (Paris, 1950).
101. See A. Fuenmayor *et al.*, *The Canonical Path of Opus Dei* (Princeton, 1994).
102. O'Neill, *Vaughan*, pp. 219–23.
103. E. R. Norman, *The English Catholic Church in the Nineteenth Century* (Oxford, 1984), esp. pp. 354, 363.
104. In Steele, *Monasteries*, pp. viii–ix. This volume is interesting in illustrating the habits of the religious orders as they were in 1903. A French compilation, *Les Ordres Religieux, la vie et l'art*, ed. G. Le Bras, in two volumes (Paris, 1980) provides a *Dictionnaire des Instituts Religieux*, vol. II, pp. 737–82.
105. See, for example, G. Moorhouse, *Against All Reason* (London, 1972), and R. North, *Fools for God* (London, 1987).

SEVEN

'WHO ARE THE LAITY?'

JAMES PEREIRO

THE AGE OF NEWMAN AND MANNING

On 22 May 1859, at the beginning of the difficulties over Newman's opinions on the laity published in the *Rambler*, Ullathorne called on him to suggest that he give up the editorship of the review after the July issue. In the course of the conversation, Ullathorne expressed regret at the disturbed state of the laity, and, at a certain point, asked Newman: 'Who are the laity?' Newman's answer, as recorded in a memorandum written the same day, was to the effect 'that the Church would look foolish without them'.[1] Mgr George Talbot's contribution to the definition of the vocation of the laity is perhaps even better remembered than Newman's: 'What is the province of the laity? To hunt, to shoot, to entertain? These matters they understand, but to meddle with ecclesiastical matters they have no right at all.'[2] It would have been interesting to witness the reaction of the Catholic working class in England, by far the largest component of the laity, and mostly Irish, to this description of their calling, had they been told about it. Talbot, however, was not far off the mark. When ecclesiastics, and even lay people, spoke about the subject they seemed to restrict the boundaries of the laity to cover only those who, whether they did so or not, were able to hunt, to shoot and to entertain. Ullathorne's question was not an idle one.

A growing interest in the laity was one of the distinctive marks of the nineteenth-century Church, one induced more by external circumstances than by internal developments. Society, science and culture were progressively, and at accelerating speed, moving away from the influence of Christian principles. The official ecclesiastical world, as a result, found itself more and more isolated from those centres where ideas, and even new forms of society were being forged. The layman, on the other hand, remained of necessity in contact with worldly realities. A new perception began to find its way into the consciousness of the Church, one that suggested it was the task of the Catholic laity to breathe

Christian principles back into those realities, and, even more pressingly at times, to respond to the challenges that society, science and culture were posing the Church.

Newman and Manning were both conscious of the need for full involvement of the laity in social life and culture. There were, however, differences of emphasis and perception between them. Manning, without ignoring science and culture, stressed the importance of social and political activism on the part of the laity; while Newman, for his part, was particularly aware of the need for the Catholic laity to be fully involved in the cultural and scientific life of the time.

The laity had not held back for an indication from the hierarchy that they should become involved in worldly affairs. Rather, that was their natural environment. In reaction to social or cultural conditions they were formulating ideas and setting in motion initiatives that Newman and Manning could not but follow up closely. In the intellectual field, one of the most prestigious initiatives in those years was that of the *Rambler* – and its successor, the *Home and Foreign Review*. Those involved in this project of intellectual journalism, inspired by the Munich school of Döllinger, were intent on introducing into this country critical methods of scientific research, particularly in the fields of history and literature, while seeking to give a considered view of current social and political questions. On the political front, on the other hand, the previous decades had seen the appearance, particularly in France, of a group of Catholic activists who, accepting wholeheartedly the new forms of government, wanted their co-religionists to be fully involved in the political life of their respective countries. Newman had hopes of the philosophical and historical movement represented by the Munich school. Although conscious of its shortcomings, he had a strong feeling for the intellectual enlargement it promised. Manning felt sympathy for the movement of Lacordaire and Montalembert. 'Each was a movement full of heterogeneous life; and they [Newman and Manning] hoped that dangerous elements might be discarded, and the life utilised for the Church.'[3] W. G. Ward, a layman and another great intellectual influence in the second half of the century as editor of the *Dublin Review*, did not share those hopes.

Manning did not want to set Church and society in opposition to each other, or to exclude Catholics from playing an active part in the political life of systems born from the principles of the French Revolution. As he put it in his pastoral letter of 1869:

> In a moment of haste and precipitation, some French writers and politicians have interpreted the condemnations in the Syllabus as a condemnation of the principles of 1789 . . . We would desire to believe, if we can, that those principles . . . are . . . reconcilable with the great laws of political morality

> which lie at the foundations of human society, and are consecrated by the sanction of the world.[4]

He could never reconcile himself to the idea of a fortress Church, hidden behind high walls, securing her intellectual and moral purity from contamination by avoiding all contact with the world. The Church, Manning thought, 'has a twofold work to do for mankind. Its first and primary, indeed, is to save souls, to lead them to eternal life. Its second, but not less true, is to ripen and elevate the social and political life of men by its influences of morality and of law.'[5] In order to carry out the latter, Catholics had to enter into the most intimate relations with society, peoples, states and civil powers. Abstention from social and, in particular, from political life had left social influence and political power in the hands of the Church's enemies, and opened the door to a string of anti-Catholic laws. This was an abdication of natural duty. It was God's will, Manning thought, that the Church should always be in dialogue with society: 'The Church never withdraws from the State as such, which would be to abandon the natural society to its own maladies and mortality.'[6] Even in the most unfavourable political situations, Catholics should use all the powers available to them as citizens: '(1) first, to guard and to conserve all the Christian faith and morals, that still remain in them; (2) secondly, to minimize all the evil of their legislation or government; and (3) thirdly, to recall them by all influences to a better condition'.[7]

Manning regretted the absence of a Catholic lay presence in English public life. It was true, he had written in 1863, that the 'social exile in which they had lived, and their exclusion . . . from public and private employments, have seriously diminished our capacity for usefulness'.[8] But that was an explanation which could be easily turned into an excuse. The situation was very much the same in 1882: Catholics had still not made any noticeable progress in the public life of the country. That pointed, in Manning's view, to a defect in either force or cultivation, or perhaps in both.[9] In 1890, in his notes on hindrances to the spread of Catholicism, he remarked how none of the recent great works of charity – the abolition of slavery, the agitation for the reform of working conditions, or the protection of children against cruelty, etc. – had been initiated by Catholics, and counted hardly any Catholics among their supporters. His own was often the only Catholic name championing such causes. They had been promoted by Dissenters, Anglicans and Quakers, but Manning did not feel that should be an obstacle: 'We are bound to co-operate with them in everything that is not contrary to faith and morals.'[10] His position found little echo among leading lay Catholics or in his successor in the see of Westminster. Catholic charity, on the whole, continued expressing itself in relief of the symptoms of poverty, while tending to ignore the need for change in the social conditions which generated many of the evils.

Lack of access to university education was, no doubt, a serious handicap for Catholics wishing to play an active role in political and cultural life. Newman's Catholic University in Ireland had been intended to provide the Church in these islands with the educated laity it required: a laity

> not arrogant, not rash in speech, not disputatious, but men who know their religion, who enter into it, who know just where they stand, who know what they hold, and what they do not, who know their creed so well that they can give an account of it, who know so much of history that they can defend it . . . An intelligent, well instructed laity . . . [who manage] to get an insight into the relation of truth to truth, to learn to view things as they are, to understand how faith and reason stand to each other, what are the bases and principles of Catholicism . . .[11]

It was the task of such an educated laity to break down the strong English anti-Catholic prejudice, and to make the Catholic case heard. Manning would have subscribed to those sentiments.

Newman considered that a Catholic university was the best possible response for that want but, after the failure of his venture in Dublin, he thought this no longer a viable proposition. The traditional universities were second-best, but the only realistic option.[12] Attendance at Oxford and Cambridge would arm Catholics with the necessary intellectual tools to compete on equal terms with Protestants in the fields of literature and science, social and political life. Besides, the personal relationships forged during those years would grant them easy access to men of future influence and power.

The bishops, however, had banned attendance at the universities in 1864 because of the dangers to which Catholic students would be exposed, given the prevalent rationalism. Manning wholeheartedly agreed with this aspect of the bishops' decision. Some argued in response that, sooner or later in their lives, Catholics in England had to enter into the atmosphere and dangers of public life, and to meet anti-Catholic prejudices, and a dominant Protestant culture and rationalism. Manning concurred: Catholics should be fully immersed in that atmosphere, but, he added, not until their Catholic formation was complete. He felt that two ideas should be safely anchored in every Christian heart at the end of the educational process: first, the existence of a divine revelation, elevating and perfecting human knowledge; second, the divine institution of an infallible teaching authority. Once Catholics had these fundamental principles well rooted in their minds, and had made of them a test for the acquisition of human knowledge, then they would be prepared to enter into dialogue with the world and with the dominant ideas and principles of the day. This preparation, Manning thought, was something which could hardly be given them during the years of school education. He also felt that, if Catholics were to attend Oxford and Cambridge, Catholic education would remain an unfinished fabric, a machinery unable to turn out a finished product, thereby rendering almost impossible the building up of a Catholic culture to which must fall the task of rescuing human culture and society from its dead-end road. He had been, therefore, sorely disappointed when, in 1864, the bishops, while banning Catholics from attending the two traditional universities, decided against setting up a Catholic one.

Manning was conscious of the influence that the general atmosphere of the country could have on the habits of mind of English Catholics. He noted the absence of an English Catholic literature in 1863, and consider it a serious disadvantage and danger when the predominant culture of the country was Protestant.[13] It was difficult for Catholics not to absorb unconsciously the prevalent intellectual and moral atmosphere while reading books or newspapers, and in daily intercourse with non-Catholics. Newman, on his part, was keenly alive to the importance of Catholic literature in the English language. He did not understand it as a literature 'which treats exclusively or primarily of Catholic matters, of Catholic doctrine, controversy, history, persons, or politics; but [one which] includes all subjects of literature whatever, treated as a Catholic would treat them, and as he only can treat them'.[14] Newman also thought of the influence that Catholic periodicals could have in creating a 'body of thought against the false intellectualism of the age, to take a Catholic view and give a Catholic interpretation of the discoveries of the age'.[15] Unfortunately, the *Rambler* and the *Home and Foreign Review*, the two initiatives in the field with which he was more closely connected, did not fare well. The scholarly level of the lay contributors associated with the periodicals partly fulfilled Newman's hope of an enlightened and confident Catholic laity in dialogue with the modern world and science. However, Richard Simpson, editor of the *Rambler* since February 1858, and Acton, his assistant, did not manage to steer clear of ecclesiastical and theological subjects, as Newman had suggested, and incurred the criticism of the English and Welsh bishops.

Newman's attempt at salvaging the *Rambler* by becoming its editor was unsuccessful. In the process, however, he left an important record of his ideas on the laity. When taking it over, he had spoken of how the bishops should naturally desire to know the opinion of the laity on those subjects in which they were really concerned, adding that even the Pope had consulted the faithful when preparing the dogmatic definition of the Immaculate Conception. Under attack from different quarters for the use of the word 'consulted' in this context, Newman defended himself in the July issue of the *Rambler* with his 'On Consulting the Faithful in Matters of Doctrine', where the term 'faithful' is used as interchangeable with 'laity'. In the article he dealt at length with the concept of *sensus fidelium* or *consensus fidelium*. He did not conceive it only as one testimony among others of Apostolic tradition. It was also an instinct of faith, welcoming truth and feeling repugnance for error, a means through which the action of the Holy Spirit manifested itself in the Church and promoted new developments.[16] The gift of discerning, discriminating, defining, promulgating and enforcing any portion of the tradition – including that represented by the *consensus fidelium* – resided in the *Ecclesia docens*.[17] Although Newman concentrated his attention in the article on doctrinal matters, he suggested that the laity should also be called to co-operate with the bishops in matters within their spheres of expertise. The *Rambler* closed in 1862. The Munich Congress of Döllinger (1863), which the *Home and Foreign* had strongly supported, marked the final act of that line in journalism. Newman could not but contemplate with dismay the failure of the project.

Newman and Manning had drawn the general lines of the possible development of lay action in this country. Each in his own way supplied the lack of lay Catholic presence in the social sphere or the field of ideas. Their disappearance left a gaping vacuum. Men of the calibre of Wilfrid Ward, Lord Acton and Baron von Hügel kept a dim light burning for a while in, on the whole, a rather sombre panorama. Ward's Synthetic Society continued from 1896 to 1910 the attempt at dialogue among widely different strands of thought and belief which had inspired the Metaphysical Society, attended by his father and Manning. Unfortunately, the 'Catholic Revival', heralded by Wilfrid Ward when writing the biography of his father, was rather short-lived. He felt that the Modernist crisis had nipped in the bud the flourishing of Catholic letters. The checking of unorthodox principles and developments was necessary, but the reaction had been too harsh, and, as a result, had put back development of true Catholic scholarship. The 'fortress church' mentality which had characterised the Catholic Church since the Reformation had reasserted itself, after a brief moment when it seemed as if it had been replaced by more open intellectual approaches.[18]

It has been said that Vaughan was more successful than Manning in obtaining the co-operation of the laity, a statement which needs a good deal of qualification. He was indeed closer to the High Toryism of the Catholic aristocracy and gentry, and he took up some of the causes they had at heart, such as permission for Catholics to attend Oxford and Cambridge or the building on a grand scale of a metropolitan cathedral at Westminster. With the exception of Catholic education, social issues and the fostering of Catholic culture and literature seem to have weighed lightly on his mind. Paradoxically, his main task force for social influence was not the English laity but the Irish Catholic MPs – the first election after the extension of the franchise had returned fifty-seven of them to Westminster – who were always ready to support his efforts to obtain fairer terms from the government for Catholic schools.[19] Bourne would continue to rely on them for similar purposes. English Catholics were hardly represented in Parliament, and the Catholic Tory peers had little leverage in an overwhelmingly Conservative House of Lords. Lord Ripon, the Liberal leader in the Lords, and the only Catholic in high office, was an isolated figure. As might have been foreseen, a serious cause of weakness at the political level in the late nineteenth century and in the early years of the twentieth century was the gulf between Irish Nationalist MPs and English Catholic Unionist Tories. The Unionist proclivities of the leading Catholic aristocrats aroused the mistrust of the Irish, and this was reinforced by the Duke of Norfolk's intervention with Leo XIII to have the Plan of Campaign condemned.[20]

The beginning of the twentieth century marked a clear change in the level of Catholic influence in the country as a whole. The dramatic achievements of the last quarter of the nineteenth century and their great protagonists were succeeded, in the opinion of many, by administrative blandness and greater insularity,[21] although others saw it as a necessary period of consolidation. One thing was obvious, that although the Catholic community in England continued growing in numbers, its influence had entered into steady decline. Beck located its peak in 1906, as a result of the influence of the Irish MPs, the still considerable importance of the Catholic aristocracy and gentry, and the afterglow of Manning's and Newman's prestige.[22]

THE INTER-WAR PERIOD: A NEW CATHOLIC REVIVAL?

The pontificate of Pius XI (1922–39) was marked from its early days by renewed awareness of the importance of the lay apostolate, accompanied by deeper theological reflection on the nature and role of the laity in the Church. The process of de-christianisation was deeply felt in traditionally Catholic countries like France and Belgium. It was even suggested that France had become a mission territory. The need for the active participation of the laity in the work of re-christianisation was unquestionable. Pius XI called on the laity to exercise their common priesthood by becoming actively involved in the work of spreading and renewing the Kingdom of Christ in the world. Catholic Action was to be the organised form of that apostolate of re-christianisation, and the encyclical *Ubi Arcano Dei* (1922) was the trumpet blast calling Catholics to that task. It opened new perspectives, although the apostolate of the laity was conceived as a *participation* in the apostolate of the hierarchy, which was still regarded as the fundamental depository of the Church's mission. In his letter to Cardinal Bertram (1928), Pius XI described Catholic Action as having 'no other purpose than the participation of the laity in the apostolate of the hierarchy'; from the hierarchy 'it receives therefrom not only a mandate, but also impetus and encouragement'.[23] The predominant mentality was one of re-entering a world from which the Church had been excluded.

The calls of Pius XI found ready welcome in many countries and peoples. New organisations grew up supported and encouraged by local hierarchies. Others, initiated by individuals concerned to meet the needs of the times, were integrated within Catholic Action. A particular phenomenon close to these shores, which had a considerable influence in this country, was the movement initiated by Cardijn in Belgium in the early 1920s to form Catholic workers for the apostolate in their work environment. It was soon acknowledged and approved as an embodiment of the ideal of Catholic Action, and, as the JOC (Young Christian Workers in this country), it was to have an extraordinary expansion and influence in Belgium and in France, where it was introduced around 1926. By the mid-1930s, there were many thousands of workers involved in those two countries.

England and Wales remained, on the whole, outside Continental developments. There seems to have been general apathy towards combination, except when some vital interest, such as Catholic schools, was at risk. Several reasons have been given for this, among them the fact that there was a dearth of organs such as Catholic universities, newspapers, trades unions or a Catholic political party. Some have added, as another reason for the failure of Catholic Action in this country, the Fascist sympathies of vocal Catholics. Organisations did proliferate in the parishes, but they usually involved the same small number of activists and tended to have a languishing life.[24] Without dismissing some of these arguments, it seems more probable that one of the fundamental reasons for the paucity of serious efforts to promote Catholic Action in England and Wales was the lack of any sense of crisis in the local Church. The general feeling was one of strength and sustained progress. If there was any de-christianisation, it seemed to affect fundamentally the Establishment and manifested itself in a steady flow of converts into the Catholic Church, among them men of the intellectual calibre of Maurice Baring, Ronald Knox and G. K. Chesterton. The number of Catholic schools went on growing, churches were filled as fast as they could be built, and there were abundant vocations for the diocesan clergy and the religious life. The mood was one of contented happiness and confidence in the future.[25] There seemed to be little need for change in a state of things that produced such results. There were also a number of initiatives that, even before the First World War, sought to mobilise the laity and gave an impression that Catholic Action, under another name, was already at work in the country, the Catholic Women's League of Margaret Fletcher (founded in 1906) and the Catholic Social Guild (1909) being two outstanding examples.

In regard to Catholic Action, as in other matters, Cardinal Bourne adopted what for him was a congenial stance, that of letting particular initiatives grow without undue episcopal interference, rather than involving himself or the hierarchy in active promotion. He granted Wilfrid Ward ample independence in the running of the *Dublin Review*, and was ready to offer similar latitude to other lay Catholic initiatives. He did not, however, neglect to intervene when he considered circumstances required him to speak. His 1918 pastoral letter continued the long line of Manning's social utterances, pointing out the excesses of capitalism, while upholding family values and rights and criticising the growth of state influence. In 1926, however, he caused a certain amount of consternation among Catholic workers, and those more directly involved in social questions, with his criticism of the National Strike. To many Catholics his condemnation of the strike was a cause of deep embarrassment, and it was received rather testily by Fr John Baptist Reeves OP in the *Christian Democrat*, the publication of the Catholic Social Guild. In the same issue of the magazine, an article by Somerville criticised the strike.[26] The following Sunday the Cardinal spoke again on the social question, leaving this time little room for complacency among employers.

The Catholic Social Guild brought together people and groups which had shown an interest in social issues along the lines of the Church's social teaching. 'Surprisingly', however, 'the Guild soon developed away from its intellectual and middle-class origins to lay the basis, with the support of some parish priests, of a committed working-class following in the years before the First World War.'[27] It was influenced by what was being done in Belgium and France but, in spite of its members' commitment, it never developed into a mass movement or reached the influence that the JOC was to acquire in those countries. There were 3,910 members in 1939. The mass of the Catholic working class – once Ireland had disappeared, for the time being, from the forefront of British politics – voted overwhelmingly Labour. The English and Welsh bishops considered the Labour Party as not strictly socialist, in spite of its rhetoric. They saw Labour as approximating in good measure to Catholic social thought and the bishops continued to show support for working-class values, together with 'a fundamental lack of sympathy with capitalism, and a tolerance of working-class radicalism – so long as it did not conflict with Catholic teaching'.[28] There had never been any attempt to create a Catholic Party, along the lines of the German Zentrum or of the more recent Italian Partito Popolare. The small number of Catholics, their dispersion, their fragmented political allegiances, and the electoral system did not offer favourable circumstances for such an undertaking. The bishops considered the three parties as perfectly legitimate political options for Catholics, and there the matter rested. When concerted political action was necessary, it usually took the form of cross-party agitation for specific Catholic issues.

During the inter-war period, the intellectual Catholic world showed considerable life and exerted a good deal of influence on contemporary English thought and letters. Frank Sheed could speak of a Catholic Revival in the 1930s. It had already started in the previous decade. The intellectual Catholic ebullience of Chesterton and Belloc had preceded and prepared the ground for it. They had made it impossible for the English public to ignore the Catholic voice, sounding so robust and confident in their writings. The next generation of Catholic writers, mostly converts, benefited from their achievements. It was probably the closest Catholics have ever been to that English Catholic literature of which

Newman had spoken eighty years before. It was very English, and certainly Catholic. English, too, were its main areas of cultivation: history, the novel and the essay.[29] Evelyn Waugh's and Graham Greene's main concerns were to write good novels. They did not necessarily treat of Catholic matters but their novels drew a picture of the crisis of the contemporary liberal society and the assumptions on which it rested, their characters being fully immersed in them. Unexpectedly, a shaft of hope enters sometimes in their lives through a faith which seemed dead and had been, perhaps, only dormant. Dawson's historical work would play on this theme more consciously: a society which has lost its religion becomes, sooner or later, a society without its culture, without bearings.

Around the same time, and in close contact with those developments, Frank Sheed and Maisie Ward set up the Sheed & Ward publishing firm with the aim of publishing not just for an existing readership, but also in order to create a public for the new ideas. With the co-operation of Tom Burns and Christopher Dawson they began to publish the works of foreign Catholic authors, Maritain and his group in particular, together with those of home-grown talents like Alfred Noyes, Dawson, Ronald Knox, and E. I. Watkin. Some late work by Belloc also featured. Through Maritain there reached England knowledge of the theology of Karl Adam and Romano Guardini. Sheed located the foundation of the new ideas in a vision of the Church as the Mystical Body of Christ, and the faithful as members of that Body, sharing in its common mission. This marked in his eyes the end of the 'siege mentality' which had dominated the Church since the Reformation: she was no longer concentrating her efforts on defending the outer walls of the citadel and living under the necessary discipline imposed by a stage of siege. The Church could hence focus on her inner nature and on the world outside.[30] The *Tablet*, brought under lay control by Douglas Woodruff and Tom Burns in 1936, set itself the aim of serving as a journalist bridge between the Church and the world; endeavouring 'to interpret not only the Church to the outside world but the outside world to those members of the Church who need[ed] a general survey'.[31] It was the beginning of an adventure in Catholic journalism which was destined to have considerable influence.

It has been remarked that the real intellectual strength of the revival lay in its 'theology of culture': 'an ordered and coherent view of the world to replace the increasing intellectual and ideological confusion evident outside the walls'.[32] Maritain's idea of a Christian humanism was complemented by Dawson's perception of the need of the spiritual, of the religious dimension, for a proper integration of culture. The message was clear: Christianity could heal what was wounded in contemporary culture; within Christianity every good and truth, every human value found a proper setting and proportion. The bankruptcy of previous cultural discourses presented a favourable time to bring Christianity to public attention as the one truly viable alternative.[33] It also offered a social programme for setting up a new and more stable order of society, based on

Christian principles.[34] However, those who promoted the revival were aware of the fact that, with all its brilliance, it hardly touched the great body of Catholics, remaining wholly an élite interest.

English lay apostolic initiatives were in some cases rather idiosyncratic. The Catholic Evidence Guild, founded by Vernon Redwood, was one of those initiatives born of a desire on the part of the laity 'to do something for the Church'. They wanted to bring religion to the streets, in dialogue with the people there, and in so doing they devised new ways of presenting the faith to the modern world. Those were not the classic lines along which Catholic Action was conceived and not until the arrival of Cardinal Hinsley was there a clear and concerted attempt on the part of the hierarchy to promote Catholic Action as understood and promoted elsewhere. In his enthronement address Hinsley proclaimed his policy: Catholic Action at home and missionary action abroad, two phases of the activity of the living Church, the Mystical Body of Christ.[35] The following year saw the publication of a Joint Pastoral Letter of the bishops of England and Wales entitled *The Apostolate of the Laity* (Advent 1936). The organized forces of the laity were called to fight against the anti-God forces, Communism in particular, which were sapping the foundations of society. The apostolate of the laity should be based 'on the sanctification of its own members'. Lay apostles should also 'acquire a sound knowledge of Christian principles which they will endeavour to apply to the problems of everyday life'. The pastoral singled out three areas for the apostolate of the laity: 'the leakage of Catholics, the spreading of the Faith, and the social question'.[36] The pastoral also described the organisation of the National and Diocesan Boards of Catholic Action, which, among other missions, had the task of encouraging the growth and co-ordinating the activities of the numerous existing Catholic societies. Most of those plans did not proceed beyond the paper on which they were written.

There was a lot to be done. C. C. Martindale SJ, at the Summer School of Catholic Studies of 1935, had remarked that although the Holy Father kept repeating that each Christian should be a Christianiser – the commercial man with the commercial man, the clerk with his fellow clerk, and so forth – little of this was happening in Britain. He saw few signs of that Catholic lay apostolate, and those as yet small: the Catholic Social Guild, the Jocist movement – then 'a tiny sacred microbe' in England – the Grail, the work among seamen of the Apostleship of the Sea, and the Legion of Mary, which had as yet found little support from the hierarchy even in Ireland.[37]

Hinsley tried to keep up the momentum. His 1937 New Year message dwelt on the same topic, and in September of that year he held a huge meeting at the Albert Hall under the title 'The Catholic Church and the Social Question'. On this occasion he accused the well-to-do and privileged sections of the Catholic community of lack of zeal in the promotion of social justice: Catholic industrialists – perhaps because of having grown up in a false tradition – seemed to condone the social evils generated by the capitalist system and ignored the principles propounded by the social teaching of the Church.[38] Fruit of the Cardinal's initiative was the 'Sword of the Spirit', born in 1940. It was conceived as a spiritual crusade involving Catholics and other Christians, with the aim of the restoration in Europe of Christian principles and values under threat from totalitarian regimes. Christopher Dawson, then editor of the *Dublin Review*, was appointed Vice-President, and the board included other lay members like Richard O'Sullivan, Barbara Ward and Professor A. C. F. Beales of London University. The initial enthusiasm generated by the common initiative was short-lived, and further progress in co-operation between Christians of different denominations ran aground on the other Catholic bishops' insistence on separate bodies for Catholics and non-Catholics. Hinsley resigned the presidency in 1942. The Sword of the Spirit was left in suspended animation, to languish through the 1940s and 1950s. It was metamorphosed in the 1960s into initiatives such as CAFOD and the Catholic Institute for International Relations (CIIR).

THE PATH TOWARDS VATICAN II AND BEYOND

The concept of lay apostolate was considerably developed after World War II by the appearance of new institutional forms and by the action of individuals. Pius XII played a significant role in acknowledging and confirming these developments. The Holy See approved in the late 1940s the first secular institutes. In 1951, his Allocution to the World Congress of the Lay Apostolate tried to broaden the concept of lay apostolate to embrace not only Catholic Action but also other forms of apostolic activity carried out by lay people. All forms of apostolate were supposed to be under the supervision of the hierarchy, to which corresponded the general supervision of the Church, but, he added, 'the dependence of the lay apostolate with respect to it admits of gradations'. It was 'strictest for Catholic Action', given that

> it is an instrument in the hands of the hierarchy. It must be, as it were, a prolongation of its arm; it is by its very fact, essentially subject to the direction of the ecclesiastical superior. Other works of the lay apostolate, organized or not, may be left more to their free initiative, with all the latitude required by the ends to be attained.[39]

Catholic Action did not exhaust, nor did it create, the lay apostolate. However, the misconception which led some to claim for Catholic Action a monopoly of the lay apostolate, or to see in this its highest manifestation, required Pius XII to come back to the subject in 1957 in his Allocution to the Second Congress for Lay Apostolate.

The Church in England and Wales was in the 1950s far behind developments of the lay apostolate on the Continent. It was still characterised by calm self-confidence. Its numbers were being increased by a considerable inflow of foreign Catholics. The traditional Irish immigration was being supplemented by many thousands of Catholics from other countries: for example, Poles and Ukrainians escaping the communist regimes established in Eastern Europe. There was also a steady and not inconsiderable influx of converts (13,735 in 1959). The Catholic middle class was becoming a visible and substantial social element, growing from the great effort of the past in Catholic education and integrating itself into the mainstream of English life. Catholics were now attaining positions of responsibility within the professions. The Church in this country retained its sense of cohesion and discipline, walking along the well-trodden paths of clerical control of its corporate life and with high lay participation in organised Church activity, particularly sacramental. The sense of community was still defined, in good measure, by the obvious contrast with a predominantly Protestant environment, which was by now losing a good deal of its former aggressive anti-Catholic propensities.

Catholic influence in society, however, hardly corresponded to its numerical strength. Catholic representation in Parliament was at one of its lowest points and Catholics, on the whole, made little impact on the intellectual life of the country. A number of the great literary personalities of the Catholic Revival were now gone, some had passed their prime, and few followed in their footsteps. In the social sphere, however, there still remained a considerable volume of life and initiative, although the Catholic Social Guild (CSG) was in terminal decline. The emergence of the welfare state had led to different reactions among those associated with the CSG. Some welcomed it as bringing gains to the working class. Others, like Fr Paul Crane SJ, the secretary and dominant force, opposed the programme of nationalisation and welfare reforms as not respecting the principle of subsidiarity, clearly defined in the social teaching of the Church. In contrast, most working-class Catholics supported the reforms and voted Labour. As a result, the CSG began to lose its natural constituency. A contributing factor was the Guild's reluctance to listen to calls for a programme of social reform and direct intervention in social issues rather than confining its activity to training. Those orientated towards direct action tended therefore to be more attracted by the programme of the Young Christian Workers (YCW) movement which insisted on action after study of the problems and on involvement in representative work to contribute to solving problems affecting young workers. From its 'microscopic' beginnings in the late 1930s the YCW had, after the war, become one of the most successful lay movements in England and Wales.[40] Its maturity was ratified by the election of Pat Keegan as its world President, while the English section of the movement was charged with promoting it throughout the English-speaking world. The *Young Worker* tried to present the

Catholic position on social issues, while being critical of what it saw as the almost purely negative anti-communist stance of organisations like the Association of Catholic Trade Unionists (ACTU), which had been promoted by Cardinal Griffin to safeguard Catholic interests, in particular Catholic schools, after the TUC voted in 1942 in favour of secular education. ACTU had become more and more involved in fighting Communist infiltration of the TUC. By the mid-1950s it was losing much of the reason for its existence, given that the threat of a Communist takeover of the trade union movement had by then receded. ACTU members, however, had a not inconsiderable influence in the TUC, and a good number of them had moved, towards the end of the 1950s, into responsible positions in it. Not all Catholic trade unionists shared the stance of ACTU; some preferred to keep a certain distance from it, as was the case of George Woodcock who became the TUC General Secretary in 1960, and held the post until 1969, having previously been Assistant General Secretary from 1947 to 1960.

Towards the late 1950s and early 1960s the work of Opus Dei, which had reached England some years before, started to make itself felt, particularly at the level of the university apostolate in places like London, Oxford and Manchester. It was welcomed and encouraged by the bishops. Some university chaplains, however, exhibited a certain anxiety in face of what they saw as an interference in their sphere of competence and a few were openly antagonistic. Bishop Petit of Menevia asked a priest of Opus Dei to take charge of the Catholic Chaplaincy at Bangor University.

Vatican Council II opened its proceedings in 1962 and dedicated a considerable amount of attention to the laity. Catholic Action and the new forms of lay apostolate and spirituality had fed and stimulated theological reflection about the nature and role of the laity in the Church, while, in its turn, theological discourse had encouraged the lay apostolate. The Council took up these developments, built upon them, and enshrined the new vision of the laity as official Church teaching. Its pronouncements on the subject constituted a substantial doctrinal corpus which found further development and clarification in subsequent magisterial documents, in particular the exhortation *Christifideles Laici* (1988), published after the Synod of Bishops held in Rome in October 1987.

The message of the Council about the laity necessarily involved a clearer concept of the relationship between the Church and the world and of the value of secular realities. The Council viewed the world not simply as an 'external and environmental framework' in which the life of the laity and the Church necessarily took place and developed, 'but as a reality destined to find in Christ the fullness of its meaning'. The 'world itself is destined to glorify God the Father in Christ',[41] and it was part of the salvific mission of the Church to orientate all worldly realities to that end by renewing the temporal order, making it increasingly more perfect, in accordance with God's design.[42] All the members of the

Church shared in this work for the salvation of humanity and the renewal of the whole temporal order, but they did so in different ways.

The Council defined the lay faithful's position in the Church on the basis of their calling to holiness, common to all Christians, and of their secular character, which is 'proper and peculiar to the laity'.[43] This secular character had a vocational dimension: 'by reason of their special vocation it belongs to the laity to seek the kingdom of God by engaging in temporal affairs and directing them according to God's will';[44] they 'contribute to the sanctification of the world, as from within like leaven, by fulfilling their own particular duties'.[45] The exercise of a secular activity, therefore, offered the laity the means to fulfil their Christian vocation to holiness and apostolate.[46] The laity received their apostolic mission directly from Christ, in the sacraments of Baptism and Confirmation, not through a delegation or mandate on the part of the ecclesiastical hierarchy.[47] The hierarchy, however, had the task of fostering and encouraging the apostolate of the laity, and of ensuring that their initiatives safeguarded good doctrine and contributed to the common good.[48]

The Council added that the laity had their proper role to play in the Church and in the world, and that, in each of these, different fields of apostolic action were open to them.[49] As some commentators pointed out, the Council did not consider these as two clearly different tasks. On the contrary, 'the layman's specific role in the mission of the Church is precisely that of sanctifying secular reality, the temporal order, the world, *ab intra*, in an immediate and direct way'.[50] Lay activity in the world had a 'theological and ecclesiological reality as well':[51] to make the Church present and active as salt of the earth in innumerable human activities and places in which she could not be present except through them.[52]

There was, however, in some quarters a certain tendency to over-stress the separation between the role of the laity in the Church and their role in the world. This tendency was not unusually compounded by a vision of the laity's role in the Church as fundamentally involving the taking over of tasks that had beforehand being reserved to the clergy, whether liturgical, financial or decision-making. The Council had clearly said that the laity had a capacity to co-operate in some functions and to a limited degree, if they were called upon to do so, in the apostolate of the hierarchy by being entrusted with certain charges more closely connected with the duties of pastors.[53] This was not infrequently translated in terms of narrowing the laity's role to a para-clerical function, which, by definition, could only involve a very small number of lay people.[54]

In England and Wales the lives of the majority of the laity were hardly affected by the Council until the late 1960s, when the liturgical reforms started to be implemented. A number of the laity openly expressed dissatisfaction. Many others felt distressed by what the saw as a lack of reverence in the way some reforms were put into practice, and, in particular, by the liturgical experiments that went on at the time. On the whole, however, lay Catholics, if not always enthusiastic about all its aspects, accepted liturgical reform without great difficulty.

The Council, however, had become a source of intense excitement for a small section of the laity. The post-war period had seen a dramatic rise in the number of Catholics being educated at university level. The Newman Association had reached a membership of 1,500 in 1950, from its meagre base of 70 in 1942.[55] From this body of educated Catholic lay people grew the self-confident groups which, having followed the progress of the Council, felt called upon to realise the vision of the Church they discerned in it. They saw themselves as different from older forms of lay organisation, like the Legion of Mary or the YCW, by their sense of independence from hierarchical control and by the conviction that they had perceived and responded to the message of the Council 'more rapidly and enthusiastically than had many of the clergy and episcopacy'.[56] The extreme clarity of their vision, fed only in part by the teachings of the Council, made them impatient not only of the bishops, who, they felt, were delaying its implementation, but also of the Council itself. It had not gone far enough. Some even thought that reform 'could only be a futile prelude to revolution, if the Church was to face up to the modern world, philosophically, politically and spiritually'.[57] They could speak of themselves as 'the natural leaders of the Church'.[58] This was a leadership founded on their vision, generated by the guiding power of the Spirit, and authenticated by marks of their own devising. The different groupings did not necessarily agree on a common policy or on the methods to follow: the Slant group might propose that the message of the gospel could only find articulation in the socialist revolution and the rhetoric of the class struggle; the Newman Association might concentrate their efforts on trying to digest recently translated works of the new theology; others focused all their energies on one-issue campaigns, with consequent loss of proportion. They shared, however, some fundamental attitudes and objectives.

The hopes they harboured for an alliance, on their own terms, of bishops, priests, theologians and lay people for the reform of the Church were soon discovered to be unfounded. Their frustration showed itself in confrontational attitudes with the hierarchy and well-publicised criticisms of the bishops. The crisis, which had been threatening for some time, burst with the publication of *Humanae Vitae*. The reaction against it brought together some who had already joined forces in previous campaigns, like the one occasioned by the removal of Fr H. McCabe OP from the editorship of *New Blackfriars* in 1966. Public dissent expressed itself now in forms that shocked many Catholics: a letter against the encyclical, signed by fifty-five priests, was published in *The Times* (2 October 1968), and seventy-five lay people had a similar letter published in the *Tablet* that same week.[59] 'Pray-in' meetings were organised at a number of cathedrals to protest against the new encyclical, and to ask for a re-examination of the way in which the authority of the Pope was exercised.[60] The organisers advanced the claim, which was to become a basic principle of their strategy, that this was the voice of the *sensus fidelium*, or, in other words, the voice of the Spirit speaking in the Church, a voice that the hierarchy could not ignore but should listen to as such.[61] This assertion started to crumble with the emergence of other groups of Catholics, which, claiming to speak for 'the silent majority', gathered under the banner of faithfulness to the teaching of the magisterium, past and present.[62]

The attention which the former groups have attracted, although disproportionate to their membership, is not totally unjustified, given the influence that they have exerted, and still exert, over the Catholic Church in England and Wales.[63] The Catholic Renewal Movement gathered together in 1968 some of those who had been associated with previous groups, and kept alive the flame of their common programme: the ordination of married men (and soon that of women); the priority of the individual conscience in defining the morality of particular acts (especially in the sexual domain); intercommunion; more lay ministries and lay participation in the ecclesiastical structures of authority and power; and entry into the British Council of Churches. The National Pastoral Congress (1980) took up most of the programme of the Catholic Renewal Movement, albeit expressing it in a more tentative way.[64] The programme has not changed much from that of the late 1960s.[65] Some of those more involved with the Catholic Renewal Movement and connected groups were later among the initiators of campaigns of criticism against forms of organised lay apostolate which did not share their particular outlook.

The 1970s also saw the full emergence in England and Wales of the crisis which had affected Catholicism elsewhere. Mass attendances diminished; congregations and orders saw their numbers plummet; vocations for the priesthood diminished; and the number of those looking for dispensations from clerical vows of celibacy grew apace. The readings provided at regular intervals by these indicators gave a perception of deepening crisis. It also became obvious that Catholics had made their own, in good measure, the values of the society in which they lived, even those values opposed to basic Christian principles. It was felt as particularly significant that marital breakdown among Catholics began to rise towards the levels of English society as a whole. Catholics were by now present at all levels of social life, business and the media, but it was questionable whether they were conscious of, and ready to carry out, a mission of christianising secular realities. Had relativism blunted the edge of the message they had to spread? England and Wales began to be perceived once again as mission territories.[66]

At about this time, new structures of consultation and advice, at diocesan and Bishops' Conference levels, began to proliferate. They tended to involve a small section of well-educated and middle-class Catholics,[67] groomed for the most part in the groups that had appeared in the late 1960s. Some saw in this signs of a growing cleavage in the Church in England and Wales between predominantly progressive activists and the bulk of Mass-attending Catholics.[68]

The National Pastoral Congress in Liverpool (2 to 6 May 1980) was a significant milestone in the life of the post-conciliar Church in England and Wales. It was a great opportunity to articulate the new vision of the Council on the role of the laity in the Church. Sector B of the Congress considered the relationship between ordained ministers, religious and laity. It pointed out the right and duty of the laity to participate in the mission of the Church, which was as much a task of lay people as it was of religious and priests. The lay role, it added, 'is specifically in the world, it has a distinctiveness of its own guaranteed by baptism, not delegated'. The laity, however, acknowledged that they were 'failing in their specifically secular apostolate'. Denys Turner, the leader of group B, when commenting on the final report, said that the laity were concerned about distinctiveness, and were afraid of the clericalisation of their calling: 'Church administration is not the primary calling of the layperson.' The lay mission 'is not a calling to self-absorption in the Church . . . but of service in the world'. In this respect, the laity were aware that their initiatives did not need organisation but felt that their formation did.[69]

There was plenty here for the bishops to work on in their response to the recommendations of the Congress. They put the final touches to the text and approved it in their meeting of 14–16 July 1980. The document, entitled *The Easter People*, did not dedicate any specific section to the laity, thereby missing a great opportunity to address this fundamental topic in a systematic and organic way. References to the laity were dispersed throughout its pages, making it difficult to gain a clear perception of the message it intended to convey.

The Church exists for the world, the bishops said. The presence of the laity in the world corresponds to their vocation 'to evangelise the society in which they live and work', extending 'Christ's kingdom to wherever they are in God's creation. For they are not simple delegates of the bishops and clergy . . . they are in their own right missionaries of Christ to the world.'[70] Almost twenty pages later, lay Catholics were reminded that they could witness to gospel truth by almost every aspect of their life at home and at work, in their leisure activities, their political involvement, the family, education and so on. The contrast of their lives, lived according to Christian values, with the standards of so much of contemporary life was part of their Christian witness.[71] Through their responsible and generous participation in the life of the community they might 'achieve positions whereby they are able to work effectively for the promotion of justice and the rejection of solutions unacceptable to the Christian conscience'. In this respect, the bishops made an important analysis of the situation in England and Wales: 'It would seem from the reports submitted in advance of the Congress that many practising Catholics are unused to making a conscious link between their faith and their daily work.'[72] Catholics had to admit, the bishops continued, that 'the awareness of our responsibility for spreading the gospel is not vivid among us at home in England and Wales'.[73] The bishops concluded there could be 'no priority more urgent, no effort more worthwhile, than the slow, patient work of forming lay people for their unique and irreplaceable task'. And this formation should be particularly aimed at forming adults for mission.[74]

The Council had based the hope of renewal in the Church on a renewed search for holiness by all the faithful, a holiness that the laity should achieve in the middle of the world. *The Easter People* repeated the Council's teaching, and added a note of concern: 'The truth is that so great is the gulf between religion and life that even practising Catholics react uncomfortably to this call to perfection.'[75] These words of the bishops' report failed to have a perceptible impact in the life of the English and Welsh laity, reflecting a negative inertia slowing down the renewal. Many people felt, not always for the same reasons, that the lasting effects of the Congress were disappointing.[76]

Apart from the already mentioned Opus Dei, several ecclesial lay realities or groups had been introduced into the country in the previous decades, such as the Focolare Movement and the Neocatechumenate. The beginning of 1981 saw the start of a long and bitter press campaign against Opus Dei. It was set in motion by Clifford Longley, with a full page article in *The Times*, and the momentum was kept up relentlessly during the following months. Cardinal Hume was in the end compelled to intervene with the publication of some recommendations for the future activity of Opus Dei within the archdiocese of Westminster. He finished them by saying: 'These recommendations must not be seen as a criticism of the integrity of the members of Opus Dei, or of their zeal in promoting their apostolate.' This disclaimer carried little weight with those who were moving the campaign. They interpreted the recommendations as a criticism, and used them repeatedly as such.[77] Opus Dei was not the only predominantly lay institution of the Church which was subject to criticism. Most of them were, the Neocatechumenate in particular. Introduced to the country in 1976, it found itself the object of a long and intense negative campaign in the mid-1990s, with a focus in the diocese of Clifton. This led Bishop Alexander of Clifton, who had welcomed them initially, to put a moratorium (January 1997) on the activities of the Neocatechumenate in his diocese.[78]

The Easter People had said that 'many of our preoccupations have to do with our internal concerns as an institutional Church and not with the "world outside" '.[79] That continued being the case in the years that followed the NPC. The only real line of development in lay activity tended to be the inclusion of more lay people in the consultative bodies of the Bishops' Conference or at diocesan and parish level. The apostolate of the laity in the midst of the world received scant attention. This seemed still to be the case in 1995 when the Bishops' Conference accepted the report entitled *The Sign We Give*, prepared by a working party, following a request from the National Conference of Priests. The report answered the call for developing 'patterns of collaborative ministry as a key feature of church life to come'. The term was used 'to describe particular relationships, ways of working and patterns of ministry which bring together lay people, religious, bishops and priests'. The relationships among them were seen by the report as 'part of the sign we give and, for this reason, we must develop patterns of collaborative ministry': the community of our Lord's disciples should appear as such by working together. The report acknowledged that there were 'many different ways of understanding and encouraging collaborative ministry'.[80] However, the practical steps it described were almost exclusively aimed at engaging lay people, at local and diocesan level, in planning pastoral strategy and in decision-making.

October 1997 saw an *ad limina* visit of the bishops of England and Wales. Their visit to Rome coincided with the publication of a document on the laity approved by the Pope on the previous 13 August 1997.[81] Its main aim was to safeguard the distinctiveness of the nature and mission of the sacred ministry, while defending the vocation and secular character of the laity: a richness of diversity and content in danger of being lost. The document started by reaffirming the particular identities of priests, lay people and religious, and their diversity of functions within the Church: all collaborate in the common mission, although they do so in different ways, proper to each. It added that, besides their proper task, the Council had considered the direct collaboration of the lay faithful with the sacred ministry of the Church's pastors. The document, however, pointed out that the functions of teaching, sanctifying and governing 'form an indivisible unity and cannot be understood if separate one from another'. It went on to say, 'Only in some of these functions, and to a limited degree, may the non-ordained faithful cooperate with their pastors.'[82] A spokesman for the Bishops' Conference, on the bishops' return to the country, spoke of how that document was not directly concerned with England and Wales. This was to a very large extent true. Still, John Paul II's message to the bishops of England and Wales at the end of their *ad limina* visit needs to be read in the context of that document. His words, when referring to *The Sign We Give*, were a thinly veiled reference to the danger of a narrow interpretation of collaborative ministry as the collaboration of the laity in the ministry of ordained priests. Partnership in the gospel, John Paul II told the bishops, requires an awareness of the diverse gifts which the Spirit entrusts to the whole Body of Christ, guaranteeing and activating the proper charisms of each section of the faithful.[83]

John Paul II stressed the importance of the parish as the place 'where the faithful normally gather as one family', to hear the word, celebrate the sacraments, and 'be inspired and strengthened *in their mission to consecrate the world in holiness, justice and peace*'.[84] Other institutions, organisations and associations were 'signs of vitality, instruments of evangelization and leaven of Christian life *as long as they contribute to building up the local community in the unity of faith and ecclesial life*'. It is in the particular Church, of which the parish is a cell, where every 'community's ecclesial character is guaranteed and its charisms activated'.[85] These words attracted considerable attention. The strength of parish life had long been one of the main assets of the Church in this country. This same strength, however, may have acted as a brake on the effort to adapt it to a more flexible and open model after Vatican II. An attempt to make the parish into an all-embracing and almost totally self-sufficient community, providing for all the liturgical, religious and spiritual needs of its members, could not fail to put considerable pressures on it and on the laity. The search for more adequate answers as to how to integrate young and old, how to accommodate different spiritualities and diverse charisms and how to build communities without neglecting mission is by no means finished.[86] The further promotion of the lay apostolate depends in great measure on this task.

The teaching of councils usually takes generations to find adequate application, and Vatican II is no exception. A great deal has been done since its closure. Still, almost forty years after the Council, it may be said that many of the vast horizons it opened for the laity remain largely unexplored.

NOTES

1. *The Letters and Diaries of John Henry Newman*, ed. C. S. Dessain, E. E. Kelly and T. Gornall, vol. XIX (London, 1969), p. 141.
2. E. S. Purcell, *Cardinal Manning* (London, 1896), vol. II, p. 318; letter to Manning dated 25 April 1867.
3. W. Ward, *W. G. Ward and the Catholic Revival* (London, 1893), p. 167.
4. H. E. Manning, *Petri Privilegium* (London, 1871), p. 17.
5. H. E. Manning, 'The Work and Wants of the Catholic Church in England' (*Dublin Review*, July 1863), in *Miscellanies*, vol. I (London, 1877), p. 29.
6. H. E. Manning, 'The Catholic Church in Modern Society' (*North American Review*), in *Miscellanies*, vol. III (London, 1888), p. 312.
7. Manning, 'Catholic Church', p. 315.
8. Manning, 'Work and Wants' (1863), p. 60.
9. Cf. H. E. Manning, 'The Work and Wants of the Catholic Church in England' (*Dublin Review*, 1882), in *Miscellanies*, vol. III, pp. 354–5.
10. Cf. Purcell, *Manning*, vol. II, p. 781.
11. J. H. Newman, *Present Position of Catholics in England* (London, 1896), p. 390.
12. Letter to Sir Justin Sheil (22-III-1867), *Letters*, vol. XXIII (Oxford, 1973), p. 101.
13. Manning, 'Work and Wants' (1863), pp. 63ff.
14. J. H. Newman, *The Idea of a University* (London, 1907), p. 296.
15. Memorandum written in 1860, in W. Ward, *Life of Cardinal Newman* (London, 1912), vol. I, p. 493.
16. Cf. J. H. Newman, *On Consulting the Faithful in Matters of Doctrine*, ed. J. Coulsdon (London, 1986), p. 73.

17. Cf. Newman, *On Consulting*, p. 63.
18. In Maisie Ward's judgement, her father and other intellectual Catholics had not appreciated the seriousness of the danger. On the other hand, she thought the Collective Pastoral of the English and Welsh Bishops in 1900 ('The Church and Liberal Catholicism') had been too negative and had had a depressing effect on many educated Catholics, both lay and clerical. It was too occupied with the disloyal minority, and did not show 'ways of service for those who were ready to serve', demanding rather a submissive laity and firmly defining their role within the Church as merely passive (cf. M. Ward, *Insurrection versus Resurrection* (London, 1937), pp. 131ff.).
19. Snead-Cox mentioned how Vaughan felt he was 'constantly calling upon the Irish members to safeguard Catholic interests in this country, and yet he had no opportunity of rendering any service in return' (J. G. Snead-Cox, *The Life of Cardinal Vaughan* (London, 1910), vol. II, p. 376).
20. For a typical example of the difficulties for co-ordinated action see V. A. McClelland, 'Bourne, Norfolk and the Irish Parliamentarians: Roman Catholics and the Education Bill of 1906', *Recusant History*, vol. 23, no. 2 (October 1996), pp. 228–56.
21. Cf. T. Buchanan and M. Conway (eds), *Political Catholicism in Europe, 1918–1965* (Oxford, 1996), p. 249.
22. Cf. G. A. Beck, 'To-day and To-Morrow' in G. A. Beck (ed.), *The English Catholics 1850–1950* (London, 1950), pp. 602–4.
23. Translation in *The Lay Apostolate: Papal Teachings* (Boston, 1961), pp. 289–90.
24. Cf. M. V. Sweeney, 'Diocesan Organisation and Administration' in Beck (ed.), *English Catholics*, p. 144. See also A. Hastings, 'Some Reflections on the English Catholicism of the late 1930s' in A. Hastings (ed.), *Bishops and Writers: Aspects of the Evolution of Modern English Catholicism* (Wheathampstead, 1977), pp. 114ff.
25. Cf. F. Sheed, *The Church and I* (London, 1975), pp. 88ff.
26. *The Christian Democrat*, vol. VI, no. 6 (June 1926).
27. Buchanan and Conway (eds), *Political Catholicism*, p. 261.
28. Buchanan and Conway, *Political Catholicism*, p. 259.
29. In these years, Catholics also made important contributions to the formulation of an English language in the musical and visual arts. Elgar's work, besides contributing to a renaissance of the English musical tradition, became emblematic of the spirit of the country at a particular moment of its history, expressing, as nobody has done before or after, one of its most characteristic moods. Eric Gill and David Jones did much the same in the sphere of the visual arts.
30. See Sheed, *The Church and I*, p. 104; also T. Burns, *The Use of Memory* (London, 1993), p. 52. Further comments in Hastings, *Bishops and Writers*, pp. 108ff.
31. Quoted in M. Walsh, *The Tablet: A Commemorative History* (London, 1990), p. 29.
32. A. Nichols, 'Christopher Dawson's Catholic Setting' in S. Caldecott and J. Morrill (eds), *Eternity in Time* (Edinburgh, 1997), pp. 27–8; quoting A. Hastings.
33. Cf. Nichols, 'Christopher Dawson', p. 35. See also A. Nichols, *Dominican Gallery* (Leominster, 1997).
34. The crisis of World War II made the new vision of society appear an imperative necessity. A. Nichols has pointed out how this 'movement' was not confined to the Catholic Church. The renaissance of a Christian concept of life, culture and society found some of its most important propagators in men like T. S. Eliot or C. S. Lewis (cf. Nichols, 'Christopher Dawson', pp. 39–40).
35. Cf. J. C. Heenan, *Cardinal Hinsley* (London, 1944), p. 24.
36. *The Tablet*, 19 December 1936, p. 866.
37. Cf. C. C. Martindale SJ, 'A Catholic Programme' in *Church and State* (London, 1936), p. 231.

38. Cf. Heenan, *Hinsley*, pp. 166–7.
39. Allocution, 14 October 1951. Translation from *The Lay Apostolate*, p. 544.
40. Some sixty thousand young workers passed through it up to the mid-fifties (cf. Buchanan, *Political Catholicism*, p. 265).
41. *Christifideles Laici* (*CFL*), 15; cf. *Lumen Gentium* (*LG*), 48.
42. *Apostolicam Actuositatem* (*AA*), 7.
43. *LG*, 31.
44. Ibid.
45. Ibid.
46. Cf. *LG*, 41; also *CFL*, 15.
47. Cf. *LG*, 33; *AA*, 3.
48. Cf. *AA*, 24.
49. Cf. *LG*, 30; *AA*, 1, 2, 5, 9, etc.
50. J. Escriva, *Conversations* (Dublin, 1968), n. 9.
51. *CFL*, 15.
52. Cf. *LG*, 33.
53. Cf. *LG*, 31; *AA*, 24; *CFL*, 23.
54. An over-concentration on involving as many of the faithful as possible as readers and extraordinary ministers of the eucharist encountered a certain amount of criticism. It was pointed out that participation, as intended by the Council, was much more than just taking part bodily in external actions. Rather it mainly depended on prayerful participation in the eucharistic mystery and other liturgical ceremonies (cf. B. J. Kelly, *Lay Spirituality: Its Theory and Practice* (London, 1980), pp. 51ff.).
55. Cf. H. O. Evennett, 'Catholics and the Universities, 1850–1950' in Beck (ed.), *English Catholics*, p. 320. Evennett calculated that in 1950 there were about 150 practising Catholic professors and lecturers teaching at university level.
56. B. Sharrat, 'English Roman Catholicism in the 1960s' in Hastings (ed.), *Bishops and Writers*, p. 133.
57. R. Haughton and Cardinal Heenan, *Dialogue: The State of the Church Today* (London, 1967), p. 7.
58. Haughton and Heenan, *Dialogue*, p. 15.
59. In 1967 Tom Burns had taken over from Douglas Woodruff as editor of the *Tablet*. The editorial line took a sharp turn as a result and the journal became the home of the dissenting groups now emerging. A later change of editor in 1982, without marking a departure from the intellectual line of his predecessor, has in time brought a greater openness to it. This was not the only welcome change. Cardinal Hume could, in 1990, breathe a sigh of relief: 'Mercifully the tone of voice has softened' (Foreword to M. Walsh, the *Tablet*).
60. This, and other issues, led to some departures from the Church, but the majority of those dissenting did not leave the Church or accept defeat, fighting on at theoretical and practical levels to impose their vision.
61. The claim did not take into consideration a clarification made to the Council Fathers in respect of the *sensus fidelium*: this is to be found in the whole community of the faithful – priests, religious and laity – not just in one of the elements of the people of God apart from the others (see note 12 to Chapter II of the Schema on the Church: cf. Vatican Council II, *Acta*, II, II/I, p. 265).
62. These groups have since multiplied. Among the first, the Faith Movement attracted a considerable number of people, and *Faith* magazine a large readership. The *Pro Fide et Pontifice* meetings, and the more recent ones of Faith of our Fathers, gathered large audiences.
63. There have been at least two D. Phil. theses completed at Oxford University concerned with radical Catholic groups. The one by P. G. McCaffery ('The Development of Catholic Rad-

icalism and Counter-Radicalism: A Comparative Study of England and the Netherlands', Oxford, 1980) is particularly useful in this respect. See also M. Clifton, *The Alliance of Dissent* (London, 1993), which follows the development of such groups to the early 1990s. There is one interesting point still in need of further study: the process by which the Bishops' Conference accepted as partners in dialogue, on behalf of their respective 'constituencies', whether clerical or lay, some of those groups. McCaffery's reasons in this respect are not wholly convincing.

64. Hastings would see in this the result of an evolution of religious consciousness among English Catholics. The principal aims of CRM had become those of the dominant group of English Catholics (cf. A. Hastings, *History of English Christianity 1980–1990* (London, 1991), p. 639). Another possible interpretation might be that these groups had become organised and dominant enough to be able to impose their agenda on the resolutions of the NPC.
65. It later reappeared in the 'We Are Church' referendum launched on 7 December 1996. By then the promoters of it could speak of long-overdue reforms. The observations of Cardinal Hume (*Briefing*, 19 December 1996, pp. 32–3), while admitting that the 'We Are Church' declaration contained a number of propositions with which all in the Church could agree, also highlighted a number of ambiguous proposals like that on conscience and human sexuality, and one other – on women priests – which, having been ruled out by the Holy Father, should have no place in a Catholic document.
66. See for example Reports B and D of the NPC, and *The Easter People*, n. 83.
67. This is a phenomenon which has its parallels in the Church of England: the House of Laity has remained essentially a middle-class and middle-aged body. As far as their professional occupations are concerned, a majority of them were connected with education (cf. G. Davie, *Religion in Britain since 1945* (Oxford, 1994), pp. 167ff.).
68. M. Hornsby-Smith, *Roman Catholics in England* (Cambridge, 1987), pp. 134–5. Hornsby-Smith spoke of the danger of alienation on the part of many Catholics, leading the Church to become 'a sect of mainly middle-class activists' (cf. M. P. Hornsby-Smith and E. S. Cordingley, *Catholic Elites: Study of the Delegates to the National Pastoral Congress* (Guildford, n.d.), pp. 32ff.). This does not seem likely. A more obvious danger is that of a 'closed-shop' mentality in the nomination of members of committees and consultative bodies.
69. Cf. *Tablet*, 31 May 1980, pp. 540ff. Archbishop Derek Worlock called the over-involvement of lay people in 'churchy' things, to the neglect of mission, an 'ever-present danger'. He thought that little attention had been paid to the formative role of lay organisations (cf. ' "Toil in the Lord"; The Laity in Vatican II' in A. Stacpoole (ed.), *Vatican II by Those Who Were There* (London, 1986), pp. 237–54).
70. *The Easter People*, n. 27.
71. Cf. *The Easter People*, n. 84.
72. *The Easter People*, n. 163; an echo of *Gaudium et Spes*, 43.
73. *The Easter People*, n. 85.
74. Cf. *The Easter People*, n. 150.
75. *The Easter People*, n. 189. M. Winter was one of those who reacted uncomfortably, on the grounds that what the Church needed was institutional change: people's lives would then change as a result, not the other way round (cf. *What ever happened to Vatican II?* (London, 1985), pp. 72–3).
76. Cf. Winter, *What ever?*, pp. 73–4; one of the reasons for his disappointment was the rather unenthusiastic response of the bishops to reconsidering questions like intercommunion, ordination of women, and sexual morality. See also Hornsby-Smith, *Roman Catholics*, pp. 40–1.
77. Several books were published on the subject in the following years. The more relevant are

probably: D. le Tourneau, *What is Opus Dei?* (Dublin, 1987); M. Walsh, *The Secret World of Opus Dei* (London, 1989), and W. O'Connor, *Opus Dei: An Open Book* (Dublin, 1991), a reply to Walsh's book.

78. For information and comment on the proceedings see *The Canon Law Society of Great Britain and Ireland Newsletter*, no. 109 (March 1997). Additional information about the nature of Neocatechumenate may be found in E. Pasotti (ed.), *The Neocatechumenal Way* (London, 1996).
79. *The Easter People*, n. 85.
80. *Briefing*, 21 September 1995, p. 3. Theologically the report was criticised for the muddled terminology used to describe the ecclesiological character of the laity, and the apparent identification of the lay person with the baptised made in the Introduction.
81. *Instruction on Certain Questions Regarding the Collaboration of the Non-ordained Faithful in the Sacred Ministry of the Priest* (Vatican City, 1997).
82. *Instruction*, n. 2.
83. *L'Osservatore Romano* (English edition), 29 October 1997, p. 3. The Vatican document, and the Pope's words to the English and Welsh bishops, seemed part of a co-ordinated worldwide effort to prevent a theological inversion of terms, where the fundamental task of the ordained priesthood, to serve the priesthood of the laity, would be, at least practically, replaced by a narrowing of the priesthood of the laity to serve the priesthood of ordained ministers.
84. *L'Osservatore Romano*, 29 October 1997, p. 3.
85. Ibid.
86. Cf. Hornsby-Smith, *Roman Catholics*, pp. 200ff.; see also *Priests and People* (June 1997).

EIGHT

FAMILY AND MARRIAGE

PETER DOYLE

Key among the themes of this chapter is the premise that attitudes to the family among English and Welsh Catholics have been traditionally determined by three fundamental beliefs: the existence of the family as the basic unit of society, indeed the archetypal ideal society in itself, with rights and duties independent of, and anterior to, any rights and duties of the State; the procreative function of marriage as its principal purpose, and the indissolubility of the marriage bond. The family, in most Catholic discourse, was viewed as a static unit, paternal and authoritarian in character, with the wife and (several) children in permanent positions of obedience and submission. In Victorian and Edwardian times this was not a peculiarly Catholic view and could be found in all English mainstream writing about society. But for Catholics it became the most important factor in determining their approach to almost every social issue and State welfare initiative, at least down to the 1960s. Sometimes there were tensions between official church teaching and the perception of pastoral needs by a parochial clergy in close touch with their people. These tensions became increasingly problematic as the Catholic body became more fully integrated into the wider society and more prosperous.

THE FAMILY

When, in 1875, the parish priest of St John's Church, Islington, established a branch of the Confraternity of the Holy Family, he asked Cardinal Manning to preach at the inauguration. The Cardinal used the occasion to underline the fundamental place of the family and to stress the value of confraternity membership:

It is meant to be a training for the family, for the home, for husband and

> wife, for father and mother, for son and daughter, for brother and sister. It is to make the homes of our people to be like the Holy House of Nazareth [where] there was prayer and praise, worship and adoration, and industry, and work and service one to another . . . It is intended that the members of the [Confraternity of the] Holy Family are to be new men, and that in the spirit of a new life, they as husbands and fathers are to rule their households.[1]

Preachers and writers who held up the Holy Family as the model for Catholics to imitate were supported in 1892, when Leo XIII encouraged Catholic families to consecrate themselves formally to the Holy Family, and in 1921 when a liturgical feast of the Holy Family was instituted for the universal Church. The model was not unproblematic: apart from its being, essentially, a 'one-child family', it could lead some writers into complex and rather unreal comparisons. In the 1940s Messenger, for example, wrote:

> The Catholic Faith teaches us that there is a spiritual but nevertheless true generation within the Godhead, for the Father . . . generates the Son. The Holy Ghost, who is the mutual love of Father and Son, completes the Trinity. Here we have the heavenly 'Family'. Further . . . this heavenly Family has its counterpart on earth in the Holy Family of Nazareth, the Incarnate Son of God, together with his Mother and his foster father. All this gives a new religious character to parenthood and to the family, and therefore also to the sex function which lies at the root of both.[2]

The importance of family was a commonplace for all Victorian writers and social commentators, and it was universally accepted that only a family built on a Christian marriage was fully a family, just as it was generally accepted that the source of authority in the family had to be the father, with the mother filling a subordinate but 'equal-in-dignity' role as the romanticised 'angel of the hearth'. Manning saw it as obvious that the Confraternity of the Holy Family in St John's was restricted to men; it was through the men in the family that the wife, mother, daughter or sister were to to be trained in the virtues of the Holy Family, though most writers attributed the role of nurturing higher instincts in the children to the mother. No one felt obliged, in the mid-nineteenth century, to argue the case for this particular view of the family, and neither the new sciences of sociology and anthropology nor the old one of theology were employed to justify or analyse it, at least until it seemed that the revival of socialism in the 1880s posed a threat to it. The family was accepted as the basic unit of society, since common sense said that the individual family must have pre-dated the coming together of families into societies and then into states; it existed prior to society and therefore enjoyed its position and rights independently of both society and the State. Nothing the State might do should ever interfere with the family's independent rights, and, indeed, the State should consider its prime duty to be the protection of the family, for society could only be successful to the extent that it was made up of a grouping of independent Christian families.

Given the centrality of the family in Catholic thought, and the parallel centrality of marriage in thinking about the family, it is surprising that no theology of either was attempted. For Catholics marriage was a sacrament and so enjoyed a place in sacramental theology, but this was itself limited. Catholic writing about marriage was dominated by canonical concerns and with making sure that the marriage was canonically valid on the wedding day – that the spouses were free to give their consent, that there were no impediments, and that the marriage ceremony took place in a Catholic church before the parish priest (or his canonically delegated deputy) and two witnesses. When the clergy discussed and wrote about marriage they were concerned with getting it right on the day and not, apparently, with the idea of a marriage as a lifelong relationship or with understanding its theology. In practice pastorally aware clergy were, of course, concerned with longer-term, more human issues, but the general lack of writing about marriage from other than a canonical point of view is striking.[3]

The issue of defending the rights of the family against interference by the State became a very contentious one in the last quarter or so of the nineteenth century, when Catholics became involved in the great education debates because they believed that parents, and not the State, had the right, and responsibility, to raise their children according to their religious beliefs. The 'battle for the schools' remained a central feature of English Catholicism for at least a hundred years, and is covered elsewhere in this volume. The concern to have Catholic schools was not, however, inspired solely by a concern for the rights of the family. The leakage of the young from active membership of the Church was a constant reality, and the clergy perceived a danger to the faith of children who would have to attend Protestant or non-denominational Board schools – theories about the rights of the family vis-à-vis the State were useful ammunition in the battle, but the main concern was pastoral. The struggle was also valuable to the English Catholic Church in creating and maintaining a sense of national unity among the diverse body that was English Catholicism: the State, and society in general, could be portrayed as the enemy, and the value of an outside threat in keeping religious minorities together is well documented.[4] There was a constant tension between this pastorally motivated desire to keep Catholics, and especially the children, separate from the wider society, and the desire to have Catholics accepted socially as an integral part of English society so that they would no longer be labelled alien and could play a full role as citizens.[5]

This tension had already manifested itself over the question of mixed marriages. In their official statements and sermons bishops and clergy condemned these strongly and unambiguously, in line with Rome's frequently expressed prohibition. The Rev. James Swarbrick of Preston said in a sermon in 1858: 'Two things are pre-eminently destructive of the welfare of offspring, heresy and adultery; these two things the Church holds in abhorrence.' He argued from the closeness of the union that should exist in a marriage, and the inevitable difficulties when there was a wide difference of opinion on the 'very first duty of man – his duty to his Creator. Is there not a broad chasm between [the partners] on those sacred and intimate convictions and sentiments of religion? Will this difference strengthen the union, will it generate love?' Moreover, 'They can have no sure hope of meeting each other in the next life.' They could not strengthen each other in faith, no matter how naturally virtuous the Protestant might be, and in bringing up the children there would be 'a bone of contention'; the children could 'hardly ever acquire thorough religious principles . . . alas! alas! many are the instances where children sprung from such marriages end their days expressing no belief . . .'[6] Swarbrick's bishop, Alexander Goss, added his condemnation:

> Mixed marriages are . . . often miserable beyond the conception of those who engage in them. The Church . . . may allow them on condition that the children are brought up Catholics, but how often is such condition violated, and the poor wife, the victim of her trustfulness, is made miserable for life, and suffers death at the birth of every child. [At best] the children are often lukewarm in their duties . . . and, at last, fall away from the faith.[7]

Notwithstanding their strong condemnations of mixed marriages the bishops were rebuked by *Propaganda* in 1867 for their lax attitude. They had been asking for too many dispensations, and their efforts to plead that conditions in England, where Catholics were in a minority, made such marriages inevitable, failed to convince Rome; they were ordered to adopt a stricter line.[8] Despite this, pastoral practice continued much as before. Bishop Goss, who refused to make any changes, had consulted his clergy; their view was that to tighten the regulations would only cause trouble. A number of priests believed the Church gained rather than lost from mixed marriages, and gave statistics to prove it. In fifty-eight missions, for example, there had been 2,716 mixed marriages, and in 859 of these the Protestant partner had become a Catholic and only 395 Catholic partners were neglecting their duties; in 1,727 cases all the children were being brought up in the Church, and in seventy-nine others at least some of the children were.[9] What is striking is the widely differing effect of mixed marriages in different missions. At Huyton there had been twelve mixed marriages and in every case the Catholic partner was neglecting his or her duties and there had been no converts. At Newton-le-Willows thirty-one mixed marriages had produced one convert, and twenty-eight of the Catholics involved had become negligent or had left the Church. On the other hand, at Great Crosby, ninety-four mixed marriages had produced forty-five converts, one apostate and none who were negligent, while the inner-city mission of St Mary's, Liverpool, had seen 155 mixed marriages, one convert, and 152 faithful Catholic partners. Mixed marriages, clearly, could have provided a fruitful apostolate, but, equally clearly, that apostolate was being neglected in many cases. This is not surprising, for the strongly worded condemnations of mixed marriages were self-fulfilling prophecies and led many to believe they were doomed to failure from the outset. The bishops felt unable to give positive guidance and had to try to impose a law that ran counter to the reality of the situation, while their clergy were left without an opportunity to discuss what might have been 'best practice' in a difficult pastoral situation.[10]

Matters did not improve: in the 1890s Bishop Bilsborrow of Salford referred to reports he had received from his priests: one claimed that nearly half of the marriages in his church were mixed and, 'knowing most intimately every family, he cannot quote a single case in which the results have not been deplorable in all respects'. Bilsborrow referred back to the survey his predecessor, Herbert Vaughan, had organised: based on it Vaughan had reported, 'It has been ascertained by returns that out of about 6,000 Mixed Marriages within ten years in this Diocese of Salford, over 5,000 have turned out unsatisfactorily or even disastrously to the faith!'[11]

Vaughan believed that a quarter of the children in his diocese who were at risk of losing their faith were in danger because of mixed marriages – 'a fruitful and growing source of danger, and one which offers the least possible hope of a successful outcome', as the report concluded. Others were at risk because of downright irreligious parents, and still others because of careless and indifferent parents. The careless and indifferent were 'more often to be pitied than blamed', suffering as they did from poverty, want of employment, and possibly drink.[12] When it came to discussing some of the external dangers, however, the bishop was much more condemnatory. In particular, he attacked the practices of the night and day refuges for children in amazingly strong terms, talking about their 'hypocrisy', their 'waging a hateful war' against Catholics, and of their only interest being in 'stealing' the children they pretended to help – they were, indeed, 'touters for souls'. Their efforts might mean 'there is one waif the less on the streets, it is true, but there is another soul robbed of its faith to swell the ranks of uncertain Protestantism'.[13] They were active in the ragged schools and the workhouses, and it was reckoned that up to 80 per cent of Catholic children leaving the workhouses were lost to the Church. Vaughan was careful not to blame the workhouse Guardians, and did not attribute any proselytising to them directly; it was just that the whole atmosphere was hostile to the faith and the children all too easily came under the wrong influences.

Vaughan was not alone in seeing the importance of dealing with the steady loss to the Church of so many young people – a loss that numerically far outweighed the increase in numbers through conversions. Nor was it just a

Catholic concern: all denominations were faced with the problem of keeping their young members if they were to continue to grow and have influence. By the last quarter of the nineteenth century denominational expansion through gaining converts from the wider society was becoming more difficult and for some churches had stopped altogether, and so endogenous growth was crucial.[14] The bitter debates over religious teaching in schools and the increasing provision of church-linked facilities such as youth clubs are witnesses to the seriousness with which the churches attempted to deal with these issues. Catholic concern about the losses led to a vast increase in social and charitable work aimed at helping families stay together. If despite these efforts the children became at risk, then there were Catholic Crusades of Rescue, Catholic reformatories and industrial schools, and Catholic emigration schemes – a complete system of Catholic provision set up and run at vast expense.[15] Victorian voluntarism encouraged the setting up of private societies to deal with any perceived social or religious need, and Vaughan urged Catholics 'not to be behind the times' in this respect; it was not just coincidence, however, that this appeal came at the end of a long attack on the Protestant voluntary societies, 'many of them merely proselytizing institutions' run by people who regarded Catholics as 'men tainted with disease', and who believed that to cure Catholic children of that disease would be a service 'to the children and to the State'. The required Catholic support was more likely to be forthcoming if there seemed to be 'an enemy without' intent on destroying the faith.[16]

Mixed marriages, careless and irreligious parents, proselytising Protestants, and a general atmosphere inimical to the practice of Catholicism: all were blamed for the leakage of young people (and adults, too) from the Church, and no doubt all were partially responsible. Even in the best of circumstances, however, some children reacted against the teaching and habits of their parents and ceased to practise their religion. The clergy were aware of this, just as they were aware that for many families it was the terrible economic and social conditions under which they struggled to stay alive that militated most of all against even a basic religious practice, let alone the development of a truly Catholic family life. Clerical reformers, both Catholic and Protestant, were often outspoken in condemning the bad housing, poor wages, awful working conditions and lack of steady employment that affected their people. Manning, for example, spoke on 'The Dignity and Rights of Labour', condemning working conditions and hours that made domestic life impossible.[17]

The most radical of English Catholic social critics was Edward Bagshawe, Bishop of Nottingham from 1874 to 1901. His pamphlet, *Mercy and Justice to the Poor: the True Political Economy* (1885), made up of three pastoral letters, was so critical of capitalism that it was denounced to Rome, and he was accused of being a state socialist. He was certainly in favour of state intervention to create a juster society, arguing it was only when the question of help for the poor was raised that the better-off began to have scruples about it.[18] Although the pamphlet was published at the request of some of his clergy and people, few followed his lead; most thought it dangerous to espouse the cause of state intervention, especially as it might damage the family. State intervention in social or economic matters was considered to be too close to emergent socialism, and every good Catholic knew that socialism and Catholicism could never be partners. These fears were given legitimacy by *Rerum Novarum* (1891): as the Pope said, socialism attacked the foundations of the family by attacking its right to private property and removing the responsibilities of parents; a socialist State might even end by taking over the care of children altogether. Socialism became a new 'enemy without', and Catholic writers united in attacking it. Two quotations from a pamphlet by Charles Stanton Devas will help to give the flavour of much of this writing. They are from a section headed, 'Socialism Immoral as being Injurious to Family Life' in his *Plain Words on Socialism* (1906). First of all Devas argued:

> The sacred union of man and woman for mutual help, for educating and supporting their children . . . the sense of mutual responsibility and care, the true and healthy communism, that of the home, the countless co-operative associations which each family forms, the thousand ties of dependence that are an occasion for the display of the best qualities of human nature – this realm of self-devotion and self-sacrifice – all this becomes unmeaning and impossible where the Socialist State provides for the nourishment and education and technical training and material and moral outfit of each child.

Devas was normally a careful and balanced writer, and there is a welcome absence from most of his writings of the simplistic dismissal of socialism frequently found in contemporary Catholic polemic. But in this case he was extreme in his condemnation, ending as follows:

> The moral office of parents is gone, the sacred enclosure of the home is violated, the sacred words father, mother, brother, sister, have been degraded to a lower meaning, and the next step is to reduce the rearing of man under approved physicians and physiologists and the latest professor of eugenics to the level of a prize cattle farm. The Christian family and Collectivism are incompatible; their antagonism is so rooted that reconciliation is impossible.[19]

The use of language in the second extract is instructive. The home has become a 'sacred enclosure', recalling its model, the home of the Holy Family, but somehow walled about to keep its members safe from outside attack and 'violation', a word in this context that has clear overtones of sacrilege. Even the words 'father, mother, brother, sister,' have become 'sacred', imbuing their holders with an air of the divine and so making them, to some degree at least, supra-human and deserving of reverence. Later we will find another writer referring to the reverence due to the 'domestic sanctuary'. Such emotive language served to link the cause of the family with the cause of religion and so imply that those who held different and opposing views must be anti-religious.[20] One of the arguments English socialists used to reject *Rerum Novarum* was that the Pope had been too sweeping in his condemnations and had failed to distinguish between moderate socialism and the extremes of communism. It was a just criticism that could be levied equally against Devas and other Catholic writers.

At the same time social surveys were indicating ever more clearly that capitalist individualism was not likely to solve the 'social question' and was, indeed, a major cause of it. Theoretical economists were beginning to question the validity of the so-called iron laws of political economy and to suggest a positive role for the State in ensuring a fairer distribution of wealth. Christian Socialists of other denominations were adopting more or less radical alternatives; what could Catholics suggest as a 'middle way' between the proven evils of Victorian capitalism and the alarming bogey of socialism? The beginnings of an answer were supplied by Devas himself, in a number of works on political economy which were generally highly regarded, especially his *The Groundwork of Economics* (1883) and *Political Economy* (1892) – Bagshawe had acknowledged the influence of the first of these. A more or less organised movement, which may be called Social Catholicism, emerged in the decade or so before 1914. It was different from the long tradition of Catholic charitable endeavour in that it wanted to change the socio-economic system, allowing the State a positive role where necessary but ensuring the independence and dignity of the individual and upholding and encouraging the primary unit of society, the family. The Catholic Social Guild, established in 1909, became the recognised leader of this movement.[21] It adopted Devas's *Political Economy* and Mgr Henry Parkinson's *A Primer of Social Science* (1913) as its theoretical foundations, and published a series of annual reports and pamphlets concentrating on problems like housing and the establishment of a living wage. The latter became the crucial testing point of all initiatives: the level of wages should be determined not by market forces but by what was necessary to allow the worker to live in dignity with a modicum of comfort and to support a family; such a 'family living wage' was a matter of justice and the only basis on which a genuine Christian democracy could be built. As a small step towards it the Catholic Social Guild welcomed the Trade Boards Act of 1909; this fixed minimum wages in some low-paid sweated industries and has been hailed as marking the break with non-interventionist economic individualism.[22]

It was not easy, however, to move Catholics towards a new view of the State. The Guild was itself accused of being socialist and one of its founders, Leslie Toke, realising the damage such labels could do in deterring Catholics, warned that its 'attempts at deeper and broader solidarities with extra-Catholic social and civic movements' would be better worked at internally and quietly.[23] During the First World War everyone accepted increased state control and intervention, but the issue became contentious again for many Catholics in 1919 with the setting up of the Ministry of Health. The controversy illustrates the almost inbred fear of state interference in some Catholics, and a related fear, that of the eugenics movement. It also showed that not all Catholics agreed with their more outspoken representatives in opposing state initiatives for social improvement.

The Ministry of Health Act of 1919 set up a single department to unite the various agencies that dealt with the nation's health. Centralisation would increase efficiency, remove overlapping agencies and allow the proper targeting of resources. From early in the century there had been increasing demand for improvement in infancy and maternity care, and war had, once again, revealed the poor physical state of many recruits to the armed forces. It had also accustomed the general population to the idea of greater governmental intervention. Opposition to the Act had come from some of those with vested interests, the Poor Law Board, for example, and the private insurance companies. The Act as passed was something of a compromise to assuage their fears, but was generally welcomed. Some English Catholics, however, had waged a campaign against it from the start and continued to see it as a danger after it came into operation.

An article in the *Month* for July 1919 summarised these Catholic attitudes. The writer, H. Robbins, began by insisting that Catholics in England were as keen about the welfare of the country as 'the most patriotic of their fellow-subjects', but had a duty to uphold Christian tradition. In particular, that duty bade them express 'alarm at the possibilities of evil contained' in the recent Act. Those possibilities were twofold: the phrasing of the Act was vague and would allow a dangerous extension of the powers of the Minister through undemocratic administrative measures, as well as allowing 'the eugenicists' to have an undue influence on its operation. More importantly, the Act was dangerous because it undermined the position of the family: 'This Ministry is another and a disastrous step towards the destruction of that idea of the home for which Catholicism stands.' Robbins stressed that the rights of the family were anterior and superior to those of the State and referred to the 1918 Education Act as another encroachment on those rights because, he claimed, it had virtually ignored parents. Now came this Health Act, allowing the State to intervene 'in all the most private matters of home life, and all but completing the destruction of parental authority'. If, instead, the State used its power to re-establish the effectiveness of the family by 'seeing that property is properly distributed, that wages are sufficient, that housing is decent, [and] that work-hours are not excessive', it would have Catholics' full support. 'But against the intrusion of a State Department, inspired and officered by godless cranks and faddists, men and women who have abandoned the Christian ideal, into the domestic sanctuary, they will fight with every weapon God has given them.'[24]

Reference has already been made to the use of terms such as 'the domestic sanctuary'; as well as implying that the home was due that reverence normally given to the holiest part of a church, it was also, perhaps, a 'sanctuary' in that it offered a place of refuge and security from the evils of a rapidly secularising society. Robbins's concluding call to arms was reminiscent of the great education campaigns; meetings were already being held in London and Lancashire at which similar views were put forward and a warning given that 'thousands of Catholic women were already being won over to Socialism'. Some moves were made to mobilise opinion by setting up a nationwide 'Conference of Catholic Organizations for the purposes of the Ministry of Health'. This petitioned the bishops in 1920 for public support, but their response was somewhat muted: they wished the new body every success but made it a condition of their support that no resolution be published or public action taken without their Lordships' consent. They also asked for a committee to be set up to advise them 'on the work of the Ministry and its dangers'.[25] Robbins's own tone became increasingly strident; in a letter to the *Tablet* he pronounced that it was for Catholics to show 'by an instant and vigorous opposition, whether they have learned anything from the fate of their forefathers under Henry VIII'.[26] He was, however, appointed to the committee, along with Rev. J. B. McLaughlin OSB and Morgan Finucane, a London doctor.

Their report was not finally ready until late 1921. Its covering letter stated that it was 'largely an agreed statement of the differences of principle which divide us, and, we think, the Catholics of this country, into two conflicting parties, each of which believes that the Catholic body ought to support it in its attitude to the Ministry'. The differences were indeed fundamental, with one side taking the traditional Catholic view of the rights and duties of parents, while the other argued that the State, as the protector of rights, was obliged to see that its citizens' health was not injured by the carelessness of individuals; therefore, 'the State is *in loco parentis* over individuals and families . . . [and] thus the individual's authority over himself is limited naturally by the State's right to intervene for the public good and his own individual good'. The author(s) of the 'pro-State' view clearly felt that Catholics were approaching the whole issue wrongly, for he (they) included the following warning:

> There is no sign of any attempt by the Ministry to attack either liberty or morality; the cry of danger has been a political stunt. The real danger is that the Catholic body will once more stand aloof in an attitude of destructive criticism; clinging to views that are antiquated, cramped, anti-national, anti-social, unpatriotic, under the guidance of amateur theologians; and that those Catholics who wish to take an active part in the national work

> will find themselves frowned on, discouraged and suspected by the Catholic body. Instead of being there as watch-dogs for their faith and principles, they will find their claim to represent the Catholic view disallowed on both sides. And the Ministry will ignore the views of a body which refuses all co-operation and rejects all attempts to meet its views.[27]

It was a timely warning, given the extreme nature of some of the Catholic opposition to welfare changes. While the committee was considering its report the Salford branch of the Catholic Federation was voicing its rejection of the Guardianship of Infants Bill that was going through the Commons. It objected that the Bill introduced 'the legal fiction, as against the natural law, that the father is not the head of the family', and claimed that the father was the only 'insuperable obstacle to the State official, and, once he is removed, the State will have less difficulty with the mother'. In fact, the Bill provided that the father and mother of every legitimate infant should be regarded as joint guardians of that infant, with joint custody and equal authority, rights and responsibilities. The Federation claimed that the Bill would encourage parents to go to court to settle differences, over their children's education for example, and then the children would effectively belong to the court. The writer ended, 'If the fathers of England will stand this Bill, they will stand anything.' The Westminster branch voiced similar objections.[28]

There were some Catholics, especially in the medical profession, who accepted that co-operation was the better policy. A CSG pamphlet of the time adopted a rather cautious approach but basically urged Catholics to co-operate with the new health authorities whenever possible without compromising Catholic principles.[29] It would be interesting to know what the Catholic working classes and the Catholic poor felt about 'State intervention'. They were among the people who would suffer the 'intrusion' and have the sanctity of their homes 'violated' by health visitors, school inspectors and the like. None of the Catholic apologists argued from what the people would or would not put up with, although the clergy were sufficiently in touch with them to know. There is some evidence that the working classes and the poor had grown used to being visited at home by voluntary and official agents from the 1870s onwards, but that they did not take kindly to it, and especially not to health visitors who told mothers what was wrong with their children but did not provide any means of putting it right. There is also evidence that mothers could feel that their position as chief organiser of the home was under threat.[30] It seems that Catholic writers who feared a growing invasion of the home by agents of the State might have had unwitting support from a large part of the Catholic population, and pulpit denunciations of undue interference in the home might have been welcomed.

MARRIAGE AND THE WELFARE STATE

Research seems to say that in practice Catholics should have felt able to co-operate with a great deal of what the Ministry tried to do in the 1920s and 1930s because its stance was rather conservative. Health authorities were very slow to think in terms of providing contraceptive advice; the main concern was in the high rates of infant mortality, and the problem was not seen in terms of general health and the socio-economics of the family, nor of the mother who was having too many children. Indeed, there was much official and unofficial 'glorification of motherhood', to encourage mothers to have children – for example, the journal *Mother and Child*, the holding of National Baby Weeks and 'Save the Mothers' campaigns. Even what organised feminist movement there was up to 1939 never questioned the place of the mother in the home; they wanted more help to go directly to the mother, and some did advocate birth control, but this was a minority voice. Despite Catholic scaremongering there was a great reluctance on the part of the Ministry to intervene in the home because it firmly believed that the best incentive for men to work was their acceptance of family responsibilities: 'Responsibility for the care of women and children was assumed to rest in the hands of a male provider. There was, therefore, great reluctance to intervene directly in the private world of the family and its economy.'[31]

Even if the Ministry was at heart conservative in its view of the family, and if much of its publicity material supported the Catholic view of motherhood, Catholics were still suspicious. The reason for this lay in the existence of a prominent eugenics movement in English social thought from about the 1880s to the 1940s. The eugenicists based their arguments on a form of social Darwinism and on the new science of genetics and heredity, and were primarily concerned with what they termed 'the quality of the race' and 'race degeneracy'. It is surprising how widespread and even pervasive these phrases became in British social discourse, especially around the time of the First World War. There were the extreme views of, for example, Sidney Webb, who warned that 25 per cent of parents were producing 50 per cent of the next generation, and went on, 'This can hardly result in anything but national degeneration, or, as an alternative, in this country gradually falling to the Irish and the Jews.'[32] The University of London set up a 'eugenics laboratory' in 1914, and in the same year the poet Wilfred Owen could accept the idea that the guns would 'effect a little useful weeding'; he was less worried, he said, by the death of British soldiers than those of their French and even German counterparts, because 'the former are all Tommy Atkins, poor fellows, while the continental armies are inclusive of the finest brains and temperaments of the land'. Even Cardinal Vaughan had spoken of 'race degeneracy' as one of the problems facing society, while in 1919

Cardinal Bourne admitted the 'enormous amount of work to be done in order to improve our race, and raise it both morally and physically . . . Those who represent the forces of the State, religious thought and social work should co-operate to bring about that effect'.[33] His reference to 'the forces of the State' is interesting: all the early eugenicists were strong State socialists, and the movement continued to press for State compulsion to achieve its ends. Finally, in the CSG pamphlet already referred to, a Dr Mooney had tried to make a distinction between 'good eugenics and bad', stating as generally acceptable the eugenicist axiom that healthy parents could be expected 'to beget healthy children', while unhealthy parents could be expected 'to beget children more or less disabled by the existence or probable development of physical and mental disability'.

Bourne and other Catholics might sometimes use the same words as the eugenicists, but had nothing in common with them; indeed, a fundamental antipathy to their position was a major reason and justification for Catholic suspicion of certain aspects of welfare reform. There were a number of reasons for that antipathy. The Irish and the poor, so often the target of eugenicist literature as 'unfit' and a 'danger to the quality of the race', were a major constituency of English Catholicism. More explicit was Catholic opposition to the methods recommended by the eugenicists to effect their revolution: birth control for the poorer and less well-endowed (both physically and mentally) parts of the population; enforced sterilisation of the worst of the unfit and irresponsible classes, coupled with prohibitions on certain 'types' marrying if their family trees suggested their offspring would probably be degenerate; and a requirement on all couples to produce certificates showing their mental and physical well-being. The willingness to impose such methods amounted to 'bad eugenics', according to Mooney; others reacted more strongly and believed all eugenicists were evil. There is no doubt that for many Catholics opposition to welfare legislation rested in large part on their fears of eugenics: whatever central government might say, the wide-ranging powers of the Ministry of Health, for example, would be exercised by local authorities, doctors and health visitors, and there were no safeguards written into the legislation to prevent a takeover by people with strongly eugenicist views intent on pushing a eugenicist programme.

Put in that way the Catholic position appears largely negative, and it does seem that when bishops or lay people wrote to the government on health issues it was to complain that Catholic principles were under attack. It must be stressed, however, that underpinning that position was a very positive view, even a vision, of the importance of the rights and responsibilities of the individual as a child of God, and of the role of parents and the family in co-operating with God in his work of creation, in the fullest sense, and redemption. For Devas, Parkinson and the Catholic Social Guild, this was the only sound foundation for a new social order, built on Christian democracy and so avoiding the evils of State socialism and competitive capitalism. For much of the time the view may have been obscured by those who concentrated on stressing what it opposed rather than what it stood for; at times its ideas were hi-jacked by faddists like McNabb and the Distributists; it could also be emasculated by those who were over-fond of pious comparisons with the Holy Family of Nazareth. Additionally, English Catholics did not hold a strong enough position in the wider society for them to become moulders of general opinion, and they probably appeared to their compatriots as unlikely champions of individual liberty, especially to a post-war society for which 'a new heaven was arriving – at least for the middle classes – full of art and new sincerity and sex and motor cars', and in which a 'confident agnosticism' was increasing.[34]

Yet increasingly in the 1920s and 1930s Catholics did look on themselves as the only reliable defenders of traditional values in English society. There is an air of having greater confidence in their position in society (a result, perhaps, of their relative success in the battles over the schools question and of their having 'proved' their Englishness during the war), at the same time as there is also a sense of greater embattlement. The Nonconformist churches were in decline, and their former much-vaunted and influential public conscience could no longer be relied on. Most members of the Church of England had shared Catholic objections to artificial birth control and divorce, and the Lambeth Conference of 1920 urged women to accept motherhood as their greatest fulfilment and surest means of salvation, condemning artificial birth control, except for 'abnormal cases'. In 1930, however, the national Church seemed to many to give up the fight, when the Lambeth Conference refused to condemn birth control and declared it was a matter for the individual conscience, although it stressed that procreation was the 'primary object of sexual intercourse'. Anglicans were also divided on a number of issues, and Archbishop Lang was not the person to provide strong leadership. In the circumstances Catholics felt it was up to them 'to stand erect amidst this moral devastation' and raise their 'voice in sight of [the Church's] divine mission to the chastity of the marriage contract unsullied by this ugly stain' (*Casti Connubii*).[35]

The practice of birth control was becoming more widespread in all classes, and a number of pressure groups were active in its cause. In 1930 local authority maternity and child welfare clinics were allowed to give contraceptive advice to expectant and nursing mothers, but not to other women. The campaign of Marie Stopes to spread her ideas on the joys of married sex brought her into conflict with a number of Catholics and led to a number of highly publicised trials; chief among these was her case against Dr Halliday Sutherland – it lasted over two years and ended in her defeat in the Lords. Another case, against Cardinal Bourne and the *Tablet*, was settled out of court when the paper apologised for publishing a letter that could be read as an attack on her integrity.[36] Catholics were supported in their views by Pope Pius XI's encyclical, *Casti Connubii*, of 1930, a straightforward reiteration of traditional teaching, and written in part as a reaction to the Lambeth Conference. Most English Catholic writing on marriage was equally traditional. G. H. Joyce SJ was masterly in his coverage of history, sacramental theology and, especially, canon law, but Richard O' Sullivan KC adopted a more aggressive tone in his attack on 'Individualism and Socialism', neither of which, he claimed, believed in the existence of the family; indeed, the so-called progressive forces in English politics had consistently attacked 'the indissolubility of marriage, the supremacy of the paternal power, the subordination of child to parent, the institution of family property'. He condemned almost every aspect of welfare legislation, including old-age pensions, unemployment benefit, state education and health insurance.[37] Fr Vincent McNabb OP, in a commentary on the papal encyclical, supported the authority of the father: 'by the physiological nature of man and woman it is the duty of the man to defend the child-bearing woman. This means for the husband *"principatum regiminis"*.'[38] It would be unfair to pretend McNabb was typical of Catholic thinkers in these years, since for him the ideal was 'family and farm', and his writing on the family was coloured by Distributist economics; but he was outstandingly popular as a speaker, preacher and writer, and his attacks on industrialism and his support of the 'home and homestead' approach to social issues influenced many who would have been appalled at the thought of joining a Distributist farm.[39]

The League of National Life, which counted Anglican bishops, Catholic priests, lay people and medical doctors among its members, and whose president was Lord Fitzalan KG, backed these approaches. At one of its meetings a distinguished Catholic doctor spoke of birth control as 'one of the greatest evils of the day . . . There was no method of contraception devised by the mind of man which was not injurious to humanity', and he called on 'all right-minded citizens . . . to fight to the last those who would undermine the integrity and morality of the nation'. He was followed by the Anglican Bishop of St Albans who, in a long and impassioned speech, attacked among others young couples who preferred to 'spend a pound on motoring than on the provision of family life'; but if everyone stood firm 'the battle for purity of life' would be won.[40]

While this public and generally sterile controversy was continuing, two debates were beginning more quietly in Catholic circles that were to be very significant. One of these concerned the use of the safe period to limit family size, the other concerned the Church's teaching on the primary and secondary purposes of marriage. *Casti Connubii* had said that those who used their right to have intercourse in the proper way 'at certain seasons' were not acting against nature; McNabb commented, a little negatively, 'Hence the difficulty of forbidding the marriage act at seasons when, according to vital statistics, conception is not likely.'[41] In the *Clergy Review* the Jesuit theologian Henry Davis commented very positively on recent developments, speaking of the duty or necessity to limit the size of one's family. He saw in the 'Knaus and Ogino Method' a 'way

[*above*] Archbishop Manning, *circa* 1870.
[*right*] Extract from Archbishop Manning's account to his former secretary, Fr John Morris SJ, dated June 1871, relating details of his visit to Pius IX to receive the *pallium*, symbol of metropolitan authority.

In the month of September, 1865, I went to Rome, to receive the Pallium. In my first audience, the night after arriving, the Holy Father began at once by saying: "I know all that has been passing in England, and I thank God for it. The loss of the Cardinal gave me great sorrow and anxiety, and the choice of a successor was made more difficult by the predic-tions of division and dissention with which I was plied on all sides. Some told me to name A., and others told me to name B.; and for a long time I was in great doubt and hesitation. I desired prayers and Masses to be said, that I might obtain light." The Holy Father then looked away from me, and looked upwards: and went on speaking, as if thinking aloud:– saying, "Ma io credevo sempre di sentire una voce chi mi diceva, Mettetelo lì – mettetelo lì – mettetelo lì." After a pause, he added: "I have heard with great consolation of the union which exists among the Catho-lics, and especially among the Bishops, in England".

[*above*] Cardinal Francis Bourne during the First World War, addressing the Dublin Fusiliers Brigade from a cart.
[*below*] Bourne, the longest-serving Archbishop of Westminster, towards the end of his thirty-one years of active ministry, officiating at the traditional ceremony of the procession of palms at the commencement of Holy Week.

The war-time leader of British Catholics, Cardinal Arthur Hinsley at Archbishop's House, Westminster, on his return to London after receiving the Red Hat from Pius XI in 1937. Hinsley was in his seventieth year when named to the see in 1935.

Pius XII being carried on the *sedia gestatoria* in St Peter's Square in 1948 before an estimated 600,000 people assembled to hear his address to Catholic Action members.

Some members of the English and Welsh episcopacy assembled in Rome in 1950, the centenary year of the restoration of the hierarchy, for the Holy Year. *From left to right*: Cyril Cowderoy of Southwark; Joseph Rudderham of Clifton; George Brunner (Auxiliary of Middlesbrough); Thomas Flynn of Lancaster; George Craven (Auxiliary of Westminster); Cardinal Bernard Griffin; George Andrew Beck (Coadjutor of Brentwood); Pope Pius XII; John Murphy of Shrewsbury; Joseph Masterson, Archbishop of Birmingham; John Petit of Menevia; Francis Grimshaw of Plymouth; Joseph McCormack of Hexham and Newcastle; Edward Ellis of Nottingham and Leo Parker of Northampton. *Bishops missing are*: Arthur Doubleday of Brentwood (sick); Michael McGrath, Archbishop of Cardiff; Richard Downey, Archbishop of Liverpool; Thomas Shine of Middlesbrough (aged); John Henry King of Portsmouth and Henry Vincent Marshall of Salford. Leeds was *sede vacante*.

William Godfrey, former Apostolic Delegate to Great Britain (1938–53) and Archbishop of Liverpool (1953–6) in Westminster Cathedral, preaching at his enthronement as seventh Metropolitan Archbishop of Westminster, 11 February 1957.

Cardinal John Carmel Heenan on 14 May 1970 in a moment of light-hearted banter with the Chief Rabbi, Dr Immanuel Jakobovits and Dr Michael Ramsey at the AGM of the Council of Christians and Jews.

[*left*] Basil Hume, ninth Archbishop of Westminster, taking possession of his titular church of San Silvestro in Capite on being created cardinal by Pope Paul VI in May 1976.

[*below*] An ecumenical procession as snow falls at the inauguration of the restructured Diocese of Menevia, 12 February 1987. Its cathedral church of St Joseph is in Swansea. (© South Wales Evening Post. All other photographs taken from the Westminster Diocesan Archives: the publishers would be grateful to hear from any copyright holders they have been unable to trace.)

forward for Catholic couples'; earlier talk of a 'safe period' had been vitiated by decidedly unsafe researches and so doctors and priests were 'incredulous' about its existence. He summarised a recent article in *Commonweal*:

> If in fact a natural method of fulfilling both the primary and secondary ends of marriage is discovered, the difficulty . . . in reconciling stern Catholic teaching on marriage with the distressing economic situation of the day, will solve itself, provided always that at least some measure of self-control is exercised . . . At present, many married persons reasonably object to a large family. Indeed, a third child may be too great a drain on the family resources.

In addition to these economic reasons, he believed 'the arguments for the regulation of births from the standpoint of the health of women are no less strong'. Thousands died in childbirth every year and 'not a few women would be doomed to die if they became mothers . . . Continency in marriage is not a practical way out of the difficulty'.[42]

Later in the same year the respected moral theologian Fr E. J. Mahoney returned to the issue in his usual cautious way. The controversy, he thought, was causing anxiety to many clergy and revolved around the issue of how widely the new approach should be promulgated; some thought the 'glad tidings' should be given to as many as possible, others that the 'exclusive use of the sterile period was, at least, venially sinful, and to be tolerated only as a lesser evil' and should not be publicised generally. The truth lay between the two extremes. Whether to publish or not was, he believed, up to the bishops; what had to be avoided was 'the scandal of the Church seeming to advertise a method which is already being spoken of as "RC Birth Control" '. English people would not be able to differentiate between the safe period and artificial contraceptives, for they 'judge actions, not as they are in themselves, but from their effects'. Mahoney's tone was altogether different from Davis's; he showed none of the latter's sympathetic understanding of the pastoral dimensions of the problem in arguing that while the safe period could be useful, disseminating knowledge about it could harm the name of the Church.[43] It is interesting that Messenger, writing in 1948, commented on such reluctance: he himself was putting forward the solution 'favoured by the Church's best theologians, if not actually taught by ecclesiastical authority. Some features in this are not so well known as would seem to be desirable.' All writers who allowed the use of the safe period stressed that parents had to have a genuinely serious reason for using it, even when they already had children.[44]

The second debate that was initiated in the 1930s concerned the ends or purposes of marriage; it may have been of less immediate practicality than that on the use of the safe period, but it had very important theoretical implications and was relevant to the emerging tendency among Catholics to control family size. The traditional teaching is that the primary purpose of marriage is procreation; other purposes, such as fostering mutual love in the partners, or satisfying their sexual desires, are secondary, and may only be enjoyed if the primary purpose is not obstructed. This did not mean that on every occasion they performed the marriage act partners had to intend to produce children (the *finis operis* of the theologians); indeed, one of the secondary purposes could well be their main intention (the *finis operantis*), but in intending the latter they must not do anything (such as use artificial contraceptives) that would interfere with the primary purpose. A passage in *Casti Connubii* was taken by some to indicate a change of emphasis:

> The mutual interior formation of husband and wife, this persevering endeavour to bring each other to the state of perfection, may in a true sense be called, as the Roman Catechism calls it, the primary cause and reason of matrimony, so long as marriage is considered, not in its stricter sense as the institution destined for the procreation and education of children, but in the wider sense as a complete and intimate life-partnership and association.[45]

A German theologian, Dr Doms, argued that one could now say that the so-called secondary purposes were at least of equal importance with the primary and could even themselves be called primary purposes. Mahoney said this view was 'attractive in many respects', though he was not wholly convinced by it, and called it 'fundamentally personalist (the complete union of two persons) rather than genetic'. Rome in the end came down against the new theory, but stressed that the secondary purposes of marriage must not be undervalued as had sometimes happened in Catholic writings.[46] Mahoney's use of the word 'personalist' is of interest here and anticipates its use by Catholic theologians from the 1960s onwards as they moved away from an overly functionalist approach to sex and marriage (see p. 212). The debate is also of interest in that it shows some Catholics moving, although very tentatively, towards the position adopted increasingly by secular writers. This pictured marriage as essentially a 'companionship', and a proliferation of marriage and sex manuals explained the role of sex in such a companionship. Compatibility between spouses would provide the required stability in a marriage, and a large number of children could make true companionship difficult.[47] Catholic discussion on limiting the size of families, however, still revolved principally around economic reasons.

Catholic books dealing explicitly with sex and its role in marriage were slower to appear. Messenger's three-volume work had some worthwhile things to say about it and he dealt in a very level-headed way with the 'pathological fear' some Catholics had of sex, a fear that all too often inhibited their enjoyment of sex in marriage. He attacked a number of well-known moral theologians (whose manuals were in use in English seminaries, it should be said) for their negative view of sex, their portrayal of it in marriage as a remedy for concupiscence, a concession to human weakness, always 'permitted' but rarely 'encouraged'. A number of books on sex and marriage (the majority of them American in origin) were published from the 1950s; they were to be generally welcomed, despite in some cases keeping the old stress on paternal authority in the family, being rather dismissive (insulting, indeed, in Trevett's case) about non-Catholics who practised birth control, and sometimes concentrating over much on the evils of company-keeping and on the duty to have as large a family as one could cope with – even Messenger spoke of the 'manifest evils' of the one-child family, evils which were to be found also in families with only two children; the ideal, he believed, was at least four children.[48] The English and Welsh bishops issued a carefully balanced statement on the necessity of sex education for both parents and children, and in 1946 set up the Catholic Marriage Advisory Council to provide advice, guidance and education, in order to promote successful Catholic marriages and parenthood; a welcome feature was that it was to work 'in harmony with and parallel to the National Marriage Guidance Council'.[49]

Meanwhile, the anti-state warriors were back. The year 1942 saw the publication of Beveridge's *Report on Social Insurance and Allied Services*, and from 1945 Labour began to establish the welfare state. Both events revived opposition to state intervention and fears about the family. The war and its aftermath justified opposition to state Fascism and Communism, and stress on the importance of individual independence was fully understandable; opposition to Beveridge and post-1945 legislation was not confined to Catholics. Catholic arguments were not new and need not detain us here in detail, but one or two features are noteworthy.[50] There was support for Beveridge in the *Clergy Review*: his *Report* fell short of the Catholic ideal on such matters as a living family wage, but offered as much as was possible. Failure to provide the security and improvements people desired might encourage that very Communism critics decried. Was there not also something pharisaical in enforcing 'counsels of perfection on others while living oneself in comfort and perhaps luxury'? Opposition seems to have been stronger among lay writers than among clerical; it is not always easy to distinguish between political and religious motivation in some of the statements. In the *Tablet* O'Sullivan wrote articles and letters attacking every change, while an extreme editorial headed 'The Salesmen of Servitude' accused the secular press of a conspiracy in keeping the worst features of the *Report* secret. There was, finally, a rather pathetic appeal to the 'Catholic voice, so eloquently heard . . . in defence of human freedom' in Europe not to be silent before 'these perils at home'. Before the 1945 election it came down in favour of the Conservatives 'to preserve freedom' and the interests of the 'ordinary poor citizen'.[51] The hierarchy were understandably concerned about the fate of Catholic voluntary hospitals under the National Health Service, but Griffin also feared that the new legislation would glorify state control and 'deprive us of those very liberties for which we're fighting'. But there was no general Catholic hostility to the welfare state, and most welcomed the greater security and better health it promised.[52]

During the 1950s the CSG, the only English organisation concerned with Catholic social theory, continued to campaign against the welfare state and, interestingly, attracted more members than ever before (though still never more than 0.1 per cent of the Catholic population), until a terminal decline set in in 1958 that led to its closure in 1967. As late as 1965 Paul Crane SJ, a former secretary of the Guild, was arguing for the restoration to the country's 'male citizens of that which is rightfully theirs – total responsibility for the welfare of their families', and 'the dismantling of the welfare state', but hardly anyone was listening.[53] It was not social theory that interested Catholics in the 1960s but the very practical question of birth control.

In the years after 1945 English society as a whole accepted birth control, not just as 'respectable' but as a moral duty to avoid global over-population. By 1967 contraceptive clinics had become part of the National Health Service and no distinction was being made between the married and the unmarried.[54] As contraception became increasingly a normal part of English family life, Catholic expectations that the Church would ease its traditional prohibition on artificial birth control were also being raised. Pope John had announced a period of 'aggiornamento' and the Second Vatican Council was reformulating many traditional positions, although Pope Paul had reserved the issue of birth control for a special advisory commission. Some continental theologians were discussing the new contraceptive pill favourably, and in 1964 Archbishop Roberts SJ formerly of Bombay wrote a widely reported article suggesting that the Lambeth Conference approach was more rational than the Catholic one and would fit in better with recent Council statements about conscience. The English bishops issued an uncompromisingly traditional statement and started a major controversy – Roberts defended himself in the *Evening Standard*, and a group of Catholic lay people wrote to *The Times* saying the bishops' statement was 'basically unjustifiable'. It was the first time English Catholics had shown dissent from a basic teaching of their Church in such a public way. In 1966 Cardinal Heenan, a member of the commission, seemed to hint at changes, and in 1967 the report was leaked: the majority of members advocated an easing of the prohibition, with couples acting according to their consciences. Catholics waited in hope for the Pope's decision.[55]

It was not just journalistic *schadenfreude* that made Catholic divisions into general news. Catholics had achieved a level of acceptance in English society not reached before; numbers were at their highest, and the geographic spread was at its greatest. During the 1960s the Secretary-General of the TUC, the Director-General of the BBC and the editor of *The Times* were committed Catholics; more Catholic students were at university than ever before, and in 1967 increased government aid to Catholic schools was granted with hardly a dissentient voice.[56] It is not surprising that this better-integrated and generally more prosperous Catholicism should be affected by the social outlook of those it had integrated with (often literally, as mixed marriages surpassed Catholic marriages for the first time in 1963) – the increasingly prosperous, and materialistic, working and middle classes of the 1960s, who had never had it so good. If small families were the norm, and something of a safeguard for the new prosperity, why should Catholics be different?

The publication of the Pope's negative decision in *Humanae Vitae* (July 1968) shattered liberal expectations but calmed conservative fears. Television and the press covered the ensuing controversy in detail, and at one stage *The Times* was receiving over a thousand letters a week on the topic. Clergy spoke openly against their bishops and were suspended – but only in some dioceses, and it was soon obvious that for all their public statements the bishops themselves were divided. Dr John Marshall, a lay member of the commission, disassociated himself from the encyclical's 'insulting' references to those who practised birth control; others quoted its call to governments to ban contraception as further evidence of its 'unreality'. In one sense, the issue of birth control became secondary – what was crucial was that a substantial body within the Church refused to accept a clear papal statement. English Catholics had always prided themselves on their loyalty and solidarity, in obvious contrast, they felt, with other denominations. Now, for many of them there was a shift to 'conscience' as the principal authority in family morality; they could claim support from ambiguous episcopal statements as bishops tried to preserve Catholic unity and keep from leaving the Church those who found the traditional teaching too difficult.[57] At the same time there was support for the encyclical, less vocal, perhaps, but still strong. The most popular Catholic paper, *The Universe*, supported it, as did many of the correspondents to *The Times*, the Catholic Priests' Association and similar lay groups; an American cardinal's commentary supporting the encyclical was published in Liverpool in 1968.[58]

Previous failure to develop a positive theology of sex and marriage was important in that it allowed opponents to talk of the encyclical's 'theological barrenness'. For much of the century the case against birth control had been linked to the case against eugenics and fears of a declining population; it was just assumed that arguments based on natural law were fundamentally sound. Birth control was portrayed as a danger to the family, leading to increased infidelity, 'sex for pleasure' and parental irresponsibility, while smaller families would deprive children of the benefits of sibling companionship. By the 1950s, however, eugenics no longer mattered, and people argued that birth control made families more stable, allowing parents to devote more time and resources to their children and improving the health of mothers. Catholics saw friends and associates who practised birth control being no less loving and responsible than themselves, with a richer understanding of the importance of a satisfying sexual relationship. Finally, when natural law as a philosophical concept was questioned, all that was left was to fall back on the authority of the Church. The notion of authority, however, was changing in the 1960s, in secular society and in the Church: the Council argued the case for collegiality, for greater involvement of the laity, and for freedom of conscience; then, at the crucial moment, authority's traditional spokemen did not speak with one voice.

The immediate controversy was over by about 1970, and a modus vivendi had been reached. From what evidence we have it seems Catholics turned increasingly to artificial methods of birth control and ceased to regard it as a matter for confession. Research continued into the safe period: the CMAC established the Family Research Trust in 1969 in response to the Pope's invitation to 'men of science to research on behalf of the family'.[59] Church leaders turned their attention to another issue on which they could speak with undivided authority, and on which they could be sure of both Catholic and wider support – abortion. This had been legalised in 1968 and by 1980 there were over 140,000 abortions annually in Britain. Catholics took the lead in opposing it but attempts to convince the wider society of its evil failed; not even all Christians supported the mild Corrie Bill of 1980 that attempted to introduce a twenty-week limit on abortions. Divorce, too, was becoming more common after the Divorce Law Reform Act of 1971, with increasing numbers of one-parent families (by 1976 there were three-quarters of a million in England and Wales) and more and more children experiencing broken homes.[60]

Neither the Catholic Church nor the Church of England recognised second marriages after divorce, but pastorally sensitive clergy knew they were becoming more common among their congregations, and wondered whether couples should be excluded from the sacraments because they re-married, even when it was clear their second marriages were much nearer to the ideal of a loving relationship than their first had been. Here was a pastoral problem that was to lead to a tentative reappraisal of the traditional approach to the theology of marriage. A similar reappraisal was taking place relating to the theology of sex and its role in marriage; since the *Humanae Vitae* controversy was proving fruitless, a new approach to the issue might provide a way forward. Theologians, clerical and lay, who were working in these areas accepted and developed a basis for morality that was essentially personalist, moving away from traditional notions of natural law. As one of them wrote, 'Morality in the full and true sense . . . is about the goodness and badness of *persons* rather than about the rightness and wrongness of *actions*.'[61]

It is too early to assess the impact of these new approaches. They have had a varied reception. When Jack Dominian began a series of articles called 'Christians and Sex' in 1976 he was accused by a priest of forgetting that the Church's tradition on sex was based on a 'refusal to let it be abused for profane gratification', but praised by a doctor-nun who complained about 'pious platitudes from pulpits from frightened or ill-informed priests' while lay people like Dominian offered 'genuine interpretations of the Gospel, relevant to life as it is'. The ensuing controversy lasted several months.[62] The National Pastoral Congress in 1980 urged the bishops to reaffirm the indissolubility of Christian marriage, but also to discover ways of 'showing compassion to those whose marriages have broken down irreconcilably, whose second marriage is a living witness to Christ and who seek to re-establish unity with the Church through the Eucharist'.[63] At the papal synod on Marriage and the Family in Rome in the same year, Archbishop Worlock of Liverpool said the bishops must listen seriously 'to the voice of experienced priests and laity pleading for consideration of this problem'; could the re-married be told only that they 'must reject their new responsibilities as a necessary condition of forgiveness and restoration to sacramental life?'[64] The 1995 English Bishops' Conference statement on the family and divorce was strictly traditional, though couched in friendly tones and acknowledging the need for pastoral care and counselling for those whose marriages had broken down.[65] When the Pope spoke on the family in Brazil in 1997 a commentator in the *Tablet* took him to task for his 'reactionary views' and the refusal of the Pontifical Council for the Family to address the questions 'present in the minds of pastors the world over'.[66]

Meanwhile, a new issue has appeared, of great concern to many parents: increasingly their children are cohabiting, apparently in good conscience, and they fear an end to traditional Catholic values. The continuity of tradition, however, is a complex notion; no one today would regard sex as inherently sinful, a not uncommon view among theologians for several centuries, and *Humanae Vitae* itself had beautiful things to say about married love that would have been unimaginable to major moral theologians of the nineteenth and early twentieth centuries. The 150 years of English Catholic experience surveyed here show that marriage does not exist in a sacred enclosure: marriage, family and society interact; its social and psychological aspects need not be considered eternal and unchanging.[67] In each age the Church must proclaim the ideal of Christian marriage, but it must also listen to the wisdom of that age.[68]

NOTES

1. Quoted in John Sharp, *Reapers of the Harvest* (1989), p. 206. See also pp. 273–4: Redemptorist missioners were keen to establish branches; by 1893, there were 193 in England.
2. E. C. Messenger, *Two in One Flesh*, 3 vols (London, 1948), vol. 2, p. 189. See also V. McNabb, *Nazareth or Social Chaos* (1933).
3. See Jack Dominian, *Marriage, Faith and Love* (1981), pp. 20ff. The Rev. C. W. Wood's popular book, *Marriage* (1887), is a good example of these concerns, as is the magisterial work of G. H. Joyce SJ, *Christian Marriage* (1933; 2nd edn, 1948), which is dominated by them. See

also Peter Doyle, 'Missed Opportunities: Clerical Conferences in the Nineteenth Century', *Downside Review* (October 1982), pp. 263–73.

4. H. McLeod, 'Building the "Catholic Ghetto": Catholic Organisations 1870–1914', *Studies in Church History*, 23 (1986), pp. 411–44, and references there.
5. For a discussion see Lynn Hollen Lees, *Exiles of Erin: Irish Migrants in Victorian London* (1979), esp. ch. 7; Sheridan Gilley, 'English Attitudes to the Irish in England' in C. Holmes (ed.), *Immigrants and Minorities in British Society* (1978); M. A. G. ÓTuathaigh, 'The Irish in Nineteenth-Century Britain: Problems of Integration' in R. Swift and S. Gilley (eds), *The Irish in the Victorian City* (1985).
6. *Marriage, A Sermon Preached at St Augustine's by the Rev. James Swarbrick . . . 1858* (1858), published by clerical request.
7. Archives of the Archdiocese of Liverpool (AAL), Goss Pastoral Letters, Lent 1863. Goss was himself the child of a mixed marriage. See also Bishop Ullathorne's synodal address, in *Ecclesiastical Discourses* (London, 1876), pp. 55–94.
8. See *Decreta Quatuor Conciliorum Provincialium Westmonasteriensium 1852–1873* (London, n.d.), pp. 315–17, for *Propaganda*'s letter; the bishops' request for lenience is in J. D. Mansi, *Sacrorum Conciliorum nova et amplissima collectio*, vol. 49, col. 302.
9. Returns in Lancashire Record Office: RCLv, Conference Reports 1863–4, and Visitation Returns, 1865.
10. Liverpool and Salford clerical conferences discussed the canon law of marriage but not pastoral practice; I believe this was also the case in other dioceses.
11. *Pastoral Letter on the Evils of Mixed Marriages by John, Bishop of Salford* (Salford, 1899). For Vaughan's survey, A. Oates, 'The Lost, Strayed and Stolen of Our Catholic Poor Children', *Dublin Review* (January 1887), pp. 157–76; also Vaughan's pamphlet, *The Loss of Our Children* (1886).
12. Oates, 'The Lost', p. 161.
13. Oates, 'The Lost', p. 163; and J. G. Snead-Cox, *The Life of Cardinal Vaughan*, 2 vols (1910), vol. I, pp. 407–8.
14. See A. D. Gilbert, *Religion and Society in Industrial England* (1976), pp. 198–203.
15. John Bennet, 'The Care of the Poor' in G. A. Beck, *English Catholics 1850–1950*, pp. 559–84, has a detailed account of provision. Also his *Father Nugent of Liverpool* (1949) on a pioneer in this work. On emigration, V. Alan McClelland, 'Child Emigration to Canada in Late Victorian and Edwardian England: A Denominational Case Study', *Children at Risk – Aspects of Education*, 50 (1994), pp. 36–53.
16. Vaughan was speaking in 1889, three years after setting up the first Catholic Rescue Society; see Beck, *English Catholics*, p. 570.
17. Manning gave the speech at Leeds in 1874.
18. Copies of the pamphlet are rare. More attention was paid to his views on the Continent; see G. McEntee, *The Social Catholic Movement in Great Britain* (New York, 1927), pp. 299–301.
19. C. S. Devas, *Plain Words on Socialism* (CTS, n.d., *c.* 1906), pp. 25–6. Also, 'Is Socialism Right After All?' in *Dublin Review* (1906), pp. 321–38, especially p. 331.
20. Devas' *Studies of Family Life: A Contribution to Social Science* (1886) argued that only the Christian family was truly a moral entity, but was criticised for being tendentious. The use of religious symbolism in connection with the family was not restricted to Catholics; see J. Lewis (ed.), *Labour and Love: Women's Experience of Home and Family 1850–1940* (London, 1986) p. 5.
21. On the origins of the CSG, see McEntee, *Social Catholic Movement*; Peter Doyle, 'Charles Plater S. J. and the Origins of the Catholic Social Guild', *Recusant History*, vol. 21, no. 3 (May 1993), pp. 401–17; Barbara Wraith, 'The English Catholic Church and the "Social Question" ', *Studies in Church History*, 33 (1997), pp. 529–45.

22. Wraith, 'English Catholic Church', p. 540.
23. Wraith, 'English Catholic Church', p. 539.
24. H. Robbins, 'The Dangers of the New Public Health Act', *Month*, vol. CXXXIV (1919), pp. 1–11. See also his article 'The Progress of the Eugenic Campaign', *Month*, vol. CXXXV (1920), pp. 101–10. Robbins was later prominent in the Land Association.
25. Low Week Minutes, Archives of the Archdiocese of Westminster (AAW), mtg of June 1920. On the Conference, see H. Robbins, 'The Ministry of Health: I: State Eugenics', *Tablet*, vol. 134, no. 27 (December 1919), and documents in AAW, Hi 2/148. Members included the CSG, the Catholic Women's League, the CYMS, the Ancient Order of Hibernians, and the Catholic Federation, among others – no mean cross-section! For the other meetings, *Tablet*, vol. 133, pp. 484, 702.
26. *Tablet*, vol. 137, 4 Sept 1920.
27. AAW, Hi 2/148; the report is undated.
28. 'Is the Father the Head of the Family? How the State will Usurp his Place!', *The Catholic Federationist* (June 1921), p. 5. For the Westminster Branch, AAW, Bourne Papers, Bo 5/43d. On the Federation, Peter Doyle, 'The Catholic Federation 1906–1929', *SCH*, 23 (1986), pp. 461–76.
29. J. B. McLaughlin OSB, BA, and Alexander P. Mooney MD, *The Catholic Attitude to the Ministry of Health* (n.d., but 1920/21).
30. Jane Lewis, 'The Working-Class Wife and Mother and State Intervention, 1870–1918' in Lewis (ed.), *Labour and Love*, pp. 109–15.
31. Jane Lewis, *The Politics of Motherhood: Child and Maternal Welfare in England, 1900–1939* (1980), Introduction and p. 16. Also Lewis, 'The Working-Class Wife and Mother', pp. 99–120, esp. p. 100.
32. In 1930 the Minister of Labour complained about the 'Irish invasion' of Lancashire and Scotland, 'a remarkable instance of a lower civilization pushing out a higher'. See *The Diary of a Dean* (n.d. but c. 1950), under February 1912, and October 1930; the dean was Inge of St Paul's.
33. For Vaughan, see the *Month* (1908), pp. 36–7. For Owen, P. Larkin, *Required Writing* (1983), pp. 235–6. Bourne was addressing a national conference on 'How to Maintain and Improve the Race'; see the *Tablet*, 31 May 1919, pp. 666–7.
34. Adrian Hastings, *A History of English Christianity 1920–1985* (1986), pp. 221, 226.
35. On Anglicanism, see Hastings, *English Christianity*, ch. 11, and A. Stephenson, *Anglicanism and the Lambeth Conference* (1978).
36. See H. Sutherland, *Laws of Life* (1935), and *Control of Life* (5th edn, 1951); Muriel Box, *The Trial of Marie Stopes* (1967). For Stopes v. Bourne see *The Times*, 14 January 1932.
37. Richard O'Sullivan, 'Some Difficulties of the Day: IV. The Assault on the Family', *Clergy Review*, vol. 4 (October 1932), pp. 261–70.
38. V. McNabb OP, *Christian Marriage: Casti Connubii, Encyc. of his Holiness Pope Pius XI on Christian Marriage, in view of the present conditions, needs, errors and vices that affect the family and society* (1933), p. 68.
39. On McNabb, see the special issue of *The Chesterton Review*, vol. 22, nos. 1 and 2, February and May 1996. Also, F. E. Nugent (ed.), *A Vincent McNabb Anthology* (1955), esp. pp. 23–9.
40. Report in the *Church Times*, 27 May 1932. The bishop 'staggered his diocesan conference' by an outspoken speech in Bedford; see *West Herts Post*; press cuttings in AAW, Bo 1/13.
41. McNabb, *Christian Marriage*, pp. 27, 72.
42. Rev. Henry Davis SJ, 'Notes on Recent Work: I. Moral Theology', *Clergy Review*, vol. 5 (1933), pp. 402–7.
43. *Clergy Review*, vol. 6 (1933), pp. 139–41.

44. Rev. E. C. Messenger, *Two in One Flesh*, 3 vols (1948); vol. 1, p. vii; vol. 2, p. 57. Also Frank Sheed, *Society and Sanity* (1953), p. 110.
45. Quoted in Messenger, *Two in One Flesh*, vol. 2, p. 165. The passage was omitted (presumably accidentally) from all English versions of the encyclical until Mahoney commented in the *Clergy Review* in 1938 (vol. 15, pp. 150–1).
46. Doms's book was translated into French: *Du sens et de la fin du Mariage* (1938). For the debate, *Clergy Review*, 15 (1938), pp. 150–1; 22 (1942), pp. 462–3, and 566–9, and Messenger, *Two in One Flesh*, who also deals with the Roman decisions of the 1940s.
47. Lewis, *Labour and Love*, pp. 150–66.
48. Messenger, *Two in One Flesh*, vol. 1, pp. 1–12; vol. 3, pp. 50, 57. Also, R. F. Trevett, *Sex and the Christian* (1960), and several titles by the American, Mgr G. A. Kelly: *The Catholic Youth's Guide to Life and Love* (1960); *The Catholic Marriage Manual* (1959); *Your Child and Sex* (1964).
49. AAW, G 1/56, for the bishops' statement; G 2/57, for the CMAC.
50. Peter Coman, *Catholics and the Welfare State* (1977), covers the issues well.
51. *Clergy Review*, 23 (1943), pp. 200–9, 433–40; *Tablet*, *passim* from December 1942 to June 1943; June and November, 1945. O'Sullivan also wrote in *Blackfriars*, 24 (February 1943), pp. 46–51.
52. Joint statement, May 1946, AAW, G 1/2b; Griffin's letter, January 1945, G 1/2a.
53. Coman, *Catholics and the Welfare State*, pp. 80–5.
54. Norman St John-Stevas, *The Agonising Choice: Birth Control, Religion and the Law* (1971), pp. 22–6.
55. St John-Stevas, *Agonising Choice*, pp. 91–129.
56. Hastings, *English Christianity*, pp. 561–3.
57. St John-Stevas covers reactions in England, Europe and USA; p. 170 deals with Heenan's famous Frost interview on conscience. Also, P. Harris, A. Hastings *et al.*, *On Human Life* (1968); Hastings, *English Christianity*, pp. 574–9.
58. St John-Stevas, *Agonising Choice*, p. 174; also B. Murtough (ed.), *The Pope, the Pill and the People* (1968). Cardinal O'Boyle, *Sex in Marriage: Love-giving, Life-giving* (1968).
59. AAW, G 2/57,94: CMAC.
60. Hastings, *English Christianity*, pp. 597, 657–8.
61. Kevin Kelly, *New Directions in Moral Theology: The Challenge of Being Human* (1992), p. 17. See also his *Life and Love* (1987), and *Divorce and Second Marriage: Facing the Challenge* (2nd enlarged edn, 1996).
62. *Tablet* (1976), pp. 1117–8, 1247, and into March 1977. Dominian published *Proposals for a New Sexual Ethic* in 1977. See also his *Marriage, Faith and Love* (1981).
63. *Liverpool 1980* (1981), p. 173.
64. *Briefing*, vol. 10 (1980), pp. 7–8.
65. *Briefing*, vol. 25 (1995), pp. 6–7.
66. F. McDonagh, 'Battling for the Family', *Tablet*, 11 October 1997, pp. 1314–17.
67. See Dominian, *Marriage*, pp. 1–5.
68. 'The Church in the Modern World' (*Gaudium et Spes*), 44; Kelly, *Divorce*, pp. 3–4.

NINE

A VIEW FROM THE BRIDGE: THE CATHOLIC SCHOOL

MAURICE WHITEHEAD

INTRODUCTION

In 1996 the bishops of England and Wales issued a statement on education in Catholic schools and colleges entitled *Principles, Practices and Concerns*.[1] The document presented the hierarchy's summary overview of various aspects of Catholic education, including the commitment of the Catholic community to Catholic schools and the distinctive nature of Catholic education. The bishops implied that current practices, in these two aspects at least, provide a continuum which has existed since 1850.

In outlining their view of the distinctiveness of the Catholic school in England and Wales, the bishops wrote that

> whatever their status – voluntary aided, special agreement, grant maintained, special or independent – Catholic schools and colleges are established to support Catholic parents in their responsibility for the academic, physical, spiritual, moral and religious education of their children in accordance with the teaching of the Church.

They went on to claim that distinctiveness is promoted by the commitment of Catholic schools and colleges in five areas:

- the education of all;
- the education of the whole person;
- the uniqueness of the individual;
- moral principles;
- the search for excellence.

The purpose of the present chapter is to test the extent to which this paradigm has or has not been adhered to consistently and coherently by the English and Welsh hierarchy since 1850. Owing to considerations of space, the focus hereafter is placed on the provision of education by the *dioceses* during the period under review: consequently, the independent sector is scarcely mentioned. Nor is the aim to analyse in detail the long and complex political and social struggle to establish the current Catholic educational system – a subject which still awaits detailed scholarly study.[2] The aim is, rather, to explore and analyse, necessarily selectively, the 'view from the bridge': that is, the bishops' own articulation of principles with regard to education in England and Wales, based on the teachings of the universal Church, as revealed in their own teachings, jointly or individually, by means of their pastoral letters and their public statements. Many of the latter have emanated from their official educational mouthpiece, the Catholic Poor School Committee (1847–1905), the Catholic Secondary Education Council (1902–05) and their joint successor bodies, the Catholic Education Council (1905–91) and the Catholic Education Service (1991 to the present day).

Throughout the chapter, particular attention is given to the leadership in this sphere offered by successive Archbishops of Westminster. Though, as will be demonstrated, the latter have not necessarily always provided the principal leadership on the Catholic education question in England and Wales, the *de jure* primacy of the see of Westminster until the sub-division of the province of Westminster in 1911, and its subsequent de facto retention of that status, as well as the physical proximity of the Archbishops of Westminster to the seat of national government, have together lent special authority to statements on education from Archbishop's House.

THE EDUCATION OF ALL

The commitment of the bishops to the education of *all* Catholics in England and Wales pre-dates the restoration of the hierarchy in 1850. The creation of the Catholic Poor School Committee late in 1847 was soon followed by a powerful joint pastoral letter of the Vicars Apostolic urging the faithful to pay heed to a pressing situation:

> We clearly see and deeply lament the very general and most pressing want of a religious education for the children of the Poor in our respective Districts; and with our united voice, we now proclaim to you with all the earnestness of our souls, that on the success of this our common effort in behalf of the children of the Poor, not only our religious progress and prosperity, but also the eternal salvation of thousands does depend.[3]

The urgency of the situation was underscored again four years later, in 1852, at the First Provincial Synod of Westminster. Catholics were warned that if they wished to see a future generation of Catholics, they must educate it, or others would 'snatch it up' before their eyes. They were instructed unequivocally by the hierarchy as to what their highest priority should be:

> Wherever there may seem to be an opening for a new mission, we should prefer the erection of a school, so arranged as to serve temporarily for a chapel, to that of a church without one. For the building raised of living and chosen stones, the spiritual sanctuary of the Church, is of far greater importance than the temple made with hands. And it is the good school that secures the virtuous and edifying congregation.[4]

Nor was the focus exclusively on the education of the poor. With the wealthiest classes of Catholics already well provided with the independent schools of Ampleforth, Downside and Stonyhurst, among others, for boys, and a host of convent schools for girls, the need in the 1850s was to develop an educated Catholic middle class. As the bishops declared, 'Where there is a sufficient Catholic population to warrant it, we earnestly recommend the establishment of a middle school . . . in which a good commercial and general education shall be given to the children of families in a better worldly position.'[5]

Though the bishops considered the creation of a Catholic university in England 'higher than we can dare', they were supportive of the enterprise then being undertaken by their brethren in Ireland in the creation of a new Catholic university in Dublin under the rectorship of Dr John Henry Newman. Their hope was that the success of the Irish venture would provide an important addition to the existing continuum of Catholic educational provision by offering the possibility of Catholic higher education to those English and Welsh students who might eventually be sufficiently qualified to avail themselves of it.[6]

From 1850 onwards, the accent from the hierarchy was continually on the 'oneness' of the Catholic community and the responsibilities incumbent on all members of the Church for the educational welfare of all their brethren, whatever their social standing. Thus, in 1854, the Catholic gentry, as well as the Catholic 'professional and trading classes in the great towns' were upbraided for their 'feeble interest in the great work of educating the poor'; and, the following year, the entire community was urged to support the establishment of Catholic reformatory schools where young delinquents might be reformed without danger to their faith.[7] Nearly twenty years later, the tone from the hierarchy, again speaking with one voice, was as firm as ever: 'We know that the education of the highest as well as of the lowest of our people is a part of the cure of souls for which we must give account. Every baptized soul, whether of the rich or poor, has a right to Catholic education.'[8]

The paramount importance of the hierarchy speaking with one voice on educational matters, in order to achieve unity of purpose in the provision of education for all, was recognised early – and put into practice to good effect. In

1893, with the prospect of major new educational legislation coming into force, the bishops resolved 'not to act separately, in promoting any fundamental change in the Public Elementary School system', but agreed that suggestions for change might be 'forwarded to the Committee of Bishops already appointed, for consideration and for report to the Hierarchy, whose decision as to policy to be followed shall be binding upon all'.[9] By acting and speaking together, the bishops were able, for example, to maintain a comprehensive geographical overview of educational provision for all, and not allow the spectacular growth of Catholic schools in urban areas to overshadow needs in rural ones. In 1898, the faithful were reminded that 'the progress of the Church in this country is not to be estimated simply by the magnitude of our schools, but also by their multiplication in what may be called the outposts of Catholicity, in the smaller towns, and in the country districts'.[10]

There is some surviving evidence that individual bishops circulated draft versions of pastoral letters on the education question to their brethren in other dioceses, inviting comments prior to publication. In 1904, for instance, the Bishop of Hexham and Newcastle, Thomas Wilkinson, sent a draft pastoral letter entitled 'The Peril to Catholic Education' to the Bishop of Salford, Louis Charles Casartelli, who was then ultimately responsible for the elementary education of 15 per cent of all English Catholic children. Casartelli's trusted educational adviser, Canon Joseph Tynan, considered the pastoral 'inappropriate' and advised that, as its content diverged from the then prevailing thinking of the hierarchy on education, its publication should be 'held back' in the interests of episcopal unity and the common good.[11]

At the organisational level, the bishops were anxious to preserve and foster the integrity of the Catholic educational system and its emphasis on 'education for all'. Though the provisions of the 1902 Education Act forced them to take rapid measures to establish a Catholic *Secondary* Education Council, this was set up merely as a temporary, necessary expedient. As soon as the opportunity arose, in 1905, the latter body was amalgamated with the existing Catholic School Committee to form the new Catholic Education Council, so that thereafter there would be 'one, and only one, strongly constituted central body to deal with Catholic Education under all the aspects which fall within the purview of the Board of Education'.[12]

The prudence of a united, long-term, national policy of education for all Catholics was vindicated in 1943 by the then Archbishop of Liverpool, Dr Richard Downey. Noting that the Church of England had lost control of over 2,700 elementary schools between 1902 and 1942, he could record with pride that during the same period the Catholic Church in England and Wales had not given up one single school: indeed, during the period from 1902 until the outbreak of war in 1939, every year had witnessed the opening of new Catholic schools.[13]

Such a record was not a matter for complacency. The policy of providing education for all Catholics since 1850 had been achieved at enormous financial cost. For decades, the Catholic laity had endured not only the normal burden of paying for education as tax and rate payers, like all other citizens, but of paying further heavy sums for school buildings to enable their children to be educated in Catholic schools. The passing of the 1944 Education Act did not remove this disability, notwithstanding the general overriding principle, asserted in the Act, that children should be educated in harmony with the wishes of their parents.

The hierarchy could see clearly that the perpetuation of such a situation, which had continued for decades up to that time, despite unrelenting efforts at negotiating for financial relief with successive governments, would be intolerable in post-war Britain. Prior to the 1945 general election, the bishops mobilised, diocese by diocese, a massive national campaign to ensure that every candidate for Parliament was fully aware of the educational disabilities still being endured by Catholics. The objective was to seek their full support to the Catholic claim that for all school building, school alterations, and school extensions, of whatever kind, the promoters of Catholic education should be assisted by grants of 85 per cent of the costs. As the bishops noted in the confidential guidance notes for the campaign:

> Our young men are coming home from war; many of them have married; they will be setting up new homes. As the [1944] Act stands they will find to their disillusionment and dismay that in addition to other grievous financial burdens imposed upon the Catholic community for the alteration, extension, or replacement of existing Catholic schools, they will also have to pay the entire cost of the provision of new schools to which they can send their children without violation of conscience.[14]

The bishops went on to urge this point should be stressed and dealt with at once, even if it resulted only in the immediate concession that brand new schools and brand new training colleges were put on an equal footing with existing maintained schools and received 50 per cent assistance for both sites and buildings.

The objective of securing 85 per cent assistance was not achieved overnight. Yet had the bishops not seized their opportunity in a concerted manner in 1945, it is highly probable that the combination of the unanticipated, extensive post-war shift of population from inner city areas to suburban housing estates and satellite towns, and post-war educational expansion, would have brought about the complete collapse of the long-standing Catholic policy of education for all in England and Wales.

If, in the period from 1850 until 1950, educational leadership had been provided principally by the Archbishops of Westminster, working in concert with their fellow bishops, leadership passed from about 1950 until the mid-1970s to a seasoned headmaster and educationist, George Andrew Beck (1904–78), successively Coadjutor and then Bishop of Brentwood (1948–55), Bishop of Salford (1955–64) and Archbishop of Liverpool (1964–76). Continuing to work collegially with his episcopal brethren, Beck, an Assumptionist, steered the policy of education for all through a momentous period of change in education in England and Wales, achieving much for the Catholic community through quiet but skilful diplomacy at the highest level of government.[15]

Beck's educational influence was destined not to be confined to England and Wales, but to help shape the educational principles of the universal Church. As a *peritus* or expert on education at the Second Vatican Council, he played an influential role in the formulation of *Gravissimum Educationis*, the Council's *Declaration on Christian Education*.[16] In a speech to the Council in Rome on 18 November 1964, he drew on his own practical experience of providing education for all Catholics in an English and Welsh context by making a wider and infinitely more far-reaching recommendation:

> In the present age the Church should show herself as the defender of the rights of *all* parents, and not only of Catholics. Neither the Church nor Catholic parents wish to claim a monopoly of special treatment from civil governments. *Every* parent has the right to bring up his children in his religious belief and according to his conscience.[17]

These ideals have long been followed, and continue to be followed today by, among others, the seventeen social work agencies of the Catholic Church in England and Wales, which together serve the twenty-two dioceses and work in close collaboration with Catholic schools and local authorities. Complementing the educational work of the Catholic community through their care for the most vulnerable members of society, many of the agencies, such as the Nugent Care Society, founded in Liverpool in 1881, work in a wide range of educational and social contexts 'with and for all people of goodwill, regardless of race, sex, age or creed'.[18]

The rights of all Catholic parents to a sound Catholic education for their children have continued to be defended by the English and Welsh hierarchy in the thirty-five years since the closing of the Second Vatican Council. In the 1990s, new pressures, fostered by radical changes in government policy, in the form of competition between schools, unfettered parental choice and an arguably undue emphasis on examination success as the sole measure of a school's performance, have again highlighted the need for the Church to provide a consistent approach in ensuring a quality education for all. As will be demonstrated, the English and Welsh bishops have not remained silent on these matters in the search for excellence in education.

THE EDUCATION OF THE WHOLE PERSON

Soon after the restoration of the hierarchy in 1850, there emerged a clear and coherent view of the manner in which Catholic education should provide for the education of the whole person. The First Provincial Synod in 1852 noted that while the bishops wished to promote in the Catholic poor schools a secular instruction equal to that available in the state system, they considered 'sound faith, virtue, and piety by far the most important elements of education'.[19] They were fully alive to the fact that in society at large, worldly knowledge was more highly prized than religious learning:

> The inspection, the rewards, the honours derived from the state, are strictly limited to proficiency in [worldly knowledge]; and the youthful mind is easily led by its own ardour, to pursue what obtains public approbation and reward, to the neglect of less prized, but far more important, acquirements.[20]

In an effort to counterbalance this tendency, a three-pronged strategy was adopted in 1853–54. First, ecclesiastical inspectors of schools were appointed to examine pupils in their religious education and to grant certificates and award prizes for excellence in learning;[21] second, in addition to pupils' daily religious education at school, the diocesan clergy in England and Wales were instructed to provide 'on every Sunday . . . a public catechetical instruction in the church, in which the mysteries of the faith, and the commandments of God and the Church, and the doctrine of the sacraments, shall be explained in a plain and clear manner'.[22] This institution of 'Sunday school', which survived on a widespread basis in England and Wales until the 1960s, normally in conjunction with Benediction on Sunday afternoons, was seen as having a dual function. While the bishops urged the clergy to accommodate their language to the understanding of young children, they also exhorted them to ensure that they should not thereby speak in a manner 'too tedious to the well instructed': indeed, by careful preparation and appropriate illustration from Scripture, it was hoped that the priest would 'attract even adults to listen and learn' from what was being taught to children.[23] Third, as a further support to the faithful beyond school age, the priest was urged to

> provide a library suited to the capacity of his people, whence even the poor and ignorant may imbibe useful knowledge by having books lent out to them for a time to read. He should also do his best to spread amongst his flock the pious works of Catholics, which are daily issuing from the press.[24]

That the education of the whole person was something which should be available to *all* Catholics, regardless of social class, was a matter of concern to the Catholic Poor School Committee. Its seventh annual report, published in 1854, just four years before Darwin's *Origin of Species*, was particularly forthright:

> We should be the last to depreciate the wonders of God in the natural world, as disclosed in the sciences of chemistry, botany, mineralogy, and so many others, objects of predilection at the present day. But what are these wonders compared to those of the supernatural world, of God deigning to become Man, to have a human Mother, and of the infinite consequences deduced from these facts? These consequences are as interesting to the poorest Irishman's most neglected child, as to the noblest blood of Howard or of Talbot . . . Should a meagre repetition of the catechism be all that is bestowed on children whose inheritance is a faith which can afford matter to exercise the noblest intellect, and devotions to satisfy the most loving heart?[25]

Writing to his flock nearly twenty years later, Archbishop Manning anticipated by decades the work of twentieth-century educationists on the 'hidden curriculum' by pointing out that true education of the whole person depended greatly on the integrity and sincerity of the teacher in every situation:

> The teacher exercises two kinds of influence, a conscious and an unconscious. The conscious influence is that which comes directly from his acts and words; the unconscious streams from him unawares, at all times, by words, acts, gestures, tones of voice, by a thousand suggestions and transparent signs. The pride, or vanity, or conceit, or scepticism, or irreverence, or impiety, or scoffing of the teacher, make themselves sensible without acts, and audible without words. They may talk all day long about humility, and faith and piety; but their pupils will become what they are, and not what they say.[26]

Bishop Thomas Whiteside, responsible for the education of 70,000 pupils in 170 schools in the diocese of Liverpool in 1901, reminded his flock that however thorough and systematic Catholic education might be, and however competently and sincerely teachers in Catholic schools might conduct themselves, parents should not imagine that the education of the whole person would be automatically achieved by sending children to Catholic schools:

> The truths they learn must not be mere abstract ideas, but if they are to bear fruit in Eternity, they must be made to touch the hearts of the children and mould their lives. The priest may, no doubt, by his preaching do something. But the duty of forming the hearts of their children rests principally with the parents, who, besides being in constant contact with them, have the authority, and also the helps both natural and supernatural, to enable them to discharge this obligation.[27]

Thirty-five years later, Archbishop Thomas Williams of Birmingham, a diocese in one of the industrial heartlands of Britain, voiced his concern that the industrialisation of society had already had a deleterious effect on the education of the whole person – and that the Catholic school was, in some measure, a bulwark against the brutalisation of humanity:

> Most of the present elementary education prepares [Man] for life as the slave of a machine, not as the servant of God; it leads to little taste for real drama or philosophy or music or architecture, it educates him to be a cog in the industrial machine. But people are not going to remain contented with education of that sort, and the hope of the nation lies in schools that make religion the basis of education. Religious schools such as ours are a real asset to the nation.[28]

With the approach of the cold war in the early 1950s, the dangers of brutalisation of another sort were highlighted by Cardinal Bernard Griffin, who widened the educational debate by warning of the dangers of totalitarianism in the education of the whole child:

> The Christian education of a child has . . . to take into account the whole child, its nature and its future purpose, and for this reason any attempt by the State to arrogate to itself the whole function of education conflicts with the rights of Christian parents and of the Church. Moreover, it is harmful to the children themselves. We have only to look at what is happening in the Communist-controlled States of Eastern Europe today, where the State is seizing the Catholic schools and is compelling parents to send their children to State schools providing secular education only, to realise how easily schoolchildren can become mere tools in the hands of unscrupulous politicians.[29]

A year earlier, in 1950, Archbishop Richard Downey, like many of his episcopal brethren before him, had attempted to provide his own definition of education in the light of the Church's teaching. As in the past, it laid great emphasis on the education of the whole person:

> Education is a cultural process which embraces the whole man – as an individual, as a member of the family, as a citizen and as a subject of the State. The first and most important consideration is the end or purpose to which the education of the child is directed. This end and purpose must be identical with the purpose of man's creation . . . The whole process of education should receive its direction from the effort to fit the pupil for the knowledge, love and service of God in this world so as to be united with Him in the next.[30]

The archbishop went on to argue that such formation cannot be attained by an occasional half an hour's religious instruction, but must be continued throughout the whole school curriculum, 'as physical education is continued throughout the day by insistence on right posture, cleanliness and the rules of hygiene in every class period'.[31]

The ends and purposes of education were to be returned to exactly forty years later by Cardinal Basil Hume. Addressing a wide range of educationists at the North of England 77th Education Conference, held in Newcastle in 1990, his comments were timely in an ambience of growing utilitarianism in the educational system in England and Wales:

> The development of vocational and technical skills, and academic achievement do not constitute the totality of what education is . . . Education in its broadest sense is concerned with lifelong inner growth, with the achieving of personal wholeness and integrity, with the development to the utmost of personal gifts and creativity. The school is but a phase in this process . . . Education is not only concerned with putting in, that is with imparting knowledge and information, but with drawing out, with the development of the whole self. There has to be release of the inner potential and personal energy of each individual.[32]

Without directly attacking the introduction of a National Curriculum which many educationists criticised as narrowly prescriptive, especially in its earliest manifestations at the beginning of the 1990s, Cardinal Hume offered a corrective to the then prevailing orthodoxy in government educational circles:

> Not all study has to be at the service of some utilitarian purpose . . . Simply to know and to rejoice in knowing is sufficient justification for study. The individual grows and is enriched by what he or she knows. In this way we grow as human beings and achieve maturity. Appreciation of what is good and beautiful, and insatiable thirst for knowledge, a fearless embracing of the truth whatever its consequences, these surely are the characteristics of an educated person.[33]

Fully aware of the ever-diminishing opportunities in state schools for pupils to have access to arts education, the Cardinal reminded his audience that

> as part of our educational endeavour we should aim to encourage people to appreciate the arts, to paint, to play a musical instrument, to design and make a thing of beauty, to be fully alive and joyfully creative. The most significant thing is not the level of competence achieved but the human and creative energies released.[34]

THE UNIQUENESS OF THE INDIVIDUAL

Implicit in the attitude of the Catholic Church in England and Wales towards the education of all Catholics over the past 150 years has been the conviction that every individual is unique. Official documents from the hierarchy have, however, often stressed the point explicitly for particular emphasis.

One of the most powerful statements on this matter was made by the Third Provincial Synod of Westminster in 1859 at a time when, as noted earlier, it was proving difficult to appeal to the financial generosity of the professional and commercial strata of the Catholic community. In an attempt to meet the problem head on, the bishops spoke plainly and concretely:

> If you enter the school to-day which you visited six years ago, you seem to see the same objects before you, and feel tempted to exclaim, 'Are we no more forward yet with this everlasting education?' 'Yes,' and 'No' might be the honest reply. Yes! you contemplate before you what looks identical: the same eyes, the same casts of countenance, the same varieties of character, the same sprightliness and the same dulness, – perhaps the very same rags, and certainly the same squalidness and destitution – And yet in the most essential respect, No! All that it profits to care for is different. These are the new immortal souls that have to be saved, and we must do for them what we have done for others.[35]

The ongoing concern of the hierarchy for the uniqueness of the individual is perhaps best illustrated by the stances taken by three Archbishops of Westminster – Manning, Hinsley and Heenan – in a variety of circumstances over the past 150 years.

One of the first actions of Henry Edward Manning as Archbishop of Westminster was to reinforce the approach outlined by the Third Provincial Synod by setting up the Association of the Sacred Heart for the Education of the Poor in London, undertaken 'in order to promote the compassion of the Faithful for the thousands of children exposed to danger and daily perishing in the streets of London, and to kindle more and more a zeal for souls among us'.[36] So concerned was Manning with this problem that he sought, and obtained, from Pius IX plenary indulgences for members of the Association fulfilling the requisite conditions.[37]

This particular solicitude for the uniqueness of the most vulnerable members of his flock was repeated in 1936 by Arthur Hinsley in his first Lenten pastoral letter after becoming Archbishop of Westminster. Noting that, despite all earlier efforts, there were still sixty-five parishes in the archdiocese without Catholic schools, and that there were 10,000 Catholic children whose faith was in jeopardy, Hinsley made a special pledge:

> As your Archbishop, we are almost daily called upon to bless Catholic projects, schemes, societies and charities. We bless them all and do all we can, within our power, to encourage them all. There remains, however, this, the principal work to which we propose to dedicate our life in a special manner, namely, the rescue of the 10,000 children from the grave and unnecessary dangers that beset their lives.[38]

Nor was Hinsley's concern confined to these 10,000 children: he was soon to confront the difficulties of unprecedented wartime conditions in his archdiocese. In meeting these challenges, he led by example. In 1939, at the first hint that individual children might soon be evacuated from their homes to avoid the danger of enemy bombing of the capital, and knowing that the stability offered both by their family life and by their Catholic schooling would be disrupted, Hinsley showed particular concern for their future spiritual well-being by ensuring that his clergy were fully briefed and that the clearest possible lines of communication were established and remained open.[39]

Nearly thirty years later, Cardinal John Carmel Heenan drew the attention of his clergy to the fact that the distinctiveness of Catholic education needed to stretch beyond the bounds of the institutional Catholic school if the uniqueness of the individual was to be respected. In an *Ad Clerum* letter to the Westminster clergy in 1967, he estimated that 50,000 young Catholics – 'roughly 40% of our children' – were being educated in non-Catholic schools and indicated that 'we are perhaps more responsible for these children than for those in our Catholic schools'. Being anxious to discover more detail about this situation, he asked the Westminster Schools' Commission to conduct a survey of the provision of existing religious instruction for these children.[40] By the end of 1967, the survey reported that there were no fewer than 67,000 Catholic children in non-Catholic schools in the diocese, and that it was practically impossible for the parochial clergy to make contact with them all. Plans were then drawn up for priests, brothers and nuns, particularly from the Archdiocese of Dublin, to help staff non-Catholic schools in an attempt to supplement the work already being undertaken in that field by a team of six priests and six nuns who had established good relations with the non-Catholic schools in which they were working.[41]

Since the mid-1960s the bishops have not ceased to pay attention to the uniqueness of the individual, but have taken account of it implicitly in a wider educational context, notably in statements on social and educational deprivation.

MORAL PRINCIPLES

The sound training in moral principles of future teachers destined to work in Catholic schools has long been a priority for the bishops. As a consequence, since 1850, the development and progress of the Catholic colleges devoted to the training of teachers has been, and continues to be, a standing item on the agenda of the bishops at their twice-yearly meetings.

The restoration of the hierarchy in 1850 coincided with the opening of St Mary's College, Brook Green, Hammersmith, for the training of Catholic schoolmasters. Early in the history of St Mary's, the bishops' own Catholic Poor School Committee noted that 'all who will take the trouble to pay a visit to Brook Green will be struck with the moral aspect of the place, the demeanour of the students, and the efficiency of the Practising School, which has been commenced but two years'.[42] An early priority for the staff of St Mary's was the writing and publication of an easily affordable series of distinctive textbooks for the Catholic poor schools of England and Wales. It was hoped the projected series would underscore, in a balanced manner, the moral principles that should characterise Catholic education:

> A Catholic spirit . . . should breathe through the whole of such a literature. It is by no means meant that religion should be introduced at every turn, whether to the purpose or not; but that from the first book upwards, the choice and the handling of subjects, their order and relation to each other, the mode in which they are illustrated and harmonised, should indicate that the writers possessed themselves the Catholic faith, and valued above all things the possession of it, as the key to all the works of God, the standard and crown of all knowledge.[43]

The aim was that such literature should contribute to the provision of good schools, capable of matching the secular education available in state schools, while religious instruction and the formation of character would be attended to proportionately. As the Catholic Poor School Committee noted:

> Assuredly there could not be, in a moral and religious aspect, a *worse* school than one in which secular instruction should be scientifically and persuasively imparted, while religious knowledge should be confined to a perfunctory repetition of the catechism, and devotional affections not cultivated at all. The mischievousness of children so educated would be in proportion to their knowledge and cleverness.[44]

In his early years as Archbishop of Westminster, Manning explored further the delicate balance between education and training and the place of moral principles in the context of Catholic education:

> Education necessarily includes instruction, but instruction is only a part, and that the lesser part, of education. Education deals with the whole moral nature, intelligence, conscience and will. It not only instructs, but trains. But the discipline of the will is impossible without religion; and therefore education, worthy of the name, without religion is impossible. This then is the duty laid upon parents. They are bound to form their children in the knowledge of the faith, and in the moral and religious obligations of a Christian life.[45]

In the build-up of the debate surrounding the passage of the 1870 Education Act, the possibility of the introduction of a system of national education, following that of the United States, from which religion was excluded, caused alarm in Catholic circles. As a consequence, Manning, anxious to preserve and develop further the distinctiveness of the Catholic education system in England and Wales, became ever more forthright in his teaching role:

> Education without Christianity is impossible; or, to use a modern phrase . . . the secular and the religious elements of education are inseparable; or, more simply . . . education is essentially religious; or . . . where religion is excluded there is no education . . . When we say that education without Christianity is impossible, we do not say that instruction without Christianity is impossible: we say only that instruction is not education, and that those who are only taught in secular instruction are not educated; and that a system of 'national education' not based on Christianity is an imposture. It is not education. It cannot educate the people. Call it national instruction, if they will; but in the name of Christianity, if not also of truth, let it not be called education.[46]

Manning's voice was not alone in warning of the dangers of a national system of schooling on the American model, and of its consequent threat to Catholic education. Shortly after the passing of the 1870 Education Act, the English and Welsh hierarchy issued a joint pastoral letter which echoed, almost verbatim, much of Manning's own pastoral letters of 1868 and 1869. The joint letter, however, made explicit to all the faithful the thinking of all the bishops:

> In whatsoever school, then, religion is not taught, morality is not taught: and where morality is not taught, the heart, the conscience, and the will of children, are not educated for the duties and conflicts of life. What can be more false, what more fatal, to men, to families, and to States, than to call this Education? It is not even instruction; for the deeper and more necessary parts of knowledge are excluded.[47]

Throughout his time as Archbishop of Westminster, Manning maintained the shared view of the hierarchy that sound moral teaching in the Catholic school is largely dependent on the moral worth of teachers:

> If we had schools without number, and money without stint, our education might still be unworthy of the name. It is the Teacher that forms the school; and the worth of the school varies according to the worth of the Teacher. We say the worth, because mere efficiency is not worth. Efficiency is necessary for instruction; but worth, that is moral goodness, influence, and power, is essential to education; for education is the formation of the mind, and will, and character of the learner; and upon the worth of our Teachers will depend in the main the character of our rising generation.[48]

Such moral education, if it were to be successful, required the monitoring and support of the clergy, and this role required careful definition. The fifteenth Liverpool diocesan synod, held in 1902, debated and deliberated on the matter.

> A priest's work . . . in the school is not, ordinarily speaking, to ask catechism, to see if the children understand its meaning, or to cram more knowledge into their heads, but it is to get the knowledge, which they already have, from their heads to their hearts; in other words, to do what St John Chrysostom considers the grandest occupation anyone can be engaged in, '*fingere mores adolescentulorum*' (to mould the character of the young).[49]

For many observers, the First World War put the moral education of the nation to the test. Archbishop Thomas Whiteside of Liverpool was careful throughout the war to collect evidence in the national press from non-Catholic observers critical of the ignorance of the average soldier in the elements of religion. Whiteside believed that for a large proportion of the children of Anglicans, for almost all those of Nonconformists, and of those who stood outside organised Christianity, religious instruction by means of undenominational Christianity in schools since 1870 had led to the fragmentary knowledge which had been witnessed in the armed services at the front. When Catholic and non-Catholic soldiers were brought together face to face with death on the field of battle, the comparative value of their early training in moral principles stood out in bold relief, in the Archbishop's view. He argued that it was only 'by careful and earnest instructions, day after day, week after week, and year after year' in the denominational school that 'the responsible leaders of a denomination can make a lifelong impression on the minds and hearts of their children, by whatever of Christian truth, by whatever of Christian power and influence still finds a home in their midst'.[50]

The exemplary character of the Catholic school in the realm of moral education was taken up publicly by Cardinal Francis Bourne in his Lenten pastoral letter for 1923:

> ... the Christian tradition of England in matters both of belief and of conduct is growing weaker every day. For this reason the responsibility of Catholics grows greater in proportion, for it will rest with them to preserve, revive, and extend that Christian tradition; and this they will be able to do only if they succeed in maintaining it, in all its purity and vigour, in themselves and in their children.[51]

Twenty years later, for Archbishop Downey of Liverpool, as he pondered the existing financial injustices with regard to Catholic schools operating in the education system, the hope was that the 1944 Education Act would bring both relief and firm support for moral discipline:

> A wise statesman, one would think, would be eager to inculcate religious principles if only as a basis for good citizenship. Let us make no mistake. Religion is the mightiest lever in the world for the uplift of mankind. The history of education proves conclusively that, in the end, mere mental training without moral discipline has always been disastrous. Let us not forget that in the Athens of Pericles the highest level of intellectual attainment went hand in hand with the lowest depth of moral degradation: and there faded from the land the glory that was Greece.[52]

In the immediate post-war period, and after the passing of the 1944 Act, in order to strengthen the teaching of moral principles in its schools, the archdiocese of Westminster formalised and published a syllabus for religious instruction for schools which had been in operation since 1942 and which was subsequently adopted by other dioceses.[53] This was supplemented and complemented, from Advent 1957, by a new, regular four-year-long course of catechetical instruction, devised under the direction of Archbishop William Godfrey, to be given at all Masses on Sunday mornings in parish churches throughout the archdiocese of Westminster.[54]

The increased secularisation of society in the second half of the twentieth century has been accompanied by a widening of the vision of the purpose of Catholic education. Addressing the Second Vatican Council in 1964, Archbishop Beck of Liverpool argued that 'the education, religious and moral, given in Catholic schools should exercise a good influence on the whole of society'.[55] His stance was taken up again by Bishop Patrick Kelly of Salford in 1987:

> To establish Catholic schools may not mean that we have fulfilled all that is our duty towards the educational enterprise in our country ... We must consider in what way we may have something to say which is for the well-being of the whole of society. Indeed I am convinced that what is precious to us is in utter truth about salvation, about wholeness, and therefore is for the well-being of all. We always sell ourselves short if we present ourselves as esoteric with self-centred and merely denominational interests.[56]

How this should be done in practice is a matter on which Cardinal Basil Hume has spoken publicly on many occasions. Speaking to a group of Catholic secondary headteachers in 1991, he noted that education and schools have a vital role to play in regenerating society. To achieve that aim they need to have regard to three interrelated objectives, 'the promotion of a personal spiritual life in pupils, a recognition and acceptance of moral norms, and a vivid sense of social responsibility'.[57]

Between 1987 and 1994, at the instigation of the hierarchy, these lines of thinking, among others, were reflected on and discussed further by parents, schools and diocesan agencies across England and Wales and culminated in 1994 in the publication of a substantial statement on social and moral education in Catholic schools from the Department for Catholic Education and Formation. This, together with fresh guidelines on education in sexuality, is currently being used to complement a range of new curricular guidance documents published by the Catholic Education Service.[58] Taken as a whole, these publications are helping to inform, and carry forward coherently, the continuing attempts of the Catholic community in England and Wales to promote and foster moral principles in Catholic schools.

THE SEARCH FOR EXCELLENCE

Following detailed discussion of the education question at the First Provincial Synod of Westminster in 1852, the hierarchy was uncompromising in its views on education in Catholic schools. Not only had education to be 'up to the mark of modern demand, and yet . . . solid in faith and piety', but the whole Catholic community was exhorted to avail itself of 'every encouragement and every improvement, which tends to raise the standard of . . . education'. Above all, there was to be 'no pretence tenable for sending Catholic children elsewhere', that is to non-Catholic schools.[59]

Within twenty years, the hierarchy could claim with justification that, burdened and hindered as the Catholic community was with poverty, 'neither in quantity nor in quality is the education of the Catholic Church in England at a disadvantage'.[60] Such a state of affairs was not achieved without constant vigilance on the part of the bishops in their own dioceses. In Westminster, for example, Manning was uncompromising in this view that 'nothing is more false and mischievous than the notion that anyone is fit to teach a poor school; nothing more dangerous and unjust than to recommend for such employment those who cannot succeed in other employments, or who have failed in any way through their own fault'.[61]

Nor was Manning convinced that high standards of teaching in Catholic schools would be realised simply by the provision of a constant supply of well-trained and trustworthy teachers. In an age in which the social welfare of teachers was not widely attended to, he had the sensitivity and foresight to appreciate that teachers, however well qualified, would flourish only if treated with respect, if properly remunerated and if adequately provided for in case of sickness and in old age. Accordingly, Manning strongly exhorted the faithful to support teachers by giving alms to the Catholic Poor School Committee.[62] The issue of the welfare of teachers, particularly the protection of their employment rights and the need for the provision of adequate pension arrangements, by creating a tax on individual dioceses, was a subject returned to again and again by the hierarchy, particularly during Manning's period at Westminster.[63]

If teachers received support for the raising of their own social standing, much was demanded of them in return by the hierarchy. In order to enhance the religious standards of Catholic schools, and to encourage children in the practice of their religion, the hierarchy in 1888 passed a resolution 'that the Masters and Mistresses of Schools should be present in church with the Children at Mass on Sundays and Days of Obligation' and that 'no Teacher should be accepted for Catholic Schools who does not explicitly engage to act as a teacher of Religion, and to assist the Clergy with regard to Children on Sundays and Days of Obligation'.[64]

The importance attached by the hierarchy to their acting together unanimously on the education question, already alluded to, formed part of their quest for the promotion of excellence. As long as Catholic schools were disadvantaged financially by government, they could not achieve their fullest potential. The full story of that struggle lies beyond the scope of the present chapter, but is exemplified by numerous key actions taken jointly by the hierarchy in petitioning Parliament for a share of money from the rates to support Catholic schools in 1893; by presenting a memorial on education to the Prime Minister, Lord Salisbury, in 1895 and by publishing a number of other public statements on education in 1895 and 1896; by the mobilising of mass meetings of Catholic parents in the Royal Albert Hall, London, in 1906 to preserve Catholic education for Catholic children at the time of the passage of the 1906 Education Bill through Parliament; and by the campaign organised prior to the general election of 1945, mentioned above.[65] These united, national efforts, reinforced regionally by the activities of diocesan Catholic federations, ensured that pressure on government for the improvement of standards in Catholic schools was unrelenting.[66]

If, at the turn of the twentieth century, pressure on government for the improvement of standards in Catholic schools was unrelenting, pressure internally on the Catholic community to assist in the development of Catholic education and to strive towards excellence was equally remorseless. In 1904 the then newly established Catholic Secondary Education Council saw that, as a result of the inevitable emphasis on the development of elementary schools since the founding of the Catholic Poor School Committee over fifty years earlier, the supply of efficient Catholic secondary schools was 'deplorably deficient', especially in the large towns. It foresaw, correctly, that 'the future of Catholicism in this country must very largely depend upon the influence which will be exercised upon their fellow-countrymen both within and without the pale of the Church by those Catholics who will receive or complete their education in Secondary schools'.[67] Furthermore, it also predicted that the opening of new secondary schools would be of prime and urgent importance in the future preparation both of elementary and secondary school teachers – and that the distinctively Catholic character of existing schools could not be maintained without a sufficient supply of Catholic teachers, themselves educated in Catholic schools.[68]

The pressure exerted on the Catholic community to improve the provision of secondary schools in the first half of the twentieth century in the search for excellence in education was not without its effect. In his capacity as chairman of the Catholic Education Council, Bishop Beck, writing in a substantial educational handbook entitled *The Case for Catholic Schools*, prepared primarily for distribution to politicians in anticipation of the general election campaign of October 1951, considered developments to be such that

> Catholics are the only body in the country *consistently* concerned with the content of education; we are the only body who have clear ideas on what education is for, and how its whole purpose is to be achieved. More than that, we find that those others who are at all deeply concerned with these questions not only agree with us but demand of the educational system of this country what, in fact, the Catholic part of it is alone providing. In that sense we are very really educational leaders at the present time.[69]

The justification of such a large claim was carefully spelled out:

> The Catholic parent, defending his right to send his child to a Catholic school, is, in fact, defending the rights of all parents; the Catholic community, maintaining its claim to just financial treatment in the matter of its schools, is not only defending a financial position. It knows that the education for which it stands is of supreme importance for the defence of all those values on which the civilisation of this country is based; and also for the toughening of its moral fibre, which this country needs in order to withstand the corrosion of godless materialism.[70]

The handbook went on to urge the Catholic community to play its full part in the search for excellence in education in two ways. In the first place, all Catholics in England and Wales were called upon, whatever their walk of life, to live up to the ideals given as the aim and purpose of Catholic education, remembering that 'we must not only claim that our educational system is the best; we must prove it to be so by the quality of our own life'.[71] Secondly, Catholics were urged to seize the opportunity, wherever they could, of bringing home to their non-Catholic friends precisely what they stood for 'in the faltering world of today'.[72]

The 1951 declaration represents the high-water mark of confidence underpinning statements on the search for excellence in Catholic education in England and Wales. When compared, for example, to the 1978 document of the bishops of England and Wales on Catholic schools, the latter lacks the conviction, passion and persuasiveness of Beck's arguments.[73] The 1978 statement, written against the depressing background of a declining school population and threats of school closures, attracted criticism in a report by a working party of the Laity Commission later that year.

The report questioned the implied logical connection in the bishops' statement between the responsibility of Catholic parents to bring up their children in the faith and uncritical support for the local Catholic school. Concluding that 'in the present context and in most places the Catholic school does represent the best choice', the report reminded the hierarchy that the educational world is not static and that, in particular, the decline in primary school population would soon require a fundamental reappraisal of how the Catholic community uses its educational resources.[74]

Since the publication in 1981 of recommendations on Catholic education, entitled *Signposts and Homecomings*, produced by a joint committee of religious and laity under the chairmanship of Bishop David Konstant of Leeds, *joint* statements by the hierarchy on education have become rare, and it has fallen to individual bishops to try and maintain the momentum of striving for excellence in an increasingly difficult political climate.[75] Bishop Patrick Kelly, for example, warned the clergy of the Salford diocese in 1987 that 'it will not be enough to give assurances that our results will be as good as those in all other schools. We must be willing to offer a vision which is really different.'[76] The problem of over-concentration on examination results as the sole measure of excellence in schools has been criticised by Cardinal Basil Hume. In 1990, he warned the educational world at large that

> pressure on schools, created by the demands of examinations, the new national curriculum, and the regular testing of pupils, encourages the tendency to place increasing emphasis on certain kinds of learning and the acquisition of specific skills. It can deaden creativity, neglect human and effective growth and lead to a somewhat lopsided educational effort. That kind of distortion does not show up in examination results; its effects are felt later in emotional and spiritual deprivation, and sometimes in anti-social behaviour.[77]

Concern for the growing pressure felt by teachers prompted Bishops John

Rawsthorne and Vincent Malone, auxiliary bishops in the Archdiocese of Liverpool with special responsibility, respectively, for Christian formation and for schools and colleges, to take an unprecedented step in 1992. In an attempt to help maintain teachers' morale and the ongoing search for excellence in education, they issued a joint letter in which they emphasised that

> some time must be taken from the pressing demands of finance, staffing, curriculum, appraisal, records of achievement and so on, to remember the end to which our whole endeavour is geared; but it is not time lost from all these important concerns, because they can only be properly considered against a coherent background of principle, and not just against a schedule of deadlines.[78]

A further pressure on teachers in the 1990s – the question of the growing competition between schools – has been addressed positively by Cardinal Hume. Speaking to Catholic head teachers in 1991, he stated:

> Competition as such is by no means a disreputable concept . . . But when it comes to competition between schools, then it is a different matter if it means that some schools will benefit at the expense of others, or some pupils be favoured when others are neglected. Thus it would be wrong for some schools to be generously funded when others are insufficiently provided with basic facilities, wrong, therefore, if the success of some schools means the failure of others . . . Every young person has the right to be educated as far as that young person's potential permits.[79]

The Cardinal's cry has not been unheeded. In April 1997, the Bishops' Conference of England and Wales published a sixty-page report entitled *The Struggle for Excellence: Catholic Secondary Schools in Urban Poverty Areas*.[80] The report was compiled after an eighteen-month process of consultation with twenty-seven schools in some of the poorest areas of the country. After examining independent evidence, largely from OFSTED reports, the study concludes positively that, on the whole, the schools in question, like the first Catholic poor schools one hundred and fifty years ago, are succeeding against all the odds.

CRITICAL ISSUES

The evidence surviving in official publications and archival sources largely supports the implication from the hierarchy that the paradigm set forth in *Principles, Practices and Concerns* in 1996 is one which has been followed consistently and coherently in the articulation of principles throughout the period under review. Detailed analysis of the extent to which those principles have or have not been put into practice historically – and are or are not currently being put into practice

– lies outside the scope of this chapter and merits further research. Serious and alarming shortcomings in the translation of educational principles into practice in the post-Vatican II period in England and Wales have already been identified.[81] Given the current, unprecedented rate of change in the world of education generally, further research on and analysis of contemporary Catholic educational practice in England and Wales ought to be a matter of the utmost importance.

Of the five areas of the paradigm under consideration, the one which shows most cause for concern, as far as contemporary statements on education from the hierarchy are concerned, is arguably *the search for excellence*. When compared to those regular, joint statements made on this subject, particularly at the apogee of the hierarchy's confidence on the education question in the early 1950s, contemporary statements by individual bishops, however well conceived and well argued they may be, simply do not carry weight in isolation. On certain major issues relevant to the future shape of Catholic education, there is corporate silence. Certain issues are dealt with outside the educational context, without any clear indication as to whether or not, when, or how they might be applied to Catholic education in England and Wales; and other issues are decided without consultation. Some examples of this phenomenon may serve to illustrate the point.

First, there already exists considerable contemporary, secular educational literature concerning global change in education. In recent years, numerous educationists worldwide have provided valuable critiques of the current place of education in society, arguing persuasively that we are standing at a turning point in history and that a major and radical shift in educational thinking is essential if we are to meet the challenges of the new millennium.[82] Given both the bishops' long involvement in education and their special position in a universal Church with a clear educational mission, it is alarming that Cardinal Hume's lead on this crucial issue has not been followed through in a dynamic statement of principles from the English and Welsh hierarchy as a joint body.[83]

Second, and closely related to the first issue, the global revolution in information technology, now rapidly transforming the developed world, has already had a profound effect on the communications policies of the Catholic Media Office in London and of a number of English and Welsh dioceses since the mid-1990s. Again, given the unique position of the Catholic education system in England and Wales, it is a cause for concern that the hierarchy has not seized the new opportunities offered by rapid developments in information technology to urge the consolidation, strengthening and further development of the existing network of schools electronically – a measure which could provide an example of excellence to the rest of the educational system as it seeks to establish a new National Grid for Learning.

Third, while the hierarchy's valuable, positive and carefully argued 1997 joint statement on European integration, made in anticipation of Britain's presidency of the European Union in 1998, was greatly to be welcomed, it raised another major question.[84] Given the unique position of Catholic schools in England and Wales in a universal network of Catholic schools, why did the hierarchy not reinforce its general statement on the question of Europe by taking the opportunity to provide specific encouragement to Catholic schools? If the future of a successfully integrated Europe, genuinely open to a wider world, is to be realised, surely Catholic schools have a leading role to play in fostering links with partner institutions in Continental Europe as part of a pan-European search for excellence in a fast-changing world.

Fourth, the hierarchy's handling of the official Catholic policy response to the 1998 Schools Standards and Framework Act, which aimed at the abolition of grant-maintained schools, attracted considerable adverse criticism from both inside and outside the Catholic Church in England and Wales, and even ridicule in the secular educational press.[85] Under the terms of the Act, governing bodies of grant-maintained schools had to decide by November 1998 between voluntary-aided, foundation or community status.

In September 1998, after together agreeing a common form of words, individual bishops sent a letter to grant-maintained schools in their dioceses warning them that they would risk losing their Catholic status if they failed to return their schools to diocesan control by refusing to opt for voluntary-aided status. Though, in the event, only two of the 150 Catholic grant-maintained schools elected to pursue the foundation status route, there was reliable independent evidence that a significant number of governing bodies of Catholic grant-maintained schools took the voluntary-aided route under duress, fearful of recrimination from the local diocese. The bishops' management of the affair, and their failure to consult the laity, was seen by some as heavy-handed and undemocratic, and their arguments for their course of action flawed and inconsistent.[86] There can be little doubt that very considerable damage to the credibility of the hierarchy as leaders on educational policy was sustained as a result of their handling of this issue.

These brief illustrations raise the larger question of why issues of this magnitude, among others, are not currently being addressed appropriately. There are at least two reasons: the enormity of the educational challenge facing not just the Catholic Church in England and Wales, but society as a whole; and the inadequacy of policy-making structures.

In an English and Welsh context, even the reorganised Catholic Education Service has been stretched in recent years in its efforts to react to and cope with rapid change as a result of increasing governmental intervention in education. This *reactive* scenario has precluded consideration of wider, global educational issues and is currently preventing *proactive* development of the type suggested. Existing policy-making infrastructures, still based essentially on those of the nineteenth century, simply cannot be expected to cope with the stresses and strains of a twenty-first-century educational challenge as great, if not greater, than any which has faced the Catholic community in England and Wales since 1850.

If, as the evidence suggests, the hierarchy's ability to pursue its long-standing search for excellence in education is in a state of rapid erosion on certain key educational issues, there is a real danger in a fast-changing world that the entire *raison d'être* of the Catholic school, in an English and Welsh context, could quickly fall into jeopardy.

A radically changed educational situation requires radical action. In the words of the Vatican Congregation for Education, looking at Catholic education on the threshold of the third millennium:

> New requirements have given force to the demand for new contents, new capabilities and new educational models besides those followed traditionally . . . Such an outlook calls for courageous renewal on the part of the Catholic school. The precious heritage of the experience gained over the centuries reveals its vitality precisely in the capacity for prudent innovation. And so, now as in the past, the Catholic school must be able to speak for itself effectively and convincingly. It is not merely a question of adaptation, but of missionary thrust, the fundamental duty to evangelize, to go towards men and women wherever they are, so that they may receive the gift of salvation.[87]

To meet that challenge in England and Wales, the 'view from the bridge' needs to be widened, radically and rapidly. The combined expertise of the very best educational thinkers – episcopal, clerical and lay – is urgently needed to provide new educational vision and leadership for the 2,000 primary and 450 secondary schools, the 17 sixth-form colleges, the 746,000 pupils and the 35,000 teachers currently working in the English and Welsh Catholic education system. The hope of the Catholic Secondary Education Council in 1904, already referred to, that the development of Catholic secondary education would eventually provide the lay Catholic leadership on which the Church in England and Wales would have to depend, was realised, potentially, long ago. Today, however, that potential, in the form of highly qualified, committed Catholic educationists, working in all sectors and all levels of the educational system nationally, has still not yet been harnessed. The urgent creation of a properly structured and adequately funded standing advisory educational forum, comprising bishops, religious and laity – on the lines of the joint committee which produced *Signposts and Homecomings* in 1981 – would do much to strengthen and enhance the work of the Catholic Education Service.

If such a forum can be instituted with the urgency which the situation demands, if all its members can genuinely collaborate in effective, long-term, realistic and proactive policy-making, based on sound research, and taking full account of the teaching of the Church on education, and if, in turn, a resultant vision for the future can be shared with the laity, and with teachers in Catholic schools through greatly improved in-service training, there is real hope that the distinctiveness of the Catholic school in England and Wales can be maintained and developed as the Church enters the twenty-first century.

ACKNOWLEDGEMENTS

For allowing access to research material used in the preparation of this chapter, I should like to thank the following: Dom Leo Chamberlain OSB, Headmaster, Ampleforth College; Fr Ian Dickie, Westminster Diocesan Archives; the Most Reverend Patrick Kelly, Archbishop of Liverpool; Fr David Lannon, Salford Diocesan Archives; Robert Newman, Director, Liverpool Archdiocesan Schools' Department; Maurus O'Donnell, Nugent Care Society, Liverpool; Brother Francis Patterson, Headmaster, St Francis Xavier's College, Liverpool; Margaret Smart, formerly Director, Catholic Education Service, London; and Fr Noel Wynn SM.

NOTES

1. *Principles, Practices and Concerns: A Statement from the Catholic Bishops of England and Wales* (Catholic Education Service, 1996).
2. A beginning has been made by James Arthur in *The Ebbing Tide: Policy and Principles of Catholic Education* (Gracewing, 1995).
3. Westminster Diocesan Archives (hereafter WDA), Joint Pastoral Letter of the Vicars Apostolic, York, 15 February 1848; *The Tablet*, 26 February 1848.
4. Synodical Letter, 17 July 1852, in *Acta et Decreta Primi Concilii Provincialis Westmonasteriensis* (Paris, 1853), p. 115.
5. Synodical Letter (1852), p. 117.
6. Synodical Letter (1852), p. 118.
7. *Seventh Annual Report of the Catholic Poor-School Committee* (London, 1854), p. 6; Synodical Letter, 15 July 1855, in *Acta et Decreta Secundi Concilii Provincialis Westmonasteriensis* (Paris, 1857), pp. 50–1.
8. WDA, *Joint Pastoral Letter of the Archbishop and Bishops of the Province of Westminster, in Provincial Council, Assembled, 12 August 1873*, p. 11.
9. WDA, *Resolutions passed by the Cardinal Archbishop and Bishops of the Province of Westminster Respecting Catholic Public Elementary Education, Low Week 1893*, resolution 8.
10. WDA, *A Joint Pastoral Letter of the Cardinal Archbishop and Bishops on the Catholic School Committee, 5 June 1898*, p. 9.
11. Salford Diocesan Archives (hereafter SDA), Box 46, Tynan to Casartelli, 26 September 1904; *Acta Salfordensia*, 1905, p. 81.
12. WDA, *Letter of the Archbishop and the Bishops of the Province of Westminster on the Catholic Education Council, 14 June 1905*, p. 4.
13. Liverpool Archdiocesan Archives (hereafter LAA), *Pastoral Letter of Richard, Archbishop of Liverpool and Metropolitan, for Lent 1943, on Education, 2 February 1943*, p. 6.
14. WDA, *Some Notes on the Education Act, 1944*, p. 4, attached to *Ad Clerum* letter of Archbishop Bernard Griffin, 28 May 1945.

15. For an analysis of part of the contribution of George Andrew Beck to education see Francis R. Phillips, *Bishop Beck and English Education* (Lewiston, NY: The Edwin Mellen Press, 1990); for a brief appreciation of his work as chairman of the Catholic Education Council, 1949–1970, see *Seventy-fourth Annual Report* (Catholic Education Council, 1978), p. 9.
16. For the English translation of *Gravissimum Educationis* see Walter M. Abbot, *The Documents of Vatican II* (Geoffrey Chapman, 1967), pp. 637–51.
17. WDA, Butler papers, Education Commission, 1964–1973, *Speech delivered by the Most Rev. George Andrew Beck, Archbishop of Liverpool, in the debate on the statement 'Concerning Christian Education'*, undated [18 November 1964] (hereafter cited as *Beck Speech*, 18 November 1964). Italics have been added to the original quotation for emphasis.
18. *Catholic Caring Agencies and Children's Societies in England and Wales*, information leaflet, 1997; *Caring*, the newsletter of the Nugent Care Society, 40 (Summer 1996), p. 4.
19. *Acta et Decreta Primi Concilii Provincialis Westmonasteriensis* (Paris, 1853), p. 116.
20. Ibid.
21. *Acta et Decreta* (1853), p. 117.
22. Robert E. Guy, *The Synods in English: Being the Text of the Four Synods of Westminster* (Stratford-on-Avon, 1886), p. 132.
23. Ibid.
24. Ibid.
25. Seventh Annual Report of the Catholic Poor-School Committee (London, 1854), pp. 26–7.
26. WDA, *Pastoral Letter of Henry Edward, Archbishop of Westminster for the Feast of the Sacred Heart, 9 June 1872*, pp. 5–6.
27. LAA, *Report of the Liverpool Diocesan Mission Fund for the Year 1900* (Liverpool, 1901), p. 7.
28. SDA, Box 216, *The Education Bill, by the Archbishop of Birmingham*, reprinted from *The Sower* (April-June 1936), unpaginated [p. 4].
29. WDA, *Pastoral Letter of Cardinal Griffin, Archbishop of Westminster, for Advent 1951*, p. 6.
30. LAA, *Pastoral Letter of Richard, Archbishop of Liverpool and Metropolitan, for Lent, 1950, on Our Catholic Schools*, p. 4.
31. Ibid., pp. 4–5.
32. Cardinal Basil Hume, 'Building Bridges': Address at the North of England 77th Education Conference, Newcastle, January 1990' in *Partners in Mission* (Catholic Education Service, 1997), p. 14.
33. 'Building Bridges', p. 15.
34. Ibid.
35. *Acta et Decreta Tertii Concilii Provincialis Westmonasteriensis* (London, 1859), p. 67.
36. WDA, Manning to Pope Pius IX, 11 October 1865, in bound collection of Manning's published pastoral letters, p. 43.
37. WDA, Pius IX to Manning, 16 October 1865.
38. WDA, *Pastoral Letter of Arthur, Archbishop of Westminster on The Urgent Need of Catholic Schools, Lent 1936*, pp. 10–11.
39. WDA, *Ad Clerum* letters of Cardinal Arthur Hinsley, 30 August 1939 and 6 March 1940.
40. WDA, Heenan papers, Pastorals and *Ad Clerum* Letters, 1962–68, *Ad Clerum* letter, 24 February 1967.
41. WDA, Heenan papers, minutes of the Westminster Council of Priests, 19 December 1967.
42. *Sixth Annual Report of the Catholic Poor-School Committee* (London, 1853), p. 10.
43. Ibid., p. 11.
44. *Seventh Annual Report of the Catholic Poor-School Committee* (London, 1854), p. 18.
45. WDA, *Pastoral Letter of Henry Edward, Archbishop of Westminster, for Septuagesima Sunday, 9 February 1868.*

46 WDA, *Pastoral Letter of Henry Edward, Archbishop of Westminster, for the Feast of the Sacred Heart, the Third Sunday after Pentecost, 1869.*

47. WDA, *Joint Pastoral Letter of the English and Welsh Hierarchy for Whit Sunday, 1871*, p. 12.
48. WDA, *Pastoral Letter of Henry Edward, Archbishop of Westminster, for the Feast of the Sacred Heart, 18 June 1882.*
49. LAA, *Synodus Diocesana Liverpolitana Decima Quinta* (Liverpool, 1902), p. 14.
50. LAA, *Report of the Ecclesiastical Education Fund for the Year Ending January 31, 1917* (Liverpool, 1917), p. 9.
51. WDA, *Pastoral Letter of Cardinal Bourne, Archbishop of Westminster for Lent of 1923* (London, 1923), p. 5.
52. LAA, *Pastoral Letter of Richard, Archbishop of Liverpool and Metropolitan, for Lent 1943 on Education*, p. 7.
53. WDA, *Syllabus of Religious Instruction for Schools*, 28 October 1947.
54. WDA, *Course of Catechetical Instruction* (Archdiocese of Westminster, 1957).
55. WDA, *Beck Speech*, 18 November 1964.
56. SDA, Bishop Patrick Kelly, *Catholic Schools: A Briefing for Priests, Especially those who are Governors of Schools, 9 December 1987* (Diocese of Salford, privately printed, 1987), p. 4.
57. Address by Cardinal Basil Hume to Catholic Secondary Head Teachers in the Archdiocese of Westminster at London Colney, 24 September 1991 (hereafter, *Hume Address*, 24 September 1991).
58. 'Social and Moral Education in Catholic Schools: Department Statement', *Briefing*, 21 July 1994; *Education in Sexuality: Some Guidelines for Teachers and Governors* (CES, 1994); *Spiritual and Moral Development Across the Curriculum* (CES, 1995); *Religious Education: Curriculum Directory for Catholic Schools* (CES, 1997).
59. *Acta et Decreta Primi Concilii Provincialis Westmonasteriensis* (Paris, 1853), pp. 115–16.
60. WDA, *Joint Pastoral Letter of the Archbishop and Bishops of the Province of Westminster, in Provincial Council, Assembled, 12 August 1873*, p. 8.
61. WDA, *Pastoral Letter of Henry Edward, Archbishop of Westminster, Fourth Sunday after Pentecost, 1871*, p. 7.
62. WDA, *Pastoral Letter of Henry Edward, Archbishop of Westminster, 9 June 1872*, p. 7.
63. See, for example, WDA, *Acta* of the hierarchy, Low Week, 1886; report on a meeting of the bishops at Archbishop's House, Westminster, 1 and 2 December 1891; and, after Manning's death, *Resolutions Passed by the Cardinal Archbishop and Bishops of the Province of Westminster Respecting Catholic Public Elementary Education*, Low Week, 1893.
64. WDA, *Acta*, 10 April 1888.
65. WDA, *Acta*, 3 October 1893, III; *Education Manifesto by the Catholic Bishops* in *Acta*, Low Week 1895; *Acta*, November 1895; *The Catholic Memorial to the Most Noble the Marquis of Salisbury, K.G., Premier, on the Elementary School Question*, 13 November 1895; *A Further Declaration by the Catholic Bishops on the Education Difficulty*, 28 November 1895; *A Declaration of the Cardinal Archbishop and Bishops of the Province of Westminster on the Government Education Bill, Low Week, 1896* (London, Burns & Oates, 1896); *The Appeal on the Education Question by the Cardinal Archbishop and Bishops of the Province of Westminster*, 10 November 1896; *Great Demonstration of the Catholics of London in Defence of their Schools in View of the Education Bill: Programme of proceedings, Royal Albert Hall*, 5 May 1906.
66. A good example of the strength of activity at the diocesan level is contained in the official organ of the Salford Diocesan Catholic Federation, *The Catholic Federationist*, vol. 17, no. 3 (May 1929), p. 3 (copy in SDA, Box 216). It provides, in summary format, an overview of the extensive lobbying activity of the Federation, notably on the education question, during the period 1906–1928.

67. SDA, Box 216, *Statement on Secondary Education*, Catholic Secondary Education Council, November 1904, p. 1.
68. *Statement on Secondary Education* (1904), p. 4.
69. *The Case for Catholic Schools* (Catholic Education Council, 1951), p. 1. For a discussion of the events leading up to the publication of the handbook, see Phillips, *Beck and English Education*, pp. 73–81.
70. *Case for Catholic Schools*, pp. 7–8.
71. *Case for Catholic Schools*, p. 9.
72. Ibid.
73. WDA, *Statement by the Bishops of England and Wales on Catholic Schools*, Spring 1978.
74. WDA, Papers of Hierarchy Meeting, Autumn 1978: Laity Commission Working Party IV (Social Teaching/Social Action) report, *The Empty School? Education 1978*, p. 1.
75. *Signposts and Homecomings: The Educative Task of the Catholic Community*, a report to the Bishops of England and Wales (St Paul Publications, 1981).
76. Kelly, *Catholic Schools*, pp. 17–18.
77. Hume, 'Building Bridges', p. 16.
78. 'A Letter to all Catholic Schools of the Archdiocese of Liverpool from Bishop John Rawsthorne and Bishop Vincent Malone', November 1992, in *Handbook for Governors of Voluntary Aided Schools* (Liverpool Archdiocesan Schools Commission, 1995), Appendix 2, pp. 6–7.
79. *Hume Address*, 24 September 1991.
80. *The Struggle for Excellence: Catholic Secondary Schools in Urban Poverty Areas* (Catholic Education Service, 1997).
81. James Arthur, *The Ebbing Tide*.
82. See, for example, Michael G. Fullan with Suzanne Stiegelbauer, *The New Meaning of Educational Change* (Cassell, 1991); Andy Hargreaves, *Changing Teachers, Changing Times: Teachers' Work in the Post-modern Age* (Cassell, 1994); Hedley Beare and Richard Slaughter, *Education for the Twenty-first Century* (Routledge, 1994).
83. See Hume, 'Building Bridges', p. 20. The Vatican's forward-looking 1994 document on 'The Presence of the Church in the University and in University Culture' might serve as a model of the type of document needed in an English and Welsh context to stimulate discussion on the future shape of the Catholic school in a fast-changing world: see *Briefing*, 21 July 1994, pp. 2–9.
84. 'Statement Regarding UK Presidency of the European Union', *Briefing*, 18 December 1997, p.10.
85. *The Tablet*, 14 November 1998, p. 1523; *Times Educational Supplement*, 6 November 1998, p. 1, satirical cartoon, p. 14; *Times Educational Supplement*, 27 November 1998, p. 3, letters, p.19.
86. Ibid.
87. Congregazione per l'Educazione Cattolica, *The Catholic School on the Threshold of the Third Millennium* (Città del Vaticano, Libreria Editrice Vaticana, 1998), pp. 35–6.

TEN

CATHOLICS AND POLITICS

JEFFREY PAUL VON ARX

INTRODUCTION

The theme of Catholics in politics during the period of the restoration of the hierarchy in England and Wales would not, from the point of view of modern historiography, seem to be a very promising subject. There is a surprising extent of agreement among historians writing over the whole range of this period, at different times, and from different points of view, that there is not much that can be said about Catholics in politics; that Catholics counted for little in British politics; and that their involvement in politics was ineffectual at best, counter-productive at worst.

The present chapter will consider the basis for this judgement. Previous historians have worked with a model of engagement in politics based on the idea of Catholic Action that led them to their conclusions. Another model for political engagement is offered here, one that emerges from the efforts of some of the principal actors in the Catholic community to articulate what they thought they were doing (and not doing) in the political arena. On that basis, it is possible to provide a new account of the political role of the Roman Catholic Church in Britain since the middle of the nineteenth century. It will become clear that the distance between intention and achievement was not so wide as it has hitherto been portrayed.

In the volume that commemorated the centenary of the restoration of the hierarchy of England and Wales, published in 1950, the editor, Bishop Beck, stated,

> It seems generally to be admitted that the influence of the Catholic community in England on public life is by no means commensurate with its size, and there seems to be a good case for arguing that, at least until very recent years, this influence has been through the greater part of this century

> steadily declining . . . Politically, since the withdrawal of the Irish members, the Catholic influence has on the whole, been negligible.[1]

The most recent treatments of political Catholicism in Great Britain in the period after the First World War offer little reason to revise that estimate, even in the interest of Beck's 'very recent years'.[2]

In a chapter on Great Britain in a recent volume on political Catholicism in Europe in this century, the political historian Tom Buchanan begins by noting that twentieth-century British Catholicism – and, a fortiori, political Catholicism in Britain – has been 'strangely neglected' by historians.[3] Buchanan's essay goes some way toward addressing that neglect. But the aim of the essay is essentially counter-historical: to explain why something that one might expect to have happened – what Buchanan describes as 'united Catholic political action'[4] – finally did not. Buchanan identifies a 'distinctive Catholic political tradition' in the stimulus to Catholic Action among working-class Catholics and their leaders offered by *Quadragesimo Anno* in the 1930s; but this tradition 'rose and fell', and 'was never able to make much impact on national politics', and 'may be judged a failure in the sense that by the 1960s Catholic social principles were no longer seen as a model for the remaking of British society'. 'The overall failure of the movement', Buchanan concludes, 'is perhaps not surprising.'[5]

The other significant recent treatment of Catholics in politics in the present century is even more straightforward in its slight estimate of Catholic political influence. In the chapter on 'Catholics and Politics' in the volume *Roman Catholics in England: Studies in Social Structure since the Second World War*, the sociologist Michael Hornsby-Smith quotes the passage from Bishop Beck cited above and offers his own conclusion: 'In sum, for historical reasons Catholics have made little contribution to politics in Britain.'[6] The explanation offered for this conclusion cites a 'profound dualism between religion and politics [that] was a characteristic feature of Catholicism in the years before the Vatican Council'. This dualism manifested itself in the reluctance of English Roman Catholics, a small minority in an overwhelmingly Protestant country, to engage in the confessional politics that characterised Catholic Action on the Continent, 'with parallel parties, trade unions and welfare organizations'. 'Catholics seem to have been happy', Hornsby-Smith adds, 'to have allowed pluralist politics take their course and concentrated on the struggle for personal salvation in "the life hereafter." '[7]

If the story told by Buchanan and Hornsby-Smith of political Catholicism in most of the twentieth century is the story of why something that should have happened – 'united Catholic political action', or confessional politics – did not, the most recent study of Catholic politics in the nineteenth century is an even more contrary account. The temptation to think with Beck that the nineteenth century was ever a period of Catholic political influence is not Dermot Quinn's.

His *Patronage and Piety: The Politics of English Roman Catholicism, 1850–1900* is a revisionist history, aimed against triumphalist accounts of nineteenth-century Catholicism from Edmund Purcell's biography of Cardinal Manning at the end of that century to the work of church historians like E. R. Norman and E. E. Reynolds closer to our own day.

If other historians have been traduced into triumphalism by the material progress and spiritual vigour of Roman Catholicism in the second half of the nineteenth century – 'churches built, parishes formed, missions preached'[8] – Quinn is not so deceived – especially when it comes to the Church's political influence and impact in the period. 'Were Catholics reliable or even predictable political allies?' he asks in the Preface and responds: 'It is here argued that the only thing that could be relied on was their touchiness, their political self-absorption and their tactical ignorance.'[9] Or in the conclusion to the study in the same vein:

> Catholics consistently failed to read the signs. They were neither as powerful as they thought, nor as sought after by statesmen. Rather they placed trust in leaders who seemed destined only to betray it. The Whigs under Russell denounced them, the Tories under Derby derided them, the Liberals under Gladstone despaired of them, the Conservatives under Disraeli and Salisbury disarmed them.[10]

Nor was self-deception their worst offence. Political patronage rather than the interests of their faith or their co-religionists was the motivation of some of the most active Catholic politicians, men like Sir George Bowyer, Edward Ryley and John Pope Hennessey. If there is a hero is Quinn's book, it is the convert Marquess of Ripon, who recognised that politics 'was the art of being properly humble in the face of complexity'.[11]

Perhaps the most revealing section of Quinn's book for what it says about the assumptions that inform the study is the concluding appendix, called 'Constituency Catholicism'. It is an attempt to estimate the strength of the Catholic (mostly, of course, Irish) vote during the 1880s and 1890s in some forty English and Welsh constituencies where it was thought to 'dominate' by one Liberal politician at the time.[12] Quinn evaluates these constituencies, and comes to the conclusion reached by other less sanguine observers at the time: that the (Irish) Catholic vote in England was quite overrated, and probably could not affect results in more than three or four English and Scottish seats.[13]

Quinn's is a devastating critique of Roman Catholic political pretensions in the nineteenth century if one accepts his premise that Catholics, in fact, operated under the delusions of grandeur that he attributes to them. It must, therefore, be an object of this chapter to determine whether Catholic leaders in the nineteenth century most interested in Catholic political engagement – especially that quintessential 'political' Catholic, Henry Edward Manning – pursued in fact the goals that Quinn attributes to them.[14]

There is a common element in the explanations offered by these commentators as to why Roman Catholics counted for so little in British politics during the last hundred and fifty years. I would like to suggest that all of them, whether implicitly or explicitly, borrowed from Continental Catholicism the idea of 'Catholic Action' as the model for the political activity of English Roman Catholics. It was against this model of Catholic Action that Roman Catholics in England were measured and found wanting.

Now Catholic Action is an ambiguous term. Narrowly defined, it refers to the programme of that name advanced by Pius XI in the 1920s in his encyclical *Ubi Arcano Dei* and elsewhere. Catholic Action as advocated by the Pope was a reassertion of the ascendancy of the Catholic faith over the values and structures of state and society. It consisted in a variety of movements of the Catholic laity acting under the direction of the clergy to bring about a re-catholicisation of modern life.[15] The Catholic Action of the 1920s and afterwards existed in an ambivalent relationship with already existing Catholic parties on the Continent, since Catholic Action, as conceived by the Pope, aimed at an explicit and undiluted Catholic witness in specific areas of social life, whereas Catholic parties were already inevitably engaged in compromise and concession over the whole range of civic existence.

Catholic Action as understood by the interpreters of the English Catholic experience considered above could, however, mean something more or less than this. It could include the notion of a Catholic political party, and we have seen that Hornsby-Smith assumed that the failure of English Catholics to produce such a party was an indication of weakness or division among them. But among other observers of Catholic involvement in politics, Catholic Action did not necessarily imply a party, but could mean, as it does for Buchanan, organised action by Catholics on principles derived from the social encyclicals. In this view the Catholic community and its leadership are thought to have 'failed' so to organise themselves adequately. Finally, Dermot Quinn offers a functionalist understanding of Catholic Action. For him, the political sophistication or maturity of nineteenth-century Catholics is measured by the ability of their leaders to produce effective political mobilisation of the community at both the constituency and national levels – for whatever purpose. Against this standard, as we have seen, Quinn believes Catholic political leadership in the nineteenth century to have failed miserably.

The idea of Catholic Action, as it has been used by all the commentators we have considered, implies concerted political action by Catholics acting as Catholics. Catholic Action in politics is thus seen as political activity apart from, and, in some cases, even over against existing politics conducted by non-Catholics. Catholic Action exists to pursue Catholic goals that are exclusive to Catholics. These goals are defined by Catholic leadership, whether clerical or lay, and the pursuit of these goals is organised and directed by this same leadership.

A question needs to be asked, however, about the appropriateness of the concept of Catholic Action, on any understanding, as a model or standard for the political involvement of Roman Catholics in England. First, was Catholic Action the only model for the engagement of Roman Catholics in political life? If not, was it the right model for the engagement of a minority religious community in the polity of a religiously pluralistic, liberal democratic state, against which the political effectiveness of that minority should be judged? Finally, was Catholic Action what the leaders of English Roman Catholicism, beginning from the first entrance of the Catholic community into British politics, intended and tried to achieve? Or were those leaders trying to work out a different, distinct and original form of Catholic politics appropriate to the conditions of political life in England, which they recognised as different from the politics Catholics confronted on the European Continent?

It is the argument of this chapter that the alternative view posed in the final question above was the case. From the time of Wiseman to the time of Heenan and beyond, it has been the policy of leaders of the Catholic community – and especially of Cardinal Manning, who, having the most opportunity to do so, really set the pattern in these matters – to engage Roman Catholics in British politics, but not as a group apart from or over against existing politics. Rather, their object was to encourage Roman Catholics to become directly involved in democratic political life through the existing parties. Certainly they expected that Catholics as electors and legislators would be concerned with Catholic interests like denominational education. But they did not think of these issues as exclusively Catholic ones, and were eager to co-operate with others to achieve them. By the time of Cardinal Manning at least, church leadership had come to recognise that liberal democratic politics, the party system, the neutrality of the State in an environment of religious pluralism, offered the best opportunity for the Church to function freely without undue interference from the State, and to realise its social mission in regard to its own good and the good of the whole community.

This object and policy is nowhere so well expressed as in a report of remarks that Cardinal Heenan addressed to a meeting of Roman Catholic Members of Parliament in March 1965, on the occasion of his elevation to the cardinalate. The Cardinal himself had called the meeting, and there was some apprehension among Catholic MPs that he would use the occasion to call for more concerted action from them in the interest of Catholic issues. It is a passage that, because it so directly addresses the issue of Catholics in politics, deserves to be quoted at length:[16]

> 'I went to the house,' Cardinal Heenan told [Scott], 'and talked to the Catholic Members of Parliament. I said, "We don't want a Catholic bloc." ' The Cardinal elaborated, 'We don't want a Catholic trade union movement. What we want is to continue as we have started: to involve Catholics in public life. If we've got something to offer it's something we offer to the community, not to the Church. We can serve the Church in our own way, but when a Catholic man has the ability to go into public life, he should do so, not for what the Church can get out of him, but for what the Church can give to the whole community. After all, with the training in social questions, for example, that any educated Catholic is given, we have a great deal to offer. In a Catholic school, the children have opportunities which are not given to others: Catholic interests immediately increase the scope and vision of children. A Catholic education is a very broad thing, and provided a Catholic goes into public life really unselfishly, as part of his apostolate, in order to give, then the less concentration of Catholic interests the better. The more they are identified with their Party and with the country the happier we are.'

A PROTOTYPE OF CATHOLIC ENGAGEMENT WITHIN THE LIBERAL STATE

Now while these remarks might be considered somewhat self-serving and overstated, they do express a distinct and clearly a very different vision of Catholic involvement in politics and public life from the 'Catholic Action' model employed by all of the commentators. Heenan's vision of the appropriate role of Catholics in politics offers us the opportunity of reconsidering the question of the 'success' of Catholics in political life. It requires, however, establishing that political involvement of the type described by the Cardinal was, indeed, 'to continue as we have started'.

That Catholics started to be involved in public life in England was a consequence of the decision of Pius IX to restore the hierarchy in 1850. Cardinal Wiseman's subsequent defence of his action in response to the controversy over 'Papal Aggression' was formative of this involvement as both an explanation of the intentions of Roman Catholics in regard to public life and as an early instance of it.

It is generally admitted by historians that the controversy over the restoration of the hierarchy was a manufactured agitation in which the Prime Minister, Lord John Russell, along with the English press, especially *The Times*, bore the greatest responsibility. The agitation drew on deep roots of English anti-papism, but was also precipitated, as far as its instigators were concerned, by more recent events. These had to do both with the failure of the government to achieve satisfactory relations with the papacy, and with developments within the Church of England. In Irish affairs, the government had experienced the disappointment of the Pope's condemnation of the Queen's Colleges and resistance to its attempts to have greater influence over the appointment of bishops there. Within the Church of England, Lord John Russell was frustrated and annoyed by Tractarian attacks on state control of the Church following the Gorham Judgement, and was looking for an opportunity to teach the High Church party a lesson. When it was published in *The Times* hard on the news of the papal brief establishing the hierarchy, Cardinal Wiseman's rhetorically over-the-top pastoral 'From without the Flaminian Gate' offered Russell the opportunity to strike out at both overt and covert Romanism, and that is what he did in his letter to the Bishop of Durham.[17]

There is, of course, an irony that Lord John Russell, of all people, should have set off the 'No-Popery' scare over the restoration of the hierarchy. As a leader of nascent political liberalism, Russell had helped to make the granting of civil rights to Catholics and Dissenters part of its creed, and had even supported the abolition of provisions of the 1829 Relief Act that had prohibited Catholics from assuming the territorial titles of bishops of the Established Church (a prohibition that the Vatican had observed scrupulously in creating the new dioceses).[18]

Russell's Durham Letter offered Wiseman the opportunity to tone down his own rhetoric, which he did in his *Appeal to the Reason and Good Feeling of the English People on the Subject of the Catholic Hierarchy*, issued immediately after his arrival in England. More than that, the *Appeal* was an occasion to confront Russell, and, in his person, English Liberalism, with the inconsistency of their position in offering Roman Catholics only a qualified and limited religious liberty. The *Appeal* was the most widely circulated tract authored by a Roman Catholic ecclesiastic since the Reformation.[19] As such, it was a manifesto both for English Roman Catholics and for their fellow countrymen to indicate the political path Catholics would follow in a new era of civil equality and full status as an ecclesial community within the emerging polity of religious pluralism.

The *Appeal* was in the first instance an unqualified claim on the part of the leader of the Roman Catholic community for the civil rights that he believed that community had been granted by Catholic Emancipation: 'liberty of conscience' and 'free exercise of religion'. Most of the *Appeal* was, therefore, a demonstration that, given their church polity, Roman Catholics had a right to a regular constituted hierarchy for the free exercise of their religion, and that this hierarchy could only be established by the pope. But beyond civil rights, Wiseman believed that relief had also guaranteed the constitutional rights of Catholics: 'The Act of Catholic Emancipation was considered . . . an act of justice, rather than of favour. It was deemed unjust to exclude from fair participation in constitutional rights any Englishman on account of his religious opinions.'[20]

For Catholics to be able to establish their Church on a regular footing was not only a matter of their rights. Wiseman was convinced that a stable and organised Catholic community would be better able to make its proper contribution to public life. To this effect, he quoted in the *Appeal* his letter of 3 November 1850 to the Prime Minister, written when the storm first broke, but before the latter's Durham Letter:

> I am confident that time will soon show what a temporary excitement may conceal, that social and public advantages must result from taking the Catholics of England out of that irregular and necessarily temporary state of government in which they have been placed, and extending to them that ordering and more definite form which is normal to the Church.[21]

In his peroration, he encouraged his fellow Catholics to 'let your loyalty be unimpeachable, your faithfulness to social duties above reproach', and complimented them, especially the Irish members of his flock, on their restraint in face of provocation during the agitation.[22]

But what is most important to notice about the *Appeal* is the form it took, the effect it achieved and the example it offered. Wiseman's appeal was made not to the Queen, the Government or the Parliament, but to the English people: to the 'manly sense and honest heart of a generous people; [to] that love of honourable dealing and fair play . . . To this open-fronted and warm-hearted tribunal I make my appeal, and claim, on behalf of myself and my fellow Catholics, a fair, free and impartial hearing.'[23] This was something new in Catholic relations with their fellow countrymen, and certainly not in the style of recusancy: a direct appeal to the forum of public opinion, in the name of liberality, over the heads of the politicians who were being untrue to their own liberal principles. Whatever the success of the *Appeal*,[24] it certainly offered a new model for Catholic engagement in public life. It was direct and unapologetic. It took for granted not only the right of Roman Catholics to participate in public life on an equal footing with other religious groups, but also the political arrangements of a State that permitted them to do so – once its bout of 'No-Popery' was over!

Let the *Appeal* stand as Wiseman's vindication of the political rights of Roman Catholics, and his handling of the 'Papal Aggression' episode as a prototype of Catholic engagement within the liberal State. For the remainder of his episcopacy, Wiseman was more absorbed, often to his great anguish, with the internal affairs of his Church than he was with public affairs. But a consequence of all his care and concern was the transformation of the Catholic Church in the course of his tenure, from the hidden Church in England that was still a legacy of penal times, to the ultramontane institution that took its place as one of the great religious forces of the Victorian age.

A NEW MODEL OF CHURCH–STATE RELATIONS

If there is a single figure who stands for the kind of political engagement that Cardinal Wiseman sought to establish through the *Appeal*, or that Cardinal Heenan wished to confirm in his address to Catholic MPs, it was Henry Edward Manning, second Archbishop of Westminster. Manning's long tenure in that see, from 1865 to 1892, offered him the occasion, first, to think through the theoretical issues surrounding Catholic political action in the non-sectarian, liberal State and, second, the opportunity to encourage and facilitate through his own leadership the participation of Roman Catholics in the political life of the State.

As Manning himself realised, the teaching of the Catholic Church about the proper relationship between Church and State, enunciated recently in the Syllabus of Errors (1864), was quite clear. He himself summarised that teaching as follows: 'The Church and the State should stand in relations of mutual recognition, amity and co-operation under the supreme direction of the Vicar of Jesus Christ, Pontiff and King.'[25] Even to begin, therefore, to reformulate the Church–State relationship in any direct or explicit way, was to come up against what Manning himself would have considered irreformable teaching of the Church.

It was, therefore, to give himself more room to think through new models of Church–State relations that Manning initially developed his ideas on this subject with reference not to the Catholic Church, but to the Established Church of England.

In the late 1860s, Manning began to argue that the Church of England had been 'morally disestablished' by the repeal of the Test and Corporations Act and by Catholic Emancipation. This legislation represented a 'change in our polity which placed its [the Establishment's] destinies in the hands of a constituency and a legislature in which Dissenters from the State religion form a very powerful element'. But it was the effect on the Church of that 'moral disestablishment' which commanded Manning's attention. For, 'from that day', he argued, 'the Church of England began to appeal to its own spiritual authority and to exert its own internal energies.' From being an Establishment with exclusive privileges, in a special relationship with the State, coterminous with the political nation, the Church of England had become, in virtue of moral disestablishment, effectively a 'voluntary body';[26] that is, it came to occupy, in relation to the State, essentially the same position as other 'voluntary' religious bodies in England: the Nonconformist denominations and the Roman Catholic Church.

The initial evidence Manning cited for the Church of England as a voluntary religious organisation was 'the multiplication of the churches dependent on voluntary offerings, the founding of schools without endowments, and the multiplication of colonial bishoprics': in other words, the initiatives the Anglican Church had taken on its own behalf, and without the aid of the State, to strengthen and build up its own structure, both at home and abroad. Manning argued that if all three established churches (the Church of England, the Scottish Kirk and the Church of Ireland) were legally disestablished tomorrow,

> the effect would be to stimulate their internal energies, and to make them exert all the powers that are in them. The religious fervour of the country would certainly be multiplied, and that not in the way of controversy, but in each body or communion upon itself. The three Establishments would somewhat more adequately do their proper work, and the sum of religious zeal and activity in the kingdoms would be increased.[27]

He predicted the effects of the regeneration of the disestablished churches in the public arena: 'The course of public legislation would assuredly not be less Christian. The public opinion of the country would be more so; and the legislature must ultimately be governed by public opinion.'[28]

In other words, as far as the Established Churches in the United Kingdom were concerned, the change in relationship to the State from one of official recognition to voluntary status would free them to act more effectively upon public opinion, the electorate and hence, on Parliament. Such a liberation of the forces of organised Christianity, given the structure of British politics, and the new susceptibility of politicians to public opinion – remember Manning was speaking a year after the Reform Act of 1867 – offered an opening of the political system to the activity of the churches for a *more*, not a less Christian society and government.

Manning added that 'it is not my purpose now, and time would forbid me to trace out the effect of all this upon the Catholic Church in this country'.[29] But having begun to develop a working theory about the new and exciting possibilities open to the churches for Christianising national life in the circumstances of a 'desecrated' or desacralised public order, Manning could now turn to the practical question of how the Catholic Church in particular might achieve these effects.

In the early 1860s, Manning had lamented the desacralisation of the public order as it manifested itself even in Catholic countries in the attack on the temporal power of the papacy, and had reacted to this phenomenon with apocalyptic alarm.[30] By 1868, he saw the same desacralisation, at least as far as England was concerned, as the condition of possibility for a *more* Christian public life through the spiritual action of the churches in the arena of popular politics on a government now virtually admitted to be secular and non-sectarian.

And could the Catholic Church now exercise that same spiritual action in face of the breakdown of the classic model of Church–State relations even in Catholic countries? If governments would no longer listen to the Vicar of Jesus Christ, Manning believed,

> the people will. And this, it would seem, may be the future. The pastors know their flocks, and their flocks know them . . . The instincts of the masses are Christian, and the tendency of political society is everywhere to the people. Of this we have no fear. The Church is nowhere so vigorous than where it is in closest sympathy with the people; as in Ireland and Poland, in America, Australia and England.[31]

In 'The Catholic Church and Modern Society', the last of the series of addresses and articles that Manning published on the subject of religion and politics, He made the following points in summary of his argument:

> 1. That perpetual hostility to the political order of any State is no duty of the Church, unless such political order should be intrinsically anti-Christian or anti-Catholic.
> 2. That indiscriminate opposition to any political order is not lawful or reasonable . . .
> 3. That perpetual abstention from exercising the duties of citizens cannot be justified.
>
> It is – (1) An abdication of a natural duty.
>
> (2) A virtual and inevitable separation of Church and State, which is condemned in the Syllabus.[32]

Now while the Church might no longer wish or be able to enter into official relations with the secularised State, there was beneath the forms of the State the 'commonwealth of natural society in all its domestic, social and civil relations'. 'The best example', according to Manning,

> of a commonwealth that has lost its Catholic perfection without losing its traditional but imperfect Christianity, and has at the same time returned in great part to the natural order . . . may be said to be the British Empire . . . The Catholic Church has all its spiritual liberties; . . . There exists, so far as I know, no bar to the participation of Catholics in any of the regions of national life, domestic, social, civil and political.[33]

This being the case, 'the withdrawal of Catholics from the active service of the commonwealth, and the non-fulfilment of the duties of citizens and patriots, is a dereliction of duty, and unlawful in itself'.[34]

'The Catholic Church and Modern Society' is the culmination of Manning's effort of two decades to work out for himself and for his fellow Catholics in Great Britain a rationale for political action in the distinctive and unprecedented circumstances of a non-sectarian state, a mass democratic polity and a religiously pluralistic society. It is to Manning's political activity as leader of the Catholic Church in England that we must now turn.

THE ISSUE OF EDUCATION

Given that the great majority of Roman Catholics in Great Britain by the time Manning became Archbishop were poor Irish, it is not surprising that education – and especially elementary education – was the public issue that first and most concerned him.

There are two presuppositions present in Manning's response to the issue of national education in England that were also basic to his vision of Catholics in politics. From the very beginning of his involvement in the education question, he tried to ally Roman Catholics with the Established Church (which had by far the largest stake in the survival of the voluntary system) and Nonconformist denominations like the Methodists who were committed to denominational education.[35] This effort was concerted and persistent and often pursued over the opposition of his co-religionists.[36] As we have seen, Manning was convinced that de-Christianised civil and political life offered unique opportunities to the churches to combat secularism. They were in a position to sustain and even to advance Christianity precisely by active engagement in the political life of the liberal State. And because the liberal State was bound to observe neutrality in their regard, the churches were free to pursue these political goals on an even playing field, and as equals. They all had equal opportunity and equal obligation to take political stands, and to form political alliances and act in concert when they shared common goals. Manning's efforts to form political alliances with the other churches in the interest of denominational education are surely best understood as an acceptance of the political forms and process of the liberal State.

Also implicit in Manning's participation in the controversies over the Bill is his distinctive and characteristic view of the relationship between the liberal State and a religiously pluralistic and secular civil society. It is clear that Manning admitted a role for the State in the matter of national education: the State had an interest in seeing that its populace was educated.[37] But he did not believe that in a religiously divided society the State could undertake the responsibility of education directly, as it might in a religiously united society:

> The State has neither the commission nor the power to educate . . . A civil power holding the balance of justice even in a firm neutrality among the religious sections of a divided people, [will] assist them to educate their children, partly by private and partly by public means, in schools proper to their respective religious convictions.[38]

But for the State to usurp the obligations of parents and religious educators by setting up and compelling attendance at its own schools was tyrannous, the deification of the civil power which Manning considered the essential perversion of the liberal State. The preservation, therefore, not only of Christianity and public morality but also of civil liberty required the 'independent action of the Church interposing itself between the State and the people' in the matter of education.[39]

There were two reasons for this. The State could not, except in extraordinary circumstances, undertake to establish or conduct educational institutions on its own in a religiously divided society because, in Manning's view, education could not be separated from religion. For the State to involve itself directly in education was to put itself in charge of an essentially religious enterprise, and in a religiously divided society, this was one of the things a liberal, secular State could not do.

The second reason the State could not have a direct role in education in a religiously pluralistic society had to do with the very identity of the liberal State as a limited form of government. If the State was to be authentically liberal and secular (in Manning's terms: neutral and even-handed among religious groups in society) it must respect and even foster the legitimate autonomy of voluntary religious associations. In the absence of religious unity, the State could not usurp parents' rights to delegate the education of their children to voluntary religious associations. In subsequent controversy over the workings of the 1870 Act, Manning's thinking on the importance of voluntarism and even of localism would develop much further (to include, for example, the right and responsibility of non-believing parents to establish non-religious schools to their liking!). Even in 1869–70, however, it is clear – in his 1869 pastoral on education, for example – that Manning believed that state support for – but not control of – the intermediate role of the churches in education was critical to the essential character of the liberal State. The State's willingness to allow the 'independent action of the Church interposing itself between the State and the people' made the difference between limited as opposed to despotic exercise of the power of the State.

RELIGIOUS PLURALISM IN THE LIBERAL, NON-SECTARIAN STATE

The efforts that Manning made both to articulate for Roman Catholics a politics of engagement with the liberal State and then to pursue it involved him in controversy: most notoriously with W. E. Gladstone over the Vatican decrees, but also with the noted jurist, James Fitzjames Stephen, over the policies of the government of the new German Empire toward the Catholic Church known as the *Kulturkampf*. Manning's involvement in these controversies led him to develop a critique of the liberal State, and to articulate a distinction between true and false liberalism that became a further guide to Roman Catholics in their relations with the British State.

Manning believed that the Vatican Council was being used by opponents of the Church like Gladstone and Stephen as a pretext for questioning the civil allegiance of Roman Catholics precisely at a time when Catholics were prepared to enter the mainstream of national political life. They did so because they feared that the participation of Roman Catholics in democratic politics was a threat to the secular character of the State. Manning argued that the inclusion of voluntary religious groups in political life was not only not injurious to the secular State, but that it was the very effort to exclude them that posed the real danger to the stability and survival of the liberal State.

English Roman Catholics recognised, Manning was perfectly prepared to admit, that the religious divisions of England required a State 'secular in legislation and action'.[40] They, above all people, had no desire to return to a religious commonwealth. 'For nearly three centuries,' Manning observed,

> we have been divided in politics because politics were mixed up with religion. Our Legislature teemed with penal laws such as the world had never seen, and that against half of the English population . . . But now for fifty years we have had peace, because we have common interests, and a solid common weal . . . And why? Because we have eliminated religious conflicts from our Legislation, because we have learned to be just . . . The late sudden and needless aggression on the Catholic religion is dangerous to the social and political tranquillity of these Kingdoms.[41]

It is important to realise that when Manning uses the term 'secular', as he now begins to do, to describe what he had earlier referred to as the 'desecrated' State, he did not mean the same thing by it as would some secularists, then or today. He did not, for example, mean a civil polity free from the explicit influence of Christianity or opposed to the participation or recognition of religious groups as such in political and civil life. England was a 'mixed commonwealth' in Manning's terms, in which religious divisions were tolerable not because religious groups were blocked from access to public life – and public funds – but because there was an 'equitable balance for our manifold uses in the midst of our manifold divisions'. The secular State in Manning's definition was a place where 'no one has a right to control this mixed administration to satisfy his private conscience, or to claim to have it all his own way'.[42]

It was essential, therefore, to the identity and ultimately to the stability of a secular State that it should be open to the involvement and participation of voluntary religious groups. To seek in any way to deny a religious community access to public life, or to call into question the fitness of members of such a community to participate in public life, was to violate the first principle of secularism as Manning understood it, and to endanger the understandings that existed among all the groups that made up civil society in a 'mixed commonwealth'. Those understandings were not only among groups, as Manning had already indicated – that no one group should seek unfair advantage over the others by attempting to engross the administration or public funds in its interest – but also within a group. As we have seen, it had long been a great object of Manning's policy within the Catholic community to encourage the engagement and responsible participation of Roman Catholics in national politics. For an important politician like Gladstone to question the civil allegiance of Roman Catholics could obviously have a chilling effect on the political involvement of that community. But for six million Roman Catholics – and it is significant that Manning has here included the Irish – to hear and possibly to internalise the message that there was an incompatibility between their religion and their loyalty was a danger not just to that community but to the stability of the State.[43] Manning believed that Gladstone was playing with fire in trying to make Catholics choose between their religion and their loyalty: 'This is playing with edged tools, and in a matter where it is hardly moral to play at all. Great public disasters might be caused by the game, and the costs of the game would fall, not on the gamester, but upon innocent men, women and children.'[44]

The controversy over the Vatican decrees reveals an important difference of understanding between the leader of English Liberalism and the leader of England's Roman Catholics about the involvement of religious bodies in the liberal State.

In his youth, William Gladstone had believed that Anglicanism and nationality were, or ought to be, coterminous, and justified the privileged and exclusive position of the Established Church.[45] In the course of the 1840s he had had to admit that the expectations the Oxford Movement had engendered – that the national church might become actually what it was ideally – were not to be realised. A situation of religious pluralism was inevitable, and would require the appropriate legislative recognition, not least to protect the Church of England from its critics.

But if national religion on exclusively Anglican terms was impossible, Gladstone came to believe that 'perhaps pluralism could be accompanied by a general movement toward [a] vision of a reunited apostolic Christendom'.[46] Located between the extremes of Protestantism and Romanism, he was convinced that reunited apostolic Christianity would look very much like Anglicanism, so that if a movement toward ecumenism could be maintained, the vision of religious nationality in England might yet be realised. From this perspective, it is easy to see why it was that Gladstone was so injured and afflicted in the 1850s by the defection from the Established Church of close friends like Manning. It is also easy to see why Gladstone would have been so hostile to developments in the Roman Catholic Church represented by ultramontanism in general and the Vatican decrees in particular. The decrees were, in effect, a declaration on the part of the leadership of the Roman Catholic Church, one of the terms in Gladstone's equation of an ecumenical movement toward Anglicanism, that they were simply not interested in playing the role he had assigned them. Instead, ultramontane Catholics had defined their identity as Church and their mission in politics and civil life according to their own perception of their needs. And Manning was in the unfortunate position of being both the local representative of this Church and one by whom Gladstone felt himself to have been personally betrayed.

In 1874–75, Gladstone and Manning understood religious pluralism in the liberal State in essentially different ways. In the 1860s, Manning had had to come to terms with the 'desecrated' or, as he came to call it increasingly in the course of this controversy, the 'secular' character of the liberal State. He accepted that the unity of a state based on religion was no more; that the 'common weal' now depended not on unity but on equity and fair dealing toward and by the manifold (religious) groups that made up civil society. And it was really the existence of pluralism in regard to religious conviction and affiliation that defined for Manning the 'liberalism' of the liberal State. All religious groups had to be free to be who they were within the limits of equity and fairness, and for Manning, the 'authenticity' of the liberal State (as opposed to its perversion in statism) consisted in its restraint: first in its resisting the temptation to set itself up as an arbitrary or artificial source of unity for civil society; second, in its willingness to permit and even to facilitate the self-expression of religious groups within the structure of politics not on sufferance but as part of its *raison d'être*.

Gladstone was at this stage still ambivalent about real religious pluralism, if by pluralism we understand accepting different religious bodies into the political nation for who and what they are, as long as they play by the rules and do not attempt to gain unfair advantage. As late as 1875, Gladstone was still seeking a unity based on religious nationality and so was less able than Manning to come to terms with the consequences of real religious diversity. At the time of the Vatican decrees controversy, therefore, it is difficult to avoid the conclusion that it was Henry Edward Manning who had the clearer understanding of how religious pluralism must work in an authentically liberal and non-sectarian state.

CATHOLICS AND PARTY POLITICS IN THE NINETEENTH CENTURY

The turn to popular politics that the Roman Catholic Church took under the leadership of Cardinal Manning inevitably raised the issue of the Church's attitude to political parties in general and to a Catholic political party in particular.[47] In August of 1885, in anticipation of a parliamentary election and with the education question very much in mind, the Bishop of Nottingham, Edward Bagshawe, suggested in a letter to the *Tablet* that English Roman Catholics abandon the two major parties and form a party of their own. Bagshawe proposed an alliance between an English and an Irish Catholic party, in which English Catholics would support Home Rule and Catholic education in Ireland, and Irish Catholics would make common cause with English Catholics in Parliament for causes like denominational education in England.[48] A possible model for such a party was, of course, the Catholic Centre Party in Germany.[49]

Cardinal Manning was well aware of the Centre Party and of its role in standing up for the Church against Bismarck during the *Kulturkampf*.[50] But it is significant that he manifested no public enthusiasm for Bagshawe's proposals for a Catholic political party in England and deprecated it in private.[51] In October, Manning issued his own election 'manifesto' – his 'How Shall Catholics Vote at the Coming Parliamentary Election?' – which was published in the *Dublin Review* and a number of other Catholic journals.[52] This would have been the occasion, had he wished, to say something in favour of an initiative to form a Catholic party. At the beginning of the article, he acknowledged the interest that had been expressed in the possibility of such a party, but it is significant that in the remainder of the article he did not return to this subject. He confined himself to advising Catholic voters in England to put questions to parliamentary candidates regarding their support of denominational education. Beyond this, it was rather pointedly stated that Catholics were free to vote as they saw fit. Now while it was true that these instructions favoured the Conservatives, more of whom could and did give the required assurances than Liberals, they assumed that Catholics would vote for candidates of existing parties, and gave no indication of support for anything like a separate Catholic party.

The question of the Church's relation to popular politics in the concrete circumstances of 1885, as even Bagshawe in his way had recognised, was inevitably connected to the existence of the Irish Parliamentary Party led by Charles Stewart Parnell. This party, while not confessionally Catholic, was overwhelmingly Catholic in its popular constituency and predominantly Catholic in the members it returned to Parliament; indeed, its members were often the only Catholics in Parliament. And everyone recognised that that party would become even stronger in its parliamentary representation as a result of the recent franchise reform upon which the new Parliament would be elected.

As head of the English Roman Catholic hierarchy, Manning could only approach this question as having been to some extent already determined. The Irish Parliamentary Party as Parnell had moulded it was a very solid historical fact, and the stance of the Roman Catholic Church toward that party was less a matter of Manning's choosing than that of the Irish hierarchy. But Manning was not without choice in his attitude or without influence in his policy toward the givens of the situation that he faced, and the choices he made are revealing.

We have seen that in October of 1885, Manning had offered advice to Roman Catholic voters in English constituencies on how they should vote in the coming parliamentary elections. They were to pose certain questions to candidates that had to do with their support of denominational education. On 21 November, Parnell had a manifesto issued to the Irish voters of Great Britain on his behalf, calling on them to vote against all Liberals and Radicals, except such as he might name. In most cases, of course, the effect of these dual instructions to Irish Catholic voters in Great Britain would be the same,[53] so the question of a conflict between the English Catholic agenda for denominational education and the Irish agenda for Home Rule did not arise.

Given the prospect, however, of the Irish party swinging their votes back to the Liberals, who were not to be counted on to support denominational education in England, conflict could and did arise. It was proposed in a number of English Catholic newspapers that the interests of the Irish movement should be subordinated to the interest of English Catholics in the question of education. Archbishop Walsh of Dublin wrote to Manning protesting at these proposals, as well as at attacks that had been made on the Irish bishops for their alliance with the Irish Parliamentary Party. Manning responded immediately: 'I will say at once that I know of no one who desires to subordinate the Irish movement to any English question.' Given what had already been said in the English Catholic press, this was, perhaps, less true than a reflection of the policy Manning himself had determined to follow, on which he proceeded to reassure Walsh: 'And you may rely on me for refusing to subordinate the Irish movement to any English question, as I believe you would refuse to subordinate the Irish movement to your own Education' – a perceptive observation on Manning's part of the constrained position in which the Irish hierarchy now found itself in relation to the Home Rule movement.[54]

Manning would follow the policy of publicly backing the Irish bishops in their arrangements with the Parliamentary Party even though, at this point, he still remained convinced that a separate Parliament in Dublin was not a good idea. Nor was Manning's deference to Walsh and the Irish bishops in the matter of subordinating English education to Irish Home Rule only for their own consumption. When the first Home Rule Bill was defeated and Gladstone's government fell, Manning wrote to Herbert Vaughan, who was probably not eager to receive them, with instructions for the coming election:

> The dissolution is on one issue. We cannot evade it, we cannot put Education before it. The Irish vote in England would be lost by doing so. We should seem to oppose Ireland. We should hopelessly divide our own people. The Education Question would not be listened to apart from Ireland. We can speak on both, but not on Education alone. . . . Education cannot be helped at this election, nor do I think it will be hindered. This will need much thought and counsel, but it is inevitable.[55]

Given what we know of the intensity and duration of Manning's campaign for voluntary education in England, his willingness to subordinate this cause to an Irish Home Rule that he did not entirely agree with is most revealing. It may well be, as Manning himself indicated, that this subordination was inevitable. But the inevitable is only so on the basis of certain assumptions. In the present case, the operative assumption for Manning was that the Catholic Church in the whole United Kingdom was ineluctably committed to popular politics. And it was committed to popular politics not in the abstract, but to the popular politics of the mass democratic political party with the exigencies that such a commitment brought with it and subject to the dynamics that a close engagement with a political party entailed. More concretely still, the Church, both in England as well as in Ireland, was committed to the Irish Parliamentary Party of Charles Stuart Parnell. This was the party to which the vast majority of Roman Catholics in the United Kingdom gave their allegiance, and if the Roman Catholic Church was to have impact and effect in the country it must work in and through that party.

The decisive and conclusive character of the Church's turn toward democratic politics as it actually existed in England and Ireland was the reason why a Catholic party on the model of the German Centre Party never got off the ground. Popular politics, by definition, can be organised from the top down only to a limited extent, and even if the bishops had wished to establish a Catholic party, most Catholics, by 1885 anyway, were already taken up in a political party – Parnell's party. This party, while composed almost entirely of Catholics and including most of the Catholics in the United Kingdom, was certainly not, despite the allegations of Protestants and secularists, a Catholic, confessional party even in the sense that the Centre Party was Catholic and confessional.

The Church – in the person of its bishops – could influence the party – to reinforce, for example, the party's commitment to non-violence and constitutionalism. It could use the party for its own ends – as, for example, standard-bearer in the Church's fight for denominational education. It could criticise and even attempt to correct the party as it did on the issue of moral leadership in the Parnell divorce scandal. But it certainly could not control or lead the party; its ability to use the party for its own ends was limited; and in some areas – the whole national question, for example – the Church had to follow or acquiesce in the party's lead. Any effort to use the Church to control the national movement, as even the papacy would discover in condemning the 'Plan of Campaign', was bound to fail.

All of this the Irish bishops – certainly Walsh – understood, and clearly Manning understood it as well. That understanding was demonstrated not simply in Manning's deference to Walsh's lead, but in his strong support for Walsh's policy in regard to the national movement – in England, in Ireland and in Rome – during the rest of Manning's life.

By 1886, the Catholic Church was committed decisively to popular politics in the United Kingdom with all the complexity and ambiguity that such a commitment entailed. It is not adequate to see this commitment of the Church by leaders like Walsh and Manning as a matter of bowing to the inevitable. The commitment was inevitable only because church leaders like Manning believed it was the right thing for the Church to do.

The path of constructive engagement with the liberal State upon which the Catholic Church had been set by Cardinal Wiseman was consolidated by Henry Edward Manning. Manning provided English Roman Catholics with a clear rationale for their participation in the democratic politics of the liberal secular State. He articulated and implemented a strategy of political co-operation between Roman Catholics and other religious groups appropriate to a religiously pluralistic society. He offered an interpretation of the liberal State in its relations with religious groups, not in terms of an artificial or imposed unity of national identity, but in terms of equity and fairness both in the behaviour and in the treatment of the various groups that made up a pluralistic society. He identified statism and, implicitly, an arbitrarily constructed nationalism, as the besetting sin of the liberal State, and offered restraint of state power, especially in the face of religious diversity, as the litmus test for the authenticity of liberalism. He resolved the question of the form of Roman Catholic political activity in the liberal State so clearly and decisively in favour of participation in existing mass democratic parties – as opposed to a confessional party – that the question simply never again arose in any meaningful way for the Catholic community. If what Manning accomplished is set against Catholic Action, defined as the Catholic laity organised and directed to achieve uniquely Catholic goals apart from and even over against existing politics, then Cardinal Manning effectively inoculated the Catholic community in Great Britain against it down to the present.

CATHOLICS AND POLITICAL ENGAGEMENT IN THE TWENTIETH CENTURY

Bishop Beck and others claim that after the end of the nineteenth century the political influence of Catholics was negligible. They make this claim on the basis of the model or paradigm of Catholic Action, rather than the model of political engagement in fact established for the Roman Catholic community by Cardinal Manning: a model of constructive but critical engagement of Roman Catholics with the politics of the liberal, secular, democratic State within a pluralistic society. In the twentieth century, Catholic politics was negligible only on the assumption that the political participation of millions of British Roman Catholics in the political life of their country was negligible. As Cardinal Heenan recognised, what Roman Catholics brought to British political life was a particular view of social questions, commitment to a vision of the common good and a willingness to collaborate within existing political forms with others of different or no religious affiliation to achieve that good. It was when church leaders attempted to conduct a politics of sectarian exclusivism that Catholic politics became a matter of public attention and led both contemporaries and later historians to the judgement that it had 'failed'. It is, of course, the contention of this chapter that such exclusivist politics was bound to fail, given the political path upon which Manning had set the Catholic community by the end of his life.

The Education Act of 1902, which placed denominational education on an equal financial footing with Board schools, achieved the single most important policy objective of Cardinal Manning still unrealised at his death in 1892. Its passage, at the hands of one of the major political parties, and with the support of the Irish Parliamentary Party, was achieved through the combined efforts of Roman Catholics and Anglicans, with appeals to public opinion in the press and at public meetings.[56] The request of the Catholic Church for the more adequate funding of its primary schools was made not on the basis of privilege, entitlement or exceptionalism, but on grounds of equity and the common good. Clearly, both the political strategy and the rationale were Manning's. The fact that the campaign was brought to its successful conclusion by Manning's successor, Herbert Vaughan, an ecclesiastic in many ways out of sympathy with his predecessor's populist and democratic ways, only serves to illustrate how powerful, even ten years after his death, was the paradigm for political action that Manning had established.

If the Education Act was a victory for Roman Catholic policy, this should not obscure the fact that its deeper significance for the Catholic community was in the means of its achievement. Subsequent successes – and even failures – of policy must be similarly judged. The continuing story of Roman Catholic involvement in education in the twentieth century is, of course, a history of successes and failures – though mostly successes – in realising policy aims: from resistance to the efforts of Nonconformists to amend the Act under the Liberals after 1906;[57] to concessions made and benefits accrued by Roman Catholics in the Butler Act of 1944;[58] to subsequent Acts of 1959 and 1967,[59] which gave Roman Catholics much of what they had campaigned for over decades. But what is important to recall – as one commentator has put it – was that 'Catholics had . . . earned this new dispensation by their convincing commitment to the very centre of the English political tradition'.[60]

Other significant 'political' developments in Roman Catholic history in the twentieth century may be evaluated according to the same criterion of whether or not they represented a constructive engagement with liberal democratic politics. For example, Adrian Hastings has argued that a peculiarly British variety of Catholic Action in the thirties inclined toward Fascism.[61] He attributes this tendency to a congruence between Fascism and the ultramontanism that, under Manning's leadership, had penetrated the Catholic Church in England during the nineteenth century.[62] The near unanimous support of Franco among Catholic churchmen and intellectuals (in the face, of course, of the Republic's murderous anticlericalism); the tendency to identify the corporatism encouraged by papal encyclicals with fascist forms of social and economic organisation; the anti-Semitism of a popular figure like Belloc; obsession with the threat of communism that led even respectable journals like the *Tablet* to express a preference for Fascism:[63] all these gave credence to the perception that institutional and intellectual English Roman Catholicism had a political tendency in this decade toward authoritarianism, if not toward Fascism. Only the war cut short these tendencies, which continued to manifest themselves, however, in certain echelons of Roman Catholicism in virulent anti-communism and suspicion of the welfare state even after the war.[64]

Hastings is correct in asserting that the tendency toward Fascism was the expression of an effort in certain hierarchical, intellectual and socio-political quarters of the Church in England to replicate Continental Catholic Action. But he is incorrect in attributing the source of that tendency to ultramontanism as it in fact emerged in nineteenth-century Britain under Cardinal Manning.[65]

Hastings asks whether ultramontane Catholicism in the 1930s was not prepared to sacrifice democratic politics in England, as it had sacrificed the Popular Party in Italy, or the Centre Party in Germany, to clerical, or, more accurately, to Vatican interests.[66] But he realises that this could never happen in England. He attributes the failure of Fascism to find any kind of a mass following among English Roman Catholics to the 'absence of a suitable ecclesiastical or political environment', and because the Catholic Church in Britain, while theologically ultramontane, was unlike other European churches 'in its wider structures and social attitudes [and] shared far more in the general pattern of contemporary Britain'.[67] Of course, Hastings makes the mistake that so many have made, of assuming that ultramontanism, even in its nineteenth-century origins, was somehow uniform and monolithic across Europe, whereas it is clear that, in its political aspect, the ultramontanism in which Manning formed the Church was adapted to its English setting from the very beginning.[68]

Hastings fails to recognise that the very resistance with which he credits British Catholics – not just to Fascism, but to any kind of exclusivist politics on the Catholic Action model – was the outcome of an historical process of commitment to mainstream politics inextricably linked to the emergence of the ultramontane Church whose political tendency he thinks was so malign. Manning, of course, had presided over both!

Against the tendencies toward Fascism of a certain segment of the Catholic community in the 1930s, Cardinal Hinsley's 'Sword of the Spirit' movement in the early 1940s was the more authentic expression of English political Catholicism. As articulated especially in the writings of Christopher Dawson in the *Dublin Review* and his *Judgment of the Nations* (1942), the Sword of the Spirit was a commitment by Roman Catholics, especially lay men and women, but with Hinsley's strong encouragement, to co-operate with other denominations in defence of democracy in the darkest years of the war.[69] Nor was it merely to right-wing versions of Catholic Action that the English Catholic community proved itself immune in the years preceding and following the war. The revival of Christian Democracy in Europe after the war and the emergence of Catholic Action in its Jocist strain provoked interest, some enthusiasm, but no widespread imitation in British Catholicism.

It has been the contention of commentators like Buchanan, Hornsby-Smith and Hastings that from the end of World War II until the present day, British Roman Catholics attracted little attention, contributed little, and maintained a low profile as far as politics is concerned. Even the great internal revolution of the Second Vatican Council did not find its counterpart in new articulations or departures for Roman Catholics in the realm of politics.[70] Once again, the perception that Catholic politics in the second half of the twentieth century were negligible has missed the forest for the trees. In the first place, there is no reason to believe that Roman Catholics as individuals were any less involved in party politics or in the political movements of the 1960s – against the Vietnam War, for example, or for nuclear disarmament – than their Protestant or secular counterparts. Secondly, the Church as an institution continued to lobby and to seek to influence public opinion on issues that were of concern to it – education, abortion, euthanasia – with greater and lesser degrees of success.

But nowhere is the misperception of the significance of a century and a half of political engagement by British Catholics more significant than in the view that there is no relationship between the Council and Catholic politics in England. That is because the obvious question to be asked about the relationship between Vatican II and the politics of British Catholics is not the influence of the Council on the politics of British Catholics, but the influence of politics as practised by British Catholics on the Council! Two of the most important and distinctive documents of the Council – the Pastoral Constitution on the Church in the Modern World, and the Declaration on Religious Liberty – simply could not have been written apart from the experience of Roman Catholics living in countries characterised by religious pluralism and liberal democratic politics: both, of course, enjoyed the overwhelming support of the British episcopate. If the Catholic Church underwent, as a result of the Council, a revolutionary transformation in its understanding of its relationship with culture, society and politics, it was mainly due to the political experience and wisdom acquired by Catholics in Britain and elsewhere in the course of over a century of critical and constructive engagement with the liberal State.

NOTES

1. George Andrew Beck, 'To-day and To-morrow' in *The English Catholics, 1850–1950* (London, 1950), pp. 602–3.
2. Tom Buchanan, 'Great Britain' in Tom Buchanan and Martin Conway (eds), *Political Catholicism in Europe, 1918–1965* (Oxford, 1996), pp. 248–74; Michael Hornsby-Smith, *Roman Catholics in England: Studies in Social Structure Since the Second World War* (Cambridge, 1987), pp. 157–81.
3. Buchanan, 'Great Britain', p. 249. According to Buchanan, 'one of the best sources for information on 20th-cent. Catholicism remains the official history ed. Bishop Beck'! The other general bibliography for British Catholicism in this period suggested by Buchanan is Edward Norman's necessarily brief treatment in *Roman Catholicism in England from the Elizabethan Settlement to the Second Vatican Council* (Oxford, 1985). See Adrian Hastings's *A History of English Christianity 1920–1990* (3rd edn, London, 1991), which, as the title suggests, treats Roman Catholicism in the wider context of all of British Christianity.
4. Buchanan, 'Great Britain', p. 250.
5. Buchanan, 'Great Britain', p. 273.
6. Hornsby-Smith, *Roman Catholics*, p. 163.
7. Hornsby-Smith, *Roman Catholics*, p. 159.
8. Dermot Quinn, *Patronage and Piety: the Politics of English Roman Catholicism, 1850–1900* (Stanford, 1993), p. xii.
9. Quinn, *Patronage and Piety*, p. xiii.
10. Quinn, *Patronage and Piety*, p. 178.
11. Quinn, *Patronage and Piety*, p. 184.
12. This was the judgement of Herbert Gladstone, Liberal Party Whip, who drew up the list of such constituencies won by the Liberals in 1886 and 1892 or presently held by Unionists but susceptible of being captured by Liberals because of the Irish vote. Quinn, *Patronage and Piety*, p. 219–22.
13. Quinn, *Patronage and Piety*, p. 249.
14. Not to be compared with Quinn's scholarly study of nineteenth-century political Catholicism is a journalistic account of the role of Roman Catholics in contemporary British life written in 1967 by political commentator and sometime Liberal parliamentary candidate, George Scott (*The RCs: A Report on Roman Catholics in Britain Today* [London, 1967]). Yet this impressionistic and anecdotal study is of interest because Scott asks some of the same questions as Quinn about Catholics in politics just after Vatican II and comes to the same conclusions. Scott conducted an unsystematic investigation of constituency politics in a number of locales where the Catholic population was significant, including his own home base of Middlesbrough. He concludes that 'the pro- or anti-Catholic vote is no longer a significant factor in most constituencies . . . Party or class allegiances will be stronger than religious ones when it comes to voting' (p. 61).

    Turning to the national scene, Scott asks, 'when a Roman Catholic is elected to the Commons, is there anything distinctively *Catholic* about his behaviour as a Member?' and answers, 'I am convinced that nothing resembling a Catholic bloc is operating in the House of Commons . . . It does not require such conversations as I have held nor the evidence of *Hansard* to appreciate how little political sympathy there can normally be between individual Catholic M.P.'s in opposing parties' (pp. 66–7).
15. Martin Conway, 'Introduction' in Buchanan and Conway (eds), *Political Catholicism*, p. 22.
16. As reported to George Scott in *The RCs*, p. 68.
17. G. I. T. Machin, *Politics and the Churches in Great Britain, 1832–1868* (Oxford, 1977), pp. 208–12.

18. Machin, *Politics*, p. 210.
19. 'The circulation of the pamphlet was enormous. It appeared in full in five London dailies on November 20th and occupied six-and-a-half columns of small close type in *The Times*, whose circulation was then 50,000. Yet by 4 p.m., not a copy of any of the papers printing it could be procured. In addition, 30,000 copies of the pamphlet were sold in three days.' Gordon Albion, 'The Restoration of the Hierarchy, 1850' in Beck (ed.), *English Catholics*, pp. 103–4.
20. Nicholas Wiseman, *An Appeal to the Reason and Good Feeling of the English People on the Subject of the Catholic Hierarchy* (London, 1850), p. 13.
21. Wiseman to Russell, 3 November 1850, quoted in Wiseman, *Appeal*, p. 23.
22. Wiseman, *Appeal*, p. 32.
23. Wiseman, *Appeal*, p. 9.
24. Over which there has been disagreement. See Albion, 'Restoration', p. 104: 'Its effect was tremendous, commanding the silence of attention on the violent agitation that had gone on in the past few weeks'; Machin *Politics*, p. 217: 'But it was too equivocal to calm matters and came too late to have much influence'; and E. R. Norman, *Anti-Catholicism in Victorian England* (London, 1968), p. 64: Wiseman's self-congratulation over his role in abating the controversy was 'an optimistic interpretation of events, for the uproar against the "Papal Aggression" continued unabated'.
25. Manning, 'Inaugural Address to the Academia of the Catholic Religion, Session 1868–9' in Manning, *Miscellanies* (London, 1877), vol. I, p. 265.
26. Manning, 'Inaugural Address', p. 261.
27. Manning, 'Inaugural Address', pp. 390–1.
28. Manning, 'Inaugural Address', p. 291.
29. Ibid.
30. See Jeffrey von Arx, 'Manning's Utramontanism and the Catholic Church in British Politics', *Recusant History*, 19 (May 1988), pp. 332–47. The most extreme statement of this alarm was in *The Temporal Power of the Vicar of Jesus Christ* (London, 1862), p. 74: 'When the civil powers of the world shall desecrate themselves and lose their relation to Christianity, they will inaugurate the beginning of the last times, and the AntiChrist shall come.'
31. Manning, *Temporal Power*, p. 101.
32. Manning, 'The Catholic Church and Modern Society' in *Miscellanies*, vol. III, pp. 312–13. The conclusion Manning reaches here is, of course, in direct contradiction to the policy of abstention from Catholic participation in the politics of the Italian State articulated by Pius IX in the *Non expedit*.
33. Manning, 'Catholic Church', pp. 316–17.
34. Manning, 'Catholic Church', p. 317.
35. His 1869 Pastoral on the subject was unusual in being addressed not only to his own clergy and faithful, but also to non-Catholics whom he hoped to win over to the cause of denominational education. He wrote to Cardinal Cullen in Dublin describing the pastoral as a '*political* declaration. I have carefully avoided giving it a predominantly Catholic character. Christian education as the *genus* and denominational as the *species* will cover all we want. And if we are to rally the Anglicans and the Nonconformists, we must, I fear, use a language intelligible to them, rather than our own' (Manning to Cullen, 15 August 1869, Cullen Papers, Archives of the Archdiocese of Dublin, quoted in D. E. Selby, 'Henry Edward Manning and the Education Bill of 1870', *British Journal of Educational Studies*, vol. 18, no. 2 (June 1970), p. 200).
36. Manning had proposed making common cause with the other donominations as early as February, 1868, when he circularised the Catholic bishops, recommending that Catholics send representatives to a public meeting organised by the Established Church to support

denominational education. The bishops were reluctant to support this proposal, but Manning requested that the (lay) Chairman and Secretary of the Catholic Poor-School Committee, the principal funding body for Catholic elementary education, attend meetings of the Anglican National Education Union (Selby, 'Manning and the 1870 Education Bill', pp. 200–1).

37. The clearest statement of this admission is from an 1882 article: 'Putting away all ecclesiastical questions, it cannot be denied that the State is justified in providing for the education of its people. It has the right to protect itself from the dangers arising from ignorance and vice, which breed crime and turbulence' (Manning, 'Is the Education Act of 1870 a Just Law?', *The Nineteenth Century*, vol. 12 (December 1882), p. 959).
38. Quoted in Selby, 'Manning and the 1870 Education Bill', pp. 204–5.
39. Selby, 'Manning and the 1870 Education Bill', p. 207.
40. Manning, *The Vatican Decrees in their Bearing on Civil Allegiance* (London, 1875), pp. 133–4. One of the earliest uses of the term 'secular' by Manning that I have been able to discover.
41. Manning, *Vatican Decrees*, pp. 135–6.
42. Manning, *Vatican Decrees*, pp. 137–8.
43. Manning, *Vatican Decrees*, pp. 138–9.
44. Manning, *Vatican Decrees*, p. 140.
45. See H. C. G. Matthew, 'Gladstone, Vaticanism, and the Question of the East' in D. Baker (ed.), *Religious Motivation: Biographical and Sociological Problems for the Church Historians* (Oxford, 1978), pp. 417–42.
46. Matthew, 'Gladstone', p. 420.
47. For the history of the idea of a Catholic party in England, see Josef L. Altholz, 'The Political Behavior of the English Catholics, 1850–1867', *The Journal of British Studies*, vol. IV (November 1964), pp. 89–103, especially p. 96. On the possibility of such a party in 1885, see Thomas R. Greene, 'The English Catholic Press and the Home Rule Bill, 1885–86', *Eire-Ireland*, vol. X (Spring 1975), pp. 18–37.
48. Greene, 'English Catholic Press', p. 21. Bagshawe's letter appeared in the 1 August 1885 issue of the *Tablet*, p. 175.
49. In 1860, August Reichensperger, who went on to become a leader of the German Centre Party, had publicly suggested, in an article in the *Rambler* ('The Theory of Party', New Series, II [1860], pp. 237–43), that English Catholics form such a party: see Altholz, 'Political Behavior', p. 96, n. 24.
50. For a discussion of the literature on the Catholic Centre Party in the social, political and religious milieu of the German Empire, see Margaret Lavinia Anderson, 'Piety and Politics: Recent Work on German Catholicism', *Journal of Modern History*, 63 (December 1991), pp. 681–716, especially pp. 705ff. For Manning on the *Kulturkampf*, see Jeffrey von Arx, 'Archbishop Manning and the *Kulturkampf*', *Recusant History*, vol. 21, no. 2 (October 1992), pp. 254–66.
51. For Manning's private opinion of Bagshawe's proposal, see Manning to Vaughan, 26 December 1885: 'We are bound as bishops to be independent of all parties as the Holy See is. Bp of Meath and Bp of Nottingham from impetuosity of character catch at the first apparent help.' Vaughan Correspondence, #278, Manning Papers (Archives of the Archdiocese of Westminster).
52. *Dublin Review*, Third Series, XIV (October 1885), pp. 401–11.
53. In the few cases where Parnell ordered the Irish to vote for Liberals who did not support voluntary education, the results were mixed. In the four cases where Liberals not endorsed by Parnell had given the assurances required by Manning, they were elected. See G. D. H. Howard, 'The Parnell Manifesto of 21 November, 1885, and the Schools Question', *English Historical Review*, 67 (January 1947), pp. 47–8; but also Quinn, *Patronage and Piety*, who

concludes on the basis of his constituency analysis that the Irish Catholic vote was overrated in general. Cf. his 'Appendix: Constituency Catholicism', pp. 217–55.

54. See Walsh to Manning, 27 December 1885; Manning to Walsh 28 December 1885, Walsh Papers (Archives of the Archdiocese of Dublin).
55. Manning to Vaughan, 11 June 1886, Vaughan Correspondence, Manning Papers. Manning also took this opportunity to inform Vaughan that he would himself look for an opportunity to speak out on the Irish question, in favour of 'the integrity of the Imperial Parliament and a legislative power in Ireland for all home matters not Imperial' – a move beyond the 'central board' scheme of Joseph Chamberlain, but still short of an endorsement of a separate Parliament in Dublin. What he proposed for Ireland, he told Vaughan, he also desired for Scotland and Wales. Manning found the opportunity he sought to express his support for this version of Home Rule in a letter published in *The Times* on 6 July 1886, after the defeat of Gladstone's Bill and in the middle of the general election. There, Manning declares that 'England, Ireland and Scotland must, in my belief, all alike have Home Rule affairs that are not Imperial. The growth of Empire and the fullness of time demand it.' Manning's letter was taken in Ireland as a declaration of support at a critical moment for Home Rule as they understood it, but as Emmet Larkin points out (*The Roman Catholic Church and the Creation of the Modern Irish State, 1878–1886* (Philadelphia, 1975), p. 381), Manning had not committed himself to more than a vague form of federal devolution, and certainly not to the existence of a separate Irish Parliament. Manning's enthusiasm for a federal, devolutionary solution to the problem of Home Rule is not surprising, given a growing commitment to decentralisation in the interest of authentically liberal government.
56. See Robert O'Neill, *Cardinal Herbert Vaughan* (Tunbridge Wells, 1997), pp. 443–7 and Marjorie Cruickshank, *Church and State in English Education* (London, 1963), pp. 69f.
57. See Cruickshank, *Church and State*, pp. 90–112 and Machin, *Politics*, pp. 284–93.
58. Cruickshank, pp. *Church and State*, pp. 137–69.
59. See James Murphy, *Church, State and Schools in Britain, 1800–1970* (London, 1971), pp. 121–5.
60. Hastings, *English Christianity*, p. 562.
61. Adrian Hastings, 'Some Reflexions on the English Catholicism of the late 1930's' in A. Hastings (ed.), *Bishops and Writers* (Wheathampstead, 1977), pp. 114–19.
62. Hastings, 'Some Reflexions', pp. 117–18: 'The one [Fascism] derided liberal parliamentary democracy as Protestant in inspiration, degenerate and phoney, and lauded Latin and Mediterranean political experience as more genuinely democratic (of a populist kind), Catholic and "counter-revolutionary". The other [ultramontanism] wholly subordinated local church to Rome and laity to clergy as a matter of divine law. Both tended to prefer Latin models to Anglo-Saxon ones, and obedience and order to freedom and public debate.'
63. Hastings, 'Some Reflexions', pp. 118–19.
64. Hastings, *English Christianity*, pp. 476, 483.
65. To whom he attributes 'hopes' for an 'ultramontane inspired society' along the lines of Catholic Action. Hastings, 'Some Reflexions', p. 115.
66. Hastings, 'Some Reflexions', p. 114.
67. Ibid.
68. See Jeffrey von Arx (ed.), *Varieties of Ultramontanism* (Washington, DC, 1998), pp. 1–11, 85–102.
69. Hastings, *English Christianity*, pp. 393–7.
70. There is, for example, no discussion of the impact of Vatican II on Catholic politics in Britain in Hastings' *English Christianity*.

ELEVEN

THE CATHOLIC CHURCH IN WALES

DANIEL J. MULLINS

THE NEW MISSION CENTRES, 1850–1895

The Apostolic Letter *Universalis Ecclesiae* decreed 'the re-establishment within the kingdom of England . . . of the Hierarchy of bishops ordinary'. The ecclesiastical District of Wales[1] was to have 'two episcopal sees, namely Shrewsbury and Menevia united with Newport'. Rome had very little perception of Wales as being anything other than a district of England. Thomas Joseph Brown OSB, Vicar Apostolic of the Welsh District since 1840, was appointed first Bishop of Newport and Menevia. Until June of the following year, he was also administrator of the diocese of Shrewsbury.

An immediate concern of Bishop Brown was to ensure the provision of priests for his new diocese. On his appointment as Vicar Apostolic of the Welsh District, he had written in 1840 to the President of the English Benedictine Congregation, Dom Bernard Barber, with the novel proposal that Benedictine monks should be professed specifically for the Welsh Mission. This was rejected out of hand. In 1850 he suggested that the Congregation should concentrate its work, for the most part, within Wales. On 19 November 1857, he wrote to Abbot Alban Molyneux with the question, 'Are you, then, willing to form the Cathedral Chapter of Newport? It will require, at least four Canons with a Dignatory, and to be increased, as means permit, to ten canons.'

He had already ensured the assent of the bishops to this proposal. Despite the persistent opposition of Ampleforth, which feared being deprived of English missions, the Abbot President and Regimen approved the scheme in meetings at Downside on 2 December and 30 December 1851. The proposal was accepted by a decree of the Sacred Congregation of *Propaganda* of 22 April 1852. Bishop Brown expected and hoped that the new monastery and cathedral church would be built at Newport. Colonel John Francis Vaughan of Courtfield offered land near Abergavenny. The convert F. R. Wegg-Prosser proposed a site outside Hereford.

After considerable debate, some of it acrimonious, Wegg-Prosser's offer was accepted and the work of building Belmont Abbey and church began in 1857. In an appeal for funds in 1859, Bishop Brown showed clearly what would be the functions of the new monastery. There was, he said, need for a seminary wherein he could train priests more cheaply than by sending them to foreign colleges or to other English colleges. There was need too for a place where the secular clergy could make their annual retreat, and which would provide temporary supply priests for the diocesan mission centres.

According to the census returns of 1851, there were sixteen places in which Sunday Mass was celebrated in the diocese of Newport and Menevia. This also gives the names of the priests and the numbers attending in each place. Already Cardiff had more Catholics than Newport, though Newport was then the largest town in Wales. For North Wales, there are returns for Holywell, St Asaph, Wrexham, Mold and Bangor.[2]

Following the persecution of 1689, the Jesuit presence in Wales had declined. Increasingly, the Franciscans took on the work of caring for a diminishing number of Catholics. By 1850, however, the English Franciscan Province was almost extinct. To help establish his diocese, the Holy See appointed Bishop Brown administrator of the Franciscan funds. These amounted to £12,000 and he succeeded in increasing this to £17,000. Some of this money, £5,000 in total, was used to build the cathedral church at Belmont. All his life, the bishop had financial worries. That so much could be achieved was due to his continuing appeals and to the generosity of some of the Catholic families and benefactors, many of them in England.

The life of a missionary priest in Wales was a difficult one. In 1801 there was one Catholic in Merthyr Tydfil. By 1827 Edward Richards, a Franciscan priest at Abergavenny, was writing to the Vicar Apostolic setting out how a mission there might be successful. Fr Patrick Portal, an Irish secular priest, was sent there in 1828 to look after some 300 Irish immigrants. Fr Portal and Fr J. Carroll, who arrived in 1835, were extraordinary apostles living in almost impossible conditions. In 1855, the number of Catholics served from Merthyr is given as 4,049. This figure covers a wide area and was later divided into the separate parishes of Merthyr, Dowlais, Pontypool and Tredegar. Conditions in the iron towns were difficult and work and wages often fluctuated.

The other centre of rapid growth was Cardiff. Fr Portal had travelled there from Merthyr to say Mass for a few Catholic families. In 1841 there were 1,200 Catholics in the town. In 1851, the number was estimated at 4,000 and for 1861 it was given as 9,800. Writing in 1893, the Rosminian Fr George Cormack wrote that 'the first step in missionary organisation was taken by the people themselves'.[3] This was to be the pattern as Irish immigration continued. Because of the poverty of the people and fear of arousing prejudice and hostility, the priests in the older centres were slow to open new missions.

An attempt to find a site for a Catholic chapel in Cardiff was rejected by the second Marquess of Bute, a decision which found favour with *The Times*. The son of that Marquess was to become the major Catholic benefactor of the Church. When a site was purchased, it provoked such opposition that it was resold. Soon afterwards, an Italian bought some land in the centre of Cardiff and transferred it to the bishop. St David's Church was built on this site. This was replaced by the present Metropolitan Cathedral in 1887. The original church was again brought into use when the cathedral was destroyed by an incendiary bomb in March 1941. It served as the pro-cathedral until St David's was reopened by Cardinal William Godfrey in 1959. The old church was finally demolished to make space for road widening.

In the discussions prior to the creation of four new vicariates, the English Benedictines had, in 1839, pointed out that in medieval times a number of cathedrals had Benedictine chapters whose members elected the bishop. From the opening of the cathedral at Belmont, the monastery was governed by a cathedral prior. Since Belmont did not, initially, have its own community, but provided for a common novitiate and house of studies, the whole Benedictine Congregation was seen as having a special role in the diocese. In 1897, the Benedictines took responsibility for St Mary of the Angels in Cardiff. For many years, they had charge of Merthyr Tydfil, Dowlais, Rhymney, Bridgend and Swansea. From these centres they established new mission centres in Morriston and Clydach outside Swansea and at Maesteg and Aberkenfig.

In response to repeated requests to the founder, Antonio Rosmini, the Fathers of Charity came to St Mary's, Newport in June 1847. Since then, they have been a very important force in the Catholic life of Newport and Cardiff. They also now look after Our Lady of Lourdes parish in Townhill, Swansea.

In a letter addressed to Fr Alfred Weld, written from St Beuno's on 24 May 1862, Fr George Porter SJ, the future Archbishop of Bombay, speaks of the Swansea mission. The Jesuits had served Swansea from Bristol throughout the second half of the eighteenth century. In the 1790s, Fr Richard Plowden began to plan for a permanent chapel in the town. By 1802, Plowden had acquired what is described as a large apartment in Swansea Castle. By 1804, there was a permanent mission in Swansea. In 1813 a chapel was built in Herbert Street. In 1847, the first part of the present St David's Church was opened. Fr Porter's letter gives an idea of the nature of mission work in Wales:

> Swansea, you are aware, is a very rising place. Within the last 30 years, several towns on the Bristol Channel have risen into importance, Cardiff, Newport, Milford etc. Swansea was the last which made any decided steps, but its prosperity promises to be more lasting. Cardiff etc. have fallen away to

> some extent, but Swansea continues to thrive and it is thought by competent judges that it will ultimately rise to the class of a first-rate port. At present, it has a population of from 40,000 to 50,000, chiefly employed in iron and copper works . . . The Catholics are marked in the Directory as 3,000. This was the number estimated many years since, at a time when the railways drew a number of Catholic workmen to the neighbourhood. At present the number is variously stated; some place it higher than 3,000; the priest, the Rev. P. Lewis, thinks it much less. If we apply the rules of the Registrar General to the number of Baptisms, 3,000 will very fairly represent the present Catholic population of Swansea. The congregation consists of a small nucleus of respectable trades-people; the immense majority are working people, some receiving high wages in the various works, more doing all the small trade of the place – selling coals, buying old clothes, chips, etc. etc. The congregation is almost entirely Irish, furnished by Cork and Waterford and the neighbourhood districts.[4]

Fr Porter with Fr Richard Payne SJ had been to Swansea preaching a mission at St David's and in the 'fine school-room' at Greenhill. The mission lasted from Passion Sunday to Low Sunday. He gives some statistics:

> The number of persons who approached the Sacraments was 1,130; of persons reclaimed, 360: of General Confessions, about 60; of adult first Communicants, i.e. from 16 upwards, about 70: Protestants received into the Church, 6. These numbers seemed to me small, but the Rev. P. Lewis told me they were high according to the Swansea standard.[5]

In conclusion, Fr Porter added an interesting comment: 'Swansea is peculiar in one respect; the men are decidedly more pious and regular than the women.' The mission crucifix commemorating the Jesuit visit may still be seen over the confessional at St David's Priory.

Fr Porter's letter of 1862 indicates the uncertainty of trade and employment during the second half of the nineteenth century. Low wages, restrictions on where money could be spent and recurring unemployment made any sustained development of parishes and missions almost impossible. In his Lenten Pastoral Letter of 1866, Bishop Brown spoke of the progress made and of the poverty of the Catholic people: 'Therefore it would have been absolutely impossible to provide clergy for even considerably below the half of an increased and increasing congregation . . . were it not for timely assistance received from religious orders.'

At the request of the bishop, the Fathers of Charity took over St David's Church in Cardiff in 1854. Their arrival marked a significant step forward in the organisation of Catholic life. In addition to the priest members of the Institute, they also brought brothers who proved effective teachers. They were soon followed by the Sisters of Providence, also a Rosminian foundation.

In 1861, the Fathers of Charity built St Peter's Church in Roath. This area of Cardiff developed rapidly in the second half of the nineteenth century and provided small housing but also more substantial properties occupied by traders and merchants. In 1865 a small school was provided at Canton and Mass was said regularly there. In this area of Cardiff were provided better built and larger terraced houses. Also in 1865 a school was established in the working-class area of Grangetown and St Patrick's Church was opened there in 1883. The Rosminian priests also began to move out of Cardiff and in 1860 began to serve the community in nearby Penarth.

As numbers increased, Irish families moved into the Tyndall Street area of Cardiff. A chapel was opened there in 1873. This was soon too small and was replaced by St Paul's Church in 1893. The small network of streets surrounding the church became a totally Catholic community and successive generations continued to think of themselves as Irish people. The area was demolished in the 1960s and the people moved to the Trowbridge and Fairwater estates. One of the new churches opened in 1965 to meet their needs was dedicated to the Cardiff martyr St John Lloyd, a witness to the changing self-awareness of Cardiff Catholics.

The Capuchin friary at Pantasaph was built in 1857. In 1860, Bishop Brown turned to the Capuchins seeking a priest for Pontypool. Fr Portal had begun saying Mass there from Merthyr. The Capuchins sent an Italian priest, Fr Elzear Torregiani;[6] and he was joined by a Fr Honorius. Irish workers were already in the mining trade at Abersychan and Mass was soon provided for them in a broken-down cottage. The Franciscans opened up another mission at Blaenavon. In 1864, the bishop invited them to take charge of Cwmbran. In the following year, Risca was begun and with the help of some benefactors, a thatched chapel was built. Abertillery was their final new foundation; they began to provide Mass there in 1875. The development in these mining areas illustrates the movement of Irish workers and their families from the coastal towns. The continuing fluctuation in trade and in employment saw many look to coal-mining as a source of reliable income. Because of the total power of the mine-owners, it would not become that for a very long time. This new supply of labour often drove down the wages paid to miners and conflict between the Irish and other workers became inevitable.

The western and rural part of the diocese of Newport and Menevia also saw some growth. Irish people were put ashore at Milford Haven and many sought and found work in the farms of Pembrokeshire and Carmarthen. The building of the naval dockyard, begun in 1814, saw Irish labourers and Irish sailors settling in the area that is today Pembroke Dock. Fr Peter Lewis was sent to the new town and began saying Mass in a public house. A church was built and opened in 1847. An Irish priest, Fr Oliver Murphy, arrived in 1850 and remained there for almost the remainder of the century.

The advent of Fr Murphy enabled Peter Lewis to move to the more Welsh-speaking parts. In the Census Returns of 1851, he had an address at Lammas Street in Carmarthen and was saying Mass in a loft over a dwelling-house in Water Street. He had a total congregation of 150 with an average attendance over five months of ninety people. Though it was his wish and that of the bishop to develop an apostolate in the Welsh language, Peter Lewis's main energy was devoted to providing for the immigrant Catholics. He opened missions at Milford Haven and Haverfordwest where he acquired a cottage in Dew Street. There were 175 Catholics in all between the two places. The original small church of St David and St Patrick was opened in 1872. Fr Lewis later moved to Swansea where he was responsible for the provision of schools and the opening of a new mission centre in Greenhill. In 1873, the Benedictines took on responsibility for Swansea. Dom Wulstan Richards was appointed parish priest in 1875. It was he who organised the building of St Joseph's, the present cathedral church of Menevia. It was opened in 1888. He was quite consciously designing the future cathedral of Swansea.

In June 1851, James Brown, rector of Sedgley Park School in the Midlands, was appointed first Bishop of Shrewsbury in the restored hierarchy. He was consecrated by Cardinal Wiseman at St George's, Southwark on July 27.

The one centre to have an unbroken Catholic presence in North Wales is Holywell. The Jesuit and secular clergy presence there and the continuing fidelity of the Mostyn family ensured that a community survived. Bangor had been made a mission in 1827 with Fr Edward Carbery in charge, a man whom Fr Louis Gerard of Llanarth Court thought would be better employed at Merthyr. John Briggs, later to become the first Bishop of Beverley, began to visit Wrexham from Chester where he had found sixty or seventy Catholics. A chapel was opened in 1828. By 1851 there were 250 Catholics at Bangor and 300 at Wrexham. An attempt had also been made to make provision for the Irish at Holyhead. This was not immediately successful. The famine in Ireland in the 1840s did not see large numbers coming to North Wales. There were many Irish labourers employed in the laying of the railway and these engaged the concern and the zeal of Fr John Tobin who served in Wrexham and later in Bangor. These men passed on to other places as the work proceeded.

In 1850 Viscount and Lady Fielding were received into the Church. As Anglicans, they had begun the building of a church at Pantasaph. Archdeacon Henry Edward Manning preached there at the laying of the foundation stone. The building was not completed at their conversion and they decided it should be a Catholic and not an Anglican church. The Bishop of St Asaph brought a court case to retain the building. The decision was that it was not in Anglican ownership until completed and therefore Viscount Fielding was free to do as he wished with his property. The architect Pugin and his builder Myers were engaged to adapt the newly named St David's for Catholic use.[7] The Capuchins went to Pantasaph in 1852. Their friary, designed by the architect J. A. Hansom, was built in 1857. From Pantasaph in 1853 the Capuchins established their first mission centre at Flint. When Fr Lawrence died of cholera in 1863 the bishop took on the responsibility of providing a secular priest. Fr Elzear, who was later to work in Monmouthshire, began to travel on Sundays to Mold as well as to Flint. The friar next turned his attention to Holyhead. The railway company provided him with a weekly free pass on the train and made a room in the Pelham Hotel available for Mass. This was in 1855. By 1860, a church had been built in the town. The Capuchins from Chester began to say Mass in Saltney, almost on the Cheshire border, in 1862.

Between 1848 and 1849, the Jesuits built a new college for their students near Tremeirchion in Clwyd and dedicated it to St Beuno. Very quickly their influence began to spread in the area. In 1854 a chapel was dedicated at St Asaph where by 1856 there were some 200 Catholics, mainly from the west of Ireland.[8]

The development of coastal resorts in North Wales created a new impetus in providing for the growing towns. A mission at Rhyl was established in 1863. The new church at Llandudno was opened with great solemnity in 1893 and Colwyn Bay became a centre in 1895. In West Wales, at Aberystwyth, the retired missionary from Mauritius, Bishop William Bernard Collier, began to provide Mass in the town. In 1888, the Passionists sent three priests to Tenby. In the following year, they took over Carmarthen and made it their main centre. For a time Tenby was served at weekends from there.

Bishop Thomas Joseph Brown of Newport died in 1880. Bishop James Brown of Shrewsbury died the following year and was quickly succeeded by his auxiliary bishop Edmund Knight. Almost a year was to elapse before the appointment of Cuthbert Hedley OSB as Bishop of Newport and Menevia. In 1873, he had been appointed Auxiliary to Bishop T. J. Brown, a role which he found frustrating and difficult. He was to become a major figure in Catholic life in England as well as in Wales. After Newman, he was the most highly regarded and prolific Catholic writer of his day.

The most imaginative and ultimately unachieveable venture of these years was the attempt at establishing the Third Order of St Dominic in the restored monastery on St Tudwal's Island off Abersoch. Henry Bailey Hughes of Caernavon was received into the Church in 1850. He went to the English College at Lisbon, a college with many Welsh connections, where he was ordained. He had a great facility for learning languages and became a well-known preacher in Portugal, Spain, Belgium and Italy. He was on the fringes of the first Vatican Council and was sent as Prefect Apostolic to the mission at Abandu in Africa. Because of ill-health, he left Africa to take charge of the Portuguese community at Boston in Massachusetts. He worked among American Indians and founded houses of the Third Order of St Dominic in Canada and South America.

In April 1885, Bishop Knight invited him to work in North Wales where his first language, Welsh, would be of missionary importance. He accepted, and decided to found a monastery. He chose the uninhabited St Tudwal's Island. It was to become 'a centre for missions to the Welsh in North Wales'. He had the idea of bringing over young men from the Breton-speaking areas of Brittany who would easily learn Welsh. While awaiting the restoration of the old monastery, he rented two cottages in Abersoch and began his missionary work there. His public Welsh sermons were not received with any enthusiasm. The idea of going in procession with a crucifix and reciting the rosary which he had found effective in Portugal did not gather crowds in Nonconformist Wales. The rigours he endured in trying to make the buildings on the island habitable no doubt interfered with his not too robust health. He was taken ill and died on 16 December 1887. The hopes that he embodied may have been romantic and foolhardy. Yet he left a memory and a challenge that to bring back the Old Faith to Wales required a recognition of the Welsh identity and the cultural distinctiveness of Wales.

TWO WELSH DIOCESES

When Fr John Burke was given the opportunity to go to Usk, an established and financially sound parish, his reason for asking to remain at Newport is significant. Not only was he of the same background and language as the Irish immigrants, but people had to be spoken to on the subject of their religious duties, he said in a letter to the bishop, and he found that the Catholics of England 'could not bear it. They want if possible an accommodating clergyman.'[9] The whole history of post-Reformation Catholicism was very different in the two countries and the relationship between priest and people was built on differing assumptions.

Bishop Hedley was very aware that in South Wales, both in his time and probably for many years to come, the missionary challenge was almost entirely an Irish problem. The older landed families and some of the recent converts had their own private means and often kept a priest. The apostolate to the Welsh he found to be 'a somewhat barren effort'.[10] His first act on taking charge of the diocese was a deliberate and significant one. He left Hereford and went to live in Cardiff. By 1881, Cardiff had replaced Newport as the principal Welsh port and much of its prosperity and its shipping was under the control of the Marquess of Bute. Hedley had sympathy for the Welsh and their culture, but no great understanding of them. He was a practical man with very real pastoral problems demanding his whole attention. Like his predecessor, he was concerned about the provision of priests for his diocese. One of his first initiatives was to revive St Joseph's High School which had opened in 1867. His aim was to make it a diocesan college that would prepare candidates for sending to seminaries. During the 1890s, J. Hobson Matthews taught Welsh and Fr Paul Hook was Prefect of Studies. The learning of Welsh was judged to be an important requirement in those who would become the diocesan priests of Wales.

In 1892, Bishop Herbert Vaughan was transferred from Salford to the metropolitan see of Westminster. It was an appointment that would have a lasting effect on Wales. Before all else, Herbert Vaughan was a missionary priest. When he first thought about priesthood, it was as a missionary in Wales that he envisaged his future. To prepare himself for that, he began as a young man to visit Fr Lewis Havard at Brecon in order to learn Welsh. Bishop Brown did not greatly encourage that; he saw a much wider role for a priest with the background and financial resources of the eldest of the Vaughan boys.

Cardinal Vaughan, as he was to become, was quite certain that the ecclesiastical provision made for Wales did not meet the need. Most of Wales did not have established parish communities that could be cared for and nurtured by diocesan priests. Wales, he believed should, like all missionary countries, come under *Propaganda* and should have its own Vicar Apostolic. In the year that the Vicariate was established he told a *Western Mail* reporter that ecclesiastically 'Wales ought to be treated as an independent State rather than as an appendage of England'.[11] He was speaking of pastoral needs and realities.

Bishop Knight was very ready to fall in with the Cardinal's proposal. The English part of the diocese, Shropshire and especially Cheshire, had seen considerable growth since 1850. The Welsh counties had not shared in this growth. Bishop Hedley was less sure. There were the travelling difficulties between North and South Wales. And Cardinal Vaughan's idea of a Vicariate clearly included Glamorgan. On that Bishop Hedley strongly disagreed. He was not happy to lose the territory of medieval Menevia, though he saw and accepted the arguments for it. The Vicariate of Wales was established by the apostolic brief *De Animarum Salute* of 4 March 1895.

The Vicar Apostolic was to be Francis Joseph Mostyn of the recusant family of Talacre near Holywell. After ordination he had served as curate and then as rector of Our Lady's, Birkenhead. The Welsh-language press was indignant at this development. Wales was a Protestant country now under attack from the Antichrist of Rome. In 1896, the ancient name of Menevia was quietly dropped. In 1881, in his letter of appointment, Bishop Hedley had been given charge of the episcopal churches of Newport and Menevia, canonically united, for ever. Canonically, *in perpetuum* means of indefinite duration.

The arrangement of a Vicariate was not likely to last. *Universalis Ecclesiae* declared that the time had come to restore 'the form of ordinary episcopal government'. Neither the new Vicar Apostolic nor Bishop Hedley found it helpful. In 1898, the ancient name of Menevia was restored and the Vicariate of Wales elevated to a diocese. The cathedral and diocesan curia would continue at Wrexham. The problem of getting around the whole of rural Wales remained until 1987. The argument that made Bishop Hedley accept the Vicariate, namely the differing pastoral needs of industrial South Wales and the rest of the country, differences so fundamental 'that no bishop or body of clergy could be either free or versatile enough adequately to cater for both at the same time' has never been fully faced.

Bishop Hedley and Cardinal Vaughan were, from two differing starting points, trying to face the reality that was illustrated in Fr Burke's letter. Catholicism is the religion of a people. It is the guide and support of those who know in their bones that its teaching is true. Because it is true, they accept the demands and the sacrifices which that truth makes on how they live out even the details of their lives. Because it is central to their whole self-understanding, the Catholic people produces its leaders, who are not always in the clerical or religious states. Without confusion of roles, a Catholic people produces or finds the clergy needed, and those who will support and advance their social and civic formation. The Catholic Church that was growing and spreading, especially in the industrial South of Wales, was very different from the recusant Catholicism of the old centres. The pastoral needs of rural Wales were also very different from those of the industrial South-East.

By 1840, even in the old centres, Irish names already predominated in the baptismal registers. By 1895, any indigenous remnants of Catholicism had been absorbed into the new communities. Irish Catholicism had been formed by fifteen hundred years of acceptance of a Catholic view of creation. Even in penal times they had found new holy places in ancient ruined churches and in keeping alive the celebrations of earlier days. They had kept their 'patterns' and they had kept the Mass and these linked them with the generations of their people. Very quickly, they began to develop public celebrations of their Catholic identity in Newport, Cardiff and Swansea. On St Patrick's Day and at Eastertime and for the Feast of Corpus Christi, they paraded publicly in the streets, carrying their banners and the badges of their religious groups. Various Catholic Benefit Societies also celebrated with public processions, particularly on the occasion of Church Holydays. The older missionary priests looked on this with apprehension.

Intermarriage among the immigrant families soon created communities bound together by bonds of blood and religion. The popular devotions and family pieties were in this way preserved and handed on. This was a piety rooted in rural Ireland. Throughout the nineteenth century, public devotions were promoted in the growing number of churches. Those that proved most popular were the public saying of the rosary and the celebration of Benediction. It was only later that these two were linked. The Catholic communities, too, liked to express publicly their loyalty to the pope.

Two matters caused continuing misunderstanding in the industrial areas. For Catholics, Sunday is a day of celebration, a day for relaxing and enjoyment. Italian families moving into the mining and seaside towns opened up small cafés. They outraged local sensibilities by opening on Sundays. The Fr Matthew temperance movement had lasting effect in the Nonconformist chapels of Manchester and Liverpool. From these cities, it had come to Wales and by 1850 became a distinguishing mark of what Catholics called chapel religion. The temperance movement had its strong advocates within the Catholic parishes. The Rosminian Fr Richard Richardson, a Derbyshire convert who came to Newport in 1857, founded what he named 'The Holy War'. Within its ranks there was place for total abstainers and for moderate drinkers. He established the Association of Our Lady of the Immaculate Conception for the Suppression of Drunkenness. Branches of this movement spread to neighbouring parishes. Other organisations with a similar purpose were the Temperance Society and the Teetotallers.

Catholic Benefit Societies were also established. The most long-lasting of these was the Ancient Order of Hibernians. There were also the United Brothers, the Catholic Women's Club and the St Patrick's Guild. These sought to promote thrift and began to develop a rudimentary form of insurance. Most were strongly church-centred, though the Hibernians was entirely under lay control. In 1868, the Rector of St Peter's in Cardiff began what he called the Penny Bank, again to promote thrift and some form of family security.

The public celebration of feasts led to the formation of parish bands. These were to be found across South Wales, where a similar development became an important element in the social life of the mining communities. League of the Cross Bands, as they were often known, became a source of great local pride and some rivalry. In addition to the adult brass bands, schools had fife and drum groups. All had their place in the public processions and celebrations of the Catholic community.

The building of a chapel or mission centre was sometimes undertaken by the men. The church erected at Dukestown in Tredegar was, until its extension and renovation, an exact replica of an Irish country chapel. It was built by Irish workers and was intended to last. Many churches were put up to meet an urgent need and so there were 'some wretched buildings put up by one generation to be repaired by the next'.[12] The little church of St Bride's at Pontarddulais was replaced in 1994. The previous, much-loved building was put up by the Irish workers who filled in a local swamp and erected a galvanised structure upon it.

In moving to live in Cardiff, Bishop Hedley widened his sphere of influence. Not only did Cardiff have the largest concentration of immigrant Catholics; it was also strongly influenced as a town and a thriving port by the Creighton

Stuart family, the Earls of Bute. The third marquess became a Catholic in 1868 and thereafter the chief benefactor of Catholic causes in the city and throughout his estates. Bishop Hedley soon became a prominent figure in public life and in 1882 was a member of the committee established to found a second college of the University of Wales in Cardiff. His support of the claim of Cardiff to be recognised as the capital of Wales did not bring universal admiration. It was typical of the man to speak out on what he thought was important in civic as well as in religious matters.

When the diocese of Menevia began in 1898, it had an estimated population of 8,500 Catholics. There were twenty-nine secular priests. In addition there were fifty-nine priests of religious orders, especially Jesuits and Capuchin Franciscans. There were Oblates of Mary Immaculate at Holyhead and Passionists in Carmarthen. The last decade of the century saw the continuing development of the seaside resorts along the North Wales coast. Missions at Rhyl, Llandudno and Colwyn Bay had already been provided and Llandrindod Wells, much favoured by Cardinal Vaughan and later by Lloyd George, was receiving some attention from the Jesuits. The hope and intention of Cardinal Vaughan to promote separate ecclesiastical provision for Wales was meant to provide the conditions needed for a Catholic mission to the Welsh people. Mostyn was very conscious of this. For potential missionaries he turned to Brittany and to the Oblates of Mary Immaculate at Quimper. With the financial support of Mrs Herbert of Llanofer, Fr Goulven Treboal and Fr Pierre Merour, recently ordained, arrived at Holyhead towards the end of August 1900. In December 1901 they were established at Llanrwst where there was one known Catholic. Merour later moved to Blaenau Ffestiniog where his reception was not friendly. He therefore transferred to Pwllheli which had not had a resident priest for ten years.

In 1910 Treboal started a parish magazine in Welsh and English. The bound copies of *Cennad Catholig Cymru* covering his years at Llanrwst make a substantial volume. Its aim was to promote devotional practices and it also contained historical and apologetic articles, notably from Mgr Paul Hook and J. Hobson Matthews. Both the Oblate priests were recalled to their own country at the outbreak of the First World War in 1914. Since their arrival at Llanrwst, the number of Catholics had grown to 120.

In 1903, Benedictines from the Breton Abbbey of Kerbeneat near Brest also arrived in the diocese. In a letter to Fr Anwyl of Cardigan, Dom John Saillour of Ramsgate gave an account of their coming: 'About our residence in Wales – the dates are very simple. We arrived in 1903 (April) and left definitely in 1921 (July), but we had promised Bishop Mostyn a foundation in his diocese some four years previously.' The monks first received the hospitality of Lord Ashburnam of Pembrey and soon rented for three years Glyn Abbey on the railway line from Burry Port to Pontyberem. Through two Catholic ladies at Llechryd they heard of the sale of Noyaddwilym near Cardigan. Some monks were sent there 'before the end of 1904 and in 1906 Glyn Abbey was completely abandoned'. According to the *Cardigan and Tivyside Advertiser* they were greeted by 'a crowd of urchins shouting "Go home to your country" and other cries of derision'. Earlier, on 29 July 1904, on hearing that Benedictines were coming to the area, the paper had said: 'The Catholic invasion of Wales appears to be almost complete . . . Protestant ministers of all denominations will have enough to do to stop the Romanish invasion.' This was quite different from their reception in Carmarthenshire, where two Baptist choirs had gone to sing carols for them at Christmas.

The foundation at Cardigan was named Caermaria. There the life of a Benedictine monastery was established and at weekends the monks went to say Mass in several parishes. In 1914, Bishop Hedley invited them to take over the parish of Caerphilly. From there, they opened Mass-centres at Senghenydd and Ystrad Mynach. The letter already quoted gives the end of this episode:

> During the 1914 War, life at Caermaria was greatly interfered with. All the young members were called to the colours by the French Government and eventually the Abbot sent the older ones either to Caerphilly or to Buckfast, and sold the place. After the war, the Superiors decided to return to the Abbey in Brittany and the Welsh enterprise came to an abrupt end.

In more recent years the Benedictine community have refounded the ancient abbey at Landevennec. They still maintain links of friendship and prayer with Cardigan.

Religious communities of women also were forced out of France. In 1902, the Breton Congregation of the Daughters of the Holy Ghost came to Wales. They established houses at Abergavenny, Pontypool, Brecon, Carmarthen, Tenby, Aberystwyth, Monmouth, Caernarfon and Pwllheli. Their apostolate was the provision of schools and the formation of the young. At the same time as the Breton enterprise, Bishop Mostyn moved to set up a college to prepare young men for the priesthood in Wales. A Miss Sankey gave a large building which had been a bank, and some land near Holywell. In 1903, Fr Paul Edward Hook was seconded from the parish of Neath in the Newport Diocese and was given Denis Quigley, also of Newport and then a deacon at Oscott, as his assistant. Bishop Hedley could not demonstrate more practically his full commitment to the foundation of the college. St Mary's College, Holywell, was formally opened in the autumn term of 1904. It was to begin as a junior seminary 'in which students for the Welsh missions could get a thorough grounding in Welsh' as well as in all the usual subjects taught in such colleges. Francis Morley of Cambridge University was engaged in both 1905 and 1906 in reporting on standards. The bishops and Mgr Hook were determined the highest levels of study and academic achievement should be the aim of the new college.

In 1921, Fr Oswald Lofthouse, an alumnus of St Mary's, was appointed Rector.

Soon after, the College transferred to Castell Brychan overlooking Cardigan Bay at Aberystwyth. The students would study Welsh and other subjects at the University College of Wales in the town. In 1929 Fr Michael McGrath, future bishop and archbishop, took charge of the College. He was an able scholar and was soon much consulted by Welsh academics in the University College. He established a lifelong friendship with the poet and scholar Professor T. Gwynn Jones.

In 1934, the College was closed. Its students had not risen beyond eighteen, nor could the building house any more. In 1936, Michael McGrath was appointed Bishop of Menevia. One of his first public acts was to invite the Calced Carmelites of Whitefriars Street in Dublin to take over the parish of Aberystwyth and to reopen the College. Fr Malachy Lynch O CARM led the group of friars to begin the work. The teaching was carried out by Carmelite priests. Welsh and French were taught by the eminent scholar, man of letters and Catholic convert, Saunders Lewis. Because the building was small and possibilities of building expansion limited, the Carmelite fathers were on the lookout for a more spacious location. In 1947, they transferred St Mary's to the old recusant mansion of Tregyb near Llandeilo. St Mary's at Aberystwyth became a college for late vocations to the priesthood. In 1954, the Carmelites left Llandeilo to open Whitefriars School at Cheltenham. The dream of a Welsh college that would grow into a seminary for Wales had come to an end.

THE PROVINCE OF CARDIFF

More than once, Bishop Hedley referred to the creation of a second diocese in Wales. It had been a difficult decision for him and one promoted by Cardinal Vaughan. The Cardinal was convinced that Wales needed separate ecclesiastical provision, because of the nature of the country, because of the weakness of Catholicism there and 'because the Welsh people had a peculiar national character of their own'.[13] By English legal practice and in Roman documents, Wales consisted of twelve counties. In the discussions leading to the establishment of the Vicariate, Bishop Hedley had opposed the inclusion of Glamorgan in the new arrangement. However, he constantly thought about the consequences of the Cardinal's view which, in principle, he accepted. In a memorandum, he wrote that it was still right to exclude Glamorgan since it differs in many ways, not least in population and in Catholic presence, from the other Welsh counties:

> It is also to be observed that if it be the object to form Wales into one diocese, it would be a mistake to leave out Monmouthshire. Monmouthshire, in the character of its population as in its history, is absolutely as Welsh as

> Glamorgan or any of the counties of South Wales. The same may be said of a large portion of Herefordshire.[14]

In the light of all this, he suggested that 'the solution of the difficulty might perhaps be found in making the two dioceses into a Welsh province, with its Archbishop at Cardiff and Menevia as suffragan'.[15]

To make progress on this suggestion required the support of the Archbishop of Birmingham, since the Welsh dioceses had been suffragans of that metropolitan see since 1911. Archbishop Edward Ilsley took up the matter and petitioned Rome on the lines proposed by Hedley. On 11 November 1915, Bishop Hedley died after thirty-four years as Bishop of Newport and, prior to that, eight years as auxiliary to Bishop T. J. Brown.

On 7 February 1916, the apostolic letter *Cambria Celtica* was issued by Pope Benedict XV. The first paragraph reads:

> Wales, a nation of Celtic origin, differs so much from the rest of England in language, traditions, and ancient customs that it would seem in the ecclesiastical order also to call for separation from the other churches and for the possession of its own hierarchy.

Wales is still seen as a part of England and continued to be so regarded by the bishops of England and Wales. It was only when the statutes for the Conference of Bishops were amended by Rome to read 'the Hierarchies of England and Wales' that any argument about one or two hierarchies was brought to an end.

The new Archbishop was John Romanus Bilsborrow, a monk of Douai Abbey and Bishop of Port Louis in Mauritius. He had spent a short time in Maesteg before going to Port Louis in 1896. His brief period in Cardiff was largely concerned with the effects of the Great War on South Wales. As Archbishop, he did not enjoy good health and submitted his resignation in 1920. Bilsborrow quickly came to the view that the new province was not best served by always having a Benedictine as bishop. During his last year, the monastic diocesan chapter at Belmont was dissolved and a metropolitan chapter of secular clergy erected at Cardiff. *Cambria Celtica* had given the Archbishop of Cardiff 'two chapters, the one secular and the other regular, and two cathedral churches'. Francis Mostyn, Bishop of Menevia, was translated to Cardiff in March 1921. He continued to administer Menevia for another five years, an arrangement which he would happily have seen continued. In 1926, Rome appointed the parish priest of St Helen's, Barry, Francis John Vaughan, a son of Francis Baynham Vaughan of Courtfield, to be Bishop of Menevia.

In the years of the Great Depression, Archbishop Mostyn developed a policy for the industrial valleys of South Wales. There was no public transport on Sunday mornings and only a few could afford a bicycle. He therefore aimed to provide a church and, if possible, a resident priest, within walking distance of every Catholic home. He regarded that distance as about one and a half miles. He therefore tried to provide a church at intervals of three miles. With a strong presence of religious in the parishes and with a significant growth in vocations to the secular priesthood, many new centres were opened. Parish incomes in these places were small and priests shared the poverty of their people.

Francis Vaughan, nephew of Cardinal Vaughan, took over a diocese covering eleven counties and with an estimated 9,880 Catholics. During his ten years as bishop, the number of secular priests more than doubled. The Jesuits, at the Bishop's request, transferred the pastoral care of Holywell, St Asaph, Rhyl, Denbigh, Ruthin and Llandrindod Wells to the diocesan clergy in 1929.[16] On the death of Bishop Vaughan, Michael McGrath was appointed in 1935 Bishop of Menevia. Formerly a priest in the Clifton diocese, and a graduate in Celtic languages of the University of Ireland, he set out to master the spoken language of Wales. He liked to recall a hill farmer in Caernarfonshire who refused to help him as he did not want to be responsible for promoting the 'Popish religion'. Archbishop Mostyn died in 1939, just before the outbreak of the Second World War. He was succeeded by the transfer of Michael McGrath from the see of Menevia. Daniel Joseph Hannon, parish priest of Penarth, was appointed to Menevia.

Bishop Hannon witnessed an unusual period in the story of Catholicism in North Wales. Many children from Liverpool, Manchester and other large English cities were sent to Wales to avoid the bombing. They were often sent to monoglot Welsh communities where the children readily acquired the language of the area. In some places, the sheer numbers of evacuee children had the opposite effect. Priests from Liverpool parishes kept in touch with these children and out of this grew the movement Cyfeillion Cymru by which parishes in England took on a financial interest in struggling parishes in Wales.

Archbishop McGrath, on his arrival, found the financial situation of Cardiff to be perilous. The attempt to meet the needs of Catholics made by Archbishop Mostyn had used up most of the diocesan funds and had left many debts. Much of his period in Cardiff is remembered for the financial austerity that he and his assistant for financial affairs, Mgr Peter Gavin, had to impose. Not all the financial restrictions were the decisions of the Archbishop.

McGrath found the level of religious lapsation among the descendants of Irish immigrants quite alarming. He attributed some of this to the effects of divided religious affiliation in families. He introduced strict regulations for the granting of mixed marriage dispensations, rules that were sometimes applied even more strictly by the clergy. Archbishop McGrath was convinced that the descendants of immigrants needed to face up to the forces of history and cultural incorporation if Catholicism was to cease to be seen as a foreign church and one unfriendly to Welsh culture and aspirations. Though there were not the Catholic teachers to meet the situation, he agreed to the introduction of Welsh into the curriculum of Catholic schools and accepted that, in the short term at least, this would require taking on competent teachers who were not Catholic. He also tried to encourage priests to learn Welsh and hoped to see parishes in Welsh-speaking areas adopt the language in the churches. In trying to convince unco-operative Irish families at Maesteg to adopt this policy, he told them that he was not attempting the miracle of changing Irish into Welsh people. 'But', he said, 'what I cannot do, history will do to your children.'

When John Petit was appointed Bishop of Menevia in 1947, Wales was given a man of strong views and great determination. Looking at the experience of his predecessors, he quickly realised that most of the growth in the rural parts of the diocese was in fact the discovery of people who had been long established in places where Catholic life and practice simply did not exist. The Lamp Society had been founded by Clement Saunders in 1946. Its initial activity was to produce leaflets that could be given away freely. Bishop Petit saw it had another potential role in Wales. In 1949 he set up the Travelling Mission to take Mass to remote areas and isolated families. Clement Saunders's offer to sponsor a Travelling Mission was gratefully accepted. Fr Patrick Crowley, a native of Cardiff and a priest of Menevia diocese, was appointed the first travelling missioner. He was sent to the Mission House in London to study ways of making the motor mission a success. For health reasons, he was unable to develop the work. In 1950 Bishop Petit turned to the Redemptorists, who had a house at Machynlleth. Under them the apostolate was launched. In 1956 the Capuchins from Pantasaph joined the Travelling Mission. Archbishop John Aloysius Ward OFM CAP, the current Metropolitan, recalls how, as bishop, he met families whom he had first encountered as a travelling missionary. In 1977, Bishop Langton Fox, as Bishop of Menevia, decided that the aims of Bishop Petit, his predecessor, had been achieved and the once isolated families were now active members of an extended provision of parishes in rural Wales.[17]

Another apostolate of Bishop John Petit's life was the bringing of Catholic education to all parts of his diocese. To help fund the work, he appointed his Secretary, Fr Philip Webb, to establish and run the Richard Gwyn Society. Named after the schoolteacher and proto-martyr of Reformation Wales, the Society appealed throughout Britain and Ireland and across the world for regular donations to the Schools Fund. He then turned to the religious orders of nuns to provide schools and teaching staff. The school would start as a private school. Once it had established its effectiveness in accordance with government requirements, application would be made for voluntary aided status. This was often difficult and could be opposed by unsympathetic Local Education Authorities and Directors of Education. Perseverance and the obvious goodness and excellent standards of the nuns have changed the perception of Catholic education and indeed of Catholicism itself.

The social upheaval and widespread destruction caused by the Second World

War brought great changes in Wales, as elsewhere. In his final report to Rome written in the last year of his life, Archbishop McGrath pointed to the decay of Welsh Nonconformity and the concomitant undermining of the Welsh language as an indication of advancing secularisation in Welsh life. Though the Catholic Church had remained almost entirely on the fringes of Welsh culture and civilisation, it could not escape the influences that would radically alter the outlook of everyone in Wales.

John Aloysius Murphy, who was transferred from Shrewsbury Diocese to Cardiff as Archbishop in August 1961, was faced with many challenges. The large urban areas of Cardiff, Swansea and Newport had suffered in wartime bombing. These ports, which had depended on the export of coal and on trade with the New World, were now in decay. In the rebuilding of the cities, the population was moved to new housing estates and the close communities of pre-war days were being broken up and scattered. New churches and schools had to be provided, as the old centres were largely abandoned. Eight new centres were opened and some thirty-two new churches built throughout the diocese of Cardiff. Many of these replaced older church-halls or buildings in poor condition. Existing primary schools were either replaced or repaired. Ten new primary schools were provided and eleven new secondary schools opened. It was an astonishing achievement. Archbishop Murphy always paid tribute to his predecessor, whose careful husbanding of resources had made it all possible. It still required vision, energy and determination and the prudent use of available funding. It was only in the final years before Murphy's retirement that inflation began to undermine the ability of the diocese to finance these developments.

During the Second Vatican Council, Bishop Petit, because of ill-health, applied to Rome for an auxiliary bishop. Langton Fox, newly-appointed Rector of Wonersh seminary, was the person chosen. He and Bishop Petit met for the first time in Rome during the Council Session of 1965. On Bishop Petit's resignation in 1972, Bishop Fox was appointed his successor in the see of Menevia. Much of his time as diocesan bishop was overshadowed by continuing illness. The faith, patience and tranquillity with which he bore his increasing disability was to become a lasting legacy and a source of strength and inspiration to all the people of Wales. In his short period as bishop, Fox sought to continue and consolidate the expansion of parish and educational provision so vigorously pursued by Bishop Petit. He was especially concerned that the Church should respond positively to the challenge of the Second Vatican Council. He took active steps to establish consultative processes and pastoral involvement of all the people in the work and mission of the diocese. He was particularly anxious to promote ecumenical encounters and promoted joint conferences with the Anglican Church in Wales. His early leadership made full Catholic involvement in Cytun in 1990 an easy and natural step.

For both Welsh bishops, the Second Vatican Council was an experience which made them examine some of their fundamental convictions. For neither was it in any sense other than the Holy Spirit at work in the Church. The liturgical outlook and practice of the decree *Sacrosanctum Concilium* was implemented. This was not without difficulty among a people who saw the Church as always unchanging in its public liturgies as well as in its doctrine. In particular, the ecumenical outlook needed careful presentation to a Catholic community which had been formed by decades of discrimination and marginalisation.

Menevia diocese since 1897 had included most of Wales. The difficulties of travel between North and South had always been a problem. The differences between both parts of Wales, the result of history, geography and public administration, made the growth of a unified diocese unnecessarily difficult. These and other pastoral considerations led Archbishop Ward of Cardiff and Bishop James Hannigan of Menevia to petition Rome for the creation of a third Welsh diocese. By the decree *Fiducia Freti* of 12 February 1987, the whole of the Welsh Church was restructured. Menevia was restored to what was almost its historic territory, though the following of present-day civic boundaries led to a small expansion eastward to include Port Talbot. A new diocese of Wrexham was created and the Archdiocese of Cardiff ceded the county of West Glamorgan to Menevia. The challenge to the Church was very clear. The evangelisation of Wales so strongly promoted by St David and his contemporaries was again to be the all-embracing need as a secularised Wales faced the third Christian millennium.

PROVIDING SCHOOLS

In 1866, Bishop Thomas Joseph Brown devoted his Lenten Pastoral to a review of developments since the setting up of the Welsh Vicariate 'at the not remote close of our prolonged administration'.[18] With gratitude and some pride he recounted a growth from 'such original desolation as we found' to what he could now describe as 'comparative prosperity'. In Lent 1881, Bishop John Cuthbert Hedley wrote in his first Pastoral Letter:

> It must be said, that in some respects, [the diocese] is worse, in spiritual matters, than it was twenty years ago . . . Churches have multiplied, but the younger people do not fill them: schools have sprung up everywhere, but the children who go out from them are, in too large a proportion, lost to us when we lose sight of them.

Already he was noting a fact which was to concern all the bishops in the last decades of the nineteenth century. Working people were becoming alienated from the churches.

Developments in the second half of the last century in Wales cannot be understood without reference to the Government Report *On the State of Education in Wales* issued in 1847. The reaction in Wales to what is still remembered as *Brad y Llyfrau Gleision,* (the treachery of the Blue Books) affected every aspect of life. The Report painted a damning picture of an illiterate and immoral people condemned to destitution because of their language and religion. The Report was commissioned following the Chartist march on Newport and the Rebecca Riots especially but not only in Carmarthenshire. Welsh Nonconformity responded by preaching and writing on the distinguishing characteristics of the Welsh nation – purity of morals and peaceful acceptance of the status quo in civil and social administration. The Welsh people should not be thought to be like the rebellious Irish.

This public consciousness had two effects. Catholics, who were predominantly Irish, were despised and to be avoided. It also meant that the churches and chapels were very wary of the beginnings of the trade union movement in the iron works and in the coalmines. The owners could count on the tacit support of organised religion in its struggles with the workers. For the Irish workers, a further complication arose. One of the effective ways of defeating strikers was to bring labour into the country. A constant source for these new workers was Ireland. This was to put enmity between those who came at the time of the Famine or earlier, and the later arrivals. The beginnings of what has been called the apostasy of the working class were already becoming apparent.

The Church has traditionally seen the provision of education as the antidote to such developments. From 1850 until the turn of the century, the provision of a mission school was seen as the first need. In a letter to the Commissioners, printed in full in the Report of 1847, Fr Patrick Millea of Cardiff speaks of the school building at that time being prepared and of the education provided:

> Up to this time we have no regular system laid down for the instructing; arithmetic, English, grammar, reading, writing etc. were the principal things in which the children were instructed. The class-books I introduced into the school a few years past were those used in the National Schools in Ireland; but for the last two years we used the class-books belonging to the Brothers of the Christian Schools, with the history of the Old and New Testament.

There is some evidence of attempts to set up schools for the children of Catholics even in the most difficult times. Bishop Brown could say, however, that when he came to the Welsh District 'there was not a single schoolroom fit for its purpose' in the whole of South Wales. The setting up of the Catholic Poor-School Committee in 1847 was to be of great significance for an area as poor as Wales. The generosity of the established Catholic families provided schools at Llanarth, Courtfield, Rotherwas, Broxwood and Belmont.[19] The converts Captain Illtyd Nicholl and Viscount Fielding provided schools at Bridgend and Pantasaph respectively. All others depended on the financial support of the Committee. Through its help school-chapels were erected in many places.

The provision of buildings did not solve the educational problem. For many parents, even the modest contribution asked for proved to be too much. Nor were the parents convinced that anything more than the ability to sign their names and simple addition and subtraction would be of benefit to their children. Fr Millea, in the letter already quoted, asked that there should be 'a well-digested system of education by which every poor man's child could benefit without scruple', that it should be free and that there should be 'a clause compelling the parents to send their children'. There was also the need to have adequately trained teachers for the schools.

Following their arrival in Newport in June 1847, the Fathers of Charity looked to the provision of schools. In August of that year, St Mary's School was opened with Bro. Spencer teaching the boys. Early the following year the Sisters of Providence took on the teaching of the girls. Following the introduction of compulsory education in 1870, the Rosminian priests sought the assistance of the Sisters of St Joseph of Annécy. The Sisters of Providence did not teach boys and so the amalgamation of schools was not possible. The Sisters of St Joseph, who had come to England from India, moved to Newport in 1873. They remain an important part of Catholic life in the Archdiocese of Cardiff.

In 1860 Bishop Brown welcomed the Ursulines of Jesus to Swansea. They too came to provide teachers for the poor Catholic children. Their early letters to the mother-house at Chavagne show the surprise of these French sisters at the poverty, poor hygiene and rough language of the Irish children.[20] Like the other orders who came to Wales, they were needed because neither the bishop nor the parishes could afford more than very uncertain modest salaries. In the ports and industrial towns, living conditions could be very primitive even when accommodation could be found. Wales was not attractive to lay teachers.

The aim in all the mission centres was to have a school for the younger children. Because of the poverty of their parents, children went to work as soon as any wage could be earned; however small, it contributed to the support of the younger children. The Carmelites, during their short period at Merthyr (1864–78), set up an academy 'for the education of the sons of artisans'. St Joseph's Grammar School was started in 1867 by Rosminian brothers – for boys and girls. The Sisters of St Joseph of Annécy in 1875 made Newport the base for their Province. In their convent on Stow Hill, they already had a private school with twenty-eight girls as boarders. In 1876, at the instigation of the Auxiliary, Bishop Hedley, the Ursulines of Jesus bought a house in Swansea, in order to open a private day school. The new convent was named St Winefride's. The school was to become the highly valued St Winefride's Day and Boarding School for Girls.

A 'high class girls' school' was opened at Roath in Cardiff in 1878. The Sisters of Providence were installed to staff and run the school. This later became Heathfield House Grammar School for girls. A Grammar School for Boys run by the De La Salle Brothers was opened at Splott in Cardiff in 1922. St Illtyd's College was to have an important role in the fostering of vocations to the priesthood and preparing Catholic boys for entry to the various professions.

A widespread provision of secondary education in Wales was slow to come. In the archdiocese of Cardiff, the building programme was promoted with vigour by Archbishop Murphy and a network of such schools was provided across the diocese. In the same period, many new primary schools were built.

In the diocese of Menevia, the scattered population made secondary school provision more difficult. It was possible to do so only in Llanelli and in the populous centres of the North-East, at Wrexham, Rhyl and Flint. It was at the initiative of Bishop Langton Fox that St John Lloyd School at Llanelli became a joint Catholic/Church in Wales enterprise. A proposed similar joint Secondary School at Haverfordwest was not realised.

More recent times have witnessed a weakening of the commitment of parents to Catholic education. Many still remember when parents sent their children considerable distances to the nearest Catholic school. Local Education Authorities were not always sympathetic and considerable financial sacrifices were accepted by families and parishes. More opulent times have brought changing values and ideals.

The contribution of the religious orders of women does not always get due recognition. Many of them were asked to take on the work of teaching. The cost of providing buildings and the funding of teachers' salaries devolved very largely on the parishes. The management of schools and the paying of the teachers had to be organised by the parish priests. This meant that salaries were low and not always certain. The orders of nuns accepted these conditions precisely because they saw themselves as missionaries. This has been just as true of the communities who opened schools in Menevia in the second half of the twentieth century as it had been in the times of Bishops Brown and Hedley in the diocese of Newport and Menevia.

The work of the Sisters throughout Wales and in every other place is largely unrecorded. Their contribution to the spread of new mission centres is still remembered by the people. They established contact with poor families, brought them and their children many small delicacies and gifts. They instructed the children and laid the foundation of many subsequent parishes. An old lady in Ystradgynlais, in remembering the visits of the Sisters in her childhood, summed up what the Sisters meant to her by saying: 'It is lovely to be a Catholic.'

NOTES

1. The county of Hereford was included in the new District in 1840. It remains part of the Archdiocese of Cardiff. It is neither possible nor sensible to exclude Hereford from this account of Catholicism in Wales.

2. G. Jones and D. Williams (eds), *The Religious Census of 1851* (Cardiff, 1977, 1981).
3. *St Peter's Magazine*, 1927.
4. *Letters and Notices*, No. 1, June 1862.
5. Ibid.
6. Fr Elzear became Bishop of Armidale in Australia in 1879.
7. Patricia Spencer-Silver, *Pugin's Builder* (Hull University Press, 1993), p. 67.
8. Francis Edwards SJ, *The Jesuits in England*, pp. 185–6.
9. G. M. Lynch, 'The Revival of Roman Catholicism in South Wales in the Late Eighteenth and Early Nineteenth Centuries' (unpublished MA thesis, University of Wales, Cardiff), pp. 158–9.
10. T. A. Wilson, *The Life of Bishop Hedley* (London, 1930).
11. D. Attwater, *The Catholic Church in Modern Wales* (London, 1935), p. 125.
12. Dom A. P. Wilson in the *Tablet*, March 1867.
13. Wilson, *Hedley*, pp. 137f.
14. Wilson, *Hedley*, p. 137.
15. Ibid.
16. Edwards, *Jesuits in England*, p. 235.
17. For the story of the Lamp Society and its role in the Travelling Mission cf. Christopher Magner, *The Lamp Society and the Welsh Travelling Mission* (published privately, 1997).
18. Bishop Brown was already considering retirement.
19. *Pastoral Letter*, 1869.
20. 'What hurts us most is the lack of care on the part of the parents . . . They will not send their children to school because they do not want the bother of washing and cleaning them' (Letter of 30 December 1861).

TWELVE

THE CATHOLIC LITERARY REVIVAL

JOSEPH PEARCE

> A great change, an awful contrast, between the time-honoured Church of St Augustine and St Thomas, and the poor remnant of their children in the beginning of the nineteenth century! It was a miracle, I might say, to have pulled down that lordly power, but there was a greater and a truer one in store. No one could have prophesied its fall, but still less would anyone have ventured to prophesy its rise again . . . The inspired word seems to imply the almost impossibility of such a grace as the renovation of those who have crucified to themselves again, and trodden underfoot, the Son of God. Who then could have dared to hope that, out of so sacrilegious a nation as this, a people would have been formed again unto their Saviour?[1]

With these words of characteristic eloquence John Henry Newman described the re-establishment of the Catholic hierarchy in England in 1850. A relative newcomer to the Church, having been received scarcely five years earlier, Newman was already a leading figure in English Catholicism by 1850 and was the effective instigator of the Catholic literary revival, the beginnings of which coincided almost exactly with the hierarchy's re-establishment. Ironically, *Anglican Difficulties*, the title given to a series of Newman's lectures published in the same year, pinpoints the central difficulty at the heart of any discussion of Catholic literature over the following century and a half. There are 'Anglican difficulties' in any such discussion because of the essentially Catholic nature of the work of some writers who belong to the Anglo-Catholic tradition in the Church of England. This tradition was responsible for the largely orthodox writing of, among others, Christina Rossetti, Dorothy L. Sayers and, most notably of all, T. S. Eliot. To what extent are these Anglo-Catholic writers to be included in any discussion of the Catholic literary revival? These problems of delineation are further exacerbated by a comparison between the orthodoxy of these writers and the relative heterodoxy of the works of Graham Greene. There is little doubt that Eliot would have considered himself a Catholic writer whereas Greene was often at pains to deny the Catholicism of his own work. Indeed, during the course of his last interview, Greene reiterated his oft-repeated disclaimer that he was 'not a Catholic writer' but 'a writer who happens to be a Catholic'.[2]

Another difficulty arises out of the anomalous position of the work of converts to Catholicism prior to their conversion. Most notably, perhaps, is the case of G. K. Chesterton, who wrote much of his best work prior to his conversion in 1922. Few would deny that Chesterton's *Orthodoxy* was primarily Catholic in nature yet it was written in 1908, fourteen years before his belated reception into the Church. Similarly, Siegfried Sassoon was a septuagenarian when he was finally received into the Church in 1957, yet much of his poetry, dating as far back as the First World War, pointed prophetically to an act of faith that he would take a further forty years to make.

It is the contention of the present writer that the substantial body of work of all these literary figures can be classified as 'Catholic' in so far as they represent an orthodox Christian response to the cynicism and materialism of the age. The underlying unity which is present, consciously or otherwise, in the literary achievement of these and many other Christian writers was summarised by T. S. Eliot in his *Notes Towards the Definition of Culture*, most particularly in his

> last appeal . . . to the men of letters of Europe, who have a special responsibility for the preservation and transmission of our common culture . . . We can at least try to save something of those goods of which we are the common trustees: the legacy of Greece, Rome and Israel, and the legacy of Europe throughout 2,000 years. In a world which has seen such material devastation as ours, these spiritual possessions are also in imminent peril.[3]

The unity was also present in the striking similarities in approach between Eliot and Newman. Compare, for instance, Newman's assertion that intellectual education was pre-eminently a discipline in accuracy of mind with Eliot's attack on the utilitarianism of modern education:

> The universities of Europe . . . should not be institutions for the training of an efficient bureaucracy, or for equipping scientists to get the better of foreign scientists; they should stand for the preservation of learning, for the pursuit of truth, and in so far as men are capable of it, the attainment of wisdom.[4]

It is clear that Newman and Eliot applied the same criteria to the practice of the arts so that their own literary achievement and that of the other leading protagonists of the Catholic literary revival should be judged appropriately. According to this view, the beauty of great literature resided in its being an expression of a common culture which was itself the fruit of the preservation of learning, the pursuit of truth and the attainment of wisdom. The highest function of art, therefore, was to express the highest common factors of human life and not the lowest common denominators; life's loves and not its lusts. This was the animus at the very core of the revival heralded by Newman.

THE EARLY CATHOLIC LITERARY REVIVAL

The critic George Levine has described Newman as 'perhaps the most artful and brilliant prose writer of the nineteenth century', but he added that this, of itself, was no guarantee of popularity: 'It is difficult to be popular when one insists on probing to the heart and on questioning all of the most popular and important moral and religious prejudices.'[5] Although Newman's highly controversial conversion did little to enhance his popularity it did inspire some of his most brilliant prose. His first novel, *Loss and Gain*, was a fictionalised semi-autobiographical account of a young man's search for faith amid the scepticism and uncertainties of early Victorian Oxford. It remains one of the classic Victorian novels. The novelist Mrs Humphry Ward later claimed that it was one of the works to which 'the future student of the nineteenth century will have to look for what is deepest, most intimate, and most real in its personal experience'.[6] It was published in 1848, three years after Newman's conversion, and the same spirit that pervaded its pages was present the following year in many of the *Sermons addressed to Mixed Congregations*, most notably perhaps in the assertion that there was no logical alternative between Catholicism and scepticism:

> . . . Turn away from the Catholic Church, and to whom will you go? it is your only chance of peace and assurance in this turbulent, changing world. There is nothing between it and scepticism, when men exert their reason freely. Private creeds, fancy religions, may be showy and imposing to the many in their day; national religions may lie huge and lifeless, and cumber the ground for centuries, and distract the attention or confuse the judgment of the learned; but on the long run it will be found that either the Catholic Religion is verily and indeed the coming in of the unseen world into this, or that there is nothing positive, nothing dogmatic, nothing real in any one of our notions as to whence we come and whither we are going. Unlearn Catholicism, and you become Protestant, Unitarian, Deist, Pantheist, Sceptic, in a dreadful, but infallible succession . . .[7]

In 1855, Newman's historical novel, *Callista: A Sketch of the Third Century*, was published. Although the setting had changed drastically, the same perennial questions confronted the characters of the third century as had beset Charles Reding, the youthful hero of *Loss and Gain*, sixteen centuries later. Agellius, a

Christian, endeavoured in vain to convince his sceptical uncle of the claims of the Church:

> 'O Jucundus,' cried Agellius, irritated at his own inability to express himself or hold an argument, 'if you did but know what it was to have the Truth! The Christian has found the Truth, the eternal Truth, in a world of error. That is his bargain, that is his hire; can there be a greater? Can I give up the Truth? . . .'

Jucundus's reply, echoing the words of Pilate more than two hundred years earlier and modern sceptics many hundreds of years later, was characterised by incredulity:

> 'The Truth!' he cried, '*this* is what I understand you to say, – the truth. The *truth* is your bargain; I think I'm right, the truth. Hm; what is truth? What in heaven and earth do you mean by truth? where did you get that cant? What oriental tomfoolery is bamboozling you? The truth!' he cried, staring at him, half of triumph, half of impatience, 'the truth! Jove help the boy! – the truth! can truth pour me out a cup of melilotus? can truth crown me with flowers? can it sing to me? can it bring Glyceris to me? drop gold in my girdle? or cool my brows when fever visits me? Can truth give me a handsome suburban with some five hundred slaves, or raise me to the duumvirate? Let it do this, and I will worship it; it shall be my god; it shall be more to me than Fortune, Fate, Rome, or any other goddess on the list. But *I* like to see, and touch, and feel, and handle, and weigh, and measure what is promised me. I wish to have a sample and an instalment. I am too old for chaff. Eat, drink, and be merry, that's my philosophy, that's my religion; and I know no better. Today is ours, tomorrow is our children's.'[8]

A similar novel, *Fabiola: A Tale of the Catacombs*, had been published the previous year by Cardinal Wiseman, who was somewhat less subtle than Newman in his use of the fictional medium for propaganda purposes:

> We need not remind our readers, that the office then performed was essentially, and in many details, the same as the daily witness at the Catholic altar. Not only was it considered, as now, to be the Sacrifice of Our Lord's Body and Blood, not only were the oblation, the consecration, the communion alike, but many of the prayers were identical; so that the Catholic hearing them recited, and still more the priest reciting them, in the same language as the Roman Church of the catacombs spoke, may feel himself in active and living communion with the martyrs who celebrated, and the martyrs who assisted at, those sublime mysteries.[9]

Whereas *Fabiola* remains Cardinal Wiseman's best-known work, much of Newman's finest work was still to come. His *Apologia*, first published in 1865, remains probably the finest exposition of a religious conversion ever written in the English language. Its candour and clarity of vision won over many who had previously been hostile to Catholicism and perhaps no book published since has been quite so instrumental in the popularising of the Catholic faith in England. In the same year he wrote his most accomplished and most beautiful poem, *The Dream of Gerontius*, a vision of the afterlife in the tradition of Dante, which was later to be set to music in an oratorio by Elgar. His *Grammar of Assent* on the philosophy of faith was published in 1870 and *Verses on Various Occasions*, published four years later, confirmed his reputation as one of the greatest of Victorian poets. Almost single-handedly Newman's genius had set the seal of respectability on a revitalised English Catholicism, and the quality of his literary output had set the standard that future generations of Catholic writers would seek to emulate.

Even as Newman was blazing a trail across the literary landscape of Victorian England, an unknown convert who had been received into the Church by Newman himself in 1866 was writing verse that would remain unnoticed and unpublished during his own lifetime. The poetry of Gerard Manley Hopkins was destined to become more popular and influential than the verse of almost any poet of his generation, but not until forty years after his death. It is a much overused cliché to say that a writer or artist is 'ahead of his time', but there are few to whom it can be applied more truly than is the case with Hopkins. His friend Coventry Patmore probably summed up the Victorian attitude to Hopkins's experimental approach when he confessed his critical reservations to Robert Bridges: 'To me his poetry has the effect of veins of pure gold imbedded in masses of unpracticable quartz.'[10] It was not until the 1920s, after 'difficult' and experimental poetry had become fashionable, that Hopkins's verse gained both critical acclaim and widespread acceptance. Since T. S. Eliot was the poet most responsible for popularising the poetic avant garde one might have expected him to be one of Hopkins's most vocal champions. It is surprising, therefore, that he is less than enthusiastic:

> Hopkins is not a religious poet in the more important sense in which I have elsewhere maintained Baudelaire to be a religious poet; or in the sense in which I find Villon to be a religious poet; or in the sense in which I consider Mr Joyce's work to be penetrated with Christian feeling. I do not wish to depreciate him, but to affirm limitations and distinctions. He should be compared, not with our contemporaries whose situation is different from his, but with the minor poet nearest contemporary to him, and most like him: George Meredith. The comparison is altogether to Hopkins's advantage . . . where Meredith . . . has only a rather cheap and shallow 'philosophy of life' to offer, Hopkins has the dignity of the Church behind him, and is consequently in closer contact with reality. But from the struggle

> of our time to concentrate, not to dissipate; to renew our association with traditional wisdom; to re-establish a vital connexion between the individual and the race; the struggle, in a word, against Liberalism: from all this Hopkins is a little apart, and in this Hopkins has very little aid to offer us.[11]

There is something almost patronising in Eliot's criticism and one is tempted to see an element of professional jealousy in his words. They were written in 1933 when Hopkins was at the very height of his fashionable popularity and when he was being lauded by many as the greatest of 'modern' poets, a position which popular critical opinion had bestowed on Eliot during the previous decade. Yet, whatever the motives behind his criticism, Eliot's appraisal fell far short of the perceptive qualities that permeated most of his critical essays. Most notable was his failure to appreciate the depths of orthodox Christian philosophy which underpinned Hopkins's work. Eliot was fully conversant with the neo-Thomism which was in the ascendancy during the early decades of the twentieth century, so it is curious that he failed to recognise the omnipresence of scholastic philosophy in Hopkins's verse. Following his conversion, Hopkins had decided to become a Jesuit priest, a fact which shaped his poetic vision to a profound extent. As a direct result of the rigours of his Jesuit training he became thoroughly conversant with the philosophy of Duns Scotus and St Thomas Aquinas. This shaped his notion of *inscape*, the central concept at the heart of all his poetry, which was itself a reflection of the teaching of Duns Scotus that everything in creation has a unique spiritual identity, its *haecceitas* or 'thisness'. Consequently, every student of Hopkins's verse needs to come to terms with this orthodox philosophical precept in order fully to comprehend his poetry. In spite of Eliot's claims to the contrary, this is Hopkins's lasting legacy and his contribution to the need in every generation 'to renew our association with traditional wisdom'.

Although Hopkins remained unknown as a poet until the 1920s, he was not wholly without influence during his own lifetime. As well as being a close friend of Robert Bridges, his critical judgement was greatly valued by Coventry Patmore. On one occasion Patmore actually burned one of his own manuscripts after it had been criticised by Hopkins. Following Hopkins's death in 1889, Patmore wrote the following words of tribute in a letter to Bridges:

> I can well understand how terrible a loss you have suffered in the death of Gerard Hopkins – you who saw so much more of him than I did . . . Gerard Hopkins was the only orthodox, and as far as I could see, saintly man in whom religion had absolutely no narrowing effect upon his general opinions and sympathies. A Catholic of the most scrupulous strictness, he could nevertheless see the Holy Spirit in all goodness, truth and beauty; and there was something in all his words and manners which were at once a rebuke and an attraction to all who could only aspire to be like him.[12]

Although Patmore enjoyed the critical acclaim that eluded Hopkins during his lifetime, it would be fair to say that his verse does not reach the sublime heights which Hopkins achieves in his greatest poems. Yet Patmore's finest poetry, which followed the death of his first wife in 1862 and his conversion to Roman Catholicism two years later, almost justifies Sir Herbert Read's judgement that much of his verse represents 'true poetry of the rarest and perhaps the highest kind'.

Perhaps Patmore's greatest champion in the final decades of the nineteenth century was Alice Meynell, herself a poet of some merit, who published popular anthologies of his verse. Together with her husband, Wilfrid Meynell, she edited several periodicals which were highly influential and which were instrumental in popularising other Catholic writers, of whom the most notable was Francis Thompson. The energy and enthusiasm which the Meynells displayed in their tireless promotion of the Catholic literati in late Victorian and Edwardian England helped to oil the wheels of, and give momentum to, the Catholic literary revival as it entered the twentieth century. This was a role which was taken up with equal vigour by Frank Sheed and Maisie Ward in the years between the two World Wars. Nonetheless, the Meynells' greatest gift to posterity was their responsibility for the rescue and rehabilitation of Francis Thompson from a life of poverty and opium addiction on the streets of post-Dickensian London. Without their timely intervention it is likely that Thompson would have died in wretched obscurity, without ever writing much of the poetry that has secured his place alongside Hopkins as the greatest Christian poet of the Victorian era. Three volumes of his poetry were published by the Meynells between 1893 and 1897 to immediate critical acclaim.

Through the Meynells, Thompson got to know the ageing Patmore shortly before the latter's death in 1896 and there are hints of Patmore's influence in some of Thompson's work. The most obvious example of this can be seen in a comparison between Patmore's greatest poem, 'The Toys', and Thompson's 'Love and the Child', both of which employ observations of a parent–child relationship as a metaphor for the relationship of man with God. There is also a remarkable affinity between Thompson's mystical vision of nature and Hopkins's notion of the intrinsic beauty, through *inscape*, of all created things. Thompson could not have been aware of Hopkins's work, of course, but the coincidental depth of affinity is clearly discernible, most notably in Thompson's 'To a Snowflake':

What heart could have thought you? –
Past our devisal
(O filigree petal!)
Fashioned so purely,
Fragilely, surely,
From what Paradisal

Imagineless metal,
Too costly for cost?
Who hammered you, wrought you,
From argentine vapour? –
'God was my shaper.
Passing surmisal,
He hammered, He wrought me,
From curled silver vapour,
To lust of His mind: –
Thou could'st not have thought me!
So purely, so palely,
Tinily, surely,
Mightily, frailly,
Insculped and embossed,
With His hammer of wind,
And His graver of frost.'[13]

One also senses an affinity in such poems with the philosophy of gratitude that characterised so much of the writing of G. K. Chesterton a few years later. It is not too fanciful to imagine that Chesterton had read Thompson's poetry when it was first published in the 1890s and, if he had done so, he would most certainly have recognised in Thompson a kindred spirit. During the years that Thompson's verse was gaining widespread recognition the young Chesterton was passing out of the period of adolescent doubt and despondency which had overshadowed his time as a student at the Slade School of Art. Writing of this period in his *Autobiography* Chesterton referred to a time 'full of doubts and morbidities and temptations; and which, though in my case mainly subjective, has left in my mind for ever a certitude upon the objective solidity of Sin'.[14] Chesterton conceded that his morbidity 'may have been due to the atmosphere of the Decadents, and their perpetual hints of the luxurious horrors of paganism' that prevailed at the Slade School of Art in the 'naughty nineties':

> . . . anyhow, it is true that there was a time when I had reached the condition of moral anarchy within, in which a man says, in the words of Wilde, that 'Atys with the blood-stained knife were better than the thing I am.' I have never indeed felt the faintest temptation to the particular madness of Wilde; but I could at this time imagine the worst and wildest disproportions and distortions of more normal passion.[15]

Perhaps it was scarcely surprising that Chesterton should have mentioned Wilde in relation to the atmosphere of decadence that prevailed at the Slade, especially as Wilde's ill-advised and abortive libel action against the Marquess of Queensbury was making the headlines in 1895 while Chesterton was still studying there. Like Francis Thompson, Wilde came to Christ and the Church via desolation and even today, a hundred years after his death, he remains a controversial figure. Indeed, such are the moral somersaults that society has performed in the century since his death that he is now vindicated for the very things for which he was vilified. Sadly, Wilde is as misunderstood today as he was in his own day, especially as the central theme of his late works has precious little to do with the role of 'sexual liberator' which posterity has thrust upon him, and everything to do with the Christian penitent seeking forgiveness. Wilde's 'heart of stone' was broken by the experience of the two-year prison sentence imposed in the wake of the libel trial and his two greatest works, *The Ballad of Reading Gaol* and the posthumously published *De Profundis*, bear witness to his eleventh-hour conversion to Catholicism. Three weeks before his death he told a *Daily Chronicle* correspondent that 'much of my moral obliquity is due to the fact that my father would not allow me to become a Catholic. The artistic side of the Church and the fragrance of its teaching would have cured my degeneracies. I intend to be received before long.'[16] In the event he was received on his deathbed.

It is indeed ironic that Wilde is only remembered for the tragedy of his life and not for its happy ending. His last will and testament remains, however, in the brilliance of *The Ballad of Reading Gaol*, a poem which bears a remarkable similarity to Thompson's masterpiece *The Hound of Heaven* in its description of the triumph of Christ through the suffering and desolation of a mis-spent life:

And thus we rust Life's iron chain,
    Degraded and alone:
And some men curse, and some men weep,
    And some men make no moan:
But God's eternal Laws are kind
    And break the heart of stone.

And every human heart that breaks,
    In prison-cell or yard,
Is as that broken box that gave
    Its treasure to the Lord,
And filled the unclean leper's house
    With the scent of costliest nard.

Ah! happy they whose hearts can break
    And peace of pardon win!
How else may man make straight his plan
    And cleanse his soul from Sin?
How else but through a broken heart
    May Lord Christ enter in?

One of the most important influences upon Wilde's descent into decadence and his subsequent repentance and conversion was the example of the French novelist Joris-Karl Huysmans. When Huysmans's *A Rebours* was published in the 1880s, its devil-worshipping mysticism was hailed as the ultimate guide to a libertine lifestyle by his decadent disciples. Wilde was one of Huysmans's most devoted followers and the influence of *A Rebours* was evident in Wilde's *A Picture of Dorian Gray*. The early indications of Huysmans's change of heart came with the publication of *Là-Bas* in 1891, in which he is simultaneously both morbidly fascinated with, and revolted by, Satanic mysticism. A year later, Huysmans professed his reconciliation with the Roman Catholic Church in his autobiography, *En Route*. This dramatic return to Christianity appears to have affected Wilde also and when, in 1898, he was informed that Huysmans had entered a monastery he responded approvingly.

Maurice Baring was another writer whose conversion to Catholicism was influenced, at least in part, by Huysmans's *En Route*. In the early years of the twentieth century, when Baring was grappling with the tenets of Christianity, the line of reasoning in Huysmans's autobiography struck him very forcefully. It was, however, another Frenchman who would have the greatest influence on Baring's conversion. In 1898 he had met Hilaire Belloc for the first time and the two men formed a friendship which would last the rest of their lives. Two years later Belloc and Chesterton met for the first time in a restaurant in Soho and, through Belloc, Chesterton became friends with Baring several years later. The friendship of these three men would later be immortalised in Sir James Gunn's group portrait which can still be seen in the National Portrait Gallery. Belloc, Baring and Chesterton, both singularly and collectively, represented the dominant force in Catholic literary circles throughout the first third of the twentieth century. Baring is the least known of the three and his own literary achievement is sadly neglected today. His *Collected Poems*, published in 1925, included many of considerable merit, most notably the sonnet sequence, *Vita Nuova*, written to commemorate his reception into the Church in 1909. Yet he was known principally as a novelist. His first novel, *Passing By*, was published in 1921 when he was already almost fifty years old and his last was published fifteen years later when his literary vocation was tragically cut short by the debilitating effects of Parkinson's disease. In between he commanded a small but passionate readership and enjoyed much critical acclaim. *C*, published in 1924, was highly praised by the French novelist André Maurois, who wrote that no book had given him such pleasure since his reading of Tolstoy, Proust and certain novels by E. M. Foster.[17] If anything, Baring was to enjoy greater success in France than in England with ten of his books translated into French, with one – *Daphne Adeane* – going through twenty-three printings in the edition of the Librairie Stock. Others were translated into Italian, Dutch, Swedish, Hungarian, Czech, Spanish and German. *Cat's Cradle*, published in 1925, was considered by Belloc 'a great masterpiece . . . the best story of a woman's life that I know'.[18] Belloc also admired *Robert Peckham*, Baring's historical saga which is so reminiscent of R. H. Benson's historical novels. 'The style,' Belloc wrote,

> which is characteristically yours, is even better in *Robert Peckham* than in any of the other books . . . Where you triumph unusually is in the exact valuation of characters which do not differ in black and white, but in every shade. You do it better in this book, I think, than in any other, even than in *Cat's Cradle* . . . It seems to me to have a more permanent quality than any other . . . All those who count will unite in its praise, except those who do not feel a subtle thing at the first shock.[19]

Not surprisingly, Chesterton shared Belloc's admiration for Baring's work. Writing to Baring in 1929, shortly after Baring's novel *The Coat Without Seam* had been published, Chesterton announced that he had been 'much uplifted' by his friend's latest book:

> It is, as you say, extraordinary how the outer world can see everything about it except the point. It is curiously so with much of the very good Catholic work now being done in literature, especially in France . . . But there are plenty of people who will appreciate anything as good as *The Coat Without Seam*.[20]

Others failed to share Chesterton's and Belloc's enthusiasm and Virginia Woolf, taking the opposite view, attacked what she perceived as Baring's 'superficiality'. Baring found such criticism frustrating, especially as he believed the failure to understand his work was due itself to a superficiality:

> It is utterly futile to write about the Christian faith from the outside. A good example of this is the extremely conscientious novel by Mrs Humphry Ward called *Helbeck of Bannisdale*. It is a study of Catholicism from the outside, and the author has taken scrupulous pains to make it accurate, detailed and exhaustive. The only drawback is that, not being able to see the matter from the inside, she misses the whole point.[21]

Largely neglected and misunderstood in England, Baring gained solace once again from the empathy exhibited by a more discerning readership across the Channel. In particular, he was 'too moved to speak' when, six months before his death in 1945, he learned of the deep admiration that François Mauriac had for his novels. Mauriac had told the Catholic actor Robert Speaight: 'What I admire most about Baring's work is the sense he gives you of the penetration of grace.'[22]

Perhaps the profundity at the heart of Baring's fiction was encapsulated in the words of one of the characters from *Darby and Joan*, his last novel:

> 'One has to *accept* sorrow for it to be of any healing power, and that is the most difficult thing in the world . . . A Priest once said to me, "When you understand what *accepted* sorrow means, you will understand everything. It is the secret of life".'

These words, which for Virginia Woolf and others represented Baring's 'superficiality', were at once both mystical and practical, so practical that Baring put them into practice, accepting his own debilitating illness with a contrite and heroic heart. In 1941, the year in which Virginia Woolf took her own life in an act of despair, Baring answered his earlier complaint that his body was 'a broken toy which nobody can mend' with the reply that his soul was 'an immortal toy which nobody can mar'.

Baring's obituary in *The Times* on 17 December 1945 regretted that 'many English readers' saw his novels as 'a form of Roman Catholic propaganda' but maintained that he was 'above all concerned to express a passionate conviction that belief in God can alone bring storm-tossed humanity into harbour'. After referring to Baring's 'friendship with the late G. K. Chesterton, and with Mr Hilaire Belloc', the obituary concluded with an assessment of Baring's literary legacy: 'Concerning his final position in literature, time may perhaps confirm the judgment of those who see in him one of the subtlest, profoundest, and most original of recent English writers.'

THE AGE OF CHESTERTON

Of the three friends, Chesterton was the most popular but, like Baring, also suffered from the public perception that his work was intended as Roman Catholic propaganda. Indeed, Chesterton would hardly have denied the charge. Works such as *Orthodoxy, The Everlasting Man, The Catholic Church and Conversion, The Thing* and *The Well and the Shallows* were unashamedly intended as expositions of Catholic Christianity. Yet this should not detract from his tremendous literary achievement. His verse was often uneven and suffered from a slapdash approach to composition but, at its best, is among the finest written this century. 'Lepanto' and 'The Secret People' represent narrative historical verse at its greatest while 'The Rolling English Road' displays that rumbustious *joie de vivre* which caused H. G. Wells to complain that Chesterton and Belloc had managed to surround Catholicism in 'a kind of boozy halo'.[23] *The Ballad of the White Horse* captured the imagination of a whole generation and influenced some of the century's greatest writers. John Galsworthy, C. S. Lewis and J. R. R. Tolkien were among its admirers, although Tolkien later became more critical of its undoubted flaws. It was also one of Graham Greene's favourite poems. In an interview published in the *Observer* on 12 March 1978 Greene called Chesterton 'another under-estimated poet'. To illustrate the point he cited the *Ballad*: 'Put *The Ballad of the White Horse* against *The Waste Land*. If I had to lose one of them, I'm not sure that . . . well, anyhow, let's just say I re-read *The Ballad* more often!'

Neither does Chesterton's reputation rest solely on his poetry. On the contrary, his genius resides primarily in his prolific versatility. His many works of literary criticism were much admired, by T. S. Eliot among others, as were his biographies of St Francis of Assisi and St Thomas Aquinas, but perhaps he deserves to be remembered above all for his handful of novels. As with his verse, these sometimes suffer from a slapdash approach, a carefree and careless disregard for structural discipline, but what they lack in technical toning they gain in sparkling spontaneity. His first novel, *The Napoleon of Notting Hill*, addressed one of the central political and cultural issues of the century, the belief that 'small is beautiful'. This was summed up by Adam Wayne, a character in the novel, with the proclamation that a place, however small, 'which is large enough for the rich to covet . . . is large enough for the poor to defend'.[24]

Chesterton's second novel, *The Man Who was Thursday*, was published in 1908. It is arguably the best and is certainly the most perplexing of his works of fiction. On a superficial level the plot is literally a plot, in the sense of the Gunpowder Plot, revolving around a group of anarchists apparently intent on destruction, yet on a deeper level it is utterly perplexing. Indeed, the book's subtitle, 'A Nightmare', seems singularly appropriate. As a dreamer has difficulty unravelling the meaning of his dreams – if, indeed, his dreams have any meaning at all – Chesterton has difficulty unravelling the meaning of his nightmare. Years later C. S. Lewis drew a surprising parallel between *The Man Who was Thursday* and the works of Franz Kafka:

> Is the difference simply that one is 'dated' and the other contemporary? Or is it rather that while both give a powerful picture of the loneliness and bewilderment which each one of us encounters in his (apparently) single-handed struggle with the universe, Chesterton, attributing to the universe a more complicated disguise, and admitting the exhilaration as well as the terror of the struggle, has got in rather more; is more balanced: in that sense, more classical, more permanent?[25]

In the light of Lewis's comments it is interesting to note that Kafka was familiar with *The Man Who was Thursday*. Discussing both *Orthodoxy* and *The Man Who was Thursday*, Kafka remarked that Chesterton 'is so gay, that one might almost believe he had found God . . . In such a godless time one must be gay. It is a duty.'[26]

Another admirer of Chesterton's first two novels is Terry Pratchett, the modern author of popular comic fantasy:

> It's worth pointing out that in *The Man Who was Thursday* and *The Napoleon*

> *of Notting Hill* he gave us two of the most emotionally charged plots in the twentieth century: one being that both sides are actually the same side; it doesn't matter which side we're talking about, both sides are the same. This has been the motor of half the spy novels of this century. The other plot can't be summarised so succinctly, but the basic plot of *The Napoleon of Notting Hill* is that someone takes seriously an idea that wasn't intended to be taken seriously and gives it some kind of nobility by so doing.[27]

Chesterton's religious faith, which was only present implicitly in his first two novels, was much more to the fore in *The Ball and the Cross*. The two heroes, a devout Catholic and a militant atheist, are ennobled by their arguments and by their adherence to the ideals they espouse. Their nobility stands in stark contrast to the cynical indifference of the world they inhabit. On one level, *The Ball and the Cross* can be seen as a parable of Chesterton's arguments and relationship with George Bernard Shaw. Chesterton and Shaw disagreed passionately on most of the issues of the day but remained good friends. Their relationship was a living embodiment of the principle to 'love thine enemy'.

Manalive is often overlooked when Chesterton's novels are discussed but it is arguably his most underrated work. It contains the charm, mystery and adventure of *The Man Who was Thursday* or *The Ball and the Cross*, but also has a depth beyond either of these, especially in its characterisation of women. In the earlier novels female characters play a peripheral role, whereas in *Manalive* they are not only central to the plot but possess a mystique which is absent, or at least only hinted at, in the earlier books. As *The Ball and the Cross* can be read as a parable of Chesterton's relationship with Shaw, *Manalive* can be read as a parable of Chesterton's relationship with Frances, his wife. The parallels between fact and fiction are obvious. The novel's hero, Innocent Smith, was Chesterton, trying always to stir the world from its cynical slumber, while the heroine, Mary Gray, was Frances, the silence on which he depended utterly, the power behind the throne. On another level, *Manalive* was a further affirmation of Chesterton's philosophy of gratitude which had found its fulfilment in Christian orthodoxy. Ultimately, the novel's whole *raison d'être* was to illustrate that the intrinsic wisdom of innocence was unobtainable to the naïvely cynical. This, of course, was the motive force behind Chesterton's creation of Father Brown and it is no coincidence that the first volume of Father Brown stories, appropriately entitled *The Innocence of Father Brown*, appeared within months of the publication of *Manalive*.

Chesterton's other novel of note was *The Flying Inn*, published in 1914, a romp across an idealised Merrie England in praise of good ale, good companionship and traditional freedoms. In some respects it bore a remarkable similarity to Belloc's *The Four Men* which appeared two years earlier. The prose in both these works was punctuated with hearty verse, or drinking songs.

By the time that *The Flying Inn* and *The Four Men* were published, Chesterton and Belloc were seen so synonymously that Shaw had dubbed them the Chesterbelloc, lampooning them as 'a very amusing pantomime elephant'.[28] For all their similarities, however, there remained many significant differences between the two halves of the Chesterbelloc, both in terms of their respective personalities and in terms of their literary achievement. Belloc's novels were never as accomplished as Chesterton's but his verse is more consistent in its quality and more considered in its construction. At its best, Belloc's poetry is as good as anything Chesterton achieved and arguably better. 'Tarantella', 'Ha'nacker Mill' and 'The End of the Road' place him among the first rank of twentieth-century poets. His 'Lines to a Don', written in defence of Chesterton, is a timeless classic of comic vitriol while 'Twelfth Night', 'Ballade of Illegal Ornaments' and 'Rose' are among the century's finest religious verse.

Besides Chesterton and Belloc, the writer most responsible for carrying the mantle of the Catholic literary revival in the early years of the twentieth century was Robert Hugh Benson. In some respects, Benson's life paralleled that of Newman. His conversion to Catholicism in 1903, and his subsequent ordination, caused a sensation on a scale similar to that which greeted Newman's reception into the Church almost sixty years earlier. In Benson's case the sensation was linked to the fact that he was the son of E. W. Benson, Archbishop of Canterbury from 1882 until 1896. Like Newman, Benson followed a literary as well as a priestly vocation and before his untimely death in 1914 at the age of forty-three he had published fifteen highly successful novels. The other obvious parallel with Newman was his writing of a lucid and candid autobiographical apologia describing the circumstances leading up to his conversion. Benson's *Confessions of a Convert* warrants a position alongside Newman's *Apologia pro Vita Sua* as one of the great expositions of the spiritual and psychological background to religious conversion.

An early admirer of Benson was Hilaire Belloc, who wrote in 1907 that he had met him once or twice 'and liked him enormously'. Belloc was particularly impressed with Benson's historical novels:

> It is quite on the cards that he will be the man to write some day a book to give us some sort of idea what happened in England between 1520 and 1560. No book I ever read has given me the slightest conception, and I have never had time to go into the original stuff myself. This is the most interesting of historical problems . . .[29]

Benson's early death ensured that he was never able to fulfil Belloc's wish and Belloc, increasingly frustrated at the Protestant bias of the Whig historians, would soon start to study the period himself. In later life Belloc would publish studies of key sixteenth- and seventeenth-century figures such as Wolsey, Cromwell, James the Second, Charles the First and Cranmer. His *How the Refor-*

mation Happened, published in 1928, would endeavour to put the whole period into context. Yet to a large extent Benson achieved the same aim in his fiction. The meticulous attention to historical detail, coupled with a patient and controlled development of character and plot, brought his novels of Tudor and Stuart England to life in a way which is hardly possible in a painstaking work of non-fiction. *Come Rack! Come Rope!* remains an outstanding work of literature, in its prose, its plot, its characterisation and its masterful control of the historical landscape in which it is set.

Neither did Benson restrict himself to historical fiction. He wrote novels which dealt with the contemporary religious and moral dilemmas of Edwardian society and, as in the case of *Lord of the World*, novels which conjured up apocalyptic visions of the future. The latter were a reaction against the optimistic science fantasies of Wells and a foreshadowing of the nightmare visions of Huxley's *Brave New World* and Orwell's *Nineteen Eighty-Four*. R. H. Benson, as a writer of fiction, was a master of the past, the present and the future. His *Poems*, published posthumously, mark him out as one of the most accomplished poets of his generation and his *Spiritual Letters*, also published posthumously, display a depth of religious faith rooted in a marriage of the mystical and intellectual. The neglect of Benson's literary achievement says more about the decline and sickness of an increasingly secularised society than it does about any alleged shortcomings in his writing.

Benson's biographer, C. C. Martindale, saw a 'disconcerting affinity' between Benson's *Papers of a Pariah* and Wilde's *De Profundis*:

> Benson had, and Wilde was resolving, so he thought, to get, that direct eye for colour, line, and texture that the Greeks possessed . . . Benson, . . . in his direct extraction of natural emotion from simple and beautiful elements, like fire and wax, as in his description of the Easter ceremonies . . . reaches, sometimes, an almost word-for-word identity with Wilde.[30]

Martindale also wrote of the 'Chestertonian quality' in Benson's work and quoted a letter Benson had written in 1905 in which he expresses admiration for Chesterton's *Heretics*:

> Have you read a book by G. K. Chesterton called *Heretics*? . . . It seems to me that the spirit underneath is splendid. He is not a Catholic, but he has the spirit. He is so joyful and confident and sensible! One gets rather annoyed by his extreme love of paradox; but there is a sort of alertness in his religion and in his whole point of view that is simply exhilarating. I have not been so much moved for a long time . . . He is a real mystic of an odd kind.[31]

The writing of both Benson and Chesterton were two of the principal constituents in the conversion of Ronald Knox to the Catholic Church in 1917. Knox was only sixteen, 'a schoolboy just beginning to think', when he had first read

Chesterton's *The Napoleon of Notting Hill.* It affected him profoundly, as he confessed to Frances Chesterton shortly after her husband's death:

> He has been my idol since I read *The Napoleon of Notting Hill* as a schoolboy; I'll only hope that you, who know as no one else does what we have lost, will find it easy to imagine as well as believe that he is alive and unchanged. Thank God for that faith; that I have it when so many of my friends lost it was due, I think, under God to him.[32]

Elsewhere Knox had written that 'Chesterton's philosophy, in the broadest sense of the word, has been part of the air I breathed, ever since the age when a man's ideas begin to disentangle themselves from his education. His paradoxes have become, as it were, the platitudes of my thought.'[33]

The fact that R. H. Benson shared the distinction with Chesterton of being Knox's idol during the formative years of his life is well documented in Knox's *A Spiritual Aeneid*:

> It was at Manchester, on Christmas Day, 1903, that I read a book written (I was told) by an Anglican who had just become a Roman Catholic (actually, in that September). It was, of course, *The Light Invisible*, a collection of stories written by Mgr Benson while he was still in the Church of England . . . Most people find it an interesting book, but free from controversial tendency . . . Yet, to me, that Christmas Day was a turning point. It was the setting of the book – the little chapel in which the priest celebrated, the terms in which he alluded to the Mother of God, the description of confessions heard in an old parish church – that riveted me even more than the psychological interest. All that Catholic system which I had hitherto known only distantly . . . now for the first time entered my horizon.[34]

Thereafter Knox always looked upon Benson 'as the guide who had led me to Catholic truth'[35] and in the last few days before his conversion, almost fourteen years after he had first read *The Light Invisible,* he read Benson's *Come Rack! Come Rope!*: 'Hugh Benson, who had set my feet on the way towards the Church, watched over my footsteps to the last.'[36]

It was no great surprise that Knox considered Benson his mentor. They had so much in common. Both were sons of Anglican bishops and were educated at Eton. They both belonged to remarkable literary families and had brothers whose literary reputations were at least the equal of their own. Both passed through Anglo-Catholicism into full communion with the Catholic Church. There was, however, one major difference. Whereas Benson's literary achievement was truly prodigious considering his early and untimely death, Knox failed to live up to his early promise. Evelyn Waugh, in his introduction to the 1958 edition of Knox's *A Spiritual Aeneid*, described the precocious and meteoric rise of the young Knox:

> He went up to Balliol in 1906 preceded by a reputation of unique lustre. While still at Eton he had written a book of light verse in English, Latin and Greek and he is still remembered there as the cleverest boy who ever passed through that school . . . At Oxford all the coveted distinctions – the Hertford and Ireland scholarships, the presidency of the Union, a first in Greats – came to him as by-products of an exuberant intellectual and social life . . . In 1910 there seemed no limit to the prizes, political, academic or literary, which a smiling world held out to him.[37]

Seen in this context, it was scarcely surprising that Knox's conversion proved almost as controversial as that of Newman or Benson, shaking the establishments of both Canterbury and Oxford. Expectations were high and many believed that Knox was destined to be a latter-day Newman. It was not to be. The reasons for the literary anti-climax were explained by Waugh:

> After *Caliban in Grub Street* (1930) and *Broadcast Minds* (1932), in which he dealt with opponents who were mostly unworthy of his attention, he decided that his vocation was not to discomfort the infidel but to work among the clergy and laity of his own Church to fortify and refine their devotion and remind them of their high calling. He drew apart from secular life with the result that the name of one of the very few prose stylists of his age was seldom mentioned in literary journals.
>
> Three books, certainly, *Enthusiasm*, *Let Dons Delight* and *God and the Atom* claim a place in the library, however small, of anyone, however indifferent to religion, who recognizes distinction in literature, but it is by his Bible that he wished to be remembered. It took ten years of his life at the height of his powers.[38]

Sadly, even Knox's translation of the Bible, painstakingly crafted into what he hoped was a 'timeless English', was very soon eclipsed by later translations which were more accomplished academically. Knox, it seemed, was never destined to reach the literary heights of which Waugh and others believed he was capable. Instead, his importance to the Catholic literary revival has more to do with his place in what Barbara Reynolds, the Dante scholar, has called the 'network of minds energising each other'.[39] He represented a significant influence on the conversions of both Chesterton and Waugh and, in Waugh's case particularly, provided spiritual succour and sustenance. Many years later, shortly before his death in 1957, Knox formed a late friendship with Siegfried Sassoon which proved instrumental in the poet's reception into the Church.

During the forty years from his own reception into the Church until his death, Knox's direct influence on his contemporaries straddled a period which saw many major changes, both in the world at large and also in the sphere of Catholic literature. The changes to the former obviously affected the changes to the latter, a fact alluded to by Mrs Graham Greene: 'Many of the later Catholic writers had a dark view, whereas Chesterton had high spirits. The later writers seemed depressed in comparison. Perhaps it had something to do with what was happening in the world.'[40] In fact, there can be little doubt that the most important single cause of the 'dark view' which replaced the Chestertonian 'high spirits' was the carnage of the First World War. The new darker spirit was captured in the sardonic sullenness of Eliot's post-war poetry, particularly in *The Waste Land* and *The Hollow Men*, which became, in a bitter twist of neo-Chestertonian paradox, iconoclastic icons.

Although Chesterton had initially mistrusted Eliot's work, mistaking the latter's anti-modern pessimism for post-modern cynicism, he eventually came to see Eliot as a major Christian literary figure, expressing admiration for Eliot's *Murder in the Cathedral* which was published a year before Chesterton's death in 1936. Neither would it be entirely correct to make such a simplistic comparison between Eliot's dark vision and Chesterton's high spirits. Chesterton and Belloc had always combined their *joie de vivre* with strident criticism of a centralist industrial system which they both despised. With the growth of the Distributist movement, under Belloc's ideological guidance and Chesterton's charismatic presidency, in the years between the wars, this criticism became more robust than ever. Also, on a purely literary level, Chesterton's response to the horror of the war was not so dissimilar to the bitterness being expressed by the war poets. His 'Elegy in a Country Churchyard' was as full of potent indignation against those responsible for the slaughter as had been Sassoon's 'Fight to a Finish'. After all, Chesterton had lost his brother and several close friends in the war. Belloc, who had lost a son as well as friends, never recovered the pre-war jollity that was the endearing feature of much of his early work. Stricken with grief, he wrote in 1920 of his own 'desire to be rid of life',[41] words of desolation, not despair. For Belloc, life after the death of his son and the earlier death of his wife would still be enjoyed on the babbling surface, most especially in the company of friends, but was endured in the still depths.

THE INTER- AND POST-WAR YEARS

It was not, however, the widespread reaction against the bloody excesses of the First World War which served as the impetus for the next wave of literary converts to Catholicism. Rather, on a deeper level, it was the reaction to the reaction. During the twenties, the post-war generation had rejected the misguided discipline and sense of duty and honour which had acquiesced in the slaughter, and had adopted an anti-authoritarian and hedonistic ethos. It was the perception of the shallowness of this 'alternative' lifestyle which had animated Eliot's grim social commentary in *The Waste Land* and even more so in

The Hollow Men. Eliot's influence was felt by other writers who followed his example in their writing of similar literary renunciations. In novels such as *Vile Bodies* and *A Handful of Dust*, Evelyn Waugh's injection of spiteful and ironic humour expressed a revulsion for modern life born out of bitter experience.

In the gossip columns of the time *Vile Bodies* was known simply as 'the ultra-modern novel', confirming Waugh's reputation as the ultra-modern novelist. This added to the controversy that accompanied Waugh's reception into the Church on 29 September 1930. How could the pillar of all things modern have turned to the pillar of all things ancient? The same incredulity had greeted Eliot's confession of Anglo-Catholicism two years earlier. Many 'moderns' clearly had difficulty in assimilating how the ultra-modern poet and the ultra-modern novelist could reconcile themselves with a creed which was almost two thousand years old. To the surprise of both the literary establishment and the literary avant garde, orthodox Christianity had once again emerged at the cutting edge of contemporary literature.

A year after the publication of *Vile Bodies*, a work in similar vein was published by the poet Roy Campbell. *The Georgiad* was a merciless verse satire of the wealthy party-set, centred around Harold Nicolson and Vita Sackville-West, of which Campbell and his wife had at one time been an integral part. *The Georgiad* steers a *via media* between Eliot and Waugh in its rejection of a modern waste land, populated by vile bodies and hollow men. Largely to escape the decadence of their life in England, the Campbells had moved to Provence and then to Spain, where they were received into the Catholic Church in 1935. Campbell's most enduring contribution to Christian literature would be his masterful translation of the poems of St John of the Cross.

Besides Evelyn Waugh, the other leading Catholic novelist to emerge during the inter-war years was Graham Greene. With *Brighton Rock* in 1938 and *The Power and the Glory* two years later, Greene made Catholic doctrine and religious dilemma the dominant force in his fiction. After the war, the increasingly heterodox nature of works such as *The Heart of the Matter, The End of the Affair* and *A Burnt Out Case* alarmed many Catholics, including Waugh, and some critics began to question whether Greene had lost his faith. None the less, his biographer, Norman Sherry, believed that he 'remained a strong Catholic until his death'.[42] Whether this is so, the fact remains that the enigma of both Greene and his fiction rests in the presence of an uncomfortable sense of doubt. Yet it is not so much the doubt that gives his novels real profundity but the ultimate doubt about the doubt. It was this doubt about doubt that kept both Greene and many of his characters clinging desperately to the Catholic faith. He and they seemed to perceive that to be anything other than a Catholic would mean becoming something less than a Catholic, a passing from inexplicable and doubtful depths to inane and dubious shallows. There was no escape from a truth which could not be proved.

Ironically, considering the allied victory over the Nazis, the same sense of pessimism accompanied the end of the Second World War as had greeted the end of the First. In part, this arose from the horror that many people felt about the dropping of the atom bombs on Hiroshima and Nagasaki and the realisation that a new and horrific weapon had emerged. The dawn of the nuclear age coincided with the world's lurch from a world war into a cold war in which the future was as bleak as it was uncertain. This spirit of gloom and despondency was captured most memorably in Orwell's *Animal Farm* and *Nineteen Eighty-Four*, but there were a host of other literary creations born of a similar anxiety, many of which were imbued with Christian disdain for the nihilism of post-war materialism.

Ronald Knox's *God and the Atom* set the cautionary tone with its warnings about the dire consequences of the triumph of scientific materialism. Edith Sitwell, whose poem 'Still Falls the Rain' had lamented the destruction of the Blitz in the intense imagery of Christ's crucifixion, had been so shocked by an eye-witness account of the immediate effect of the atomic bomb upon Hiroshima that she composed her poem, *The Shadow of Cain*, the first of her 'three poems of the Atomic Age'. The poem's imagery was as chilling as its subject. 'The first two pages', Sitwell explained, 'were partly a physical description of the highest degree of cold, partly a spiritual description of this.'[43] Her words had the mark of prophecy, reflecting the fears of many as the world emerged from world war to cold war. *Après le déluge* . . . the Cold.

The horrors of Hiroshima also inspired Siegfried Sassoon, writer of some of the finest poetry of the previous war, to new heights of creativity. In 1945 he wrote 'Litany of the Lost', a verse which echoed the concerns expressed by Sitwell and which employed similar resonant religious imagery as a counterpoise to post-war pessimism and alienation. By the middle of the following decade, these concerns had led both Sassoon and Sitwell into the arms of the Catholic Church.

In the same year that Sitwell and Sassoon were expressing their nuclear reactions, Waugh's *Brideshead Revisited* was published. Written over a year before the bomb was dropped but not published until 1945, Waugh's novel of hope among the ruins of a vanishing civilisation was none the less animated by the same post-war pessimism and anxiety which permeated the poetry and prose of Sitwell, Sassoon and Knox. It sold exceedingly well on both sides of the Atlantic. In England, the *Tablet* acclaimed it as 'the finest of all his works, a book for which it is safe to prophesy a lasting place among the major works of fiction'.[44] In America, *Time* described Waugh as a stylist unexcelled among contemporary novelists.

The praise was tempered by a vociferous minority who disliked *Brideshead Revisited* on both political and religious grounds. It was deemed politically incorrect for its nostalgic swan-songing of a rapidly vanishing aristocratic way of life and Waugh was vilified for being a reactionary and a snob. Meanwhile other critics, such as Edmund Wilson, had criticised the religious dimension. Replying to Wilson, Waugh remained unrepentant: 'He was outraged . . . at finding God introduced into my story. I believe that you can only leave God out by making your characters pure abstractions.' Modern novelists, Waugh continued,

> try to represent the whole human mind and soul and yet omit its determining character – that of being God's creature with a defined purpose. So in my future books there will be two things to make them unpopular: a preoccupation with style and the attempt to represent man more fully, which to me means only one thing, man in his relation to God.[45]

This paralleled the view of Graham Greene who believed that only the existence of God gave eternal significance to human actions and therefore an added depth to human characters which was unattainable in the novels of non-believers:

> I think I was in revolt against the Bloomsbury School, E. M. Forster, Virginia Woolf, and I thought that one of the things that gave reality to characters was the importance of human beings with a future world: it made the characters far more important . . . I found a certain flatness in the Bloomsbury circle of writers. There was something missing.[46]

With the publication of *Brideshead Revisited* Waugh completed the metamorphosis from ultramodern to ultramontane and in so doing had passed from fashion to anti-fashion (before the latter had become fashionable!). The transformation also invited comparisons between the works of Waugh and those of the disappearing old guard of the Catholic literary revival. Certainly, the influence of Chesterton on the writing of *Brideshead Revisited* is patently obvious. Its central theme of the redemption of lost souls by means of 'the unseen hook and invisible line . . . the twitch upon the thread', was taken from one of Chesterton's *Father Brown* stories.

The combination of Catholicism and aristocratic high society in *Brideshead* also invites comparisons with the novels of Maurice Baring who died in the year of the novel's publication. Less obvious but probably as powerful was the subliminal influence of Hilaire Belloc who had been one of Waugh's heroes since his days as a schoolboy at Lancing. Waugh was attracted to Belloc's militantly aggressive and traditional approach to Catholicism but was equally impressed by the matter of fact, almost humdrum way in which he practised his faith. It was the simple unaffected faith of cradle Catholics like Belloc, as distinct from the arriviste zeal of converts, which shaped the characterisation of the Flytes in *Brideshead*. Another Catholic writer who probably influenced aspects of the writing of *Brideshead Revisited* was Compton Mackenzie, whose evocative description of life in Oxford in *Sinister Street*, a book which Waugh had read and enjoyed at Lancing, found resonant echoes in Waugh's own atmospheric treatment of Oxford undergraduate life.

Another novel which displayed an orthodox Christian response to the dilemmas posed by post-war modernism was C. S. Lewis's *That Hideous Strength*, published in July 1945. At the time of its publication Lewis's friend, J. R. R. Tolkien, was in the midst of writing *The Lord of the Rings*, and there are certain distinct similarities between the two books. Lewis's ascribing of demoniac powers to the men of science in *That Hideous Strength* bore more than a marked resemblance to Tolkien's treatment of the same issues. Indeed, Lewis's description of *That Hideous Strength* to an American correspondent in 1954 could almost serve as a description of *The Lord of the Rings*: 'I think *That Hideous Strength* is about a triple conflict: Grace against Nature and Nature against Anti-Nature (modern industrialism, scientism and totalitarian politics).'[47] This triple conflict between the supernatural, natural and unnatural was arguably the key to both books and it is an indictment of the ignorance of the post-war world that many of Tolkien's millions of readers remain entirely ignorant of the orthodox Catholic theology at the heart of his sub-creation.

Perhaps it would be appropriate to end with Tolkien, especially as the emergence of *The Lord of the Rings* as 'the greatest book of the century' in several recent polls allows this short appraisal of the Catholic literary revival to end on a note of triumph. There are of course many sins of omission, almost too many to mention, but this in itself is a testimony to the extraordinary range of Catholic literature which the last century and a half has produced. One feels guilty at having overlooked the achievement of Muriel Spark, and even more so at the failure to give that extraordinary writer George Mackay Brown the attention his work deserves. Then there is the Welsh connection: Saunders Lewis, David Jones, R. S. Thomas . . .

Then again, there are the other issues that are raised by the mere mention of George Mackay Brown, Saunders Lewis, Jones and Thomas, such as nationalism, regionalism, ruralism, decentralism, and the whole 'small is beautiful' debate at the heart of their work. One wishes to chart the history of ideas which led to their ideological positioning: from Pope Leo XIII's groundbreaking encyclical, to Chesterton's *The Napoleon of Notting Hill*, Belloc's distributism and E. F. Schumacher's vision of society based on the social teaching of the Church as espoused in his hugely influential *Small is Beautiful*. All of this lies beyond the scope of the present study but does at least illustrate some of the questions at the heart of the Catholic response to the dilemmas raised by modern society.

Perhaps, however, the enduring nature of Catholic literature goes beyond any modern dilemmas. The ultimate questions are not concerned with virtual reality, however technological and clever, but with the bedrock reality which is rooted in unchanging human nature in relation to an unchanging God. One goes back to the dialogue from Newman's *Callista* with its reiteration of Pilate's perennial question: 'What is Truth?' Ultimately, this is the question which great Catholic literature both asks and answers. It is, to end with echoes of Chesterton, the everlasting response of the everlasting man.

NOTES

1. J. H. Newman, *Occasional Sermons*, pp. 173–4, quoted in William Samuel Lilly (ed.), *A Newman Anthology* (London, 1949 edn), p. 181.
2. *The Tablet*, 23 September 1989.
3. T. S. Eliot, *Notes Towards the Definition of Culture* (London, 1962 edn), pp. 123–4.
4. Eliot, *Notes*, p. 123.
5. George Levine, *The Boundaries of Fiction: Carlyle, Macaulay, Newman* (Princeton University Press, 1968), p. 165.
6. Alan G. Hill, introduction to John Henry Newman, *Loss and Gain* (Oxford University Press, 1986 edn).
7. J. H. Newman, *Discourses to Mixed Congregations*, pp. 283–4, quoted in Lilly (ed.), *Newman Anthology*, pp. 274–5.
8. John Henry Newman, *Callista: A Tale of the Third Century* (London, 1885 edn), pp. 248–50.
9. Cardinal Wiseman, *Fabiola: A Tale of the Catacombs* (London, 1962 edn), p. 172.
10. Bernard Bergonzi, *Gerard Manley Hopkins* (London, 1977), p. 139.
11. T. S. Eliot, *After Strange Gods* (London, 1934), p. 48.
12. G. F. Lahey SJ, *Gerard Manley Hopkins* (Oxford University Press, 1930), pp. 52–3.
13. Francis Thompson, *Collected Poems* (Fisher Press edn, Sevenoaks, 1992), p. 274.
14. G. K. Chesterton, *Autobiography* (London, 1936), p. 80.
15. Chesterton, *Autobiography*, pp. 92–3.
16. Richard Ellmann, *Oscar Wilde* (London, 1987), p. 548.
17. Paul Horgan, *Maurice Baring Restored* (New York, 1970), p. 49.
18. Robert Speaight (ed.), *Letters from Hilaire Belloc* (London, 1958), p. 213.
19. Speaight (ed.), *Belloc*, p. 214.
20. Emma Letley, *Maurice Baring: A Citizen of Europe* (London, 1991), p. 217.
21. Maurice Baring, *Have You Anything to Declare?* (London, 1936), p. 147.
22. Laura Lovat, *Maurice Baring: A Postscript* (London, 1947), pp. 4–5.
23. Alfred Noyes, *Two Worlds for Memory* (London, 1953), p. 260.
24. G. K. Chesterton, *The Napoleon of Notting Hill* (London, 1904), pp. 90–1.
25. D. J. Conlon (ed.), *G. K. Chesterton: A Half-Century of Views* (Oxford, 1987), pp. 71–2.
26. *Chesterton Review*, vol. III, no. 1, p. 161.
27. *Chesterton Review*, vol. XVIII, no. 3, p. 457.
28. *New Age*, 15 February 1908.
29. C. C. Martindale, *The Life of Robert Hugh Benson*, vol. II (London, 1916), p. 45.
30. Martindale, *R. H. Benson*, vol. II, pp. 90–1.
31. Martindale, *R. H. Benson*, vol. II, p. 90.
32. Evelyn Waugh, *Ronald Knox* (London, pbk edn, 1959), pp. 197–8.
33. Claude Williamson (ed.), *Great Catholics* (London, 1938), p. 548.
34. Ronald Knox, *A Spiritual Aeneid* (London, 1958 edn), pp. 31–2.
35. Knox, *Spiritual Aeneid*, p. 161.
36. Knox, *Spiritual Aeneid*, p. 215.
37. Knox, *Spiritual Aeneid*, Introduction by Evelyn Waugh.
38. Ibid.

39. Barbara Reynolds, interview with the author, Cambridge, 19 September 1996.
40. Mrs Graham Greene, interview with the author, Oxford, 20 August 1996.
41. Hilaire Belloc, from an unpublished letter in the author's possession.
42. Professor Norman Sherry, letter to the author, 26 September 1996.
43. Victoria Glendinning, *Edith Sitwell: A Unicorn Among Lions* (London, 1981), p. 260.
44. John A. O'Brien (ed.), *The Road to Damascus* (London, 1949), p. 11.
45. *Life*, 8 April 1946.
46. *The Tablet*, 23 September 1989.
47. Roger Lancelyn Green and Walter Hooper, *C. S. Lewis: A Biography* (London, 1987), p. 179.

THIRTEEN

THE CATHOLIC CULTURAL CONTRIBUTION: ARCHITECTURE, ART, LITURGY AND MUSIC

EDWARD YARNOLD

> 'The Roman Catholics;' – not a sect, not even an interest, as men conceived of it, – not a body, however small, representative of the Great Communion abroad, – but a mere handful of individuals, who might be counted, like the pebbles and the *detritus* of the great deluge . . . Such were Catholics in England, found in corners, and alleys, and cellars, and the housetops, or in the recesses of the country; cut off from the populous world around them, and dimly seen, as if through a mist or in twilight, as ghosts flitting to and fro, by the high Protestants, the lords of the earth.[1]

Thus John Henry Newman in 1852 directed the thoughts of the bishops at the first Synod of Westminster back to the time of their birth, say half a century before the 'Second Spring'. Even if one allows for a degree of rhetorical exaggeration, the influence of the Catholic Church on the cultural life of the nation at the end of the eighteenth century must have been negligible. The Parliamentary calculation of the Catholic population in 1767 was a mere 69,376.[2] Until the Relief Act of 1791 it was still a penal offence to build a public chapel; and even after the Act Catholics were forbidden to construct steeples or ring church bells. As late as 1835 Nicholas Wiseman could write that the English Catholic Church was 'just emerging from the catacombs'.[3]

Nevertheless, the Church was growing, steadily at first, and then sharply. By 1780 it had risen to about 80,000 according to John Bossy's calculations,[4] from which figure it increased dramatically to 452,000 in 1837–40, and to about three quarters of a million by 1850.[5] This growth was due largely, but by no means entirely, to Irish immigration, which began in significant numbers about 1790;

Bossy concludes in fact that there was a 'continuous and self-generating [English] growth underlying what was added by recruitment from outside'.[6]

The cultural influence of English Catholics, like the head-count, had already begun to develop long before the restoration of the hierarchy; the reaction provoked by Wiseman's letter from the Flaminian Gate would not have been so hysterical if the Catholic community had been still as downtrodden as Newman claimed it was about 1800. In no other field is this more evident than in the spectacular number of churches that were built after 1791. Before that date congregations were accommodated in private chapels on the estates of the Catholic nobility and gentry, in Newman's 'alleys, and cellars, and roof-tops'; in embassy chapels like the Sardinian embassy in Lincoln's Inn Fields and the Bavarian embassy chapel which eventually became Warwick Street Church; and in illegally constructed new buildings. At first such buildings had to be unobtrusive, like the Benedictine St Peter's, Seel Street, Liverpool,[7] built in 1788 with the exterior disguised to resemble a warehouse. Even as late as 1863 the church in Ramsey, near Huntingdon, was built to look from the street like an ordinary house, for this was an area in which Catholics were still aliens; the census of 1851 indicates no churches or priests at all in Huntingdonshire, and a resident population of 268 native Irish people. *Loss and Gain*, the semi-autobiographical novel of 1848, the first book which Newman wrote as a Roman Catholic, paints contrasting pictures of Catholic churches in large towns with High Mass complete with deacon, subdeacon and Gregorian chant, but at the same time of an inconspicuous Catholic chapel in Oxford, which the hero Charles Reding mistakes for a dissenting place of worship or a museum.[8]

CHURCH ARCHITECTURE

Already by 1823 there were 358 churches and chapels in England and Wales, by 1837 433, by 1851 nearly 600, by 1880 more than 1,100, and by 1949, 2,821.[9] The second of these dates is significant, because it is two years after Augustus Welby Pugin became a Catholic in 1835. While Pugin's influence on church architecture, both inside and outside the Catholic Church, was immense, Denis Gwynn did scant justice to the heroic and imaginative achievements of the first third of the nineteenth century when he spoke of Pugin's predecessors as 'a Catholic community which had ceased to possess any churches worthy of the name'.[10] For example in the 1790s John (later Bishop) Milner built St Peter's, Winchester, which was the first Catholic neo-Gothic church in England. St Patrick's, Soho was built in 1793 for an Irish congregation, and St Mary Moorfields in 1820 in a classical style, for a while serving as a pro-cathedral for the London district; Bloxwich in Staffordshire acquired a 'beautiful Grecian chapel' in 1825. By 1834 there were five chapels in Liverpool, all of them large enough to cater for communities of 6,000 people or more.[11] Irish immigration was the cause, but not the only cause, of this titanic programme of church-building; the general growth of the industrial towns was no less responsible. It was to meet the latter need that a parliamentary Act of 1818 provided a million pounds for the building of churches for the established religion; the sum paid for 214 churches, all but forty in what Pugin regarded as a debased version of Gothic.[12] The Catholic Church of course received nothing.

Whatever view one takes of the architectural and religious merits of the Catholic churches constructed before Pugin, there can be no doubt concerning the enormous influence he exerted on ecclesiastical building both within his own communion and outside it. Pugin was born in 1812, the son of Auguste Charles Pugin, a French émigré draftsman, whose drawings of medieval buildings and decorations 'marked a new stage in the progress of the Gothic Revival toward archaeological accuracy'.[13] This was a time when Scott's Waverley novels were stimulating the taste for things medieval which had emerged in the eighteenth century with Walpole's Strawberry Hill and the general fashion for 'Gothick' follies. Pugin *père* took boarding pupils in the family home in London, among whom the son gained such a precocious mastery of the draftsman's skills that at the age of fifteen he was commissioned to design furniture for the new apartments at Windsor Castle, which he conceived in an antiquarian style that he later came to regret. By the time he was twenty he had turned his hand to sailing ('There is nothing worth living for,' he is said to have declared, 'but Christian architecture and a boat'; and all his life he enjoyed dressing as a sailor), the antique trade, stage-designing and furniture-making, and had had a spell in a debtor's prison. A legacy from his aunt gave him leisure to train himself as an architect by the simple expedient of travelling widely in Britain and on the Continent and studying medieval architecture at first hand. In 1835 he became a Roman Catholic, presumably inspired by his love for the Middle Ages; he had met no Catholic priests, and despised contemporary Catholic churches:

> Going into Catholic chapels (there were no churches then) what did I see? The very tabernacle a Pagan temple, the altar a deal sarcophagus, over which a colossal eye with rays looked down from a flat ceiling, artificial flowers under glass shades between the altar candlesticks, costly marbles produced in cheap papers, brackets painted with sham windows supporting nothing; and vestments, who can describe?[14]

Three years earlier the Roman Catholic Earl of Shrewsbury had been so impressed by the young Augustus Welby's drawings that he employed him to make alterations at Alton Towers, the earl's Staffordshire seat. This commission was only the first in a fruitful partnership between the nobleman and the architect which was to continue until both men died within a few months of one another in 1852. Pugin later developed the site of the ruined Alton Castle for the earl into a little Christian community including a 'Hospital' for the aged, a girls' school, a chapel, a priest's residence, and a Guildhall, which doubled as a boys' school and a Mechanics' Institute. His skill as a designer of Gothic interiors earned him a series of commissions for Charles Barry, the most notable of which was to collaborate in the designing of the new Houses of Parliament. However his early reputation was based above all on his book *Contrasts*, which in its first edition of 1836[15] carried the subtitle: 'a parallel between the architecture of the fifteenth and nineteenth centuries'. This little book began with several chapters in which he set out the principles which proved the superiority of Gothic (his preferred term was 'Pointed') architecture over other forms, especially for the building of churches. First, the design should be so manifestly fit for its purpose that the spectator may at once perceive what that purpose was; second, Christianity should possess an architecture capable of symbolising 'its sublime truths . . . its stupendous mysteries'. Gothic architecture met this requirement: 'from Christianity has arisen an architecture so glorious, so sublime, so perfect, that all the productions of ancient paganism sink, when compared before it, to a level with the false and corrupt systems from which they originated' (p. 2). Thus the cross expresses the doctrine of the redemption, the triangular form of the pointed roof and arches symbolises the Trinity, and the height of the building and its vertical lines represent the resurrection (p. 3). In his Oscott lectures of 1841 Pugin added two corollaries: a church should carry no unnecessary features, and all ornament should be an enrichment of the building's essential construction.[16] In the early 1840s he focused his vision more sharply, and came to regard the pointed arches of the Decorated period rather than the flattened arches of the Perpendicular as the perfect expression of Gothic principles. For all the vigour of Pugin's polemical prose, the power of the book lay with the concluding series of pairs of drawings contrasting modern buildings with their medieval counterparts. Not content with depicting the supremacy of medieval over contemporary construction, Pugin sketched in background details indicating the superiority of the medieval way of life which produced the architecture. Thus the medieval episcopal monument is matched by one of 'the Right Reverend Father in God John Clutterbuck, D.D. [wearing wig, bands and round spectacles] *aetatis suae* 72: also of Caroline and Lydia his two wives' (one of whom looks down her nose at the other). A notice nearby reads: 'Persons are desired not to walk about and talk during Divine Service nor to deface the walls.' (The picture shows this last injunction to have been ignored.)

Contrasts produced an immediate impression on the public and, together with the support of Shrewsbury and the enthusiastic convert Ambrose Phillipps, led to a series of commissions. In 1837 Pugin began alterations on Scarisbrick Hall in Lancashire (including a clock-tower which may have provided the inspiration for Big Ben); and in the same year he designed the furnishings of the chapel at the college and seminary at Oscott, near Birmingham (where he served for several years as Professor of Ecclesiastical Art), and drew the plans for the Cistercian monastery at Mount St Bernard's in Leicestershire, which had been endowed by the munificence of his two patrons. From 1839 he was engaged in a whirlwind of activity designing one church after another, beginning with St Mary's, Uttoxeter for Lord Shrewsbury. For the magnificent St Giles's, Cheadle, the earl placed unlimited funds at Pugin's disposal; many of the architect's other churches were constructed under severe financial constraints. The frontispiece of the 1843 work *An Apology for the Revival of Christian Architecture in England* depicts an amazing composite townscape of twenty-five ecclesiastical buildings which he had already designed in the space of four years (though some of them would take several more years to be built); five of them were to become cathedrals: St Chad's, Birmingham (the first English cathedral to be built since the Reformation); St George's, Southwark (destroyed in World War II); St Mary's, Newcastle-upon-Tyne; St Barnabas', Nottingham; and Killarney in Ireland (Enniscorthy Cathedral was to follow later). Denis Gwynn gives a list of about thirty-six Catholic churches in England alone,[17] not including his work in Ireland and for the Church of England, and many chapels for religious houses and colleges. He sent plans to Australia for three cathedrals, and designs for simple churches which could be adapted to meet local requirements (though one wonders what his reaction would have been to corrugated-iron roofs). Pugin's creativity prompted *Punch* to print a mock advertisement of the work of 'A. W. Pugsby': 'Designs for Cathedrals made in five-and-forty minutes; superior ditto in one hour; ditto ditto for Churches in twenty-six minutes. Episcopal chapels in fifteen minutes – and, to save trouble, no Dissenters need apply.'[18]

Pugin's work went far beyond the planning of his buildings. He designed every detail of decoration, and entrusted its execution to a trusted group of craftsmen. Together with these collaborators he devoted enormous energy to a display of their work, which they named the Medieval Court, at the Great Exhibition at Crystal Palace in 1851. Gradually the frantic pace of his work took its toll. 'My mind has been deranged through over-exertion,' he wrote in his last winter. 'The medical men said I had worked one hundred years in forty.'[19] After a short period in Bedlam he was allowed to return to the house he had built for himself at Ramsgate, where he died in 1852. He was buried in the same town in his beloved St Augustine's Church, which he had built at his own expense.

Pugin's influence on nineteenth-century architecture was immense. A reviewer wrote that his early work at St Mary's, Derby marked for Roman Catholics 'the transition from chapel to church architecture'.[20] However he met with opposition within his own Church, especially because of his use of rood-screens to enhance the sense of liturgical mystery by separating the priest from the people.[21] Bishop Peter Augustine Baines sought a ruling from *Propaganda* against the use of Pugin's enfolding Gothic vestments. Many resented what seemed to them an attempt by the triumvirate of Pugin, Shrewsbury and Phillipps to dictate the general taste. Newman, while admiring Gothic – he described Pugin's Lady Chapel at Cheadle as 'Porta Coeli'[22] – rejected the exclusive claims made for it, and retained an affection for the classical style of Trinity College, in which he had made his first communion as an Anglican. He regretted that what began as a 'living architecture of the nineteenth century' after twenty years had become 'a sort of antiquarianism'.[23] D. Watkin judges that Pugin's principles 'found wider acceptance in the Anglican than in the Catholic Church'.[24] They inspired a generation of Anglican architects, such as W. Butterfield, A. Waterhouse and G. E. Street. Yet in advocating Gothic architecture Pugin's was not a lone voice: neither the Cambridge Camden (or Ecclesiological) Society nor John Ruskin derived their commitment to the Gothic from him. Andrew Saint's assessment of Pugin's unique contribution seems just: 'By the end of the 1830s, then, the concepts of structural truth and Gothic rationalism were *au courant*. It wanted only someone with Pugin's energy and genius for invective to kindle the fire.'[25]

Pugin's work was carried on by his two sons, Edward Welby and Peter Paul. Edward was responsible for more than seventy churches in England and Scotland, in addition to several in Ireland. He had the originality to modify some of his father's principles, discarding screens so as to allow an unrestricted view of massive Benediction altars, and often adopting an apsidal design for the sanctuary.[26] Peter Paul did much of his work in Scotland and for the Benedictines, for whom he produced plans for Fort Augustus, Belmont, Princethorpe and Stanbrook. It has been estimated that he designed more than 450 altars.[27]

A. W. Pugin's ambition to establish the Pointed style as the prevailing Catholic architecture was not realised, though the fifteenth Duke of Norfolk (1847–1917), who continued the tradition of the munificent endowment of churches, chose Gothic for his churches at Norwich and Arundel, which were deservedly chosen later to become cathedrals for the two new dioceses of East Anglia, and Arundel and Brighton. For Arundel he employed the Catholic architect Joseph A. Hansom, who achieved an impressive volume of work for patrons of his own church, but whose name is linked rather in public memory with the design of the 'Patent Safety Cab'. Hansom and his sons Charles and Joseph S. H. worked prolifically for Catholic organisations, building for the Jesuits St Beuno's College, near St Asaph, the Holy Name, Manchester, and St Walburg's, Preston (its slender spire rising gracefully to the height of 306 feet was the tallest to be built in England since the Reformation) as well as Plymouth Cathedral. The architect of St John the Baptist, Norwich was George Gilbert Scott II, yet another convert, whose more famous father of the same name had produced distinguished work for the Church of England, as well as public structures like the Albert Memorial. Two of George Gilbert II's sons, themselves Catholics, followed their father in designing churches mainly in the Gothic manner. The elder, Giles Gilbert Scott, designed the church at Ampleforth, but is however probably best known for his work on the Anglican cathedral at Liverpool, a Gothic building of imposing and uncluttered masses. For the churches of the two Oratories in London (Brompton, 1884) and Birmingham (1909), however, the Italian style (which Newman variously termed 'Grecian', classical or 'Palladian') was chosen out of respect for St Philip Neri's Oratory in Rome.[28] The respective architects were E. Doran Webb and the convert Herbert Gribble; both churches benefited from the munificence of the Duke of Norfolk.

Even more significant was Cardinal Vaughan's choice of a Byzantine form for the cathedral at Westminster. Manning, who lived in personal austerity in what according to his biographer 'could be mistaken for a Dissenting Chapel doing duty as a railway waiting-room',[29] had acquired the site for the cathedral and appointed the Catholic architect Henry Clutton, who published Gothic plans based on Cologne Cathedral; but the task of building was left to the next archbishop, Herbert Vaughan. Vaughan had the vision to recognise the opportunity of doing more than build a cathedral for the Catholics of London:

> We want the Empire to possess in its very centre a living example of the beauty and of the majesty of the worship of God . . . fully presenting the cosmopolitan faith and devotion of the Catholic Church . . . Now that nearly one-fourth of the population of the world is subject to the British Crown, there are duties commensurate with our national influence.[30]

To reduce expense and to avoid competition with Westminster Abbey and St Paul's, he decided against both Gothic and classical styles. Clutton's plans were accordingly discarded, and a new commission was entrusted to John Francis Bentley, yet another in the line of distinguished convert architects; it seems to have been taken for granted that an architect should be found within the Church. Bentley's previous work included the seminary at Hammersmith, the Jesuit preparatory school St John's near Windsor, and the Redemptorist monastery at Clapham. Like Pugin he worked in close association with his own team of craftsmen; he was one of the founders of the Guild of SS. Gregory and Luke, a Catholic organisation aimed at raising the standard of ecclesiastical art and liturgy.

Although Vaughan had envisaged a 'basilican' building in the style of Constantine's Old St Peter's in Rome, Bentley, though he favoured the Gothic style himself, developed an 'Italo-Byzantine' design inspired by Hagia Sophia, Constantinople, and San Vitale, Ravenna. According to his daughter, the style commended itself to Bentley because it was not confined to any particular nation, but 'was, up to the ninth century, spread over many countries'. Not quite consistently, a Byzantine architecture seemed to him appropriate for London, which was the capital of a modern empire and of a world of commerce.[31] The English Catholic Church's conception of its vocation had indeed developed since Wiseman in his Appeal to the English People had claimed Westminster's 'nests of ignorance, vice, depravity and crime' as his mission-field. Nevertheless, the visitor to the cathedral, however awe-struck by its massive proportions and splendid decorations, may well feel that a vernacular style would have better symbolised the Catholic Church's mission to the nation and the Empire. On the practical level, Vaughan was impressed by the unimpeded view of the sanctuary which the new plan provided for the congregation.

The exterior is built with orange-red bricks banded with Portland stone, and is constructed with four main domes, turrets and a dramatic campanile, which from many viewpoints is a feature of the London skyline. Within, eight columns of yellow marble support the richly gilded *baldacchino*. Although the original intention was to cover the internal brickwork with marble and mosaics, to save expense the upper bricks have been left bare, which has the happy result of drawing the eye upwards into a mysterious gloom. The marble stations of the cross were carved by Eric Gill. The most recent mosaics, which decorate the Blessed Sacrament chapel, are the work of Boris Anrep, completed in 1962.

The main structure took a mere seven years to finish, so that it was ready in 1903 to house its first ceremony, which was poignantly the funeral of its founder Cardinal Vaughan. The consecration took place in 1910, once the debt of more than £250,000 had been paid off. *The Times* of 10 April 1910 devoted nearly two columns to a description of the ceremony. Originally the cathedral, for all its size, was tucked away out of sight behind the shops of Victoria Street; its aspect was immensely improved when in 1975 the Westminster Council knocked down some of the shops and opened up a piazza – a step which aroused vociferous opposition, to which remaining anti-Catholic sentiment probably contributed.[32]

Non-Gothic styles were also chosen for the three most recent Catholic cathedrals, Liverpool, Clifton (Perry Thomas Partnership, completed 1975) and Brentwood (a classical building with a novel central placement for the altar, architect Quinlan Terry, 1991). The principle of employing a Catholic architect had by now been abandoned. For the first of these buildings Sir Edwin Lutyens (1869–1944), the most distinguished architect of the day, designed a massive edifice in the monumental classical style he had employed so successfully for the Viceroy's House in New Delhi; it would have held ten thousand people, and, with its elevated site and with a dome larger than that of St Peter's, would have provided a spectacular sight from the Mersey. Unfortunately World War II intervened when work had not progressed beyond the crypt; when peace returned it was judged that the original design would be too expensive to complete at post-war prices. Nevertheless, according to one commentator, Lutyens's grand project, though never realised, 'will survive as an architectural creation of the highest order, perhaps as the latest and supreme attempt to embrace Roman, Byzantine, the Romanesque and the Renaissance in one triumphal and triumphant synthesis'.[33] Consequently Archbishop Heenan commissioned Adrian Gilbert Scott, the younger brother of Giles, to prepare a scaled-down version of Lutyens's plans, but even this proved too costly. Finally it was decided to complete the original crypt, but to build over it a cathedral to a new design. After a competition the commission was awarded to Frederick Gibberd for a circular concrete design, with a central lantern crowned with spikes; one of its best features is its stained glass. It was completed in 1967, but defects in the concrete have already caused great trouble.

The enormous energy that went into the ambitious church-building programme we have described is all the more remarkable because it occurred at a time when the Church's resources were stretched to the limit by the need to build and maintain schools for the growing Catholic population, many of whom were penniless Irish people who had been forced to seek relief in England from the potato famine. In this period the aristocracy took on a new role. In penal days they had kept the faith alive by supporting private chapels in the country where the Masses celebrated by their personal chaplains were attended by the neighbouring Catholic population; now they helped to provide, out of their own pockets and by organising subscriptions, public churches served by priests appointed by the bishops. We have fixed our attention on the two great church-founders of the period, the 16th Earl of Shrewsbury and the 15th Duke of Norfolk, who in addition to the churches he built on his own initiative was described as the 'lay-founder' of Westminster Cathedral; but there were many others whose names have not been mentioned here. Nor have we given much space to the religious and collegiate buildings which numbered among the more worthy examples of Catholic architecture, such as the seminaries (sometimes combined with schools) at Ware, Wonersh, Oscott and Ushaw; and monastic buildings (again sometimes combined with schools) like Mount St Bernard's, Downside, Ratcliffe, Ampleforth and Stonyhurst. Here again much was due to the munificence of wealthy patrons. However, the dramatic urban development of churches would hardly have been possible without the generously donated 'pennies of the poor' and the contributions (in manpower and money) made by the religious orders. For example, the quality of the many churches of Preston owes much to the Jesuits, while the beautiful church of St Francis, Gorton, Manchester was built by E. W. Pugin for the Franciscans; after lying derelict and vandalised for some years, it has now been listed by the World Monuments Fund among the four most endangered buildings, and there are hopes for its restoration.[34]

Since Vatican II the bishops of England and Wales have taken steps to promote worthy liturgy and church architecture. In 1976 Bishop Alexander of Clifton was responsible for setting up a Department of Art and Architecture of the hierarchy's Liturgy Commission. The bishops issued three Directories, namely *The Parish Mass: A Resource Book for Clergy, Religious and Laity* (1981), *Music in the Parish Mass* (1981) and *The Parish Church – Principles of Liturgical Design and Reordering* (1984).[35] The *Clergy Review* (now *Priests and People*) ran a quarterly supplement on Church Art and Architecture, edited for many years by a priest-architect Kenneth Nugent SJ. A *Catholic Building Review* was established, and in

1984 became the *Church Building Magazine*, produced jointly with the Church of England.

GRAPHIC AND PLASTIC ARTS

In this survey of architecture, we have found one dominant figure, A. W. Pugin. When we turn our attention from architecture to the graphic and plastic arts, we again find one outstanding personality: Eric Gill.[36] Like Pugin, Gill was a convert whose faith profoundly influenced his art, who saw that his work was intimately connected with a view of life and a way of living, expressed his philosophy of the religious function of art in a number of controversial and passionate books, believed that art required sound and honest craftsmanship, and sometimes experienced strained relations with the authorities of the Catholic Church.

The entry on Gill in the *Dictionary of Art* lists a long roll of his accomplishments: 'sculptor, letter-cutter, typographic designer, calligrapher, engraver, writer and teacher', to which list 'portraitist' and 'architect' should be added; however, the epitaph he chose for the tombstone he designed for himself shows which of these avocations he regarded as central: 'PRAY FOR ME ERIC GILL STONE-CARVER 1882–1940'. When he turned to the carving of figures, his letterer's instincts led him first to work in low relief rather than in solid forms; critics observed that he was always more interested in surface than in volume.

Gill's father was a dissenting clergyman, who eventually took orders in the Church of England. After studying at Chichester Art and Technical Schools and finding employment in an architect's office, Gill became disillusioned with his work. Not only was it 'hateful to be employed drawing carvings and mouldings and ironwork for other people to make';[37] he was dissatisfied with a conception of architecture which concentrated on decoration rather than the making of a building to fulfil a function. 'That the way you live and pray in any radical sense determines the very existence of architecture is an idea, or it was in the 1900's, unheard of in any but revolutionary circles.'[38] Pugin, however, would have agreed wholeheartedly.

Accordingly Gill began to study lettering, an interest that first grew from his fascination with the names on the sides of railway locomotives (at the end of his life he painted the nameplate for the 'Flying Scotsman'). He began to receive commissions, including an inscription to be cut for the Medical School at Cambridge, and lettering to be painted, such as the Ten Commandments for Byfield Church, Northamptonshire, and signs for the booksellers W. H. Smith. More diverse work followed, as he took to engraving titles for books and teaching lettering at the Paddington Institute. Later a period of continence occasioned by his wife's pregnancy prompted him to his first experiment in the naturalistic sculpture of the female form.

In 1907 he took his wife and daughters to live at Ditchling, Sussex, where a group of like-minded craftsmen gradually developed around him: such as Edward Johnston, the letterer, Hilary Pepler, who in 1916 set up the Ditchling (later St Dominic's) Press for hand-printing work, Desmond Chute (later ordained) and the many-sided David Jones, who will reappear in our story. The word 'craftsman' is chosen deliberately: Gill aimed at good construction; 'let art take care of itself as it very well can'.[39] Later he wrote: 'I think it would be a good thing if all art education were done away, and all men became workmen and made *things*.'[40] He returned to this theme in his *Autobiography*:

> All workmen are artists in so far as they are men and not mere tools, and therefore are ministers of the truth; but in those days [of his youth], as in these, this fact was denied. The artist had become a special class of person – a lapdog or mountebank, refined or vulgar.[41]

Apprentices followed in due time. Following the lead of William Morris and the Distributists, the community tried to supply their own food, and to wear clothes they had sewn for themselves from cloth they had woven from wool they had spun. Gill wore smocks even in cities, explaining that this style of garment did less violence to the cloth.

As a young man Gill had moved in rationalist circles. However, although at this time he had made almost no Catholic contacts, there grew in him at Ditchling the conviction that 'the Roman Church is the right answer to modern England', which was in a 'devilish state'.[42] (When he came to know the Church better, however, he concluded that contemporary church leaders were far from finding the answer.) Though the beauty of Catholicism formed part of the attraction – he had been transported by the sight of Chartres and the sound of plainchant sung at Mont-César – social considerations seem to have been decisive. He was received into the Church with his wife Mary Ethel in 1913; his daughters followed in the next few months. Fr Vincent McNabb OP, who shared many of Gill's social ideas, became a frequent visitor to Ditchling, and received him into the Dominican Third Order with Mary and with Pepler, who had also joined the Church. The community set up a private chapel, where they recited Compline every evening; later they added the other offices of the liturgical day. Gill's spirituality and his thought continued to develop along Dominican lines for the rest of his life. His writing sometimes resembles a scholastic disputation; he participated in the translated edition of *Art et Scholastique*, Jacques Maritain's neo-Thomist study of the philosophy of art. Besides the Dominicans, another priest whose advice he often sought was Fr (later Monsignor) John O'Connor, a parish priest in Bradford, whose unconventional thinking and capacity for empathy had given G. K. Chesterton the idea of Father Brown. Gill and his family remained at Ditchling until 1924, when they moved to a more remote home at Capel-y-ffin in the Black Mountains; four years later they moved once more to the less Spartan setting of Pigotts near High Wycombe, which remained their home until Gill's death in 1940.

Shortly after his reception into the Church Gill received an invitation to carve the stations of the cross for Westminster Cathedral. Although he disapproved of the marble and mosaic decorations, and would have preferred to see the walls whitewashed, he was impressed by the building itself, and accepted the commission, which he completed in 1918; his call-up was deferred until he finished the work. His next large work was a war memorial for Leeds University which represented Christ driving out of the temple the money-changers, who were shown as a top-hatted pawnbroker, his fashionable wife and his clerk, a politician and two financiers, with a dog (symbolising St Dominic – the *Domini canis*, the Lord's dog) at their heels;[43] not surprisingly the work raised a storm of controversy. Other public work included panels for the Underground station at St James's Park; a large panel for the League of Nations at Geneva, representing the rebirth of man, and echoing Michelangelo's Sistine *Creation*; a series of Ariel figures for the BBC in Portland Place; and ten panels for the Palestinian Archaeological Museum in Jerusalem. To a colossal female torso he gave the name 'Mankind'; he took special pleasure in his carving of the 'Deposition'. He carved a statue of St John the Baptist for the new Anglican cathedral at Guildford. He did not live to put the finishing touches to a marble altarpiece for the English Martyrs' Chapel in Westminster Cathedral; the authorities there provoked public outrage by presuming to cut away St Thomas More's monkey. (After Gill's death they also saw fit to improve his Stations by colouring the lettering red.) He carved war memorials and designed postage stamps. The year before his death saw the opening of the only building he created, the Catholic Church at Gorleston, built on original lines in the shape of a cross with pointed arches springing directly from the floor and with whitewashed walls; the altar was placed at the crossing under the tower. He despised neo-Gothic, and believed in the use of modern materials and techniques. His beautiful typefaces alone would have been sufficient to keep his fame alive; while he chose for them the names of saints – Perpetua, Felicity – or of his daughter Joanna, the profession knows one of them, Gill Sans, by his own name.

Gill was as adept as Pugin in writing theoretical justifications of his work. When people complained of the lack of realism in his Westminster Stations, he replied that his treatment was 'diagrammatic' (perhaps one might say 'iconic'), and compared the carvings to plainchant, or 'a sentence without adjectives', or the beads of a rosary, which arouse piety not emotion.[44] He explained that what he modestly described as his 'inability to draw naturalistically' led him 'to concentrate upon something other than the superficial delights of fleshly appearance. It compelled me to consider the significance of things rather than their charm.'[45] 'Naturalism,' he wrote later, 'has always and everywhere been the sign of religious decay.'[46] 'The only kind of work I can do or wish to do is of some sort more allied to that of children . . . than to that of the more obviously grown-up old masters.'[47] He later described his Ariel carvings for the BBC as 'a work of art only in the low sense of the word'. It was a 'useful object' as a 'sign or symbol', like a pawnbroker's three balls.[48] His experience in letter-cutting and his insistence on the importance of the act of making gave him the confidence to carve directly on the stone, without the use of a plasticine model.

Although Gill remained a devout Dominican Tertiary throughout his life and died a holy death with the last sacraments, he was in frequent conflict with the Catholic authorities over two issues. The first concerned his political views, which he expounded vigorously and aggressively in a series of essays, lectures and books, such as *The Necessity of Belief* (1936). He never abandoned the socialist convictions which led him as a young man to frequent meetings of the Fabian Society and the Independent Labour Party. He waged a persistent campaign against the modern industrial and mechanised society; but if the 'machine state' could not be abolished, he wrote in 1935, 'Communism seems the only just politics . . . it seems clear that justice is more likely to be achieved when ownership is vested in men as workmen rather than in men as men of business.'[49] Cardinal Hinsley sent Gill gentle rebukes for the communist leanings of his writings.

Even more damaging to Gill's reputation in his own Church was the frank eroticism of many of his engravings and writings (the unconventional nature of his family life did not become public knowledge until many years after his death[50]). He illustrated *Lady Chatterley's Lover*, the Song of Songs, and Powys Mathers's semi-pornographic *Procreant Hymn*. While preparing to join the Catholic Church, he had continued carving a phallus. Gill himself wrote to a friend: 'I know my constant tendency to incontinence – immodesty – the physical nature of man and woman seems to me so utterly delightful and good . . . therefore I find it difficult to see uncleanness where most people see it and where Holy Church bids us see it.'[51] A German associate described Gill as 'a completely innocent mixture of religion and eroticism', and wrote of his 'peculiar godliness, which is an all-embracing eroticism, his rejection of ethics, his erotic asceticism'.[52] A woodcut of Christ embracing the Church, represented as a female figure, led to a temporary breach with Vincent McNabb.[53]

His understanding friend Fr John O'Connor gave a succinct defence of Gill's erotic art: 'Whatever tends to make sexual attractions normal, and to keep them so, deserves well of the commonweal.'[54] Gill himself justified his erotic works in various ways. Nudity was natural, and the naked body beautiful. Art which sprang from a healthy delight in the human body was a defence against contraception, as it expressed fertility as well as sensuality; contraception was disrespect for the human being *as an artist*. Chastity and purity were not 'merely negative values'.[55] More theologically he explained that a nude could be an 'ikon', deepening our love for God's creation, 'its infinite beauty and subtlety, its grandeur and its solemnity, its sweetness and its terrors, even its comicality, and, so to say, its Rabelaisian buffoonery and pig-style coarseness. All these things are good and holy . . .'[56] To say 'I love the roundness of thighs' was a way of saying 'I love God'.[57] Echoing St Paul he wrote to Fr Bede Jarrett OP: 'I hold that as Christ loves the Church, so a man shd. love his wife. It does not appear that Christ loves the church only in order to beget Christians but also because she is adorable and delightful and lovely.'[58]

Another unique Catholic artist who entered Gill's circle more than once, both at Ditchling and Capel, was the engraver, water-colourist, calligrapher and poet David Jones (1895–1974), yet another convert. Although Jones was born in Kent, his imagination was inspired by his father's Welsh origins. Both his art and his poetry bore the scars of his war experiences with the Royal Welch Fusiliers; he was wounded in 1916 in the Battle of the Somme, and later suffered three breakdowns. After conventional training at art schools, a meeting with Eric Gill changed the direction of his life. Gill introduced him to Fr John O'Connor, who received him into the Church in 1921. Although he had first begun to feel the attraction of Catholicism under the stresses of the Western Front, he also found in the Catholic belief in sacramental signs a basis for the understanding of art. Later he joined Gill's community at Ditchling, learning engraving, and followed him to Capel, where he found the Welsh mountains inspiring. Jones's water-colours and paintings, even when they depict mythological subjects, carry an undercurrent of Christian mysticism; he developed a unique style of epigraphy, combining English, Welsh and Latin expressions. For all the mystical power of his visual art, it is probable that posterity will remember him more for his poems, among which his epic *In Parenthesis*, based on his war experiences, and *Anathemata*, a meditation on the Eucharist, are outstanding.

The Ditchling community survived Gill's departure in 1924 as a centre producing hand-crafted vestments, chalices and altar-furnishings. The partnership between the Dominicans, Christian Socialism and art which had flourished there was also continued in the Spode House meetings organised by Fr Conrad Pepler OP, the son of the Hilary who had been Gill's associate at Ditchling.

It would serve little purpose to list all the leading Catholic artists of the period, but mention should, however, be made of a few. The Irish stained-glass painter Evie Hone (1894–1955) was another convert whose faith influenced her work profoundly; she is best known in England for her large window in the Eton College chapel. Simon Elwes (1902–75), a lifelong and devout Catholic, after fighting in the desert campaign and serving as an official war artist in World War II, suffered a stroke which made his right hand useless and forced him to learn to paint with his left; despite his disability he rose to become an RA and Vice-President of the Royal Society of Portrait-Painters. Criticism rather than creation was the field of influence of John Rothenstein (1901–92), another convert, and the son of the painter William; he was Director of the Tate Gallery from 1938 to 1964, and recorded his experiences in a three-volume autobiography.[59]

An account of Catholic artists of the period would be incomplete without mention of Aubrey Beardsley, whose exquisite drawings, often grotesque and erotic, made him an influential figure in the world of art at the end of the nineteenth century. Described by one critic as the 'Fra Angelico of Satanism',[60] he was received into the Church a year before his death at the age of twenty-five in 1898. Such a conversion, however striking and sincere, was far from unique: several literary figures in the 'Decadent' movement, such as André Raffalovich (later a patron of Eric Gill), John Gray (who became a priest) and Oscar Wilde, took the same step; the first two at least influenced Beardsley in his decision.

Religious orders have acted as patrons of the arts. Thus Aylesford Priory, the historic Carmelite foundation restored under the leadership of Fr Malachy Lynch as a shrine for pilgrims, has become a showcase for the ceramic work of the Polish artist Adam Kossowski. When the Jesuits needed to build a new Campion Hall at Oxford, Fr Martin D'Arcy, with the encouragement of his superiors, imaginatively offered the commission to Lutyens, and once the building was opened enriched it with an art collection (which became known as the *objets d'Arcy*); outstanding in the collection are the dramatic Stations of the Cross by Frank Brangwyn and a series of murals by Charles Mahoney in the Lady Chapel, the latter paid for by Evelyn Waugh's donation of the royalties earned by his biography of St Edmund Campion.

LITURGICAL CELEBRATION

The culture of a church is embodied in its liturgy. Throughout our period there were places where the full ceremonial flourished. Although Newman's experience was very limited when he made a character in *Loss and Gain* describe Mass in an English or Continental city church, his picture is presumably accurate, even if not typical:

> The celebrant, deacon and subdeacon, acolytes with lights, the incense, and the chanting . . . The laity on the floor saying their beads, or making their acts; the choir singing out the *Kyrie*; and the priests and his assistants bowing low, and saying the *Confiteor* to each other. This is worship, and it is far above reason.[61]

Robert Gradwell described perhaps a more typical Sunday Mass of the 1820s as follows:

> The priest reads devotions in the vernacular tongue, *Pater, Ave, Credo, De profundis*, Acts of the Theological Virtues, Litany of the B.V.M., or select Office. Then he reads the Epistle and Gospel of the day, and preaches or leads an instruction on them. Then follows Mass [in Latin] and catechistical

> instruction, unless the Catechism forms part of the afternoon devotions and instructions.[62]

A Welsh bishop describes Mass celebrated in a country town in a loft over the public slaughter-house to the accompaniment of the bellowing and the stench of the animals; but the form of service may have been the same.[63]

John Bossy gives an account of several manuals which contain public devotions in English before Mass conforming more or less closely to the pattern Gradwell described.[64] The practice seems to have flourished in the last years of the eighteenth century and the early decades of the nineteenth, and was perhaps adapted to a congregation whose members were either too poor or too illiterate to use a prayer book. In 1838 the bishops issued a form of prayers to be recited publicly before and after Mass. Quite a different approach to the Mass was recommended in Bishop Challoner's *Garden of the Soul*, which was first published in 1740, and remained in use into the twentieth century, though later editors allowed themselves the liberty to make drastic revisions. Although lengthy prayers are proposed for the family to recite at home, no church service preparing for the Mass is given; instead there are meditative prayers in harmony with what the priest is doing or saying at the altar. The emphasis is on private devotion: on entering the church the Mass-goer is recommended to choose 'a place to kneel in, where you may be most recollected, and least disturbed'. The manual *Hierurgia* compiled by the Earl of Shrewsbury's learned chaplain Daniel Rock gives the complete Ordinary of the Mass in both Latin and English; but the publication was not so much a prayer book as a work of instruction designed especially for inquiring Protestants.[65]

What this way of celebrating Mass lacked in colour and warmth was supplied by paraliturgical services, many of which were introduced from the Continent, first by émigré French priests at the time of the French Revolution, and later by the Italian missionaries, such as Gentili and Barberi, and converts of ultramontane leanings like Faber. In 1838 the Vicars Apostolic had forbidden the use of English prayers even at evening service, though English hymns were allowed; Vaughan, reversing this decision when Bishop of Salford, composed an English service of psalms and hymns.[66] In the second half of the nineteenth century a fierce debate broke out between the 'Old' or 'Garden of the Soul' Catholics, who favoured traditional 'English' devotions (such as Vespers), and the supporters of 'Italian' forms of worship, such as Benediction and the Forty Hours, which were practised with especial exuberance at the London Oratory under Faber. Well into the twentieth century Sunday evening services, consisting of 'Rosary, Sermon and Benediction', *Bona Mors* devotions (prayers for a holy death), and Holy Hour, were well attended even in small churches.

The standard of music varied at different times and in different places. There was no tradition of vernacular hymn-singing during the Mass such as flourished in Germany. The more fashionable Catholic churches set themselves ambitious standards. Pugin poured his sarcasm on the spectacle

> exhibited to the afflicted Christian . . . surrounded by a scoffing auditory of protestant sight-seekers who have paid a few shillings a head to grin at mysteries which they do not understand, and to hear the performances of an infidel troop of mercenary musicians, hired to sing symbols of faith they disbelieve, and salutations to that Holy Sacrament they mock and deny.[67]

Pugin and his associates wanted to replace elaborate music with Gregorian chant, Pugin most passionately so. As he wrote to Faber, complaining of the liturgy at the London Oratory: 'A man may be judged by his feelings on Plain Chaunt. If he likes Mozart he is no chancel and screen man. By their music you shall know them . . .'[68] The Anglican characters in Newman's *Loss and Gain* enthusiastically discuss methods of performing the chant: 'I think', one says, 'the perfection of sacred music is Gregorian set to harmonies; there you have the glorious old chants, and just a little modern richness.'[69] At the beginning of the present century Pius X brought more uniformity and restraint into liturgical music by two *motu proprio* pronouncements (1903–04), which declared plain-chant to be the ideal form (though classical polyphony also received commendation), and entrusted the task of producing new editions to the monks of Solesmes. The Society of St Gregory organised summer schools aimed at developing the singing of plainchant.[70] Generations of schoolchildren became familiar with it through the selection entitled *Plain Song for Schools*. Meanwhile Richard Terry, the Organist and Director of the Choir at Westminster Cathedral, helped to raise the general level of singing with his handbook *Catholic Church Music* (1907) and his *Westminster Hymnal* (first edition 1912), which remained for decades the standard collection of English hymns.

Although the Second Vatican Council (1962–65) was largely responsible for the dramatic changes which the performance of the liturgy has undergone in the last decades of the century, the process had got under way some years before, particularly in France and Germany. The reform of the Holy Week services, inspired by pastoral as well as historical concerns, was the work of Pius XII in 1955; to him also was due the relaxation of the eucharistic fast which encouraged more frequent communion, thus continuing the process begun by Pius X's lowering the age for first communion. Imaginative efforts were made in the years before the Council to involve the people more fully in the Latin Mass. Readers were allowed to read the epistle and gospel in English while the priest read them *sotto voce* in Latin. 'Dialogue Masses' became common, in which the whole congregation was invited to recite the Latin responses normally spoken by the server. Permission was given for a commentator to provide the congregation with a running explanation of the priest's actions at the altar.

It is undoubtedly the authorisation given at Vatican II for the vernacular to be used at Mass and in the other sacraments which has had the greatest impact on Catholic worshippers. In the event, the permission granted by the Council, which appeared so daring at the time, now seems timid. The use of Latin is to be preserved. While confirming the privileged place of Latin, the Council decreed that:

> since the use of the vernacular, whether in the Mass, the administration of the sacraments, or in the other parts of the liturgy, may frequently be of great advantage to the people, a wider use may be made of it, especially in readings, directives and in some prayers and chants.[71]

Unfortunately changes were too often introduced insensitively and without adequate explanation; the Catholic anthropologist Mary Douglas pointed out the importance of continuity in the use of symbols as a means of maintaining values and social identity, and indignantly described the liturgical innovators as 'colour-blind signalmen'.[72] Many worshippers, while welcoming or at least accepting the use of English, disliked the 'chopping and changing' and the 'bobbing up and down'. Moreover the new form of Mass is often celebrated with so little ceremony that an excessive emphasis is attached to the spoken word. The complaint of the young that the Mass is 'boring' should not be dismissed out of hand.

The Latin Mass Society has campaigned for the retention of the pre-Vatican II Mass (commonly known as the 'Tridentine Mass'); the same cause has led some to support the schismatic Society of St Pius V founded by Archbishop Marcel Lefèbvre; the Association for Latin in the Liturgy, on the other hand, advocates the use of the Latin text of the Vatican II liturgy. Nor has the impact been confined to Catholics alone. Members of other churches and of none have joined dissatisfied Catholics in protesting against the changes, regarding the loss of the Latin as a betrayal of a national cultural heritage and fearing that the classical Latin motets will no longer be performed. The new translations have been compared unfavourably with Cranmer's work in *The Book of Common Prayer* – though this last is a problem which also faces Anglican liturgical revisers. One cannot, it seems, emerge from the ghetto without washing one's dirty linen in public.

The work of translating the liturgy was entrusted to a specially constituted body named the International Commission on English in the Liturgy (ICEL).[73] Their English Missal was published in 1973, three years after the Latin original; an interim translation brought out in England in the years 1970–73 was superseded by ICEL's work. Although the Commission's workload, which included the co-ordination of suggestions made from all round the world, was enormous, by the end of the 1970s they had published a stream of liturgical translations, including the rites for baptism, confirmation, adult initiation, penance, the liturgy of the hours, the Pontifical, and many more. Though at times successful, the ICEL translation, especially that of the collects of the Mass and other prayers in similar form, has incurred considerable criticism, though the charge of disproportionate American influence is unfounded. The Commission's aim of making the prayers readily intelligible to the listener was admirable, but the devices adopted for this purpose were sometimes ill-conceived. The decision to discard the periodic structure of the Latin in favour of short, parallel clauses and sentences often led to bathos. The decision to avoid relative clauses naming the attributes under which God was invoked ('O God, who . . .') sometimes made a prayer sound like the imparting of information to the Almighty. Moreover the decision to omit rather than to adapt images or expressions not immediately intelligible to the English-speaking listener has often made the prayers bare and uninspiring. John McHugh wrote a detailed and trenchant criticism of the ICEL translation of the Mass; the Vatican had issued a sensible set of suggestions for the guidance of translators, but these do not seem to have been heeded.[74]

Heeding such criticisms ICEL has produced a new translation of the entire Sacramentary, which as I write is undergoing the lengthy process of scrutiny leading to publication. Meanwhile some specimens of their work have been revealed to the public, which lead one to expect that the new English Missal will be much more satisfactory than its predecessor. Eamon Duffy has analysed a few examples, comparing the old and the proposed new ICEL translations with Cranmer's version.[75] Here is one:

Cranmer	*Old ICEL*	*New ICEL*
O God, the strength of all them that put their trust in thee,	Almighty God, our hope and strength,	O God, the strength of all who hope in you,
mercifully accept our prayers;		accept our earnest prayer.
and because through the weakness of our mortal nature		And since without you we are weak
we can do no good thing without thee,	without you we falter.	and certain to fall,
grant us the help of thy grace,	Help us	grant us the help of your grace,
that in keeping thy commandments we may please thee,	to follow Christ	that in following your commands we may please you
both in will and deed.	and live according to your will.	in desire and deed.

The introduction of the vernacular liturgy has led to a flowering of hymn-writing and musical composition. In the 1950s the Grail translation of Jean Gelineau's French psalms, written in a kind of sprung rhythm and set to easy tones, quickly and deservedly gained popularity outside as well as inside the Catholic Church. Since then the Grail psalms have been somewhat eclipsed by other forms of psalmody devised for the new Lectionary of 1969, such as the compositions of the Benedictine musicians Laurence Bévenot and Gregory Murray. In less liturgical contexts the meditative repetition of the Taizé chants composed by J. Berthier is often practised. Frequent use is made of hymns written in a 'folk' style for guitar accompaniment, which are often charismatic in inspiration; though some are sentimental or jejune, others have a genuine poetic quality and theological content. The compositions of the American 'St Louis Jesuits' have made a successful crossing of the Atlantic, as have the works of M. Joncas and M. Haugen (once described tartly as 'sub-Hollywood'), which bridge the gap between the traditional and the folk styles. New collections of hymns have proliferated, of which the compilations published by Geoffrey Chapman and by Kevin Mayhew and Joan McCrimmon have probably been the most frequently used. In order to combine a level of musical sophistication with congregational participation W. Tamblyn and P. Inwood led the way in devising new styles of liturgical singing, in which the congregation repeats phrases sung by a cantor or sings refrains punctuating more complicated music for the choir. The St Thomas More group of composers under Inwood's leadership set a worthy standard for liturgical composition, not least by the publication of *Music for the Mass* (ed. G. B. Smith and C. McCurry, London 1993); the Pastoral Centre named after the same saint and founded by Harold Winstone helped to make the new resources generally available until it closed down in the late 1980s. The use which the denominations make of one another's hymns is one of the most evident ecumenical gains of recent times: Catholic congregations happily sing 'Amazing Grace', Charles Wesley's richly theological words, and the productions of the Iona community, while happily seeing some of their own hymns spread in the opposite direction.[76]

The new liturgy has called for drastic architectural changes. New churches are regularly built without altar-rails to separate the sanctuary from the congregation, with a free-standing altar enabling the celebrant to face the people, a font placed in full view of everyone, and an ambo or lectern replacing a pulpit. The Blessed Sacrament is often reserved in a side-chapel, thus enabling the congregation to exchange greetings before and after services without inhibitions. Confessionals have frequently been replaced by 'reconciliation-rooms' enabling face-to-face contact between priest and penitent.

Churches, however beautiful, are not museums: they exist for worship, and may need to be adapted for the worship of the post-Vatican II era. Often changes have been made very successfully, as at Ogle Street, London, where the worshipper cannot fail to be impressed by the large cruciform font let into the floor (though the altar has less merit). Adaptations are not however always so successful. The removal of Pugin's screen from St Chad's, Birmingham caused perhaps as much of an uproar as its original construction. Old altars too grand to remove still stand to eclipse the new ones facing the people which have replaced them. The glorious *baldacchino* at Westminster Cathedral now over-arches an altar which is rarely used. Side altars have become redundant. Statues have been removed, sometimes with a thoroughness which bears comparison with that of the Puritans. Babies are baptised in undignified little basins while the old fonts stand neglected at the back of the church. Occasionally in fact the beauty of a church calls for an adaptation of the liturgy, rather than *vice versa*; for example, an imaginative celebrant can find ways of ensuring the participation of the congregation even if the altar does not face the people.

MUSIC

When we turn from liturgical music, written for pastoral use, to the general musical life of the nation, for much of our period the outstanding figure, Catholic or otherwise, was Edward Elgar (1857–1934). Unlike most of the people we have been recalling, Elgar was a Catholic from the beginning of his life, though his parents were both converts. Elgar's father was a piano-tuner in Worcester, where he later ran a music-shop with his brother; for some forty years he served as organist at St George's, the Jesuit church, where his son succeeded him for three years in 1885.

The first half of Edward Elgar's life gave few signs of the greatness that was to come. Although he had little formal musical training, picking up from the family his ability to play several instruments, he eventually took violin lessons in London, and played among the strings in the orchestra for the Three Choirs Festival; he never received any lessons in composition. A number of early works failed to gain much notice, until in 1899 his *Enigma Variations* met with immediate acclaim. This was the beginning of a wonderfully prolific fourteen years, in which he completed a series of major works: *The Dream of Gerontius*, which survived a disastrously under-rehearsed first performance in Birmingham in 1900; two oratorios, *The Apostles* and *The Kingdom* (1903 and 1906) (the projected third in the series, *The Last Judgement* was begun but not completed); the *Introduction and Allegro for Strings* (1905); the two symphonies (1908 and 1911); the violin concerto, the first performance of which was given by Kreisler in 1910; another oratorio, *The Music Makers* (1911); and the symphonic study *Falstaff* (1913). The period also included minor works which have gained a place in the repertoire: *Sea Pictures* (1899); the *Cockaigne* overture (1901); and the Military March No. 1, the first of the *Pomp and Circumstance Marches*, which

Elgar foretold would 'knock 'em flat', and which, coupled with Arthur Benson's words 'Land of Hope and Glory', continues to do so on the last night of the Proms. Although during the war he gave his attention to patriotic music of lesser weight, he then returned to serious work, with three chamber compositions (1918–19) and his last masterpiece, the cello concerto (1919). After the death of his wife Alice in 1920, however, inspiration deserted him until his last months. He was engaged on a third symphony when he died of cancer in 1934, to be buried next to his wife at the Catholic church in Little Malvern.[77]

Although Elgar remained a Roman Catholic to the end, receiving Extreme Unction in his last illness, and even excluding from his will the one nephew who had left the Church, it is only in *Gerontius*, apart from minor liturgical works, that the influence of his Catholic faith is easy to discern. He wrote to his friend Jaeger (who was the subject for the 'Nimrod' variation in the *Enigma*) that he had written the *Dream* 'out of my insidest inside'. At the end of the score he transcribed a quotation from Ruskin: 'This is the best of me; for the rest I ate, and drank, and slept, loved and hated, like another; my life was as the vapour, and is not; but *this* I saw and knew: this, if anything of mine, is worth your memory.'[78] Perhaps Elgar felt an affinity with the character of Gerontius, whom Newman drew not as a dying saint, but as a man going to face his God with his love of the world not yet fully integrated with his faith. The work was far too Catholic for some tastes: before it could be performed in Worcester Cathedral in 1902, the Worcester Festival Committee required the omission of the Litany of the Saints, and the removal of the words 'Masses' and 'Purgatory'.[79]

Yet with a man so subject to abrupt swings of mood and to outbursts of self-pity as Elgar such religious sentiments could not last. 'Providence denies me a decent hearing of my work: so I submit,' he wrote to Jaeger after the fiasco at Birmingham. 'I always said God was against art and I still believe it . . . I had my golf in good style yesterday and am not ill or pessimistic – don't think it, but I have allowed my heart to open once – it is now shut against every religious feeling and every soft, gentle impulse *for ever.*'[80]

Despite his self-centredness, his insecurity, his depressions, his neurotic anxiety over money and his frequent ingratitude, Elgar could experience deep and lasting attachments. Apart from *Gerontius*, his most passionate music seems to have been inspired by these friendships. The tragedy of the Great War left little impression on his music, though he dramatises himself as 'cursing God for allowing dumb beasts to be tortured – let him kill his human beings but – how CAN HE? Oh, my horses.'[81] Instead he directed his musical talents to composing morale-raising pieces with titles like *Follow the Colours*, *The Spirit of England* and *Fight for the Right*. The Military March No. 1, which had been linked with Benson's poem as early as 1902, now enjoyed a new vogue.

For several decades Elgar was regarded, and deservedly so, as the leading composer in England, or even in the world. Although for a while the jingoistic tone of some of his music led to a decline in his popularity, his place in the standard concert repertoire is assured. His Symphony No. 1 was the first to be written by an Englishman. His works gained a high reputation in Germany, where they were often performed, thanks largely to his friend the conductor Richter. Elgar himself felt at home in that country, and, for all its Englishness, his work reveals German Romantic influence – too much so, in fact, for Thomas Beecham's taste.[82] Public honours were showered on him: knighthood, baronetcy, Order of Merit, honorary doctorates, though he never received the peerage after which he hankered. He was chosen to compose the music for Edward VII's coronation in 1902. In 1924 he was delighted to be offered the appointment of Master of the King's Musick. Another Catholic, Malcolm Williamson, an Australian who has settled in London, followed Elgar in the same post in 1975.

Two other Catholic composers of national reputation, both converts, whose music has been deeply influenced by their faith, should be mentioned. Edmund Rubbra (1901–86), while attracted to Buddhism, wrote a Mass in honour of St Dominic and settings of words by St John of the Cross and Gerard Manley Hopkins; his Symphony No. 8 bears the title 'Homage à Teilhard de Chardin'. Lennox Berkeley (1903–89), a friend and collaborator of Benjamin Britten, besides a *Stabat Mater*, a *Magnificat* and several Masses, composed for Kathleen Ferrier a setting of four poems by St Teresa.

There have also been Catholic performers whose lives and work have revealed a deep faith, such as the tenor Gervase Elwes (1866–1921), who was the leading exponent of the role of Gerontius until his tragic death in a rail accident in the USA, and his fellow tenor, Count John McCormack (1884–1945), who, though Irish by birth and American by naturalisation, was a frequent performer in Britain. Without Eric Fenby, the young Scarborough church organist who offered the blind and paralysed Delius his services as amanuensis from 1928 to 1934, the composer's last masterpieces would never have been written. Mention must also be made of the high standard of the singing of the Westminster Cathedral choir, especially under George Malcolm (1917–97), who was its Master of Music from 1947 to 1959. Malcolm drew from his choir a 'continental sound', which an obituarist, with unflattering evenhandedness, described as a 'natural sound', a 'direct, vibrant, screechy timbre', in contrast with the 'inhibited and smooth hooting' characteristic of English boys' choirs.[83] When Malcolm invited Benjamin Britten to a performance of *A Ceremony of Carols*, the composer admired the Westminster tone so much that he chose the choir to give the first performance of his *Missa Brevis* in 1959.

We may conclude this survey of the Catholic contribution to English cultural life with two observations. First, the century and a half has witnessed the Church emerging so fully on the national scene, that, although there are today many Catholic artists and musicians, there is no longer a specifically Catholic movement in the arts in the way that Catholicism had been inseparable from the work of Pugin or Gill and their associates. Secondly, the majority of the leading figures in our account have been converts. This fact suggests that social or educational factors may have prevented the full flowering of artistic talent among those baptised in the Catholic Church and brought up in its schools; but on the other hand the influx of so many distinguished artists into the Church speaks highly of the power of Catholicism to provide inspiration and fulfilment to the most gifted individuals.[84]

NOTES

1. J. H. Newman, *Sermons Preached on Various Occasions* (London, 1857), pp. 171–3.
2. See J. Bossy, *The English Catholic Community 1570–1850* (London, 1976), p. 184.
3. Quoted in D. Gwynn, *Lord Shrewsbury, Pugin and the Catholic Revival* (London, 1946), p. 21.
4. Bossy, *English Catholic Community*, pp. 184–5, 298.
5. This figure is consistent with Philip Hughes's estimate of more than 679,067 out of a total population of just under 18 million at the time of the census of 1851 (P. Hughes, 'The English Catholics in 1850' in G. A. Beck (ed.), *The English Catholics 1850–1950* (London, 1950), p. 44). The estimate for 1837–40 was made by the English bishops (Hughes, '1850', p. 44). All of these figures are based on a degree of guess-work, and are therefore not strictly comparable; nevertheless they are reliable indicators of rapid growth.
6. Bossy, *English Catholic Community*, pp. 306–7.
7. See Bossy, *English Catholic Community*, pp. 311, 340, 344.
8. J. H. Newman, *Loss and Gain* (World Classics, Oxford, 1986), pp. 63–4.
9. P. Hughes, 'The Coming Century' in Beck (ed.), *English Catholics*, p. 19n; D. Gwynn, 'Growth of the Catholic Community' in *English Catholics*, p. 435.
10. Gwynn, *Shrewsbury*, p. xv.
11. See Bossy, *English Catholic Community*, pp. 311–12, 317, 426.
12. Cf. Horton Davies, *Worship and Theology in England from Newman to Martineau, 1850–1900* (London, 1962), vol. iv, pp. 43–4.
13. Rosemary Hill, 'Augustus Welby Northmore Pugin: A Biographical Sketch' in P. Atterbury (ed.), *A. W. N. Pugin: Master of Gothic Revival* (New Haven and London, 1995), p. 37.
14. Manuscript quoted in Davies, *Worship*, pp. 32–3.
15. In the second edition of 1841 Pugin modified his views a little, and came to regard paganism rather than Protestantism as the ultimate enemy of sound architecture.
16. A. W. Pugin, *The True Principles of Pointed or Christian Architecture* (London, 1843), p. 1.
17. Gwynn, *Shrewsbury*, p. 115.
18. *Punch* 9 (1845), p. 238, reproduced in Atterbury (ed.), *Pugin*, p. 34.
19. Quoted in Gwynn, *Shrewsbury*, p. 139.
20. *Dublin Review* (1839), p. 244, quoted in P. Atterbury and C. Wainwright (eds), *Pugin: A Gothic Passion* (New Haven and London, 1994), p. 63.
21. '. . . the mystical separation between the sacrifice and the people, with the emblem of redemption carried on high and surrounded with glory', A. W. Pugin, *True Principles*, p. 42.
22. Letter to Lord Shrewsbury quoted in Atterbury and Wainwright (eds), *Gothic Passion*, p. 76.
23. J. H. Newman, *Letters and Diaries*, XII.460–2, quoted by D. Meara, 'The Catholic Context' in Atterbury, *Pugin*, p. 60.
24. D. Watkin, *English Architecture: A Concise History* (London, 1979), p. 158.
25. A. Saint, 'The Fate of Pugin's True Principles' in Atterbury and Wainwright (eds), *Gothic Passion*, pp. 272–82; quotation on p. 278.

26. On the work of Pugin's sons see R. O'Donnell, 'The Later Pugins' in Atterbury and Wainwright (eds), *Gothic Passion*, pp. 259–71.
27. See O'Donnell, 'Later Pugins', pp. 269–70.
28. Cf. R. O'Donnell, 'The Architecture of the London Oratory Churches' in M. Napier and A. Laing (eds), *The London Oratory Centenary 1884–1984* (London, 1984), pp. 21–47; H. Tristram, *Cardinal Newman and the Church of the Birmingham Oratory* (Gloucester, 1962), pp. 31–3. The Birmingham church was constructed on the site of an earlier edifice hastily erected in 1853, which consisted originally of four plain brick walls with a second-hand roof (Tristram, *Birmingham Oratory*, p. 27).
29. S. Leslie, *Henry Edward Manning* (London, 1921), p. 473.
30. H. Vaughan, 'Westminster Cathedral: A Monument and Memorial', quoted in A. Wharton, 'Westminster Cathedral: Medieval Architectures and Religious Difference', *Journal of Medieval and Early Modern Studies*, 26 (1996), pp. 525–57; quotation on pp. 539–40.
31. W. De L'Hôpital, *Westminster Cathedral and its Architect* (London, c.1919), vol. I, p. 26, quoted in Wharton, 'Westminster Cathedral', p. 539.
32. For an illustrated description of the cathedral and an account of its construction, see K. Powell, 'A Hymn to Byzantium', *The Architects' Journal*, 22 June 1995, pp. 24–37. See also P. Doyle, *Westminster Cathedral 1895–1995* (London, 1995).
33. J. Summerson, 'Arches of Triumph: Sir Edwin Lutyens's Design for the Roman Catholic Cathedral, Liverpool' in *The Unromantic Castle* (London, 1990), pp. 245–56; quotation on p. 256.
34. Reported in *The Times*, 16 September 1997.
35. Distributed by the CTS, London. S. and C. Johnson, *Planning for Liturgy* (Farnborough, 1983), offers further guidelines.
36. The best documented biography is Fiona MacCarthy's *Eric Gill* (London, 1989).
37. E. Gill, *Autobiography* (London, 1940), p. 113.
38. Gill, *Autobiography*, p. 100.
39. Letter of 6 September 1909, quoted in Robert Speaight, *Eric Gill* (London, 1966), p. 44.
40. Letter of 28 February 1915, quoted in Speaight, *Gill*, p. 82.
41. Gill, *Autobiography*, p. 39.
42. Letter of 18 January 1912, quoted in Speaight, *Gill*, p. 61.
43. See Gill's own commentary on the work in 'A War Memorial', *Art-Nonsense and Other Essays* (London, 1929), pp. 110–14.
44. *Westminster Cathedral Chronicle*, March 1918, quoted in Speaight, *Gill*, p. 80.
45. Gill, *Autobiography*, p. 164.
46. Gill, *Art-Nonsense*, p. 51.
47. Letter of 28 February 1915, quoted in Speaight, *Gill*, p. 82.
48. *The Listener*, 15 March 1933, quoted in Speaight, *Gill*, p. 217.
49. Letter to *Time and Tide*, 1 September 1935, quoted in Speaight, *Gill*, p. 238.
50. Gill's diaries testify to his sexual relations with his daughters in their youth; see MacCarthy, *Gill*, pp. 156–7.
51. Letter of 21 November 1924, quoted in Speaight, *Gill*, p. 160.
52. H. Kessler, *The Diaries of a Cosmopolitan*, tr. C. Kessler (London, 1971), p. 256.
53. Speaight, *Gill*, pp. 200–1.
54. Letter of 21 January 1941, quoted in Speaight, *Gill*, p. 181.
55. Gill, *Autobiography*, p. 44.
56. Gill, *Drawings from Life*, quoted in Speaight, *Gill*, p. 292.
57. Gill, *Art-Nonsense*, p. 36.
58. Letter of 25 July 1926, quoted in Speaight, *Gill*, p. 177.
59. *Summer's Lease* (1965), *Brave Day, Hideous Night* (1966), *Time's Thievous Progress* (1970).

60. Roger Fry, quoted in S. Weintraub, *Aubrey Beardsley, Imp of the Perverse* (University Park, Pennsylvania and London, 1976), p. 261. Recent studies include S. Calloway, *Aubrey Beardsley* (London, 1998), and M. Sturgis, *Aubrey Beardsley, a Biography* (London, 1998).
61. Newman, *Loss and Gain*, p. 33.
62. Gradwell, *Home Thoughts from Abroad*, quoted in Davies, *Worship*, p. 32.
63. Letter of Bishop Thomas Brown OSB, quoted in Beck (ed.), *English Catholics*, pp. 276–7.
64. Bossy, *English Catholic Community*, pp. 370–7, 383–5.
65. See Davies, *Worship*, p. 31.
66. Bossy, *English Catholic Community*, p. 385; E. Norman, *The English Catholic Church in the Nineteenth Century* (Oxford, 1984), p. 351.
67. Pugin, *Apology*, pp. 24–5. Elsewhere he complains of 'the theatrical quaverings of a Warwick-street choir' (*Contrasts* (1836), p. 55).
68. Quoted in Gwynn, *Shrewsbury*, p. 125.
69. *Loss and Gain*, pp. 198–9.
70. Cf. (John) Bernard McElligott, *The Society of St Gregory* (Exeter, 1952).
71. Decree on the Liturgy, *Sacrosanctum Concilium*, 36, tr. A. Flannery in *Vatican Council II: The Conciliar and Post-Conciliar Documents* (Leominster, 1975 and later).
72. M. Douglas, *Natural Symbols: Explorations in Cosmology* (London, 1970), p. 42.
73. For a survey of ICEL's work, see P. C. Finn and J. M. Schellman (eds), *Shaping English Liturgy* (Washington, DC, 1990).
74. J. McHugh, *On Englishing the Liturgy: An Open Letter to the Bishop of Shrewsbury* (printed privately, 1983); Consilium for the Implementation of the Constitution on the Sacred Liturgy, *Instruction on Translation of Liturgical Texts*, Eng tr. ICEL (Washington, DC, 1969).
75. E. Duffy, 'The Stripping of the Liturgy', *The Tablet*, 6 July 1996, pp. 882–3.
76. For an account of recent changes in Catholic worship, see J.D. Crichton *et al.* (eds), *English Catholic Worship* (London, 1979).
77. An 'elaboration' by Anthony Payne of the 'sketches' Elgar left of the Third Symphony received its first performance in 1998.
78. See M. De-la-Noy, *Elgar: The Man* (London, 1983), pp. 85, 91.
79. De-la-Noy, *Elgar*, p. 84.
80. De-la-Noy, *Elgar*, p. 92.
81. Letter to F. Schuster, quoted in De-la-Noy, *Elgar*, p. 167.
82. De-la-Noy, *Elgar*, p. 151.
83. *The Times*, 15 October 1997.
84. I would like to thank the many people who have helped me write this chapter, especially Ronald Creasman, Barbara Dorf, John Elwes, Paul Inwood and Kenneth Nugent SJ.

FOURTEEN

CATHOLICS, SOCIETY AND POPULAR CULTURE

MICHAEL J. WALSH

COMMUNITY AND SUBCULTURES

The area around Brick Lane, in the East End just across the road from Spitalfields Market, has been home to a series of waves of immigrants into London – Huguenots, Jews and most recently a Bangladeshi community. Once famed for its bagel shops, it is now far better known for its curry houses. Eating there with my family one November evening in 1997 I overheard a conversation across the room. Three men, two in middle age, one much younger, were discussing football. The youngest was a Glaswegian, a supporter of Glasgow Rangers. They were debating the skills of individual players. In Scotland, said the Rangers fan, all two-footers are left-footers. His companions nodded with interest, and the conversation passed on. The remark was made without rancour, but as an apparent (to him) statement of fact. Football players, at least in Scotland, were known as much by their religious denomination as by their skills with their feet. Catholics were still distinguishable as a group.

The conversation had, of course, been about Scotland, where the sectarian divide runs deeper than anywhere else in mainland Britain. But even within England and Wales in the last fifty years, Catholic beliefs and customs marked them off to some degree from the rest of the population of the country, as was demonstrated by the analysis of a Gallup survey of Roman Catholic opinion, published in 1979,[1] or by George Scott's generally sympathetic study of the English Catholic community published in 1967.[2] Catholics constituted, as Peter Coman put it,

> a subculture by virtue of their specific norms and values in sexual, marital and familial morality, their allegiance to Rome, the importance attached to

> the Mass, their belief in life after death and their numerous distinguishing symbols such as Friday abstinence . . . [Catholics endeavoured] to preserve that subculture by segregating the young in educational terms through the maintenance of a separate denominational educational system. Similarly, group endogamy sought to provide an all-Catholic milieu within the family. Such educational segregation and marital endogamy in combination with an array of Catholic associations, such as the Association of Catholic Trade Unionists, were designed to protect the Catholic subculture.[3]

The same perspective has been expressed by many other commentators. As Sebastian Flyte tells Charles Ryder in Evelyn Waugh's most overtly Catholic novel, *Brideshead Revisited,* Catholics have 'got an entirely different outlook on life – everything they think important is different from other people'.[4]

Sebastian Flyte's description of the Catholic community ('at least four cliques all blackguarding each other half the time'[5]), even allowing for literary licence, presents a subculture not quite so homogeneous as some of the historians and sociologists tend to suggest it to have been. On the other hand the Flyte family was an exception, Catholic, in any case, only by marriage. There may have been a considerable diversity of social strata, representing practically every rank in English society with the obvious exception of the royal family, but the vast majority were Irish immigrants. Statistics of the Catholic community before 1850 are notoriously unreliable – one has only to read John Bossy's hesitations written into his attempts to quantify the community for the years before 1850.[6] Currie, Gilbert and Horsley express much greater confidence, though whether it is entirely justified one may doubt.[7] What is certainly the case, however, is that the demography of Catholicism was decisively altered towards the end of the eighteenth century by a massive influx of Irish into England, and especially into Lancashire. They came to work in the mills, and to live in towns and, as John Wolfe comments, they made of the poor Irishman the 'normative image' of Roman Catholicism.[8]

They were not the only Catholic immigrants. Very large numbers of émigré clergy arrived from France and presented a very different picture. Their arrival considerably strengthened the Catholic clergy in London and the South of England, as well as reinforcing the image of the Catholic Church as a bulwark against revolution. But the French, for the most part, returned to France: the Irish kept coming. In 1841 the number of Irish-born residents of England and Wales was just over 289,000: a decade later it was all but 520,000; in 1861 it was well over 600,000. From then on the Irish-born decreased in numbers. England, though it was close, was not the favoured destination for those who wished to emigrate from Ireland. The favoured destination was the United States, and it was only when immigrant quotas were imposed there that, in the 1920s, the numbers coming to England began once more to rise.

Though so much has been written about the Oxford Movement and its converts, it was, at the beginning of the period covered by this book, the Irish who made up by far the larger part of the Catholic community in this country. Not only were 520,000 of the 679,000 Catholics in England and Wales Irish-born, a considerable number of the remainder would have been only first-generation English. As will be seen, one effect of this on the political life of this country has been the significantly different voting pattern of the Catholic community, a characteristic which Hornsby-Smith identified.[9]

It would be quite wrong to infer, however, that the dominant religious culture of the Catholic community a hundred and fifty years ago was, by sheer weight of numbers, an Irish one. Very many of those who crossed the Irish Sea had only a marginal association with Catholicism, at least as it was understood in the middle of the nineteenth century. A major task of the clergy was, therefore, a process of conversion, followed closely by a campaign of education. The notion of a 'fortress mentality' among Catholics, bolstered by the sort of structures described by Peter Coman in the quotation given above is, I think, of doubtful validity before the twentieth century. But in so far as it existed it did so to take special care of the immigrant Irish community. The real problem to be addressed, however, is into what brand of Catholicism they were spiritually and culturally inducted.

It has rather been taken for granted that, in nineteenth-century Catholicism in England, there were two brands of devotional life struggling for supremacy. One of these was a retiring, subdued form of worship as practised by those with a recusant tradition, used to keeping themselves very much to themselves, the other a far more flamboyant, Italian-inspired version of Catholicism which was promoted by the ultramontanes. According to this account of what was going on in Roman Catholic churches and chapels, it was the latter, the ultramontane, version which triumphed, introducing into English Catholic life a wholly alien form of the faith.

It was, as Edward Norman has pointed out, in the interests of the ultramontane party to suggest that the devotional life of English Catholics was 'at a particularly low ebb',[10] and he points out that there had long been nothing particularly secretive about their churches. He does, however, go on to insist that the 'old Catholics' rejected '"continental" devotional practices'.[11] This was Nicholas Wiseman's view, who found the traditional devotion of English Catholics short on 'the fervour of love overflowing the heart and lips, in glowing, affectionate, impassioned addresses'.[12]

Mary Heimann's remarkable study, *Catholic Devotion in Victorian England*,[13] has criticised this understanding of English Catholic worship on a number of grounds. She has pointed to important continuities in devotional practice, particularly in saying the rosary, certainly not itself a nineteenth-century import, and in the preference for a form of Benediction of the Blessed Sacrament which went back to Richard Challoner's *Garden of the Soul* of c. 1740 rather than the more Italianate *Quarant' Ore*. It was these two devotions, she argues, which were of overwhelming importance in the life of English Catholics during the nineteenth century, and there was nothing particularly ultramontane about either of them.

That there was a revival of devotional life during the period, she does not deny, but she does not attribute this, either, to the ultramontane connection – at least, not solely. There was a revival of religious fervour throughout Europe in the nineteenth century, most obviously exemplified by the sudden expansion both of religious congregations, especially those for women, and of missionary activity. In England, Heimann points out, from the middle of the century onwards more Catholics went to Mass, received communion and went to confession than had been customary hitherto. Confraternities grew in number and in size, and parish missions and retreats flourished.[14] But this, she argues, was typical of Catholicism elsewhere in Europe. And though these manifestations of increasing religiosity possibly owe something to the centralising tendency of the papacy, the prayers and devotions which were taken up by English Catholics came mainly from France rather than from Italy – something, one might add, which was equally true of Catholicism in the United States.[15]

This is perhaps not surprising. Many, if not most, of the clergy had been educated in France or the Low Countries (which makes one wonder about Dr Heimann's assertion that England had been spared the Jansenism of pre-Revolutionary France[16]). On the other hand, the preachers of missions and retreats, Passionists and Redemptorists in particular, came from a more Italianate tradition. In contrast, and despite the emotional intensity of Frederick William Faber, English devotional language remained restrained and relatively simple, drawing its inspiration from other English churches, Heimann believes, rather than from the Continent.[17] In keeping it simple there was a concern to appeal to the poor who, as has been seen, made up a large proportion of Roman Catholic congregations. The poor were held in particular esteem. 'The notion of holy poverty', she remarks, 'certainly became a commonly held pious maxim',[18] and the social and ethnic mix within congregations became a matter of pride and, Heimann adds, made them distinctively different from the majority of their fellow churchgoers of other denominations in England.[19]

Members of other denominations did not necessarily share this perspective. What upset his mother most about his conversion to Roman Catholicism, George Tyrrell revealed in his autobiography, was 'that a son of mine should go to Mass with the cook'.[20] As Newman commented in the introduction to the third edition of *The Via Media*, 'there are those, not a few, who would be Catholics, if their conscience would let them; for they see in the Catholic religion . . . a power of sympathy and resource in view of the various ailments of the soul, and a suitableness to all classes and circumstances of mankind.'[21]

The first edition of this book was published in 1836. By the time he came to produce the third edition (1877) he had his hesitations: 'It is so ordered on high that in our day Holy Church should present just that aspect to my countrymen which is most consonant with their ingrained prejudices against her, most unpromising for their conversion.'[22]

Newman was, I take it, referring to the recent Vatican Council with its declarations of papal supremacy and infallibility, which he regarded as inopportune. But that the Church should appear in a guise unappealing to Newman's fellow countrymen was not something that the large Irish contingent would be alarmed about. After all, as refugees from a famine which they blamed, rightly or wrongly, on the English, they had very little reason to admire the British State, its trappings and its culture. If Catholicism was different, then all the more reason for belonging to it, especially because it showed concern for the poor.

Perhaps nowhere is this concern more evident than in Cardinal Manning's intervention in the London Dock Strike, which began on 14 August 1889 – certainly no other initiative of the Cardinal's brought him, and the Catholic Church, to greater political prominence. His was a very direct approach. Manning had the advantage of already being acquainted with the docker's leader, Ben Tillett. In the midst of the strike Tillett returned to his lodgings in Poplar to be told there was an old priest (Manning was then eighty-one years old) waiting to speak to him. Tillett found him reading the latest episode of a Sherlock Holmes story in the *Strand Magazine*.[23] The full story of Manning's intervention, and success in gaining the dockers their 'tanner' despite considerable odds can be found elsewhere.[24] It became the stuff of legend, perhaps not least among Catholics because Frederick Temple, then the Bishop of London, having first been persuaded to join Manning's committee of conciliation, withdrew because he thought the whole process was doomed to failure, and returned to his holidays.

Manning's motives were no doubt various. He was certainly alarmed by the thought that the strike might get out of hand, and lead to something like the Paris Commune (not forgetting its murdered archbishop) of 1871. But he was also aware that very many of those who worked on the London docks were Irish and, nominally at least, members of his diocese. His views on social issues in general were shared by hardly any of his colleagues among the Catholic hierarchy, though he found a ready audience abroad – not least with Pope Leo XIII himself. The Italian Cardinal Capecelatro wrote of him, 'I know none among Catholic Socialists (let the name be permitted me) braver than my late beloved friend, Cardinal Manning, a social student fearless in speculation, effectual in enterprise.'[25] He had, of course, expressed similar concern for the poor, particularly for those who worked the land, in his days as a member of the Church of England, and the attitudes he adopted towards the welfare of the poor have been described as 'Anglican' and contrasted with the attitudes of the majority of Catholics at that time.

Sheridan Gilley has argued elsewhere[26] that, for Catholics, charitable giving was an obligation for the wealthy, who thereby saved their souls, rather than an effort to ameliorate the lot of the poor. Though there may be much truth in this, it seems to me that it is difficult to disentangle motives, and there was a considerable culture of charitable activity which grew up in the nineteenth century and continued on into the twentieth. Of the charitable organisations, without doubt the Society of St Vincent de Paul was the most important. The first branch ('Conference') was formed in London on 12 February 1844, in the course of a meeting presided over by Frederick Lucas, the editor of the *Tablet*, though Lucas refused to become the SVP's first English president: that title went to a Mr Pagliano, in whose hotel in Leicester Square, La Sablonnière,[27] the meeting had been held. By the end of the year there were five conferences in London, and they were soon founded elsewhere in England. The SVP may have been the most potent charitable body, but there were many more. 'The multiplication of organisations', as Hugh McLeod says, 'intended to champion the interests of Catholics as a body, and to meet the special needs, spiritual, economic or recreational, of every identifiable group within the Catholic body.'[28] They engaged in proselytising and the defence of the Church, as well as philanthropy, 'blending the explicitly devotional with either the socially useful or the pleasantly sociable'.[29]

It would, I think, be wrong to see this, at least in the nineteenth century, as a nascent 'pillarisation' of the Catholic community such as emerged in Holland, where Catholic societies (and Calvinist ones) formed an alternative social structure. In this country the clergy seized upon devotional, and other, societies, as a means of saving souls which would otherwise be at risk. The Boys' Brigade, for instance, which began in Southwark in the 1890s, was meant to be 'a Centre of Catholic loyalty and Catholic activity; each a refuge from the allurements of Socialism, the temptations of the streets, [and] the poisonous companionship of the loafer'.[30] Uniforms, whether for the Boys' Brigade or the Scouts, were expensive, and the two organisations appeared linked to the British Army, which did not commend them to Irish youth. On the other hand, attempts to promote Gaelic sports among the Irish, again a movement beginning in the 1890s, did not have much success either.[31]

The Boys' Brigade and the Scouts were both eminently worthy British institutions. As the advertisement in the 1911 edition of the *Catholic Directory* describes it, the purpose of the Brigade was 'to safeguard the faith and morals of our Catholic Lads when they leave school . . . Drill and the military aspects are attractive it is true, but represent only a small proportion of what the Brigade does for the boy' – there were gymnastic exercises, what were described as ambulance lessons, cricket and football teams. As Steven Fielding remarks,[32] the clergy attempted to impose upon their flocks 'a more respectable form of civic conduct'. The chief offence against civic conduct was, of course, drunkenness – and the street-fighting which often accompanied it. This was something which Manning took particularly seriously. He instituted 'the truce of St Patrick', attaching special indulgences to sobriety on 17 March: 'I ask any man whether the drink that maddens and degrades this land is not a preparation for what we saw and wondered at in the drunken commune of Paris?' he remarked.[33] His concern, however, was not only for the stability of the State but for the betterment of his own flock.

At first Manning co-operated with a broad, though largely Nonconformist, alliance of churchmen against intemperance – he even became Vice-President of the United Kingdom Alliance which campaigned against alcohol abuse, and despite its Nonconformist origins regularly spoke at its meetings. But in 1872, the year in which he himself became a total abstainer from alcohol, he founded, for Catholics, The League of the Cross. The League established a network of branches, and drew upon revivalist techniques similar to those employed by the Salvation Army – an organisation for which he had considerable respect – an approach which brought Manning into public ridicule, even from some of his fellow Catholics. Unfortunately, as Derek Holmes remarks, 'the rallies of the League were not wholly abstemious',[34] and there were drunken brawls in 1891 among League members returning from their annual gathering.

Manning made a number of contributions to English public life – he had, as Newsome remarks, 'a definite programme of "practical Christianity" to set before his own flock and the whole nation'.[35] He hoped other members of the Church would do likewise but, with the exception of Edward Bagshawe of Nottingham, few if any of the other English bishops shared what Cardinal Capecelatro had described as his 'Catholic Socialism'. Manning had been a friend of W. E. Gladstone, the Liberal Party leader and four times Prime Minister, from his Anglican days, but in general was rather more sympathetic to the Tory leader and twice Prime Minister, Benjamin Disraeli.

There were always a number of political issues on which the Catholic community might have been thought to have views. When, in 1859, the temporal power of the papacy was under siege, Cardinal Wiseman suggested that such English Catholics as had the vote should cast them against Lord Palmerston, because neither he, nor Lord John Russell who became his Foreign Secretary, were at all sympathetic to the papal cause. Catholics, of course, had little reason to like Russell after his promotion of the Ecclesiastical Titles Act of 1851 which forbade English Catholic bishops, under penalty of a fine of £100, to use the territorial title of their sees. This Act, repealed two decades later by Gladstone, was oddly out of keeping for someone who otherwise had been generally sympathetic to Catholic interests.

Sir John Acton, elected as a Liberal Member of Parliament in 1859, was obviously not of that frame of mind, nor subscribed to the notion that there was a natural alliance between Catholics and the Tory Party, as Lord Derby once put it. The Oxford convert, W. G. Ward, was of like mind with Lord Derby, arguing in the *Dublin Review* that the Tories should look upon Catholics as guarantors of social stability. On the other hand in the *Rambler*, the monthly magazine which he for a time edited, Acton urged the Liberal position on the temporal sovereignty, much to the irritation of Wiseman and Manning. In 1865 Ward was even prepared to vote for a 'no-popery' candidate rather than for a Catholic of a liberal persuasion – though the issue here, convenient enough for the naturally Tory Ward, was liberalism of a theological, rather than of a political, kind.

The temporal sovereignty apart, there were two issues in particular which affected the way Catholics voted. They were, however, contradictory, and also divisive along class lines. The first was education, the second Irish Home Rule. 'No Catholic can vote for any candidate [i.e., the Liberal Party candidates] who proposes to saddle the country with a secular and godless system of education,' instructed Bishop Vaughan in a letter to the people of the Salford diocese in 1874. 'Better suffer a little tyranny from the Tories', wrote the future Cardinal to Lady Herbert a little later, 'than vote for the Radical programme in Education.'[36] Six years later Lord Bury wrote in the *Tablet*,

> The Board School, with its secular education and its legal prohibition to pronounce the name of God in school hours, will be the fate of our children if Mr Gladstone is returned to power. The Conservatives have at least this in common with Catholics, that they dread the complete secularisation of education.[37]

That, then, was one issue – the secularisation of education – which many Catholics regarded as a threat. On the other hand there was the problem of Ireland. Despite his early friendship with Gladstone, Manning seemed closer to Disraeli, until, that is, the Liberal leader announced in 1868 that he was going to disestablish the Church of Ireland. This Manning welcomed warmly. Not so other Catholics, who saw this as yet another step in the direction of secularisation. The *Tablet* led the attack. It had been published in Dublin, where its founder Edward Lucas had located it after he had enthusiastically embraced the Irish cause. John Wallis, who acquired the paper on Lucas's death in 1855, promptly moved back to London.

Wallis was a Tory of trenchant views. As Snead-Cox, a later editor, observed:

> Wallis rammed his political opinions down the throats of his readers with a fine unconcern whether for their wishes or his own interests. And not altogether without success. Indeed, it may be said that it was Wallis's advocacy of Tory views in *The Tablet* which, in some sort, prepared the way for

> that conversion from Liberalism which has been a distinguishing feature in the history of English Catholic opinion during the last fifty years.[38]

This was almost certainly to misread the situation. The natural political home of *Tablet* readers was the Tory Party: if there had been a drift to Liberalism stemmed by Wallis it was only because Liberals had been sympathetic to Catholic emancipation. Wallis would have none of this, but it may have been his opposition to Irish disestablishment which finally brought his downfall – he had made an enemy of too many of his potential readership.[39] He sold the paper to Herbert Vaughan. Vaughan was most certainly no Liberal, but sided with Manning in supporting Gladstone over disestablishment. On Home Rule, however, when Gladstone embraced it, he was adamant. His reasons for opposing it may even have had something to do with his opposition to Liberal plans on education. He feared that Catholic influence in the House of Commons, which was almost wholly dependent on Members returned from Irish constituencies, would be lost, and the Church thereby become vulnerable.

But though Cardinal Vaughan, as he became in 1892 a year after succeeding Manning at Westminster, may have been against it, a great many of his flock were equally firmly in favour as was, again out on a limb, Bishop Bagshawe. In 1892 the *Tablet*, still controlled by Vaughan (it remained in the ownership of the Westminster diocese until Hinsley sold it to a lay consortium in February 1936 because it was losing money[40]), called for Irish voters in England to be disenfranchised. Many of the clergy urged their flocks to vote Tory, because of the Liberal Party's perceived 'secularism' in education, particularly so in the 1906 election. Four years later the Liberal Party was obliged to rely on Irish Nationalist Members at Westminster and showed themselves more favourable to Home Rule, which had rather slipped from their agenda, than they had been for a long time.

Home Rule protagonists, however, were well aware that they could not carry the day on their own. Only in the Scotland Road Division of Liverpool were the Irish present in such numbers as to elect an Irish Nationalist MP, T. P. O'Connor. They needed to win English votes as well, and it was believed that the English working class was by far the most sympathetic group to Home Rule. This belief, when acted upon, served to integrate Irish Catholics into working-class politics, which in any case was much more naturally their place – a priest reported in 1907 that when a Communist march passed a Catholic church, half those in the procession doffed their caps.[41]

There were other reasons why Catholics might be sympathetic to the emerging Labour Party. One could certainly interpret the papal encyclical, *Rerum Novarum*, published in 1891, as being critical of capitalism. There was an attachment to the medieval gild system in the encyclical which fitted conveniently with English Catholic culture. Had the gilds not been destroyed by the 'cupidity' of Henry VIII, argued the Bishop of Salford addressing the Co-operative Society in 1897,

> we would not have required workhouses for the poor, we would not have had employers engaged in bitter strife, we would neither have had strikes, nor their calamitous consequences to our national industries; for from the highest to the lowest all were locked together in bonds of natural fellowship.[42]

This was an appeal to a romanticised version of the Middle Ages which might have been expected to win support from right across the Catholic community that had been taught to believe that capitalism had emerged in England, to the detriment of the workers as the bishop pointed out, as a result of the destruction of the Catholic Church during the Reformation.[43] There was a sense among Catholics in England that, however much they had been marginalised by society as a consequence of the Reformation, they were gradually coming back to take their rightful place.

This was the burden of Newman's famous 'Second Spring' sermon delivered on 13 July 1852 before the hierarchy assembled at Oscott. But it did not happen. Catholics tended to point as signs of hope to the occasional elevation of some Roman Catholic to high office, as, for example, the *Tablet* did on the appointment of Stuart Knill as Lord Mayor of London in 1892, hailing it as the end of bigotry. But, as *The Times* commented in September 1874 about the conversion of Lord Ripon,

> A statesman who becomes a convert to Roman Catholicism forfeits at once the confidence of the English people. Such a move involves a complete abandonment of any claim to political or even social influence in the nation at large, and can only be regarded as betraying an irreparable weakness of character. To become a Roman Catholic and remain a thorough Englishman are – it cannot be disguised – almost incompatible conditions.[44]

There is something faintly absurd at the thought of Cardinal Vaughan being driven past the building in Cambridge he was going to buy as a home for the future St Edmund's House in a closed carriage so that the Reverend Mr Ayerst, from whom the property was to be purchased, should not know that he was selling it to Catholics. This seems to have been a pointless anxiety as the following year Mr Ayerst showed no embarrassment in asking whether the Master of St Edmund's would allow him and the final year of his students of his private hostel to be photographed outside the now Catholic institution.

That was early in 1896.[45] *Apostolicae Curae*, Pope Leo XIII's bull condemning Anglican ordinations as invalid because defective both in form and intention, was issued the following September. Four years later a 'Joint Pastoral Letter' for the English and Welsh hierarchy was issued, condemning 'liberalism'. Both the bull and the pastoral were very largely the achievement, if such they can be described, of Vaughan himself.[46] They marked a watershed, a change in the self-perception of English Catholics, persuading them that they were after all an isolated, discriminated against, minority who needed to cling together if they were to survive. And if anything was calculated to reinforce this belief it was the holding of the Eucharistic Congress, for the first time in an English-speaking country, in London. The Congress itself went off well, but at the very last minute the Government banned the carrying in procession of the Blessed Sacrament. There was also some trouble on the streets, with fears for the safety of the papal legate.[47]

PAPERS AND JOURNALS

But the real threat was from within, rather than from without, the Church. As Peter Doyle has remarked, there was a 'richness of Catholic letters' but what intellectual activity there was in the study of religion 'was soon to be snuffed out by the dead hand of the Modernist crisis'.[48] John Moore Capes, an Oxford Movement convert in 1845, found the cultural and intellectual life of his new Church distinctly wanting. He eventually reverted to Anglicanism, but in the meantime had founded the *Rambler*[49] which, especially after Richard Simpson had taken over the editorship in 1856, became the voice of liberal Catholicism. It was partly because Simpson, a layman, was perfectly ready to stray into the clerical preserve of doctrine, that the monthly ran into trouble with Wiseman. After articles by Simpson on original sin Wiseman suggested that Simpson should turn his attentions away from religious topics. The Cardinal was again irritated when Acton, part-owner and co-editor, described St Augustine as the father of Jansenism. Simpson's resignation from the post of editor was demanded by Wiseman when a contributor to the journal asserted that the hierarchy's attitude to the government's attempts at educational reform was uncooperative. Newman himself was then briefly editor, in which time the *Rambler* published his article 'On Consulting the Faithful in Matters of Doctrine'. Acton took over from Newman after only two issues. Opposition to the stance of the journal by the hierarchy continued. Its name was changed in 1862 to *Home and Foreign Review*, and it became a quarterly of rather more scholarly approach, but with the same claim to intellectual freedom. It survived only two years in an increasingly hostile climate.

Much more to the taste of the hierarchy was its great rival the *Dublin Review*, founded in 1836 by Wiseman himself, though in 1863 the Cardinal passed it over to Manning, who appointed the convert theologian, and ultramontane, W. G. Ward to the editorship. The *Universe* was started as a popular Catholic weekly in 1860, inspired by Wiseman and managed by the Society of St Vincent de Paul. It, too, had an ultramontane editorial policy, being modelled explicitly on the trenchantly pro-Roman *L'Univers*.[50] Apart from the *Rambler*, the only major

Catholic journal of theologically liberal sympathies was the *Catholic Standard*, founded by a Frenchman in 1849 but taken over by the convert Henry Wilberforce, son of William Wilberforce, who merged it with the *Weekly Register*, which name it took. Its owner saw it as a rival to the *Tablet*. It remained in the hands of converts for the rest of the century, being acquired by Manning at one point to prevent its demise – or falling into the hands of the Jesuits. Manning passed it on to Wilfrid Meynell, an act which Vaughan, by this time owner of the *Tablet*, regarded as an act of betrayal.[51] Meynell edited it with his wife Alice until 1899, when it was acquired by Robert Dell, who involved it in the Modernist controversy. It closed in 1902.

The Jesuits had their own journal, the *Month*, started in 1864 by Fanny Margaret Taylor, a vicar's daughter who had been with Florence Nightingale in the Crimea and who went on to become Mother Magdalen Taylor, founder of the Poor Servants of the Mother of God. It was acquired by the English Province of the Society of Jesus in 1865, sold by Fanny Taylor because it was losing money. In the nineteenth century it had a number of distinguished editors, and published significant literary, as well as historical and theological, pieces, the most famous of them being Newman's *Dream of Gerontius*. It turned down, however, Hopkins's *Wreck of the Deutschland*. It also published a large number of articles by George Tyrrell, a staff writer on the *Month* from 1896 to 1900, when he was banished to Richmond in North Yorkshire because of a piece on the doctrine of hell entitled 'A Perverted Devotion' which had appeared not in the *Month* but in the *Weekly Register*. The *Month*, wrote the Jesuit General of the day, Fr Luis Martin, in his memoirs, 'was a rather bland journal, which had no stomach for battling the Protestants and Liberals. I blamed this on the English spirit that is little inclined to break lances over doctrinal issues and is habituated to tolerating Protestant errors.' The periodical further incurred his wrath by taking Dreyfus's innocence for granted, and the priests at Farm Street, where the *Month* was located, likewise caused him annoyance by letting out their hall to Archbishop John Ireland of St Paul, Minnesota, leader of the 'Americanist' party within the United States Catholic hierarchy.[52]

The *Month*, therefore, at least by the end of the century, was something of an heir to the *Rambler*. Its writers fell under deepest suspicion in Rome, and the English Province chose safer paths to follow from then on. George Tyrrell himself died excommunicate. A possibly greater scandal at the time was the case of St George Mivart who also died excommunicate after refusing to sign a profession of faith tendered him by Cardinal Vaughan. Mivart was a scientist, and a convinced evolutionist, though not a radical one. He, like Tyrrell, had fallen foul of the doctrinal authorities for writing on hell, in his case in *The Nineteenth Century*. He had been placed on the Index in 1893, a fact of which he became aware only in 1899 when a new edition of the Index was published. He had also attacked the French Church's attitude to the Dreyfus affair. Mivart demanded to know the specific charges against him, and the names of his accusers. The Jesuit Cardinal Prefect of the Congregation of the Index refused. Mivart was formally excommunicated on 18 January 1900. He died the following 1 April.

As Patrick Allitt has written,

> Tyrrell was the last of the English or American converts to argue that the Catholic Church was an intellectual pioneer. In the new century the Church would continue to win converts of the highest intellectual stature, but henceforth they would generally steer away from theology and find the Church's strength in its *resistance* to intellectual novelties and its deference to an enduring tradition and a strong authority principle. The condemnation of Modernism therefore marks a watershed. Convert intellectuals remained dominant in English and American Catholic churches for the next fifty years but no longer as theological pathfinders. Most of them were, on the contrary, pillars of orthodoxy, willing to accept the lessons of the Vatican Council and *Pascendi* and to act as apologists in their defense.[53]

These sentiments re-echoed the views of Abbot (later Bishop) Christopher Butler expressed in 1958 in an article in the *Dublin Review.*[54] English Catholics had made many distinguished contributions to the intellectual life of the country – Adrian Hastings singles out Dom David Knowles's history of the monastic and religious orders and Frederick Copleston's impressive history of philosophy, half of which was complete by the end of the 1950s – but, he adds, the 'more distinguished components remained, as had long been the case, emphatically non-theological'.[55]

By the 1990s the criticism would no longer be true, certainly not for the United States which has produced some notable scholars in both theology and Scripture, and not true either in Britain, at least for theology. An impressive number of university professors in the religious disciplines are from the Roman Catholic community in this country. But it is also the case that, with one exception (and she is German by origin), these professors have come out of a predominantly clerical, rather than a purely lay, culture. They are also from what might be called the liberal wing of the Church, which represents the mainstream of theological scholarship. They are likewise supported by an array of religious journals which are, for the most part, in the same tradition.

Meanwhile the Catholic newspapers have altered their stance. The *Tablet*, which had become a highly conservative journal under the editorship of Wallis, and had continued in the same style for over a century until the end of the editorship of Douglas Woodruff in 1967, became theologically far more liberal under Woodruff's successor Tom Burns, while remaining politically conservative. After Burns's retirement the paper became more liberal, both politically and theologically. Although the Dominican journal (*New*) *Blackfriars* had represented a left-wing stance almost all its life, other publications such as the *Month* reverted to a more liberal approach only in the 1960s, in the aftermath of the Second Vatican Council. From the late 1940s and throughout the 1950s, however, the *Month* had achieved a degree of fame in Britain as a literary and historical journal under the editorship of Philip Caraman. Caraman was adept at persuading distinguished converts to Catholicism to contribute to its pages. It was an approach, incidentally, which Tom Burns had adopted in the magazine *Order* he began in 1928. *Order* ran for only four issues, but attracted a particularly distinguished group of contributors.[56] There was among Catholics a remarkably high literary culture during the late 1920s, through the 1930s[57] and 1940s and into the 1950s.

But those appreciative of the literary accomplishments of Greene, Waugh, Knox and others were a very small part of the Catholic community. There were very many more readers of publications such as the *Universe*, created in 1860 by the SVP at the request of Cardinal Wiseman to provide a cheap newspaper for the poor, the *Catholic Times* and the *Catholic Herald* – this last begun as the organ of 'Catholic Industrial Democracy' in 1884, under the inspiration of Cardinal Manning.[58] From 1934, under the editorship of Michael de la Bedoyère, this last became a mass circulation paper, competing with the other two. All were out of step with their working-class readership over the civil war in Spain – Catholic workers, like the generality of their class, were supportive of the Republic.[59] Only the *Catholic Worker*, founded in 1935 by a member of the Catholic Guild and sold on the streets in the 1930s, especially in Northern towns in direct competition to the Communist *Daily Worker* and the Fascist *Action*, represented the views of the Catholic working class. It closed in 1959.[60] The remaining papers came into their own, however, in the early 1960s, with the coverage of Vatican II. Circulation soared, the *Universe*, owned at the time by the *Liverpool Echo*, achieving more than 300,000 weekly sales, making it the world's largest Catholic newspaper.

These massive circulation figures did not long survive the Council. Only the *Tablet* has increased its sales in the 1990s, both the *Universe* and the *Catholic Herald* dropping to numbers that cannot in the long term guarantee their survival. The *Catholic Times*, which for a time went out of existence, was revived by the owners of the *Universe* as a somewhat more up-market weekly of decidedly right-wing views, though still with circulation figures which make it scarcely viable.[61] In their heyday, however, they were one of the more important structures maintaining in being the sense of identity within the Catholic community. That identity is gradually being eroded, and with it the props which had kept it in being.

The rise and fall of these institutions can be charted in the pages of the annual publication the *Catholic Directory*. For most of the nineteenth century the *Directory* carried basic information of a civic nature – about recent legislation, postal services and the like – in the manner of an almanac, suggesting that

Catholics were an integral part of the nation. By 1910 this had entirely disappeared, to make room for the increasing numbers of confraternities, associations, crusades, guilds, benefit societies. Lists in the *Catholic Directory* bear witness to the way in which Catholic organisations burgeoned in the last years of the nineteenth century and into the early decades of the twentieth. The Catholic Association, later renamed the Catholic Church Extension Society, was first mentioned in the *Directory* for 1893. It was founded on 2 July 1891 'to organize Catholics on purely Catholic lines, in the cause of Catholic progress'. The Society for the Maintenance of the Apostolic See first appeared in the *Directory* in 1929, the year that the Vatican City State was established. Its objects were 'to obtain more prayers for the Holy Father's intentions; to make the prerogatives of the Sovereign Pontiff better known; to increase the moral prestige of the papacy; to help the Holy Father in his universal work of the Apostolate and in his constant endeavour to establish the Kingship of Christ and his peace among the Nations'. There was even an English League of Catholic Esperantists which claimed in the *Directory* in 1929 that there were 1,400 Catholic Esperanto-speakers in twenty-six countries.

The numbers of people in such organisations in Britain never rose much above 20 per cent of the Catholic population according to Fielding – though that seems a significant proportion – and he also insists that, unlike Mass attendance, there was a preponderance of men.[62] Their purpose was chiefly to protect the membership and had little proselytising zeal. That was reserved for overseas missions.

SOCIETIES, GUILDS AND THE WELFARE STATE

Perhaps the most significant of the mushrooming societies was the Catholic Federation, founded in Salford in 1906 by Catholic trade unionists at odds with the TUC's policy of backing the Labour Party's policy on secular education – though obviously this stance made them equally opposed to the Liberals. Its journal, the *Federationist,* described it as a 'powerful Catholic organization knit together in unity and solidarity, with the spirit of the Maccabees and the spirit of faith sending an electric current of living and vital Catholicity into the soul of every unit, and calling them to action against the growing hosts of enemies of God, Religion and Social Democracy'. Or, to put it another way, 'to marshal the forces of the Catholic Church against the rising tides of Freemasonry, Socialism and an anti-Christian Democracy', as the *Federationist* insisted in November 1910.[63]

The political enemy was unclear. Irish nationalists backed the Liberals, especially from 1908 when Churchill was promoted to the Cabinet, because of his, and the general Liberal support for Home Rule. The Federationists, however, were forced to lend their backing to the Tories who alone, it was thought, were safe on the non-secular nature of education. Despite this right-wing leaning, Federationists supported the miners in their strike of 1912 because they approved of the closed shop and the right to picket, and while they opposed a minimum wage they were in favour of a 'living wage', in line with Catholic social doctrine. They were also behind the votes for women movement,[64] promoting a greater role for women in the unions.[65]

Unions were, of course, very much part of Catholic social thinking in the aftermath of Pope Leo XIII's encyclical *Rerum Novarum*. On the other hand, Leo had condemned socialism. Thomas F. Burns was a leading Federationist and also secretary of the National Confederation of Catholic Trade Unionists which annually, and successfully, opposed the TUC's attempt to pass a resolution in favour of secular education. In 1914 he publicly quarrelled with the Dominican Vincent McNabb, accusing him of confused thinking when he claimed that Leo had not condemned all forms of socialism. It was part of a much wider, and nastier, controversy that had arisen in the wake of the foundation, in September 1909, of the Catholic Social Guild.[66] Its object, as defined on 1 November that year, was 'to facilitate intercourse between Catholic social students and workers'. From the beginning it had the active support of the hierarchy, and was effectively led by a series of Jesuits including Fr Charles Plater, the moving spirit behind its foundation and its major protagonist until his death, at the age of forty-six, in January 1921.

Despite this apparently unimpeachable pedigree, the CSG was promptly denounced as socialist and a priest could remark at a CSG meeting in 1911, 'I know of no single instance of a Catholic becoming a socialist who did not speedily become an atheist'.[67] A wealthy industrialist engaged a lawyer to examine all the CSG's publications to find evidence of socialism of the sort believed condemned by the Holy See. A report was sent to the hierarchy, who chose to ignore it, making it abundantly clear that however socialist the British Labour Party might be, it was not socialist in the sense declared anathema to Roman Catholics. Burns's controversy with McNabb revived the issue momentarily, and it once more became live when, in 1918, Arthur Henderson reorganised the Labour Party and it formally adopted both secular education and nationalisation as part of its policy. Again Burns appealed to the hierarchy to forbid Catholics to join Labour, and again his appeal was rejected. In his pastoral letter for that year Cardinal Bourne insisted that in the labour movement he 'had detected the true lineaments of the Christian spirit';[68] both the *Universe* and the *Catholic Times* supported Labour, at least as a possible option for their readers. The Federation eventually gave up its anti-Labour crusade after a final attempt by Burns, during the 1921 general election campaign, to persuade Catholics that voting Labour was contrary to their faith. Instead it concentrated in the 1920s on issues of public morality such as contraception and the censorship of films. In 1922 the Federation objected to the Care of Infants Bill on the grounds that it would make the mother joint head of the family with the father.[69]

The Federation went out of existence in the late 1920s, and Burns's National Confederation of Catholic Trade Unionists did likewise. In the early 1940s, however, the Association of Catholic Trade Unionists was established, first of all in the diocese of Hexham and Newcastle and then nationally, after a meeting in Manchester in 1947. Its concern was principally to support the continuance of Catholic schools in the face of TUC opposition.

The CSG pursued a much more left-wing line than did the Federation. This was evident in its annual Summer Schools, Yearbooks and occasional publications, and especially, after its first issue in January 1921, in its periodical the *Christian Democrat*. One faithful reader of the *Democrat* – and there tended always, and especially in the 1950s, to be far more subscribers than there were members of the CSG – always burned her copy before the servants could see it.[70] On the General Strike of 1926, however, the CSG was ambivalent. Its magazine printed an article by a Dominican after the strike had collapsed criticising Cardinal Bourne who had condemned it as immoral. The strike was, said the Cardinal in a remarkable sermon in Westminster Cathedral on 9 May 1926, 'a sin against the obedience we owe to God'. The BBC carried the message that same evening.[71] The *Democrat*, however, also had in the same issue an article by the editor denouncing the General Strike in terms similar to those of the Cardinal.

The CSG proved more united on the virtues of democracy. Don Luigi Sturzo, the founder of Italy's *Partito Popolare*, after being forced by the Vatican to abandon his posts within the Party and emigrate to London at the end of 1925, effectively to make way for the rise of Mussolini, was welcomed by Guild members and became a regular contributor to the *Democrat*. One of the earliest denunciations of Hitler was similarly delivered, by a Dutch senator, to one of the CSG's Summer Schools in 1933, and printed in the *Democrat* for September that year.

Such opposition to Fascism was not generally shared by English Catholics, or at least by those most in the public eye. Cardinal Hinsley had a signed photograph of Franco on his desk. And it was an English Catholic intellectual, Douglas Jerrold, who hired the plane to fly Franco home from exile in the Canaries to launch the Nationalist crusade in Spain. Both Chesterton and Hollis praised Mussolini, Hollis even endorsing the Italian invasion of Ethiopia on the ground that it could do the Ethiopians a great deal of good to be exposed to Italian scientific know-how.[72] 'The fear of Communism', Adrian Hastings has remarked, 'easily blinded them to the evils of Nazism, and the pro-Fascist lobby, mounted by a powerful section of the English Catholic intelligentsia, easily covered Germany too. There was far too much anti-Semitism among them already for the Nazi attacks on the Jews to matter very much.' Even after Pius XI's encyclical attacking Nazism had been published, the English Catholic publishing house of Sheed and Ward brought out *Fascism and Providence*. Catholics who condemn the Nazis, claimed the author J. K. Heydon, 'and there are some few who are busying themselves considerably, may be found to be fighting against God'.[73]

Among those thus busy were the members of the CSG, and the contributors to the Dominican monthly *Blackfriars*. Eric Gill and his Distributist colleagues embraced an ideology, which called down (almost equal) plague on both capitalism and socialism, while being more sympathetic to the latter than the former. It owed much to Hilaire Belloc's *The Servile State* of 1913, the same year that Gill, the son of an Anglican clergyman, converted to Catholicism. As the name indicates, it propounded a belief in a wider distribution of property as a safeguard of political liberty, the decentralisation of control, and a guild system made up of master craftsmen rather than unions consisting of employees. There was a veneer of medieval romanticism about it all, but as a creed it blossomed thanks to the incisive writing of Belloc, the undoubted wit of Chesterton, and the fame of Eric Gill. At their height the Distributists could count about three times the membership of the CSG but, their peace campaigning and unremitting opposition to Fascism (which they shared with the CSG) apart, they were of much less consequence in the corridors of Catholic power than the Social Guild.

Though some, such as Michael de la Bedoyère at the *Catholic Herald*, were warning even as late as 1940 that Stalin was a more potent enemy than Hitler, English Catholics were rallied behind the war effort by a new organisation, inspired by Cardinal Hinsley but entirely lay-led, the 'Sword of the Spirit'.[74] Its object, as described after the first meeting of its executive committee on 2 August 1940, was

> a campaign of prayer, study and action. Its fundamental aim is the restoration in Europe of a Christian basis for both public and private life, by a return to the principles of international order and Christian freedom: for these principles are rooted in the Law of Nature which is common to all mankind and recognizes no absolute superiority of race or colour.

The Sword had been intended to attract members from all Christian denominations, but hierarchical fears of ecumenical activity frustrated this end.[75] Early hopes were dashed, successes were not continued into the closing stages of the war. Even so there were high points, such as the mass meetings at the Stoll Theatre in London on 9 and 10 May 1941, with the Archbishop of Canterbury in the chair for the first, and the Archbishop of Westminster for the second. Many Catholics associated themselves with the movement; there were groups among the armed forces not only of Britain but of the Czechs, the Poles, the French and the Belgians. Its *Bulletin* was printed in French and Polish. The Ministry of Information produced its leaflets, and the RAF dropped them over Germany and occupied Europe.

Only part of the movement's troubles sprang from differences with the hierarchy. There was a lack of clarity about what it ought to be doing and there were serious internal divisions among executive members. These became most evident over the Beveridge Report of 1942. Not only the Sword was affected: the Catholic Social Guild was similarly divided, and, unlike the Sword, ultimately failed to survive the disagreements. There were members of both the Catholic Federation and of the Catholic Social Guild who had wanted to move more effectively into action by creating a Catholic, or at least a Christian, political party. Thomas F. Burns started the Centre Labour Party in 1918 in protest against Arthur Henderson's remodelling of the Labour Party, but it never achieved the backing of the hierarchy beyond that of his own bishop in Salford. Time and again, over the General Strike, over Fascism, over Beveridge's proposals, it became clear that however firmly Catholic social principles might be held, there were many divergent interpretations of how they should be put into practice. A political party was out of the question.

Cardinal Hinsley read the Beveridge Report as he lay dying. He approved of it because it was intended to help the poor and the aged. He hoped that Parliament would pass it, even though he was unhappy with the increased state intervention which was entailed.[76] As has been seen, not all Catholics were so sympathetic. Beveridge could be presented as a major step toward the 'servile state' about which Belloc had warned Catholics, a warning many took very seriously. 'From the age of five, if not of two,' wrote Douglas Woodruff in the *Tablet* of 14 August 1943, 'until the age of sixty-five, the rails are being laid down for an Englishman's life. He is ordered by the State to learn, and then he is ordered to work, under the Charter of the New Age.' The problem with the welfare state as conceived by Beveridge was that it could be presented as a radical contradiction of the principle of 'subsidiarity' enunciated by Pope Pius XI in his encyclical *Quadragesimo Anno*.

The task of coming to terms with the legislation subsequent to the Report fell to Hinsley's successor, Bernard Griffin, Archbishop of Westminster from the end of 1943 and Cardinal three years later. He had the advantage, unusual among the hierarchy, of coming from a fairly left-wing family, and had the benefit of advice from a senior Labour MP, Richard Stokes. He backed in principle the establishment of the National Health Service – though he thought it 'would be a sad day for England when charity becomes an affair of the State'[77] – while managing to maintain the independence of the Catholic hospitals. In this last he had the firm support of most of the Catholic press except the *Catholic Herald* whose editor, Michael de la Bedoyère, became the Cardinal's biographer.

Like British doctors at large, Catholic doctors feared for their livelihoods under the new NHS. Their organisation, the Guild of SS. Cosmas and Damian, also expressed alarm at the thought that the new service might 'encourage practices against their conscience and the laws of God', as the *Herald* quoted their spokesman as saying in February 1948. In the end they were mollified by a conscience clause, and like many, if not quite all, Catholics they rallied behind the changes the Labour Government was introducing. Outright rejection came, as might have been expected, from, on the left, the Distributist League whose nostalgia for a vanished, or rather never existing, Arcadia made them of little significance in a massively industrial society, and on the right from the *Christian Democrat* under the editorship of the Jesuit Paul Crane. Crane was in charge of the CSG from 1952 to 1958, but the Guild's concern at what its leadership saw as growing totalitarianism went back to the first publication of the Beveridge Report. It was supported by the economist Colin Clark, whose *Welfare and Taxation*, published by the Guild in 1954, was a favourite text for Conservatives to quote when attacking Labour policy.

The CSG achieved its highest membership under Crane, and the *Christian Democrat* easily its highest circulation, demonstrating that the opposition to the welfare state it expressed found a resonance in the Catholic community. However, the Jesuit Provincial replaced Crane as secretary of the CSG in 1958, and R. P. Walsh took over as editor of the *Christian Democrat*. Both the Guild and its publication subsequently languished, and were wound up in 1967. Crane, however, went on to found *Christian Order*, identical in format to the *Christian Democrat*, and expressing increasingly shrill criticism of the welfare state and, after Vatican II, of changes in the Church. But, even before Vatican II had met for its final session, a group of left-wing Catholics had produced a riposte in the Marxist-oriented journal *Slant*. It was short-lived, but for a time injected a new excitement into such Catholic intellectual life as there was in England.

Adrian Hastings has commented that the 1960s marked the height of Catholic penetration of the establishment, with George Woodcock in charge of the TUC, Charles Curran as Director General of the BBC, Rees-Mogg at *The Times* and Shirley Williams as Secretary of State for Education with Norman St John-Stevas as her shadow on the opposition benches.[78] One might have added to the list Paul Johnson at the *New Statesman*, and in 1965 Fritz Schumacher published his immensely influential *Small is Beautiful* – and became a Roman Catholic.

The decade of the Council, which was constantly on the front pages, partly at least because of the popularity of Pope John XXIII, was also probably the height of Catholic expansionism. About one in ten of the population of England was a practising Catholic, which meant, given the unevenness of the spread throughout the country, that in some areas around 80 per cent of church attendance was made up of Catholics going to Mass. Of all live births 15 per cent were to couples – married couples in those days – in which one partner was a Roman Catholic. Over 12.75 per cent of all marriages in England in 1961 were before a Catholic priest. And well over 50 per cent of the Catholic population of the country lived in London – an enormous change, for only half a century earlier more than 50 per cent of Catholics lived in the ecclesiastical province of Liverpool.

THE PUBLIC IMAGE

And in London, at least north of the river, there presided Archbishop Heenan, appointed in 1963, Cardinal from 1965. Heenan is a significant figure in English Catholicism because he was well known to non-Catholics as well as Catholics because of his wartime broadcasts, and also, perhaps particularly, because of a High Mass from Leeds Cathedral in the run-up to the coronation of 1953. As a study of the churches and the BBC puts it:

> The Protestant Truth Society predictably declared itself scandalized at 'the elaborate ceremonial' which was a grave offence to the conscience of Her Majesty's loyal Protestant subjects. Even a leader in the *News Chronicle* bellowed 'Call it off!' But Cardinal Heenan [he was then merely a bishop] basked in an otherwise positive response from non-Catholics, and it was clear . . . that the broadcast had a singularly fruitful impact, over and above Heenan's own popularity as an accomplished talker.[79]

Heenan, as a radio performer, had been promoted by Fr Agnellus Andrew OFM, who was himself extremely popular. But both owed their access to the air largely to the work of A. C. F. Beales, who was drafted into the BBC in 1941 from King's College, London, to organise the Corporation's programme of talks during the war. He was responsible for introducing a significant number of Catholics to listeners, including Barbara Ward, later to be Lady Jackson, who in 1946 became the youngest-ever governor of the BBC. Martin D'Arcy SJ, the Catholic representative on the Central Religious Advisory Council, was irritated by Beales's influence over religious broadcasting, not least because he was a layman, and resigned at the same time as Beales returned to King's. This left a major gap which Andrew was called upon to fill. He did it expertly, and gained the confidence of the BBC management as much as of the hierarchy. On one occasion he was asked by Cardinal Griffin to write a letter of protest to the BBC's Director General, and by the Director General to draft a reply.

Andrew had to tackle the debate over whether the Mass should be a regular form of Catholic worship for listeners – and later viewers. It had been broadcast occasionally, especially during the war, but as an exception. The original remit had been for non-denominational Christian services. There were some Catholic priests who excelled as preachers at such events – Bede Jarrett OP, Ronald Knox and Cyril Martindale SJ, who was D'Arcy's rather more perceptive predecessor on the Central Religious Advisory Council. Polemic was out – one priest caused scandal in 1927 by praying for the conversion of England[80] – but even after denominational worship was allowed it was not general policy to broadcast the Eucharist. This policy Andrew had a hand in changing. But he was also aware that too few Catholic clergy were skilled in broadcasting. In the mid-1950s, therefore, he founded a residential training centre at Hatch End, on the outskirts of London, of which he became warden.

The Church's self-confidence in this period, which Heenan exemplified, was bolstered by the fact that it alone of the major denominations had continued to grow in the years after the war. The Nonconformist denominations were in decline, the Church of England at best stable. But in 1959 the Catholic Church registered its highest ever conversion rate in this country of 334 per million of the population. A dozen years later it had dropped dramatically to 89 per million, which was just about what it was in 1850. In between, of course, Vatican II and the controversy over *Humanae Vitae* had occurred, but the drop in this, as in church attendance and membership of Catholic organisations should be seen more in the light of the earlier decline in the other denominations.

Nonetheless it was sudden, and clearly shook the confidence of the Church. In England, and of course elsewhere as well, the rapid collapse in Mass attendance was regularly attributed to the effects of Vatican II – opinions differed as to whether they were directly the result of the Council, or of misinterpretations of the Council by radical Catholics. Some organisations, such as the Latin Mass Society, have survived; several have disappeared. The strength of division, however, was obvious at the Faith of Our Fathers conference on 4 May 1996, when some 2,000 'traditionalists' met in Central Hall, Westminster, under the benign gaze of a bust of John Wesley, to bemoan changes in the Church and to applaud the American tele-evangelist Mother Angelica.

The Faith of Our Fathers gathering was in a sense a response to the National Pastoral Congress, held at Liverpool in May 1980. It, too, had some 2,000 attending, but in their case representatives of organisations and dioceses. It was chaired by the Archbishop of Liverpool, the late Derek Worlock. For those who went, which included a good number of the bishops, it was a moving experience. Its conclusions were progressive, though not radical. Even so the *Universe* chose to describe them as 'a snub to the Holy Father'[81] and the bishops, though formally welcoming them, failed to respond in practice.

Popular Catholicism was much in evidence when Pope John Paul II came to Britain in the early summer of 1982. He was greeted with enthusiasm by, it seemed, every style of Catholic in the country. Yet even then they were not enthusiastic enough to purchase souvenirs licensed by the church authorities in sufficient quantities to cover the costs of the trip. It is difficult to imagine that now, when John Paul has himself become such a controversial figure, another visit by the Pope would persuade similar-sized crowds to turn out. The role of Rome has once more become, as it was a century and a half ago, a divisive issue in the life of English Catholicism.

NOTES

1. M. P. Hornsby-Smith and R. M. Lee, *Roman Catholic Opinion: A Study of Roman Catholics in England and Wales in the 1970s* (University of Surrey, Guildford, 1979).
2. Hutchinson, London.
3. Peter Coman, *Catholics and the Welfare State* (Longman, London and New York, 1977), pp. 4–5.
4. Folio Society edition, 1995, p. 67.
5. Ibid.
6. John Bossy, *The English Catholic Community 1570–1850* (Darton, Longman & Todd, London, 1975), pp. 405–29.
7. R. Currie, A. Gilbert and L. Horsley, *Churches and Churchgoers* (Oxford University Press, 1977). They justify their claims on pp. 9–20. However, the table on p. 28 seems to me seriously to underestimate the RC population in 1850.
8. J. Wolfe, *God and Greater Britain*, (Routledge, London, 1994), p. 34.
9. Hornsby-Smith and Lee, *Roman Catholic Opinion*; but see more specifically M. P. Hornsby-Smith, *Roman Catholics in England* (Cambridge University Press, 1987), pp. 165–7. Regular Mass attenders are more likely to support the Labour Party than are the lapsed; cf. Steven Fielding, *Class and Ethnicity* (Open University Press, Buckingham, 1993), p. 130.
10. Edward Norman, *The English Catholic Church in the Nineteenth Century* (Clarendon Press, Oxford, 1984), p. 4.
11. Norman, *English Catholic Church*, p. 4.
12. Quoted by Anthony Archer, *The Two Catholic Churches* (SCM Press, London, 1986), p. 24.
13. Mary Heimann, *Catholic Devotion in Victorian England* (Clarendon Press, Oxford, 1995).
14. Heimann, *Catholic Devotion*, pp. 35ff.
15. Cf. Colleen McDannell, *Material Christianity* (Yale University Press, New Haven and London, 1995), pp. 133–62 and, on the nineteenth-century *l'art Saint-Sulpice*, pp. 167–70.
16. Heimann, *Catholic Devotion*, p. 168.
17. Heimann, *Catholic Devotion*, p. 169.
18. Heimann, *Catholic Devotion*, p. 158.
19. Heimann, *Catholic Devotion*, p. 178 – given this paean of praise for English Catholicism with which the book ends, it is perhaps worth remarking that Heimann herself is not a Catholic!
20. Quoted Nicholas Sagovsky, *On God's Side* (Clarendon Press, Oxford, 1990), p. 10.
21. Quoted from H. D. Weidner's edition of J. H. Newman, *The Via Media of the Anglican Church* (Clarendon Press, Oxford, 1990), p. 22.
22. Newman, *Via Media*, p. 23.
23. David Newsome, *The Convert Cardinals* (John Murray, London, 1993), pp. 332–3.
24. Newsome, *Convert Cardinals*, pp. 331–3 and J. Derek Holmes, *More Roman than Rome* (Burns & Oates, London, 1978), pp. 177–8.
25. Quoted Newsome, *Convert Cardinals*, p. 331.
26. Sheridan Gilley, 'Papists, Protestants and the Irish in London, 1835–70' in G. J. Cuming and D. Baker (eds), *Studies in Church History* 8 (Cambridge University Press, 1977), pp. 259–66.
27. 'The Sandpit'!
28. Hugh McLeod, 'Building the Catholic Ghetto' in W. J. Sheils and Diana Wood (eds), *Studies in Church History* 23 (Blackwell, Oxford, 1986), p. 412.
29. Heimann, *Catholic Devotion*, p. 133.
30. Quoted in Fielding, *Class and Ethnicity*, p. 65.
31. Fielding, *Class and Ethnicity*, p. 17.
32. Fielding, *Class and Ethnicity*, p. 46.
33. Quoted Newsome, *Convert Cardinals*, p. 335.

34. Holmes, *More Roman than Rome*, p. 168.
35. Newsome, *Convert Cardinals*, p. 335.
36. Quoted in Dermot Quinn, *Patronage and Piety* (Stanford University Press, Stanford, CA, 1993), p. 29.
37. Quinn, *Patronage and Piety*, p. 134.
38. From J. G. Snead-Cox, *Life of Cardinal Vaughan* (London, 1910), vol. I, p. 188, quoted in Michael Walsh, *The Tablet* (Tablet Publishing Company, London, 1990), p. 13.
39. Walsh, *The Tablet*, p. 15.
40. Walsh, *The Tablet*, pp. 39–45. There is no evidence for the suggestion, often made, that Hinsley sold the paper to the consortium because he thought it ought to be in lay hands. Rather oddly, Tom Burns suggests in his autobiography that Douglas Woodruff, appointed editor in 1936, was Hinsley's choice as purchaser of the paper. That is not so. Hinsley, who had been out of the country for a long time, did not know the English Catholic community, and relied for advice in this instance on his solicitor, Joseph Weld. Weld proposed Burns as the appropriate person to take the *Tablet* over. Cf. Tom Burns, *The Use of Memory* (Sheed & Ward, London, 1993), pp. 144–5.
41. Fielding, *Class and Ethnicity*, p. 108.
42. Quoted (from the *Manchester Guardian* of 25 January 1897) by Fielding, *Class and Ethnicity*, p. 110.
43. Ibid.
44. Quoted Quinn, *Patronage and Piety*, p. 91.
45. For the foundation of St Edmund's, see Michael Walsh, *St Edmund's College Cambridge* (St Edmund's, Cambridge, 1996), pp. 26–55.
46. For the Bull, cf. J. J. Hughes, *Absolutely Null and Utterly Void* (Sheed & Ward, London, 1968); for the pastoral, David G. Schultenover, *A View from Rome* (Fordham University Press, New York, 1993), pp. 131–60.
47. Peter Doyle thinks that the degree of disturbance may have been overstated; cf. his *Westminster Cathedral* (Geoffrey Chapman, London, 1995), pp. 48–9.
48. Doyle, *Westminster Cathedral*, p. 11.
49. Josef L. Altholz, *The Religious Press in Britain 1760–1900* (The Greenwood Press, New York, 1989), pp. 101–3. Chapter 11 is devoted to Roman Catholic periodicals.
50. For the significance of *L'Univers*, see Owen Chadwick, *The History of the Popes, 1830–1914* (Clarendon Press, Oxford, 1998), pp. 323–7.
51. For the rivalry, see Walsh, *The Tablet*, pp. 14–21.
52. See Schultenover, *View from Rome*, pp. 203–4.
53. Patrick Allitt, *Catholic Converts* (Cornell University Press, Ithaca, NY and London, 1997), p. 126.
54. Quoted Adrian Hastings, *A History of English Christianity, 1920–1985* (Collins, London, 1986), p. 486 from the Summer issue, pp. 117–18. Similar views had been expressed for American Catholicism by the distinguished historian John Tracey Ellis: 'American Catholics and the Intellectual Life', *Thought* (Autumn 1955), pp. 351–88. Ellis's view was even more despondent than Butler's.
55. Ibid.
56. Burns, *Use of Memory*, pp. 44–8.
57. Cf. in particular Adrian Hastings, 'Some Reflections on English Catholicism in the late 1930s' in Adrian Hastings (ed.), *Bishops and Writers* (Anthony Clark, Wheathampstead, 1977), pp. 107–25.
58. Altholz, *Religious Press*, p. 106.
59. For a brief summary of attitudes, cf. Thomas Moloney, *Westminister, Whitehall and the Vatican* (Burns & Oates, London, 1985), pp. 63–82.

60. J. M. Cleary, *Catholic Social Action in Britain 1909–1959* (Catholic Social Guild, Oxford, 1961), pp. 173–4.
61. At the time of writing, the *Universe* and the *Catholic Times*, both owned by Gabriel Communications, are battling for survival. They claim print runs of 75,000 and 20,000 respectively, but 'in both cases circulation is significantly lower' (*Tablet*, 22 August 1998, p. 1105). The *Catholic Herald*, struggling with a very small circulation, has apparently been boosted by the support of Conrad Black, the Catholic owner of the *Daily Telegraph*. One of the *Telegraph's* columnists, the convert Anglican Dr William Oddie, has been appointed editor of the *Catholic Herald*.
62. Fielding, *Class and Ethnicity*, p. 52.
63. Quoted by Peter Doyle in 'The Catholic Federation 1906–29' in Sheils and Wood (eds), *Studies in Church History* 23, p. 462.
64. A Catholic Women's Suffrage Society was formed at a meeting in Alan's Tea Rooms in Oxford Street in March 1911. Representatives were given a warm welcome at the National Catholic Congress held at Newcastle the following June. The CWSS campaigned for an extension of the franchise in general, as well as votes for women. The hierarchy, however, refused either to back or condemn the movement while the *Month*, though in principle supportive, complained that the CWSS had not protested against militant action by suffragists – window-breaking in Dublin. Renamed St Joan's Social and Political Alliance in 1923, the CWSS continued to campaign for women's rights even after the vote had been granted them in Britain.
65. Doyle, 'Catholic Federation', p. 467.
66. For a detailed history of the CSG, see Cleary, *Catholic Social Action*. Within its limits, this is almost a complete account, for the CSG did not long survive the changes related at the end of the book.
67. Cleary, *Catholic Social Action*, p. 14.
68. Quoted Fielding, *Class and Ethnicity*, p. 111.
69. Cf. Doyle, 'Catholic Federation', p. 476.
70. Cf. Cleary, *Catholic Social Action*, p. 113.
71. Hastings, *English Christianity*, p. 188.
72. Allitt, *Catholic Converts*, p. 221.
73. Hastings, *English Christianity*, p. 326.
74. Michael Walsh, *From Sword to Ploughshare* (Catholic Institute for International Relations, London, 1980). After the war Sword of the Spirit campaigned for human rights and survives as the Catholic Institute for International Relations.
75. Cf. Michael Walsh, 'Ecumenism in Wartime Britain', *Heythrop Journal*, 23 (London, 1982), pp. 234–58, 377–94.
76. J. Derek Holmes, 'English Catholicism from Hinsley to Heenan', *Clergy Review* (1977), p. 42.
77. Holmes, 'English Catholicism', p. 49.
78. Hastings, *English Christianity*, p. 562.
79. Kenneth Wolfe, *The Churches and the British Broadcasting Corporation 1922–1956* (SCM Press, London, 1984), p. 500.
80. Wolfe, *Churches*, p. 37.
81. Quoted in Hastings, *English Christianity*, p. 645.

FIFTEEN

FAITH IN CRISIS: FROM HOLOCAUST TO HOPE, 1943–2000

EDWARD HULMES

THE UNFINISHED MISSION

Cardinal Wiseman's pastoral letter, 'Without the Flaminian Gate of Rome', was published on 7 October 1850. Addressing the Catholics of his new diocese of Westminster, he included the following passage:

> . . . your beloved country has received a place among the fair churches, which, normally constituted, form the splendid aggregate of Catholic communion: Catholic England has been restored to its orbit in the ecclesiastical firmament, from which its light had long vanished, and begins anew its course of regularly adjusted action round the centre of unity, the source of jurisdiction, of light, and of vigour.

A century and a half later it is clear that the course of Catholic action in England and Wales has not been so easy to regulate 'round the centre of unity' as the Cardinal anticipated that it would (or, perhaps, should) be. Freedom to practise the faith outside the narrow confines of the ghetto was to liberate the Catholic community from centuries of post-Reformation subservience in this country, but it was also to encourage Catholics to think and to decide for themselves on matters of faith and morals in ways that would have pained a man who, as Rector of the *Venerabile,* had already introduced prayers for the reconversion of England to the Catholic religion. In the years since the Cardinal's celebrated pastoral letter, Catholic emancipation has proceeded at a remarkable pace, so much so that it is no longer permissible to review the period in a merely domestic way.

Future generations may think it curious, to say the least, that at the end of the twentieth century, in societies which claim to be civilised and pluralist (not to say, post-Christian), it is thought barbaric to hunt foxes and deer, to execute a convicted murderer, yet acceptable to abort an unborn child as much for the convenience of 'caring' adults as for any other consideration of the health and welfare of those most intimately involved. At the end of the century the Catholic Church's uncompromising stand on the uniqueness of Christ, on the particularity of the Catholic faith, and on the need to decide the social and ethical issues of today by having recourse in the first instance to Scripture and Tradition, raises questions about the permissible limits of human freedom. This is especially true in deciding how to respond to recent developments with regard to human reproduction and sexuality, genetic engineering, organ transplants and cloning. Euphemisms and circumlocutions are increasingly employed to lessen the impact of the actual as well as the potential threats to Catholic beliefs, values and standards. Human rights, for example, now focus on the individual's *right to choose*. The disposal of unwanted 'human material' becomes *embryo-reduction*; techniques designed to eliminate socially disturbing handicaps and congenital weaknesses play their part in *eugenics*; assisting the terminally ill and the world-weary to end their lives is the 'compassionate' justification for *voluntary euthanasia*. Despite the bitter experience of the last five decades, genocide continues in various parts of the world under the term *ethnic cleansing*. Unborn children are deprived of the most basic human right – to life, that is – in *Planned Parenthood Clinics*; not a few medical practitioners feel insulted when accused of killing human beings by aborting them, when they claim that they are 'simply terminating pregnancies in the same spirit that they strive to treat any other medical problem'; sexual promiscuity is *responsible* so long as it is *protected*, but *irresponsible* if it is not *safe*.

In the future, as in the past, Christ's word is: 'Be not afraid. I have overcome the world'.[1] This is reassuring, but for Catholics – the word is used intentionally, though not to give offence either to other Christians or to those who belong to different faiths – there are some acute, and probably embarrassing, questions to be asked about our human response to Christ's comforting promise. This chapter, which focuses on the themes of *evangelisation, education* and *ecumenism*, is a personal response to some of these questions as the millennium approaches. From a Catholic point of view, the years 1943–2000 are too full of incident, not to mention controversy, to allow for more than a personal and selective response to some of the developments in their course. At first sight the choice of the year 1943 seems arbitrary, while locating the *terminus ad quem* in the year 2000 – given the lack of foreknowledge with which any human being faces even the immediate future – looks like imprudence. The words 'From Holocaust to Hope' epitomise the theological crisis through which the Church is still passing. The phrase suggests the anguish with which believers attempt to sustain their belief in a loving God, knowing that within living memory unspeakable evil has brought inexcusable suffering to millions. On the eve of the new millennium Catholics are obliged to consider how the Catholic faith can be transmitted to a generation that will inhabit a world very different from the one in which they themselves grew up. How, in the light of what has happened during the past half-century, are Catholics to remain faithful to the Gospel when the prevailing climate of opinion encourages indifference rather than hostility to its claims?

The word 'holocaust' is already charged with fearful emotions as a result of the policy of genocide, ruthlessly practised against the Jews by Hitler's National Socialists. The appropriateness of the word 'holocaust' for the suffering endured by the Jews during the time of the Third Reich has recently been questioned on the grounds that it almost sanitises a unique human catastrophe by failing to describe it for what it was, a deliberate programme of mass murder, carried out in the extermination camps set up for the purpose in many parts of Nazi-dominated Europe. By the end of this century, however, sanctioned by a law passed by the majority of members of the Houses of Parliament in 1967, several million unborn children have already been aborted in what is being described as another holocaust, one which Catholic opinion has consistently striven to prevent.

The coming millennium is associated with happier expectations (neither utopian nor chiliastic, necessarily) that human rights will be respected as never before, and that justice, reconciliation and peace will prevail in a better world. The reference to hope in the title signals the optimism with which Christians look forward to the future in the light of faith. Despite the tragic reality of so much that has happened this century, Christians have grounds for continuing to give reasons for the hope that is in them.[2] Here it is assumed that theirs remains the task that has always been and always will be the work of Christians, namely, that of bearing witness to Christ in what is a manifestly sinful and fallen world. In this task the Catholic Church has a vital role to play in bearing witness – as the adjective 'catholic' implies – to a *comprehensive* and *inclusive* understanding of God's revelation in Jesus Christ, a revelation that is capable of making *whole* all that is created.

In 1943 two events occurred, each of which was to influence the course of Catholic life and witness in this country. The first was the death of Cardinal Hinsley, the leader of the Catholic community in England and Wales, who died on St Patrick's Day. The second was the publication in that year of Pope Pius XII's historic encyclical *Divino Afflante Spiritu*. This document confirmed its author as the patron of faithful but fearless biblical study.[3] Both these events heralded change in the development of the Church's mission in and to the world. With the death of Cardinal Hinsley a discrete chapter in the history of the Church in England and Wales came to an end. The Church was about to be challenged from inside as well as from outside, and in ways that were to promote anxiety as much as satisfaction among the faithful. Further afield the Catholic Church in particular was beginning to be condemned for what a minority of vociferous critics described as its complicity in the evil of the Nazi Holocaust against the Jews. This criticism, which continues to be rehearsed at the end of the twentieth century, was directed towards the author of the encyclical *Divino Afflante Spiritu*. In 1943, a generation before the Second Vatican Council, Pope Pius XII was instrumental in reviving for Catholics everywhere the study of the Bible as a key to personal spiritual growth and ecumenical endeavour among all Christians. With the publication of the encyclical, fresh impetus was given to the Church's search for an understanding of the relationship between Tradition and Scripture, and for a blue-print for ecumenical action. Pope Pius XII reminded his readers in that seminal document that the Catholic way of life is always to be a *Catholicismus in Scripturas mensuratus* – in other words, a faith rooted in (and thus to be measured by) Scripture – informed and reinvigorated by reference to ancient Christian tradition in the light of contemporary Christian knowledge and experience.

In retrospect, the passing of Cardinal Hinsley marks a caesura in the continuum of Catholic life rather than the beginning of a radical discontinuity. The transmission of ecclesiastical authority from one archbishop to another at that time came at a moment when many changes in the life of the Church were about to be made. Few who had been brought up a generation earlier can have imagined the scale of the changes that were to come with increasing rapidity and with such disconcerting effects on many of the faithful. Successive cardinal archbishops of Westminster must have sensed, if not actually feared, the impact of the changes that were only becoming apparent. Under Cardinal Bernard Griffin (1943–56), who served as papal legate for the centenary celebrations of the restoration of the English hierarchy in 1950, and Cardinal William Godfrey (1956–63), the life of the Church continued in comparative tranquillity. Appointed in 1963, the eighth Cardinal Archbishop of Westminster, John Carmel Heenan, was to experience more troubled times. For the next twelve years he saw his principal task as one of preserving the unity of the Church in England and Wales. There is no doubt that the unity of the Church was threatened by the differences of opinion within the Catholic community occasioned by the publication in the summer of 1968 of Pope Paul VI's encyclical *Humanae Vitae* on the subject of contraception. Nor was his work made easier when critics of the ecclesiastical status quo began to see in the decisions of the twenty-first ecumenical Council of the Church, called by Pope John XXIII at the end of 1962 and closed by Pope Paul VI in December 1965, fresh opportunities for dissent and for radical reinterpretations of Catholic orthodoxy. By the time that Cardinal Basil Hume assumed the leadership of the Catholic hierarchy in England and Wales in 1973, Catholics throughout the world had been thrust rather than led into an era of accelerating and sometimes bewildering change.

Some of the change has been yeast-like in its effects; some has had less catalytic and edifying consequences.

From 25 to 31 October 1942, at the height of the Second World War, Angelo Giuseppe Roncalli, the future Pope John XXIII, was on a spiritual retreat together with his clergy in the Apostolic Delegation in Istanbul. At the time he wrote some words in his diary, which were to help set the agenda for his pontificate from 1958 to 1963 and for the Catholic Church ever since:

> The two great evils which are poisoning the world today are secularism and nationalism. The former is characteristic of the men in power and of lay folk in general. The latter is found even among ecclesiastics . . . We are living through great events, and chaos lies ahead. This makes it all the more necessary to return to those principles which are the foundation of the Christian social order, and to judge what is happening today in the light of what the Gospel teaches us, recognising in the terror and horror which engulf us the terrible sanctions that guard the divine law, even on earth.[4]

On the night of 23 October the same year, eight hundred miles to the south of Istanbul, a thousand Allied guns of the Eighth Army began an artillery barrage that signalled the start of the battle of El Alamein. A similar distance to the east, the Red Army was engaged in bitter fighting against German forces in and around Stalingrad. The ensuing Allied victories against Rommel's forces in North Africa and against von Paulus' VIth Army at Stalingrad were two of the great turning points of the Second World War in the struggle against Nazi aggression. Twenty years later Pope John XXIII was to summon his senior colleagues to attend the Second Vatican Council.

In 1943 the French philosopher and religious writer, Simone Weil took her own life while working for the French resistance movement in London. At a time when others were suffering persecution and death under the Nazis in Europe, she chose to identify with workers in France by eating no more than the starvation rations offered to them. Born into a Jewish family in Paris in 1909, she developed a profound mystical understanding of Catholicism towards the end of her short life, but never felt able to commit herself to the institutional Church. She believed that the supreme greatness of Christianity derives from the fact that it does not seek a supernatural remedy against suffering but a supernatural use of suffering. Rabbi Albert H. Friedländer expresses a Jewish point of view on the theological problem:

> Suffering is part of human life. The easy definitions of early Reform Judaism rejected any notion of the evil resident in man. To this day, we make facile comparisons with our neighbours, explaining that they believe in original sin and we believe in original goodness. The rabbis had a different understanding. They appraised humanity in terms of what they could see, and

> they saw evil. Evil led to suffering, and the Jews were not exempt from this. Contemplating the destruction of Jerusalem, they did not enumerate the political and military factors which led to the burning of the city. They found the reasons in the moral decay of the populace.[5]

Mention may also be made of the political activity which, to the surprise of those who considered that the nation already had enough to do to defeat Nazi aggression, was proceeding in the fields of social action and educational provision. In 1943 the Beveridge Report appeared as a blueprint for change in the provision of a comprehensive scheme of social insurance, without income limit, for all the people of Britain. This report and the development of the welfare state in the years that followed owe a largely unacknowledged debt to the social teaching of the Catholic Church, which is associated particularly with the work of Pope Leo XIII. In 1944, the Butler Education Act appeared, after much preliminary consultation. Among its many innovative provisions was one that sought to give religion a more prominent place in the curriculum of state schools. This was something that Catholics could support, *ex animo*, while continuing to argue the case for special arrangements to be made in order to meet the needs of Catholic education.

At the end of the century the Church is still engaged in three essential activities, each of which retains a social dimension. The first is the work of evangelisation. The second is the work of education. The third is the work of ecumenism. In each case this service to and in the world recognises the importance of what has been called the option for the poor, an option to which papal calls for the reconsideration of the best possible use of available resources consistently draw attention. It is the option for the poor, as understood by the followers of Christ, which offers to the needy what the consolations of secular ideologies have been incapable of providing. This work of love needs to be reviewed in the light of Dominical imperatives. The mission of the Church is unfinished. It begins as it will end with Jesus, the Christ, true God and true Man, the same yesterday, today and for ever. Three interrelated commands of Jesus serve to remind his followers that the Church – as the Second Vatican Council confirmed in *Ad Gentes Divinitus* (1965) – is missionary 'by her nature'. None of these imperatives can be disobeyed, ignored, or changed by the followers of Christ without betrayal. The first is *The Evangelical Imperative*. 'Go, therefore, and make disciples of all nations . . .' (Matthew 28:19). The second is *The Educational Imperative* ' . . . teaching them to observe all that I have commanded you' (Matthew 28:20). The third is *The Ecumenical Imperative*, derived from the High Priestly prayer, which promotes the unity for which Jesus himself prayed:

> 'I do not pray for [my disciples] only, but also for those who believe in me through their word, that they may be one; even as you, Father are in me, and

I in you, that they may also be in us, so that the world may believe that you have sent me.'[6]

THE EVANGELICAL IMPERATIVE

During the period of crisis and change in the second half of the twentieth century, the Church's missionary task has been subjected to scrutiny and criticism from inside as well as from outside. Reinterpretation of the theory and practice of the Church's teaching mission has had to be undertaken with proper regard for the challenges presented to faith in Christ by the problems of evil, scepticism, doubt, uncertainty, other religious systems, unbelief, nationalism, secularism, materialism, and by theological liberalism. The dark side of society is exposed by the sights and sounds of poverty and deprivation in many places, but it is with human depravity as well as social deprivation that the Church has to deal in undertaking its task of evangelisation. The perpetrators of violence in all its many forms against persons and property are as often as not, it would appear, unable to distinguish between good and evil. In the early days of the Second World War Dorothy L. Sayers wrote:

> While there is a superficial consensus of opinion about the ethics of behaviour, we can easily persuade ourselves that the underlying dogma is immaterial. We can, as we cheerfully say, 'agree to differ'. 'Never mind about theology,' we observe in kindly tones, 'if we just go on being brotherly to one another it doesn't matter what we believe about God.' We are so accustomed to this idea that we are not perturbed by the man who demands, 'If I do not believe in the fatherhood of God, why should I believe in the brotherhood of man?' That, we think, is an interesting point of view, but it is only talk – a subject for quiet after-dinner discussion. But if the man goes on to translate his point of view into action, then, to our horror and surprise, the foundations of society are violently shaken, the crust of morality that looked so solid splits apart, and we see that it was only a thin bridge over an abyss in which two dogmas, incompatible as fire and water, are seething explosively together.[7]

The moral ambivalence remains. Consensus of opinion about 'the underlying dogma' no longer exists, or if it does it is insufficiently explicit. Faced with so much invincible ignorance of the spiritual and moral claims of the Gospel, Catholics will not easily be persuaded that they are not living in a post-Christian society. Yet the century does not approach its conclusion in a miasma of despair. It ends with the message of hope insistently expressed by Pope John Paul II in his repeated calls to mission, to reconciliation, and to the fullest possible understanding by all Christians of the mystery of the Holy Trinity. From the

Church's point of view, the Second Vatican Council provided the ideas and the instruments for faithful development and change. The darkness of events is illuminated by the light of Christ through the constant witness of a Church which, despite appearances, has in this century demonstrated the right to be called an *ecclesia semper reformanda*, with a universal and inclusive Gospel still to proclaim. The mission of the Church continues to be opposed by widespread human indifference to and ignorance of the faith, by atheistic ideology, secularism, apostasy, materialism, and by the growth of neo-paganism.

Millions of people who have known what it means to live under repressive regimes of one kind or another for most of the twentieth century are learning about the uncertainties that follow liberation. Some totalitarian dictatorships have collapsed. Economic and moral confusion has attended the political débâcle. Many long-established moral and spiritual values have been questioned and abandoned in the pursuit of personal freedom. Other dictatorships and one-party states remain, tottering but intact. New and even more menacing political systems may yet emerge. For the moment the threat of nuclear holocaust has apparently receded. The manufacture and the acquisition of chemical and biological weapons still pose threats to world peace. In the last fifty years astonishing scientific discoveries and potentially beneficial advances in applied technology have been made. Many of these innovations have been beneficial, but during the same period there have been unprecedented acts of violence, mass murder and genocide in many different parts of the world. A century ago few could have foreseen the uses, for evil as well as for good, to which these discoveries would one day be put. Fewer still could then have imagined the depths to which large numbers of their descendants would sink in applying themselves so assiduously to the spiritual, physical and mental destruction of their fellows.

Belief in human self-sufficiency, in the power of unaided human reason, and in the selective application of the instrument of methodological doubt, was sanctioned by the Enlightenment. It has not been sufficient to take us through the darkness of the twentieth century. The proffered substitutes to theism have proved to be gods that failed. The monolithic structures of atheistic communism erected in the Soviet Union began to crumble in the 1980s. A decade later the USSR collapsed. The stability of its new elements, as of its former client states, is uncertain. Whether or not religion will provide a firm basis for stability there remains to be seen. Marx's dictum that religion is the opium of (not *for*) the people begins to sound more like a nostalgic than an openly hostile observation about religion in the light of his further comment: 'Religion is the sigh of the oppressed creature, the heart of a heartless world, the soul of a soulless environment.' Many people in this country today know what it is to live in a heartless world and a soulless environment. Marxism itself, however, had already brought millions under the influence of a powerful opiate, namely, the superstitious belief that human reason is potentially sufficient of itself to make any recourse to traditional metaphysics, let alone to a revealed theism, superfluous. Throughout the century, however, the Church has been obedient to the evangelical imperative, often in face of the harshest persecution.

From the early 1930s right through the second half of the twentieth century countless numbers of victims suffered under totalitarian dictatorship, but in the case of the 'Final Solution' that led to the *Sho'ah*, the 'calamity, devastation and ruin' of the Holocaust – planned and all but carried out by the National Socialists – it was the Jewish people who suffered uniquely. Not all the victims were Jews, but all Jews were (and in a real sense still are) victims. Part of the tragic legacy of the Holocaust is the crisis of theism. For the inheritors of the biblical revelation, for Christians as well as Jews, the crisis is one of belief in a loving and merciful Creator who permits suffering on such a scale. For unbelievers with no God to defend or to blame, the crisis is one of continuing to believe that human beings are capable of delivering themselves from the consequences of their evil inclinations.

After the collapse of the Third Reich in 1945 some profoundly disturbing theological and anthropological questions were raised by the genocide practised in Bergen-Belsen, Auschwitz-Birkenau and the other extermination camps scattered across Europe. The question, 'Where was *God* at Auschwitz?' is not the only one to disturb us. 'Where was *man* at Auschwitz?' also demands an answer. Both questions bear witness to the sense of dereliction felt by many in the closing years of this century. Similar questions are being raised more recently as the horrors of the Soviet Gulag and the 'Cultural Revolution' in China begin to be revealed. At a different level, but no less disturbing for thoughtful Catholics is the charge – still to be heard at the end of the century – of Catholic indifference under the leadership of Pope Pius XII to the sufferings of the Jews and others during the Holocaust, and even of Catholic collusion with their torturers. Few details were generally known at the time about the scale of the tragedy that was being enacted in the concentration and extermination camps of Europe. With the liberation of the camp at Bergen-Belsen on 15 April 1945 by units of the British army, and the subsequent discovery of other extermination camps across Europe, a hitherto unsuspected level of human wickedness was revealed. The story of the persecution, internment, and extermination of millions on grounds of their race, religion and disabilities is grim and not to be forgotten. On a scrap of paper found at Ravensbrück concentration camp a woman prisoner had written the following prayer:

> O Lord, remember not only the men and women of good-will but also those of ill-will. But do not only remember all the suffering they have inflicted on us. Remember the fruits we bought, thanks to the suffering: our comradeship, our loyalty, our humility, our courage, our generosity, and the greatness

> of heart which has grown out of all this. When they come to judgement let all the fruits that we have bought be their forgiveness.

At the end of the twentieth century it is confidently asserted that the modern mentality, not to mention its brasher post-modern sibling, is now liberated from the traditional supports provided by the humanistic legacies of Greece and Rome, together with the contingency-affirming monotheisms of Judaism, Christianity and, more recently, Islam. The present Pope presents a different picture, however:

> *As the year 2000 approaches, our world feels an urgent need for the Gospel.* Perhaps we feel this need precisely because the world seems to be distancing itself from the Gospel, or rather because the world has not yet drawn near to the Gospel. The *first* case – the move away from the Gospel – is particularly true of the 'Old World', especially of Europe; the *second* is true of Asia, the Far East, and Africa.[8]

In the 'post-modernist age' there is, apparently, no authoritative basis for the religious beliefs, the moral values, and even the natural sciences of yesterday. There is a moral 'black hole' at the heart of our universe. There may never have been a time when playing games with words was so confusing as it now is. The widespread use of terms such as 'pluralism' and 'multi-cultural' is a case in point. The word 'pluralist' is a singularly inaccurate adjective to use in describing the society in which we live in this country. The extent of cultural enrichment of 'pluralism' in any society can be overstated. The potentially disruptive effects of the juxtaposition of differing religious, cultural, political and economic traditions is too easily ignored. Scepticism and uncertainty about the validity and relevance of religious belief in general (and of Catholicism in particular) are common. Religious and cultural diversity in this country have transformed – some would say, secularised to the point of irreversible superficiality – the theory and the practice of religious education. This is a point to be taken up later. The secular basis of what is described as 'pluralism' has been made virtually inaccessible to criticism. Those with alternative world-views about how education is to be organised in order to reflect the beliefs of their believing community keep silence, or make their own arrangements for the education of their children. To be specific, there are considerable numbers of Jews, Sikhs, Muslims – and Christians – for whom the extent of cultural enrichment is restricted. The result is the substitution of what Chief Rabbi Jonathan Sacks has called 'narrowcasting' for 'broadcasting'. By the former term he means addressing the converted: the exchange of commonly held beliefs in ghetto-like communities where only the opinions with which we agree are to be heard. 'Pluralism' ought properly to allow for the free interchange of conflicting beliefs, not least about the philosophy, the theory and the praxis of education. The cohesion of any society depends upon the setting of the *tolerable* limits to personal freedom. The rhetoric of pluralism offers little practical help either in distinguishing the intrinsic quality of the *differences* which make each human being and each community of human beings unique, or in helping to reconcile the differences that threaten the integrity of the society in which they are to be found. The freedom of all is undermined if there are no commonly accepted restraints on the exercise of personal liberty. This is where a sense of history and an awareness of tradition are of importance for the preservation of order and for the integrity of society.

In the twentieth century, as in the nineteenth, Modernism remains *un mouvement catholique dévié*. Less interested in the reinterpretation of Scripture and the renewal of Catholic Tradition, its devotees look to eclectic new forms of spirituality which do not offend the modern 'scientific' temper. Such critics continue to express their dissatisfaction with Catholic orthodoxy. They have difficulty with claims for the historical reliability of the Gospels, with the accounts of 'events' in the life of Jesus, and with the miracles. The distinction between the *doctrines* of the Church and the *teaching* of the Church is sometimes overlooked. The former are the unchangeable truths about God's revelation of himself in Christ. They are the essential elements, the truths, which are of the essence of Catholicism. The teaching of the Church may be open to modification and change in the light of experience, as more and more is revealed by the Holy Spirit and by research in many fields. Even so it is the spirit of Christ which helps the Church to reformulate the teaching for our own time. Doctrines are thus reinterpreted, not displaced. Only through the same spirit of Christ is the link maintained in the Church between revealed doctrines and authentic teaching. Only thus is authentic development to be distinguished from inauthentic innovation. In the case of some critics, still prepared to call themselves Christian, the shift has amounted to an abandonment not only of Tradition as understood by orthodox Catholics in the phrase 'Scripture and Tradition', but also of Scripture, as the biblical record is subjected, not to the investigation of readers, whether scholarly or lay, in the way advocated by Pope Pius XII in the encyclical mentioned earlier, but to the scepticism of secular scrutiny. It is not easy to discover just where some critics do stand on many theological issues because they are in the habit of claiming that they are misunderstood whenever their words are taken at face value.

What is the future of Christian mission undertaken in obedience to the evangelical imperative in a 'pluralistic' 'multi-faith' world? Twentieth-century attempts to solve the problem of religious diversity in terms of cultural relativism or by the doctrine 'my religion is true for me; your religion is true for you' are unconvincing. But the questions remain. Are there not other proven paths to enlightenment? How is the evangelical imperative to be reconciled with the claims of Hindus, Buddhists, Sikhs, Jains, and the adherents of lesser known religions? What is to be said about the religions of China and Japan? Are they not all of them concerned with delivering their adherents from darkness to light? Hinduism promises an ultimate deliverance from ignorance to knowledge of the real, providing for the purpose a strategic plan of progressive salvation. In doing so its adherents claim that it satisfies a universal human need. Catholicism, too, offers a way of life which promises 'more light', which opens the eyes of the blind so that they can perceive the Truth; which enables us to see infinity in a grain of sand, and which points to a present as well as a future salvation. The mystery of God is unfathomable, but Catholics are not left groping blindly in the dark. We would know nothing were it not for the enlightenment given *in Christ*. Ultimately it is the hiddenness of God that is most disconcerting for the believer, although the God who hides himself is also the God who reveals himself on his own terms. What Martin Buber called *Gottesfinsternis*, the darkness which surrounds the mystery of God, is a phenomenon known in all the great monotheistic religions, Judaism, Christianity and Islam. Yahweh, God-in-Christ, Allah, identify the God who is otherwise an absent God, the *deus absconditus*. Despite all our efforts our concepts of God are less adequate than we like to think. Martin Luther spoke for many when he identified the paradox of the *deus absconditus*, who is also the *deus revelatus*, the God who reveals himself. 'Can you find out the deep things of God? Can you find out the limit of the Almighty?' asks Zophar the Naamathite of the forlorn Job.[9] What we would like to know will be made manifest, Paul writes to Timothy, 'at the proper time by the blessed and only Sovereign, the King of kings and Lord of lords, who alone has immortality and dwells in unapproachable light, whom no man has ever seen or can see'.[10] To 'take leave of God' suggests the beginning of a journey that starts with the realisation that our present conceptions of God are too limited. It does not mark an arrival at the end of that journey with the somewhat rueful conclusion that we are, after all, alone in the universe and must, therefore, courageously 'take leave' of the *reality* of God. The response to the divine initiative for the salvation of all is still an integral part of the Gospel that the Church is charged to preach up to and after the millennium, and to the end of time.

During the course of the last 150 years some notable intellectual movements have helped to erode the belief, of primary importance in all the great monotheistic religions, that individuals are morally responsible for their actions. Darwinism ascribes animal status to human beings. As products of evolutionary process our actions follow animal impulses, however sophisticated our animal natures have mysteriously become. Sigmund Freud made human beings the helpless puppets of suppressed sexual feelings. Karl Marx made us the victims of social and economic forces. Materialism, monetarism, scientism, post-modernist analysis, behaviourist psychology, have all contributed to a widespread popular belief that the actions of individuals are determined by environment and by the countless stimuli to which human beings are subjected and for which they are not personally responsible. The belief that individuals are accountable for what they do has, nevertheless, survived this philosophical onslaught.

To judge from the number of books and articles that are available, there is still great interest in Jesus, despite widespread indifference to the claims of the mainstream churches which exist solely to further his earthly mission. Who was he? Who *is* he? His personality and his message still attract the attention of many who would not consider themselves to be religious in the usual sense of the word. A hundred years ago it was Albert Schweitzer who gave impetus to the renewed search for the historical Jesus. A century later orthodox Catholic Christology continues to promote belief in the two natures of Jesus, in his humanity and in his divinity. The temptation to think of Jesus as no more than a human creature, though in possession of unique spiritual gifts, yet explicitly or tacitly to deny his divinity, has proved to be difficult to resist for some Christians during the last fifty years. The Christ of faith has been separated from the Jesus of history, with predictable consequences. We have thus seen the emergence of a human figure clad in different sets of clothing according to the imagination and fancy of his interpreters. By the end of the 1940s, after the global catastrophe of the Second World War, and in the wake of the Holocaust, Jesus begins to appear in some circles as an anti-Semite, a betrayer of his own culture, the progenitor of a religion that has consistently down the centuries connived at the destruction of the Jews, when and where it did not actually provoke it. A decade later the emphasis begins to be on the Jewishness of Jesus. Jews claim him for their own, as a rabbi, albeit one who was sadly mistaken about many things. In another guise Jesus is presented as an archetype of the collective unconscious. Then he appears as a revolutionary, as a social reformer, as an anti-establishment figure and as a commendably belligerent pacifist. And lurking beneath the surface throughout this period there have been other suggestions, not to say claims, about his humanity. Why did he elect to be celibate? What was his relationship to some of the 'publicans and sinners' with whom, according to certain passages in Scripture, he apparently preferred to consort?

In the closing years of the century the word *theology* has been qualified by a series of adjectives, 'black', 'liberation', 'feminist', for instance, each of which bears witness to the sectional interest of its protagonists. For Catholics who choose to think about these things this fragmentation, this specialisation, can be unnecessarily disconcerting. Holding the line against those who would emphasise one aspect of the ministry of Jesus remains an important part of Christian witness as the millennium approaches. This is not to say that in proclaiming the Catholic faith in times of crisis, Christians give up their attempts to interpret the significance of their spiritual heritage in and for their own times. At a time when Christians of all churches and denominations constitute only a minority of the population, the task becomes one not just of outreach in missionary terms but of encouragement within. The task is to make better-informed Christians rather than more Christians. It is to offer Jesus as the Saviour of the world. The *new evangelisation,* which Pope Paul VI's apostolic exhortation *Evangelii Nuntiandi* (1975) outlined, involves both a continuing evangelistic endeavour throughout the world in the service of those who have not heard the Gospel and a more spirited *rediscovery* of the treasures of the same Gospel by those who are already within the fellowship of Christian believers.

THE EDUCATIONAL IMPERATIVE

The questions raised so far require a reassessment of the ways in which the Catholic faith is presented to the young, to those of all ages who continue to question, and to the cultured despisers of all revealed religion. The constant call today is for more and better education, but what kind of education will serve? Catholics have a distinctive part to play in meeting this need, but only for as long as the education they help to provide is explicitly grounded in Christ, and sustained by an authentically Catholic spirit. It is not difficult for teachers – in the Church, as well as in schools, colleges and universities – to isolate themselves from the real world and thus to overlook the questions which individuals are asking (or would like to ask if given the opportunity), and to provide them instead with answers – answers that are fashionably tentative, partial or provisional – to questions which few are bothering to ask. For a long time secular institutions of higher education have assumed proprietary rights to decide what is to count as knowledge, and how such knowledge is to be acquired, assessed and disseminated. With variations of style, method and presentation, the formal lesson and the even more formal lecture remain the stock-in-trade of the professional educator. The lecture pattern (and to change the location, the sermon or homily pattern) persists, with questionable efficacy in so many instances. At the end of the century even the printed word is in danger of being superseded – in popular thinking at least – by the progress of information technology. The nature of this revolution in communications is still only dimly understood by all save the initiated. Its impact, whether we understand it or simply decide to ignore it, is already far-reaching and profound. The scale and the rate of the changes that are now being introduced into our lives are hard to comprehend. Ignorance of the social as well as the technological implications of the changes brought about by electronic innovation engenders feelings of powerlessness. Nadezhda Mandelstam once observed: 'The future has one marvellous advantage: it always elusively recedes – particularly when it promises happiness.'[11]

Since the mid-point of the century, in this country as elsewhere no doubt, the erosion of Christian apologetics from the curriculum has met with an ambivalent response by those who know what once was and what now is. In the last fifty years this task of equipping those involved in Catholic education appears to have been a less important priority than before. It may be time to change that, using a maxim of St Peter, which shows not merely *what* the educational task is, but *how* it is to be undertaken:

> In your hearts reverence Christ as Lord. Always be prepared to make a reasoned defence (*apologia*) to any one who calls you to account for the hope that is in you, yet do it with gentleness and reverence.[12]

The often perfunctory learning and thoughtless repetition of formal catechetical formulae, the playing of sterile games with words and borrowed phrases, the uncritical reliance on an imperfectly understood Magisterium, the rehearsal of stock answers, the disposition to engage in 'theological' encounter with other Christians and non-Christians alike, are all easy to caricature and to condemn. But Catholics in this country have emerged from the ghetto. The need for self-defence, self-preservation, self-justification and self-conscious triumphalism has passed. The recognition that the ancient formula *extra ecclesiam non est salus* is to be patiently reinterpreted under present conditions in a multi-faith society has had its effects on the way in which the *uniqueness* of the Catholic faith is now to find expression. The neglect of thoughtful apologetics, however, as an integral element in Catholic education has led to a situation in which many – perhaps most – younger Catholics are left doctrinally defenceless, philosophically inept, and in ignorance of the faith they are otherwise encouraged to profess. Dialogue with other Christians and with members of other faiths, or of none, can only be less fruitful than it otherwise might be, when Catholics are incapable of contributing something of the unique particularity of Catholicism.

Education, for the thoughtful Catholic (no matter what 'subject' is being studied, and at whatever level), is a lifelong process of 'learning to know Christ and his benefits'. How could it be anything else and deserve to be described as Catholic? Catholic education as a whole, not just in its elements of religious education, is intended to reflect a view of the world that is illuminated by faith in Christ, as understood and interpreted in the Catholic community, even when the intention is not explicitly expressed. Catholic education claims to be more than a tentative search for God in the still uncharted and apparently fathomless sea of faith and unbelief. The primary purpose of Catholic education is not to encourage individuals 'to choose a faith for themselves', if and when and how they feel disposed so to do. Catholic education is about *discovering* Christ, or it is nothing. It is about holy living and holy dying, or it misses the mark.

At a time when a loss of faith in religion as well as in science is often indicated by an indifference to the claims of both, and when there are signs that surprising numbers of people are turning for solace to drugs, cults, superstition and fantasy, Catholic education can still present the unity and the diversity of the historic Christian faith in such a way as to make a compelling appeal to the mind as well as the heart. Given the opportunity and the skill, it can do this without resorting either to coercion or indoctrination. It offers an all-embracing way of life, an alternative prospectus, to that provided by the increasingly forthright advocates of secularism, materialism and hedonism. The Catholic option will fail to attract the attention it deserves, however, if its methodology is unsystematic, if its content is intellectually undemanding, and if its presentation lacks the essential elements of critical and enthusiastic advocacy. Catholic education is in danger of becoming too indistinct, too narrowly defensive, and too little apologetic in the classical sense of the word. The reasonable and reasoned case for faith in Christ and for membership of the Mystical Body which is the Church, is so easily ignored when personal experience is made the touchstone of theological and doctrinal relevance. Experience and imagination, though unquestionably important, are not the ultimate criteria for testing the authenticity of Catholic life and thought in any age, least of all in our own. This is nowhere more true than in liturgy. The Englishing of the Liturgy has, as yet, done little to awaken – still less to preserve – a sense of mystery and awe in our post-Conciliar celebrations of Holy Mass.[13]

The Catholic view of human beings as potentially rational and responsible creatures of God needs to be re-affirmed. The *discovering* of the truth, of the beauty, of the coherence and of the integrity of faith in Christ is a divine gift, but this does not mean that education has no part to play in preparing individuals to find a treasure that lies hidden. Catholic education, to change the metaphor, is a pilgrimage with a definite goal in mind, not an invitation to set out on a speculative journey in search of a God who may or may not exist. If the talk is of a search for God, the search has to be presented in the Catholic tradition as a human response to the divine initiative, not a human venture into the unknown. 'We shall not fully understand the meaning of our calling, however, if we do not bother to learn the spiritual tradition in which it comes to us.'[14] This does not exclude human questioning, uncertainty and doubt from the learning process, but it does set them in perspective within the life of the whole Catholic community. If the talk is of love, the love is that which is revealed in Christ's own life, death and resurrection. We learn of that love not by speculation about what may be in the mind and heart of God, so to speak, but in response to what God has already done in the person of Jesus, the Christ. And in so far as we are ever given the grace to do it, 'We love because he [God] first loved us'.[15]

Faith in Christ continues to suffer from widespread ignorance of its origins, history and development. Yet an acquaintance, if not a familiarity, with Christianity tends to be assumed, not questioned, by many people. Childhood experiences are, apparently, sufficient to turn some individuals away from the Church for ever. They 'know' what religion is and do not care to consider the matter further. It is said that one can live 'a good life' easily (and even comfortably) without the unnecessary weight of religious obligation. In consequence, rejection of the faith can be based upon self-seeking pragmatism rather than sophisticated metaphysical insight. Ignorance of institutional and organised religion, generally, gives rise to the silliest criticisms of what believers are supposed to be obliged to think and do. So far as the *Catholic* school is concerned, one might reasonably expect that teachers, if they are to be effective, are involved primarily as learners themselves, however diffident their personal approaches to questions of faith may be. Whether they wish it or not, they will be taken as examples of faith and belief in action. As much can be said of parents, catechists, religious and clergy – in fact of anyone who admits to even a tenuous link with the Church. We are all to be learners in the school of Christ. Catholic education, in the broadest sense of the term, therefore, should help us to make progress in that demanding school. Yet on the eve of the millennium it seems that we are far less sure than our predecessors were about how the education provided in our schools is to serve us. There is much to be uncertain about at a time when institutional religion is under insistent attack and its leaders contemptuously dismissed because their convictions fail to reflect the spirit of the age. Even in some parts of the Church uncertainty about matters of faith and morals is commended as evidence of a thoughtful and maturing Christian commitment. It is not surprising, therefore, that concern about the characteristic value of Catholic education is on the increase. The process of *discovering* (not of inventing, or re-inventing) the faith may or may not start in school. What happens there, as well as what does not happen, will inevitably influence the way in which personal experience later in life is interpreted as confirming an early disposition to faith or an early inclination to unbelief. The important question is whether the faith or the unbelief that emerges has been critically informed as an educational priority during the formative years of statutory schooling.

What place can the Church's teaching authority continue to have (or be allowed to have) in so complex and rapidly changing a world as ours, a world in which individuals are expected 'to think for themselves' and 'to make their own decisions' about matters of belief and action? Catholic education cannot simply be reduced to presenting a broad spectrum of possible options with regard to religious belief and moral action, which individuals may choose or reject as they feel inclined. It must also provide a sturdy framework within which 'choice-making' can be sympathetically supervised and evaluated. If I am never shown how informed choices are made, if I never get any advice or practice about how to choose for myself, it should surprise no one if I assume that what I am already doing is what I ought to do when told to 'think things through for myself'. And before rejecting the authority of the Magisterium out of hand in favour of spiritual self-help it might be worth the effort to ask some questions about the nature of the secular authority most likely to replace it, with the latter's emphasis on what are so often claimed as 'neutral', 'descriptive', 'objective' and 'non-directive' approaches to the complexities of human experience. Inadvertently rather than intentionally, no doubt, the theory and practice of Catholic education may come to be unduly influenced by secular principles of education. In a predominantly secular society such as ours it is to be expected that questions of religious faith will be regarded as matters for private consideration, and that religion is best regarded in education as a specialist minority-interest subject. In one sense it *is* a special subject, but in a Catholic school it cannot be confined to one section of the curriculum, as if it were but one option among many others. Religion – the faith – must inform and direct the whole Catholic educational enterprise.

Private interpretation, so often little more than a euphemism for uninformed prejudice in matters of theological opinion, moral judgement and political preference, is not denied to those who submit to the teaching authority of the Church, although the readiness – even the eagerness – to make 'thinking for oneself' the hallmark of an educated person tends to exaggerate the capacity of human beings to think for themselves without considerable outside help. It also underestimates the continuing value of religious tradition and the influence of environment. Private interpretation may be important, but it is only part of the story. The notion of 'liberation', especially when it is identified with the real material needs of individuals and groups in the world today, tends to be interpreted too exclusively in terms of emancipation from *their* oppression and material poverty, rather than inclusively as deliverance from *my* sin and spiritual deprivation.

It is said that the search for a credible set of religious beliefs is growing, and not only among the young. As often as not the implication is that the Church has somehow to rid herself of the 'incredible' things and the 'outdated' rules which her members are still expected to believe and to keep on the eve of the twenty-first century. It is said that increasing numbers of people are looking for a coherent set of values, which will enable them to cope with feelings of inadequacy, loneliness and alienation in an often hostile world. If this is true there is still a worthwhile task ahead for Catholic education. The task is not to promote a vague interest in different sorts of spirituality, a task for which other kinds of education are better suited. The task is to open up the treasury of the Catholic faith for those who, despite their links with the Church, may be unaware of the richness of its contents. In a 'pluralist' society, in which *every* kind of religious belief, at least in theory, is accommodated sympathetically though none given priority, it may seem to be invidious to insist that for Catholics – however readily they learn about (and from) other religions and non-theistic 'life-stances' – the priority is still to explore their own tradition, not least with the aid of greater doctrinal precision. This is where the newly published *Catechism of the Catholic Church* will help. The cause of ecumenism and the course of inter-faith dialogue can lose momentum if the case for the particularities of different belief-systems (including the particularity of the Catholic faith) are simply ignored in the attempt to avoid controversy.

The multiplicity of theistic and non-theistic religious options in the world, though confusing, provides Catholic teachers with an opportunity to explore the unity which may well underlie the perceived diversity. The challenge presented to Catholic teachers is to undertake this task without neglecting either the uniqueness of Christ or the particularity of the Catholic faith. For centuries there has been something quaintly English about the notion that religion is a private matter, better left unexposed to public scrutiny. But concealment of this kind is not always appropriate. If it were, the Gospel would never have been shared, let alone preached. Faith then would be left as a matter of personal preference, temperament and feeling. The historic Catholic religion still needs to be made accessible in its fullness – not least to Catholics and to potential Catholics. It is undeniably true that many students leave their Catholic schools incapable – though perhaps unwilling in any case – to counter the misinformed criticisms which are made by critics of contemporary Catholic life, belief and thought.

Despite all the official teaching of the Catholic Church, despite all the discussion, and despite the production of some excellent teaching material, Catholic teachers are as likely to be unaware of the opportunities presented by religious and cultural diversity to Catholic education itself, as they are indifferent to the wider ecumenism to which a study of world religions can fruitfully contribute. If asked, they might reply that there is already too much to be done in Catholic schools to allow time and space for what they take to be an additional distraction. They could even argue that at a time when a chilling ignorance of its beliefs and practices is often assumed to be a sufficient reason for rejecting the Catholic religion, it would be more sensible to concentrate on teaching (or at least teaching *about*) the Catholic faith in the limited time available.

Children deserve to be equipped to live in a rapidly changing world in which religious faith is often seen as a purely personal and private matter. The problem for Catholic teachers in Catholic institutions is that of allowing for the widest possible exploration of what it means to be an adherent of any religion, without failing to discharge faithfully the responsibility of ensuring that the characteristic imprint of Catholic education is not abandoned. Catholics are not at liberty to question the centrality of Christ in *any* part of education. Christocentric education cannot be confined to those parts of education which flourish (or which sometimes languish in strange isolation) under the name of *religious* education. If, for whatever reason, Catholics do allow the Christocentric focus of attention to become blurred, they help to compromise the essential and distinctive nature of the whole Catholic educational enterprise. Catholic education is pre-eminently a lifelong process of consecration into the mystery of

Christ, not an effortless ritual initiation into an ethnic minority or a private social club.

Teachers are rarely opposed in principle to the inclusion of teaching about world religions in Catholic schools, but understandably sceptical about the educational value of undertaking a task for which many of them are not equipped to deal competently. Even today only a few specialist teachers in comparative theology or religious studies are to be found in the profession. More are needed if justice is to be done within Catholic education to the faiths by which others live, especially those faiths represented in Britain today. Clergy and parental opinion is, admittedly, more cautious and even critical, but some of the documents of Vatican II, notably *Nostra Aetate*, leave little room for doubt about what the Fathers in Council had in mind. Leadership and direction are certainly required, because teachers cannot simply decide arbitrarily what they will do in the classroom. On this particular question of curriculum content and development it would be helpful to have, first, some new contributions to the philosophy of education, and to the theology of education, written from the perspectives of a Catholic world-view. Second, it would be useful if teachers in Catholic schools could have access to some carefully graded and co-ordinated introductory manuals, student work-books, teachers' handbooks, visual and audio aids, not to mention computer programmes, which facilitate a discussion of the relationship between Catholics in different parts of the Catholic world, as well as between Catholics and those who belong to other religions. Nor would a representative reader of Catholic Education be out of place. Here is an opportunity, not to speak of a growing market, for publishers.

It would be unreasonable to deny today's students access to accurate information about the major world religions, a number of which are already well established in Britain. This must necessarily include teaching about Christianity as a major world religion, and teaching about Catholicism as one of the major branches of Christianity. From a purely pragmatic point of view students need to learn that the integrity of a society depends upon an understanding of the common dangers or threats, as well as the opportunities for co-operation, faced by its members. In a 'pluralist' society religious and cultural differences may just as easily promote disaffection as mutual enrichment. The monitoring of such possibilities, however, cannot be given as the most compelling reason for a systematic approach to world religions in Catholic education. What makes the inclusion an integral part of the process is the faith that beneath the outward differences of name, form, belief and practice, which appear to divide us, lies the unity to which Christ is the key.

By the 1990s it became apparent that the system of higher and continuing education was in need of radical reform in order to meet changing needs and circumstances. What kinds of qualifications would increasing numbers of students require for life in the twenty-first century? Endless discussion about standards in education have concentrated on resources, both human and material. This was and is to be expected, but there is a further aspect that has received less attention than it ought to have been given. It may be disputed, though the demurrals lack conviction, that our expectations of the young – whether in the formal educational setting of school, at work in industry and commerce, in the Church more generally, and no doubt elsewhere – have been too low. It is often the case that minds remain unstretched and abilities unused. This lesson is one to be learned not least by those in the Church who are engaged in the vital task of catechesis. Banal liturgy, undemanding theology, well-intentioned attempts to attract unbelievers by assuring them that the Church's doctrinal foundations, social teaching and moral absolutes are negotiable, provoke lasting derision and indifference.

THE ECUMENICAL IMPERATIVE

For Catholics there is no lack of papal guidance about the importance of ecumenism and about how, under the Holy Spirit, it is to be conducted. The guidance is offered not only to Catholics involved in inter-faith dialogue with members of other religious communities, with those having no religious beliefs, or those who profess atheism. It is also for Catholics who choose to engage in intra-faith encounter with those who belong to other Christian denominations. This is clear from Pope John Paul II's encyclical *Ut Unum Sint.*[16] In answer to one of a series of questions put to him in 1993 by the Italian journalist, Vittorio Messori, Pope John Paul II gave a reply which leaves little doubt that Catholics who seek to deepen their own faith are to be encouraged to learn something about the faiths by which others live. He was asked:

> But if God who is in heaven – and who saved and continues to save the world – is One and only One and is He who has revealed Himself in Jesus Christ, why has he allowed so many religions to exist? Why did He make the search for the truth so arduous, in the midst of a forest of rituals, of beliefs, of revelations, of faiths which have always thrived – and still do today – throughout the world?[17]

These are good questions, which continue to puzzle non-Catholics as well as Catholics today. With so many different religions in the world, many claiming to be unique, if not exclusive, it is tempting to treat them all as equally valid or to dismiss them all as equally irrelevant in the closing years of the twentieth century. With apparently little to choose between them, it is not immediately apparent to a casual observer that any of them is worth choosing in preference to another, or that any one of them speaks more realistically than the rest to the needs of modern men and women. Do not most people manage to live reasonably happy lives without the aid of any form of institutional religion?

The word 'doctrine' is often associated with what is considered to be the dead weight of tradition and with oppressive ecclesiastical authority. This is a pity because doctrine is an essentially neutral term, signifying simply 'that which is taught'. More specifically 'that which is taught' in the Catholic community is the accumulated knowledge, based upon collective as well as personal experience, of the truth of the Gospel. In that sense Catholic doctrine is incremental. The edifice of doctrine is enlarged, not replaced, by present experience. In doctrine we recognise a distillation of accumulated and still accumulating Christian experience, and find the key in our own time to *discovering* Christ. Faith and reason are still the foundations upon which the Church reaches up to Christ. Thoughtful inquiry into the sacred mysteries is not inimical to the spirit of faith. Sharing the faith remains the primary task, but we need to know what the faith is before we can proceed to communicate it. Doctrine – the clear presentation of what is believed in a community of believers, and the grounds for such belief – is important in furthering fruitful ecumenism.

The pursuit of learning, in Catholic terms, 'learning to know Christ and his benefits', is assisted by the work of creative writers, philosophers, theologians, social scientists and natural scientists, even when they venture – and not always tentatively – beyond the boundaries of their respective disciplines. From the point of view of a believer in a transcendent, immanent, creative and re-creative God, be the believer a Hindu, a Jew, a Christian or a Muslim, there can be nothing in the universe that is not already, or potentially, a source of revelation and insight. For such a person all that is worth knowing is of God, in two senses, in that it both comes *from* God and is ultimately *about* God. To gain knowledge of God from whatever source is, thus, the responsibility of the Christian, the objective of the Christian life, and the *raison d'être* of Catholic education. From their own different perspectives the same can be said of Jews and Muslims, for instance, about the strategic aims of education.

In October 1992, Pope John Paul II echoed some words of Pope John XXIII, reminding his hearers of a remark made by the Pontiff at the opening of the Second Vatican Council. Pope John XXIII stated that the principal task entrusted to the Council was to guard and to present in more appropriate ways 'the precious deposit of Christian doctrine in order to make it more accessible to the Christian faithful and to prepare people of goodwill'. From a Catholic point of view, therefore, questions about ecumenism, inter-faith dialogue, spiritual formation, catechesis, religious and moral education at all levels will ultimately be decided by the extent to which the matter under review and the methods by which it is to be considered contribute to the progressive deepening of faith in Christ. The rich diversity within the worldwide Catholic community has a potential for enlivening the ecumenical enterprise. It is often ignored. The novels of Shusako Endo, the Japanese Catholic writer who died in 1996, are a rich source of contemporary theological awareness, literary merit, social criticism and moral insight that is largely ignored in this country. From his experience of living as a member of the minority Catholic community in Japan, he once said:

> It seems to me that Catholicism is not a solo, but a symphony . . . If I have trust in Catholicism, it is because I find in it much more possibility than in any other religion for presenting the full symphony of humanity. The other religions have almost no fullness; they have but solo parts. Only Catholicism can present the full symphony. And unless there is in that symphony a part that corresponds to Japan's mud swamp, it cannot be a true religion. What exactly this part is – that is what I want to find out.[18]

It is painfully true that little more than lip-service is paid to the documents of the Second Vatican Council by many Catholics, whether the subject is education, the mission of the Church, ecumenical activity between members of the different branches of the Christian Church, or the wider ecumenism between adherents of different faiths and of none. Of crucial importance is *Nostra Aetate*, 'In Our Time'.[19] As Pope John Paul II has since affirmed, this document makes it clear that the primary task of the Church remains what it always has been, namely, to ensure that the tradition of the Catholic Church is received and passed on to the next generation:

> From the beginning Christian Revelation has viewed the spiritual history of man as including, in some way, all religions, thereby demonstrating the unity of humankind with regard to the eternal and ultimate destiny of man. The Council document speaks of this unity and links it with the current trend to bring humanity closer together through the resources available to our civilisation. The Church sees the promotion of unity as one of its duties: '*There is only one community and it consists of all peoples*. They have only one origin, since God inhabited the entire earth with the whole human race. And they have one ultimate destiny, God, whose providence, goodness, and plan for salvation extend to all . . .' Men *turn to various religions to solve mysteries of the human condition*, which today, as in earlier times, burden people's hearts: the nature of man; the meaning and purpose of life; good and evil; the origin and purpose of suffering; the way to true happiness; death; judgement and retribution after death; and finally, the ultimate ineffable mystery which is the origin and destiny of our existence.[20]

It would be a pity if the impressive new reference work of Catholic thought, belief and practice, the *Catechism of the Catholic Church*,[21] were to become little more than a hidden treasure in Catholic circles, neglected by those unaware of its riches. It provides for Catholics who believe that the ecumenical pursuit of unity in the light of the prayer offered by Jesus for his disciples does not excuse them from taking seriously the words of the Divine Commission recorded at the end of Matthew's Gospel. *Lumen Gentium* places Jesus, the Christ, 'the light of humanity', at the centre of all authentically Catholic belief and action, including evangelisation, education and ecumenism. Inter-faith dialogue thus presents difficulties as well as opportunities for Christian ecumenism.

After 1945, when the events of the Second World War had accelerated the eventual demise of British empire and British colonialism, the number of immigrants from former colonies and dependencies increased in this country. The 'melting-pot' theory depends for its success in resolving potentially divisive religious and cultural differences in the community on the disposition and continuing willingness of individuals and groups to assimilate with the host community. Neither in Britain nor in the United States has this proved to be the case as the century draws to its close. Despite formidable opposition and strident calls from some quarters for further immigration control in order to prevent 'the erosion of British – more specifically of English – values and traditions', there is still considerable good-will and fellow-feeling for those who have come to these shores in the recent past, and in more recent days for those who seek asylum here as a result of the conflicts in their own countries. For first-generation immigrants the prospect of British citizenship, comparative security, employment and access to the benefits of the welfare state, may just be sufficient *at first* to compensate for the likelihood of discrimination on grounds of colour, race or religion. For their successors it is not enough. When do the descendants of immigrants cease to be immigrants? For the immediate descendants of first-generation immigrants racial discrimination is proving to be a continuing problem that may yet lead to serious instability in the community. In many cases personal identity is less a matter of ethnic origin than of religious affiliation. In the next century it may not be enough to express personal identity in terms such as 'Asian', 'African' or 'West Indian'. There are signs that it is religion rather than race which is beginning to define the identity of the children of former immigrants. Having spent much of my career studying the world of Islam, I know what is meant by those who in this country today no longer identify themselves as being of Asian or Arab origin, for instance, but as 'Muslims'. And more than that, I understand what they mean when they assert, even as British citizens, 'My nationality is Islam'.

Half a century after the end of World War II, it is difficult to convey to anyone too young to have known it the sense of euphoria that followed the collapse of the Axis Powers. It did not take long for the euphoria to give way to scepticism about utopian ideologies of any kind. Disillusion with spiritual as well as economic and political nostrums has proceeded as the century progresses towards its end. Institutional religion is in process of being bypassed rather than studiously ignored by many whose sentiments are expressed in terms of the need to save the world by preaching a gospel of universal compassion and fellow-feeling, based upon convictions about a common humanity. This is secular ecumenism. No less utopian than any other twentieth-century secular dream, this vision of the future presents its own challenge to the Church's ecumenical vision. The wider ecumenism, involving adherents of different faiths and of none, must provide for discussion about the relationship between religion and science. For the Christian, whether a scientist or not, the work of creation and re-creation is predicated on the initiating action of the Creator God who calls upon men and women to co-operate with him and, recognising the responsibility delegated to mankind, to be co-workers with God in the creation and re-creation of the worlds. In Christian terms responsibility is always a delegated responsibility, *de haut en bas*, so to speak. Never to be equated with temporal power as the world may understand it, its source is God. Its function is exemplary in the self-sacrificial way demonstrated by Christ in his service to and for others.

The 150th anniversary, in 1997, of the restoration of the Latin Patriarchate of Jerusalem by Pope Pius IX passed almost unremarked by Catholics in this country. His Brief *Nulla Celebrior* appeared on 23 July 1847. In the closing years of the twentieth century the Christian minority in the Holy Land, which traces its ancestry back to the time of Christ, is under the increasing threats of persecution and expulsion. Some Christians choose to emigrate; others feel obliged to leave their homeland because of the pressures exercised by Jewish immigration and resettlement, especially around towns like Bethlehem and Nazareth. Will eyes be on Britain at the time of the millennium, or on Bethlehem? And if on the birthplace of Jesus, will it be because of what happened there 2,000 years ago, or because of the violence that is taking place there between Jews, Christians and Muslims – those whom the Qur'ān calls 'People of the Book', not least because as believers in the one true God they *ought to have* so much in common? What will Bethlehem look like then? There is an Arabic proverb which can be translated into English like this: 'Relatives are scorpions'. Sad to say, there is more than a grain of truth in this. Those who ought to have so much in common can often be divided from each other by the bitterest antagonisms and the fiercest mutual hostility. Jews, Muslims and Christians have a long history of disagreeable relationships but they can all claim to be spiritual descendants of Abraham, their father in faith. Despite this family relationship, they still experience difficulties in recognising each other's rights in what is the Holy Land for all of them. Ecumenism, like charity (or love, if the more recent translation is preferred), starts in the family.

It is ironic that at a time when ecumenical co-operation and inter-faith dialogue is encouraged at every level, a disturbing resurgence of anti-Catholicism is to be noted. This anti-Catholicism – described only half in jest as the anti-Semitism of the liberal intellectual – has become evident in the strident criticism that is being directed not so much against the Church's social and economic teaching as against her determined stand against abortion, euthanasia and unfettered permissiveness. This anti-Catholic sentiment frequently lurks behind the words and actions of the critics, whenever Catholics are caught making the mistake of sounding like faithful ones. One of the consequences of this is that Catholics have now to contend less with cultured infidelity and refined agnosticism than with uninformed hostility, blinkered scientism, and even a feeling that the hallmark of the mature Christian living at the end of the century is uncertainty rather than conviction. Ecumenism is an integral part of the authentic mission of the Catholic Church. It is for this reason that Christians cannot fail to be involved in ecumenical activity. To the criticism that this is not *ecumenism* but *mission* (and furthermore, mission of an obsolete kind), the reply must be that in whatever she does the Church must always be obedient to the Great Commission recorded at the end of Matthew's Gospel. In recent times Christian mission has been re-defined in terms of service rather than of evangelisation and proselytism. Missionaries do have to tread carefully in many parts of the world in which they now find themselves, but ecumenism – as the word itself suggests – implies universalism throughout the inhabited world. It cannot, therefore, be intrinsically inimical to the Catholic spirit. The ecumenical question is one of deciding the limits of inclusiveness and the reasons for exclusiveness.

Fundamentalism has a bad name and it gets a bad press. Is it a sickness from which 'religious' people suffer uniquely or can 'non-religious' people catch it too? And if it is a sickness, what is the cure? There are different kinds of fundamentalism, some of which are more acceptable than others. In an ecumenical age the task is to distinguish between them. One of the easiest ways of dismissing the beliefs and ideas of those with whom we disagree is to label them as 'fundamentalist'. If we do this without much thought we may just fall into the trap of being too selective by half, by which I mean that we may overlook the unexamined assumptions upon which our own ideas and beliefs are founded. Some kinds of fundamentalism, however, are more socially acceptable than others. In the past, religious fundamentalism of the kind associated with minority Christian groups has been virtually ignored in Britain. In this country, in particular, religious enthusiasm has usually been treated with amused tolerance, except in circles in which it has been considered to be in bad taste. Shorn of political power, religious fundamentalists have posed no threat to a society which, as in the case of Britain, has become more and more secular during the twentieth century. In the United States, however, Christian fundamentalism has already become powerful politically. Politicians who campaign for office have to take the religious convictions of large numbers of their potential supporters increasingly seriously. The 'moral majority' lobby cannot be disregarded. And once in office, politicians have to be careful about what they say, do, and enact, if they wish to be re-elected. Elsewhere in the world religious fundamentalists have been making the running, not because they constitute a 'moral majority' in their own countries, or because they represent a significant number of the population, but because they are prepared to resort to terrorism in order to further their cause. Nor have their activities been limited to the countries in which they live. The spirit of fundamentalism and the actions that spring from its promptings are much more widespread than we sometimes suppose. Religious believers generally, and the Christians among them in particular, have no monopoly of 'fundamentalist' bigotry. Secularists, too, have a commitment for which to account. The notion, still critically unexamined in educational circles – that those without religious beliefs are capable of being objective, fair and balanced in ways that religious believers cannot hope to match because of their religious convictions – remains to be exposed for the specious claim that it is. A more vigorously Christocentric anthropology has to emerge in order to meet the challenge presented by secular humanism and to reinvigorate mission, education and ecumenism.

POSTSCRIPT

In 1968, only a few years after the concluding session of the Second Vatican Council, Frank Sheed's book with the title *Is It the Same Church?* insisted that the answer to the question was assuredly in the affirmative. Not even his spirited advocacy was sufficient to reassure some of his readers that their fears of betrayal and discontinuity were groundless. The Church today may be leaner and fitter for its mission in this country than it was fifty years ago, although it is not out of nostalgia that questions are now being raised about what may have been prematurely abandoned in the ensuing process of change and innovation. In every age the question is: *What is the Spirit saying to the Church now?* The waters that have flowed down the Tiber and the Thames may have carried with them much that needed to be swept away. The counsels of the Church are said to be more open to scrutiny. Few will mourn the passing of ecclesiastical pomp, or regret the decline of obseqious deference to clerical precedence. The apostolate of the laity is rightly emphasised, though still imprecisely defined and imperfectly understood. The decline in the number of priests and religious – at least in the West – presents the Church with obvious practical problems.

Yet some things of value may have been prematurely abandoned, unnecessarily neglected, inadvertently lost, or temporarily mislaid. Will the overwhelming *mystery* of the Church as the Body of Christ continue to inspire Catholic life and action? How can an understanding of distinctively Catholic beliefs about the Real Presence of Christ in the Eucharist be nurtured? Do we need further linguistic revision of the Liturgy, or is there not rather a need to employ the traditional as well as the modern liturgical resources of the worldwide Church in more consistently sensitive and joyful ways? Is there a new role in

Catholic education for a systematic approach to apologetics? Is the promotion of ecumenical activity among Christians, adherents of other faiths, or those of no faith, weakened or strengthened by affirmations about the particularity and coherence of Catholic life and belief? Will Catholic particularism make an indispensable contribution to fruitful ecumenism, or will it conceal the kind of triumphalism that frequently marred the faithful expression of Catholic conviction in earlier days by its intolerant exuberance? Or will it assume yet another guise, in the tone (if not the content) of the strident expressions of Catholic dissidence? How is the nature of the authority by which the Church continues her mission to the world until the Lord comes to be reinterpreted and understood in the twenty-first century? There is no shortage of questions to be considered or questionings to be reassured. On the eve of the millennium Catholics continue to pray in the Name of the Holy Trinity, upon whose creative and re-creative activity everything depends.[22] 'When you send forth your Spirit, they are created, and you renew the face of the earth.'[23] 'Even so, come, Lord Jesus!'[24] 'Come, Holy Spirit, fill the hearts of your faithful people and kindle in us the fire of your love.'

NOTES

1. John 16:33.
2. 1 Peter 3:15.
3. Pope Pius XII's encyclical *On Promoting Biblical Studies*, published in 1943, commemorated the 50th anniversary of Pope Leo XIII's encyclical *Providentissimus Deus*, sometimes described as 'the Magna Carta of Catholic Biblical Studies'.
4. Pope John XXIII, *Journal of a Soul*, tr. Dorothy White (Geoffrey Chapman, 1965) p. 260.
5. Albert H. Friedländer, *Riders Towards the Dawn: From Ultimate Suffering to Tempered Hope* (Constable, 1993), p. 49.
6. John 17:20.
7. Dorothy L. Sayers, *Creed or Chaos?* (Hodder & Stoughton, 1940), pp. 11–12.
8. Pope John Paul II, *Crossing the Threshold of Hope*, ed. Vittorio Messori, tr. Jenny McPhee and Martha McPhee (Jonathan Cape, London, 1994), p. 114.
9. Job 11:7.
10. 1 Timothy 6:15ff.
11. Nadezhda Mandelstam, *Hope Abandoned*, tr. Max Hayward (Collins-Harvill, 1989), pp. 483–4. The English title of the book uses her first name, *Nadezhda*, which means 'Hope' in Russian, to obvious effect. Her husband, Osip Mandelstam, is regarded by some as the greatest Russian poet of the twentieth century. Exiled to the *Gulag* in one of Stalin's purges, he died there of a heart-attack in 1938.
12. 1 Peter 3:15.
13. See John McHugh, *On Englishing the Liturgy: An Open Letter to the Bishop of Shrewsbury*, (published privately from Ushaw College at Darlington Carmel, 1983). Hopefully, by the year 2000 a revised Missal may be approved for use, one which will claim to address points raised here.
14. Edward Norman, 'Image of the Rock', *The Daily Telegraph*, 13 June 1998.
15. 1 John 4:19.

16. Published on 25 May 1995.
17. John Paul II, *Crossing the Threshold of Hope*, p. 78.
18. In an interview in the magazine *Kumo*, translated by F. Marthy, 'Shusako Endo: Japanese Catholic Novelist', in *Thought* (Winter 1967). His works include *Silence* (1966) and *The Samurai* (1982), novels that will be of interest to teachers in search of a Catholic critique of the contemporary world from a different cultural perspective. Shusako Endo has been described as the Japanese Graham Greene.
19. See Austin Flannery OP, general editor, *Vatican Council II: The Conciliar and Post Conciliar Documents* (Dominican Publications, Dublin, 1975), pp. 738–42.
20. John Paul II, *Crossing the Threshold of Hope*, pp. 78–9, quoting from *Nostra Aetate* 1.
21. *Catechism of the Catholic Church* (Geoffrey Chapman, 1994).
22. *Catechism* (quoting St Irenaeus), para. 292: 'The Old Testament suggests and the New Covenant reveals the creative action of the Son and the Spirit, inseparably one with that of the Father. This creative co-operation is clearly affirmed in the Church's rule of faith: "There exists but one God . . . he is the Father, God, the Creator, the author, the giver of order. He made all things by himself, that is, by his Word and by his Wisdom", "by the Son and the Spirit" who, so to speak, are "His hands".'
23. Psalm 104:30.
24. Revelation 22:20.

INDEX OF PROPER NAMES